Bernice Chesler's
BED & BREAKFAST
IN NEW ENGLAND

"The most detailed and extensively researched guidebooks available."
—*Country Almanac* **magazine**

"My husband and I read your book aloud to each other for the pure enjoyment of it. I feel that each of the hosts are almost long-forgotten friends that are coming back into my life." **—Anne Taylor, Philadelphia, Pennsylvania**

"We have perused several other books . . . but always come back to yours, which gives us exactly all the information we are looking for."
—George and Mary Rose Sokorai, Woodbine, New Jersey

"We appreciate your books for their integrity and accuracy."
**—Kay and Peter Shumway, Moose Mountain Lodge,
Etna, New Hampshire**

"Most reliable reviews of what's available and charming, and reasonably priced."
—Ilene Spiro and Ira Schor, Newton, Massachusetts

"Bible to the industry." **—***The Cape Codder*

"[Guests] come clutching a dog-eared and loved Bed & Breakfast in New England.*"*
—Sandy Knox-Johnston, Corner House, Nantucket, Massachusetts

"The travel philosopher . . . [whose] words I often recall." **—***Spy* **magazine**

"Your book was the final encouragement needed to begin my own B&B."
—Beverly Bainbridge, Remembrance, Plymouth, Massachusetts

"Your wonderful book allowed us to find a vacation paradise."
—Eric Cheerer, Elizabethtown, Pennsylvania

"Your excellent book . . . proved invaluable . . . made our holiday even more enjoyable."
—Karen Barnes, London, England

"Especialmente informativa." **—***El Nuevo Dia,* **Puerto Rico**

"We had fun reading it and making our plans. . . . [Hosts were] caring, helpful, better than museum guides. . . . One of the best vacations that we've ever spent together!"
—Susanne Müller, Allgan, Germany

"The amount and quality of information provided to the reader are unmatched in any other guidebook." **—The American Country Collection**

"The bed & breakfast guru." **—***Travel Agent* **magazine**

By Bernice Chesler

Author
In and Out of Boston with (or without) Children
Mainstreaming through the Media
Bed & Breakfast Coast to Coast
Bed & Breakfast in the Mid-Atlantic States
Bed & Breakfast in New England

Coauthor
The Family Guide to Cape Cod

Editor and Coordinator
The ZOOM Catalog
Do a ZOOMdo
People You'd Like to Know

Bernice Chesler's *Bed & Breakfast in New England* and *Bed & Breakfast in the Mid-Atlantic States* are accessible in searchable electronic format at the Online BookStore (OBS) (e-mail address: obs@editorial.com). For information call 508/546-7346.

Bed & Breakfast in New England

Connecticut, Maine, Massachusetts, New Hampshire, Rhode Island, Vermont

Fourth Edition

by Bernice Chesler

A Voyager Book

The Globe Pequot Press

Old Saybrook, Connecticut

Library of Congress Cataloging-in-Publication Data

Chesler, Bernice.
    Bed & breakfast in New England: Connecticut, Maine,
Massachusetts, New Hampshire, Rhode Island, Vermont / by Bernice
Chesler. — 4th ed.
        p.   cm.
    "A Voyager book."
    Includes index.
    ISBN 1-56440-364-5
    1. Bed and breakfast accommodations—New England—Guidebooks.
2. New England—Guidebooks.   I. Title.
TX907.3.N35C47 1994
647.947403—dc20
                                                                93-44013
                                                                    CIP
Editorial and production services: Editorial Inc. of Rockport, Massachusetts.
Cover design: Steven Bridges.
Cover photo: Courtesy Wadsworth Atheneum, Hartford, Connecticut.
    Gift of Mrs. Frederic J. Agate. Photo by E. Irving Blomstrann. Cover
    shows detail of quilt; entire quilt is reproduced on page 405.
Text design: Penny Darras-Maxwell.
Maps: Geoffrey Mandel.
Composition in Meridien on the Ventura 3.0 system.

Manufactured in the United States of America
Fourth Edition / Third Printing

To David

CONTENTS

INTRODUCTION

"Those hosts would be great for a documentary film," I said to my husband. We were leaving a Vermont bed and breakfast, a genuine farmhouse; the farmer had offered me cow salve to soothe leg muscles that ached from pedaling over the hilly terrain.

That was over a dozen years ago. (I had been working as a documentary film researcher for public television.) Who would have guessed then that bed and breakfast was to become the hottest trend in American travel? The acceptance of B&Bs on this side of the ocean came at just the right time for us—just as our youngest left for college, just as we were to discover the joys of pedaling from B&B to B&B, and from one interesting experience to another, in what is now a total of 14 states and 6 countries.

In the 1990s bed and breakfast has come to be recognized for its personalized style, for hosts who help to give a sense of place. Now many B&B hosts have plotted back-road routes for guests. With the advent of bed and breakfast reservation services, bed and breakfasts are in the city and suburbs as well as in rural areas. In addition, B&Bs have opened in restored everything—from churches to schoolhouses, from beach cottages to mansions.

To distinguish private homes from inns, this book has introduced a symbol (♣) for private homes that have one, two, or three guest rooms. B&B inns are likely to be larger, are a full-time profession, and in some cases have one or more hired staffers. Other symbols—in answer to travelers' requests—will lead you (quickly) to a romantic place, a spot that is great for kids, or a B&B where your group, family, or colleagues might book the entire place. See the key to symbols that appears at intervals throughout the book.

In documentary film style, *Bed & Breakfast in New England* tries to focus as much on the memorable hosts as on their homes and B&B inns. In addition, each description aims to save travelers' time by anticipating questions: Located on a main road? What time is breakfast? Sample menu? Size of bed? What floors are rooms on? Shower *and* tub? Is smoking allowed? Any pets in residence? What's the difference between the $60 and the $90 room?

Research for my first B&B guide began in 1980. Nine B&B books and about 2,000 interviews later, this latest edition reflects the wide range of possiblities that fit into my original interpretation of bed and breakfast: generally, a home setting with an owner in residence; a maximum of about 10 rooms; a common room; breakfast included in the rate, but no public restaurant or bar on the premises.

So what's changed? New owners are in residence. Lots of new places have opened. Many gazebos are on the outside. Many more private baths are on the inside. New layers of regulations have added to costs and rates. Old-timers (more than five years in business) find themselves adding a few rooms to keep B&B economically viable. Some move across the street or next door. They learn to hire an inn-sitter now and then. And always, there is a steady stream of dreamers who see B&B—after all, it's only breakfast, they say—as a fantasy lifestyle.

And what about you, the traveler? The art of letter writing is alive! Excerpts from some of the thousands of enthusiastic letters written to me are included in this book. There really is a letter of the day, usually one that reinforces the concept of a people-to-people program—and makes you feel good all over.

Accuracy is a hallmark of this book. Every detail was confirmed just before press time. But please keep in mind that successful hosts sometimes make *changes in rooms, beds, menu, or decor—and yes, in rates too.*

It is a joy to work with Jay Howland, my editor who remembers everything and everyone. My thanks also go to Robert Carson, Annie Balasa, and Fernando Corredor, who handled more than 30,000 pieces of paper, deciphered floor plans, and decoded hieroglyphics. Quilter Sandra Keller of Needham, Massachusetts, gave much-appreciated help with cover research. Additional support and encouragement have come from my agent, Laura Fillmore, and the staff of Editorial Inc. including Cathleen Collins, David Eales, Mary Helen Gunn, and Tim Evans. And once again, David, my husband, has planned all our trips by plane, car, and bicycle. He listens, offers judgment when I solicit objectivity, and acts as my computer expert in residence.

Suggestions about people and places are welcome for consideration in the next edition. Please address them to me at The Globe Pequot Press, 6 Business Park Road, P.O. Box 833, Old Saybrook, CT 06475.

Bernice Chesler

Answers to Frequently Asked Questions

What is bed and breakfast?

It is a package arrangement that includes overnight accommodations and breakfast. Although embellishments (amenities) are offered at many American B&Bs, the keynote is hospitality. Think of it as a people-to-people program.

Are baths shared?

Some are—usually with just one other room. But depending on the number of guests, a shared bath could be private for you. Many American B&Bs have followed the trend to all private baths, sometimes with a shower but no tub, sometimes with a whirlpool bath and a sauna too.

How much do B&Bs cost?

Rates range from about $50 to well over $100 (including breakfast) for two people. The season, location, amenities, food, length of ownership, maintenance costs, taxes—all affect the rate. Remember: Nothing is standardized at B&Bs. In this book, check under "Rates" to see what credit cards are accepted at a particular B&B. Many small places prefer cash or travelers' checks. And it's a good idea to check on deposit requirements; refund policies differ. Required local and/or state taxes vary from place to place and are seldom in the listed rates. Suggestion: Consider paying upon arrival. Good-byes will be that much smoother, and you really do feel as if you have visited friends.

To tip or not?

In a private home, tipping is not a usual practice, *but* times may be changing. In a private home where B&B is rather constant, owners realize that extra help helps. Those B&B owners also know that some remembrance is appreciated by the part-time folks who contribute to your memorable stay.

In a B&B inn, treat staff as you would in a hotel. *Some inns, particularly those in resort areas, add gratuities to the tab*—or else they couldn't keep their help!

An interesting phenomenon: An amazing number of travelers write heartfelt thank-you notes to surprised and delighted hosts.

Is B&B like a hotel?

Not at all! It's not intended to be. You are greeted by a family member or an assistant, or occasionally by a note. Every room is different in size, layout, and decor. A B&B may not provide the privacy—or the loneliness—of a hotel. Because business travelers have discovered B&Bs, however, there may be a phone jack or even a private phone in the room. (Reminder: There is no desk clerk. Please call the B&B during reasonable hours.)

If you must have things exactly as they are in the hotel you usually go to, go to the hotel!

Is B&B for everyone?

Many B&Bs are perfect for unwinding and a change of pace, for romantics, or for a home-away-from-home environment. If you seek anonymity, B&B may not be for you. As one host said, "Guests who come to B&Bs are outgoing; they want to be sociable and learn about you and the area."

Among all the wonderful guests, a few hosts can recall an occasional "memorable" demanding guest (it's fun to see the change that frequently takes place overnight) or a first-timer who arrived with considerable luggage—cumbersome indeed on the narrow steep stairs to the third floor of a historic house.

Tastes and interpretations differ. Take charm, for example. "Tell me," said the older guest, "what's so charming about a tub on legs? I was so glad when built-ins finally became the fashion."

Recommendation: Tell the host if this is your first time at a B&B. When making the reservation, if privacy is a real concern, say that too. Hosts' listening skills are usually well tuned.

How do B&Bs on this side of the Atlantic differ from those in the British Isles or other countries?

The style of B&B-and-away-you-go is not necessarily the norm in North America. Although there are B&Bs with just one room and many where you are expected to leave for the day, guests are often invited to spend more time after breakfast "at home"—by the pool or fireplace, on the hiking trails or on borrowed bicycles. Even hosts are amazed at what they do when they get involved in others' lives! They worry about late arrivals. They have been known to drive someone to a job appointment or to do laundry for a businessman whose schedule changed or to prevail upon the local auto mechanic when the garage was closed.

Can I book through travel agents?

Many travel agents have caught on to the popularity of B&Bs. In this book B&Bs with the ◆ in the "Rates" section pay commissions to travel agents. And some agents will make arrangements for you, whether or not they receive a commission from the B&B.

Do B&Bs welcome children?

In this book B&Bs with the symbol ✚ are always happy to host children. Some B&Bs without the symbol also welcome children, though not necessarily by the houseful! Although there are B&Bs that provide everything from the sandbox to the high chair—and a babysitter too—some B&B hosts have been known to say (tactfully), "Children find us tiresome." Check the "Plus" section in the descriptions in this book. Consider the facilities, the room and bath arrangements, and the decor. Are your kids enticed by candlelit breakfasts? Are they used to being around "don't touch" antiques? Do they enjoy classical music? Are rooms limited to two persons? Is a crib provided? Are there lots of animals on the farm? Is there a built-in playmate, perhaps an innkeepers' child? Remember what you looked for B.C. (before children). If you do bring the kids and still wish for some private time at the B&B, please arrange for a sitter. Be fair to yourself and your children, to other guests, and to the host/chef/gardener/interior designer/historian—who really does love children.

What about facilities for physically handicapped persons?

Rooms that are handicapped accessible are noted in the detailed "Bed and bath" item of each B&B description in this book. In addition, each writeup mentions the floor locations of guest rooms.

Are there B&Bs that prohibit smoking?

Many do. (Note the ⊁ symbol in this book.) Among the B&Bs that do allow smoking, many limit it to certain areas or rooms.

If you like people and enjoy company and cooking, isn't that enough to make you a happy host?

It helps. But experienced hosts all comment on the time and work involved. Guests who ask, "Is this all you do?" would be surprised to realize that there is more to hosting than serving tea and meeting interesting people. Even I have fallen into the trap of multiplying a full house by the nightly rate, only to hear my husband say, "That's 600 sheets!"

What do you recommend to those who dream about opening a B&B?

For starters, attend one of the workshops or seminars given by adult education centers, extension services, innkeepers, or B&B reservation services. Apprentice, even for a weekend, or sign up with a reservation service and host in your own home. Many prospective innkeepers attend Bill Oates and Heide Bredfeldt's seminar, "How to Purchase and Operate a Bed & Breakfast or Country Inn." Contact Oates & Bredfeldt, P.O. Box 1162, Brattleboro, VT 05302, 802/254-5931; fax 802/254-3221. For a free aspiring innkeeper's packet that includes a list of innkeeping workshops conducted in various parts of the country, contact the Professional Association of Innkeepers International, P.O. Box 90710, Santa Barbara, CA 93190, 805/569-1853; fax 805/682-1016. For an overview of everything from suppliers of products and services to B&B/inn publications and organizations, I recommend

Country Inns Yellow Pages, a thorough information resource book available at a special rate of $10 if you mention *Bernice Chesler's Bed & Breakfast in New England.* For a copy of the *Yellow Pages* and for a free sample of *Inn Marketing* (a what's-going-on newsletter with a focus on marketing), contact Norm Strasma's Inn Marketing, P.O. Box 1789B, Kankakee, IL 60901; 815/939-3509; fax 815/933-8320.

Every host in this book enjoys what they call "the great emotional rewards of a stimulating occupation." Some remind couples who wish to make hosting a vocation that it helps to have a strong marriage. One who encourages prospective innkeeepers to "Just do it!" adds, "but be aware that you have to be more gregarious than private. You have to learn to carve time out for yourself. Hosting requires a broad range of talents (knowledge of plumbing helps), a lot of flexibility, an incredible amount of stamina, and perseverance. And did I mention you might need some capital?"

Can a host or reservation service pay to be in this book?

No. All selections are made by the author. There are no application fees. And all descriptions are written by the author; no host or service proprietor can write his or her own description. A processing fee is paid after each selected B&B and reservation service reviews its writeup. The fee offsets the extensive research that results in highly detailed writeups reflecting the individual spirit of each B&B. The processing fee for an individual B&B is $125. (For those with one or two rooms and a top rate of $50, it is $100.) The fee for a reservation service is $125; for a reservation service host $40. The author pays for all her stays.

What are some of your favorite B&Bs?

Even when you stay in hundreds, you tend to remember the hosts of each B&B more than the place. We have arrived on bicycles and been greeted with the offer of a car to go to dinner. There's the horticulturist, a septuagenarian, whom we could hardly keep up with as she toured us through her spectacular gardens. There's the couple who built their own solar house. Multifaceted retirees—some who have restored several houses. The history buffs who filled us in on the area and recommended back roads. The literary buffs who suggested good books. Hosts in a lovely residential section just minutes off the highway. Hosts we have laughed with. Yes, even some we have cried with too. Great chefs. People who are involved in their communities and trying to make this a better world. People whose home has been a labor of love and who love sharing it with others. We have enjoyed rather luxurious settings and some casual places too. It is true that each B&B is special in its own way. That's why the place to stay has become the reason to go. It's wonderful.

B&B RESERVATION SERVICES

A reservation service is in the business of matching screened hosts and guests. Although it can be a seasonal operation, in some areas the service is a full-time job for an individual, a couple, partners, or a small group. For hosts, it's a private way of going public, because the host remains anonymous until the service (agency) matches host and guest. This unique system allows hosts in private homes to have an off-and-on hosting schedule.

Listings may be in communities where there are no overnight lodging facilities, or they may provide an alternative to hotels or motels. Although most services feature private homes, some include B&B inns with 6–10 guest rooms. And some services now offer stays in unhosted homes.

Each service determines its own area and conducts its own inspections and interviews. A service may cover just one community, or a metropolitan area, or an entire region.

Advance notice is preferred and even, with many services, required. Length-of-stay requirements vary. Some services stipulate a one-night surcharge; some require a minimum of two nights.

Rates are usually much less than at area hotels. The range may cover everything from "budget" to "luxury." Deposits are usually required. Refund policies, detailed with each reservation service description in this book, differ.

Fee arrangements vary. Many services include their commission in the quoted nightly rate. For public inns the services' quoted rate may be the same as what the inn charges, or it could be a total of the inn's rate plus a booking fee (about $5–$15).

Write for printed information or maybe, better yet, call. Before calling, think about bed and bath arrangements, parking, smoking, pets, children, air conditioning—whatever is important to you.

A reservation service acts as a clearinghouse and frequently provides an opportunity to stay at a B&B that would not be available any other way.

KEY TO SYMBOLS
♥ Lots of honeymooners come here.
♯ Families with children are very welcome. (Please see page xii.)
♠ "Please emphasize that we are a private home, not an inn."
♣ Groups or private parties sometimes book the entire B&B.
♦ Travel agents' commission paid. (Please see page xii.)
✖ Sorry, no guests' pets are allowed.
✗ No smoking inside *or* no smoking at all, even on porches.

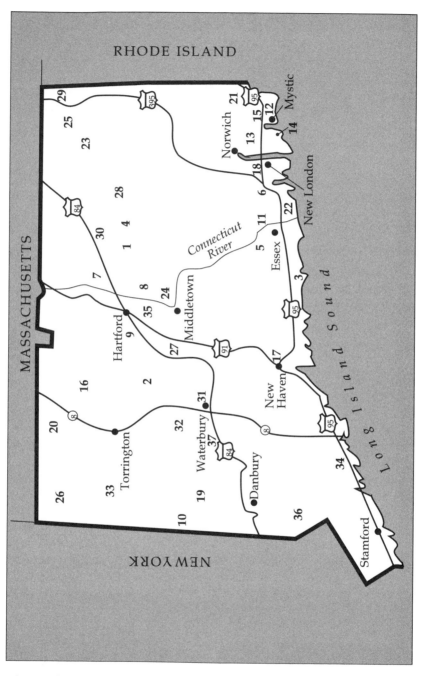

The numbers on this map indicate the locations of B&Bs described in detail in this chapter.

CONNECTICUT

__ Connecticut Reservation Services __

Bed and Breakfast, Ltd.
P.O. Box 216, New Haven, CT 06513

Phone: 203/469-3260 During the academic year (Jack teaches full time), 5–9:30 p.m. weekdays; anytime weekends or summer months.

Listings: Over 125. "From elegantly simple to simply elegant." Located throughout Connecticut. Some listings in Massachusetts and Rhode Island; new listings constantly added. Mostly private residences. A few inns and unhosted private residences.

Reservations: For one day or up to three months. Same-day service usually available. "A quick phone call encouraged to discuss availability and appropriate placement." Thereafter, guests have direct advance contact with host.

Rates: $45–$50 singles, $50–$75 doubles. Suites and deluxe accommodations slightly higher. ◆

Jack Argenio emphasizes variety—in types of homes as well as in price range. Many are historic residences filled with antiques. He selects knowledgeable and congenial hosts and tries to personalize matches to suit guests' needs and budget.

Plus: In-ground pools, Jacuzzis, gourmet dinners, hiking trails. Some hosts meet guests at airports or train stations.

Covered Bridge
Maple Avenue, P.O. Box 447, Norfolk, CT 06058-0447

Phone: 203/542-5944, 9 a.m.–6 p.m. daily; other times, answering machine.

Listings: 70. Most are hosted private residences in Connecticut's Litchfield County and shoreline communities, in the Berkshires of Massachusetts, in Rhode Island and New York towns bordering Connecticut, and in Southern Vermont. A few are unhosted and some are inns. A free sample list is available. Directory (booklet), $3.

Reservations: One to two weeks' advance notice preferred. Two-day minimum for weekends, three for holidays. Available through travel agents.

Rates: $60–$150. Some family, senior citizen, and weekly rates available. Prepayment in full is required. Cancellations received at least 10 days before expected arrival date will be refunded less a $15 handling charge. With less than 10 days' notice, entire prepayment may be forfeited unless room is rebooked. ◆

Hank and Diane Tremblay, former corporate executives, are experienced travelers and innkeepers (Manor House, page 20) who work with travelers on an individual basis to try to accommodate their needs. Most of their selected hosts live in antiques-furnished historic homes that are sometimes featured in major national publications. Many are in idyllic settings. Hearty breakfasts are a feature, as is the "free to come and go" atmosphere.

Nutmeg Bed & Breakfast Agency

P.O. Box 1117, West Hartford, CT 06127-1117   Fax 203/232-7680

Phone: 800/727-7592 or 203/236-6698, Monday through Friday, 9:30–5, year round; machine at other times.

Listings: 200. Located throughout Connecticut—near all major cities and towns and along the shore—and in the Berkshires foothills of Massachusetts, in bordering Rhode Island towns, and in New York. Hosted private residences and some inns. Directory ($5) has general characteristics of each area as well as house descriptions.

Reservations: One week's advance notice preferred. Two-night minimum on holidays and graduation weekends and at other times at some locations.

Rates: $45–$125 single; $55–$150 double; average $75–$95. Family and weekly rates available. Amex, MC, Visa to hold reservations. $15 charge for confirmed cancellation. One night's lodging charged if notice received less than 7 days before expected arrival; 14 days for holidays and special events. Five percent credit card fee. ◆

Michelle Souza, a B&B convert who has traveled extensively, offers quality accommodations for tourists and business travelers. Her well-established service specializes in finding temporary and permanent housing for relocating executives; she also works with colleges, private schools, and hospitals to provide lodging for visiting faculty, parents, and patients in private homes.

Other reservation services with some B&Bs in Connecticut:
Bed & Breakfast/Inns of New England, page 259
Bed & Breakfast of Rhode Island, page 307

KEY TO SYMBOLS
♥ Lots of honeymooners come here.
⋈ Families with children are very welcome. (Please see page xii.)
◖ "Please emphasize that we are a private home, not an inn."
⁂ Groups or private parties sometimes book the entire B&B.
◆ Travel agents' commission paid. (Please see page xii.)
✖ Sorry, no guests' pets are allowed.
✦ No smoking inside *or* no smoking at all, even on porches.

Connecticut B&Bs

Jared Cone House

203/643-8538

25 Hebron Road, Bolton, CT 06043

Hosts: Jeff and Cinde Smith
Location: Fifteen miles east of Hartford; 15 west of University of Connecticut; 7 west of Caprilands Herb Farm; 2 to Lake Bolton. On the Green in rural community (population 5,000) with farms and woodlands. Near fine cuisine, pick-your-own farms, hay and sleigh rides.
Open: Year round. Reservations requested.
Rates: Single $45 shared bath, $55 private. Double $60 shared bath, $70 private. Rollaway $10.
🏠 🛄 🛏 🍴

The Palladian window in the second-floor hallway is a dramatic introduction to the guest floor in this traditional post-and-beam center hall Georgian colonial, which has wide board floors and a kitchen with a huge hearth. Architecture buffs are delighted with an invitation to see the hand-hewn beams in the attic and the hand-stacked rock foundation in the basement. Jeff, a furniture maker, and Cinde purchased their treasure in 1985. Built by a wealthy farmer in the late 1700s, and once the library and the town's post office, the house is now registered with the U.S. Department of the Interior Office of Archeology and Historic Preservations.

The spacious rooms in the historic home have print wallpapers, antiques and reproductions, and a light, airy, uncluttered look. This is the land of antiquing (right here at the B&B, if you'd like), fall foliage, and canoeing (with the hosts' canoe).

In residence: In family quarters on first floor—Julie, age eight, and Drew, age five. Two cats, Groucho and Wilma.
Bed and bath: Three second-floor queen-bedded rooms. One with private full bath en suite. Two share a full bath. Crib and twin rollaway available.
Breakfast: Usually 8–10. Juice, homemade pumpkin bread, cream cheese, jellies and marmalades. Eggs with toast, pancakes, or French toast with homemade maple syrup. Fresh fruit in the summer. Served in dining room or on the porch.
Plus: Upstairs sitting area next to Palladian window. Porch. Patio. Use of bicycles, stroller, playpen. Pinball, Ping-Pong, darts, and ring toss in barn game room.

---

*U*nless otherwise stated, rates in this book are for two and include breakfast in addition to all the amenities in "Plus."

Chimney Crest Manor   203/582-4219
5 Founders Drive, Bristol, CT 06010

Hosts: Dan and Cynthia Cimada-more
Location: On a hilltop overlooking Farmington Valley. In historic Federal Hill area, one-quarter mile from Bristol Clock Museum, 1 mile from New England Carousel Museum; 14 miles from Litchfield Hills. Twenty minutes west of Hartford, 15 east of Waterbury.
Open: Year round. Two-night mini-mum stay on holiday weekends and in foliage season.
Rates: $75, $80, $95, $105 single; $85, $90, $105, $115 double. $10 child, $15 age seven and older. Weekly and monthly rates available. Corporate, senior citizen, and Lovers' Weekend (two-night stay) discounts. MC, Visa.
♥ ⁂ ◆ ✈ ⊬

British royalty, honeymooners, and many business travelers have walked along the 40-foot-long arcade in this sprawling 32-room Tudor mansion. There's a cherry-paneled library, a Spanish-tiled sun room, six handcrafted fireplaces, and ornate plaster ceilings. Much of the house is carpeted; furnishings are traditional.

When a television crew filmed a B&B segment here, they pointed the camera at the tile roof, arches, gardens, and multiflue chimneys. Then they came into the huge dining room, where a roaring blaze was in the fireplace and the table was beautifully set. The estate was built in 1930 by the Barnes family, known locally for specialty steels and springs. Since Cynthia's parents bought the house in the mid-1950s, it has seen use as a preparatory school. After the second Cimadamore child was born, Cynthia was ready for "something else to do at home." The residence for three generations became a B&B offering privacy and warm hospitality, large full guest suites and meeting room space.

In residence: Diana, age 17, and Dante, age 9. Buffy is the family's bichon frise.
Bed and bath: Five suites. Large very private garden suite (great for families or meeting leaders) with fireplaced living room, queen-bedded room, wet bar. Three second-floor queen-bedded suites, each with private full bath, sitting room; one suite with working fireplace, two with full kitchens. One first-level apartment with private parking and entrance.
Breakfast: Full, 7–8; continental until 9; weekends an hour later. Fruit salad, homemade breads plus yogurt pancakes, French toast, or eggs. Served with linen, china, and crystal in fireplaced dining room. Dan or Cynthia joins guests.
Plus: Bedroom air conditioning. Fan, clock radio, television with cable, telephone in each suite. Garden. Large patio.

From New York: *"The place is beautiful. . . . Our first B&B experience and we are won over. Cynthia was terrific, the food excellent."*

---

*D*id you hear about the salesman who left a B&B breakfast
with five good leads?

Captain Dibbell House

203/669-1646

21 Commerce Street, Clinton, CT 06413-2107

Hosts: Ellis and Helen Adams
Location: Two blocks from harbor, on a historic residential street. One mile south of I-95, just off Route 1. Two miles to Hammonasset State Beach; 10 to Essex; 40 to Mystic; 23 to Yale University; 3 to Salt Meadow National Wildlife Refuge.
Open: February–December. Two-day minimum stay on holiday weekends. **Rates:** Queen-bedded rooms $85 double, $75 single. Twin-bedded room $75 double, $65 single. Three-night discount. Weekly, senior, corporate, and off-season (November–May) rates. Amex, Discover, MC, Visa.
♥ ♣ ♦ ✈ ⊬

A triumph! For three consecutive years, the hosts of this small B&B won first prize in *Yankee* magazine's Great New England Inns Apple Pie Contest. Their restored 1866 Victorian, "not the ornate kind," is furnished with family pieces and auction finds. Much of the original art work is done by "up and coming" traditional artists. Classical music is almost always playing. And the perennial gardens are flourishing.

"After spending summers in the area on our sailboat, we knew this would be a marvelous place to open our kind of B&B, a small friendly place in a small friendly coastal town with wonderful sunsets viewed from the beach." And so it has been for the Adamses since they left their Poughkeepsie, New York area jobs as child welfare caseworker and public health inspector. "Now, seven years later, we have hosted some of the greatest people in the world. Some breakfasts last more than two hours, and people who arrived here as strangers to us and to the other guests leave as friends."

In residence: Two cats: "very shy" Mister Max, and Ramses (Abyssinian).
Bed and bath: Four second-floor rooms, all private baths. Three with queen bed; two with shower bath, one with tub/shower bath. One room with king/twins option, shower bath.
Breakfast: 8:30–10. An egg dish or baked treat such as scones or breakfast version of the prize-winning pie. Juice, fresh fruit, teas and freshly ground coffee. In summer, served in gazebo bordered by gardens and brick walk.
Plus: Bedroom ceiling fans. Fruit. Flowers. Freshly baked snack. Guest refrigerator. Lawn games. Puzzles, games, and cards. Borrowables include bicycles, beach chairs with umbrella, cooler, rain umbrella.

From Massachusetts: *"Attention to detail . . . everything was wonderful."*

Innkeeping may be America's most envied profession. As one host mused, "Where else can you get a job where, every day, someone tells you how wonderful you are?"

Maple Hill Farm Bed & Breakfast

365 Goose Lane, Coventry, CT 06238-1215   203/742-0635
                                                 800/742-0635

Hosts: Tony Felice and Mary Beth Gorke-Felice
Location: Rural. Four miles from I-84 and from Caprilands Herb Farm, 7 miles west of University of Connecticut, 20 miles east of Hartford. On seven acres with apple orchard, stone fences, birds, flowers.

Open: Year round. Two-night minimum stay on University of Connecticut's graduation, homecoming, and parents' weekends.
Rates: $50 single, $60 double, $5 crib, $10 extra person. MC, Visa.
♥ ♨ ⚓ ❖ ✕ ⚷

A real B&B. An experience. A trip through 260 years. A great setting for a wedding—or for a ride in the Amish buggy. In back, there's still a three-seat outhouse; the original dwelling, which predates the house; and a well. And there are horses, an in-ground swimming pool, hammocks, and a picnic area under a huge maple tree, alongside an English garden. Inside the Cape-style house there are gunstock posts, wide board floors, and lots of collectibles and family memorabilia, all blending with skylights and a solarium with hot tub and huge winter-flowering jade. The keeping room has been recreated complete with beehive oven in cook-in fireplace built with original hearthstone and lintel. The window seat awaits (while Tony cooks breakfast) in the restored kitchen, which has original wood floor and, now, countertops from a 1740 building. "When the children left, we felt that the space was meant to be shared," explains Mary Beth, an independent pediatric nurse practitioner. For the curious (and most guests are), Tony, an industrial salesman, and Mary Beth share fascinating and fun information about the history of the house and its former owners. All this, with breakfast by candlelight accompanied by classical music.

In residence: Brandy Alexander, "an extremely affectionate miniature poodle."
Bed and bath: Four second-floor double-bedded rooms (one also has a single bed, one also has a crib) share two full baths (one is Victorian with claw-foot tub).
Breakfast: 7:30–9. "A feast." Fresh fruit dish. Homemade bread. Their own farm-fresh eggs. Bacon or ham, French toast or hotcakes. Cereals. Served on heirloom china, crystal, and silver.
Plus: Tour of house. VCR movies with fresh popcorn. Board games. Therapeutic massage by appointment. Jacuzzi in solarium.

> Many guests wrote: *"Relaxing . . . authentic . . . beautiful countryside . . . hosts who embrace guests with open arms and warm hearts . . . memorable."*

Wedding guests love to stay at a B&B.

Riverwind   203/526-2014
209 Main Street, Deep River, CT 06417-1704

Hosts: Barbara Barlow and Bob Bucknall
Location: Adjacent to the town green, in a small Connecticut River Valley village between Essex and Chester. Minutes to Goodspeed Opera House, Gillette Castle, Hammonasset Beach; half hour to Mystic Seaport.

Open: Year round. Two-night minimum, Saturday inclusive, April 15–January 2.
Rates: Per room. $90 (the one with unattached bath) to $150 ("Champagne and Roses"). Additional occupant, 50 percent of room rate. MC, Visa.
♥ ⁂ ✦

Perfect for several magazines, including *Country Living* and *Country Inns.* Recipient of a "ten best country inns" award. The site of small weddings. (Barbara is a justice of the peace.) Romance also plays a part in this inn's history.

Barbara, a Virginia junior high school learning-disabilities teacher who had experience restoring three other houses, came north for a week and found and bought the abandoned 1850 house. She uncovered fireplaces, hand sanded floors, wired, tiled, and stenciled. In 1984 she drove a truck from Smithfield, Virginia, filled with family and other country antiques. Placed throughout the inn, they show a love of folk art, a sense of display, imagination, and whimsy. A garden rake handle holds the hanging over one mantel. Carpenters' tools are towel racks. Pig items acknowledge the innkeeper's growing years on a farm in the ham capital of the world. Color schemes are taken from quilts.

When it was time to expand, Barbara planned an authentically styled 18th-century keeping room along with four more guest rooms, some quite luxurious. She hired Bob Bucknall, a local contractor, a Deep River native. And in fairytale fashion, they fell in love, they married (in Virginia), and Bob became full-time co-innkeeper.

In residence: Miss Hickory, "an affectionate tabby."
Bed and bath: Eight rooms on first and second floors. All private baths. Each room quite different. Queen or double beds. Some are canopied; some, four-posters. "Champagne and Roses" features queen canopied bed, bath with Japanese steeping tub, separate shower, private balcony, complimentary champagne.
Breakfast: Usually 9–10:30. (Coffee and tea for early risers.) A southern buffet in fireplaced dining room. Hot entree, Smithfield ham, pig-shaped biscuits, fruit compote, coffee cake, juices, coffee, tea.
Plus: Bedroom air conditioning and ceiling fans. Welcoming drink. Game room. Library. Guitar. Complimentary beverages. Mints. Flowers. Piano; old sheet music. Plant- and wicker-filled wraparound (glassed-in) porch—with ceiling fans. Bocci. Hibachis. Picnic baskets. Directions to "best-kept secret" nature preserve.

Guests wrote: *"Charming . . . relaxing . . . warm hospitality."*

The Red House

203/739-5327

365 Boston Post Road, East Lyme, CT 06333-1402

Hosts: Harlan and Joan Sturgis
Location: A rural setting on three acres. On a two-lane road, 5 minutes from I-95, 3 to the shore, 20 to Essex and Mystic. Midway between New York City and Boston.
Open: April through February;

closed Thanksgiving and Christmas. Reservations preferred.
Rates: Per room. $60 single, $75 double. $7 cot. Special rates for families using both rooms.

From Rhode Island: *"Great people. Harlan (justifiably) takes great pride in the berries he grows and serves for breakfast . . . Joan's wonderful too . . . their 1760s house, a real charmer."* From Australia: *"Interesting and comfortable."*

A gem of a B&B is another way of putting it. The Sturgises bought the 1760 center chimney colonial, all restored, in 1982. Inside you'll find wainscoting, small-print wallpapers, seven (nonworking) fireplaces, and, in the living room, exposed ceiling beams and a beehive oven. Part of the family room is a greenhouse where most of the plantings are started. It also has a wood stove and sliding doors to a welcoming wood deck.

Outside are thriving gardens, stone walls, two "mugs," a goose pen, and circular rock outcroppings, all with stories. Archeologists think the mugs, or outdoor cellars, are is similar to caves discovered nearby, carbon tested to circa 900 B.C.

Harlan, a selectman and retired school principal, has lived in town for over 40 years. Joan, a native, is a massage therapist (right here, if you'd like). They share good hints for interesting back roads to area attractions.

In residence: Sherman and Midnight, "friendly and talkative cats."
Bed and bath: Two rooms with nonworking fireplaces, private adjoining baths. First-floor room has king/twins option, wide board floors, exposed beams, tub bath. Second-floor room has heirloom double bed, shower bath. Cot available.
Breakfast: 6:30–9:30 weekdays, Sundays until 10. Coffee for early risers. Menu varies. Often, Harlan's blueberry pancakes with buttermilk and his blueberries. Served with sausages or bacon or French toast made from Joan's sourdough bread. Homemade jams. Unlimited coffee. Hosts usually join you in the sunny dining room overlooking the gardens, or on the deck.
Plus: Refreshments. House and garden tour. Sometimes, opportunities to pick raspberries. Family room with TV and wood-burning stove. Bedroom window fans. Passes to private beach. Outdoor hot/cold shower.

Unless otherwise stated, rates in this book are per room for two and include breakfast in addition to all the amenities in "Plus." As for taxes and gratuities, please see page xi.

The Stephen Potwine House   203/623-8722

84 Scantic Road, East Windsor, CT 06088

Hosts: Bob and Vangi Cathcart
Location: Overlooks a pond, sweeping lawn, and willow trees on rural Route 191. Two miles from Route 91. Between Hartford, Connecticut, and Springfield, Massachusetts. Adjoins 100 acres of undeveloped state property. Near

cider mills, antiques shops, theater.
Open: Year round. Reservations required.
Rates: Main house room—$65 single, $75 double. Guest wing—shared bath $45 single, $55 double.
♥ ◢ ⁂ ✖ ⊬

Weddings have been held by the pond. Some honeymooners have opened their presents in the living room. Other travelers return for rest and renewal weekends, scheduled periodically by Vangi, a stress management/wellness counselor who teaches yoga and conducts Reiki sessions. Her career switch, from retailing and fashion, coincided with empty-nest time. Husband and cohost Bob is an insurance office manager.

The homestead, built in 1831 for Stephen Potwine and occupied by family members until 25 years ago, is the Cathcarts' sixth restoration. (Others have been in Rochester, New York, and in Hartford and Boston.) In 1986 Vangi stenciled walls, curtains, and "charming crooked floors." She repaired Grandmother's crocheted bedspreads, hung family portraits, and arranged country collectibles. And one Mrs. Potwine, a 91-year-old East Windsor resident, came to tea.

In residence: Chaun-see, "a very friendly Himalayan cat who is not allowed in guest quarters."
Bed and bath: Three second-floor rooms. One in main house has queen bed, air conditioning, nonworking fireplace, private full bath with Jacuzzi. In guest wing, reached through carriage house, two double-bedded rooms (one is air conditioned) share a full bath with claw-foot tub and a sitting room.
Breakfast: 7–9. Garnished with Vangi's herbs. Juices, eggs, granola, cereal, cottage cheese, homemade muffins, bagels, English muffins. "Healthy eating encouraged!" Served in dining room.
Plus: Coffee in fireplaced keeping room or on screened porch. Picnic table, canoe, TV, VCR. Cross-country skiing, ice skating, and fishing right here.

From Virginia: *"We were treated like friends in a beautiful home and peaceful setting."*

Butternut Farm   203/633-7197

1654 Main Street, Glastonbury, CT 06033-2962   fax 203/633-7197

Host: Don Reid
Location: On two wooded and landscaped acres. "Within 90 minutes of most of Connecticut." Ten minutes from Hartford by expressway; 1.6 miles south of Glastonbury Center to Whapley Road. Enter by first hole in

the bushes on left. "Don't run over the chickens, please."
Open: Year round.
Rates: $65 room. $75 suite. $85 apartment. Amex.
♥ ◢ ⁂ ✖ ⊬

From Michigan: *"Everything about this amazing place, from the lovingly restored old house and farm buildings to the antique furnishings and exotic animals, from the homemade breakfast jam to the bedtime sherry, conspires to make a couple of nights and breakfasts quite unforgettable."*

Other family members attending our nephew's wedding agreed with the mother of the bride from Michigan.

Don restored this 1720 center entrance architectural gem with its eight wide fireplaces, pumpkin pine floors, and paneled walls while he was a banker. (Then he was a schoolteacher for seven years.) Along the way, in the 1970s, he was asked to accommodate a neighbor's guests. Ever since, he has been sharing his home with travelers—including famous chefs.

Everywhere you look, there's an 18th-century treasure—a cherry highboy, a gateleg table, banister-back chairs, and English delft—in addition to hand-hammered hinges, exposed beams, and 12-over-12 windows. Outside, there are tulips in the spring, herb gardens, and Adirondack chairs on a stone patio. And those animals. All appreciated by first-time as well as repeat guests.

In residence: "The neighborhood petting zoo—Abyssinian cats Chester, Rupert, and Millie crave attention." Fifteen goats with names, 50 pigeons without names, 50 chickens with eggs! And Harry, the goose, two ducks, "one gorgeous golden pheasant."

Foreign languages spoken: French, some German and Italian.

Bed and bath: Two rooms—one with two twin "hired man's" beds and one with a double canopied bed, each with full bath. Two suites—one with a four-poster double, private full bath; one with double sofa bed, shower bath, private entrance. Barn apartment has double canopied bed, full bath, kitchen, private garden.

Breakfast: Usually 8:30; flexible for business travelers. Juice and fruit. Fresh-from-the-barn eggs and milk. Toast. Homemade jam. Don's honey. Cheeses. Goat's milk, coffee, tea. Served in intimate breakfast room or in early 18th-century dining room.

Plus: Air conditioning. Individual thermostats. Private phone, TV, and VCR in some rooms. Late-afternoon wine or soft drinks. Guest refrigerators. Apples. Several common rooms.

Nutmeg Bed & Breakfast Agency Host #449

West Hartford, CT

Location: On a quiet residential street. Minutes' walk to West Hartford Center; seven-minute drive to St. Joseph College and UConn West Hartford. Fifteen minutes to downtown Hartford.

Reservations: Usually long-term bookings; occasionally one- or two-night reservations. Year round through Nutmeg Bed & Breakfast Agency, page 3.

Rates: $55 single. $65 double.
✭

The Dutch Colonial house, furnished traditionally with a Victorian flair, is the home of an elementary school teacher/professional singer and her husband, a flugelhorn, trumpet, and violin player who also teaches. Both natives of West Hartford, these community activists offer friendly hospitality in a

(Please turn page.)

fashion adopted from their own B&B stays—providing privacy, directions, and suggestions to guests who tend to stay several months, sometimes on weekdays only.

In residence: One dog, "an important member of the family."
Bed and bath: On second floor—one large room with brass double bed, private full bath, phone, cable TV. Adjacent smaller room with twin four-poster Civil War bed booked alone only if larger room isn't booked.
Breakfast: Continental. Bagels, muffins , cereals, juice, hot beverages. "All set up for early risers." Prebreakfast coffee brought to your door, if you'd like.
Plus: Fresh flowers. Use of kitchen, laundry, garage space.

Nutmeg Bed & Breakfast Agency Host #322
Kent, CT

Location: On brook-bordered two acres along Route 7 in Litchfield County. In season, sheep in pastureland across the street. Three miles north of Kent center. Five-minute drive to Kent School; 3 miles to Kent Falls State Park and Appalachian Trail; 20 to Lake Waramaug. Near Audubon sanctuary, wineries, antiquing.
Reservations: Year round through Nutmeg Bed & Breakfast Agency, page 3. Two-night minimum on holidays.
Rates: $85 Blue Room. $90 Rose Room or cottage.

♥ ✪ ✗ ✄

"We don't want to leave," say many guests who come for a getaway. "Royal treatment" is just what the hosts envisioned when they moved here seven years ago from another part of Connecticut. That's when the host, a retired engineer who dreams of being a full-time innkeeper, found this 1860 house. Its 1930 addition, built from an old barn, is perfect for their antiques (collectibles) shop and for the hostess's stenciling studio. Her lovely work is evident throughout the main house, where she has many carefully arranged collections, including dolls, Quimper, cranberry glass, and Wedgwood. The cottage, too, has stenciling, antiques, and designer linens.

Bed and bath: Two rooms plus a cottage. Up a private staircase to two quiet double-bedded rooms in back. Rose Room has beamed cathedral ceiling, private tub and shower bath, sitting room. Blue Room has private tub and shower bath (two steps from room). Private cottage has queen-bedded room, pullout sofa in living room, kitchen, bath.
Breakfast: Presented 7–noon. Fresh fruit, juice, breads and muffins, natural cereals, hot beverages. With fine china, linens, and glassware. Cottage guests have option of eating there at any hour or in main house in the morning.
Plus: Afternoon tea. Beverages always available. Specialty soaps. A hallmark—plenty of towels, including bath sheets. Special occasions acknowledged; "let us know."

From Bernice's mailbag: "The last straw was the classmate from 1935, whom I hadn't seen in 50 years, who read about us in your book. He's been here twice."

Hidden Meadow

40 Blood Street, Lyme, CT 06371

203/434-8360

fax 203/434-3328

Hosts: The Brossard family
Location: In a quiet country area, good for walking. Near antiques shops, fine restaurants. Three miles to Old Lyme village, 15 minutes to Essex, within half hour of Mystic, Stonington, state beaches.

Open: Year round. Two-night minimum on holiday weekends, May 15–30, month of October.
Rates: Per room. $90–$110 king, queen, or twin beds.
♥ ❀ ⊁

There's even room to stable your horse here on the idyllic property. The house began in 1760. Additions were made by well-known Lyme residents, a Broadway actor, and an author who specialized in New England historic houses and barns. The changes in the 1930s resulted in a colonial with Georgian entry, circular driveway, multiple stone terraces, iron railings, and reflecting pool. And there are lawns, gardens, stately trees, a small orchard, two horse barns (tours given), and other small buildings. Restoration, of course, is constant.

Karen, a U.S. Pony Clubs riding instructor (and tennis player) and her daughters have lived here since 1986. They started B&B in 1991 by "spoiling guests," using china, silver, and linens in a fireplaced dining room decorated with antiques, chintzes, and still-life paintings. They mark maps and give touring suggestions—all to appreciative "new friends."

In residence: In hosts' quarters, Nancy, age 20, and Kate, 15. One dog, Nutmeg, is "our hostess with the mostest." Dusty, a Labrador, enjoys wading in the reflecting pool. Four horses.
Foreign language spoken: French, a little by Karen; fluent by daughters Lucie and Anne, who visit frequently.
Bed and bath: Three second-floor rooms, attached private full baths. Two could be a suite: one with king bed and fireplace, one with twin four-poster beds/king option and sitting area. One has queen bed.
Breakfast: 8:30–10 (earlier for bird-watchers). Fresh fruit, homemade breads, muffins. Brandy French toast, farm-fresh eggs, country sausage or bacon, blueberry pancakes, walnut waffles. In dining room or on covered terrace.
Plus: Tea, sherry, or lemonade. Homemade cookies. Living room with fireplace and beehive oven. Library. Help yourself to raspberry crop (in July). Fresh flowers. Thick towels. Mints. Window fans.

Nutmeg Bed & Breakfast Agency Host #513

Mystic, CT

Location: On 1½ acres, surrounded by stone walls and fruit trees. Half mile off I-95, along the street that leads into Mystic. Five-minute drive to Mystic Seaport; 20 to Rocky Neck Beach in New London.
Reservations: Year round except

Christmas Eve and New Year's Eve through Nutmeg Bed & Breakfast Agency, page 3. Two-day minimum for holiday weekends.
Rates: Per room. $95–$125. $20 third person.
♥ ❀ ✈ ⊁

(Please turn page.)

Outside there's a Scottish flag, sign of the hospitality offered inside by a Scottish-born hostess and her Connecticut-born husband, a mechanical engineer who is looking forward to becoming a full-time host.

During one of their many trips to Mystic, after having lived all over the country, they chanced upon a FOR SALE sign in front of this rambling 15-room Victorian (with attached barn and outbuildings), which had been meticulously restored two years earlier. The house deed, dated in the 1800s with Charles Hancock's signature, hangs in the hall. Was he a relative of John Hancock? Such research is ongoing—as is the search for "just the right antique."

Some day this house, where Victorian teas, seminars, and family reunions are held, may be the setting for a novel. The hostess, a writer, has formed an area writers' workshop.

In residence: One son in his twenties. One dog and two cats.
Foreign language spoken: "A little high school French."
Bed and bath: Four air-conditioned bedrooms, all private baths; plus one additional room for party booking a second-floor room. First floor—queen-bedded room with working fireplace, private full en-suite bath. Honeymoon suite with double bed, private shower bath en suite, TV; French doors lead to private deck. Second floor—king/twins option, private full bath or room with king bed, private shower bath.
Breakfast: 8:30–9:30. Fruit compote. Eggs, bacon, sausage. Strawberry walnut pancakes or French toast and scones. Muffins or nut breads. Bagels and cream cheese. Served in large, many-windowed dining room or in garden.
Plus: Beverages. Candy. Garden flowers. TV room, books, games, VCR (lots of movies). Chairs under dogwood tree.

Applewood Farms Inn   203/536-2022

528 Colonel Ledyard Highway, Ledyard, CT 06339-1608

Hosts: Frankie and Tom Betz
Location: On 33 acres. A colonial farm surrounded by stone walls, lawn, and a neighboring breeding farm for prize Arabians. Five miles north of Mystic. Six miles south of Foxwoods Casino.
Open: Year round. Two-day minimum stay on weekends.

Rates: Shared bath—$65, $90. Private bath—$115 double bed, $125 king. Suites—$150 two rooms, $250 three rooms. Discounts for four or more days. $25 third person in room. Amex, MC, Visa (but check or cash preferred).
♥ ♦ ✥ ♦

Thank goodness. Thank the Betzes, and many do, for buying this farm, which was considered for condominiums in the 1980s. A guest from New Hampshire dubbed it "a real discovery," one that is now on the National Register of Historic Places. Five generations of Gallups lived in the 1826 house until it became a horse farm in 1964. When the Betzes bought it in 1985, they restored everything. Most walls are simulated whitewash. There's stenciling and hand-hewn chestnut floor boards. And antiques, primitives, a grandfather clock, a large pewter collection, and lots of indoor plants. Next door there are about 50 Arabian horses. The Betzes have one of their own, plus sheep "for local color."

Tom's farming days started at age 11, long before he had a marine electronics business (and a home in Mystic with a greenhouse). Here, he wears a cowboy hat, rides a tractor, grows vegetables and roses, and dreams up special Valentine's Day arrangements. Tom and Frankie, known for her award-winning jams, are the grandparents of four and have linked their interests in horticulture, birding, and travel.

In residence: Milton, a Hungarian sheepdog. Wiggles, the cat.
Bed and bath: Six rooms, four with working fireplaces and private baths. Two share a tub/shower bath. Rooms are on second and third floors and have king, canopied four-poster double, or double bed.
Breakfast: 8–10. Juice, tropical fruit dish with sherbet, eggs with bacon and toast. "Other surprises." Hot beverages. Can last as long as two hours.
Plus: Beverages. Air conditioning in some bedrooms. Two common rooms. Parlor baby grand piano. Fruit, mints, seasonal wildflowers. Hiking trails. With advance notice, pickup at stations or Groton–New London Airport. "Polite pets welcomed; kennel and stable provided."

The Palmer Inn   203/572-9000
25 Church Street, Noank, CT 06340-3611

Host: Patricia Ann White
Location: In a quiet fishing village, two miles southwest of Mystic. One block to Long Island Sound beach. Within walking distance of tennis, art galleries, and a renowned casual lobster-in-the-rough restaurant.
Open: Year round. Two-night mini-

mum on summer and fall weekends.
Rates: $115–$135 third floor; $125–$165 second floor; $165–$175 room with fireplace. Package rates include sailing lessons with certified captain in Noank.
❀ ✠ ⊱

"Connecticut's best" for a *Yankee* magazine apple pie contest is also almost famous for Dickens and Arthur. In their honor, one guest, a Long Island baker, brought cakes shaped like dachsunds and decorated with "authentic" faces.

Pat is an ardent sailor who loves her home port. And she loves her home, this Southern plantation–like house located on just an acre of land. It has 30-foot pillars in front and a main hall with 13-foot ceilings, mahogany beams, brass fixtures, and original wallcovering.

Until 1984 Pat was director of a nonprofit agency. Here, surrounded by family heirlooms and antiques, she greets first-timers and many returnees, who come for holiday theme weekends, a crackling fire, the sound of a foghorn, a nearby winery, dinner sails, and hot-air ballooning.

In residence: Dickens and Arthur, miniature dachshunds, "real charmers."
Bed and bath: Six (large, some huge) second- and third-floor rooms, some with water views. King, queen, and twin beds available. All private full baths.
Breakfast: 8:30–9:30. Fresh fruit salad. Homemade granola (featured in *Yankee* magazine), breads and muffins—especially banana walnut—and jellies, jams. In the Grand Salon, "our parlor."

(Please turn page.)

Plus: Tea or sherry, 4–6. Ceiling fans in all rooms. Library. Games. Fresh flowers year round. Veranda. Bicycles. Shop with antiques and works by local artists.

The Old Mystic Inn   203/572-9422

58 Main Street, P.O. Box 634, Old Mystic, CT 06372

Hosts: Mary and Peter Knight
Location: On a two-lane main street (Route 27) in the village. Five minutes north of Mystic Seaport.
Open: Year round. Two-night minimum May–November weekends.

Rates: May–October $135 weekends, $110 weekdays. November–April $115 weekends, $95 weekdays. $20 rollaway. Amex, MC, Visa.
♥ ♫ ♣ ♦ ✈

It didn't take long for Peter to be dubbed "the mayor of Mystic." And just a year after the Knights, parents of five grown children, fulfilled their dream of becoming innkeepers, Peter bought the country grocery/morning muffin/sandwich store across the street. There's more: Peter, an ordained Episcopal minister who is also an estate and tax planner, travels to several pulpits during the year. Mary was an executive secretary and real estate office manager before becoming a full-time innkeeper.

The inn's painted sign recalls the years that the 1794 house, restored as a B&B in 1986, was a landmark bookstore. A carriage house was built in back in 1988. In 1991, after B&B research in England and throughout New England, the Knights moved from western Massachusetts, decorated in colonial colors, and furnished without clutter, with reproductions and antiques.

In residence: Duke, an English black Lab.
Bed and bath: Eight air-conditioned, carpeted rooms (three with working fireplaces); all queen beds (five are canopied), all private baths. In inn—one first-floor room, three (one with porch) on second floor. In carriage house—four ground-floor rooms, two with whirlpool tubs.
Breakfast: Usually 8:30–9:30. Fresh fruit. Homemade muffins and breads. Eggs, waffles, pancakes, or French toast. Hot beverages. At tables set for four in fireplaced dining room.
Plus: Fireplaced living room. Porches. Afternoon refreshments. Saturday evening wine and hors d'oeuvres. Train station pickup service. Chocolate kisses.

Cobble Hill Farm   203/379-0057

Steele Road, New Hartford, CT 06057

Host: Jo McCurdy
Location: On 40 magnificent acres. Two hours from Manhattan and Boston, 20 minutes to Litchfield, 30 to antiques shop on Route 7, 40 to Great Barrington or Lake Waramaug.

Open: Sorry, no longer in business (as of midyear 1994).
Rates: Per room—$95 with full breakfast; $455 weekly rate. $170 suite.
♣ ✈ ✂

Guests wrote: *"We felt like we were dreaming. . . . My husband says that the breakfast alone is worth the drive . . . a little piece of paradise."*

A *Country Living* magazine spread featured the old cooperage, now a summerhouse, and the grounds. Those grounds! Filled with gardens, paths, privacy, and a sense of freedom. No wonder that some guests enjoy a walk, sit by the spring-fed pond, or on the patio "where you can hear the chatter of the birds and the rush of the water over the dam."

The McCurdys brought up five children—"I loved that role," Jo says—here in this marvelous 1796 house filled with interesting antiques. When you finally move from the country kitchen cum attached greenhouse (I took many pictures right there), you'll see Jo's decorating skills in beautiful rooms without clutter or formality but with warmth and wonderful themes and colors. When husband Don returns from his business (controlling heat and air conditioning by computers), he too enjoys the farm and guests.

In residence: Bingo, a Jack Russell terrier. Buddy, a black Labrador. Horses, chickens, and other barn animals.

Bed and bath: Five very private second-floor rooms; some can be suites. All private baths. One with queen waterbed, shower bath. Four-poster canopied double bed, shower bath. High double bed, tub bath. Room with queen canopied bed and room with twins/king option, full bath.

Breakfast: 9:30. An event. Full menu—fresh fruit or baked apple, homemade muffins, bacon and fresh eggs, toast and homemade jam; maybe custard with raspberry sauce, pumpkin bread, raspberry-filled French toast. Juice, coffee, tea. Served in dining room by fireplace or on screened porch.

Plus: Swimming in pond. Gather your own breakfast eggs. Fireplaces in guests' living room and library. Bedroom floor fans. Big bath sheets. During the day, tea and coffee in dining room.

Nutmeg Bed & Breakfast Agency Host #210

New Haven, CT

Location: A quiet neighborhood of late 19th-century homes, one-half block from buses and Yale shuttle. Half mile from Yale's science campus. **Reservations:** Year round through Nutmeg Bed & Breakfast Agency,

page 3. Three-day minimum on Yale graduation and parents' weekends. **Rates:** Suite with private bath $90 for three, $80 double, $70 single. Semiprivate bath $55.

♥ ✗ ✗

In addition to guests who come for nearby Yale University, "many, especially foreign travelers, come to this 'gateway to New England' before going to the coast, to Cape Cod, and on up to Maine. They enjoy our symphony, theater, museums, antiques shows, and concerts."

The host is prepared with maps and books about New Haven—and on New England too. The century-old house is attractively and comfortably furnished.

In residence: Two cats.

Bed and bath: Third-floor suite has room with antique iron double bed, alcove with single bed, private full bath, convenience (microwave and refrig-

(Please turn page.)

erator) kitchen. Second-floor room has double brass and iron bed, shared bath.
Breakfast: Fresh fruit salad, baskets of homemade breads and muffins, cereals, coffee, tea, milk. Buffet style, with flowers and linens, in formal dining room.
Plus: *New York Times.* Beverages. Bedroom window or table fans. Front porch. Rear deck overlooks large perennial garden.

Queen Anne Inn

265 Williams Street, New London, CT 06320-5721

203/447-2600
800/347-8818

Host: Tracey Rose Cook
Location: In a residential neighborhood, one-quarter mile from I-95. Within walking distance of restaurants, Connecticut College, and the Coast Guard Academy. Ten-minute drive to Mystic Seaport, Eugene O'Neill Theater, Nautilus Museum.
Open: Year round. Two-night weekend minimum, May–October.
Rates: Double occupancy. Shared bath $78 or $90. Private bath $94, $110, $120, $135, or $145 (varies with size of bed, canopy, TV, working fireplace). Suite $155. Extra person $20. Singles $5 less. Amex, Diners, Discover, MC, Visa.
♥ ❖ ♦ ⚲ ⚵

A restoration award winner. A turreted 1880 Queen Anne Victorian with many fireplaces, a paneled foyer, intricate oak woodwork, and stained glass windows at the circular landing.

All restored. All in a town on the water, a feature Connecticut-born Tracey missed while she was an advertising manager for a Rochester, New York, newspaper. So here she is, managing the established inn, surrounded by Victorian antiques and a collection of nautical artwork—pampering honeymooners and tourists, dignitaries who are visiting the Coast Guard, and visiting professors at Connecticut College.

In residence: Husband Jim, weekend cohost, is a microbiologist, a Brown University research assistant. One cat "lives in our quarters only."
Bed and bath: Eight rooms, including two suites. On three floors. All private baths. Some with wood-burning or freestanding fireplace. Bridal room also has a balcony. Tower suite has kitchen and telephone. Twin/king, queen, and double beds; some canopied and antique four-posters. Rollaway available.
Breakfast: 8:30 and 9:30. Fruit, freshly made breads, muffins. Stratas, baked French toast casserole, or fruit-filled phyllo. Presented at individual tables in parlor by fireplace.
Plus: Jacuzzi on third floor, sign-up basis. Air-conditioned bedrooms. Private phone, desk, TV in some rooms. Flowers.

---

*If you've been to one B&B, you haven't been to them all.
If you have met one B&B host, you haven't met them all.*

The Homestead Inn

203/354-4080

5 Elm Street, New Milford, CT 06776

Hosts: Rolf and Peggy Hammer
Location: In the village center near village green, shops, restaurants, movie theater.
Open: Year round. Two-night minimum holiday and May–October weekends.

Rates: In the inn, $70–$80 single, $80–$90 double. In Treadwell House, $62–$70 single, $70–$80 double. Amex, Diners, Discover, MC, Visa.
♯ ♦ ✈

Unique! This inn, discovered by business travelers as well as vacationers, is really two buildings: an 1850 Victorian, an inn since 1928, and the neighboring Treadwell House, a former motel with inn decor.

The Hammers had restored two other older homes when, in 1985, they refurbished this property and decorated with antiques, reproductions, wallpaper, and traditional fabrics. And still they redo inside and garden outside.

Before becoming an innkeeper, Rolf had been in corporate sales and marketing. Peggy, a physical and massage therapist, collects children's books. Both hosts are experts on hiking trails, scenic drives, wineries, historic sites—"so much in these beautiful Litchfield Hills!"

In residence: Keeley, a golden retriever, and Candy, the cat, are not allowed in guest rooms.
Bed and bath: All private baths; most are tub and shower. Eight inn rooms on two floors. Rooms have one or two twin beds, one or two double beds, or a double and one twin. The six Treadwell House rooms have queen or two doubles. Rollaway and crib available.
Breakfast: Buffet 8–10 weekends; 6:30–9 weekdays. Fresh fruit, juice, English muffins, cereals, dark bread, coffee cake, yogurts, cheese. In beamed and fireplaced living room.
Plus: Air conditioners, telephones, TV in bedrooms. Wicker-furnished front porch. Soft drinks and ice in guest refrigerator.

From Massachusetts: *"In all our travels, one of the best for cleanliness, atmosphere and service . . . warm, friendly hosts . . . a successful 'inn' experience!"*

Covered Bridge Host #2NOR

Norfolk, CT

Location: Secluded estate on five acres. Ten-minute walk to town center, Yale School of Music; 20 to Music Mountain, 40 to Tanglewood. Near lakes, antiquing, skiing.
Reservations: Available year round

through Covered Bridge, page 2. Two-night minimum on holiday weekends.
Rates: Queen bed $90–$110. King bed $85–$100. Suite $125–$150.
♥ ♯ ❀ ✈ ✂

A horse and carriage will pick you up under the stone-pillared portico and take you along the circular driveway and the gorgeous grounds to the quiet tree-lined street and a restaurant on the other side of the town green. The hostess who arranges the garden flowers—iris, peonies, and lilacs—will make

(Please turn page.)

custom bouquets. And lined picnic baskets, coordinated with each room, are available to guests in this 1903 Colonial Revival house.

The English country look—throughout—was created with antiques, family heirlooms, and auction finds through the talents of the hostess, a former gift buyer who works in interior design, and her husband, a former paperhanger and painter.

Bed and bath: One suite plus two rooms; all private full baths. On second floor, spacious garden view suite with canopied queen bed, working fireplace in sitting room. Fireplaced peach room has canopied queen bed. Blue room has king/twins option.
Breakfast: 8:30–11. Full. Maybe omelets or eggs Benedict with bacon or sausage, homemade muffins and breads, fresh fruit and juice. Served in guest rooms.
Plus: Welcoming beverage. Fireplaced living room. Spacious sun porch. Terrace. Candy. Silver beverage bucket. Robes. In each room, tape player, radio, (hidden) alarm clock. Special occasions acknowledged.

From New York: *"Don't tell. We want to keep this for ourselves."*

Manor House   203/542-5690
Maple Avenue, P.O. Box 447, Norfolk, CT 06058-0447

Hosts: Diane and Hank Tremblay
Location: On five beautifully landscaped acres, within walking distance of quiet village, historical society, antiquing, Yale chamber music concerts. On a side street off Route 44. Twenty miles to Tanglewood. Two and a half hours from Boston and New York.
Open: Year round. Two-day weekend minimum, three days on holiday weekends.

Rates: Double occupancy. $85–$95. $110–$160 with balcony. $110–$140 two-room suite. $120–$135 with two-person soaking tub. $135–$150 with Jacuzzi. $135–$160 with fireplace. $20 additional person. Less in March, April, and midweek. $10 one-night surcharge. Amex, MC, Visa.
♥ ❧ ◆ ✗ ✄

The perfect getaway. With hosts who "spoil their guests with unflappable affability" (*Philadelphia Inquirer*). They live in a very large antiques-furnished English Tudor, built in 1898 by Charles Spofford, designer of London's underground system. Often dubbed "romantic and elegant," the inn has the original cherry paneling, Tiffany stained glass windows—and, for one room, a private elevator. In another baronial-sized guest room there's a king-sized lace-canopied bed, a sitting area, a working fireplace, and a balcony. Manor House may be the only B&B in the world that offers free accommodations with the purchase of a harpsichord.

Beekeeper/gardener/chef Hank was a hit in a 1993 Abraham & Strauss (Manhattan) cooking demonstration. Until 1985 both hosts (the staff) were executives with a large Connecticut-based insurance company. Their commitment to personalized quality B&Bs carries over to their reservation service (page 2) for other B&Bs in the area.

In residence: "Mineau is our friendly and affectionate cat."
Foreign language spoken: French.
Bed and bath: Nine rooms on second and third floors. All with private bath; most have shower without tub; one has two-person soaking tub; one has two-person Jacuzzi. King, queen, double, or two twin beds; some rooms with daybed too. Some with private balcony.
Breakfast: Usually 8:30–10. Blueberry pancakes, orange waffles, stuffed French toast, or poached eggs with lemon chive sauce. Homemade muffins and Hank's yeast breads, Tremblays' honey, local maple syrup, homegrown vegetables, herbs and berries, special teas and coffee brewed with spring water. Served in dining room, on porch—or in bed!
Plus: Bedroom ceiling fans. Enormous fireplace with grand piano, 78-rpm record collection, and CDs (most were produced by Grammy award–winning guest). Library. Flannel sheets. Down comforters. Huge bath towels. Those garden flowers. Guest refrigerator. Town lake passes. Christmas sleigh rides. Horse-drawn historic tours. Possible tour of harpsichord builder's studio.

From Connecticut: *"Five stars! . . . a retreat from hustle and bustle of daily living . . . romantic decor . . . fantastic hosts . . . great breakfasts. . . . Perfect."*

Antiques & Accommodations
32 Main Street, North Stonington, CT 06359

203/535-1736
800/554-7829

Hosts: Ann and Tom Gray
Location: In a village center with 18th- and 19th-century homes and a meandering stream (where children fish). Fifteen minutes to Mystic, Stonington, and Watch Hill (Rhode Island) beaches. One mile from casino.
Open: Year round. Two-night mini-mum on summer and fall weekends.
Rates: Victorian midweek $95, $110, $125 with fireplace; weekends $155, $175, $195 fireplace. Single room $69. Cottage $125–$155. Suite $145–$195. Package rates for wine tasting or festival weekends.
♥ ♯ ❋ ♦ ✖ ⅄

From 26 trips to England, Ann and Tom—"we feel like Anglophiles"—have filled this 1861 Victorian with 18th- and 19th-century antiques, including furniture, sterling silver accessories, Oriental rugs, and lamps, that are all for sale. Since the Grays, parents of six grown children, opened the B&B in 1988, just about the time Tom had considered attending culinary school, they have acquired the neighboring 1820 center chimney colonial, their "garden cottage" with beautifully stenciled furnishings and floor-length curtains. Separating the two houses are brick-lined gravel paths and gardens with flowers, raspberries, strawberries and blackberries. Many international travelers stay at this B&B, which is praised by romantics including honeymooners, families who appreciate the cottage accommodations, and many who enjoy being pampered.

In residence: Two outdoor cats, Spur and Merlin. Britt, a black Labrador.
Foreign language spoken: Elementary German.
Bed and bath: Five rooms and one suite. In Victorian, private baths (one full, one shower only) for two air-conditioned second-floor rooms, each with a canopied double bed. (One room has adjoining single.) First-floor room has queen four-poster, working fireplace, private en-suite full bath. Cottage

(Please turn page.)

accommodations on ground level—two queen-bedded rooms, each with large full bath, share a fireplaced keeping room. Three-bedroom suite with kitchen, living room, full bath, covered patio. (And more changes to come.) **Breakfast:** 8:30–9:30. Full. Ever-changing menu. Eggs fresh from the chickens next door. Fresh fruits. Juice. Quiches, omelets, French toast with pecans. Homemade muffins and jams. By candlelight. With classical music. **Plus:** Complimentary sherry. Plant-filled porch. Courier service for touring shops. Fresh flowers (wild ones in season). In cottage, crib, high chairs, toys. Sometimes, babysitting.

Helen and Donald Janse   203/434-7269

11 Flat Rock Hill Road, Old Lyme, CT 06371-1503

Hosts: Helen and Donald Janse
Location: On a quiet country road lined with stone walls and old maple trees. Ten minutes from I-95. Twenty minutes from Goodspeed Opera House, half hour west of Mystic Seaport.

Open: Year round. Reservations suggested.
Rates: $60 single. $75 double. $15 rollaway for third person. Amex, MC, Visa.
♥ ⬛ ♦ ✠

The first guests came here as overflow from the local inn. Built just 20 years ago, the Williamsburg-style saltbox was designed for world travelers and antiques collectors who were retiring. Since the Janses purchased the wonderful property in 1977, they have not only maintained the parklike acre but developed extensive gardens that have become the basis for a mail-order business for their own crafts, foods, and how-to books. "Wreath making is our most popular one." They also have a shop in the garage with their own items, such as ornaments, preserves, and wood products.

Inside there's an unhurried gracious atmosphere with artwork everywhere, Orientals, and antiques. Don recently retired as director of cadet musical activities at the Coast Guard Academy. He now teaches music and drama, part time, at Fishers Island School. He is a poet and published composer. Helen, how-to book coauthor, is a retired executive secretary of Kodak and IBM.

In residence: Both hosts smoke. Twinkle, "a gentle, affectionate cocker."
Bed and bath: One room with double bed, adjoining private full bath. Four windows provide views of the grounds and adjacent woodlands. Rollaway available.
Breakfast: Juice or seasonal fruit, sausage, ham or bacon, eggs, toast, freshly baked muffins and homemade jams, coffee. Served in dining room or on the porch or patio.
Plus: Air conditioning throughout. Beverages. Fireplaced living room. Library/den. Fresh bouquets. Garden tour. Annotated list of restaurants (reservations made) and sightseeing attractions.

🏠 *"Please emphasize that we are a private home, not an inn."*

Clark Cottage at Wintergreen

354 Pomfret Street, Pomfret Center, CT 06259

203/928-5741
fax 203/928-1591

Hosts: Doris and Stan Geary
Location: Quiet. On parklike grounds in this semirural New England town. Set way back from Routes 44 and 169, next to Pomfret School and half mile south of Rectory School. Thirty minutes to Sturbridge Village, Worcester, Providence; 45 to Hartford, New London, and Mystic Seaport. Six minutes to Golden Lamb Restaurant; necessary advance reservations (months, sometimes) made by Gearys.
Open: Year round.
Rates: Double occupancy. Private bath $65, with fireplace $75. Shared bath $60. MC, Visa.

Four acres of rolling lawns and extensive oft-photographed gardens surround the 18-room house that was once part of the 1,000-acre Clark estate. Although many guests come for the area private schools, the hosts of this B&B, an 1885 Victorian with six fireplaces and five porches, introduce other travelers, including antiques dealers and those looking for a getaway, to an unspoiled area—a place with marvelous old homes, lots of open space, and wonderful valley views.

Stan, an Oyster Bay, Long Island, native and sailor (now business manager at Rectory School), was in business in New York and in other Connecticut towns before he and Doris moved here ten years ago. The grandparents of seven have been restoring the house "room by room." Furnishings include 18th- and early 19th-century antiques.

Guests wrote: *"I would go out of my way to stay in this place . . . very private setting . . . wonderful breakfasts . . . lovingly restored . . . immaculately maintained . . . amicable hosts . . . good directions to Brimfield . . . felt at home."*

Bed and bath: Four large second-floor rooms. One with Italian antique queen bed, working fireplace, private adjoining shower bath. One with queen, hall shower bath. One with two twin beds, working fireplace, hall full bath. One with queen brass bed, private bath. Rollaway available.
Breakfast: Upon request. Fresh fruit, freshly baked bread or muffins. Pancakes, stuffed French toast, omelets, or bacon and eggs. In breakfast or dining room, or on screened porch.
Plus: Three bedrooms air conditioned. Ceiling fans. Desk, private phone, and TV. Beverages. Down comforters. Flannel sheets. Robes. Fresh fruit. Turndown service. Guest refrigerator. Garden flowers. Adirondack chairs. Spectacular sunsets.

From the country: "Rural living is great. Did I tell you about the night the cows came? A farmer neighbor up the road had left a gate unlatched. About 10 p.m. I had 22 Holsteins and one bull milling around the backyard, peering in the windows, mooing and munching! The garden was unhappy, but the guests loved it."

The Croft

203/342-1856

7 Penny Corner Road, Portland, CT 06480-1624

Host: Elaine Hinze
Location: On a residential street in a rural community. On four acres with open fields, barns, and gardens. Near golf course. Three miles to Wesleyan University on the other side of Connecticut River; 20 minutes to Hartford; 40 to beaches. Within 30 minutes of Goodspeed Opera House, Valley Railroad (steam train), Mark Twain's house, Wadsworth Atheneum.
Open: Year round. Reservations required.
Rates: Larger suite—one bedroom, $75 double, $60 single; two bedrooms, $85 two people, $105 three people. Smaller suite, $55 double, $45 single. $15 rollaway or trundle.

Although Wesleyan is a major draw, Elaine's guests come to stay in this old shipbuilding and quarrying (brownstone) town. They relax on the grounds, take day trips, and come "home" to their own comfortable quarters.

Elaine, an administrative assistant at Wesleyan, restored this low-ceilinged 1822 Federal colonial. The first house built on the street, it has had many changes and additions, including her small solar greenhouse "where I keep my rose geraniums going from cuttings." She grows her own bay plant (bay leaves), starts her herb plants, and has an extensive perennial flower garden on the property that winds behind the neighboring houses. And many of her guests seem to enjoy gathering eggs.

In residence: Cory, a sable collie. Chickens. Lambs.
Bed and bath: The entire second floor; two suites with private exterior entrances. Larger suite has a room with a double bed, one with twin bed, sitting/dining room, kitchen, full bath, rollaway. Other suite has double bed, dining nook, private shower bath; trundle bed available.
Breakfast: In your own quarters. In larger suite, stocked refrigerator. Juice. Bagels, sweet buns, English or homemade muffins, breads. Cream cheese, jams. Eggs and Canadian bacon. Tea, milk, coffee, herbal teas. In smaller suite, full breakfast served (until 8:30, later on weekends) with coddled eggs, omelets, or Finnish pancakes with sweet breads or muffins. Juice, fruit, cereals, coffee, tea.
Plus: Air-conditioned bedrooms. Refrigerator, private telephone, and television in each suite. Gas grill in picnic area. Down and polyester pillows. Screened porch. Hair dryer. Setups provided.

> From Pennsylvania: *"Clean, comfortable, and cozy. Beds were terrific. Kitchenette used for preparation of economical dinners."* From Michigan: *"Elaine is friendly, caring, and ever so helpful."*

In this book a full bath includes a shower and a tub. "Shower bath" indicates a bath that has all the essentials except a tub.

The Felshaw Tavern

203/928-3467

Five Mile River Road, Putnam, CT 06260-3104

Hosts: Herb and Terry Kinsman
Location: In rural country known as "Connecticut's quiet corner." On Route 21, 3½ miles from Putnam, 1½ miles from Route 395, 2 miles from Route 44. Sturbridge is 30 miles away; Mystic, 50; Boston, 65. Within 10 minutes of Pomfret, Rectory, and Marianapolis Schools.
Open: Year round.
Rates: $80 per room, includes tax.
♥ ⬛ ♦ ✄ ⅄

The magnificent restoration is worth a thousand pictures. Still, it is the hospitality that is remembered by many poets, business people, honeymooners, travel writers . . . and at least one young man who subsequently booked a weekend for his parents.

Thanks to an *Antiques* magazine advertisement, the Kinsmans found this center chimney colonial with five working fireplaces. Built in 1742 as a tavern, it had seen many changes by 1979, when Terry and Herb, after 30 years in Los Angeles, "fled east."

The hosts greet you on the granite steps at the handsome mahogany raised-panel front door made by Herb. Among the many rooms in the large, gracious home furnished with fine antiques is the Keeping Room with beehive oven. The skylit breakfast room, the English oak–paneled study, and the recently completed 28-by-17 "library/music room/run-away-from-the-world room with leaded and stained glass, French doors, and a Palladian window" are also Herb's creations. And it is hard for the untrained eye to tell that his slant-front mahogany desk and black walnut lowboy are reproductions. On the grounds, there's a stone wall, a pergola leading to an enclosed gazebo, and high fence with perfectly scaled finials.

What a setting for Terry to write copy for classical record liner notes! What a setting for "rediscovering oneself and each other"—and the Kinsmans with their global concerns.

Bed and bath: Two very large second-floor rooms, each with queen four-poster bed, sitting area, working fireplace, private bath. One full bath; one shower bath.
Breakfast: Full. Served at guests' convenience (within reason!) in breakfast room overlooking meadow and woods. Perhaps eggs scrambled with cheese, beef sausages, homemade muffins, coffee or tea.
Plus: Welcoming beverage. Books. Periodicals. Television. If you'd like, Herb's expertise, backed by examples of pitfalls and experiences. Suggestions for a lake or historic home or for spectacular routes by foot, bicycle, or car.

According to guests (many are preservationists and/or house restorers), there ought to be a medal for the meticulous work—everything from research to labor—done by B&B owners. Indeed, many have won preservation awards.

Thurber House

203/928-6776

78 Liberty Way, Putnam, CT 06260-3113

Hosts: Betty and George Zimmermann
Location: Rural and quiet. On a hill overlooking the village common and white-spired church. Good cycling and hiking area. Ten minutes to Putnam and Pomfret, 30 to Worcester, 45 to Sturbridge.

Open: Year round.
Rates: Per room. $70 private bath, $60 shared. Learning weekend (Christmas Past or Refinishing-and-Antiquing) package rate includes country inn dinner.
🛏 🖤 ✗ ⌦

Some extraordinary sunsets are enjoyed from the back porch of this handsome Federal colonial house—but the Zimmermanns haven't forgotten the guests who tarried so long watching the celestial fireworks that they were late for the wedding that brought them to town.

"The Kinsmans of Felshaw Tavern (page 25) suggested that we would like hosting, and they were correct." Many come for area private schools, or to enjoy the countryside, Sturbridge Village, and antiquing.

Originally a summer house built in the early 1800s for artist T. J. Thurber's family, this became a year-round residence around 1870. Twenty-seven years ago, the hosts bought it—in need of complete restoration. Throughout there are fine antiques, Oriental rugs, drapes and swags on the windows, and many Thurber paintings. And then there's that porch, the one that overlooks gardens, long vistas, and many a long-remembered sunset.

In residence: Elsie, the cat.
Bed and bath: Two second-floor rooms with working fireplaces. Larger room with two twin four-poster beds. One room with double four-poster. Baths are private or, sometimes, shared.
Breakfast: 7–9. Fresh fruit, juice, "and a hearty main dish and home-baked goods." In semiformal dining room; sometimes on porch.
Plus: Piano. Bicycles for guests' use. Window fans. Usually, afternoon hot or cold drink, evening wine, cheese and crackers.

> From Louisiana: *"Warm, accommodating hosts . . . immaculate and comfortable house . . . fabulous food."*

Nutmeg Bed & Breakfast Agency Host #324

Salisbury, CT

Location: Rural with lake frontage; three minutes' drive to launch area, eight to swimming. On 36 acres in Berkshire foothills. Tanglewood, 45 minutes; Catamount and Butternut ski areas, 12 miles; half hour to Music Mountain, Norfolk, and Yale Music Festival; 15 minutes to Lime Rock Park racetrack.

Two hours northwest of Manhattan.
Reservations: Year round through Nutmeg Bed & Breakfast Agency, page 3. Two-night minimum preferred on weekends and holidays.
Rates: $85 semiprivate bath. $130–$150 private bath.
🖤 ✗ ⌦

"There's something compelling about the land in this area," said the host, a writer who covers a wide range of topics—from taxes to art. Before opening the B&B, this Ohioan's jobs included one that took her to 48 states.

The wonderful house, furnished with English, German, and American antiques, is an 1780s Federal with an 1830s Georgian/Victorian addition. The front door, framed by leaded glass fan and side lights, has the original key and bolt. And there's that land—with the lake, the sheep in the pasture, and the blooms in the gardens.

In residence: One dog, a midsize (45 pounds) Australian shepherd.
Bed and bath: A variable combination of five rooms; some overlook gardens and lake. Option of private or semiprivate bath. Suite arrangement; queen, double, or twin beds.
Breakfast: 8:30–9:30. Fruit, coffee, toast and muffins or croissants, cereals. Served under chandelier in fireplaced dining room.
Plus: Down pillows. Blankets woven from wool from host's sheep. Screened porch. Fireplaced library. Picnic baskets.

Yesterday's Yankee

Route 44 East, P.O. Box 442, Salisbury, CT 06058

203/435-9539
fax 203/435-4586

Hosts: Doris and Dick Alexander
Location: On main road at the edge of a colonial village in Berkshires foothills. Forty minutes' drive to Tanglewood. Near antiques shops, fine restaurants, outdoor activities, old cemeteries, and historic sites.
Open: March–December. Two-night minimum on weekends and holidays,

Memorial Day through October.
Rates: $65 smaller queen room; $70 large. $70 twin beds. $75 king. $20 rollaway. Seventh consecutive night free. Ten percent less for three-night stay midweek (Sunday–Thursday) and for senior citizens (no minimum stay) midweek. MC, Visa.
♥ ❖ ♦ ✗ ⅙

From New York: *"I wish I could stay on, permanently! . . . Dick and Doris make everyone feel so comfortable . . . everything, every detail, is 'right' . . . a peaceful atmosphere . . . delicious breakfasts . . . an extensive library . . . interesting conversations about Early American antiques . . . help with travel plans. If I were an artist I would love to capture the lilac at the front door, the herb garden (fresh breakfast garnishes), the large, old trees, the flower beds."*

Dick, a retired architect and builder who restores and builds fine furniture, and Doris, a writer and calligrapher who taught junior high English, have lived in town for 30 years. They're volunteers with the library, the travel commission, and the local historic society. Nine years ago they restored this treasure and started B&B. The only original (1744) Cape Cod–style home in Salisbury, the house has wide board floors, whitewashed walls, small-paned windows. Throughout there are collections—many antiques, books, silhouettes, and mirrors. Braided rugs are in the guest rooms. And the acclaimed host may offer a suggestion for a private spot with panoramic sunset view.

Bed and bath: Three second-floor rooms share one full modern bath. One with queen bed. One with queen and rocking chairs in sitting area. One with twins/king and rocking chairs in sitting area.

(Please turn page.)

Breakfast: 6–9 (usually at one seating). "Prepared with an eye toward healthful living." Four courses may include juice without added sugar, peach soup, figs with lime cream, 20-grain porridge, homemade granola and breads, Norwegian "munka," fresh herb omelet, French toast, ham and apple bake, or Doris's latest invention—"Magic Dragon Puff." Dick serves by 250-year-old keeping room fireplace.
Plus: Air-conditioned bedrooms. Thick towels. Robes. Fruit, cheese, candy. Bocci court. Lawn croquet. "Games and books galore."

Chaffee's B&B   203/628-2750

28 Reussner Road, Southington, CT 06489-3310

Hosts: Milt and Kay Chaffee
Location: In a quiet residential area, two miles from I-84. Ten minutes from the Mount Southington (downhill) ski area. Close to four large Southington apple orchards;

20 minutes south of Hartford.
Open: Year round except Christmas. Reservations preferred.
Rates: $40 single, $50 double.
◆ ✕ ⊭

According to Milt and Kay, they used my first B&B book for their own travels, then came home and observed that the Southington area was lacking in personalized accommodations. Their family is grown, and Kay enjoys crafts, cooking, and baking. Milt, a retired banker, has been an active amateur radio operator for over half a century. Since 1985 they have been offering a relaxed environment in their six-room colonial ranch house located in an area that is "s-o-o quiet."

Bed and bath: Room on first floor with two twin beds, private full bath.
Breakfast: Usually about 8:30. Juice, fruits, eggs any style, cereal, and Kay's specialty, muffins. Served in dining room overlooking the large yard, or on screened porch. Hosts join guests.
Plus: Central air conditioning. Hosts' living room with books, organ, cable television.

From Maryland: *"More than a place to stay. . . . From the moment we walked into their home, Milt and Kay made us feel welcomed . . . concern for guests showed in the many conveniences provided in our large, private room and bath."*

Storrs Farmhouse on the Hill   203/429-1400

418 Gurleyville Road, Storrs, CT 06268

Hosts: William and Elaine Kollet
Location: Rural. Less than 2 miles to University of Connecticut campus, 7 miles to Caprilands Herb Farm, 15 to Sturbridge Village.

Open: February–December. Advance reservations required.
Rates: $35 single. $55 double. $15 rollaway or crib.

Although many guests come with a planned agenda, this is a place where you may help feed the sheep (whose wool has been woven into guests' blankets), feed chickens, and collect eggs. The Kollets, grandparents of six, feel that they could fill a book with stories about memorable guests who have come from all over the world. One who stayed here during a sabbatical wrote, "Warmth, care, and love are what the Kollets offer."

Elaine, a hotel and food management graduate and a former town council and zoning board member, and Bill, a retired insurance company electrical engineer, built most of their center chimney Cape farmhouse 20 years ago. (As a youngster, Elaine learned from her father about carpentry, bricklaying, and tiling.) They furnished with some antiques, a grandmother clock, and Oriental rugs. One room has huge tropical plants hanging from a half-glassed roof and many windows that look out on sheep pastures and flower gardens— and, in the spring, bluebirds.

In residence: Chables, a golden retriever. Columbian sheep. Chickens.
Bed and bath: Four large rooms. All private baths (some full, some shower only). Two double-bedded rooms on first floor. On second, one room with two twin beds, one with double bed.
Breakfast: 7–9. Almost-famous muffins. Fresh eggs. Cereals. Fruit. Plenty of coffee or tea. Served in "white and bright" kitchen, on sun porch, or in dining room. High chair available.
Plus: Wool mattress pads. Flannel sheets in winter. Coffee and tea almost anytime. Loan of bicycles and canoe. Greenhouse exercise room with hot tub, exercise equipment, plants.

From New York: *"Great! Comfortable. Immaculate. Friendly. Breakfast included the best muffins I have ever had."*

Folkstone Bed & Breakfast Host #277A
Thompson, CT

Location: On one acre with stone wall and informal perennial gardens. Along a country road just off of pretty Thompson Common in a National Register district. Five-minute walk to fine dining at historic inn.

Reservations: Available year round through Folkstone Bed & Breakfast Reservation Service, page 222.
Rates: $65 double. Singles $15 less.
♥ ♯ ♠ ✄

The theme is Irish. In a country home—a 1½-storied 1763 house with wide floorboards, low ceilings, and many colonial antiques. From Ireland there are lace curtains, contemporary paintings and photographs, linen and lace table-cloths, teapots and cozies, walking sticks, and a wide selection of music. A highlight for many: a three-mile walking or cycling tour that the hostess led for a National Corridor Heritage weekend. The route is all on undulating country roads and goes by the studios (visits arranged) of a basketmaker and a craftsman who makes wooden jigsaw puzzles; also a gallery, some garden shops, and farms.

The host is a high school English teacher who conducts student tours to England, Ireland, and Wales. His wife, a nurse, enjoys sharing her family heritage.

In residence: Mother of the hostess.
Foreign languages spoken: French. A bit of Gaelic.
Bed and bath: Two carpeted queen-bedded rooms; private baths. First-floor room has queen bed, shower bath, TV, phone, French doors leading to private

(Please turn page.)

deck overlooking gardens and stone walls. Second-floor slanted-ceilinged room has shower and Jacuzzi tub.
Breakfast: 7–9. Choose from menu with omelets, French toast, eggs, sausage, bacon. Irish soda bread (a major hit). Muffins. Barre's (Irish) tea. Served at table set in traditional Irish B&B style.
Plus: A great yard for pets. Welcoming beverage. Recipes shared and exchanged. Fireplaced living room. Extensive library of Celtic literature and tapes. Fresh fruit in rooms. Loan of bicycles.

Nutmeg Bed & Breakfast Agency Host #468
Thompson, CT

Location: On three acres in wooded area. With 325 feet of lake frontage. Within walking distance of convenience store. Fourteen miles from Sturbridge Village; minutes to antiques center in Putnam; four miles to Thompson Raceway and from I-395.

Reservations: Year round through Nutmeg Bed & Breakfast Agency, page 3.
Rates: $65 per room. $15 less for single. $15 each extra person.
♥ ♯ ♠ ⁂ ✄

"Sometimes we host getaway guests. This weekend we have a family with three children who are swimming, using the canoe, and visiting with grandparents who live nearby. When we retired from the FBI and teaching we looked in many states and decided to settle right here in my home area—and to build a B&B. In 1990 we built this post-and-beam-house with the perfect layout for guests who come with or without children, with or without a dog!"
The antiques-furnished house is built on a hill overlooking the lake. The atmosphere is relaxed. Guests are treated like family. Sometimes rug-hooking workshops are scheduled. Breakfast is a big hit.

In residence: One dog. (It's okay if you bring yours.)
Bed and bath: Private lakeside entrance to two first-floor rooms. One with double bed and one with twin share full bath, large sitting room with queen sofa bed, cable TV, VCR, videos for all ages, big deck, phone. Rollaways available.
Breakfast: Usually "whenever you like." Fresh fruit. Quiche with ham, blueberry pancakes and sausage, or fruit-filled crepes. Homemade breads and muffins. With silver and china in dining room overlooking lake.
Plus: Use of refrigerator—and canoe and rowboat too. Picnic area with grill.

The Tolland Inn   203/872-0800
P.O. Box 717, 63 Tolland Green, Tolland, CT 06084-0717

Hosts: Susan and Stephen Beeching
Location: In historic district facing the village green. Steps from country store and genealogical library. Three minutes from Interstate 84. Seven miles to University of Connecticut, 20 to Hartford and Old Sturbridge Village, 22 to vineyard, 6 to Caprilands Herb Farm.

Open: Year round. Two-day minimum stay on some key spring and fall weekends.
Rates: Shared bath $50 double, $40 single. Private bath $60 double, $70 king or twin beds, $50 single. Amex, DC, MC, Visa.
♦ ✄ ✄

"I was totally enchanted," wrote one guest after visiting with the Beechings. Steve, a designer and maker of custom fine furniture, has examples of his work throughout the inn. Susan, a teacher of special education, is a third-generation innkeeper, with experience at a family guest house on her native Nantucket Island.

When they moved from Boston in 1985, the Beechings bought The Steele House, known for its lodging accommodations from the 1800s until 1959, the year it was sold to its last registered guests as a private home. They renovated, refurbished, and renamed the white clapboard inn. Now the peaceful ambiance is enhanced by a recently enlarged sun porch that has hand-planed raised panels, a coffered ceiling, a Rumford fireplace, and pierced tin sconces.

Bed and bath: Eight rooms, six private baths. On first floor (air conditioned), one room with double bed, shower bath, strobe fire alarm for the hearing impaired. One room with queen canopied bed (by Steve), working fireplace, sunken hot tub with view of lawn. Upstairs, low-ceilinged rooms with chestnut beams. Two double-bedded rooms; one with "an amazing curved wall" and one with exposed beamed ceiling share a full hall bath. Room with king/twins option, beamed ceiling, private shower bath. One with a high handmade double bed, one with brass double bed; each with private shower bath. Two-room suite overlooks gardens; double bed, full kitchen, sitting area, private shower bath.

Breakfast: Full: 8–10. "Susan's fabulous orange rolls." Juices, seasonal fruit, muffins, breakfast cakes. Belgian waffles, cinnamon/raisin French toast. Inn-made jams include grape made with inn's arbor fruit. Brewed coffees; tea. Served at trestle dining room table or on wicker-furnished sun porch.

Plus: "Books everywhere—for readers of any sort." Beverages. Classical music.

House on the Hill   203/757-9901
92 Woodlawn Terrace, Waterbury, CT 06710-1929

Host: Marianne Vandenburgh
Location: High on a hill in historic residential district. One mile from I-84 and Route 8. Within 10 minutes' drive of University of Connecticut branch, Teikyo Post University, Westover and Taft schools, Cheshire Academy. Ninety miles from Manhattan; 20 to Litchfield.

Open: Year round.
Rates: $65 shared bath. $75 suite; $100 suite with queen bed, fireplace. Romantic dinner, custom-designed menu, presented by fire or on a silver tray in your room; by arrangement only, $150 for two.
♥ ✲ ♦ ✄

This award-winning B&B, a *Victoria* magazine "set," has put Waterbury back on the map. Painted in six colors (the neighbors sent thank-you notes), the 20-room Victorian is surrounded by glorious perennial gardens. Inside, the natural woodwork—mahogany in the library, cherry in the main parlor, oak in the main entrance—has never been painted since the house was built in 1888 by Wallace Camp, a brass manufacturer and inventor.

From the wicker-furnished arched porches to the redone kitchen (complete with island that has a base of 1920s department store mahogany drawers

(Please turn page.)

topped with old marble) and all the way to the turret suite, there is a sense of joy—created by Marianne. She is a Renaissance woman with an eye for display and color—a home economist/former Soho antiques shop owner and elderly services administrator turned house restorer/freelance decorator/garden designer/community activist/caterer extraordinaire. Throughout, there's an interesting mix of crafts, antiques, and modern pieces. Go and experience. I did, for one night, during a B&B promotion tour. Jane Fonda did, for several weeks, during a filming. Business travelers, house hunters, and wedding guests also appreciate the welcoming environment.

Bed and bath: Suites. On second floor, canopied double bed, sitting area, tub bath, porch; room with double bed, full bath can be a suite with double-bedded room, full bath. On third floor, double bed, full bath, kitchen, TV, air conditioning; turret suite has queen bed, fireplace, full bath.
Breakfast: Flexible timing. Most frequently requested menu: pancakes (made with cornmeal ground by hand by Marianne's parents on their Ohio farm), smoked sausages, homemade "four-berry/barb" sauce, orange juice, coffee (freshly ground beans) or tea. Served in fireplaced dining room.
Plus: Refreshments upon arrival. Mints or cookies on pillow. Flannel sheets. Turndown service. Extensive library. Window fans. Second-floor guest microwave and refrigerator. Weddings (catered by Marianne) and small corporate seminars booked at Seventy Hillside, an elegant English mansion in Waterbury. Inquire about cooking classes and winter concerts.

From Massachusetts: *"A wonderful warm experience."*

The Clarks   203/274-4866

97 Scott Avenue, Watertown, CT 06795-2518

Hosts: Richard and Barbara Clark
Location: One block from the main street in Watertown. Three blocks from the Taft School; within a 10-minute drive of Routes 8 and 84.
Open: January and April–December.
Rates: $40 per room.

This traditional B&B filled a need. Taft School parents were having difficulty finding accommodations in the area, so the Clarks began hosting in 1983. Since then, others—particularly business people and those "passing through"—also find the Cape-style home a convenient and comfortable stopping point.

Barbara is a retired elementary school teacher. Richard, who has retired twice, is an active Lions Club member. They are both active in community and church activities. As for B&B, "We have been privileged to meet so many interesting people. It is fun!"

Bed and bath: Two rooms. One large first-floor room with two twin beds, adjoining guest den, private half bath, large deck. One second-floor double-bedded room. Both share second-floor shower bath with hosts.
Breakfast: 6–8 weekdays, 6–9 weekends. Usually a continental menu, but eggs are also available. Served in the dining room.
Plus: Bedroom ceiling fans. Afternoon or evening beverages. Use of entire house, including kitchen and laundry facilities, front and back porches, barbecue grill.

From Massachusetts: *"Although smaller (than B&B inns) . . . comfortable, clean . . . felt like we were visiting friends.* From New York: *"Wonderful. Felt very welcome in their beautiful home."*

Covered Bridge Host #2WC
West Cornwall, CT

Location: On a 64-acre wooded estate with breathtaking views of mountains and valley. Three miles to Marvelwood School; about 10 to Hotchkiss, Kent, Salisbury, and South Kent schools; 1½ miles from historic covered bridge, unspoiled village, antiquing, and restaurants—including one with deck overlooking a "delightfully noisy (babbling)" brook.

Reservations: Available year round through Covered Bridge, page 2. Two-night minimum on holiday and fall weekends.

Rates: $95 per room.
♥ ⬛ ⁂ ♦ ✈ ⚞

First there's the 200-degree, 75-mile, all-the-way-to-the-Catskills view. One-nighters have been known to take a look and ask to stay for a week. The setting is complete with a sharp drop, amidst pine, hemlock, oak, ash, birch, hickory, and walnut trees—and wild turkeys too. Then there's that stone (inside and out) library, built in 1930 by the host's father, who traveled extensively and lived in China for several years. And all the wonderful antiques, rugs, and chandeliers collected by the host while he restored large Victorian residences in Washington, D.C. Since making the family homestead his permanent residence nine years ago, this host has become full-time tree surgeon/road repair man/bottle washer/bell captain/butler.

Area residents search for miles around and feel as if they have discovered this place in their own back yard. One couple who came in search of lodging for wedding guests decided that this would be their honeymoon site.

Bed and bath: In a guest wing with private exterior entrance, two double-bedded rooms without a common wall, each with private full bath and air conditioning.

Breakfast: 7–9:30. Freshly squeezed orange juice, freshly ground coffee, Grand Marnier French toast or blueberry pancakes with bacon. By wide stone library fireplace or on 50-foot-long flagstone terrace.

Plus: Living room. Sun room. Lots of books. The terrace with wrought iron furniture—and that compelling vista.

Can't find a listing for the community you are going to? Check with a reservation service described at the beginning of this chapter. Through the service you may be placed (matched) with a welcoming B&B that is near your destination.

The Cotswold Inn

203/226-3766

76 Myrtle Avenue, Westport, CT 06880

Hosts: Richard and Lorna Montanaro
Location: Not visible from the road but right in town, amidst historic homes. On a small lot surrounded by gardens. Five-minute walk to designer shops, restaurants, Westport

Country Playhouse. Five-minute drive to Long Island Sound beach; 55-minute drive from Manhattan.
Open: Year round.
Rates: Per room. $175–$225 depending on size. Amex, MC, Visa.
♥ ❖ ♦ ✈

Pure luxury. In a gabled English cottage that Richard built with authentic materials (wide plank maple floors and used brick for fireplaces) on a vacant lot in 1982. Now it has a guest book filled with well-known names (many actors who have performed at the Westport Country Playhouse), honeymooners, business travelers, "and plenty who come for and seem to get relaxation."

Considered a sophisticated, elegant version of country decor, the intimate inn, named by the *Fairfield County Advocate* as "the best place for your rich in-laws to stay," is furnished with fine reproductions—Chippendale and Queen Anne wing chairs, love seats, and sofas; highboys; and four-poster beds. The rooms, "all romantic," were decorated with the help of the Laura Ashley folks in New York and Westport. And in 1992 the Montanaros were married here.

Richard, who has lived in the area all his life, has built many large beautiful homes in Westport and New Canaan. Before becoming fulltime innkeeper, Lorna was in marketing research. For peaceful walks, they'll direct you to Devil's Den, a 1,500-acre wildlife santuary that has hiking (and cross-country ski) trails.

Bed and bath: Four soundproofed, air-conditioned second-floor rooms, each with individual thermostat, telephone, desk, cable TV, clock radio. All with queen bed (two with canopy), private full bath; one room also has a single sleigh bed and working fireplace.
Breakfast: 8–10:30. Earlier by request. Fresh fruit salad, orange juice, cereals, bagels and pastries, yogurts. In kitchen with sliding doors leading to garden patio. "Can last up to three hours!"
Plus: Flower arrangements everywhere. Specialty soaps and shampoos. Evening cognac and wine. Mints and Godiva chocolates. Access to health facility, two blocks away.

From Illinois: *"Almost museumlike but still homey. The small gardens are among the finest I have seen in New England."*

---

*T*he place to stay has become the reason to go.

Chester Bulkley House Bed & Breakfast

184 Main Street, Wethersfield, CT 06109   203/563-4236

Hosts: Frank and Sophie Bottaro
Location: In 1634 village, within walking distance of shops, restaurants, three historic homes open to the public, 1700s meeting house. Less than a mile to a boating park (for picnics and sunsets) on a pretty cove.

Minutes from I-91 and I-84. Ten minutes to Hartford and to Trinity College; 90 to Boston or New York.
Open: Year round.
Rates: Shared bath $65. Private bath $75 double or twin beds; $85 king. ♯ ♣ ♦ ✈

"It's absolutely gorgeous," reported the well-established Rhode Island B&B owner who visited after the Bottaros opened in 1989, shortly after they had restored the entire 1830 brick Greek Revival house complete with brick patio surrounded by wonderful gardens. Some retirement project!

Earlier, while Frank had an office machines business, he transformed the family home, a 1950s ranch. Because of their B&B stays during their own trips, the Bottaros were inspired to become hosts in the lovely village—perfect for history and architecture buffs—where they have lived all their married lives. Now Sophie still works part time as an American Airlines trip planner. They greet many guests who are enchanted with the house, the village, and Frank's breakfasts.

Foreign language spoken: Italian.
Bed and bath: Five large antiques-furnished second-floor rooms. King, queen, and double-bedded rooms with private shower baths. Room with double bed and room with two twin beds (can be a suite) share a full bath. Rollaway available.
Breakfast: 7–10; earlier upon request. Fresh fruits, freshly baked muffins, and breakfast cakes followed by "entree of the day." Freshly ground coffee. With china and silver in fireplaced dining room.
Plus: Air conditioning and ceiling fans in bedrooms. Fireplaced living room. Refreshments. Turndown service. Fresh flowers. Robes. Forgotten items basket. Pillow chocolates. Use of bicycles. Walking tour brochure. Takeaway maps.

From Florida: *"Gorgeous house . . . friendly helpful hosts . . . delicious breakfast."*

Nutmeg Bed & Breakfast Agency Host #119

Wilton/Ridgefield area, CT

Location: Secluded. In woods overlooking pond, stream, and small waterfalls. Near fine restaurants, antiquing, tennis and racquet ball, hiking trails. An hour from Manhattan.

Reservations: Available year round through Nutmeg Bed & Breakfast Agency, page 3.
Rates: $90 for two. ♥ ♯

Maybe you'll arrive to the romantic scene of candles and kerosene lamp at the end of the path. The Oriental pavilion–like cottage, created from a rustic cabin, was designed by the host with a carpenter friend. Almost hidden from the main house three seasons of the year, it has glass-sided cupolas and a

(Please turn page.)

24-by-16-foot main room with cedar ceiling and oak floor. Glass walls and wide decks overlook a suspension bridge, waterfalls, woods with deer, phlox in the spring, flaming colors in the fall. Furnishings are a blend of contemporary and antiques. Mexican tile is on the floor of the kitchen, which has granite counters.

Explore the area or stay right here. The well-traveled hosts, a hospital administrator and a school administrator, know that it's a great place to "just hang out." They are avid gardeners who enjoy cooking, sports, and photography. Here they have had the fun of seeing newlyweds arrive in bridal clothes. A budding cartoonist who arrived with a unique idea (which, subsequently, he worked on with the host) has returned several times with reports of "close to a contract." And some guests take advantage of the glass-topped private spa room on the property, just up the hill.

Bed and bath: Queen bed plus a double futon, skylit shower bath.
Breakfast: Full. Your choice. Gourmet meal prepared and delivered to you; or prepare your own with provided items you request; or join hosts in their spectacular kitchen.
Plus: Welcoming beverage. Swimming. Use of float, tennis racquets, bicycles. Hiking trail map. Well-behaved dogs are welcome.

Covered Bridge Host #1WOD
Woodbury, CT

Location: On Woodbury/Southbury line. On four wooded acres along Route 6, a main road in historic district of town that likes to say "where New England began." Next door to veterinarian (in inn's original carriage house) with several horses outside. Within 10 minutes' drive of 40 antiques shops and several restaurants.
Reservations: Available year round through Covered Bridge, page 2.
Rates: $72–$92 single. $80–$100 double. $20 third person.
♥ ⁂ ✖ ✂

A "famous dinner" changed the lifestyle of the hosts, a Manhattan architect and a fashion designer who had often reminisced about their stay at a Bath, England B&B. There they were at their Connecticut weekend cottage when neighbors mentioned an "ancient inn," a nearby Colonial Revival place that was in need of serious redoing. Next chapter: It was all done in time for a 1992 opening in English country style with chintzes, antiques of several periods, refinished floors, and flowered wallcoverings. Some guests ask if the hostess will stencil or sponge their walls in a similar 18th-century French style. Many express gratitude for antiques shop recommendations, a good night's sleep, and the hospitality.

In residence: One cat in hosts' quarters only. One six-year-old daughter who appears in B&B occasionally. And her new sibling, due as this book went to press.
Foreign language spoken: "A little Parisian French."
Bed and bath: Four rooms and one suite, all with insulated walls and drapes. On second floor—two rooms, each with antique double spool bed, share connecting full bath. One room with king/twin option, private full bath with

claw-foot tub, ring shower. One room with queen brass bed, private full bath, private porch. Third-floor air-conditioned suite has painted Eastlake queen bed, sitting room, private full bath.

Breakfast: 8–10. Fresh juice and fruit, homemade muffins, coffee, tea. Entree—maybe egg dish or flavored French toast—from 20-year *Gourmet* magazine collection. With silver, antique china, and linen in fireplaced dining room or on porch.

Plus: Complimentary tea, coffee, and biscuits always available. Fireplaced living room (with TV) and library. Chocolates on pillow. Fresh flowers in season. Before-and-after restoration album. A chance to visit Bailey, veterinarian's pet pig. Due in 1994—walking trails along three acres down to the river. Honeymoons acknowledged.

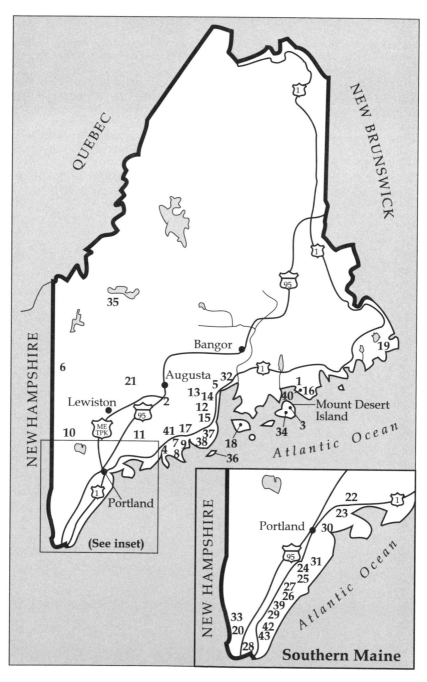

The numbers on this map indicate the locations of B&Bs described in detail in this chapter.

MAINE

KEY TO SYMBOLS
♥ Lots of honeymooners come here.
♯ Families with children are very welcome. (Please see page xii.)
● "Please emphasize that we are a private home, not an inn."
⁂ Groups or private parties sometimes book the entire B&B.
♦ Travel agents' commission paid. (Please see page xii.)
✘ Sorry, no guests' pets are allowed.
✄ No smoking inside *or* no smoking at all, even on porches.

—— Maine Reservation Services ——

Bed & Breakfast of Maine

RFD 1, 377 Gray Road, Falmouth, ME 04105

Phone: 207/777-5540.

Fax: 207/772-1184.

Listings: 70 and still growing. Most are hosted private residences; 3 are inns. They are along 250 miles of coast (but few are actually on the waterfront), in inland cities, in the mountains, near lakes, on working farms, and in the woods. Directory ($5).

In the 25 years that Donna Little has lived in Maine, she has been an architectural student, environmental educator, and (for 20 years) historical society president. As host in her own historic home, a former stagecoach stop that is minutes from Portland and the airport, Donna serves with china and silver—and wears jeans. Since buying this established reservation service in 1993, she has added many listings, including several hosts who are naturalists. "Most are older homes. All are inspected, clean, and pretty—and they offer a friendly atmosphere. Most have two or more guest rooms; many with a private bath. And the hearty breakfasts are a trademark."

Reservations: Two weeks' advance notice suggested; two months' notice for July and August, busy months that also have minimum stay requirements in resort areas.

Rates: $40–$50 single. $50–$150 double. Deposit equal to first night's lodging required in most cases. A few resort places have $5 or $10 one-night surcharge. Cancellations made within one week of reservations with private hosts receive refund less $10 service charge; refund for B&B inns varies. MC, Visa for holding reservation.

Bed & Breakfast Down East, Ltd.

39 Cedar Street, Belfast, ME 04915-1443

Phone: 207/338-9764, Monday–Friday, 10–5.

Listings: 90 in about 80 communities. "They are all over the state in every possible setting—oceanfront, lakeside, beach, mountain, rural, coastal village, city, suburban, inland village, on working farms, wilderness lodge. . . ." Mostly hosted private residences. A few inns. Directory (45 pages, $5) is organized according to region with full description and detail.

Reservations: Advance notice of three to four weeks preferred, but will try to accommodate last-minute callers. Some hosts—particularly those in resort areas—require two-night minimum weekends, especially during the summer months.

Rates: $40–$70 single. $45–$105 double. Deposit equivalent to one night's stay required. $10 surcharge, July–October 15, for one-night stay. Deposit

(Please turn page.)

less $15 processing fee refunded on cancellations with at least two weeks' notice. With less notice, a refund is at the host's discretion. Amex, MC, Visa.

With a very traditional view of B&B, filled with down-home hospitality, good value and an opportunity to "meet the locals," Sally Godfrey began her personalized service in 1983. She knows all her (varied) hosts and carefully matches travelers with compatible hosts in surroundings of comfort and hospitality.

Plus: Some homes offer babysitting, laundry, or other services. Some will pack lunches. "Most offer the spectacular Maine scenery, clean air, peace and quiet."

Other reservation services with some B&Bs in Maine:
Bed and Breakfast/Inns of New England, page 259
Bed and Breakfast of Rhode Island, page 307

Maine B&Bs

Green Hill Farm   207/422-3273

RR 1, Box 328, Ashville, ME 04607-9731

Hosts: Ted and Nuna Cass
Location: In a rural coastal community, 17 miles northeast of Ellsworth, 45 minutes to Acadia National Park.

Open: Mid-May through mid-October.
Rates: $40 room with ¾ bed. $45 twin beds; $5 third person.

Intentionally an informal place, this is a traditional B&B, "sharing our home" style. Before coming here in 1985, Nuna, a spinner and knitter, worked as a historic home guide and with a New Hampshire logging museum. Ted, the gardener, originally from Iowa, served in the Merchant Marine and the Peace Corps and was a Spanish teacher. A lighted sign helps to identify the house for latecomers. Sag-wagon service is provided for cyclists "who misjudge distances or energy."

In residence: Junior, a reasonably friendly black cat. Some sheep. Ted is "a pretty well-trained pipe smoker." (Smoking area restricted.)
Foreign languages spoken: Fluent Spanish and Danish; French and German "on a make-do basis."
Bed and bath: Two second-floor rooms—one with antique ¾ cannonball bed and one with two twin beds—share modern shower bath. Rollaway available in twin room.
Breakfast: Juice or fruit. Hot or cold cereal, eggs, homemade muffins, toast, blueberry/oatmeal pancakes, French toast. In kitchen at table set with flowers.
Plus: Window or floor fans. Tea, coffee, or cocoa. Clothes dryer.

> From New York: *"An unpretentious, eclectically furnished Maine farmhouse with charming antiques, old wallpapers, modern plumbing, delicious breakfasts."* From Canada: *"Unusually warm welcoming atmosphere . . . friendly, humorous, and honest discussions. . . . We wanted to learn and 'feel' Maine and its people. . . . Knowledgeable hosts recommended secluded coves that had no tourists (other than us) and local fishermen and lobstermen who told great stories for hours. We give Green Hill high marks . . . rural, quiet, and so pleasant."*

Maple Hill Farm B&B Inn   207/622-2708

Outlet Road, RR 1, Box 1145
Hallowell, ME 04347

(U.S./Canada) **800/622-2708**

Host: Scott Cowger
Location: Serene. On 62 acres with fields, woods, swimming hole. Adjacent to state wildlife management area. Five minutes to Augusta, Maine Turnpike, Hallowell center ("great dining"), Cobbossee Lake; 10 to off-beaten-path five-star restaurant.
Open: Year round.

Rates: Shared bath $53 small double, $58 large double. Private bath $68; $83 queen with whirlpool. Singles $10 less. $12 extra person. $5 crib. Weekly rates. Government rates and off-season discounts. Amex, CB, Diners, Discover, MC, Visa.
♥ ♨ ❖ ♦ ✕ ✍

(Please turn page.)

Acquired at auction in 1992 by a civil engineer, a native Mainer with an interest in ecology, gardening, music, theater, photography, and people. Scott was the buyer of this Victorian farmhouse, restored and enlarged as a B&B in the 1980s. Now he meets business, wedding, and conference (some right here) guests as well as cyclists, vacationers, and families.

In residence: Robert Audet, assistant innkeeper. George, "a friendly independent cat."
Foreign language spoken: Some French.
Bed and bath: Seven rooms, all with phones. First-floor handicapped-accessible double-bedded room with private bath and exterior entrance, deck. Three second-floor rooms with one or two double beds share a large full bath. Three third-floor rooms in newer wing—double bed, private shower hall bath; double bed, en-suite shower bath; queen bed, en-suite shower bath, separate whirlpool (for two) room. Cots and crib available.
Breakfast: 7–9. Fresh fruit cup, orange juice. Eggs Benedict, plain or blueberry pancakes, or French toast. Cereals. "Robert's famous home fries." Teas. Freshly ground coffee.
Plus: TV in some rooms. Beverages. Garden or field flowers. Covered porch. Croquet. Horseshoes. Art gallery.

From Massachusetts: *"Wonderful place. On top of a hill surrounded by big fragrant hay fields, wooded trails behind them. . . . Friendly easygoing hosts. . . . My six-year-old son said, 'It's a good place to catch frogs, all the rooms are nice and pretty, and they have beds.'"* From Rhode Island: *"Immaculate, unpretentious . . . excellent food, nearby theater and restaurants . . . classical music. . . . Farmer mowing hay in the field. Ah."*

Black Friar Inn   207/288-5091
10 Summer Street, Bar Harbor, ME 04609

Hosts: Barbara and Jim Kelly
Location: On a quiet in-town street, next to municipal parking lot, 1½ blocks from Frenchman's Bay.
Open: May through October. Two-night minimum, mid-June–mid-October.

Rates: Double occupancy. In season, $95–$105 second floor, $85–$90 third floor. Off-season, $75–$85 second floor, $65–$70 third floor. Singles slightly less. MC, Visa.
♥ ✖ ✢

"A little like the home everybody wishes they had," wrote one guest, who liked "to hang around the kitchen and chat. As a New Yorker, I can't tell you what a balm this was to my soul. . . . Jim and Barbara suggested the hike to Bar Island at low tide. I think they consider themselves permanent tourists." Other guests added comments about the food, the immaculate inn, its convenient location, and the innkeepers (again and again).

As Barbara says, "It seemed natural—after years of traveling throughout Maine and after careers in the textile business, to choose innkeeping (in 1986), when we decided to do something together in a place we really love." Architectural features from old Bar Harbor mansions were used when this Victorian house was completely rebuilt in the early 1980s. In one room there's a mantel used as a headboard. The pub was a private library. The wicker-furnished breakfast/sun room has cypress and tin walls that came from a Maine church. The other common room, complete with fireplace, is a replica of a small English pub.

Bed and bath: Six queen-bedded rooms on second (Victorian decor) and third (Laura Ashley patterns) floors. One with skylights. All private baths; some down the hall. Pedestal sinks in three rooms.
Breakfast: 8–9:30. Entree changes daily. Could be eggs du jour, Belgian waffles, or French toast. Homemade breads and muffins. Baked apples. Breakfast meats. Served in sun room.
Plus: Spring sea kayak school. Guided kayaking and fly-fishing programs. Ceiling or oscillating fans. Cozy third-floor rear sun deck. Robes for hallway baths. In summer, flowers in rooms and window boxes; afternoon refreshments. Off-street parking.

Castlemaine Inn
39 Holland Avenue, Bar Harbor, ME 04609

207/288-4563
800/338-4563

Hosts: Norah O'Brien and Terry O'Connell
Location: On a quiet street, two blocks from waterfront. Five-minute walk to shops and restaurants. One mile from Acadia National Park and Bluenose ferry terminal.
Open: May–October. Two-night minimum July and August and on holiday weekends.

Rates: Double occupancy. $98 or $105 double bed. $118 queen, $135 with fireplace or balcony. $148 two-room suite, canopied queen, fireplace, air conditioning. $25 third person. Less May, June, September, and October. MC, Visa.
♥ ♣ ✖ ✁

From Maryland, New York, Delaware, New Jersey, Colorado, California: *"A treat to stay there . . . Norah goes beyond immaculate. . . . Lovely furnishings and comforters, pillow shams, starched Irish table linens . . . I'm a picky lady with great taste! . . . Cheerful and helpful . . . felt at home . . . Norah knows about walking and hiking trails. . . . And, by mail, we still exchange information on new or newly discovered mystery writers. . . . Beautiful restoration with Victorian atmosphere."*

The walk is canopied. The baths and fireplaces have been redone. And handmade quilts are on the beds of this rambling Victorian, which the hosts converted to a B&B in 1981. They knew the area from vacations. When they lived in Ohio, Norah was a teacher. Terry dovetails cohosting with work for a Chicago construction company.

Bed and bath: Ten air-conditioned rooms, most with canopied queen beds, on three floors. All private baths; most have tub and shower. Some rooms with working fireplace and a private balcony. One suite on first floor. Third-floor suite has two bedrooms—one queen, one with two twin beds—and parlor with VCR, balcony, one shower bath, and a half bath.
Breakfast: 8–9:30. Muffins, coffee cake, scones, cereal, homemade bread, fresh fruit bowl, bagels with cream cheese, preserves, cheese, juices, imported

(Please turn page.)

teas, gourmet coffee. Buffet in breakfast room, in fireplaced parlor, or on veranda.
Plus: Wicker-furnished front porch. Cable TV in each room.

Graycote Inn   207/288-3044
40 Holland Avenue, Bar Harbor, ME 04609-1432

Hosts: Joe and Judy Losquadro
Location: On a quiet side street one-acre lot with large lawn and shade trees. Two blocks to waterfront. Five-minute drive to Acadia National Park.
Open: April–November. Two-day minimum Memorial Day to mid-October.

Rates: Memorial Day weekend and mid-June to mid-October $80–135, suites $175 (for four). Off-season $65–95, suites $125. MC, Visa.
♥ ✗ ⅄

"We loved B&B as guests, took an innkeeping course, and conducted a search until [in 1992] Graycote Inn found us!"

In Washington, D.C., Judy, a registered nurse who is an accomplished needleworker, was an executive assistant to the president of an executive search firm. Joe, a retired naval officer "all around the world," was a computer marketing executive.

They bought this Victorian, an inn since the 1930s; it had been restored in 1986 by the previous owners, who found ceiling moldings in the basement rafters and oak flooring strips in the attic. Pastel backgrounds give a light and airy feel to rooms furnished with country and Victorian pieces. Romantics come here. "And many just want to unwind, maybe hike to the top of Cadillac Mountain or sit on Schooner Head cliffs, read a book, drink in the solitude, and enjoy the peace."

In residence: Miko, blue point Siamese cat, in hosts' quarters.
Bed and bath: On three floors—10 good-sized carpeted rooms. Plus two two-bedroom carriage house suites, each with king and queen bed and living room with TV. All private baths; some full, some shower without tub. Beds are king or queen; most are canopied. Amenities vary: balcony, sun porch, skylight, sitting room with daybed, working fireplace, air conditioning, window or ceiling fans.
Breakfast: 8–9:30. Quiche, sausage and egg strata, or oven-baked caramel French toast. Homemade muffins. Fresh fruit, juice, cereal, hot beverages. At tables for two on sun porch with ceiling fans.
Plus: Fireplaced living and dining rooms. Upright piano. Air conditioning on third floor. Five o'clock refreshments. Guest refrigerator. Double hammock and outdoor chairs. Coffee and tea always available.

Guests wrote: *"Make you feel so welcome. . . . Judy and Joe greet you with morning menu, delicious and relaxing breakfast, the weather, and a day-trip recommendation. . . . I'm very fussy and can't wait to return."*

Hospitality is the keynote of B&B.

Hearthside Inn
207/288-4533

7 High Street, Bar Harbor, ME 04609-1816

Hosts: Barry and Susan Schwartz
Location: On a quiet side street. Two blocks from the waterfront. Five-minute drive to Acadia National Park.
Open: Year round. Two-night minimum July and August and on holiday weekends.

Rates: Per room. First floor—queen bed, fireplace, whirlpool tub, $125. Upper floors—$75, $85, $100, $115 depending on room size, amenities. MC, Visa.

From Connecticut: *"Far better than the description in your book. Barry and Susan put their hearts in everything, from pancakes to the impeccable restoration."* From New Mexico: *"A wondrous tapestry combining clean, delightfully appointed rooms, with touches of Victoriana . . . vivacious conversation, good suggestions."* From Pennsylvania: *"A sanctuary. . . . Like home, yet you feel pampered."*

All those guests' letters confirm that the couple who, seven years ago, just "upped and moved" are pretty happy with their decision. The Schwartzes— "We can't imagine ourselves doing anything else"—left New Jersey, where Barry was a corporate executive and Susan a teacher.

A before-and-after album chronicles the restoration efforts in this 1907 house, originally built as a doctor's home. Winston Churchill, Romeo and Juliet, Queen Victoria, and Emily Dickinson are some names of the guest rooms. The carpeted inn is furnished with Victorian and country antiques. The list of suggestions includes kayaking—and, for honeymooners, "one place that would get us in a lot of trouble if it ever got into print!"

In residence: Pennie, 15, and Josh, 13.
Bed and bath: Nine queen-bedded rooms on three floors; some with working fireplace and/or private porch. All private baths—some full, some shower only, some with whirlpool tub.
Breakfast: 8–9:30. Buffet style. Hot dish may be pancakes, French toast, or eggs. Fruit salad, strawberry or other homemade breads, maybe poppyseed cake, muffins, bagels, homemade granola, hot/cold cereal, juice, tea, coffee.
Plus: Afternoon tea or evening refreshments.

Holbrook House
207/288-4970

74 Mount Desert Street, Bar Harbor, ME 04609
800/695-1120

Hosts: Jeani and Jack Ochtera
Location: On the road to and 1.5 miles from main entrance of Acadia National Park. One mile to golf course. Ten-minute walk to restaurants, shops, waterfront.

Open: May–October.
Rates: $110–$115 per room. $125 per suite. Packages and special rates, May–mid-June.

It's just the way the Ochteras planned when, in 1989, they bought this B&B in a matter of days. The late 1800s cottage has been a haven for vacationers for over a century. Jeani, a former Christmas Tree Shops manager and a teacher before that, did all the painting, papering, and window treatments.

(Please turn page.)

She added antiques, dolls, and Victorian and personal touches. Jack, "another super people person," is a worldwide traveler who was in corporate real estate with McDonald's; now he's an executive with Shaw's Supermarkets' English-based corporation. The parents of five grown children have spent decades of summers in this area. In the winter they live and ski at Sunday River (Bethel, Maine). As one L.L. Bean shopper said while I was signing books there: "Holbrook House has flair everywhere. It belongs in your book."

In residence: Molly, a Wheaton terrier.

Bed and bath: Twelve carpeted rooms (mostly canopied beds) on first and second floors; all private baths. Handicapped-accessible room with queen four-poster, shower bath. One room with canopied queen, private exterior entrance, shower bath. Other rooms have queen beds (one has double), some with sitting room. Most baths are en-suite—with shower, without tub.

Breakfast: An event. Presented 8–9:30. (Coffee and teas at 7.) Belgian waffles with blueberry/raspberry/strawberry puree with whipped cream; an egg dish; hashed brown potatoes with tarragon, cheddar cheese, corn bread with tomato horseradish sauce. Juices in crystal. Fruit plate with seasonal sauce. Homemade breads, muffins, pastries, granola. Cooked by Jeani and served at tables (for two or more) set with floor-length cloths, china, and crystal in plant-filled sun room.

Plus: Tea at 5 p.m. with homemade brownies, macaroons, or Grandmother's maple nut cookies. Guest refrigerator. Porch rockers. Creative rainy and foggy day suggestions. Restaurant reviews.

> From Scotland: *"Perfect in every respect."* From Pennsylvania: *"A dream come true, where the hospitality was surpassed only by the accommodations and THE FOOD. Jeani will forever be remembered for her caring, thoughtful, and gracious manner."* From Virginia: *"Absolutely delightful—breakfast, decor, hosts."*

The Inn at Canoe Point   207/288-9511

Box 216, Bar Harbor, ME 04609

Hosts: Don Johnson and Esther Cavagnaro

Location: Secluded. Along two acres of pine forest on the rocky coast of Frenchman's Bay. One-quarter mile from Acadia National Park entrance. One mile to Bluenose ferry. Two miles to Bar Harbor.

Open: Year round.

Rates: Memorial Day–Columbus Day $115, $125, $135, $160, $210. Off-season $85–150. (Lower rates Sunday–Thursday, January–March.) Package rate for early December Christmas tree–trimming weekend.

♥ ❖ ✻

Extraordinary. At the edge of the ocean, with an enormous wraparound deck that juts out above the water. With intentionally simple interior design featuring neutral colors "to allow the large windows to create a feeling of being surrounded by natural beauty." (You are.) There's a floor-to-ceiling granite fireplace in the Ocean Room that has those mesmerizing views of the bay and the mountains beyond. It's all in a stucco Tudor summer cottage, built as a private home in 1889 and converted to this intimate inn (Don's fifth on Mount Desert Island) in 1986. It's a perfect and unforgettable setting for privacy and for very small weddings. Inspired dreamers should inquire about the innkeeping seminars that are held here twice a year.

Don, the Bar Harbor Chamber of Commerce president who first became acquainted with the island on a summer job after college, had a career in Chicago retailing. Esther, who hails from New Hampshire, has been in the hospitality industry for over a decade.

In residence: Nikki, a nine-year-old German shepherd.
Bed and bath: Three queen-bedded rooms; smallest, the most popular, has windows on three sides. Plus two suites—one with king/twins option occupies entire third floor; one has queen bed, fireplaced living room with French doors, and deck. All private baths with shower and tub or shower only.
Breakfast: 8–9. Entree repertoire includes French toast, stuffed French toast, blueberry pancakes, cranberry and walnut pancakes, quiche. In Ocean Room or on deck.
Plus: Great hints for hidden places. Hot tea by the fire. Iced tea on the deck. Down comforters. Grand piano. Stereo. Individual thermostats. No TV. Beach towels. Fresh flowers. Robes. Guest refrigerator. Hiking lunches (extra charge).

The Maples Inn   207/288-3443

16 Roberts Avenue, Bar Harbor, ME 04609

Host: Susan Sinclair
Location: On a quiet, tree-lined residential street. One and a half blocks to ocean; 3- to 10-minute walk to restaurants and shops; two miles to Acadia National Park.
Open: Year round. Two-night minimum on three-day holiday weekends.

Rates: June 15–October 15, $90–$130. Rest of year $60–$90. Extra person $15. Christmas Trim-a-Tree Weekend package rate. Discover, MC, Visa.
♥ ❖ ✦ ✂

Everyone in town knows the Victorian house with the rose-painted porch, the color chosen by Susan, a Wells Fargo Bank teller who became vice president in charge of corporate training. And they know Susan, who is active in the community and with Friends of Acadia. She sails and hikes, and in the winter she takes piano lessons and teaches tap dancing.

In 1991, following an apprenticeship with Don Johnson, page 48 (now she co-leads innkeeping workshops with him), she bought The Maples Inn and drove her belongings from California in an 18-foot moving van. Since, she has redecorated—and has been praised in person by Walter Cronkite.

In residence: Bailey, an energetic miniature schnauzer "adored by guests."
Foreign language spoken: Spanish. "Plan to learn French this year."
Bed and bath: Six rooms (five with queen beds), all with private shower baths. Second floor—two-room suite with modified-canopy queen bed, fireplaced living room with queen hide-a-bed; one queen-bedded room with separate treetop sitting room and twin hide-a-bed; one with bay window, detached bath (robes provided). Third floor (individual thermostats)—two queen-bedded rooms (one under eaves) and one double-bedded room with skylight and deck.

(Please turn page.)

Breakfast: 8–9. (Some recipes published by *Gourmet* and requested by *Bon Appetit.*) Blueberry stuffed French toast, overnight caramel strata, or chocolate chip pancakes. Served in candlelit dining room.
Plus: Four o'clock tea and cookies by fire or on rocker-filled porch; 6 p.m. wine and cheese. Upright piano. Down comforters. Guest refrigerator; complimentary sodas. Beach towels. Trail books for borrowing. "Fabulous" picnic baskets, $8.50 per person. Special occasions acknowledged. Games, cards, puzzles, audiocassettes, give-and-take books.

> From California: *"Although all the little touches were there, it is Susan's personality that makes the inn work so well."*

Nannau-Seaside B&B   207/288-5575

P.O. Box 710, Lower Main Street, Bar Harbor, ME 04609-0710

Hosts: Ron Evers and Vikki Erickson Evers
Location: In Compass Harbor, a mile from town center, down a long private driveway in a quiet wooded area adjoining Acadia National Park.
Open: Year round. Two-night minimum Memorial Day–October.
Rates: With fireplace—$125 bath en suite, $95 private nonadjoining bath. Third floor $95 for one room; two-bedroom suite $115 for two, $130 for three, $145 for four. MC, Visa.
♥ ✗ ⊱

If you have ever wanted to stay in one of the area's famed summer "cottages," here is your chance. From the grand front hall your eyes focus ahead to the enormous full-length window with ocean views. To the left is the living room with huge fireplace (with crackling fire many mornings and most nights) and walls covered with a wonderful coral-colored hand-printed William Morris paper. The house, listed on the National Register, is furnished with many period pieces, auction finds, a William Morris stairway runner, and Japanese and 20th-century Maine woodblock prints.

With prompting, Ron and Vikki, the first year-round residents of the house built in 1904, will share their unlikely experience of taking a hike 10 years ago, seeing an empty house without a FOR SALE sign, and finally buying the place, which was "way too big for the two of us." The art history major turned researcher and fine wallpaperer, together with her husband, a talented carpenter and baker, have done all the restoration work except the plumbing. They greet guests who come for the beauty of the island, for the chance to see a whale from the beach right here, and, as many returnees say, "to feel refreshed and relaxed in 'the Nannau Time Zone.'"

In residence: Misty, their mixed terrier/corgi.
Bed and bath: Four queen-bedded rooms with ocean views, private baths. Second floor—bay-windowed room, working fireplace, claw-foot tub and hand-held shower. Room with working fireplace, nonadjoining bath with claw-foot tub and hand-held shower. Third floor—room with new tiled full bath; two-bedroom suite with queen bed, two twins, large full bath with hand-held shower.

Breakfast: 8–9. Maybe omelets and homemade croissants, almond-filled French toast with maple syrup, eggs Florentine with English muffin, or Belgian waffles with whipped cream, fresh berries.
Plus: Down comforters. Screened porch. Croquet court. Private beach.

Fairhaven Inn   207/443-4391

North Bath Road, RR 2, Box 85, Bath, ME 04530-9304

Hosts: George and Sallie Pollard
Location: Quiet. On 24 acres of trees, meadows, lawns, bordered by the tidal Kennebec River. Birding, snowshoeing, and cross-country skiing right here. Five-minute drive to town center and Maine Maritime Museum, 20 to Freeport. Twelve miles to Popham Beach, eight to Bowdoin College.

Open: Year round. Two-night minimum on July, August, and holiday weekends.
Rates: $50–$60 single. $55–$75 double. Special rates for stays longer than three nights and for whole-inn bookings. Cross-country ski packages. MC, Visa.
♥ ✿ ♦

> From Pennsylvania: *"Lovely. . . . Nicely decorated, meticulously clean . . . spacious and comfortable common rooms . . . breakfasts are delicious, imaginative, and plentiful. The combination of Sallie's infectious enthusiasm and George's dry wit, plus their friendliness and helpfulness, left us with warm, happy feelings that lasted for the rest of our vacation."*

The winning combination works for the Pollards, who, as guests in 1988, expressed their love of this inn and its quiet country setting—with birds and wildflowers and nearby beaches that have sand, dunes, and tidal pools. "Why don't you buy it?" asked the previous owners. Within two months the Pollards sold their home of 30 years in Wilbraham, Massachusetts, where Sallie was a human service program director and George a manufacturer's representative. The inn, restored in the 1970s, is a 1790s shingled Georgian colonial furnished with antiques and country pieces.

In residence: Two cats.
Bed and bath: Eight rooms with queen, double, or twin beds. First-floor queen-bedded room has private full bath. Seven second-floor rooms; baths (five are private, two rooms share a bath) are full or with shower and no tub. Rollaway available.
Breakfast: 8–9 (coffee available at 7). Fruited hot cereals, yogurt or granola, blintzes with bananas and strawberries, fruit soups, baked grapefruit. Served in fireplaced dining room with river view.

B ed and breakfast gives a sense of place.

Glad II

207/443-1191

60 Pearl Street, Bath, ME 04530

Host: Gladys Lansky
Location: In historic area. Eight-minute walk from center of town; 1½ miles to Martime Museum. Ten minutes to Bowdoin College, 20 to Freeport, 40 to Boothbay Harbor; 25 to Popham Beach or Reid State Park; 45 minutes north of Portland.

Open: Year round. Reservations appreciated. Two-day minimum on holiday weekends.
Rates: $50 per room. Ten percent less for seniors and returnees. Discount for seventh night of weekly stay. Amex, MC, Visa.
♨ ♦ ✈ ⚓

"I worked for a large insurance company in New York City as an adminstrative assistant, and I also gave piano lessons for many years. I have stayed in B&Bs and can't think of a nicer thing to do. Since opening here in 1984, it has proven to be exactly what I had hoped for."

The Victorian house that once had layers of wallpaper is now decorated with painted white walls, cheery accents in primary colors, and a blend of furnishings. Now Gladys is giving piano lessons again. Her long list of suggestions includes combining the Maritime Museum with a visit to the working shipyard, where you can take a boat ride down the river. "And there are beaches, a state park with varied topography, picnic and playgrounds, classical music performances, local band concerts, and festivals."

In residence: Nicholas, "a four-legged dog person." Knack, the four-inch parakeet "who walked here one day."
Foreign languages spoken: "A bit of French and Spanish."
Bed and bath: Two carpeted second-floor rooms share one full bath. One large double-bedded room. The other room has two twin beds with wicker headboards.
Breakfast: 7:30–9. Juice, fruit, cereal, homemade muffins and jam, beverage. Served in dining room or on screened porch.
Plus: Air conditioning. Grand piano. Cable TV. Parlor. Bedroom window fans. Porch.

> From Florida: *"Comfortable beds. Spotless house . . . I got the recipe for the wonderful blueberry muffins. . . . A warm, generous hostess who provided many suggestions for the state of Maine. Best of all is Nicholas."*

The Inn at Bath

207/443-4294
fax 207/443-4294

969 Washington Street, Bath, ME 04530

Host: Nicholas H. Bayard
Location: In historic district on main street with lovely old well-kept homes. Ten-minute walk to town. Fifteen minutes to Bowdoin College or Wiscasset, 18 miles to L.L. Bean.

Open: Year round.
Rates: Canopied double $65; very large bath $70. Other rooms $75, $85, $90 (fireplace). Suite $130. Amex, Discover, MC, Visa.
♥ ♨ ♨ ⚓ ♦ ⚓

The year was 1990. The Pollards, page 51, longtime friends, drove by this for-sale 1810 Greek Revival and mentioned that it would make a wonderful B&B. And that's how Nick, a Wall Street investment banker for 27 years (who also worked on Third World industrial development projects), became an innkeeper. Nine months of renovations later, Nick opened here surrounded by family portraits, fine antiques, and comfortable sofas. The fly fisherman who loves "books, language, hiking (nearby Morse Mountain), harbors, and Maine" is, as guests can tell, a contented innkeeper.

In residence: Inspector Clouseau, a male Shih Tzu.

Bed and bath: Five spacious second-floor rooms with air conditioning, telephones, and color TV; all private baths. Three rooms have double beds— one is canopied, one a four-poster, one with extremely large bath. Largest room with king/twins option can be a suite with adjoining smaller double-bedded room. Renovated barn hayloft with beamed ceiling, queen bed, sofa, working fireplace, cable TV.

Breakfast: Usually, one sitting at 7:45, another at 9. Fresh fruit, juice, homemade bran muffins, cut-to-order bacon from nearby farm, eggs, home-made granola, hot cereal. Or French toast. Locally made jams.

Plus: Fireplaced parlors. Six p.m. beverages. Turndown service. Guest refrigerator. Beach towels. Individual thermostats in three rooms. Babysitting. Laundry facilities.

> From New Jersey: *"Much more than a place to sleep . . . immaculate . . . newly appointed bath with fine quality soaps and towels . . . wonderful breakfast in elegant dining room."*

Packard House   207/443-6069
45 Pearl Street, Bath, ME 04530

Hosts: Vincent and Elizabeth Messler
Location: In historic district, one block from the Kennebec River. Within walking distance of shops and restaurants. One and one-half miles from the Maine Maritime Museum; 15 minutes from Bowdoin College, 20 from L.L. Bean, 40 from Portland.

Open: Year round. Two-night minimum weekends, July–October. Reservations required January–March.
Rates: Double occupancy. $65 queen or twins. $80 suite. $15 third person in suite sitting room. MC, Visa.
♥ 🛏 ♣ ◆ ✗ ✂

> From Maryland: *"Pampered!"* From Massachusetts: *"A quick (too quick) look into Maine living. Excellent breakfasts and hospitality."*

Since moving from Connecticut in 1985, the Messlers have hosted receptions for the Maritime Museum and have become involved with many organizations, including Hospice and the Fourth of July Art Show. Guests from all over the world appreciate their enthusiasm for Bath—and for the history of shipbuilder Benjamin F. Packard's house. Thanks to fifth-generation descendants (who have visited), old Packard family photographs and commemorative plates are on display in the restored rooms.

Their B&B is a "dream come true" in the state where Elizabeth's family had spent many summers. Host/chef Vincent, a former health insurance executive, sells real estate and refinishes furniture and collectibles. Elizabeth enjoys painting, interior decorating, and, most of all, walking the beaches. The 1800s Georgian house is furnished with antiques, reproductions, historic paintings, and family heirlooms.

(Please turn page.)

In residence: Benjamin Basset, a basset hound, "in rear of house."
Bed and bath: Three second-floor rooms. One with queen four-poster and one with two twin spool beds share a full hall bath. Suite has queen cannonball bed, adjoining private shower bath, sitting room with love seat/twin bed.
Breakfast: 8–8:30; usually 8:30–9 in winter. "Special" French toast; blueberry buttermilk pancakes; baked Swiss eggs with bacon or homemade sausage and homegrown herbs; applesauce; toasted Irish soda bread, a family tradition. Served in formal dining room.
Plus: Music room with baby grand piano. English garden in enclosed courtyard. Dinners—if guests are snowed in!

1024 Washington B&B   207/443-5202

1024 Washington Street, Bath, ME 04530

Host: Michele Valdastri
Location: In a mansion-lined historic district. Five-minute walk through park overlooking river to shops, galleries, and restaurants. Near Maritime Museum and beaches; 15 minutes to L.L. Bean.

Open: Year round. Two-night minimum Friday–Sunday.
Rates: $65 shared bath, $80 private, $125 suite. Off-season, $50 shared, $60 private, $90 suite. MC, Visa.
♥ ✿ ◆ ✗

Four gorgeous *Colonial Homes* pages pictured the restored brick Italianate mansion decorated with Victorian antiques. Leaded windows, cherry dining room wainscoting, a light and bright parlor—all are part of the B&B opened in 1987 by Michele, who moved here from Florida with her husband, a consultant for an international corporation. She grew up in a family of innkeepers and has been cooking "since I was old enough to stir the sauce. Here, I think breakfast is absolutely magic. People—some timid, some gregarious, all strangers—leave as friends." Many write thank-you notes acknowledging Michele's suggestion to slow down and not miss "the good stuff, the real Maine, the hideaway spots."

In residence: One dog not allowed in guest areas.
Bed and bath: Five second-floor rooms (one with gas fireplace) plus a two-room suite with working fireplace, 7-foot tub. Queen beds except one room with two twin beds. All with 12-foot ceilings, ornate wood floors, air conditioning, individual heat control. All baths (five are private) except one have European soaking tubs with showers (some hand-held).
Breakfast: Presented 8:30–9:30. Crepes, gourmet egg "McMuffin," croissants, fresh fruit mix, Italian frittata. Served on antique china in breakfast room overlooking gardens. Background chamber music.
Plus: Mints. Robes. Fresh flowers. TV (hidden in cabinet) in guest rooms. Guest refrigerator with complimentary beverages. Special occasions acknowledged. Babysitting.

From Massachusetts: *"Luxurious tub deeper than your shoulders . . . fine quality sheets . . . watched the moon through enormous bedroom windows . . . sunlit in morning . . . exquisite sitting and breakfast rooms . . . breakfast a treat."*

The Horatio Johnson House   207/338-5153

36 Church Street, Belfast, ME 04915

Hosts: Helen and Gene Kirby
Location: In historic district, a neighborhood of lovely old homes (good walking territory), 20 miles north of Camden. Five-minute walk to shops, antiques centers, restaurants, and waterfront.

Open: Year round. Reservations recommended.
Rates: $40 single, $45 double. $10 third person.
♥ ♨ ✽ ♦ ✗

"Why did you move the dress that was hanging in my room!"

Returnees find that Helen sometimes changes the vintage clothing hanging on the back of a door or on the walls of this home, which the Kirby's made "close to the way it was when built in 1842." In the kitchen are Gene's punched tin cabinet doors, as well as a wood stove, a beamed ceiling, and hanging baskets. The Kirbys share all their expertise and can tell you about creating a bathroom out of three closets or teach you the ways of counted cross-stitching—all in a very relaxed, welcoming atmosphere.

Helen, a hat collector who had an antiques shop here, was a university administrative assistant. Gene, formerly a Massachusetts vocational school superintendent, makes animal and Santa Claus carvings that are sold in shops from Camden to Bar Harbor.

Bed and bath: Three large rooms, all with private baths. One has twin beds, one has queen; another with queen has adjoining room with single bed.
Breakfast: 8–8:30. Fresh fruit. Homemade granola, egg-free muffins and dishes. Hosts usually join guests.

The Jeweled Turret Inn   207/338-2304

16 Pearl Street, Belfast, ME 04915-1907   (in Maine) **800/696-2304**

Hosts: Carl and Cathy Heffentrager
Location: Residential. Two blocks from Victorian downtown. Half mile from "super park overlooking ocean," 17 miles north of Camden, within 20 miles of four state parks.

Open: Year round.
Rates: June 15–October, $65–$85. November–June 14, $55–$75. Honeymoon rooms $85. Singles $5 less. $10 third person.
♥ ✽ ♦ ✗ ✍

"A bed and breakfast vacation in beautiful historic Maine" is the answer to "What brought you from Anchorage, Alaska, where you were born and raised?" Several trips and years later, the young couple, still in their twenties, found Belfast, a "stepping-back-in-time town with this house and its stone verandas and gables and turrets." Now on the National Register of Historic Places, the house has been restored—all the woodwork too—by Carl, who grew up doing carpentry and construction, and Cathy, a piano teacher. They have filled the house with Victorian antiques, lots of lace, and their knick-knack collections.

(Please turn page.)

In residence: Daughter Megan, age 12. Renegade, a Yorkshire terrier, "a toy dog who occasionally introduces himself."
Bed and bath: Seven rooms on first and second floors, private baths. (Ceiling fans in two rooms.) Queen-bedded and double-bedded rooms with full bath. One room with queen bed, fireplace, full bath, hand-held shower. One with two twin beds, shower bath. Rollaway available.
Breakfast: At 8 and 9. Poached cinnamon pears, fruit cup, or baked apples. German pancakes, sourdough gingerbread waffles, Belgian waffles, quiche, or French toast. Scones are house specialty. Teas and freshly ground gourmet coffee.
Plus: November–May, Victorian tea at 3 p.m. In summer, iced tea on veranda. Mints. Garden.

Guests wrote: *"A magnificent grand old Victorian lady . . . memorable breakfasts . . . spotless. . . . I'll always remember the sun streaming through, throwing colorful prisms on the wall."*

Chapman Inn   207/824-2657

Corner Church & Broad Streets, P.O. Box 206, Bethel, ME 04217-0206

Hosts: Sandra and George Wight
Location: Facing the town green in historic district. Across from cross-country trails, 18-hole championship golf course, historical society. Ten minutes to Sunday River and Mount Abram ski areas.
Open: Year round. Two-night minimum on winter weekends.
Rates: Include use of sauna and, in summer, private pond beach four miles away. For winter weekends and vacation weeks, add $20. Private bath $55 single, $65 double, $20 extra adult, $10 child under 12. Shared bath $45 single, $55 double, $15 extra adult, $5 under age 12. Amex, MC, Visa.
♥ ♨ ✳ ♦

"Guests often say they feel like they live here," says Sandra, who talks about "living out a fantasy" in this big, casual, homey Federal-style house built by a sea captain in 1860. Sandra and George, who "runs a slasher that cuts and loads trees" have lived in the Bethel area all their lives. "We're related to half the town!"

The former home of William Rogers Chapman—composer, conductor, and founder of the Maine Music Festival—was converted to an inn in 1984 by Robin and Doug Zinchuk, the current owners, who now live nearby with their four young sons.

Bed and bath: On three floors. Six traditional rooms (two have private shower baths; four share two baths) with double or both a double and a single bed. Plus three full apartments. And, in winter, dorm facilities.
Breakfast: 7–9. Juice, fresh fruit, whole-grain cereal and bread. Homemade granola. Hot dish served in summer; buffet style in winter—"for skiers anxious to get to slopes." Special diets accommodated. In dining room with lace cloths and curtains, soft music.
Plus: Living room fireplace. Late-afternoon snacks. Bedroom fans. Game room, TV room, two saunas in converted barn. Use of canoe and beach chairs. Group dinners arranged. Babysitting with advance request. Toys, cribs,

booster chairs. A Maine touch, a souvenir. Some pets allowed. With advance arrangements, pickup at Portland Jetport.

From Maine: *"We are fussy about clean, comfortable accommodations and were delighted. They made us feel right at home."* From Oregon: *"Personable hosts. . . . Leaving was not easy."*

The Douglass Place   207/824-2229
HCR 61, Box 90, Bethel, ME 04217-9501

Hosts: Dana and Barbara Douglass
Location: On Route 2, a mile northeast of the village. Six miles to Maine downhill ski areas, 30 to foot of Mount Washington in New Hampshire; 72 miles from Portland, 180 to Montreal.

Open: Year round except for two weeks in April and last two weeks in October. Two-night minimum on holiday weekends.
Rates: $45 single, $55 double. $20 extra bed.
♥ ♙ ♟ ❖

From Florida: *"My husband and I and Maria, our parrot, live aboard a sailboat for most of the year. We all have never experienced such a warm at-home feeling as we had at the Douglasses'."*

The Douglasses brought up four daughters in this comfortably furnished home. The house was built in the early 1800s by the Twitchells, successful farmers whose descendants put on a Victorian addition in 1880s. Those flower gardens, the hobby of Dana, a semiretired land surveyor, are the reason that some tour buses stop here. "Sharing this 20-room home [since 1982] is a marvelous way to meet people from all over the world," says Barbara, a retired social worker. Visitors from England summed it up, "The friendliest welcome to strangers, a lovely house, comfortable beds—just a half mile from Bethel center."

In residence: Husband occasionally smokes ("Shouldn't!").
Foreign language spoken: A little French.
Bed and bath: Three twin-bedded rooms and one with queen bed and queen sofa bed share two second-floor full baths plus a half bath downstairs. TV in all rooms. Rollaway available.
Breakfast: 7–9:30. Beverage, fruit in season, dry cereals, homemade muffins and preserves.
Plus: Gazebo. Tour of huge pegged barn. Game room with piano and pool table. Cross-country ski trail starts in back yard. Cookies and cool drinks in summer; hot tea or cocoa for skiers. "Hiking trails and antiques shop for our summer guests."

---

*U*nless otherwise stated, rates in this book are for two and include breakfast in addition to all the amenities in "Plus."

The Hammons House   207/824-3170

Broad Street, P.O. Box 16, Bethel, ME 04217

Hosts: Sally and Richard Taylor
Location: In historic district, 1½ blocks from Main Street. On a tree-lined street, across from an 18-hole golf course and groomed ski trails. Six miles to downhill and cross-country ski areas.
Open: Year round. Advance reservations required. Two-night minimum on holidays and school vacation weeks.

Rates: Holidays and school vacation weeks, $65 single, $80 double, $150 suite. Weekends and ski season, $55 single, $70 double, $125 suite. Mid-week off-season (April until week before Christmas, except for one week in October), $45 single, $55 double, $90 suite. Additional person $30; 12 and under $20. MC, Visa.
♥ ✪ ✈ ✄

Perfect for peace, tranquillity—and special occasions. Since Sally opened this B&B in 1986, her perennial gardens have been the site for several beautiful weddings, including her own in the summer of 1991. Dick teaches English, Latin, and German at Gould Academy, where he is also running and cross-country ski coach.

The Greek Revival house, built for the Honorable David Hammons, member of the thirteenth Congress, is on the National Register of Historic Places. It is decorated with soft colors, traditional prints and furnishings, and braided rugs, a craft Sally teaches. A plant-filled conservatory overlooks the mountains. In winter, a fireplace beckons. As for special events, Sally reports that "the Hammons House Novel-in-Progress is being written by guests. The adjacent 1920s theater–now–antiques shop is open June–October."

In residence: Riff Raff, "a small lovable version of a Maine coon cat who stays outdoors."
Bed and bath: Four rooms. One corner room with two twin beds and one large room with a double and one twin bed share sitting area and full bath. Two-room corner suite with private stairway, full bath, and window seats includes one room with two twins, one with extra-long double bed. Rollaway available.
Breakfast: 8–9. Baked apples, French toast, whole wheat pancakes, or cheddar omelets. Homemade muffins, lemon or brown sugar corn bread. Fresh fruit. Juice, coffee, tea. Served in dining room or conservatory.
Plus: Heat lamps in baths. Beverages. Lots of books. Shaded porches. Open patios.

From Massachusetts: *"Very quiet and relaxing . . . two of the nicest people you'd ever want to meet."* From New York: *"Superb and beautiful breakfasts."*

Guests come from as close as 10 minutes away or from around the world.

Hodgdon Island Inn   207/633-7474

P.O. Box 492, Barter's Island Road, Boothbay, ME 04571

Hosts: Sydney and Joe Klenk
Location: Rural and residential. Six-minute drive from downtown Boothbay Harbor. On an island, "but you don't see water all around." Overlooking Sheepscot Cove.

Open: Year round except three weeks after Columbus Day (late October) and six winter weeks.
Rates: $70 or $75 queen bed. $80 or $85 king. $10 less in winter.
♥ ❖ ✙ ⅄

When the youngest of seven Klenks called to say, "Mom, I've found your B&B" he was right! As college roommate of the youngest Hodgdon (a big family that still lives on the island), he learned that his roommate's parents were selling their 240-year-old family home—just about the time the Klenks wanted to become innkeepers.

Sydney and Joe made major changes, added six new baths, furnished with their eclectic collection of heirloom oak, pine, and wicker, and opened here in 1990. As Sydney says, "My mother was from Maine. We always had a big cottage with a lot of company. I remember summer as fun time. It still is! Occasionally we go out to dinner, leave a a note telling our guests where we are, and return to find a guest's message: 'OK Mom!' We draw maps, suggest restaurants, plan day trips—and enjoy sharing this beautiful home."

Bed and bath: Six rooms, all with private baths. First floor—king/twins option, shower bath. Second floor—king/twins option, full bath. Queen- or king-bedded rooms, each with shower bath.
Breakfast: 8–9. (Continental thereafter.) Fresh fruit. Hot muffins, orange juice, homemade granola and other cereals. Blueberry pancakes and sausage; quiche and bacon; French toast or egg dish. Freshly brewed coffee and decaf. Herbal and regular teas. A very leisurely meal.
Plus: In summer, chlorine-free heated outdoor pool; lemonade on the porch. Old-fashioned lawn swing on rollers. Adirondack benches for two by the water. In cooler weather, help-yourself instant hot beverages. Gas log stove in parlor.

> From Massachusetts: *"Delightful. . . . A little off the beaten path. . . . Easy drive to Boothbay Harbor. A good candidate for your book. . . . Done a lot of tasteful remodeling to a house built in the early 1800s. . . . Almost 100 years later [1873] the whole house was raised, a new first floor inserted, and voila!—a Victorian with lots of interesting decorations."*

Kenniston Hill Inn   207/633-2159

Route 27, P.O. Box 125   (U.S./Canada) **800/992-2915**
Boothbay, ME 04537-0125

Hosts: Susan and David Straight
Location: Two miles north of bustling Boothbay Harbor, set back from the road on a hill, surrounded by maple and oak trees.
Open: Year round.

Rates: Double occupancy. $65–$75 double beds, $85 twin beds, $85–$95 queen or king beds. Fireplaced queen-bedded $90–$95, king-bedded $95. MC, Visa.
♥ ❖ ◆ ✙ ⅄

(Please turn page.)

"How old is this house?" is the usual question asked by guests as they enter the beamed living room, which has a huge hearth with two bake-ovens and a David-reproduced mantel. Period wallpapers, stenciling, wainscoting, and country primitives are in some rooms. The handsome 1786 center chimney Georgian colonial has seen several remodelings—"yes, its history is complete with a ghost story"—and is now being restored "one room at a time to its original simple formality."

Susan, who was working in banking, and David, a cabinetmaker (reproduction early country pieces) purchased the established inn in 1990. Many of their guests linger and enjoy the house and grounds. Others go antiquing, seal watching, or sightseeing. In winter they have the option of a five-course fireside dinner right here.

In residence: Jack, a Yorkshire terrier, "a good napper."
Bed and bath: Ten rooms (six with individual heat control); all with private attached bath. Three rooms with private exterior entrance. Arrangements include rooms with working fireplaces and full baths (other baths are shower, no tub). Beds (many four-posters) include king, queen, double, or two twins. Queen and one twin bed in carriage house.
Breakfast: Coffee and tea at 8. Intentionally special at 9. Perhaps bacon-and-three-cheese pie, ham and Swiss wrapped in puff pastry, eggs Benedict, peaches and cream French toast. Fruit. Home-baked goods. Family style on fine china with starched and pressed napkins at table surrounded by hand-crafted Windsor chairs.
Plus: Special occasions acknowledged. Seasonal afternoon refreshments. Fans. Perennial gardens.

Seawitch Bed & Breakfast   207/633-7804

Route 27, Box 27, Boothbay, ME 04537-9807

Hosts: Claire and Bill Hunt
Location: Secluded. On 10 wooded acres on a country road halfway between Route 1 and Boothbay. A short walk to quiet cove where seals visit. Ten-minute drive to harbor.

Open: Year round. Two-day minimum on holidays.
Rates: $120 Memorial Day–Labor Day. $100–$110 September–October. $95 rest of year. $15 third person.
♥ ❖ ✈

While this expanded Cape Cod–style sea captain's house that the Hunts designed was being built, they stayed a total of 100 days at a Boothbay B&B, the inspiration for Seawitch. Since moving here from Grosse Pointe, Michigan, in 1990, Bill and Claire have expanded the grounds, "and we're constantly developing new menu ideas." Both enjoy sharing their love of the area, gardening, and their home, which is filled with antiques, ship prints, and artifacts from all over the world.

Foreign languages spoken: French and German.
Bed and bath: Two spacious double-bedded (one is a four-poster) second-floor rooms, each with attached private full bath, working fireplace, sitting area. Private guest entrance. Rollaway available.

Breakfast: Usually 9. Almond crepes with raspberry puree, Spanish omelets, thick slab French toast, or egg-and-cheese pie. At dining room table set with Battenberg lace linens, crystal, fine china, antique silver.
Plus: Late-afternoon beverage with hors d'oeuvres in library. Coffee and juice at 7:30 a.m. Fresh flowers. Candy. Amenities basket. "Piles of pillows." Down comforters. Flannel sheets. Lace and cutwork duvet covers in summer.

Five Gables Inn

207/633-4551
Murray Hill Road   (outside Maine) 800/451-5048
East Boothbay, ME 04544

Hosts: Ellen and Paul Morissette
Location: On a hill overlooking a lobstering bay. On narrow road off Route 96. In a small shipbuilding village, three miles from Boothbay Harbor.
Open: May through mid-November. Two-night minimum on holiday weekends.

Rates: On first and third floors, $80–$90 double bed, $95 queen bed. Fireplaced rooms $100 or $110 with queen bed, $130 with king bed. MC, Visa.
♥ ♣ ♦ ✈ ✗

Here they are—the Morissettes, who became innkeepers in 1983 when they redid a 200-year-old house that had become apartments. (Previously, Paul had been a renowned Vermont restaurant owner and chef for a quarter century.) When Ellen and Paul learned that the region's only remaining Victorian hotel, built in 1845 and last used in 1978, was about to meet the fate of similar structures, they, together with extended family members, took on the two-year restoration. A before-and-after album shows the transformation from a building that had 22 guest rooms and 3 baths. Ellen's daughter decorated with reproduction country and traditional furnishings. Once again the wide veranda with hammock, Lifecycle bike, and lots of wicker is filled with guests enjoying the view and serenity. Some take a lovely walk through the woods to the summer commmunity of Bayville. And should you come by sea, the inn has two moorings.

Bed and bath: Sixteen rooms (five with working fireplace) on three floors. All private baths; some with tub and shower, some shower only. King, queen, double, twins available.
Breakfast: 8–9:30. Eggs Florentine or chili-cheese strata. Rosemary potatoes, apple crisp, homemade muffins, fresh fruit, homemade granola, juices, meats. In dining room or on porch. (Lasts for up to two hours.)
Plus: No TV. Afternoon tea or lemonade with homemade chocolate chip cookies. Fresh flowers. Glycerine soap. Oscillating fans. Golf clubs available.

Can't find a listing for the community you are going to? Check with a reservation service described at the beginning of this chapter. Through the service you may be placed (matched) with a welcoming B&B that is near your destination.

Anchor Watch

207/633-7565

3 Eames Road, Boothbay Harbor, ME 04538-1005

Hosts: Captain Bob and Diane Campbell
Location: One hundred feet from ocean—facing lighthouses, islands, lobster boats, and yachts. On a dead-end street, a five-minute walk to town's shops, restaurants, and boat trips.

Open: Valentine's Day through December.
Rates: Summer $75–$95 (view of the ocean determines rate). $15 third person. Less in winter. Package rates include boat ride and dinner. MC, Visa.

♥ ✿ ◆ ✖ ⊱

Rave reviews have come from a CEO who had never stayed in a B&B before—"We usually stay in The Williamsburg Inn (Virginia) or The Greenbrier Hotel (West Virginia)"—and from guests who have slept in every room, guests from England, guests who have returned with in-laws and babes-in-arms. They remember "the pink light of morning reflected off the ocean," fresh flowers, neat plantings, spotless everything, hot breakfast breads, the wicker-furnished porch, and the abundant evidence that "Diane, who has a warm and friendly touch, likes what she does."

In 1985 the Campbells left their jobs as English teacher and design engineer to return to the town where they grew up. To accommodate their ferry passengers (to Monhegan and Squirrel islands), they bought the house next door, decorated in country cottage style, and became innkeepers. And now they have a pier and float overlooking the outer harbor. In summer, Diane's dad is official porch greeter.

In residence: Two outside cats, Skeesix and Smokey.
Bed and bath: Four Monhegan Island theme rooms on second (with ceiling fans) and third (with air conditioning) floors. All private baths, one full, the rest shower without tub. Third-floor rooms have ocean views and shared deck. Views of ocean or garden from second-floor rooms. Two queen-bedded rooms. Two with both a double and a twin bed.
Breakfast: 8:30. Could be apple pancakes and blueberry muffins; orange/pineapple or blueberry blintzes and bran muffins; banana/strawberry popovers with warm applesauce and rhubarb muffins; or baked orange French toast. Served in breakfast nook with ocean view; in summer, tray tables for porch or deck.
Plus: Afternoon tea table. Pillow favors. In season, discount coupons for harbor tour. Pier and float great for sunning or feeding ducks or watching lobster boats. Laundry facilities.

---

*O*ne out of five guests leaves with the dream
of opening a B&B.

The Noble House   207/647-3733
37 Highland Ridge Road, P.O. Box 180, Bridgton, ME 04009-0180

Hosts: Dick and Jane Starets and family
Location: Set back on a hill overlooking (across street from) scenic Highland Lake. Minutes' walk to antiques and crafts shops. "Near romantic restaurants" and Sabbathday Shaker Village. Five miles to Shawnee Peak at Pleasant Mountain ski area, 30 to North Conway (New Hampshire) outlet shopping. Near swimming, hiking, skiing, golf, tennis.
Open: June through October; two-night minimum on weekends. Rest of year by advance reservation only.
Rates: $74 shared bath, $84–$115 private bath. Third person $15 child, $25 adult. No charge for portacrib.
♥ ♦ ❖ ♦ ✕ ✂

Guests paint the sunset. They fall asleep in the lakeside hammock. They write to me about the family that came from California in 1984 to the house built for a senator in 1903: "Enjoyed the hospitality, the location, and all the great food!"

When the Staretses, parents of four, bought the big Queen Anne–style house from Dr. Noble, the town dentist for 40 years, little restoration was needed in the main house. When they converted the carriage house, Jane decorated with wicker and antiques, comforters and color-coordinated linens.

Dick is a commercial airline pilot. Jane has been a special education teacher in three states.

In residence: Son Jonathan is 12. One smoky gray coon cat.
Bed and bath: Nine rooms. Queen four-poster or double bed in three second-floor rooms that share a large full bath and porch. Huge third-floor suite with two twin beds and a double bed, private shower bath. In converted barn, two adjoining ground-level rooms; one room with queen bed and Jacuzzi; one with two twin beds, private shower bath. Lakeview honeymoon suite has queen brass bed, whirlpool bath. Rollaway and bassinet available.
Breakfast: 8–9. Freshly squeezed orange juice, fruit, eggs, homemade bread. Cheese strata, blueberry or whole wheat pancakes with Noble's own maple syrup, or rum raisin French toast. By fireplace in Victorian dining room.
Plus: Grand piano. Antique organ in fireplaced parlor. Porch rockers. Special attention for honeymooners. Use of pedal boat and canoe.

Middaugh Bed & Breakfast   207/725-2562
36 Elm Street, Topsham, ME 04086

Hosts: Mary Kay and Dewey Nelson
Location: In the historic district, one mile from downtown Brunswick and Bowdoin College. Ten miles from Freeport and L.L. Bean, 30 miles north of Portland. The yard adjoins the Topsham Fairgrounds.
Open: Year round. Advance reservations preferred.
Rates: $60–$70 per room. $10 hide-a-bed. MC, Visa.
♠ ✕ ✂

The Nelsons found most of the interior restoration done when they bought the Federal/Greek Revival house in 1987. Their own decorating touches include stenciling and swags. "Our search for background has taken us back

(Please turn page.)

to 1820. We have been gathering oral history documentation too. Gardening has become a great hobby. We are having fun working on the iris, daylilies, peonies, roses, quince, lilacs, and honeysuckle."

Dewey, a retired aviator, is a contractor, tax consultant, and full-time host. Mary Kay teaches second grade, enjoys walking, and assists guests in planning coastal Maine day trips.

In residence: George, "a very friendly nine-year-old black and white cat." Molly, an "aloof five-year-old springer spaniel."
Bed and bath: Two large second-floor rooms, one with king bed, one with queen; private full baths. Sofa bed on first floor. Crib available.
Breakfast: 7–9. Fruit. Homemade breads and muffins. Blueberry pancakes, waffles, or French toast. Served in dining room or on sun porch.
Plus: Fireplaced living room with plenty of reading material. Family room with TV and games. Mints. Bedroom ceiling fans. Large yard.

Blackberry Inn

82 Elm Street, Camden, ME 04843-1907

207/236-6060
800/833-6674
fax 207/236-4117

Hosts: Vicki and Ed Doudera
Location: On U.S. Route 1 with good view of Mount Battie. Easy walk to harbor, village center.
Open: Year round. Two-day minimum on holiday weekends.
Rates: Double occupancy. Mid-June through late October: $75–$80 double, private half bath. Private baths $130 king with whirlpool, fireplace, TV; $95–$100 queen (one with fireplace); $95 twins; $75–$80 double. Carriage house $110. Third person $10 under age 13, $20 adult. Mid-May–mid-June and late October–January 2, $10–$20 less. January 3–mid-May, $30–$40 less. Weekend cooking-class packages. MC, Visa.
♥ ⚶ ✗ ✶

There's a sense of place in this restored Victorian, which was featured in Pomada and Larsen's book, *Daughters of Painted Ladies: America's Resplendent Victorians*. It has polished parquet floors, antiques of the 1800s, some country pieces, ceilings with intricate plaster decorations—and two guest parlors, one with a wood stove. The friendly attention-to-detail innkeepers are former Bostonians who love the Camden area with its theater, chamber concerts, and opportunities to sail, ski, and hike "and to enjoy our young sons!" Ed, the creative chef, is an attorney and a hospital trustee, and he's active with the schools. Vicki, a food and travel writer who is now working on her first novel, helped to save the old Camden post office.

In residence: Matthew, age six; Nathan, age four. Mookie, a lovable black Labrador retriever, "everyone's favorite innkeeper!"
Foreign language spoken: "Bienvenue! Ici on parle francais."
Bed and bath: Ten rooms (two are air conditioned); eight with private full baths, two with private half bath. King, queen, double, or twin beds. Two with private garden entrance, wood-burning fireplace, whirlpool tub, cable TV. First-floor double-bedded room has wood-burning fireplace, private half bath, upstairs shower (robes provided). On first floor of perfect-for-families

carriage house—queen-bedded room, one with two twin beds, TV/sitting area, full bath, full kitchen.

Breakfast: 8–9:30. (Coffee earlier.) In Ed's repertoire—cheese blintzes with blackberry sauce, brie souffle, and apricot crunch toast. Breads, muffins, coffee cakes, fresh fruit, juices, yogurt, granola. Freshly ground blended coffee. In courtyard or fireplaced dining room.

Plus: Afternoon hospitality hour. Blackberry candies. Pickup at Owl's Head Airport or Camden bus stop. Special occasions acknowledged. Sprinkler system.

Edgecombe-Coles House

HCR 60, Box 3010, 64 High Street
Camden, ME 04843-3501

207/236-2336
fax 207/236-6227

Hosts: Louise and Terry Price
Location: Overlooking the ocean. Set back from Route 1, behind a huge hedge. A half mile north of the center of Camden.
Open: Year round. Two-day minimum on June, July, August, and fall weekends. Reservations required weekdays November–May.

Rates: July–October, twin and queen $120, king $150/$170. Rest of year, twin and queen $80, king $100/$120. Third person $25. Amex, Diners, Discover, MC, Visa.
♥ ❖ ♦ ⋈

The ocean view—with or without the porch telescope—is remembered almost as much as the innkeepers. The Prices found the property on their way to Bar Harbor, on their way to a lifestyle change; their find was a New England farmhouse that had become the gatehouse to a mansion that is no more.

Terry, an engineer/designer, and Louise, an illustrator/designer, had already restored 12 houses in California. Since coming to Camden in 1982, they have spent several winters restoring other houses, which they sold. Because they are avid collectors, the inn is filled with various types and styles of antique furniture, Oriental rugs, and original art—all admired by "people who require lots of attention and others who wish privacy."

In residence: Three show dogs—"the very friendly one greets guests."
Bed and bath: Six second-floor rooms; three with ocean views; all with private en-suite baths. King, queen, or twin four-posters. Twin room has a shower bath; all others have a tub and shower. Cot available.
Breakfast: 8:30. (Coffee available at 7:30.) Juice. Fresh fruit. Home-baked muffins, bread, and maybe cake too. Waffles, blueberry pancakes, or eggs with bacon or sausage. Homemade jams. Tea. Freshly ground and brewed coffee. In dining room or on porch.
Plus: Three fireplaces. Bicycles. Chocolates. Flowers. Imported toiletries. Champagne for celebrations. Afternoon beverages. Window fans. Transportation from Camden bus or Rockland/Owls Head Airport. Local laundry service provides next-day return. Option of dinner during severe weather. "No pipes or cigars, period!"

The Maine Stay

207/236-9636

22 High Street, Camden, ME 04843-1735

Hosts: Peter and Donny Smith and Diana Robson
Location: On Route 1, among homes on the Register of National Historic Places. Two blocks from the harbor.
Open: Year round.
Rates: Mid-June through late October $75 shared bath, $90–$110 private. May–mid-June $60 shared, $70–$85 private. Winter $55 shared bath, $70 private, $85 huge room with wood stove. Singles $10 less. Two third-floor rooms for three to five guests, $75–$160 depending on number of guests and rooms booked. Amex, MC, Visa.
♥ ♣ ♦ ✈ ✂

An award winner. Popular year round. There's an antique coal stove in the country kitchen. A deck outside the dining room looks out onto parkland and Mount Battie. Period furnishings, Oriental rugs, wide board floors are here too.

What to do? Printed suggestions galore. Activities measured in blocks and miles from the door. Places you've heard a lot about. Places you've never heard a word about. A walking tour. Gardens. Hints: "Don't sit next to the foghorn." Bicycle tours. Driving tours. Stitchery weekends. Maps. Small business meeting arrangements. Recipes at the touch of a computer key. Sometimes, a song or two with guests in the kitchen. (Peter sang with barbershop quartets. His wife, Donny, a registered nurse, and her twin sister, Diana, a music major and librarian, have competed in Sweet Adelines groups.) It all happens in the house that began in 1802 and continues to see changes to this day. As Peter says, while announcing that the inn is well on its way to having all private baths, "After 36 years in the navy, we wanted to drop anchor in a nice spot and let the world come to us." Guests have summed it up: "Delightful."

Bed and bath: Eight rooms; four with private bath. All with individual thermostats. First-floor very private 16-by-19-foot room has queen bed, wood stove, views of woods, private patio. Second- and third-floor rooms have queen, twins, or double bed. (One double-bedded room with twin bed in adjoining room booked as a single room for two people only.)
Breakfast: Usually 8:30, as early at 6:30, as late as 10:30. Fresh fruit. Egg dish, waffles, French toast, or whole wheat pancakes. Breads, muffins, or popovers. Served on English china with sterling silver and crystal.
Plus: Afternoon tea. Freshly baked cookies. Flannel sheets. Some ceiling fans. Two fireplaced parlors. TV room with VCR. Transportation to/from airport.

Windward House

207/236-9656

6 High Street, Camden, ME 04843

Hosts: Jon and Mary Davis
Location: In historic district, one-half block above Camden Harbor, shops and restaurants. With gardens, orchard, views of Mount Battie.
Open: April through December.
Rates: Tax included. July–mid October $90 double, $100–$135 queen, $135 suite. Off-season $65 double, $100 queen or suite. Amex, MC, Visa.
♥ ⛵ ♣ ✈

From Massachusetts: *"We have enjoyed many of the B&Bs your book has introduced us to, but none have matched the Windward."* From California: *"Breakfast alone is worth the trip."* From Pennsylvania: *"Decor is excellent taste [mostly antiques] with a homey atmosphere. Grounds and gardens are breathtaking."* From Georgia: *"Jon and Mary exude the vitality and serenity that come from loving what they do."*

B&B travels throughout the United States and in Europe, Australia, and New Zealand inspired these avid sailors to create their own in this 1854 Greek Revival. They restored (see before-and-after album), opened in 1987, and were listed on the National Register in 1989. Several of their guests have also resettled in the area. In New Jersey Jon was a director at AT&T's national headquarters. Mary, a registered nurse, was co-owner of The Gourmet Touch, a catering firm.

In residence: Muffy, 15-year-old calico cat, "available upon request."
Bed and bath: Seven rooms and one suite, all with individual thermostats, private baths, designer bedding. First floor—queen canopied bed, skylights, full bath, private entrance. Second floor—queen beds (one is canopied; one room has twin bed also), all shower baths. Plus suite with private entrance, queen bed, ceiling fan, sitting room, full kitchen. Third floor—large room with queen bed, another "under the eaves" with double; each with skylight, full bath.
Breakfast: 8:30. (Coffee at 7.) An event. Broiled grapefruit-or-pear apple blueberry crisp; peaches-and-cream French toast; orange yogurt pancakes; or egg puff. Fresh juices. Homemade muffins and baked goods. Served family style at table set with silver and fine china.
Plus: Fireplaced living room. Library with TV and stereo. Teas, hazelnut coffee, and cider always available. Guest refrigerator. Beach towels. Deck and rear lawn. Mints. Fruit. Garden flowers.

Blanchard Bed and Breakfast   207/763-3785

Route 235, HC 62, Box 702, Hope, ME 04847

Hosts: John and Betty Blanchard
Location: On two acres of fields (stargazing at night) and ever-expanding gardens. Pick-your-own apple orchard across street. Neighboring cows. Minutes' walk to general store (pizza and sandwiches too) at Routes 235/105 intersection; and to spring-fed pond for swimming. Seven miles inland from Camden.
Open: Year round. Two-day mini-

mum for advance reservations on July and August weekends.
Rates: $60 queen with private bath; $70–$80 queen plus twin in adjacent alcove; $100 queen together with double-bedded room. $155 entire floor—two queens, one double. $10 extra person (two maximum). Air conditioning $5 per night. Discover, MC, Visa.
♥ ♧ ♠ ♣ ✗ ✗

From Massachusetts, Illinois, Michigan, Maine, Canada, New York, California: *"Treated our children as grandchildren. . . . felt pampered . . . breakfast was a highlight . . . exceptionally helpful with suggestions for activities and restaurants . . . spacious and gorgeous room . . . clean and comfortable. . . . On prebreakast walk with Mr. Blanchard and Buddy, the true master of house—four feet of packed*

(Please turn page.)

snow, mountain views, a brief but colorful history of the area. . . . We book with our family reunion overflow. It has become a lottery to see who 'wins' the Blanchards' rooms."

The Blanchards settled in this restored Greek Revival, "a living tribute to Yankee thrift, ingenuity, industry, and skill" in 1979 when John retired as a Coast Guard commander. (His earliest journey was at age 19, when he sailed around the world on the *Yankee*.) Through a decade of hosting, they have met honeymooners, cyclists, genealogists, travelers who "do everything on land and sea and others who stick to back roads," and plenty who write to me.

In residence: Buddy, "our golden retriever, a canine Mr. Rogers who makes everyone feel special." Two outdoor cats.
Bed and bath: Entire second floor—three rooms and two private baths (one tub/shower, one shower only). Two queen-bedded (one is canopied) rooms; either can be booked for same party with a smaller double room (robes provided). Twin bed, rollaway, and crib available.
Breakfast: 8–9. Blueberry buttermilk pancakes. Muffins, breads, coffee cake. Cereals, juice, fruit, hot beverages. Fruit milkshakes with nonfat yogurt. Special diets accommodated.
Plus: Fireplace, piano, and cable TV in living room. Window fans. Flannel sheets. Beach towels. Use of refrigerator, iron and board. Garden tours. Outdoor games. Screened gazebo tent. Children's books, games, high chair, booster seats, playpen.

The Spouter Inn   207/789-5171
U.S. Route 1, P.O. Box 270, Lincolnville Beach, ME 04849-0270

Hosts: Paul and Catherine Lippman and sons Matthew and Grant.
Location: On the main road, across from sandy beach and small harbor in center of village. On two acres with extensive gardens. Five-minute drive to Camden. Two minutes' walk to Isleboro ferry.

Open: Year round. Two-night minimum on weekends, June 15–October 15.
Rates: June 15–October 15, $75 double, $75–$95 queen, $125 suite. Off-season, $55 double, $55–$75 queen, $95 suite. Discover, MC, Visa.
♥ 🏡 ❄ ✕ ✕

Everywhere there are signs of Paul's creative thinking and Catherine's decorating. It feels like a well-kept old house, but the inside is all redesigned and rebuilt, with some original lighting fixtures, floorboards, and windows— and with a walk-in kitchen hearth.

"When we were looking for a place to live in 1985, we could see that this house, in a great location, had possibilities for blending our interests, experiences (which include catering), and goals." In Pennsylvania Paul was an engineer and Catherine a registered nurse.

Now the Lippmans are at home for work and school. Matthew, age 13, and Grant, age 11, have always been home taught and are involved in many sports. Paul offers sea kayak tours—great for closeups of sea life—that leave right from here. And there are plenty of suggestions for touring, cycling, and hiking.

Bed and bath: Six rooms with ocean views and all-new private shower baths. One double-bedded room. Four with queen bed (three with working fireplace; one with Jacuzzi and air conditioning). Suite with queen bed, queen sofa bed, fireplace, Jacuzzi, wet bar, ceiling fan. Rollaway available.
Breakfast: 7–9. Quiche, crepes, omelet, puffed pancakes, strata, or French toast; with homegrown herbs and vegetables. "Our own sausage." Fresh fruit dish, homemade pastries. Juice, coffee, tea.
Plus: Porch rockers face Penobscot Bay. Fresh flowers. Mints on pillow. Beverages. Two common rooms—"site of amazing stories and tall tales"—one with fireplace, one with wood stove. Individual thermostats.

> From Massachusetts: *"Amazing restoration work . . . beautiful hardwood floors and cherry stairs . . . charming . . . impeccable . . . great breakfast."* From New York: *"Light, bright, airy. . . . We will recommend this place a lot . . . warm, friendly hosts."*

Bed & Breakfast of Maine Host #32

Rockport, ME

Location: Serene. High on a ledge overlooking the harbor. Two miles south of Camden.
Reservations: Year round through Bed & Breakfast of Maine, page 41.

Rates: $85 double with shared bath. $175 king. $115 for two on the sloop with stocked galley. Less in off-season.
♥ ⛵ ✿ ✈ ⚲

Rare and wonderful. Built in 1988. From the street the exterior resembles a dormered Cape Cod–style clapboard house. From the harbor it's a spectacular structure with towering gables, lots of glass, balconies, and gardens. Stone terraces lead all the way down to the water, where the hostess's 30-foot sloop is moored. (The sloop is available for overnights that include a stocked galley, and for day sails and week-long charters.) The house has wood floors, Oriental rugs, and period furnishings. And the piece de resistance: in the center of the house, a cool, windowless screening room with an entire wall, 9 feet by 12 feet, waiting for your video selections.

The hostess is a film scriptwriter who has traveled extensively for location filming and for seminars she teaches.

Foreign languages spoken: French and Spanish.
Bed and bath: Double with shared bath, French doors leading to terrace and hammocks. King with private bath, Jacuzzi, fireplace, balcony.
Breakfast: Full. With that view, of course, from circular deck.

---

*T**he place to stay has become the reason to go.*

Twin Gables Bed and Breakfast   207/236-4717
4 Spear Street, P.O. Box 189, Rockport, ME 04856

Hosts: Don and Nina Woolston
Location: In a quiet residential neighborhood. On grounds with arched hedges, rose bed, gardens. Faces a "not very busy" private golf course. One block to harbor. Ten minutes' walk to village, Opera House, Photo Workshop.
Open: June to mid-October. Two nights preferred.
Rates: $85 double or twin beds, $120 suite. $20 additional person.
♥ ⬛ ✗ ✄

From Texas: *"A wonderful honeymoon . . . returned to our newfound friends a year later."* From New York: *"I travel alone . . . a special B&B . . . elegant yet homey . . . people-oriented proprietors who know when to further conversation or be listeners."* From Missouri: *"Beautiful, quiet, clean, and nostalgic . . . a gem."* From Florida: *"Fell asleep to sound of foghorn . . . great location, spacious house, delicious food . . . hosts who seem genuinely to delight in figuring out what their guests want and then supplying it . . . a history book, directions or a ride to a valley, restaurants."* From Maryland: *"Felt pampered."*

And that's the way it has been since 1989, when another B&B asked the Woolstons to take overflow guests. In Maryland Nina worked for the Department of State and as a legal secretary. When Don retired from NASA in 1978, they moved here, established a custom picture-framing business, restored this nine-bedroom added-on-to farmhouse, and decorated with many antiques, hooked rugs, and traditional pieces.

Foreign language spoken: Limited French.
Bed and bath: One suite and one room (choice of three). Private baths with footed tub and hand-held shower. Suite has double poster bed, adjacent sitting room with TV, VCR, phone, and sink; attached bath. Other room booked has double bed and sink or twin beds (high windows); hall bath. Rollaway available.
Breakfast: At 8. Juices. Fruit (often baked). Egg casserole, French toast a l'orange, cooked cereals, or blueberry pancakes with Maine syrup. Homemade muffins, coffee cake, or toasts with Don's homemade jams. Served on different china and glassware each day. On sun porch (ceiling fan), in dining room, or in eating room off kitchen.
Plus: Fireplaced living room with upright piano. Afternoon tea a l'orange or lemonade with cheese and crackers. Candies. Fresh flowers. Robes. Lots of books.

Many B&Bs that allow smoking restrict it to certain rooms and/or public areas. Although some of those B&Bs that have the ✄ symbol allow smoking on the porch and/or patio, others do not allow smoking anywhere on the property.

The Black Duck on Corea Harbor

Crowley Island Road, P.O. Box 39   207/963-2689
Corea, ME 04624-0039

Hosts: Barry Canner and Robert Travers
Location: In a small fishing village. Overlooks harbor, lobster cooperative, outer islands. On 12 acres with rock outcrops and berry bushes. Minutes' walk to sand beach; 800 feet to salt pond and marsh. Five miles to Schoodic section of Acadia National Park. Ten-minute drive to restaurants.
Open: Year round.
Rates: Ocean view $70 with private or shared bath. Forest view $55, shared bath. Suite $115. $10 third person.

From New York: "Innovative, healthful breakfasts . . . well maintained . . . gracious, helpful, and knowledgeable hosts." From Pennsylvania: "Few shops . . . inviting rooms . . . the most relaxing atmosphere with gorgeous natural beauty . . . gave our nine-year-old daughter and her friend ideas for blueberry picking, marsh finding, animal care. . . . Our seven-day stay will be ten this year—with the friend's parents as well."

Definitely off the beaten path. A rambling 1800s fisherman's house that is freshly decorated and furnished with the hosts' antiques, Oriental rugs, contemporary art, oil lamps, and tin toy collection. "Guests find the area so calming that many who arrive for one or two nights stay longer when space is available." In Massachusetts Barry was a city planner in Newton and Brockton; Bob sold security systems. (Bob now sells real estate.) They vacationed in the area for five years before opening here in 1991.

In residence: Two dogs. Three cats. Dolly Bacon, a potbelly pig.
Foreign languages spoken: Danish and limited French.
Bed and bath: Four rooms; two with ocean view. First floor—room with one double and one twin bed, private shower bath, private entrance and deck. Second floor—double brass-and-iron bed, private full bath. One queen and one double room (can be a suite) share a full bath. Rollaway available.
Breakfast: At 8. Blueberry pancakes; "Eggs Black Duck" (low fat and cholesterol); orange-glazed French toast; or baked Victorian French toast. Homemade breads and muffins. Fresh fruit. Cereal. Juice, coffee, teas. Can last for two hours on foggy or rainy days.
Plus: Fireplaced living room. Wood stove in TV/sitting area. Library. Outdoor lounge chairs. Guest refrigerator.

The tradition of paying to stay in a private home—with breakfast included in the overnight lodging rate—was revived in time to save wonderful old houses, schools, churches, and barns all over the country from the wrecking ball or commercial development.

Brannon-Bunker Inn 207/563-5941
HCR 64, Box 045C, Route 129, Damariscotta, ME 04543-9503

Hosts: Jeanne and Joe Hovance
Location: Rural, with spectacular sunsets. Five-mile drive from Route 1 on the road to Christmas Cove. Five miles to Damariscotta, 15 minutes to Pemaquid Point, 45 to Camden or Boothbay.
Open: Year round. Advance reservations preferred.

Rates: Double $55 shared bath, $65 private. Suite $75 for two, $95 for three, $115 for four. Singles $5 less. Third person, $10 adult, $5 child. Amex, MC, Visa.
♥ ♨ ❖ ♦ ✕ ✌

The layout of the barn-turned-inn is fascinating. It is attached to a Cape-style house and has a wide interior staircase and a low ceiling on the first floor, creating a wonderful gathering area in the Publyck Room with its huge fieldstone fireplace. Actually, the first conversion of the barn was as a 1920s dance hall called "La Hacienda."

Joe is host, antiques dealer (with shop at the inn), and refinisher who also does caning and other seat repair. Before the family moved here in 1984 he was director of an environmental center and historic sites in New Jersey. Jeanne, an experienced house restorer, has decorated each "deliberately old-fashioned" room with antiques of a different era, with stenciling, print wallpapers, homemade quilts, and country crafts. One sitting area reflects Joe's interest in World War I military collectibles. The hosts welcome children ("we know what it is like to travel with them") and offer suggestions—everything from restaurants to "a gem of a canoeing place."

In residence: Daughter Beth assists. Summers, Mike and Beth are home from college. Jamie is 11.
Bed and bath: Seven rooms; five with private bath. Queen, double bed, or twin beds. Two handicapped-accessible rooms—one has twin beds; the other has queen bed, shower bath, kitchenette. In second-floor suite, one double-bedded room, one with twin beds, living room area, kitchen. Cot and crib available.
Breakfast: 8–9:30. Early-bird special available. Juices, fresh fruit, homemade muffins, toast, cereal; coffee, tea, or milk.
Plus: TV, games, and books. Picnic table and outdoor seating. Kitchen facilities. Babysitting.

Bed & Breakfast of Maine Host #58
Deer Isle, ME

Location: Rural. On an island. Quiet. Minutes' drive to Blue Hill, concerts, Haystack School of Crafts, sailing, sea kayaking, galleries, trips to other islands.
Reservations: May–December through Bed & Breakfast of Maine,

page 41. Two-night minimum reservation.
Rates: Per room. $60 shared bath. $80 double bed, private bath. $90 queen suite, private bath. Less in off-season.
♥ ♨ ♣ ✕ ✌

Come over the bridge and drive down to the end of a lane to this very large restored 1850s farmhouse with landscaped grounds, orchards, and its own private beach. From the Great Room there's a 180-degree view of the ocean, of sailboats, of serenity—with no other houses in sight. The host had such a good time redoing this house that he has changed careers and become a contractor. He and his wife and two young children live in their own private quarters.

Bed and bath: In guest wing, seven antiques-filled rooms with queen, double, and twin beds. All with private baths. Throw rugs on highly polished floors.

Breakfast: Continental. Varies. Perhaps freshly squeezed juice, fruit cup, blueberry bread pudding, beverages.

Todd House   207/853-2328
1 Capen Avenue, Eastport, ME 04631-1001

Host: Ruth McInnis
Location: At Todd's Head on Passamaquoddy Bay in this coastal fishing village.
Open: Year round.
Rates: $35 single, $45 smaller double, $55 double with fireplace, $70 or $80 queen with private bath, furnished kitchenette. $10 additional person. $5 less, six or more days.
♥ ♩ ♫ ♪ ⋈

Guests wrote: *"Like an imagined visit with one's favorite relative. . . . I enjoyed meeting [Ruth's] grandchildren and the assorted cast of nice characters who wandered in and out of the place . . . blueberry muffins a high point. . . . Rooms are exquisite—all the modern conveniences in a 200-year-old setting."*

With advice from the Maine Historic Preservation Commission, Ruth has become a restoration expert. When the chimney was rebuilt, she learned that this house was, in 1775, a cabin before becoming a Cape. You can almost follow the history of the house through the Indian Room and the Cornerstone Room and into a 1990 addition. As the house is on the National Register, the street side of the addition looks almost as it did years ago; but the water side is all glass. Also taking advantage of the view: an eight-foot-tall fieldstone barbecue and a deck.

Until 1980, when she returned to Eastport to teach in her hometown, Ruth taught in Portland. B&B is her way of sharing her love of old houses, history, and Eastport.

In residence: Kitty, the cat, "a hit with many guests." (Well-behaved guests' pets are welcome; the "most unusual" award goes to a large parrot.)

Bed and bath: Six rooms on two floors. First-floor queen-bedded room with private bath. One second-floor room with a queen and a twin bed, private bath. The four that share two baths have a double or two twins beds. Some have working fireplaces, cable TV, sitting areas, view of water. Some on first floor are handicapped accessible. Two trundle beds.

Breakfast: 7:30–9. Juices, coffee, tea, milk, cereals, granolas, homemade muffins, fruit. Served at antique table by huge fireplace with bake-oven and views of the ocean.

(Please turn page.)

Plus: Tours of the house and area. Books on local history. Will meet guests at the airport or bus. Kitchen privileges. Cookout equipment.

Weston House Bed & Breakfast　　207/853-2907
26 Boynton Street, Eastport, ME 04631-1305

Hosts: Jett and John Peterson
Location: On a hill overlooking Passamaquoddy Bay and Campobello Island. In easternmost U.S. city, seven miles southeast of Route 1.

Open: Year round.
Rates: Per room. $50 single, $55 double. $60–$65 queen, $70 king. $15 extra bed.
♥ ⬛ ✿ ✈ ⅙

Acclaimed Vermont innkeepers wrote: "Worth traveling to the end of the earth for." That's just what the Petersons thought when they came from northern California to this well-maintained 1810 Federal house listed on the National Register of Historic Places. They learned its history and furnished with a mixture of antiques and family treasures, with antique clocks and Oriental rugs. They experimented with orchids. And watched a lemon tree flourish (last year's harvest: 30) in the living room.

John was with the U.S. Forest Service. Jett, a former junior high school teacher, supervised legal caseworkers in the district attorney's office. Moving to the East Coast has meant more time to work with foods (a hit at a Fisherman's Forum) and needlepoint; to do woodworking and gardening; to offer (by reservation) high tea in December or candlelight dinners for special occasions; and "to meet great people who come here for business or pleasure."

In residence: Fala Delano II is a Scottish terrier. Landseer is a West Highland white terrier.
Bed and bath: Five large second-floor rooms share (robes provided) one tub/shower and one shower bath. King-bedded room has working fireplace, color cable TV, bay view. Two rooms each with a queen bed. One double-bedded room. One room with single brass bed. Rollaway available.
Breakfast: "A holiday every day." Accompanied by classical music. Could be fish-shaped puff pastry filled with smoked salmon and topped with dill, poached egg, hollandaise sauce. Hallmark dish—pancakes with brandied apricot sauce and bacon curls. Cinnamon bread pudding with fresh berries and "a fabulous raspberry sauce." Wild blueberry or cranberry walnut muffins. In dining room or on porch.
Plus: Afternoon tea or sherry. Mints. Flowers. Kitchen wood stove. Fireplaced living room. Croquet. Lawn chairs. A list of 16 reasons to come to Eastport.

　From Missouri: *"Delightful sunrise, house, hosts, food, and garden."*

Innkeeping may be America's most envied profession. As one host mused, "Where else can you get a job where, every day, someone tells you how wonderful you are?"

High Meadows

207/439-0590

Route 101, Eliot, ME 03903-1210

Host: Elaine Raymond
Location: A wooded country hillside. Four miles from Kittery/Route 1 factory outlets. Six miles to Portsmouth, New Hampshire.

Open: April through October.
Rates: Tax included. $60 shared bath, $70 private bath.
♥ ⱴ ✿ ✦ ⚬

Can't think of a better reason to go off the beaten path. Even the approach, up a shaded lane, gives a sense of anticipation. There are meadows, a tree growing through an old wagon wheel, granite from a barn foundation made into a wonderful stone wall. And perennial gardens and manicured lawns and, everywhere, views. Guests stay in an antiques-filled home built in 1736 by a merchant shipbuilder and captain. "I tell them about camping with the children here in 1960 when there was no water, no electricity, no roadway," says Elaine, who designed and planned the restoration of all 11 rooms. She made all the curtains, hooked the rugs, and furnished with handsome period and country pieces. Kitchen cabinets are made from 200-year-old attic floorboards. What started out to be "a place to keep my horses" has become a haven, a B&B since 1981, where occasionally Elaine, a justice of the peace, officiates at small weddings. Her husband, Ray, is genial cohost and grounds-keeper.

Bed and bath: Five rooms, three with canopied beds. On first floor, queen bed, private full bath. Upstairs, a private shower bath for room with a queen and another with two twins. Two double-bedded rooms share a shower bath.
Breakfast: 8–8:30. Entree varies. Fruit, pancakes or quiche, homemade muffins and breads, beverage. In summer, on large screened porch or patio facing woods.
Plus: Large terrace. Barn porch with rockers. Living room fireplace that is high and shallow and draws beautifully. Half-hour walking trail with wild raspberries in July.

From Massachusetts: *"A welcome retreat from the everyday hustle and bustle . . . thoughtfully prepared food."* From Illinois: *"My bride of 48 years and I found love at first sight for Elaine, her family, the place. In Germany, they would say* 'Ausgezeichnet!'"

Home-Nest Farm

207/897-4125

Baldwin Hill Road, Fayette, ME
Mailing address: Box 2350, Kents Hill, ME 04349

Hosts: Arn and Leda Sturtevant
Location: In hill and lake country with a 65-mile panoramic view to White Mountains. Eighteen miles west of Augusta, 1½ miles from Route 17, "beyond a small stretch of gravel, a small annoyance that blesses us with relative isolation."

Open: Year round except March and April. Reservations and two-night minimum stay required.
Rates: Main house $50 per room. The Red Schoolhouse $80. Lilac Cottage $95. East wing $80 one floor, $95 two floors.
♥ ⱴ ⱴ ✦ ⚬

(Please turn page.)

More than an experience, Home-Nest gives the feeling of discovery—all because of Mainers who share their "love of history and one of the prettiest spots on planet Earth with new friends." Arn is a sixth-generation resident; the family homestead restorer; a retired bank president; a farmer; and a cofounder of Norlands, a nearby living history museum where you can churn butter, cut ice, milk cows. He and Leda can direct you to waterfalls, to abandoned orchards in woods, or to private local swimming holes. If you'd like, they'll show you slides of all the possibilities and help plan day trips. You are invited to picnic in the meadow, pick berries, fish, ski from the door, enjoy their sheep, peruse the published 500-page Sturtevant family history. It's no wonder that guests speak of "an oasis" and "down-home hosts."

In residence: Two riding horses; 25 sheep (each has a name).
Bed and bath: Seven rooms in three antiques-furnished historic buildings, each with kitchen and oil and electric heat. In hosts' residence (1817 Greek Revival)—on second floor, canopied queen bed, private tub bath, private living room, working fireplace, separate entrance. East wing (1784 saltbox)— first floor, canopied queen, private bath, fireplaced parlor with TV, living/dining room with old cooking fireplace, kitchen; two bedrooms and bath on second floor. Lilac Cottage (1800 Cape)—three bedrooms (on two floors), two baths, wood stove. Red Schoolhouse (1830 Greek Revival)—a large bedroom (double), a twin sleeper couch in living room, shower bath, wood stove. Rollaway available.
Breakfast: In hosts' residence only, full buffet 7:30–10; otherwise prepared by guests from well-stocked larder that includes fresh berries, muffins made with homegrown blueberries, fresh eggs, homemade bread and oatmeal, jellies and jams.
Plus: Window fans. Laundry facilities. Canoes (no charge) at nearby lakes. Yacht club beach privileges. Sailboat rentals.

From Washington, D.C.: *"Thoroughly restful, bucolic and regenerating."*

181 Main Street B&B   207/865-1226
181 Main Street (U.S. Route 1), Freeport, ME 04032-1418

Host: Ed Hassett
Location: On a quiet end of Main Street. A five-minute walk to L.L. Bean and outlets.

Open: Year round.
Rates: Double occupancy $95. Third person $15. MC, Visa.
✳ ✮ ⅏

Guests wrote: *"We like as many comforts as possible. 181 Main Street has them all. . . . The innkeepers know where to get bargains, what to see and do, where to find a garage (and dentist) in an emergency . . . and they can cook, too."*

Country Home featured this 150-year-old Greek Revival Cape house and its many country and Empire antiques, Maine oil paintings, local crafts, and hand-hooked rugs. Wide pine floors are refinished. The many quilts—some with dates sewn into them—were all made by the mother of Ed's cohost, David Cates.

Ed, the full-time innkeeper, is a former mental health administrator who hadn't been in Freeport in 20 years when "the search" (300 houses in five states) brought him to town. His "worst shape of all" discovery opened in July

1987 as a totally renovated—from roof to furnace, from baths to in-ground pool—and immaculate B&B. David, a former flight attendant who has degrees in English and French, is working on his graduate degree in nursing.

In residence: Mae, a golden Labrador, "loves to walk with guests."
Foreign languages spoken: French. Very little Spanish.
Bed and bath: Seven air-conditioned second-floor rooms; all private shower baths. Queen or double beds; some canopied or four-posters.
Breakfast: 7:30–9. (Tea and coffee at 7.) Could be heart-shaped French toast or house frittata, garnished with fruit or fresh flowers. Fresh fruit, juices, lime and other homemade breads. In adjoining dining rooms with a table for each guest room. A very sociable time.
Plus: Parking. In-ground 18-by-36-foot pool, brick deck. Large backyard, Adirondack chairs. Perennial gardens. Bedside homemade goodies.

Porter's Landing Bed & Breakfast

70 South Street, Freeport, ME 04032-6426   207/865-4488

Hosts: Peter and Barbara Guffin
Location: A quiet country setting with woods and a small stream. Less than a mile from downtown and L.L. Bean. Within 10 minutes' drive of hiking trails and beaches.

Open: May–December.
Rates: $95 Memorial Day weekend–October. $80 off-season. Singles $10 less. Third person $15. MC, Visa.
♥ ❖ ♦ ✖ ⌣

The Guffins from New Jersey fell in love with Maine on their camping honeymoon in 1974. They returned to the state when they bought their 1830 Greek Revival house in 1985. With fond memories of British Isles B&B experiences (on a bicycling trip), they renovated the 1870 attached carriage house as a B&B; it's a perfect arrangement for guests hosted by a family. In the large living/dining room is a photographic documentation of the Guffins' efforts, which have been acclaimed for attention to historical and architectural detail. A loft library is over the second-floor bedrooms. Throughout, there's an uncluttered blend of new with traditional furnishings, Oriental rugs, some balloon shades, some swags and jabots.

Peter is a lawyer who has recently taken up kayaking—"launching just down at the end of Cove Road." Barbara, a quilter and school volunteer, has become an avid gardener.

In residence: In hosts' quarters—Megan, 10; Katherine, 8; Emily, 3.
Bed and bath: Three rooms. One with queen four-poster bed and another with a double bed each have a private shower bath. One double-bedded room with full bath. Rollaway available.
Breakfast: 8:30. Could be pancakes—blueberry or baked sausage and apricot; Belgian waffles; or raisin bread French toast. Fresh fruit salad. Homemade breads and muffins. Granola. Fresh-ground/brewed coffee.
Plus: Living room Rumford fireplace. Afternoon tea or lemonade with homemade breads, cheese and crackers, or fresh fruit. Floor fans. Phone jack. Guest refrigerator.

White Cedar Inn   207/865-9099

178 Main Street (U.S. Route 1), Freeport, ME 04032-1320

Hosts: Carla and Phil Kerber
Location: Two blocks north of L.L. Bean.
Open: Year round. Two-night minimum on holiday weekends.

Rates: Memorial Day weekend–November 1, $95. Off-season, $75. $15 third person in room year round.
♥ ⊁ ⅍

As Phil tells it, "We've always wanted to run an inn, so I sold my restaurant in Berkeley Springs, West Virginia, and bought this century-old house, which had belonged to Arctic explorer Donald MacMillan when he accompanied Robert Peary to the North Pole. Carla is a nurse (part time) at the Maine Medical Center. Innkeeping is enhanced by the friendly guests, people who make us feel as if we have one of the world's largest extended families." As Carla tells it, "Phil is the reason guests return!"

To Maine the enthusiastic couple brought interests in skiing, hiking, fishing, and snowshoeing—and added carpentry, wallpapering—and parenting. Many guests wrote to me about "impeccably neat, clean, cozy, and comfortable rooms; excellent hosts; and fantastic food."

In residence: In hosts' quarters—Alice, six, and Robin, five.
Bed and bath: Six rooms with antique brass or painted white iron beds—queen, double, double and a twin. Two first-floor rooms each have private shower bath. Upstairs, four rooms with private full bath.
Breakfast: 7:30–9. Juices, homemade muffins and jams, fresh fruit, wild Maine blueberry pancakes, French toast, scrambled eggs, bacon or sausage or ham, waffles, coffee cake, coffee. Served in sun porch with floor-to-ceiling windows facing town and spired church.
Plus: Common room with wood stove and TV. Picnic table. Outdoor grill.

Atlantic Seal B&B   207/865-6112

25 Main Street, P.O. Box 146, South Freeport, ME 04078-0146

Hosts: Captain Thomas and Gaila Ring
Location: Quiet neighborhood overlooking Freeport Harbor (excursion boats depart here). Minutes' walk to open-air/indoor lobster restaurant. Three miles to L.L. Bean and outlets.

Open: Year round. Two-day minimum for some holidays.
Rates: Shared bath $65 double, $85 queen. (January–May 1, $55, $65.) Private bath with Jacuzzi and shower $125 per room; off-season $95. $15 third person.
♥ ⅰ ⅰ ⁘ ♦ ⊁ ⅍

Guests wrote: "A homey atmosphere ... rest, peace, and pampering ... our base camp for day trips. ... And the food! Took a walk in the morning (with their dog) just to work up an appetite ... served on antique china ... warm and friendly hosts ... a slice of heaven."

Many people, including some interested in Tom's spring-through-summer excursion boat (for island visits, seal watching, and lobstering demonstrations), suggested that the Rings' seaside 1850s Cape Cod–style house would make a great B&B. Now one guest room features a Jacuzzi. The guest parlor is furnished with family pieces—nautical memorabilia, Victorian sofa, oil paintings, and spinning wheel. The "haven," as some guests call it, is Gaila's dream come true. "Before," she worked as a dental assistant. Captain Tom, also a native Mainer, is a Maine Maritime Academy graduate.

In residence: Samantha, an English springer spaniel, "loves people and boat rides with Tom." Sadie, a black cat, "loves bird watching and wood stoves."
Bed and bath: Three second-floor rooms, all with water view. Room with one queen and a double, Jacuzzi for two, shower, cable TV. One double-bedded room shares full bath with a room that has double four-poster, window seat. Rollaway available.
Breakfast: Usually 8–9:30. Lobster omelet is seasonal house specialty. Fresh fruit, sausages, homemade muffins, orange juice, fresh-brewed coffee, teas. In dining room on antique china.
Plus: Afternoon tea in parlor. Down comforters. Beach towels. Picnic tables. Window fans.

The Alewife House   207/985-2118
1917 Alewive Road, Kennebunk, ME 04043-9739

Hosts: Maryellen and Tom Foley
Location: On rural Route 35, which connects area beaches, villages, and exit 3 of Maine Turnpike. On six acres with gardens, orchards, woods, and a brook. Ten minutes to Dock Square.
Open: Year round.
Rates: $75–$80. MC, Visa.
♥ ⛵ ♦ ✈ ⌛

From New York: *"Loaded with history, Asian antiques, and collectibles . . . hospitable innkeepers proud of the house's history . . . helpful . . . beautiful convenient location . . . delicious breakfast."* From Connecticut: *"Loved it. After this I have no inclination to want to find better."*

This large 1756 house of post-and-beam construction, owned by the same family for 200 years, was purchased by the well-traveled Foleys in 1986. Tom is a bank personnel director and retired army officer who has worked in the computer industry. Maryellen, a former curator for the Kennebunkport Historical Society, is a teacher and writer, and she has an antiques shop on the premises. Their own most recent trip was to Egypt.

In residence: Marchesa, "a friendly retired (greyhound) racer, experiencing 'couch potato' stage."
Bed and bath: Two second-floor double-bedded rooms. One is a suite with two working fireplaces, private stairway to first-floor sitting room and shower bath. Other has private first-floor tub and hand-held shower bath, access to private fireplaced sitting room.
Breakfast: Usually 8–9. Fresh fruits, homemade muffins, vanilla yogurt, freshly brewed coffee, tea. On sun porch overlooking gardens and forest.
Plus: Large screened porch. Expansive rear lawns. Window fans. Beach passes. Fresh flowers in season. Turndown service upon request. Three guest sitting rooms, including colonial kitchen with cast iron and enamel stove.

Lake Brook Bed & Breakfast Guest House

57 Western Avenue, Lower Village   **207/967-4069**
Kennebunk, ME 04043-2865

Host: Carolyn A. McAdams
Location: On a tree-lined main street. One mile from beach, half mile from Kennbunkport's Dock Square. Facing a tidal brook that ebbs and flows. "Quite an array of wildlife; a moose last Thursday at 6:30 a.m.!"
Open: Year round. Two-night weekend minimum Memorial Day–Columbus Day; three nights on holidays.
Rates: Late June–October and Christmas season, $75–$90. November–June, $65–$75. $15 third person in third-floor suite. Singles $10 less, year round.

♥ ⚓ ⛵ ⁂ ♦ ✈ ✂

> From Massachusetts: *"A peaceful B&B . . . homey . . . wonderful conversations . . . a warm, caring hostess . . . 'our hideaway' . . . a different, creative menu each day."* From "B. Franklin" (actor Bill Meikle): *" . . . (over)indulging with but a modicum of chagrin in her estimable comestibles. Indeed, despite the press of business, I have yet to stay less than two days."*

Spectacular gardens. Fresh wallpaper. And now, all private baths in this colonial farmhouse where Carolyn changed the floor plan and hung Maine seacoast watercolors. A former Peace Corps member, Carolyn returned to Costa Rica in 1988 and stayed with some of the same families she had lived with 20 years earlier. "In many ways, the Peace Corps (and B&B too) makes us realize we are all the same."

In residence: Cali, a "very friendly double-pawed calico cat."
Foreign language spoken: Spanish.
Bed and bath: Four rooms. Three on second floor, each with private entrance and ceiling fan. One with a queen brass bed and full bath; two double-bedded rooms with shower baths. July and August only—third-floor suite (three ocean-facing windows) with kitchen, double bed and a single daybed, shower bath.
Breakfast: 8–9. Fresh fruit, juice, tea and Carolyn's own special blend of coffee. Repertoire includes homemade English muffin bread; boeuf a la Newburg on toast; Finnish puff with fruit poached in sherry, sausage on side; Mexican torte; baked French toast; asparagus/cheese strata. In dining room or on wraparound porch overlooking tidal brook.
Plus: Porch rockers. In summer, refreshing beverage. Ceiling fans in second-floor rooms. Down comforters. Free loan of beach parking passes.

*T*hink of bed and breakfast as a people-to-people concept.

Arundel Meadows Inn   207/985-3770

Route 1, Arundel
Mailing address: P.O. Box 1129, Kennebunk, ME 04043

Hosts: Murray R. Yaeger and Mark Bachelder
Location: On 3½ acres next to Kennebunk River with meadows and perennial gardens. Ten minutes to Kennebunk Beach and Kennebunkport. Eleven miles to Ogunquit; five to Rachel Carson Reserve or to quiet paths, woods, and ocean at Laudholm Farm.

Open: Year round. Two-night weekend minimum, Memorial Day–October 15.
Rates: Doubles $75–$95; with fireplace $85–$95. Suites $100–$110. Additional guest (up to two) $20. Less Columbus Day–Memorial Day except for holiday weekends. Inquire about special packages.
♥ ✻ ♦ ✈ ⚹

From Illinois: *"This inn is a must! . . . many services beyond the call."* From Massachusetts: *"Enhanced by antique furnishings and Murray's art . . . wonderful afternoon tea."* From Connecticut: *"Rooms are perfectly done . . . ambiance clearly sophisticated without any sense of hauteur."* From everyone (seemingly) about breakfast: *"Phenomenal . . . attractively presented . . . French toast not to be missed . . . homemade croissant . . . out of this world . . . sumptuous."*

Before becoming an innkeeper, Mark studied with Madeleine Kamman and cooked for her as well as at other Boston area restaurants. He was also an administrator at Boston's Parker House and Copley Plaza hotels. Murray is a professor emeritus at Boston University's College of Communications and president of a presentational skills consulting firm. The 1830 farmhouse, just about rebuilt before its 1986 B&B opening, continues to change with redecoration, creation of a suite that can be converted to a conference room, rooms made larger here, addition of sliding glass doors there.

In residence: Hildie, "a schnauzer who 'knows' she's a person."
Bed and bath: Seven air-conditioned rooms, three with working fireplaces. All private baths; five full, two shower (no tub). Two rooms with private entrances. Queen beds in most rooms. One suite with queen-bedded room and a room with two twin beds. One suite with king bed, sitting room. One room with two double beds.
Breakfast: At 8 and 9. Eggs Benedict, quiche, fresh vegetable tart, seafood crepes, or amaretto French toast. Juices, fruit compote (homegrown berries). Homemade muffins, coffee cakes, croissants. In dining room overlooking patio.
Plus: Fireplaced living room. French doors leading to patio. Cable TV in several bedrooms.

From Massachusetts: *"Great! Charming place with attentive owners. . . . Breakfast is a bit overwhelming. . . . We loved the Oriental room . . . big suite is a great deal and very quiet."*

---

*B*reakfast *is where the magic happens.*

The Ocean View   207/967-2750

72 Beach Avenue, Kennebunk Beach, ME 04043

Hosts: Bob and Carole Arena
Location: Directly on Kennebunk Beach, one mile from center of Kennebunkport. In a neighborhood of private homes.
Open: April–December.

Rates: Mid-June through mid-September, $125 double, $165–$175 suite. Off-season, $85–$95 rooms, $110–$130 suites.
♥ ✷ ✿

"We live in a tourist area. Carole had years of inn experience while managing the White Barn Inn in Kennebunkport, so opening our own place seemed natural. For a long time this property, built in the 1800s, was all we dreamed about."

Since they opened in 1985, the Arenas have made *many* changes to the original guest house, decorating with a light, airy, "beachy" feeling. And since the flood of 1991, they have completely renovated their "painted lady," which has Oriental rugs on the original hardwood common room floors. Due credit is given to the Arenas' three sons, all athletes, for making the whole project possible.

Carole is full-time innkeeper. Bob is still employed in human resources. The big reward comes in the form of enthusiastic guests (many returnees), who call this "bed on the beach." Some say the location gives them a feeling of being on a boat. One from Connecticut wrote: "The atmosphere is wonderful inside and out. An ocean lover's paradise."

Foreign language spoken: A little French.
Bed and bath: Nine oceanfront carpeted rooms. All private baths; some tub and shower, some shower only. In main house, smaller rooms with queen, double, or twin beds. Next door, in Ocean View Too (where you might have breakfast in bed), four suites with queen bed, sitting area, color cable TV, wet bar/refrigerator, and small individual terrace.
Breakfast: 8:30–10. In main house oceanfront breakfast room. Fresh fruit. Croissants. Granola. Yogurts. Biscuits with honey, French toast, blueberry pancakes, or waffles. Continental breakfast delivered to Ocean View Too rooms.
Plus: Main house fireplaced living room. TV room, porch, yard. Fresh fruit, coffee, tea, soft drinks always available. Garden flowers. Day-trip itineraries.

Bufflehead Cove   207/967-3879

P.O. Box 499, Kennebunkport, ME 04046

Hosts: Harriet and James Gott
Location: On five acres of woods and an orchard. On the tidal Kennebunk River. In view of Kennebunkport.
Open: April–December. Two-night minimum on weekends.

Rates: $75–$95 double bed. $85–$115 queen bed, small balcony. $110–$140 suite with queen, a single bed, balcony. $115–$125 queen with private entrance. $130–$160 Hideaway.
♥ ✳ ✷ ✿

Ecstatic guests wrote: *"Bufflehead Cove is the serenity and beauty that one seeks to feel in Maine . . . a spot that you can place inside you and reclaim once you return to your own chaos . . . wonder and anticipation down the wooded private road [to a] sea captain's home with wraparound porch smack dab on the river. . . . Decorated with flair and attention to detail . . . makes you feel as if at a favorite aunt's . . . the most amazing breakfast served with such style . . . freshly picked flowers in every corner. . . . Harriet and Jim are special people with superb intuition . . . [know] the best secret picnic spots, hidden coves, perfect beaches. . . . From the dock we paddled upstream as adventurous as Lewis and Clark. . . . Like being in a fairy tale."*

Long lyrical guests' letters reminisce about the Gotts, Maine natives, and their style of sharing this house on the cove "where even the gulls find shelter during an ocean storm." L.L. Bean was here for a catalog location shoot. And this B&B has been featured in *Country Inns* magazine.

In 1991 all three Gotts lived in a small Mexican fishing village for four months. Just before this book went to press, Harriet hiked in Costa Rica; Jim, a commercial fisherman, searched for his roots in Ireland.

In residence: Erin, 18. One cat.
Foreign language spoken: Nonfluent Spanish.
Bed and bath: Six rooms with king (Hideaway), queen (three with private balcony—one, as a suite, also has a room with twin bed), or double bed. All private baths. Very private Hideaway has king bed, fireplace, whirlpool tub, vaulted ceilings, ceiling fan, many windows. All but queen-bedded studio (private entrance and view of apple orchard and woods) have river view.
Breakfast: 8:30–9. A typical example: freshly squeezed orange juice, fruit plate, asparagus cheese strata, bread stuffed with sausage and spices, home-made cranberry muffins. Served in dining room or on the porch. If requested, continental breakfast served in room.
Plus: Some rooms have ceiling fans. Tea or mulled cider by fireside in spacious beamed living room. Private dock right here.

The Captain Fairfield Inn

207/967-4454
800/322-1928

Pleasant and Green Streets, P.O. Box 1308
Kennebunkport, ME 04046

Hosts: Dennis and Bonnie Tallagnon
Location: In historic district. Surrounded by elm trees, gardens, and other sea captains' homes. Across from Village Green. One block from river. Five-minute walk to Dock Square, restaurants, shops, galleries.
Open: Year round. Two-day minimum on weekends.

Rates: Mid-June–October $85–$140. Late October–mid-June $75–$105. Fireplaced rooms—fall, winter, spring $125–$149. Winter and spring packages. Discounts for three-day midweek stays. Ten percent less for seven days or longer. Amex, MC, Visa.
♥ ⁂ ♦ ✗

From many guests in New Jersey, Massachusetts, Connecticut: *"A first B&B experience that has put our plans for the Rockies on hold. . . . We were married there by the light of the fireplace and a few candles. It was perfect—simple, sacred, and beautiful. . . . Exquisite interior decorating, a large old-fashioned very deep*

(Please turn page.)

tub, glycerine soap, hazelnut coffee, waffles, omelets, Kennebunkport history. . . . Bonnie and Dennis are awesome! It is obvious that they are happy doing what they do. . . . Beautiful rooms . . . delicious food with pretty garnish . . . exceptional."

"Alas, we missed innkeeping and couldn't resist the challenge of this 1813 Federal colonial mansion. After almost two years of restoring and redecorating, we opened in 1991."

This lovely inn has handsome wallcoverings, antiques, period furnishings, and window treatments. And it has Bonnie, a former teacher, and chef Dennis, a former restaurateur, known from 1977 until 1986 for their Red Clover Inn, created from a farmhouse in the Killington, Vermont, area.

Foreign languages spoken: Limited French and German.

Bed and bath: On first two floors—nine large queen-bedded rooms (some with twin bed also). All with individual thermostat, private full bath. Some with working fireplace, air conditioning, or fans. Handicapped-accessible room has canopied bed, working fireplace, private porch.

Breakfast: 8:30–9:30. (Coffee at 7.) Dennis offers a choice from varying daily menu. Fresh fruit and juice. Omelets, crepes, apple or blueberry pancakes, eggs Benedict. Homemade granola, muffins, and bread. Yogurt. Gourmet coffee. Fine teas. Hot chocolate in winter. By huge hearth, in breakfast room overlooking gardens, or on patio. By request, continental served in bedroom.

Plus: Fireplaced living room. Library with TV. Piano. Afternoon tea or mulled cider and snacks. Guest refrigerator stocked with ice, spring water, and iced tea. Down comforters. Beach passes and towels. Fresh flowers. Special occasions acknowledged.

The Captain Lord Mansion

207/967-3141

Pleasant and Green Streets, P.O. Box 800   (outside Maine) 800/522-3141
Kennebunkport, ME 04046-0800   fax 207/967-3172

Hosts: Rick Litchfield and wife, Bev Davis
Location: Set back from road with huge lawn in front. Across from Kennebunk River. Three blocks from shops and restaurants.
Open: Year round. Two-night minimum on all weekends.
Rates: Vary according to season, week-

day, weekend, fireplace (or not), size (third-floor rooms are about 16 feet square; others, 25 feet square) and river view. January–April, midweek $75–$149 (fireplaced $159 weekends). May–December, $129–$199; Hideaway $249 high season. Discover, MC, Visa.
♥ ❖ ◆ ✗ ✄

Countless "best" awards. Magazine picture perfect for many major publications. An elegant welcoming 1812 Federal mansion, on the National Register, that has period wallpapers, fine antiques, and many personalized touches— also carried out in the neighboring house (four rooms) and in the Hideaway, a two–guest room secluded cottage. All created by innkeepers, almost a legend in their own time, who personally did everything—sanding, plastering, and carpentering—from the first day of ownership in 1978 until 1983, "when we could afford to hire a painting crew!"

Bev was a McDonald's advertising manager and Rick an account manager at an advertising agency. Today they live just down the street from the inn and they have a staff. Five days a week, Rick, Brick Store Museum trustees' board president, greets guests, serves breakfast, and shares the history of the mansion. Bev dovetails behind-the-scenes work (including all the decorating decisions) with her newly purchased horse farm (she built a new arena for lessons), and with mothering of two junior high school–aged daughters.

Bed and bath: Sixteen rooms, 11 with working fireplaces. All private baths; some tub and shower, some shower only. Four-poster bed (many are king) and sitting area in each room. Hideaway rooms have whirlpool tub baths, candlelit breakfast.

Breakfast: 8:30 and 9:30. Coffee earlier. Blueberry or apple-cinnamon pancakes, French toast, ham quiche, or cheese strata. Fresh fruit, muffins, yogurt, muesli cereal, eggs. Family style in air-conditioned country kitchen.

Plus: Beach parking passes, towels, mats, umbrellas. Afternoon tea and sweets. Window fans. Lawn chairs. Chocolates. Cookies. Directions to the horse farm, four miles away.

The Chetwynd House Inn   207/967-2235

Chestnut Street, Box 130, Kennebunkport, ME 04046-0130

Host: Susan Knowles Chetwynd
Location: Across street from whale watch excursion departures. Fronted by porch and driveway. Within walking distance of everything.
Open: Year round. Two-night minimum on weekends and holidays.
Rates: January–mid-June $75–$95,

$89–$99 with TV and air conditioning, $105–$115 suite. Mid-June–mid-September $100, $125 with TV, $160 suite. Fall $75–$95, $89–$110 with TV, $105–$140 suite. Spring and fall specials.

♥ ♦ ✹ ⅍

You'll be well fortified for the day after an exotic Chetwynd breakfast. After this festive hallmark, some summer guests sit around on the porch and enjoy the river breezes. They scribble recipes on index cards; they exchange addresses and business cards and routes to destinations. Those who make advance winter reservations return from walks along the ocean to a high tea by candlelight—"the more Victorian the better."

In Connecticut Susan was an English teacher. She came to this tall-windowed 1840 sea captain's house in 1972 and opened it as the town's first B&B. Area carpets cover the wide pine floorboards. Throughout there are antique and traditional furnishings with lots of blue, Susan's favorite color.

Foreign languages spoken: Some French and Italian.
Bed and bath: Four carpeted rooms; all private baths. On second floor—queen four-poster, hall bath. Two-bedroom air-conditioned suite with queen four-poster, a double bed, cable TV, full bath. Third floor—king bed, air conditioning, cable TV, shower bath.
Breakfast: At 9. (Coffee earlier.) Fresh fruits, blueberry muffins, egg dishes, filet of sole or haddock, crabmeat souffle, quiches, oyster stew, Belgian waffles. "A different vegetable every day for non–egg eaters." Served with china, crystal, and silver.
Plus: Classical music. Bedroom fans. Living room/library. Fruit basket. Tea or hot chocolate. On-site parking.

Cove House Bed & Breakfast   207/967-3704

RR 3, Box 1615, South Maine Street, Kennebunkport, ME 04046

Hosts: Kathy and Bob Jones
Location: Residential street with houses from early 1700s to contemporaries. On a tidal cove. Ten-minute walk to Dock Square or beach.
Open: Year round. Two-night mini-
mum July and August and on holiday weekends.
Rates: Shared bath $60; $15 third person. Private bath $70; $60 single. Amex, MC, Visa.

🏠 🛥 ♣ ✈

> From Massachusetts: *"Charming spot, away from traffic but within walking distance of beach. . . . Atmosphere is so cozy that I feel like I'm staying with friends. . . . Homey, rather than like a museum. . . . Large screened porch is great."*

This farmhouse—the oldest part was built in 1793—was just what Kathy was thinking about after experiencing home-style B&B stays in the British Isles and after spending four decades of summers in Kennebunkport. Since the family moved here in 1982, they have done much restoration work and furnished with their antiques collection. The large yard has blueberry bushes (guests can pick their own) as well as an English garden. In Masssachusetts Kathy was a high school English teacher and antiques dealer. Bob works in Harvard University's police department.

In residence: Son Barry, age 15. Two cats, Peppy and Mischief. "Nutmeg is a Heinz 57 variety dog."
Bed and bath: Three second-floor rooms with individual thermostats. One with double bed, private shower bath. Room with three twin beds shares a tub/shower bath with queen-bedded room.
Breakfast: 8–9:30. Fresh fruit. Blueberry muffins. Cinnamon French toast or chipped beef on toast.
Plus: Wood stoves in living room and den. Window fans. No TV. Afternoon/evening tea. Fresh flowers. Lawn chairs.

The Inn at Harbor Head   207/967-5564

RR 2, Box 1180, 41 Pier Road   fax 207/967-8776
Kennebunkport, ME 04046-9793

Hosts: Joan and David Sutter
Location: Quiet. In Cape Porpoise. On the harbor with private dock. Set back from a picturesque winding road, 2½ miles from Kennebunkport.
Open: Year round. Two-night minimum on weekends and holidays.
Rates: January–mid-May $95–$160. Mid-May–mid-June $110–$175. Mid-June–December $125–$195. King-bedded suite (available mid-May–mid-October) $160–$195. MC, Visa.

♥ ♣ ✈ ⚄

> Guests wrote: *"A piece of paradise . . . an uncovered treasure . . . hosts who have an extraordinary ability to make guests feel welcome . . . lovely linens, antiques . . . unreal baths . . . exquisite view. . . . Breakfast is an experience."*

This is a peaceful waterfront showplace on an intimate scale. The Sutters have turned their 1898 home, their residence for a quarter century, into a designer's dream, a favorite for media attention too. Audiences everywhere gasp when I show slides of Joan's murals and trompe l'oeil effects, the floral arrangements, the harbor setting. In a Bloomingdale's cooking demonstration, shoppers marveled as Joan and David simultaneously stuffed French toast, garnished with violets, and chatted. Here, the gulls swoop. The bell buoy beckons.

Bed and bath: Five imaginative antiques-furnished rooms, none sharing a wall; all private baths. On first floor, water-view room with queen bed, shower bath, French doors, and private deck; one with queen iron bed, bath with Jacuzzi and shower. Upstairs, queen-bedded room, shower bath. Suite with canopied four-poster queen-bedded room, tiled gas log fireplace, sitting room, skylit shower bath. Most popular suite (air conditioned)—king bed, sitting area, large bath with Jacuzzi and bidet, cathedral ceiling, skylight, "unparalleled view."
Breakfast: At 9. (Coffee and tea at 7:30.) Freshly squeezed juice in stemmed glasses. Fruit (maybe poached pears with custard sauce). Sweet or savory entree, perhaps vegetable medley or Belgian waffles with amaretto-flavored whipped cream; stuffed French toast; fruit stratas with fresh-fruit sauces; or chicken dish with shallots, mushrooms, asparagus, or broccoli. At table set with flowers, linen, and silver in dining room with wood stove.
Plus: Music (often classical). Ceiling fans. Down pillows and comforters. Phone jacks. Special occasions acknowledged. Beverages, cheese and crackers. Hammocks. Library, games, puzzles. Beach passes, towels, chairs.

The Inn on South Street   207/967-5151
P.O. Box 478A, South Street, Kennebunkport, ME 04046

Hosts: Eva and Jacques Downs
Location: On a quiet tree-lined street in the historic village area, within easy walking distance of shops, restaurants, and beaches.
Open: February. April–December. Two-night minimum on weekends and holidays.
Rates: June, July, September $95; $99 ($105 single night in August, also October for some rooms) weekends and holidays. November–June $85. With firewood, October–June $125; $135 weekends and holidays. Suite/apartment June, July, September $155; August and October $165; holidays $175; off-season $155–$165. MC, Visa.
♥ ♣ ♦ ✂

Guests wrote: *"A gem . . . that special something you long to come back to . . . exquisite traditional furnishings . . . gracious hosts."*

"Gracious" also applies to the 19th-century Greek Revival house, which became a beautifully decorated and impeccably maintained B&B when the children were in college. There are wonderful window treatments made by Eva, an Oriental influence in the living room, attractive gardens (now with bordering stone wall), and "presented" cuisine that inspires poets. Plus a room arrangement that provides much privacy.

(Please turn page.)

Jack, an extraordinary bread baker, is a professor of American history at the University of New England; he is also an expert on the early American trade with China. Before becoming full-time innkeeper—"with just four rooms so that we can carry out our personal style," Eva, a great source for all kinds of area information, was an occupational therapist and child care administrator.

Foreign languages spoken: Spanish and German fluently; some Russian.
Bed and bath: Three spacious rooms, one per floor, plus an apartment/suite; all with in-room phones. On first floor, four-poster canopied queen bed, a single daybed, shower bath, working fireplace, small refrigerator. On second, queen brass bed, full bath, small refrigerator. On third, queen bed, a twin sleigh bed, full bath. First-floor apartment/suite (perfect for honeymooners or a family) has private entrance, kitchen, room with queen four-poster bed, fireplace stove, living room with double sofa bed, full bath with Jacuzzi.
Breakfast: Intentionally special. 8:30–9; 9–10 in winter. Jack's incredible breads. Souffle-omelets with fruit sauces, filled German pancake, or blintzes. Juice. Fruit. Homemade jams. Served in country kitchen; sometimes in garden.
Plus: Coffee at 7:30. Afternoon beverage. Living room with fireplace/Franklin stove, balcony. Fresh flowers. Floor fans. Down comforters. No TV. "Valet jogging."

Kylemere House 1818   207/967-2780

South Street, P.O. Box 133, Kennebunkport, ME 04046-1333

Hosts: Ruth and Helen Toohey
Location: In quiet historic district within walking distance of shops, galleries, restaurants, ocean.
Open: May–December. Two-night minimum on July–October weekends and holidays.

Rates: Vary according to season, weekday/weekend. $75–$95. $95–$135 very large room ($20 extra person). $110–$135 fireplaced room. Singles $5 less. Amex, Discover, MC, Visa.
♥ ♣ ♦ ✗ ⚓

In 1992, after more than 20 years of coming to Kennebunkport from Montreal for vacations, Ruth and her daughter, Helen, bought this 1818 National Register Federal home, an established B&B complete with antiques and period furniture, Oriental rugs, attractive wallcoverings, and beautiful perennial gardens. Ruth was looking for a new career/challenge after retiring early from education. Helen, who had a management position in the fashion industry, wanted "to change direction and try a mother/daughter partnership." Now they meet "lovely people from all over the world" and direct guests to their favorite beach, nearby sanctuaries, and "the real Kennebunkport, which offers so much historically and naturally."

Foreign language spoken: French.
Bed and bath: Four rooms with sitting areas, cross-ventilation, en-suite baths. First floor—canopied queen bed, working fireplace, shower bath. Second floor—overlooking garden, two rooms with shower baths; one king/twin option, one king. Plus extra-large room with queen four-poster, double sofa bed, tub/shower bath.

Breakfast: 8:30. Fresh juice/fruit, yogurt, compote, homemade sausage, quiche, specialty egg, seafood dishes, homemade muffins, breads, hot croissants. Special diets accommodated.
Plus: Window fans. Radios. No TV. Afternoon refreshments. Down comforters. Lawn chairs. Open porch off dining room.

> From Massachusetts: *"Authentically preserved . . . comfortable . . . plenty of hot water . . . fabulous gardens."*

Maine Stay Inn and Cottages   207/967-2117
34 Maine Street, P.O. Box 500A   (U.S./Canada) **800/950-2117**
Kennebunkport, ME 04046-1800   fax **207/967-8757**

Hosts: Lindsay and Carol Copeland
Location: On a main street in a residential historic district. On two acres of lawn. Five-minute walk to Dock Square and harbor.
Open: Year round. Two-night minimum on most weekends.
Rates: Inn rooms and one-bedroom cottages $125–$140. Suites, fireplace cottages, and two-bedroom cottages $150–$190. Mid-October–late June $85–$125, $100–$160. "Romance renewed" package, November–June, includes dinner at fine restaurant. Discount for stay of seven or more nights. Amex, Discover, MC, Visa.
♥ ♨ ❖ ♦ ✄

It's romantic. It's historic. And families are comfortable here too. It's all according to the plan that evolved when Lindsay, who was in bank marketing for 17 years, and Carol, who was in strategic planning and product management, decided to make a living "in a hands-on way, in a small year-round town that has a diversity of culture." Since moving from Seattle five years ago, the Copelands have redecorated most of the inn with a Victorian flavor—using Laura Ashley and Waverly wallcoverings, wicker and brass and iron headboards. During breakfast and at tea, Lindsay and Carol are often asked about restaurants—including some that are kid-friendly—and about off-the-beaten-path suggestions such as apple picking, back roads, cycling routes . . . "full concierge service!"

Built in square block Italianate style around 1860, the inn is on the National Register of Historic Places. The main house has had many additions—including bay windows, porches, a cupola, and a suspended flying staircase.

Foreign language spoken: Carol speaks a little German.
In residence: "A neighbor's playful black Lab is practically a member of the family." Occasionally Sara Copeland, age 10, and Lizzie, age 7, visit. (The family lives in another Kennebunkport property.)
Bed and bath: All private baths; tub and shower or shower only. Six main house rooms—four corner rooms with queen bed; one with private deck and entrance. First-floor suite has queen bed, fireplaced parlor with double sofa bed. Second-floor suite has queen canopy bed, parlor with double sofa bed. Ten cottages, three with fireplace, all with kitchenettes; one is two-bedroom, rest have one bedroom. Plus queen-bedded cottage without kitchenette but with sitting room and fireplace. In cottage, option of breakfast brought in a basket.

(Please turn page.)

Breakfast: 8–9:30. Sumptuous. Varies daily. Entree repertoire includes baked omelet, apple bread pudding, apple or blueberry blintzes, French toast. Fruit. Muffins, breads, or scones. Homemade granola. Yogurt. In dining room set with lace cloths, china, and mugs—or on wraparound porch.
Plus: Beach passes. Table fans. Color cable TV in each room (hidden in armoires in main inn). Setups. Afternoon tea, coffee, lemonade, or cider with homemade cookies or brownies. Swing set. Access to nearby private pool ($2 per person).

Old Fort Inn

P.O. Box M, Old Fort Avenue
Kennebunkport, ME 04046-1688

207/967-5353
800/828-3678
fax 207/967-4547

Hosts: Sheila and David Aldrich
Location: Secluded and quiet. On three acres in an area of large summer estates. One block from the ocean.
Open: Mid-April through mid-December. Three-day minimum July–Labor Day, and on Memorial Day and Columbus Day weekends. Two-day minimum mid-September through mid-October.
Rates: Double occupancy. June–December: $120–$135 standard, $148 superior, $165–$230 deluxe. $20 third person. Spring and November midweek package rates. Amex, MC, Visa.
♥ ♣ ♦ ✈

When the Aldriches created an intimate inn and miniresort—with freshwater heated pool, tennis court, and shuffleboard—they converted an 1880s barn to a lodge with a massive brick fireplace, exposed beams, and weathered pine wall boards. A turn-of-the-century brick and stone carriage house now has antiques-furnished guest rooms, each with electric heat, wall-to-wall carpeting, color TV, a refrigerator, and a direct dial phone.

This has been home to the Aldriches since 1980, when David left the oil industry and Sheila, a former flight attendant, brought antiques-shop experience. She decorated with country pieces, Laura Ashley papers and prints, and stenciling. David oversees construction and maintenance—and spends time in the antiques shop, where he's always ready to discuss tennis or skiing, or maybe the restoration of antique cars.

In residence: Shana, 17. A large gray fluffy female cat called Samantha.
Bed and bath: Sixteen large rooms, each with a private bath. Most with canopied or four-poster bed—king, queen, two doubles, or two twins.
Breakfast: 8:30–10. "Deluxe buffet." Juice, fresh fruit, cereals, yogurt, homemade granola, muffins, croissants, hot beverages.
Plus: One hour of free tennis daily. Cookies. Chocolates. Window fans. Babysitting. Laundry. Bicycles for rent. No pipe or cigar smoking in the guest rooms.

If you have met one B&B host, you haven't met them all.

The Welby Inn   207/967-4655

P.O. Box 774, Ocean Avenue, Kennebunkport, ME 04046-0774

Hosts: David Knox and Betsy Rogers-Knox
Location: In a quiet residential neighborhood, a five-minute walk to town (Dock Square) or hosts' favorite little beach.
Open: May–October plus weekends in April, November, and December.

Reservations preferred. Two-day minimum in July and August.
Rates: Mid-June through October, $80–$95, depending on size of room. Rest of year, $60–$70. Singles $5 less, third person $15. Amex, MC, Visa.
♯ ⅄

Betsy's touch is everywhere, starting with the sign on the lawn and on into the kitchen with its hundreds of hand-painted counter tiles. A published botanical illustrator, she now has her work reproduced by a national greeting card company. Here, every room is enhanced with an original illustration.

David's touch is everywhere too. An Air Force captain before he was a Vail, Colorado, high school teacher, he learned everything about the building trade by doing. The gambrel-roofed captain's house, built in 1900, had been a guest house for 38 years when the Knoxes bought it in 1985. And all because they followed up on a *Down East* magazine ad that they saw during their fifth Maine vacation!

(Marathoners) Betsy and David grew up in New England, but Betsy's grandparents come from Welby, England. (Hence the name of the inn.) The extension of this blend can be seen in the Laura Ashley wall prints, old New England beds, English wardrobes, and old quilts. Outside, there's a recently built awning-covered patio of reproduction cobblestone and, in front, a New England stone wall assembled in traditional style without mortar.

In residence: Daughter Jessica Ann, 15, is "wild about horses."
Bed and bath: Seven rooms. All private baths, some with shower, no tub; all but one are en suite. On second floor, double or queen beds (full bath). Two third-floor skylit rooms; one with king bed, one with double and one daybed. Cot available.
Breakfast: 8:30. (Coffee at 7:30.) Homemade breads and muffins, an egg dish, and a variety of fruit. Juice, coffee, tea, milk, toast and cold cereal. In country-style dining room or enclosed sun room. Continental breakfast in bed upon request (9–10).
Plus: Evening beverage. Mints, flowers, and fans (table or floor) in rooms. Fireplaced living room. Guest pantry. Yard. Small gallery with paintings and tiles for sale.

From New York: *"House is beautiful . . . food, great . . . comfortable . . . made us feel right at home."*

B &Bs *offer the opportunity to get away without going away.*

Gundalow Inn
207/439-4040
6 Water Street, Kittery, ME 03904-1641

Hosts: Cevia and George Rosol
Location: On the town green and the banks of the Piscataqua River. Fantastic cycling country. Ten-minute walk across bridge to Portsmouth, New Hampshire (80 restaurants, Strawbery Banke, arts festival, concerts); 15 minute scenic drive to ocean beaches, 20 minutes to University of New Hampshire.
Open: Year round.
Rates: Mid-May through mid-October—$95 double, $85 single. Off-season, $20 less. $15 additional person. MC, Visa.

♥ ❖ ✖ ⅒

Very much the feeling of Grandmother's house, this 1889 brick Italianate Victorian was "rediscovered" when Cevia, a former editor/writer/antiquarian bookseller, and George, an electrical engineer, created the inn in 1990. There's a story for everything, including the hidden good-morning staircase, the builder's self-portrait with handlebar mustache, and the inn's name (gundalows are workboats). If you're visiting locals, they are often invited for breakfast. If you're a guest when the innkeepers host their choral group after a concert, you are invited to the party.

Foreign languages spoken: Some French, Slovak.
Bed and bath: Six rooms, private full baths. Queen-bedded room on first floor. On second, two double-bedded rooms, river views; another one with two extra-long pineapple twin beds. On third, one with queen bed, one with two twins, skylit river views, claw-foot tubs, hand-held showers. Rollaway available.
Breakfast: An event. Usually 8–9:30. Freshly squeezed juice. Maybe peach yogurt soup. Exotic homemade scones. Egg dish, meat, or maybe George's smoked salmon, garnished with fresh fruit or herbs. Served on patio or in breakfast room with fireplace and river view.
Plus: Completely sprinklered. Piano. Ceiling fans. Individual thermostats. Beverages. Phone jacks. Perennial and herb gardens. Rockers on porch overlooking river. "Lots of great books."

> From Pennsylvania: *"A real treat . . . combining a warm, welcoming personal touch with an oasis of seclusion and privacy. . . . Antiques, memorabilia, immaculately clean. . . . Breakfast prepared beautifully by Cevia and served graciously by George is an event in itself."* From Connecticut: *"Thought of every detail."* From Virginia: *"Fresh flowers, extra large pillows and towels, blueberry scones to die for."* From Wisconsin: *"Delightful, fascinating hosts."*

The Gazebo
207/646-3733
800/486-3294
P.O. Box 668, Route 1, Ogunquit, ME 03907-0668

Host: Tony Fontes
Location: On Route 1, one mile north of Ogunquit village center. Ten-minute walk to beach. At trolley stop—to shops, restaurants, Perkins Cove.
Open: Year round except for the month of January. Two-night minimum July–September.
Rates: Per room. $95–$115.
♥ ✖

Every day Tony hears, "What are we having for breakfast tomorrow?" It's a big feature here in the 150-year-old Greek Revival house that Tony gutted and rebuilt in 1987 when he decided to leave his job as supervisor of an airlines complaint department. Perhaps you've heard nationally syndicated Gene Burns talk on the radio about The Gazebo. Or maybe you know some honeymooners who have been here. Or have seen the recipe for ham and egg croquettes with tomato and basil sauce in *Gourmet* magazine. Some weekends there are popular packages that include cooking demonstrations with the Arrows Restaurant.

The latticed gazebo, a landmark on the trolley stop, has hanging geraniums in each of its eight archways. Window treatments—balloon shades, jabots, and swags—are often a source of comments from guests, who say that the inn feels like Grandmother's place. In the summer the pool surrounded by gardens is a peaceful place for predinner (bring your own) drinks. "And winter guests love the quiet pace of off-season."

Bed and bath: Nine air-conditioned rooms on first and second floors. All private baths—some tub and shower; most shower only. One room with two twin beds. A double or queen bed in all other rooms (one is a suite).
Breakfast: 8:30–9:30. Maybe stuffed French toast with apricot-orange sauce, homemade turkey sausage, poached pear with raspberry sauce, eggs Benedict, homemade apple-walnut muffins. Served on china and crystal in fireplaced dining room or on deck overlooking the inground swimming pool and gardens.
Plus: Second-floor sun deck. Guest refrigerator available.

The Pine Hill Inn   207/361-1004

14 Pine Hill South, P.O. Box 2336, Ogunquit, ME 03907

Hosts: Charles and Diana Schmidt
Location: Secluded, "with just the sound of birds." Five-minute walk to Perkins Cove, restaurants, shops, beginning of cliff walk. Two-mile trolley ride to sandy beach, 10 minutes to Kittery outlets.

Open: Mid-May through mid-October.
Rates: $85–$95 double, $75–$85 single. $25 additional person. MC, Visa.
♥ � ♣ ✻ ✗ ✓

Eight years in coming—to Maine and to innkeeping! This Victorian house, converted to a B&B in 1986, was the dream place that in 1991 inspired the Schmidts to take early retirement. Wicker chairs, a love seat, ottomans, and tables are in the common room surrounded by tongue-and-groove pine walls and ceilings. In Ohio Charles and Diana were self-employed in their own network-marketing business.

Bed and bath: Four rooms plus two-bedroom cottage; all private baths, individual heat control, ceiling fans. One double-bedded room has bath across the hall (robes provided). Other rooms—king; queen and two twins; two twin beds. In cottage, a double and two twin trundles.

(Please turn page.)

Breakfast: Usually 8–9. Freshly squeezed orange juice, fruit cup, homemade granola, yogurt. Homemade muffins, breads, pastries, jams, and jellies. Served in common room or on screened porch.
Plus: Beverage. Down pillows. Forgotten items.

From Massachusetts: *"Diana has an eye for detail . . . fresh flowers . . . gorgeous (50-foot) screened porch that runs length of house . . . felt pampered."*

West End Inn   207/772-1377
146 Pine Street, Portland, ME 04102-3541

Hosts: Tom and Hilary Jacobs
Location: Residential. In historic Western Promenade area. Within walking distance of restaurants, art galleries, shops, Old Port.
Open: Year round.

Rates: Memorial Day weekend–Columbus Day weekend, $90 double, $80 single. Off-season, $10 less. Amex, MC, Visa.
♥ ⬛ ⁑ ♦ ✈ ⅟

The gracious restored brick townhouse, built in 1871, is the home of transplanted New Yorkers—a nurse and a banker. Their interests in sailing, art, auctions, and the coast brought them in 1990 to Portland, "where there are lighthouses, parks, and beaches—spectacular and unexpected." Hilary, a New Zealander, brought walking sticks (borrow one, if you wish) and paintings to remind her of her native country. As hosts in Maine they've become known for their warm welcome and their freshly baked chocolate chip cookies.

Bed and bath: Four carpeted rooms, all private modern baths. Three rooms on second floor, all with full baths; two are attached, one across the hall. One third-floor room, shower bath. King, queen, or twin beds. Rollaway available.
Breakfast: Flexible hours. Blueberry pancakes with Maine maple syrup. Home-baked muffins and breads. Dining room table set with china, silver, and fine linen.
Plus: Ceiling fans. Phone jacks in some rooms. Tea and cookies. Fresh fruit and flowers. Mineral water. Transportation to/from airport.

From Massachusetts: *"The best."*

Crown 'n' Anchor Inn   207/282-3829
121 North Street, P.O. Box 228, Saco, ME 04072-0228

Hosts: John Barclay and Martha Forester
Location: On two acres of landscaped lawns in historic district. One mile from I-95, exit 5. Five-minute walk to museum, library, Thornton Academy. Two miles to

Saco Beach, 10 to Kennebunkport.
Open: Year round.
Rates: $60 (smallest), $70, or $85. Third person $15. Discover, MC, Visa.
♥ ⁑ ♦ ⅟

Adult children give their parents a gift weekend here. Honeymooners return for anniversaries. Weddings are held in the formal antiques-appointed double parlor with its magnificent floor-to-ceiling marble-based gold leaf mirror. Furnishings range from Victorian rococo to primitives. Over four thousand volumes are in the barn library. The grounds, too, are of particular interest, because the property, on the National Register, was once owned by Dr. George Lincoln Goodale, the botany professor who was responsible for acquiring the Harvard University glass flower exhibits made by the Blaschka family of Germany.

The elegant Federal/Greek Revival house had been vacant for four years before John, a book jobber and retired banker, worked on the restoration in 1991 with Martha's husband, Jim, a retired Louisiana professor who didn't live to see his dream. Since Martha and John opened in 1992, the inn has been discovered by genealogists, historians, house tour goers, and delighted guests.

Foreign language spoken: Some French.
Bed and bath: Six rooms; all private baths. First floor—double bed, whirlpool bath. Five on second floor (smaller rooms in earlier-built ell with lower ceilings); three with working fireplace, one with Jacuzzi.
Breakfast: 7–10. Elaborate. Freshly squeezed orange juice, fresh fruit—perhaps with ice cream, home-baked bread, meat and egg dishes, tea, Louisiana dark roast coffees. In candlelit dining room on Royal Doulton china.
Plus: "Books that have followed us home." TV. VCR. Beverages. Special occasions acknowledged. Guest refrigerator. Dinner by advance reservation only. Small pets welcomed by prior arrangement only.

Guests wrote: *"Superb suggestion for jogging area [local cemetery] without fumes. Came for one day and stayed for four. . . . A warm and magical atmosphere."*

Brass Lantern Inn
81 West Main Street, P.O. Box 407, Searsport, ME 04974

207/548-0150
800/691-0150

Hosts: Pat Gatto, Dan and Lee Anne Lee
Location: On a rise of U.S. Route 1, overlooking Penobscot Bay, 1½ miles north of Moose Point State Park. Next to woods with path to stream. Within walking distance of Penobscot Marine Museum, restaurants, and shops.

Open: Year round.
Rates: Oceanview rooms $70 Memorial Day weekend through October; rest of year $50. Other rooms $65; off-season $50. Third person $10. MC, Visa.
♥ ♦ ✗ ✔

The elegant 1850 Victorian, a tourist home in the 1930s, was a private home when the two sisters and Lee Anne's husband bought it in 1991. Their extensive changes include new baths, redecorating, and interior shutters. Several rooms have the original wide plank floors. The dining room has an intricate tin ceiling. Collectibles, family treasures, and antiques are throughout.

In addition, right here the innkeepers have opened a collectibles and antique train shop—featuring Lionels—that has become a big hit. Pat's late husband was a serious train hobbyist. In New Jersey Pat was a Sears credit supervisor; Lee Anne, a sales manager; Dan, a general manager in the plastics industry. Fond memories of Maine vacations brought them here in search of a B&B.

(Please turn page.)

In residence: In hosts' quarters—David, 22; Katie, 17; Jonathan, 15.
Bed and bath: Four second-floor rooms; two with ocean view. All with double bed (one is canopied); two rooms also have an additional twin bed. All private new shower baths. Rollaway and cradle available.
Breakfast: 8–9. Blueberry pancakes with Maine maple syrup or ham and eggs. Fruit cup, orange juice, muffins, rolls.
Plus: Fireplace and spinet piano in one parlor, TV in another. Videos. Free pass for Penobscot Marine Museum, one mile north.

From Maine: *"Beautiful. Great hospitality. Knowledgeable host family."* From New Jersey: *"Tastefully decorated and well maintained. Highly recommended!"*

Thurston House Bed & Breakfast Inn
P.O. Box 686, 8 Elm Street, Searsport, ME 04974-0686   207/548-2213

Hosts: Carl and Beverly Eppig
Location: A quiet neighborhood. One block in from Route 1, known for its antiques shops and flea markets along a six-mile stretch. One block to bay and to Penobscot Marine Museum; three blocks to playground, picnic area, and beach.
Open: Year round.

Rates: Tax included. $40 single, $45 extra long double, $50 twins, $60 double with private bath. $10 additional person. $105 five in carriage house. Seventh night free. November–May, $5 less for shared bath, $10 less for private bath. MC, Visa.
♥ ♨ ❖ ◆ ✹ ✁

From New York, Massachusetts, Florida: *Carl dons his chef's toque and prepares a potpourri of delights, a feast fit for kings. . . . Alters recipes for guests with allergies . . . a great 'yarn spinner' . . . impressive knowledge of regional history . . . shared suggestions that lived up to expectations. . . . Carriage house ideal for our family . . . a vacation our two little boys will never forget . . . like it more than many inns two or three times the price. . . . Impeccably clean . . . a warm and generously hospitable respite from the world outside."*

Guests are grateful that the Eppigs settled into their "Penobscot paradise." When Carl was an air force colonel, the family lived "everywhere." Their 1831 house is comfortably furnished with some antiques and reproductions. The front hall with spiral staircase has century-old hand-screened wallpaper. Bev works for the federal government. Carl extends his experience as director of morale, welfare, and recreation by answering all inquiries with a personal note and very useful enclosures including a good map.

In residence: Daughter Christine. Two cats—not in guests' area.
Bed and bath: Four rooms. Carriage house sleeps five in two first-floor rooms (individual thermostats) with exterior entrance plus access from house; room with two twin beds and single daybed shares a full bath with room that has extra-long double bed. On main house second floor, large double-bedded room has anteroom with trundle bed, shower bath. Other double-bedded room (with bay view) has claw-foot tub, hand-held shower.
Breakfast: 7:30–9; sometimes, two seatings. "Forget about lunch" menu

includes prepared fresh fruit, freshly baked hot breads, entree of the day.
Plus: Fireplaced living room with upright piano. Window fans. Afternoon refreshments.

Academy Street Inn   207/384-5633

15 Academy Street, South Berwick, ME 03908-1506

Hosts: Thomas and Edith Boogusch
Location: Overlooking the town square. Ten miles from York Beach, Portsmouth, outlet shopping; 45 minutes from Boston and Portland.

Open: Year round.
Rates: $45–$50, double occupancy. $10 each additional person.
♥ ♨ ⌂ ⚹ ✕ ⅙

The Boogusches love this small town. "We're away from the hustle and bustle." They love their house. "Over an eight-year period, we restored and decorated elegantly." And guests can tell that B&B as a family venture is another good match. Once a restaurant in addition to being a Berwick Academy headmaster's house, the colonial Victorian has Austrian chandeliers, three carved oak fireplaces, paneled oak wainscoting in the dining room—and the piece de resistance, a 65-foot screened wraparound porch overlooking revitalized gardens.

In residence: Jeremy and Shawn during college vacations. Andrew, 10; Kelsey, 6. One friendly golden retriever, Honey.
Bed and bath: Four very large second-floor rooms, two with queen bed, one with double and a twin bed, and one with a double share (robes provided) two full hall baths; private bath possible. Rollaway and crib available.
Breakfast: 8–9. Bacon or sausage with eggs; waffles; blueberry pancakes or French toast. Fresh fruit. Juices. Coffee cakes and muffins. In formal dining room, in plant room, on screened porch, or "at the kitchen bar, watching us cook."
Plus: Fresh garden flowers. Piano. Room phone and TV by request. Window fans. Laundry. Kitchen privileges. Guest refrigerator.

Harbour Cottage Inn   207/244-5738

Clark Point and Dirigo Roads, P.O. Box 258, Southwest Harbor, ME 04679-0258

Hosts: Ann and Mike Pedreschi
Location: Across the road from harbor and lobster wharves. Two-minute walk from oceanarium and town dock.
Open: Year round except November.

Rates: $60–$95 twins or queen, $65–$105 king, $85–$140 suite, depending on season. Single $5 less. Winter dinner packages arranged. Amex, Discover, MC, Visa.
♥ ⌂ ✕ ⅙

From Alabama, New Jersey, New York: *"Decorated with some absolute treasures from Ann's family in England . . . most luxurious B&B bath I've seen . . . fabulous gourmet breakfasts and lively, kind young couple . . . a gem."*

Mike traveled from Poughkeepsie, New York, to Mount Desert Island in 1989 and fell in love with the area, "and within six months we were here, undoing

(Please turn page.)

four apartments in the 1870 structure, installing a sprinkler system, and furnishing with some antiques, including a German piano." Since, they have walked every trail on the island, cross-county skied on many, and pedaled mountain bikes on the carriage paths. Ann, a ceramicist, now paints with watercolors.

Bed and bath: Eight rooms on three floors. All private baths with hair dryers and heat lamps; some with steam shower, seated steam bath, or double whirlpool; one with claw-foot tub and separate shower. King (one is canopied), queen (one is suite with daybed in sitting room), or twin beds. **Breakfast:** 7:30–10. Buffet of home-baked breads and muffins, fresh fruit salad, juice followed by served (at individual tables) chef's special such as eggs Benedict, fruit rollups, or waffles with homemade raspberry or blueberry sauce plus cream. (Please request special diet accommodation before breakfast.) Coffees and herbal teas.
Plus: Ceiling fans/individual thermostats (except ground-floor king room). Tea or coffee with homemade nibbles at 5:30. Fresh flowers in season. Thick bath sheets. Turndown service. TV with VCR. TV or phone in room (extra charge).

The Island House   207/244-5180

Box 1006, Clark Point Road, Southwest Harbor, ME 04679-1006

Host: Ann Gill
Location: Across street from harbor. Ten-minute walk to village center; five minutes to lobster docks, Oceanarium, and Coast Guard station. Five-minute drive to Acadia National Park and ocean.
Open: Year round.

Rates: Shared bath—April–June $55 double, $45 single; July–October $60 double, $55 single; November– March $45 double, $35 single. Private bath $10 more. Cot $20. Suite $120. Loft apartment $95 for two; $115 for three; $135 four.
♥ ⊶ ⁂ ♦ ✄ ⅍

"Everything has changed, yet nothing has changed," said Ann's son when he saw the latest renovation in the family home, which was once part of Mount Desert Island's first summer hotel. Today the freshly decorated house has much of the original pine woodwork. There are old photos and a page from an old register. Furnishings reflect Ann's childhood years in Southeast Asia. Ann enjoys gardening, hiking, and assisting with all kinds of outing plans. Among grateful guests: one who arrived just in time to get directions to the mountaintop—for his marriage proposal at sunset.

Bed and bath: Second-floor rooms could be two two-room suites, each with private full bath, or four rooms sharing two full baths plus first-floor full bath. Rooms have twin beds, a double, or a queen. Cot available. Loft efficiency apartment sleeps up to four (who eat breakfast in main house).
Breakfast: Usually 7:30–9. (Coffee and tea at 7.) Fresh fruit or juices. Home-baked muffins, Danish, or coffee cake. Eggs Florentine, a vegetable omelet, blueberry pancakes, or French toast with homemade blueberry sauce. Granola and dried cereals. Served in dining room or on veranda.
Plus: Piano, books and music, TV with VCR. Porch glider, large garden with picnic table.

From Massachusetts: *"Like staying at your loving auntie's house."* From Tennessee: *"Iced tea on arrival, night lights, Hershey kisses, spotlessly clean baths, a newspaper, exquisite breakfasts."*

Island Watch   207/244-7229
P.O. Box 1359, Freeman Ridge Road, Southwest Harbor, ME 04679

Host: Maxine M. Clark
Location: Quiet. High atop Freeman Ridge, overlooking harbors of Southwest Harbor and Mount Desert. Five-minute walk by graveled road through woods to the village, 15-minute walk by paved town road. Within walking distance of Seal Cove's narrow graveled Acadia National Park Road with scenic winding trails.
Open: April–November. Two-night minimum required.
Rates: $65 per room. $15 third person in room.

♥ ♯ ✓ ☆ ♦ ✗ ✗

The grandmother of four (ranging from age 15 to 26) likes to hike, motorcycle, snowmobile, sail, sew, and cook. Maxine, a professional Realtor, spent her early years on an island; and as a teenager, when her father was a lighthouse keeper, she lived in Bass Harbor Lighthouse.

With its white walls and clear, uncluttered space, the family-built (1967) house uses the great outdoors as its primary decor. The floor-to-ceiling windows give the feeling of living above the treetops. (The songbirds love the area too.) And the sunrise was a treat right from here! There are plenty of comfortable chairs in front of the enormous fieldstone fireplace, which was built with stones from the family farm site. Likely to be around are native-born friends who offer sailboat rides, tell fish stories, and help with maps.

In residence: Heidi, a black standard poodle, seldom with guests.
Bed and bath: Six rooms. All private baths (one with tub, rest with showers); five are en suite. Two handicapped-accessible rooms (suites) each have a double and a single bed. King, queen, or double beds plus cot available.
Breakfast: 7–9. French toast, pancakes, waffles, or bacon and eggs. Homemade breads. Coffee, juice, and cereal. Maxine cooks in a marvelous arrangement that allows her simultaneously to work in the kitchen, socialize with guests in the dining area, and point out the Bluenose ferry rounding the tip of the island. One table is on outside deck.
Plus: Those decks—for sun, shade, harbor views, and stargazing. Barbecue. Will meet guests at Bar Harbor airport. Storage space for bikes, skis, camping equipment, snowmobiles.

---

*U*nless otherwise stated, rates in this book are for two and include breakfast in addition to all the amenities in "Plus."

The Kingsleigh Inn   207/244-5302

100 Main Street, P.O. Box 1426, Southwest Harbor, ME 04679

Hosts: Tom and Nancy Cervelli
Location: At edge of village, 100 yards from harbor. Near restaurants, shops, museums, art galleries. Minutes to Acadia National Park.
Open: Year round.
Rates: January–mid May and mid-October through December $55–

$65, $95 suite. Mid-May through June and post–Labor Day through mid-October $75–$85, $125 suite. July through Labor Day $85–$95, $155 suite. Singles $5 less. Amex, Discover, MC, Visa.
♥ ✖

The kitchen as well as the fireplaced living room—and the wicker-furnished, flower-bedecked porch too—are gathering spots for guests. Many are returnees and enjoy visiting with the innkeepers, who left Long Island and computer jobs in 1990 "for a people-related activity in a beautiful area." For about a dozen years, the Cervellis had vacationed here. "We ate lobster, hiked, biked, played golf, and took boat excursions." (They still do.)

Their house, built in 1904, was converted to a B&B in 1984. Hardwood floors are refinished. The sitting room is carpeted. Furnishings—with an uncluttered look—are country Victorian and traditional.

Bed and bath: Eight rooms, all private baths, all with ceiling fans. Two first-floor rooms and five second-floor rooms have queen beds (one has daybed also), shower baths. Turret suite with harbor view has king bed, working fireplace, turret room with telescope, TV, large tub and shower bath.
Breakfast: 8–9:30. Omelets, quiche, blueberry pancakes, French toast, stratas, or eggs Benedict. Juice, homemade breads and muffins, fresh fruit. In candlelit dining room or on porch.
Plus: Late-afternoon tea, wine, cheese and crackers. Coffee and tea always available.

Penury Hall   207/244-7102

Box 68, Main Street, Southwest Harbor, ME 04679

Hosts: Toby and Gretchen Strong
Location: In the village, "just 2¾ miles from Echo Lake and Acadia Mountain Trail."
Open: Year round. Two-night

minimum June–September.
Rates: June–September $50 single, $60 double. October, April, and May $5 less. November–March $15 less.
☀ ✖ ✖

Turn the old bell on one of the etched-windowed double doors of this 1830 house-with-additions. You will be warmly greeted by horn-rimmed Toby and, very likely, Patches, who may assist in escorting you to your room.

A 1981 trip to Cape Breton and Nova Scotia inspired the Strongs to become one of the first "quiet side" B&Bs. In summer their porch is blossom-filled by Gretchen, who has just retired as the Tremont Town Manager. Toby's diverse professional experiences include newspaper editing, innkeeping, his own software company, and, most recently, the duties of chamber of commerce president.

Since moving here in 1978 with their two teenage sons, the Strongs have been restoring the comfortably furnished house. "And don't forget to mention the forest green living room walls with pure white trim." (Everybody does.)

In residence: Patches, a 16-pound Maine coon cat, "brought up with guests."
Bed and bath: Three second-floor rooms. One with twin beds, two with double beds. Two shared baths, one with shower and one with tub.
Breakfast: 7:30–9. Juice, fresh fruit, maybe eggs Benedict, blueberry pancakes, omelet, date-walnut French toast, assorted eggs with muffins, homemade jams and jellies, pure maple syrup. Prepared and served by Toby, who usually joins guests.
Plus: Tea. Sauna. Laundry. Kitchen privileges in winter. Use of canoe, windsurfer, 21-foot day sailer. Very helpful printed information about the area.

Putt's Place Bed & Breakfast   207/246-4181
P.O. Box 126, 8 Main Street, Stratton, ME 04092   800/862-6720

Hosts: Elaine and Jim Poitras
Location: Along the main road in a quiet rural area. With view of mountains and lake. Snowmobile and cross-county ski trail through the

yard. Seven miles to Sugarloaf U.S.A.
Open: December–May.
Rates: Tax included. $50 double, $75 triple.
🏷 🏷 ⚜ 🏷 🏷

From Canada, New Hampshire, Maine, New Jersey: *"Felt like part of the family. . . . Entertaining hosts. . . . Feather beds a welcome treat. . . . After skiing, loved coming 'home' into room heated by a wood stove. . . . Spacious and comfortable family room. . . . Bathroom is a piece of artwork and graffiti (encouraged). . . . A different breakfast each day. . . . Hand in hand with Sugarloaf, best eastern ski vacation! . . . a bountiful country breakfast with everything homemade."*

Jim, who owns a carpet business (even some walls here have carpets on them), built this modifed A-frame in 1972 as a ski vacation home for the family. Elaine, who does counted cross-stitching "almost every night," has experience as a summer guide and as a bookkeeper on the coast. Since opening as a B&B—"the greatest job of all"—in 1987, the ardent snowmobilers have been having just as much fun as their guests in this "take-off-your shoes-and-talk" kind of place.

Bed and bath: Four second-floor rooms (and the hosts) share two first-floor baths. Two with double beds; one with two twin beds; one with three twins; all with feather beds.
Breakfast: 7:30. Juices. Fruit cup. Dessert breads (recipes shared). Homemade muffins. French toast with cinnamon raisin bread; blueberry pancakes; Belgian waffles; or ham baked with pineapple. Served by wood stove at six-foot oak table made by Jim.
Plus: Fireplaced living room with cable TV. Individual thermostats. After-ski cup of hot chowder or soup. Hot chocolate and tea always available. Down comforters. Flannel sheets. Guest refrigerator. Fresh fruit. Sometimes "moose out back."

Fox Island Inn   207/863-2122

P.O. Box 451, Vinalhaven ME 04863

Host: Gail Reinertsen
Location: In an island fishing village, a 75-minute ferry ride from Rockland. Twelve-minute walk from ferry landing. Within two blocks of restaurants and summer activities. A little

over a mile to swimming quarries.
Open: May–October.
Rates: $40 single, $50 twins, $45–$50 double, $60 large double. $10 extra person.
🛪 🌿

"Everyone tells me that they come to get away, and that's just what they do on an island like this. It's a fishing village with about 1,200 year-round residents. The summer population is close to 5,000, and there are art shows, concerts, and charming restaurants. Guests enjoy the outdoors—nature preserves; quiet woodland walks; the rocky shoreline; the spring-fed warm-water quarries for swimming; church suppers; flea markets; the lack of shops; and 39 miles of paved roads (good for cycling) plus many that are unpaved (used by mountain cyclists). This comfortable place with shared baths fits right into the simple style here."

Gail is a Tallahassee, Florida, resident who is married to a law professor. A former law librarian, she now travels two out of three weeks during the winter as a representative for a Canadian publisher of law books. Her B&B stays inspired her to become a bed and breakfast manager, first on Cape Cod and then in Florida, before she bought this B&B in 1991.

In residence: Dixie, a golden retriever, "in guests' area only by popular demand."
Bed and bath: Six rooms; all shared baths. First floor—one large shower bath and one half bath shared by small single room with three-quarter bed, two small double-bedded rooms, and a large room with two twin beds. Second floor (can be a suite)—one small double-bedded room and a large room with a double and one twin bed share a large shower bath. Rollaway available.
Breakfast: 8–10. Fresh fruit, juice, homemade granola, homemade breads, muffins, scones, gourmet coffee. Buffet style in kitchen.
Plus: Upright piano in living room. No TV. Beach towels. Guest kitchen for preparing picnics/light meals. Fresh flowers and robes in rooms. Several old bikes loaned; rentals available on island.

Broad Bay Inn and Gallery   207/832-6668

P.O. Box 607, 1014 Main Street, Waldoboro, ME 04572

Host: Libby Hopkins
Location: In residential neighborhood, a half mile off U.S. Route 1. Short drive to Monhegan Island, Islesboro, and Vinalhaven ferries. Close to Audubon wildlife sanctuary, Damariscotta Lake, Medomak River, Camden.
Open: Year round. Two-night mini-

mum on July and August weekends.
Rates: Per room. May–October, $70 Victorian double, $75 Canopy Room, $60 and $45 second- and third-floor rooms. Other months, 20 percent less. Thanksgiving and Christmas packages. MC, Visa.
♥ 🍴 ⁂ ♦ 🛪

Waldoboro reminds Libby of North Carolina summer stock days, when she ran art shows at the theater and met one Jim Hopkins, a designer/actor/puppeteer/singer. Three decades later, having been artists with Princeton University, the Educational Testing Service, and the *Wall Street Journal*, the Hopkinses settled here, opened an art gallery, established summer workshops (still ongoing) with renowned instructors, and became professional caterers as well as community leaders—with the reopened Waldo Theatre, the library and schools, the Lions Club, and much more. Guests remember sleigh rides, a wedding in the garden, the decor, the food (one recipe published in *House Beautiful*)—and the hosts.

Foreign language spoken: Some French.
Bed and bath: Five rooms, three shared (robes provided) full baths. First-floor double-bedded room shares hosts' bath. Two second-floor baths are shared by second-floor double-bedded room, one room with canopied four-poster double (floor-to-ceiling windows overlooking garden), one with two twin beds, and third-floor room (reached by steep stairs) that has two twin beds.
Breakfast: 8–9. Host's whim. Maybe blueberry muffins, homemade breads; frittata, Parmesan baked eggs, meats, pancakes, crepes, fresh fruit ambrosia. (Special diets accommodated with advance notice.) Served on English china on starched hand-embroidered white tablecloths, in dining room or by kitchen wood stove.
Plus: Sun deck. Screened porch overlooking garden. Hammock. Evening tea or sherry. Fresh flowers and fruit. VCR; musical film tapes. Art and theater library. Fans. TV, games, piano.

Guests send accolades: *"Breakfasts are hearty, subtle, and delicious. . . . A woman of great kindness and extraordinary thoughtfulness. . . . One feels both comfortable and a sense of occasion. . . . Charm, charm, charm all the way."*

Le Vatout B&B (Gallery & Sculpture Gardens)

207/832-4552

218 Route 32 South, Waldoboro, ME 04572-6003

Host: Don Slagel
Location: Four-tenths mile south of Route 1 on Route 32, the road to Pemaquid Point with superb water views all the way. Near the Old German Meeting House and Waldo Theatre.
Open: Year round. Advance reserva-

tions required November through April; preferred May–October.
Rates: $55 shared bath, $70 private. Singles $5 less. $10 each additional person in room. No charge for babes in arms or use of portacrib.
♥ ♫ ⌂ ♣ ♦ ✗ ⚘

From a continuous flow of letters, from South Africa, Holland, Canada, England and many states: *"Enchanting garden setting . . . attractive and comfortable house . . . imaginative and delicious fare . . . superb recommendations for restaurants and a bicycle route. . . . Gallery alone is worth the visit. . . . Owned and deftly run by a man of wit, gentle manners, and artistic scholarship. . . . A gift for making guests feel at home."*

Before returning here in 1986, this popular host lived in many places from Maine to Mexico as musician, teacher, composer, conductor, author, actor, singer, artist/sculptor. He filled his pre–Civil War expanded Cape house with

(Please turn page.)

family pieces and much art. And he converted the attached barn to a lovely 1,500-square-foot art gallery (with Palladian window) that features five new exhibits each summer. The 1½ acres of gardens attract visitors from miles around and provide a beautiful and dramatic backdrop for sculpture.

In residence: CioCioSan and Kino, two friendly cats who spend summers in the gardens. Small flock of Cochin bantams.
Foreign languages spoken: "Vestigial German, Spanish, French."
Bed and bath: Five rooms. First floor—room with queen bed, private full bath. Second floor—room with twin beds, room with double bed and cot, and room with double and one twin bed share 2½ shower baths. Available for minimum three-day stay—large room with double bed, three twins, private entrance, shared shower bath.
Breakfast: 7:30–9. Perhaps gougere, fruit cobbler, asparagus on toast, quiche—"something not found in a restaurant." Freshly brewed coffee/tea, orange juice and/or fruit, homemade breads, muffins, jams/jellies, cereals.

The Barn Bed and Breakfast   207/832-5781

2987 Friendship Road, South Waldoboro, ME 04572

Host: Helen Power
Location: "The only humanly in-habited barn along this country road." Not far from a barn depicted in one of Andrew Wyeth's paintings. Six miles from Waldoboro (and Morse's sauerkraut), three from

Friendship, where one of the original sloops departs for summer morning and afternoon cruises.
Open: May–November 1. Advance reservations appreciated.
Rates: $50 double, $40 single. $10 cot.
♥ ♯ ♠ ♣ ⊁

Pages and pages! Guests' letters written to me from all over the world extol everything from the wildflowers at the doorstep to the tasteful decor, from the sense of humor to discussions about poetry, health care systems, cycling routes. From Canada: "I learned a lot from Helen about Maine, but even more importantly, about enjoying life fully, wherever I happen to be. Bravo Helen!"

First built across the road about 1793, the barn has been moved, divided, added to, and finally reconstructed into a well-insulated architectural gem. Helen, too, loves this place, and the fields and open sky, "the blue smile of the firmament." In 13 years of hosting, this grandmother, a potter, has had the pleasure of seeing the growing children of many repeat visitors.

Foreign languages spoken: "Could perhaps struggle with French and German."
Bed and bath: Three rooms share one full bath and an upstairs skylit living room. One large room with double bed and space for cot, one medium-sized room with two twin beds, and one small room, Helen's favorite, with single bed. Cot available.
Breakfast: Usually at 8 or 8:30. Fruit (maybe blackberries picked that morning in the lane) or juice. "Blintzes are my specialty. Give me a bit of warning." Bacon and eggs, crepes, omelets, or buckwheat pancakes; cinnamon crumb cake or homemade blueberry muffins served in old-fashioned cast iron muffin pans. Served on her own blue-and-brown pottery in brick-floored kitchen.

Plus: Garden flowers. Wood stoves for heat. Plenty of books. Comfortable outdoor chairs. Back porch with picnic table and incredible view of long fields, birds, daisies—and, at night, stars and fireflies.

From Minnesota: *"A delight to the senses . . . exquisitely set table . . . a gift."*

Tatnic B&B   207/676-2209

Tatnic Road, Wells, ME
Mailing address: Box 518A, South Berwick, ME 03908-9607

Hosts: Tin and Jane Smith
Location: Secluded. On 63 acres, across a footbridge, at the end of a five-mile uphill road off of Route 1. Six miles to Ogunquit's beaches, 15 to Kennebunkport

and to Durham, New Hampshire.
Open: Year round.
Rates: $30 single, $48 double. $10 each daybed. Children's special—$55 for one family in a room. MC, Visa.
⚓ ♨ ⚄

This warm, inviting environment is enhanced by two people who haven't changed their outlook since building their passive-solar, almost maintenance-free home "with the help of all our friends" in 1978–80. It heats with about 3½ cords of wood in the winter. Insulation and cross-ventilation keep it cool "like a cave" in summer.

Tin, in addition to being a talented builder-by-doing and gardener (130 fruit trees plus crops), is a Maine Organic Farmers and Gardeners board member. And he works with the Laudholm/Wells Reserve, a fabulous place to walk. Since being featured in *Family Circle* for her ingenious patterns and "Quilt-in-One-Day" presentations, Jane, a professional quilt maker and teacher, travels nationwide to give workshops. (Guests may arrange for private lessons right here.)

As in an expanded New England farmhouse, a solar addition was built in 1986 for Tin's mother, Marie-Louise Smith, who plants hundreds of flowers each year.

In residence: "Ben and Jake, Percheron workhorses, who help farm, gather wood, and give us cart rides."
Foreign language spoken: Marie-Louise speaks Danish.
Bed and bath: Two "treetop" rooms—reached via open curved oak staircase from two-storied living room—share first-floor full bath. One room with extra-long queen bed and space for three cots; one with two twin beds. (Small TV in each room.)
Breakfast: Flexible hours. Fruit; corn pancakes with real maple syrup; homemade blueberry muffins or bread; granola or eggs. Tatnic's honey. Cheerios for kids. Yogurt. Served in dining area by fireplace and windowed walls that overlook beautiful gardens (and hummingbirds, too, when we were there).
Plus: Custom map according to your interests. Tree swing. Outdoor furniture (and maybe mosquitoes too). Screened porch. Ideas for a floor plan with well-designed built-ins. Kitchen facilities for dinner preparations. Evening swim at Ell Pond, seven miles away.

From California: *"Comfortable, interesting, and quite beautiful . . . encouraged to pursue my own dreams and plans."*

The Sunset House

207/963-7156

Route 186, HCR 60, Box 62, West Gouldsboro, ME 04607   **800/233-7156**

Hosts: Carl and Kathy Johnson
Location: On Schoodic Peninsula near Flander's Bay. Bordered by Jones Pond. Forty minutes "down east" of Bar Harbor.
Open: Year round. Two-night minimum August weekends.
Rates: Double occupancy. Novem-

ber–April 15, $39–$59; April 16 through June, September 16 through October, $59; July–September 15, $69. Singles $10 less. $10 extra person. Seventh consecutive night free. MC, Visa.

♥ ⋔ ⁂ ◆ ✹ ⅄

From Massachusetts: *"The view was breathtaking, the sea air invigorating, Carl's feast memorable. . . . Highly recommended for a place to get away and renew yourself."*

Mesmerizing sunsets. Moonlit nights on the pond. There's swimming "warmer than local salt water," fishing, canoeing, cross-country skiing, ice skating and ice fishing. A mill stream with babbling water running to the bay. Kathy's dream of a small farm. And Carl, an executive chef at a large seasonal hotel, who uses locally grown products.

The Johnsons, active community members, came from Cape Cod in 1989 to this aptly named Victorian B&B, which "has only been modernized by heat, electricity, and running water." The country decor changes with ongoing projects.

In residence: Mason, 16. Matthew, 14. Tammy and Maggie, "official greeters," toy apricot poodles. Smokey and Slash, mother/daughter cats. Dairy goats in pasture.
Foreign language spoken: Some German.
Bed and bath: Seven rooms on second and third floors. One room overlooks pond; four have ocean view. On each floor, two shared (robes provided) full baths. Double or twin beds.
Breakfast: 7–9. Specialties include sour-cream cinnamon-raisin French toast, yeast-raised sourdough waffles, omelets. Special diets accommodated.
Plus: Tea or coffee with homemade goat milk cheeses, pastries or breads. Parlor wood stove. Beach towels. Window quilts. In winter, dinners (extra charge).

From Australia: *"We enjoyed it very much. And still talk about the beautiful cheese cake and waffles."*

The Squire Tarbox Inn

207/882-7693

RR 2, Box 620, Wiscasset, ME 04578

Hosts: Karen and Bill Mitman
Location: "Down a country road to nowhere." Surrounded by woods on Westport Island, a small rural area. Ten miles south of Wiscasset and Route 1. Within 30-minute drive of beaches, antiquing, museums,

lobster shacks, harbors, L.L. Bean.
Open: Mid-May through October.
Rates: $70–$90 double, $90–$110 small queen room, $110–$130 large queen room, $130–$150 king/twins option. Amex, Discover, MC, Visa.

♥ ◆ ✹

One of a kind. Featured in many publications, including *'GBH, Yankee,* and the *Washington Post.* The very style of country living envisioned by the Mitmans when they were administrators (Copley Plaza Hotel marketing and hospital personnel) in Boston. Their handsome rambling colonial farmhouse—the oldest part was built in 1763—has original beams, moldings, fireplaces, and carvings. There are antiques, rocking chairs, candles (at dinner), quilts, books—and good reading lights. A pine-needled path leads to a screened house by the saltwater marsh. And the immaculate barn, moved here and restored in 1990, is a story in itself.

Karen, a quilter, and Bill, a private pilot, are cheese makers who produce a ton a year from the milk of their award-winning, scene-stealing, "wonderfully responsive" Nubian goats. Since buying the inn in 1983, they have continued to share their lifestyle "surrounded by nature" with many grateful guests.

In residence: Fourteen goats, two donkeys, one horse, eight chickens, two barn cats.
Bed and bath: Eleven rooms on first and second floors with double, queen or king/twins option; all private shower baths. Four are large, more formal main house rooms with working fireplaces. Seven are more informal carriage barn rooms (connected to house); three have private entrance.
Breakfast: 8–9:30. Fresh fruit. Juice. Granola. Home-baked breads and cakes. Yogurt. Quiche. Hot beverages. Buffet style. Eat in dining room or on sundeck.
Plus: All those fireplaces. Player piano in music room. Wood stove in barn sitting room. Window fans. Individual thermostats. Full liquor license. Beach towels. Rowboat, bikes, and swings. Beverages available all day. By reservation, dinner at 7, $29 per person, with creative entrees, homegrown vegetables and herbs, homemade pastas, rolls made with goat's milk whey.

Hutchins House   207/363-3058

209 Organug Road, York, ME 03909

Hosts: Linda Hutchins and daughter Liz Barrett
Location: On a hill overlooking the river and the country's oldest pile-driven drawbridge. Across street from many guests' wedding reception site—York Golf and Tennis Club. Surrounded by lawns, gardens, and large oak trees. "Twenty-minute walk up river through a wooded park, passing by boats and shorebirds, to York Harbor Beach." Within walking distance of downtown.
Open: May–October. Two-night minimum on weekends.
Rates: (Include continental breakfast; hot entree $5 extra.) June weekends, holiday weekends, and July–October, $79 shared bath, $89 private. Saturdays, $4 one-night surcharge. Off-season, $65–$69. Third person $25. Suite $130. Picnic baskets $5.50/person.
♥ ⬛ ⁂ ✹ ⅄

From Massachusetts: *"Spacious rooms—with a view! A lovely home with loving people."*

"I raised six kids in this 17-room turn-of-the-century house, and I am so very happy to have a reason to stay here and keep it beautiful!"

(Please turn page.)

Linda is a registered nurse, a massage therapist, an avid gardener, and an adventure traveler who spends almost two winter months a year traveling all over the world. Often, breakfasts here have a Caribbean flavor, a holdover from Linda's days as owner and operator of a charter boat in the Virgin Islands.

In residence: "O.J. Ole! is our large orange coon cat. Mickey is a blond cockapoo with a husky voice."
Foreign language spoken: College French.
Bed and bath: Four large tall-ceilinged rooms overlooking the river. Two second-floor air-conditioned queen-bedded rooms have private full baths. On third floor, one queen with air conditioner and one room with two twin beds share a shower bath. Rollaway available.
Breakfast: 8:30–9:30. Buffet with juice, fresh fruit, hot cereal, homemade breads. On flower-filled riverview deck with awning or on wicker-furnished sun porch.
Plus: Guest refrigerator. Down comforters. Mints on pillow. Extensive movie library. Outdoor four-person hot tub overlooking water. Canoes for rent.

The Wild Rose of York B&B   207/363-2532
78 Long Sands Road, York, ME 03909

Hosts: Fran and Frank Sullivan
Location: One mile from the ocean. On a hill in a quiet area near center of the historic village. Just down the road from a game preserve with trails for hiking or cross-country skiing. Fifteen minutes north of Portsmouth and south of Ogunquit.
Open: Year round except for some times in the winter. Two-day mini-mum on summer and holiday weekends.
Rates: June–October 15, single $55, double $65. Rest of year, single $45; double $55 one night, $50 two consecutive nights. Extra person $20; child age 11–15 $10; 1–10 $5. Year round, seventh night free.
♥ ⌂ ⛵ ✿ ✈

Captain Rufus Donnell built this columned colonial mansion in 1814 for his bride. In 1985 Fran and Frank, authors of *Budget Dining and Lodging in New England,* moved here from Massachusetts "for the fun of meeting new people, making them comfortable, and helping them to appreciate an area." Fran is still a nurse/counselor who works with older persons. In addition, she is a watercolor artist and quilter. Now that Frank, a retired biology professor, has completed work on a science education project, he and Fran are writing a book on B&Bs in Ireland. Here, they tell guests about tide pool areas and York's mile-long cliff walk. Winter brings cross-country skiing and hot soup by the fire.

Foreign languages spoken: French and some German understood.
Bed and bath: Three rooms, all private baths. One first-floor room with double bed, unattached private shower bath. On second floor, one room with queen bed and working fireplace, full bath. One with a double four-poster and enclosed sun porch with single bed and room for a cot; full bath.

Breakfast: 8–9. Belgian waffles, fruit-filled crepes, apricot French toast, peach pancakes, a Dutch puff (popover with apples). Juice, fruit, coffee or tea. Served in dining room fashioned after a tavern, or on large front porch. **Plus:** Welcoming beverage. Two large common rooms, fireplaced living room. Piano (spontaneous concerts and sing-alongs encouraged). Library/TV/game room. Window fans. Wraparound partially screened porch. Hibachis. Huge yard with swing, bocci ball, picnic areas.

Canterbury House   207/363-3505
432 York Street, P.O. Box 881, York Harbor, ME 03911-0881

Host: James T. Pappas
Location: Overlooking York Harbor. Within walking distance of soft sand Harbor Beach. Near restaurants, outlets, deep-sea fishing, antiques shops.
Open: Year round. Two-night minimum on holiday weekends and all weekends in season.
Rates: $69 double, shared bath; $85 private. $10 less with continental breakfast. $20 extra person. Weekly rates and weekend packages. MC, Visa.

R&R accompanied by classical music is the order of the day in this century-old Victorian hosted by James, a retired travel agent (for 28 years in Thunder Bay, Ontario) turned drapery designer and (trained) culinary expert.

Theme weekends are featured for most holidays. Winter Sunday brunches are available to the public by advance reservation. And candlelit dinners are arranged too.

In residence: One cat, not allowed in guest quarters.
Foreign languages spoken: Greek and French.
Bed and bath: Seven rooms, some with harbor view, on second and third floors. One with private bath, double bed, sofa bed. Other baths shared (robes provided) by three rooms. Two doubles, a twin, or a double bed and a twin bed in each room.
Breakfast: 8–9:30. Fresh orange juice, fruit salad, fresh hot muffins. Full includes Belgian waffles, French toast, or casserole. At separate tables set with china, crystal, sterling silver, linens.
Plus: Tea time at 4, munchies and cocktails at 5. Down comforters. Turndown service. Third-floor ceiling fans. Mints on pillow. Fresh flowers and fruit. Beach towels and chairs. Guest refrigerator. Transportation to/from airport, bus, and train station.

Guests wrote: *"Terrific breakfast . . . loved the [porcelain] dolls . . . loved our stay."*

"A genial greeting? The only person around was a workman on a ladder, so I left," read one complaint. "Bernice, I was the workman," replied the innkeeper/handyman/chef.

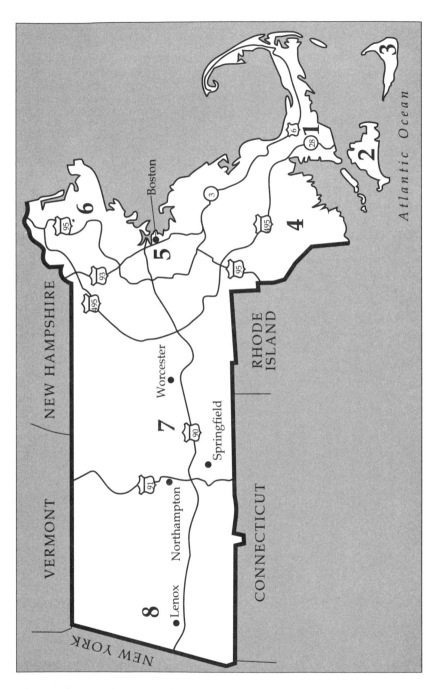

The numbers on this map indicate the areas for which there are detailed sections.

MASSACHUSETTS

Massachusetts
_____ Reservation Services _____

Although most Massachusetts-based services concentrate on one area, several
have hosts in neighboring regions. (Some refer you to other services throughout the country and in England too.) The services, going east to west, are:

Cape Cod, Martha's Vineyard, and Nantucket
Bed & Breakfast Cape Cod. Please see page 118.
Destinnations. Please see page 118.
House Guests Cape Cod and the Islands. Please see page 119.
Orleans Bed & Breakfast Associates. Please see page 119.

Boston and Just a Little West
AAA Accommodations. Please see page 189.
A Bed & Breakfast Agency of Boston (and Boston Harbor B&B). Please
    see page 189.
Bed and Breakfast Associates Bay Colony, Ltd. Please see page 190.
Bed & Breakfast Cambridge & Greater Boston/Minuteman Country.
    Please see page 191.
Boston Reservations/Boston Bed & Breakfast, Inc. Please see page 191.
Greater Boston Hospitality. Please see page 192.
Host Homes of Boston. Please see page 192.
University Bed & Breakfast, Ltd. Please see page 193.

North of Boston
Bed & Breakfast Folks. Please see page 208.
Bed & Breakfast Marblehead & North Shore/Greater Boston & Cape Cod.
    Please see page 208.

Central Massachusetts
Folkstone Bed & Breakfast Reservation Service. Please see page 222.

Berkshires
Berkshire Bed & Breakfast Homes. Please see page 234.

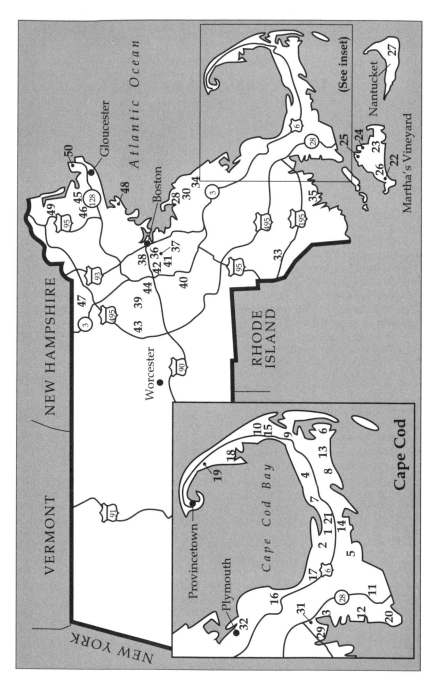

The numbers on this map indicate the locations of eastern Massachusetts B&Bs described in detail in this chapter. The map for B&Bs in Central Massachusetts, Connecticut River Valley, and Berkshires is on page 220.

Cape Cod, Martha's Vineyard, and Nantucket; Southeastern Massachusetts; Boston; Just a Little West; North of Boston

In this book, areas of Massachusetts are arranged roughly from east to west. Please see page 221 for Central Massachusetts, Connecticut River Valley, and Berkshires.

KEY TO SYMBOLS
♥ Lots of honeymooners come here.
⚓ Families with children are very welcome. (Please see page xii.)
⚐ "Please emphasize that we are a private home, not an inn."
⁂ Groups or private parties sometimes book the entire B&B.
♦ Travel agents' commission paid. (Please see page xii.)
✗ Sorry, no guests' pets are allowed.
✄ No smoking inside *or* no smoking at all, even on porches.

Cape Cod, Martha's Vineyard, and __ Nantucket Reservation Services __

Bed & Breakfast Cape Cod

P.O. Box 341, West Hyannisport, MA 02672-0341

Phone: 508/775-2772. Year round. Best time to call is 8:30–5. Mail requests answered by return mail. Answering machine calls returned next business day.

Fax: 508/775-2884.

Listings: 90. Located mostly on Cape Cod and the islands of Martha's Vineyard and Nantucket. A few are in metropolitan Boston, in the north shore area including Gloucester, and in south shore communities including Scituate. All are hosted residences or inns.

Reservations: Two-night minimum stay in season and on weekends. "Cape Cod is a popular destination year round. Advance reservations suggested as early as your dates are firm."

Rates: $40–$60 single, $50–$185 double. $5 surcharge for one-night stay, when available. $10 nonrefundable booking charge. Deposit required is 25 percent of total charge. Deposit less $20 is refunded if cancellation is received at least one week prior to arrival. Amex, Discover, MC or Visa for deposit; balance to be paid in cash or traveler's check. Five percent surcharge for balance payment by credit card.

Guests booked through this service receive extensive information before arrival, "ensuring that guests know what to expect, leaving no room for surprises." Available accommodations—all inspected annually—range from modest to luxurious and include houses built in the seventeenth century as well as contemporary beachfront properties with many amenities.

Plus: Studios, carriage houses, or apartments available for weekly rental.

Destinnations

P.O. Box 1173, Osterville, MA 02655

Phone: 508/428-5600 or (from U.S. or Canada) 800/333-INNS (4667).

Fax: 508/420-0565.

Listings: 30 and growing (rapidly). Located on Cape Cod and on the islands of Martha's Vineyard and Nantucket. Most are open year round. They include small B&Bs and inns—some with restaurants. Properties throughout New England can accommodate corporate events and group meetings.

Reservations: At least two weeks' advance notice is recommended, "especially in August, usually the busiest month of the year." Most have a two-day weekend minimum Memorial Day–Columbus Day; three-day minimum during holiday and Christmas Stroll weekends.

Rates: $60–$225 for two. Packages include winter rates, dining, antiquing, golfing. Amex, Discover, MC, Visa. ♦

This expanded reservation service personalizes each inn booking and then some. They will plan an itinerary according to your interests. They book air and ground transportation and suggest restaurants, attractions, historical sites, and shops. A consortium that features "high standards in accommodations, guest service, and consumer value," this service was established in 1992 by Bill DeSousa, a banker when he lived in New York, and Glenn Faria, who has extensive experience with hotels, restaurants, and meeting planning.

House Guests Cape Cod and the Islands
Box 1881, Orleans, MA 02653

Phone: 508/896-7053 (information). 800/666-HOST (or 4678) reservations only. Live 9–9 daily Memorial Day–Columbus Day; 9–6 rest of year except January. Answering machine all other times.

Fax: 508/896-7054.

Listings: 100. Half are hosted private homes; half are inns. Located in every Cape Cod town plus Edgartown, Vineyard Haven, and Oak Bluffs on Martha's Vineyard, and on Nantucket. Free directory is a 50-page booklet including descriptions and rates.

Reservations: Two-week advance notice suggested. Two-night minimum Memorial Day–Columbus Day, three nights on all three-day (holiday) weekends.

Rates: $35–$68 single. $40–$250 double. $15 one-night surcharge at some locations. Some weekly rates and senior citizen discounts. $15 booking fee. Fifty percent deposit required; full prepayment for one-night stays. Ten days' advance notice required for refund of deposit less 10 percent service charge (minimum $12) on private home reservations. If less than 10 days, deposit refunded, less processing fee, only if accommodations can be rebooked over entire reserved period. Inns and guests houses have individual cancellation policies. Amex, Discover, MC, Visa. ♦

Charles DiCesare and Richard Griffin are B&B innkeepers in addition to being the owners of the Cape's original bed and breakfast reservation service. Previously, Charles, a Swiss-trained hotelier, had a career in London and Saint Moritz. Richard managed a large professional association. On the Cape, they take pride in their efficient and recognized service.

Plus: Guided tours of the Cape arranged. Several hosts provide pickup and return service to airport, train, and bus stations. Short-term (over seven days) arrangements available for unhosted cottages, studios, houses, and apartments.

Orleans Bed & Breakfast Associates
P.O. Box 1312, Orleans, MA 02653-1312

Phone: 508/255-3824 or 800/541-6226. Daily, 8–8, year round except holidays. Answering machine at other times.

Fax: 508/255-2863.

Listings: 75. Mostly nonsmoking private one- to three-bedroom host homes; a few country inns and select self-catering accommodations. Located in the area known as the Outer or Lower Cape, "from the elbow to the wrist of the arm that juts out to sea," including only the towns of Harwich, Chatham, Brewster, Orleans, Eastham, Wellfleet, and Truro. Call for annual directory.

Reservations: Ten days' advance notice preferred. Day-before reservations accepted if arrangements can be made. Two-night minimum stay.

Rates: $65–$175 per room. Deposit of two nights' rate required, plus a $10 reservation handling fee. For cancellations, notification is required 10 days prior to scheduled arrival date; deposit is then refunded, less a $20 service charge. For less than 10 days' cancellation notice, deposit is refunded if accommodation can be rebooked. Discover, MC, Visa.

What Mary Chapman began on a kitchen table in 1983 is the basis to this day for her reservation service: she is dedicated to the people-to-people concept of B&B. (Callers can tell.) She and her staff know the hosts. And—what is rather unusual for private home hosts—they know each other, from semi-annual gatherings. Sharers all, they offer warm hospitality and a love of the area.

Other reservation services with some B&Bs on Cape Cod:
Bed & Breakfast Marblehead & North Shore/Greater Boston & Cape Cod, page 208
Bed and Breakfast Associates Bay Colony, Ltd., page 190
Host Homes of Boston, page 192

All the B&Bs with this ✦ symbol want you to know that they are a private home set up for paying guests (rather than an inn). Although definitions vary, these private home B&Bs tend to have one to three guest rooms. For the owners—people who enjoy meeting people—B&B is usually a part-time occupation.

Cape Cod B&Bs

Many Cape Cod hosts report that guests come to see all of Cape Cod in a weekend. "Please remind them in your book that Cape Cod is 90 miles long." The following B&Bs are in alphabetical order according to the towns and villages where they are located. B&Bs on the islands of Martha's Vineyard and Nantucket are on pages 161–178.

Ashley Manor   508/362-8044

P.O. Box 856, 3660 Old King's Highway (Route 6A), Barnstable, MA 02630

Hosts: Donald and Fay Bain
Location: On two acres of parklike grounds, set back from Route 6A, up a sweeping driveway behind huge privet and boxwood hedges. Within walking distance of harbor, beach, village, whale watch excursions.
Open: Year round. Reservations recommended. Two-night minimum on weekends, more on some holidays.
Rates: Double-bedded room $115; $135 with working fireplace. Suites with working fireplace $160–$175. Cottage $175. Third person in suite or cottage 25 percent extra. Amex, MC, Visa.

♥ ❖ ♦ ✈ ⚵

Guests wrote: *"Enchanting . . . charming . . . Donald's gourmet breakfast kept us going into the afternoon . . . special coffee . . . constant supply of logs . . . delightful innkeepers."*

The whole scene—"we keep making it more romantic"—is just what Fay, a former advertising executive, and Donald, a lawyer, were ready for when their children were grown. In 1986 they left Manhattan and came with their antiques, Oriental rugs, grand piano, and comfortable sofas to a "special property originally built in 1699" that has seven fireplaces, wide floor boards, the original steep stairway, and Cape Cod blown glass windows. The secret passageway that now connects two suites was probably used as a hiding place for Tories during the Revolutionary War. Restored in 1964, the house has been an inn since 1985. Outside there's a gazebo and a 44-foot brick terrace facing two acres of manicured lawns, a tennis court, a fountain garden, and age-old plantings including cherry and pear trees.

Foreign language spoken: French.
Bed and bath: Six spacious air-conditioned rooms, all private baths. Five with working fireplace. Downstairs suite with queen canopied bed. Two second-floor suites; one with canopied king bed, one canopied queen. Two double-bedded rooms. The Garden Cottage, a separate building, has queen bed, sitting area, kitchenette, fireplace, bath.
Breakfast: 8:30–9:30. Freshly squeezed orange juice, coffee, teas, homemade breads and muffins, cereals including homemade granola. French toast with bacon, quiche, omelets, Swedish pancakes. Served on terrace or in fireplaced formal dining room by candlelight.
Plus: Complimentary wines. Fresh fruit. Candies. Flowers. Coffee and tea in rooms. Fine linens. Free loan of bicycles. Hammock. Croquet. Romantic fountain garden.

Beechwood

508/362-6618

2839 Main Street, Route 6A, Barnstable Village, MA 02630

Hosts: Anne and Bob Livermore
Location: Behind tall hedges in historic district. Half mile to village, harbor, small beach, whale-watching boats.
Open: Year round. Two-night minimum on weekends.

Rates: First floor $140 queen-bedded room, $130 double. Second floor $105 except room with king and single ($135). Third floor $105. Third person $20. Less November–April, excluding holidays. Amex, MC, Visa.
♥ ❖ ♦ ✗

Gourmet magazine called it "elegant." Guests dub it "romantic, beautiful, and relaxing." Featured in a National Trust for Historic Preservation calendar, this Victorian is a wonderful example of fanciful Queen Anne style—from the lighting fixtures to antique furnishings to hand-cut tricolored exterior shingles.

In 1987 the Livermores—a Connecticut innkeeper and an engineering sales manager—realized their dream by buying the restored step-back-in-time Beechwood. They both enjoy cooking, classical music, sailing, and "real Cape" walks.

In residence: One cat restricted to hosts' quarters.
Bed and bath: Six rooms. All private baths; some full, some shower only. Two first-floor rooms, each with working fireplace—one with double, one with queen canopied bed. Second floor: one room with double bed, handpainted cottage furniture, stained glass windows; one with two doubles, view of harbor and bay; one with a king and a single bed. Third floor: panoramic bay view in air-conditioned room with double brass bed, sloped ceilings, double sinks in bath. Rollaway available.
Breakfast: 8:30–9:30. (Flexible for early ferry.) Apple-filled pancake, eggs in puff pastry with cheese sauce, crepes, or waffles. Breakfast meats. Fresh juice and fruit, freshly baked breads and muffins. Served in fireplaced dining room on tables for two with flowers and small oil lamps.
Plus: In summer, lemonade on wraparound veranda furnished with wicker, hammock, rocking chairs; other seasons, tea with sweets. Bedroom fans. Beech-shaded lawn chairs. Croquet. Badminton. Gardens.

Charles Hinckley House

508/362-9924
Old King's Highway (Route 6A) and Scudder Lane   fax 508/362-8861
P.O. Box 723, Barnstable, MA 02630

Hosts: Les and Miya Patrick
Location: Fronted by those gardens. A short distance from Route 6, exit 6. Five-minute walk down a lane to bay.
Open: Year round. Reservations recommended. Two-night minimum

stay on weekends. Three-night minimum on holidays.
Rates: $119 room with double bed, $139 queen. $149 suite.
♥ ❖ ♦ ✗ ✗

> From New York: *"Lived up to our expectations for a perfect honeymoon . . . beautiful, cozy, homey . . . incredible breakfasts . . . special people."*

Miya is a caterer/landscape gardener; Les, a contractor who specializes in period restoration. Ten years ago, inspired by the inn restoration they did for someone else, they purchased this unoccupied hip-roofed Federal colonial built by shipwright Charles Hinckley in 1809. Featured in both *Country Living* and *Country Home*, the house has an oft-photographed hip-high wildflower garden that lines the granite steps to the front door. Floors are a pumpkin pine. Country furniture is painted or refinished. Flower arrangements—gladioli, cosmos, lilies, daisies, in baskets or vases—are replenished daily in season. The paint colors (often mixed by the Patricks themselves) and fabrics all blend and say "country" in the warmest sense.

In residence: Daughter Eryn is two. Zydako, a mild-mannered Great Dane.
Bed and bath: Four rooms; one with private exterior entrance. All with antique beds, working fireplaces, private baths. One double with tub-only bath. Three queens (two are four-posters) with shower (no tub) bath.
Breakfast: 9–9:30. Coffee, tea, or espresso; fresh orange juice, homemade pastries, fresh fruit plate garnished with flowers, crepes, omelets or French toast. In dining room by the fireplace.
Plus: Beverages. Chocolates. Fresh fruit. Special occasions acknowledged (let Les and Miya know). Will meet guests at the airport. With advance arrangements, dinner ($50 per person) for overnight guests (only).

The Thomas Huckins House   508/362-6379

2701 Main Street (Route 6A), P.O. Box 515, Barnstable, MA 02630

Hosts: Burt and Eleanor Eddy
Location: In historic district. Fifteen minutes to Cape Cod Canal, 5 to whale watch departure area. A short walk to a saltwater inlet overlooking 10 miles of Sandy Neck Beach dunes.

Open: Year round. Two-night minimum on holiday weekends.
Rates: Per room. $75–$95. $15 per extra person beyond two in room or suite. MC, Visa.
♥ ♨ ✿ ♦ ✈ ✂

A fascinating old place. Guests from every state, and many foreign travelers, think so too. They comment on the paint colors. And features seen in *Early American Life:* 18th-century hinges, latches (no doorknobs), paneling, flooring, three cooking fireplaces—one with beehive oven, and nine-over-nine window panes. Occupied by the Huckins family from 1705 to 1956, the house was purchased by the Eddys in 1979, the year they started to take it apart (structurally) and put it back together again. In 1984, with the restoration done and the children grown, they began B&B.

Burt, a furniture maker who sometimes carves birds, and Eleanor, a historian who is researching early Barnstable, have traveled extensively with their antiques business.

In residence: O'Malley Sue, an Irish setter, a semipermanent resident while son is abroad; Anabel, a Maine coon cat. "All pets, kept from the guest areas, are not a problem unless a guest has severe allergies."
Bed and bath: Three large rooms, all modern private baths. First-floor room—canopied double bed, full bath, working fireplace. Second floor—double-bedded room, private staircase, sitting area, oversized shower and seat in bath. Room with queen canopied bed, fireplace, large shower bath; a double-bedded room can be added to make a suite (good arrangement for families).

(Please turn page.)

Breakfast: 8–9. Fresh fruit; juice; eggs any style, French toast with maple syrup, or banana pancakes; cranberry muffins, maybe Swedish coffee cake. Homemade jams and jellies. Served in keeping room, opposite a 10-foot walk-in fireplace.
Plus: Tour of the house. Parlor with fireplace and TV. Patio. Portable telephone. Brick patio overlooking "old-fashioned" perennial garden. (Many guests leave with cuttings.) Croquet.

A guest wrote: *"Not only is the house charming, but so are the proprietors."*

Honeysuckle Hill

591 Main Street, Route 6A, Old King's Highway
West Barnstable, MA 02668-1126

508/362-8418
800/441-8418

Host: Barbara Rosenthal
Location: In National Historic District with sheep, meadows, cranberry bogs, and salt marshes. Five-minute drive to Sandy Neck Beach. Fifteen minutes to whale watching and Hyannis.
Open: Year round. Two-night mini-

mum on some holiday weekends.
Rates: $110 year round for room with working fireplace. Other rooms $90 or $95 summer, $80 or $85 offseason. $20 third person in room. Amex, Discover, MC, Visa.
♥ ⚬ ◆

Guests wrote: *"A treasure trove of historical information . . . saw places we might have missed . . . our own cozy retreat with a fire in the fireplace, homemade cookies by the bedside, sherry on the hall table, lovely decorating touches."*

Pampering is intentional at Honeysuckle Hill. From "the best B&Bs in England" Barbara borrowed ideas that include everything from needle and thread to feather beds (which everyone wants to buy!). Her weathered-shingled Victorian farmhouse—restored by former owners, a well-known Cape family of weavers— "is at least 175 years old." A recent addition is a cathedral-ceilinged Great Room with huge windows overlooking gardens and lily pond.

In St. Louis, Missouri, Barbara taught art. She is active in historic groups and helps produce videos of old Cape Cod.

In residence: Two dogs: "Chloe, a Cavalier King Charles spaniel, loves to check guests in. Annie strikes glamour poses and hopes you won't mention her pedigree (none)."
Foreign languages spoken: A little French and Italian.
Bed and bath: Three air-conditioned rooms, private full baths. Two firstfloor queen-bedded rooms, one with working fireplace. On second floor, very private room with king bed.
Breakfast: 8:30–10. A highlight. Juices, fruit, hot breads and muffins, cinnamon rolls. Souffles (recipe from Salmon River rafting trip), blueberry pancakes, or French toast. Served on whimsical china.
Plus: Afternoon tea with cakes, cookies, or scones. Wide-screen TV, VCR, tape library. Mountain and 10-speed bicycles, car rack. Beach towels, chairs, umbrellas, pails. Binoculars. Inn-to-inn bicycling. "Please call about arrangements for small children and pets."

The Pond House   508/759-1994

44 Monument Neck Road, Bourne, MA 02532

Host: Bernice Van Dam-Blodgett
Location: Serene. Countrylike. Overlooking a pond and woods across the street. Gardens include hundreds of lilies in season. Short walk to one beach; four-minute drive to two others, including one on an island (with homes that have beautiful gardens) reached by two-mile causeway. Eight-minute walk to Cape Cod Canal. Within 20 minutes of Heritage Plantation, Thornton Burgess Museum, Plimoth Plantation, Martha's Vineyard ferry.
Open: Year round. May 15–September 15, two-night minimum preferred.
Rates: $65–$80. Singles $50. Extra person, $15 over age 12.
♥ ♠ ❖ ◆ ✖ ✄

Home was never like this. You return to a room (as many times as you return in a day) that is picture perfect with fresh towels and folded clothes. Bicycles are provided for rides along the picturesque Cape Cod Canal, where the scene changes every minute. For special occasions there's wine in crystal glasses on a silver tray and fresh flowers. Antiques include furnishings, a Dutch rocking horse, "and my grandfather's huge Dutch shoes."

Bernice, a mother of grown children, is a former coloratura who also has experience doing everything from plastering to tiling to cabinetmaking. She lives in a hip-roofed Federal colonial built in the 1980s. As one guest said, "There's something wonderful everywhere you look."

In residence: Gin-Gin, a purebred golden retriever.
Foreign language spoken: A little Holland Dutch.
Bed and bath: Three carpeted second-floor rooms; egg-carton foam on all beds. One room with antique high-back double bed, private bath with Jacuzzi, view of pond. Another with antique high-back double bed and one with king/twins share a full bath. Rollaway available.
Breakfast: 9–11. Announced by music box. Juices. Fruits. Homemade muffins, cinnamon rolls, or Dutch apple cake. Hot beverage. Special diets accommodated. Full breakfast with eggs Benedict or cheese strata served with one day's advance request. Served on fine china in candlelit dining room.
Plus: Fireplaced den. Spinet piano in living room. Window fans or air conditioners available. Robes. Mints. Guest refrigerator. Beach towels. Gas grill; outdoor tables and chairs. Fishing poles. Bus pickup service at Bourne Circle, one mile away.

---

*I*s B&B like a hotel? How many times have you hugged
the doorman?

The Brewster Farmhouse Inn

508/896-3910
716 Main Street, Route 6A   (U.S./Canada) 800/892-3910
Brewster, MA 02631-1035   fax 508/896-4232

Hosts: Bob Messina and Joe Zelich
Location: In historic district. Across from Brewster Windmill and Drummer Boy Museum. Minutes to fine restaurants, Cape Playhouse, Rail Trail. Short walk to Cape Cod Bay.
Open: April–November for sure. Sometimes in other months. Two-night minimum July–Labor Day.

Rates: July–Labor Day $125 queen, $140 king, $155 suite ($85 per separate room with shared bath). Off-season $85 queen, $95 king, $115 suite ($65 separate room). Dining, golf, whale watching packages. Amex, Carte Blanche, Diners, Discover, MC, Visa.
♥ ♦ ✠ ✂

From a huge stack of long, detailed letters: *"I don't think we've stopped talking about it since being there in 1992! . . . Felt like a princess on huge, raised, rice-carved bed. Bedside brandy . . . Ghirardelli chocolates . . . breakfast is an event. (How did they find fresh raspberries in October?) . . . Warm robes for our return from cold whale watch. . . . Met the most interesting people. . . . Warm, helpful, knowledgeable hosts . . . one loves to bake, they both love to cook . . . outdoor Jacuzzi with light mist falling, autumnal smells of Eden moss, apples, leaves, orchard grass . . . cathedral ceiling in fireplaced gathering room with Mexican tile floor, Oriental rugs, glass sliding doors that lead to flower-bedecked deck encircling a heated in-ground pool. . . . Felt as if I was experiencing a page out of* Architectural Digest *or* House Beautiful.*"*

In upstate New York Bob taught social studies; Joe, special education. They became Cape restaurateurs and motel owners and operators in 1986. Before opening the inn in 1992, they revitalized this 150-year-old farmhouse and decorated with antiques, reproductions, and traditional pieces.

In residence: Rosemary, Sarah, and Lilly—miniature dachshunds.
Foreign languages spoken: A bit of Italian and Spanish.
Bed and bath: Three rooms and one suite, all with air conditioning, private bath, wall-mounted dryers. First floor—queen bed, working fireplace, shower bath. King four-poster, full bath, private entrance, sun deck, access to spa and pool. Second floor—queen bed, shower bath. Two-room suite, queen bed in each room, shower bath.
Breakfast: 8–9:30. Fresh fruit (homegrown berries), homemade breads, croissants, muffins. Repertoire includes Florentine quiche with sautee of spinach and julienne ham or Portuguese French toast topped with apple sautee and bacon or sausage.
Plus: Fireplaced living room. Phone jacks in rooms. Afternoon tea and wine with homemade baked goods. (Could be kale soup with freshly made Italian bread.) Poolside cold drinks. Picnic baskets prepared.

In this book, areas of Massachusetts are arranged roughly from east to west.

Isaiah Clark House

1187 Main Street (Route 6A)
Box 169, Brewster, MA 02631-0001

508/896-2223
800/822-4001
fax 508/896-7054

Host: Charles DiCesare
Location: Two minutes from well-known and much-photographed general store. On historic Old King's Highway, with five acres of gardens, fruit trees, wild berry patches.
Open: Year round. Two-night mini-

mum Memorial Day–Columbus Day. Advance reservations required.
Rates: May 24–October 7, $85–$115. October 15–May 23, $75–$95. Honeymoon package available. Amex, Discover, MC, Visa.
♥ ❖ ♦ ✴

From Connecticut: *"The house is furnished in a quiet, understated style, inviting us to put our feet up. Charles, the trained and world-traveled hotelier, intuitively knows when to join the conversation, to discuss choice of English teas or, if you know enough to ask him, how it was when he presided over the Hilton opening in London."*

Exposed beams, stenciling, colonial colors, and antiques are throughout this beautifully restored rambling sea captain's house, which is deceptively small from the outside. Since opening as a B&B in 1986, it has won the Brewster Garden Club's Outstanding Landscape Design award. Two rooms that "you can't tell" are new have been added.

As host, Charles brings 200 years of family experience in the hospitality business to B&B. In addition, he runs a reservation service (page 119)—and enjoys history, opera, jazz, skiing, swimming, and Scrabble.

In residence: One cat, Miss Olga, "kept in private quarters but available for pictures."
Foreign languages spoken: French, Italian, some German and Spanish.
Bed and bath: Seven air-conditioned rooms, all private full baths. First floor—one room has queen, TV, en-suite bath. Two rooms have canopied queen, working fireplace, across-hall bath. Second floor—two queen-bedded rooms (one is beamed and skylit), each with working fireplace, across-hall bath. One queen and one king/twin option, en-suite baths, parlor with TV.
Breakfast: 8:30–10 (coffee earlier). Homegrown fruits and herbs. Homemade muffins. Smoked Nova Scotia salmon, broiled ham, frittata, Belgian waffles, cheddar omelet, or blueberry pancakes. In dining room or on deck overlooking gardens.
Plus: Welcoming refreshments. All rooms have air conditioning. Robes. Turned-down beds. Bedtime cookies and milk. Fireplaced parlor. Upstairs parlor with TV, VCR, stereo, library. Bicycles. Beach chairs and towels. Complimentary transportation to/from airport, train, bus, private beach. "Narrated" tour of house. In summer, iced tea and lemonade, 3–5 p.m.

---

*B*ed and breakfast is the hottest trend in American travel.

Quail Hollow
Brewster, MA

Location: Peaceful. On spacious grounds between two ponds. Two miles to bike trail. A mile from mid-Cape highway, four to Orleans.
Reservations: March–December through House Guests Cape Cod and the Islands, page 119.
Rates: $70 queen room. Fall weekends, $100 for two nights. $25 per extra person in nearby double room.
♥ ⚘ ⚘ ✗ ⚮

Drive along the unpaved "cartway" and around the carriage barn to the rear of this old farmhouse, a 200-year-old Cape with 19th-century addition. Walk across an expanse of lawn to the front of the house, which faces a lake. And then it's through an old-fashioned porch (where breakfast is served) into the antiques-furnished house, home of a Cape resident who will direct you to a park area with walking paths and to bike paths, whale watching, fishing charters, and shopping. She provides maps of nearby towns and a list of various recommended restaurants. "And many guests use our canoe or kayak to paddle over to another lake, the largest on Cape Cod, and enjoy a swim."

In residence: "Two well-behaved cats."
Bed and bath: On second floor, one room with queen bed, private shower bath. Across the hall, a room with a double bed for up to two others of traveling party.
Breakfast: Fruit, homemade muffins, hot beverages. Served on large screened porch overlooking the water.
Plus: Badminton, croquet, large yard. Games for children.

From Vermont: *"A wonderful spot. Delightful hostess. An undiscovered treasure."*

Copper Beech Inn   508/771-5488
497 Main Street, Centerville, MA 02632-2913

Hosts: Joyce and Clark Diehl
Location: In historic district. On property with tall trees including, they say, the largest European Beech on Cape Cod. A half mile to warm-water Craigville Beach and renowned ice-cream store. Five-minute drive to Hyannis and island ferries.
Open: Year round. Reservations required. Two-night minimum, mid-May–mid-October.
Rates: Mid-May–mid-October, $80 double bed, $90 queen or king. Off-season, $10 less. Suite for three, $130. Amex, MC, Visa for deposit only. Weekly rates available.
♥ ✣ ✗

The original graceful stairway and wrought iron latches are part of the appeal of this three-quarter Cape–style house built by Captain Hillman Crosby in 1830.

For 30 years the Diehls had vacationed and visited in all areas of the Cape. When they opened their B&B here in 1985, they retained the character of this National Register property—and furnished with a blend of antiques and traditional pieces. This is a home away from home remembered for warm hospitality and Joyce's breakfasts.

Clark is a former field executive for a major corporation. Joyce has a special interest in education for women. Through their reservation service, Bed &

Breakfast Cape Cod, described on page 118, the Diehls have even more contact with B&B travelers, as well as with other hosts who appreciate Cape Cod.

Bed and bath: Three air-conditioned rooms with private baths. On first floor, one room has queen four-poster bed, private bath with shower, Oriental carpets. Another room with double bed, full bath. Second-floor suite has a pencil-post king bed, bath with shower, and adjoining room with twin bed.
Breakfast: 8–10. Fresh fruit, pastries, and house specialties including berry bowl with whipped cream; pancakes, eggs with breakfast meats. Served family style in dining room or in kitchen next to 1898 wood cookstove.
Plus: Refreshments in family living room or parlor. Beach mats. Outdoor hot-water shower. Lounge chairs overlooking pond. Wicker-furnished porch. By prior arrangement, will meet guests at Hyannis airport, bus, or train.

From Kansas: *"A beautiful home and a warm heart."*

Bed & Breakfast Cape Cod Host #12
Chatham, MA

Location: Residential. About a mile from the village and its restaurants, shops, scenic lighthouse, fishing pier, windmill, and, in summer, Friday night bandstand concerts.
Reservations: Available year round through Bed & Breakfast Cape Cod, page 118.

Rates: $65 for two, $15 third person. For up to four guests, $105 for two adjoining rooms, each with a double and a twin bed.

From Massachusetts: *"Charming folks, perfect for kids, a homey welcoming atmosphere."*

Built in 1980 by the host, a former college professor, with the help of sons, this is a reproduction bow-roofed house with a fireplaced living room, lots of exposed wood, wide board floors, and skylights. Now the host is a management consultant and auditor. His wife, a nurse, comments: "When our [nine] children were young, we moved to a New Hampshire farm for a few years. As vacationers, when we camped at Nickerson State Park, Chatham became our favorite town. Even now, we join the tourists and walk along the main street every night. Morning walks are usually by the ocean; it's such a mystery, always with something new to see. Guests often ask: Where to swim? Where to eat? And do we ever get bored in the winter? (No.) We love sharing this wonderful area with bed and breakfast travelers."

Bed and bath: On first floor, room with double bed, private full bath. On second floor, queen-bedded room and adjoining room with a double bed and a twin bed share a full bath.
Breakfast: 8–9:30. Juice, muffins, baked goods, cereal, beverage. Served in dining room or on deck.
Plus: Shells collected by hostess are "for the taking" by young guests. A menu collection from area restaurants.

The Old Harbor Inn

22 Old Harbor Road
Chatham, MA 02633-2315

508/945-4434
(U.S./Canada) **800/942-4434**
fax 508/945-2492

Hosts: Tom and Sharon (Tootie) Ferguson
Location: One house in from Main Street rotary. On two-lane quiet-at-night residential part of Route 28. In a seaside walking town surrounded by water on three sides. Minutes from galleries, museums, shops, National Seashore beaches, wildlife refuge, and "every kind of food emporium from picnics to fine dining."

Open: Year round. Two-night minimum July 4–Labor Day and on holidays.
Rates: October 15–March $85–$110 single, $95–$120 double; April–mid-June $95–$130 single, $95–$140 double; Mid-June–Labor Day $105–$145 single, $115–$155 double. September–October 14 $85–$130 single, $95–$140 double. Packages offered. CB, Diners, Discover, MC, Visa.
♥ ❖ ♦ ✈ ✂

Many international travelers are among the guests who come to this gracious and comfortable inn, which was built as a doctor's home in 1936. Tootie—"Dad's nickname for me"—has decorated in English country style with chintzes, florals, and small patterns. She paints watercolors. And furniture that Tom built. She stenciled the breakfast floor. And on summer Fridays, she plays baritone horn in the famous Chatham Band gazebo concerts. Tom, sometimes called the breakfast moderator, is a golfer, sailor, horologist (clocks and timepieces), and real estate agent. When he retired from AT&T as operations manager in 1988, he and Tootie moved to this "enchanting village." Guests can tell that the Fergusons consider innkeeping "an extension of our Connecticut lifestyle as a host family for organizations and conferences."

Bed and bath: Seven rooms on first and second floors. King, queen (some four-posters), or twin beds. All with private baths and decorator fabrics and linens. First-floor rooms have private exterior entrances.
Breakfast: 7:30–9:30. Buffet style in sun room or on outdoor deck. Blueberry, beach plum jam, chocolate chip muffins—"no variety repeated as long as you are here!" and scones (maybe cranberry), fresh fruit salad, yogurt and granola, cereals, juices, gourmet coffee and teas, hot chocolate. Baked egg dish or cinnamon orange French toast in winter.
Plus: Afternoon tea on Friday, Saturday, holidays. No TV. Popular dessert buffet on spring and fall weekends. Some rooms have air conditioning and/or individual thermostats. Window fans. Baby grand piano in fireplaced gathering room. Beverages. Turndown service. Oversized towels. Fresh flowers. Candy. Potpourri. Board and parlor games.

I'll just sleep in the morning," said one college-age son,
until the next day when he smelled the muffins.

Isaiah Hall B&B Inn

152 Whig Street, Dennis, MA 02638

508/385-9928
800/736-0160
fax 508/385-5879

Hosts: Marie and Dick Brophy
Location: In a quiet year-round residential area on the historic bay side. A half mile from the beach and one-third mile from the village and Route 6A. About 15 minutes from Hyannis.
Open: April–mid-October. Two-day minimum in July and August and on holidays.
Rates: Vary according to room or bed size, balcony, fireplace. Mid-June–Labor Day, double $75–$108 private bath, $57–$59 shared; single $64–$97 private, $50–$52 shared. Off-season, double $68–$98 private, $52–$55 shared; single $58–$88 private, $46–$48 shared. $12 extra person. Amex, MC, Visa.
♥ ♟ ♣ ♦ ✗

Inside and out, "the real Cape" was all there one weekend in May, when we took a short prebreakfast bicycle ride to the accompaniment of bird songs—to the endless beach where quahogs were being harvested; past sand dunes; and back to the 1857 Greek Revival farmhouse (and attached/renovated carriage house).

Since the Brophys came here in 1983, they have made major changes but retained the ambiance of another era, with beams and antique rockers, white curtains, and wicker. In the kitchen and dining room there is some artwork done by former owner Dorothy Gripp, whose work can be seen in museums all over the country.

Marie, a B&B consultant, was a school counselor and then a high-tech compensation analyst. Dick hosts when he is at home from his job as a high-tech personnel manager.

In residence: "Clyde, our 17-year-old black cat, minds his own business."
Bed and bath: Ten rooms, all with cross-ventilation, on first or second floor. Five rooms in main house, five in carriage house. Queen, double, or a queen (or double) and a single bed. Nine rooms with private bath; one with working fireplace; four in carriage house with balconies. Extra bed available.
Breakfast: 8:30–10. At 8 by request. Cereals. Fruit, English muffins, homemade breads and muffins, jams, jellies, raisins, yogurt. Juice, coffees, teas. On a 19th-century buffet in antiques-filled dining room made for camaraderie.
Plus: A good brochure with guest-chosen photographs. Guests' parlor with Victorian coal stove. Great Room in converted carriage house. Table games. TV. Porch rockers. Terry robes. Forgotten items. Clock radios. Bedroom fans. Ironing boards. Large yard with gardens, lawn chairs, badminton, volleyball, croquet. Use of refrigerator.

From a flood of letters: *"Charming all around . . . peaceful . . . lovely grounds . . . everything fresh and clean . . . great innkeepers who know the area . . . felt fortunate to stay there."*

---

*M*any B&Bs are perfect for family reunions.

Weatherly House   508/385-7458

36 New Boston Road, Dennis, MA 02638-1902

Hosts: Krista and Christopher Diego
Location: "Semiquiet in season."
Fronted by neat white fence. One
block from main street. Surrounded
by other older homes, shops, restaurants. Walk to playhouse, homemade ice cream, old cemetery (rub-
bing allowed), Cape Cod Museum of
Fine Arts, village green concerts.
Open: Year round.
Rates: $95 Memorial Day–Columbus Day. $75 off-season. Amex.
♥ ⬛ ✣

From New Jersey: "Classic seashell driveway . . . a small charming bed and breakfast close [a mile] to beach . . . fresh flowers . . . impeccable . . . prettily shaped soaps . . . chocolates on pillows . . . beautiful rooms with antiques, wing chairs, traditional wallpapers, and colonial colors . . . Krista is a bubbly, cheerful mother of two darling boys . . . delicious breakfast . . . presentation is lovely too with handmade baskets."

Krista makes those baskets. And jams. And she spins wool from those sheep. A native Cape Codder, she met Vermonter Chris, now Chatham Bars Inn chief operating officer, as a fellow University of New Hampshire hotel administration student. In New York, she worked for Hyatt; Chris, for Marriott. In 1988, still in their mid-twenties, they restored this c. 1835 house "that had nothing, not even a furnace." Now they lend bikes to guests "and send them to scenic, unspoiled, and uncommercial Cape Cod"—and answer questions from many who dream of this lifestyle.

In residence: In hosts' quarters, son Nicholas is five ("Guests always say they like my red hair and glasses."); Tucker is two. Golden retriever, Max; cockatiel, Annie; bunny, Flopsy-Mopsy; cat, Dexter; sheep, Ella, Elsie, and Jessie.
Bed and bath: Two rooms. First floor—canopied queen, private full bath, sitting room with TV. Up steep staircase to entire second floor with canopied queen bed, private shower bath, private sitting room, TV.
Breakfast: 8–8:30. Cranberry and orange juices, fresh fruit, freshly baked muffins or fruit breads. French toast, pancakes, or eggs (fresh from neighbor's chickens) any style. Bacon. Cereal. Coffee, tea. Served on china in fireplaced dining room under pierced tin chandelier.
Plus: Fireplaced living room. Window fans. Beach towels. Patio. "Garden flowers our specialty!"

The Rose Petal B&B   508/398-8470

P.O. Box 974, 152 Sea Street, Dennis Port, MA 02639-2405

Hosts: Dan and Gayle Kelly
Location: On a residential (through) street that ends at a sandy Nantucket Sound beach. Several restaurants within walking distance. Seven miles east of Hyannis.
Open: Year round. Two-day minimum for holiday weekends. Please
make advance arrangements for young children.
Rates: Mid-June through mid-September $59. Rest of the year $45–$55. Extra person $12. Family rates available.
♥ ⚄ ✣ ♦ ✄

From New York: *"Sunshine was here, even with wind, fog, and rain outside. Splendid hosts, scrumptious breakfast, and a quiet haven made our stay remarkable and relaxing."*

Dan's daily baking results in wonderful aromas. Sometimes you have an opportunity to see him decorate a three-tiered or other special occasion cake. Trained at the Culinary Institute of America, he now bakes for a local bakery/restaurant as well as for the B&B. Both Dan and Gayle, a substitute teacher in winter, have experience in university (Princeton and Rutgers) food service administration. Their impeccably kept house, built for early Dennis Port settlers, was a summer retreat for a church when they bought it and expanded their talents to include plastering, stenciling, and landscaping. (Passersby stop to photograph the roses in the yard.) Furnishings are family pieces and colonial reproductions.

Foreign language spoken: Gayle speaks "rusty" French.
Bed and bath: Four second-floor rooms (three are air-conditioned), each with one queen or two twin beds. Three rooms share tiled second-floor shower bath. Fourth room shares first-floor full bath (restored footed tub) with hosts. One twin-bedded room has private staircase from kitchen and private entrance from deck. Rollaway twin bed available.
Breakfast: Usually 8–9:30. Homemade muffins, croissants, strudels, coffee cake, Danish. Eggs Benedict, crepes, omelets, or French toast with toppings. Juice, fruit, cereal, granola, cranberry butter, freshly ground coffee, specialty teas. Buffet style in dining room.
Plus: Beverages. Complimentary homemade pastries "to go" for excursions. Window fans. Guest parlor with TV, piano, regional magazines, daily newspaper. Simmering potpourri. Sun porch. Guest refrigerator. Beach towels and mats. Collection of restaurant reviews.

The Nauset House Inn 508/255-2195

143 Beach Road, P.O. Box 774, East Orleans, MA 02643-0774

Hosts: Diane and Al Johnson; Cindy and John Vessella
Location: Residential. On two acres, a half-mile walk to Nauset Beach. Three-minute drive to town center.
Open: April–October. Two-night minimum on weekends.
Rates: $65–$75 shared bath. $95 private bath. $105 cottage or honeymoon suite. $55 single. MC, Visa. ♥ ✗ ✁

From Pennsylvania: *"More important than the serenity and beauty of the greenhouse, the perfect attention to detail . . . the ideal location within walking distance to the beach and away from town, are the innkeepers who have an uncanny ability to know which guests will like what and also to know when guests want solitude and when they want conversation."*

This inn is the answer to those who want a home-away-from-home ambiance—with a hint of fantasy (the conservatory)—yet not a *very* small B&B. It is owned and operated by two generations who garden (flowers arranged in every room); go whale watching; explore the area (great hand-drawn annotated map provided); go to auctions and hand-paint furniture; make dinner

(Please turn page.)

and theater reservations; cook (whimsical sketches in cookbook); experience spontaneous bagel-making and guest chef sessions; and, everywhere, display arts and crafts including their own stained glass, quilts, pottery, and stenciling. Camellias and a weeping cherry tree grow in the 1910 conservatory (from Connecticut) that was added to the 1810 Cape-style dormered farmhouse. The family's 10-year dream was discovered by *Country Living* in 1983, shortly after Al left his executive position at Beechcraft Airplanes, just after Cindy graduated college.

In residence: In hosts' quarters, Nicholas, age five. Winny, a bearded collie, "a real lover." Roo, a quiet cairn terrier, "equally loving."
Bed and bath: Fourteen rooms. Eight with private baths; three rooms with private tub and shower bath. Three first-floor rooms share one bath; three upstairs room share one bath. Queen, double, twins, and one single available. One cottage with queen bed, sitting room. Honeymoon suite (accessed by separate staircase) with double bed, private balcony.
Breakfast: 8–9:30. Varies daily. Always muffins and omelet-of-the-day. French toast and sticky buns are specialties. Family style in fireplaced, brick-floored publike beamed room that opens onto a terrace.
Plus: Wine and cranberry juice with hors d'oeuvres at 5:30. Fireplaced common room. Bedroom table fans. Guest refrigerator. Beach towels. Herb and perennial gardens. Picnic table.

The Parsonage Inn   508/255-8217

202 Main Street, P.O. Box 1501, East Orleans, MA 02643-1501

Hosts: Ian and Elizabeth Browne
Location: In the village, on the road (1.3 miles) to Nauset Beach on the Atlantic Ocean. Within walking distance of fine restaurants and shops. Two miles from Route 6.
Open: Year round. Two-night minimum on June–September weekends and holidays.

Rates: June–September $80–$105 queen, $75–$85 double. $10 less April–May and October–November. $20 less December–March. $10 additional person. MC, Visa.
♥ ♨ ✽ ✈ ⊁

Sit by the fire or on the patio and listen to Chopin, Mozart, or Liszt played by Elizabeth, a piano teacher who grew up in Kenya and lived in England—all before going to Chicago, where she taught 40 students and met Ian, an English-born accountant and medical group executive director. When they decided to purchase an inn, they remembered their first inn experience right here in Orleans.

In 1991 they bought this B&B, a full Cape house, a parsonage in the 1880s, built c. 1770s. Despite all the remodeling over the years, the house retains the feeling of history, of old Cape Cod. Today its uncluttered, fresh, crisp look is embellished with country antiques and some art from Africa, England, and California.

Foreign language spoken: "A little French and a smattering of Swahili."
Bed and bath: Eight rooms (five air conditioned), all with private bath. Seven with queen bed, one with double. Cedar Room has canopied bed and

TV. Willow Room has private entrance, kitchen, TV, queen and futon bed. Spacious Barn Room has vaulted ceiling, sitting area and TV.

Breakfast: 8–9:30. Hearty and healthy ("I'm always looking for low-fat and -sugar alternatives") Scones with Devonshire-type cream, fruit breads, muffins, yogurt and granola, juices, Colombian coffee, teas. Served in dining room, on patio at umbrella tables, or in your room.

Plus: Hors d'oeuvres 6–7 p.m. Fresh flowers. Guest refrigerator.

> From New York: *"Hospitality, courtesy, and good fellowship are outstanding.... The Parsonage Inn is a paragon."*

The Red Geranium

East Orleans, MA

Location: Residential. On a rural main street. On landscaped grounds with gardens and reflecting pond. One and a half miles to Nauset Beach, two miles to bayside beach. Short walk to shops and fine dining.

Reservations: January–November through Orleans Bed & Breakfast Associates, page 119. Two-night minimum stay.

Rates: $75 per room. $110 guest wing. ♥ ◀ ⁂ ✘ ⅄

For many guests a stay here is the highlight of a Cape visit. The charming English-style (larger) Cape furnished with family heirlooms, collectibles, and original oil paintings is the home of Peggy, a painter (and craftsperson with a sense of whimsy) who always wanted to be an innkeeper, and her husband, Marcus, a restorer of antiques. When they settled here in the late 1970s, they made authentic restorations, wallpapering and stenciling in the New England tradition. With every changing season Peggy changes decor in the colonial dining room. Special occasions, including yours, are celebrated. Everywhere, in many ways, there's a strong sense of old-fashioned caring in this warm and friendly B&B.

Bed and bath: Double or twin beds in airy second-floor rooms furnished comfortably with period antiques. Large full semiprivate bath. Plus a spacious guest wing with queen-bedded room, private bath, living room, full kitchen. Guests who book this wing are welcome to join others for breakfast in the main house.

Breakfast: 8–9:30. "Lavish and imaginative," with fruits, juices, cereals, homemade breads and muffins, coffee, brewed tea.

Plus: Private guest entrance. Fan/air conditioner and TV in each bedroom. Second-floor sitting room with a desk, games, and refrigerator. Hot water for tea or coffee. Tour of house.

From Bernice's mailbag: "Guests tell us that your book answers all the questions they usually ask on the phone. Still, it's kind of amazing to have them arrive as old friends because they know so much about us."

The Over Look Inn

508/255-1886

P.O. Box 771, County Road (Route 6)   (U.S./Canada) 800/356-1121
Eastham, MA 02642

Hosts: Nan and Ian Aitchison, son Mark, and Tania, his wife.
Location: Way back from road, across from entrance to main Cape Cod National Seashore visitors' area. Bike paths (and bicycle rental shop) right here; three miles to Orleans and fine restaurants.

Open: Year round. Reservations required.
Rates: Per room. $125 July–August. $75–$125 off-season. Packages available. All major credit cards accepted.
♥ ♣ ♦ ✄

> From England, New Jersey, Massachusetts: *"This is one popular inn—and for good reason . . . an elegant Victorian world . . . lovely tranquil retreat. . . . Meals are a treat to the palate, appealingly presented. . . . Interesting family. . . . Recommendations for fun beaches, historic sites, good places to eat . . . everything arranged for guest's comfort . . . a great experience."*

For twenty years the Scottish ("our accents give us away") couple had a Cape summer home. After Nan, director of development at a Toronto girls' school, and Ian, a chartered surveyor, bought this Queen Anne Victorian house, a long-established lodging establishment, their college-age sons spent two years on restoration. In 1985 the inn opened with brass beds, down comforters, antiques, African and Eskimo art, and Ian's collection of Churchill's works. In 1988 the Aitchisons built an addition with large bedrooms, more baths, and a "Hemingway Billiard Room" decorated with Victorian antiques. Business and international groups meet here. Wedding parties—and cross-country skiers—love it too. Now son Mark and his wife, Tania, a Brazilian tour guide, run a riverboat tour company on the Amazon in the winter. Son Clive, who had his studio in the 18th-century barn, is also married; he's an art teacher in Toronto.

In residence: Sandie, outdoor Lab/shepherd. Winnie, basset hound.
Bed and bath: On second and third floors, 10 rooms (5 are air conditioned) with ceiling fans. All private baths (some with shower, no tub); most are en suite (terry robes for hall bath). Queen, double, or twin beds. Honeymoon suite has fireplace, private porch. Cottage with kitchen. New: Handicapped accessible/family suite.
Breakfast: 8–10. Scottish fare. Maybe kedgeree—finnan haddie, rice, onions, chopped eggs, raisins sauteed in butter, plus dab of mango chutney.
Plus: Afternoon tea, hot scones. Five common rooms, including Winston Churchill library with books and Victorian card table. Four fireplaces. Expansive lawn. Porches. New Year's celebration that has become an inn tradition.

Some executives who book a meeting at an inn return on a weekend for a getaway. Some on a getaway return with colleagues for a meeting.

The Penny House Inn

508/255-6632

4885 County Road (Route 6)   (U.S./Canada) 800/554-1751
P.O. Box 238, North Eastham, MA 02651-0238

Hosts: Bill and Margaret Keith
Location: Hidden behind a high wooden fence and tall privet hedge. On 1½ acres of lawn. In Cape Cod National Seashore area, midway between Hyannis and Provincetown. Minutes to bike trails and Massachusetts Audubon Society sanctuary.

Open: Year round. Three-night minimum on holiday weekends.
Rates: Late June–early September $95 (second-floor rooms) to $120 (suite with working fireplace). Off-season, $65–$100. Amex, Diners, Discover, MC, Visa.
♥ ⁙ ♦ ⍻

The 1751 captain's house with bow roof and wide-planked floors reflects the shipbuilding techniques of the year it was built. Newer rooms added in the 1980s are also furnished with country antiques and collectibles. In 1987 the Keiths, world travelers—Bill's work with General Motors took him to Antarctica, Indonesia, New Zealand, and Japan—found this "right place," as Margaret calls it. They decorated with paintings from Australia, Margaret's homeland, and with porcelain and some Chinese artworks. It's right for travelers, too, people who often exchange travel experiences as well as conversations about food, sailing, the outdoors, and cycling from inn to inn.

In residence: Beau, a Maltese terrier.
Bed and bath: Ten rooms (five are air-conditioned) on two floors. One with private entrance and balcony. All private baths; robes provided for two in hall. King (one with working fireplace); queen (two with cathedral ceiling, skylight, and ceiling fan; two with bow roof ceiling and air conditioning); double; or twin beds.
Breakfast: 8–10. French toast, eggs in toast cups, or waffles served with bacon, sausage, or ham. Fresh fruit. Juice. Cereals. Homemade muffins. Served in 1751 dining room that has 200-year-old beams, Oriental rug, clothed tables for two.
Plus: Afternoon tea. Oversized bath towels. Rear grass patio with tables and chairs.

> From New York: "*Enjoyable.... Cozy, very clean and tastefully decorated rooms ... good breakfast ... appreciated extras such as beach towels and restaurant menus ... ideal location for National Seashore.*"

If you've been to one B&B, you haven't been to them all. If you have met one B&B host, you haven't met them all.

The Whalewalk Inn
220 Bridge Road, Eastham, MA 02642-3215

508/255-0617
fax 508/240-0017

Hosts: Dick and Carolyn Smith
Location: Residential back street. Three acres of lawn, gardens, meadows. Ten-minute walk to beaches; 100 yards to bike path. Ten-minute drive to National Seashore; five to galleries, shops, restaurants.
Open: April–December 1. Two-night minimum June–September week-

ends; three nights on Memorial Day, July 4, Columbus Day weekends.
Rates: $90 guest house queen or main inn first-floor queen. $105 main inn upstairs rooms. $135 cottage queen or main inn king. $150 guest house or barn suites. April–May 21 and October 12–December 1, $15 less.
♥ ❖ ◆ ✘ ⅙

From Massachusetts: "Perfect.... Absolutely gorgeous ... simply elegant ... I even asked for a recipe ... gracious, friendly hosts."

Devotees abound. First-timers feel like discoverers. Intentionally, it is "simply elegant" (request brochure with photos)—with casual, happy innkeepers, former Boston advertising executives. Now Dick is an acclaimed cook. Carolyn's interior design talents were recognized as one of the top 10 in a Waverly Country-Room-of-the-Year contest.

The main house, a Greek Revival built for a whaling captain, became a farm before being converted to an inn in 1953. The saltbox honeymoon cottage was a chicken coop. Major renovations were done in the 1980s. Since buying the inn in 1989, the Smiths have decorated with country antiques from the United States, France, England, and Denmark—and some reproductions. Rooms are light and airy with soft colors: peach, rose, or blue. "And to think we're here just because, upon departure as guests, we told the innkeepers that we were thinking of doing this some day!"

Bed and bath: Twelve rooms, private baths. Main inn first floor—queen bed; king bed, full bath with oversized tub, private entrance. Second floor—twin, double, or queen beds. Two barn suites (one has private deck), each with king/twin bed, living room, kitchen, full bath. Two guest house suites (room with queen can be added to either), each with queen bed, kitchen, living room, working fireplace, full bath; one has a loft with twin beds. In cottage—queen bed, full bath, kitchen/dining area, private patio, working fireplace.
Breakfast: Usually 8:30–9:30. Grand Marnier French toast, blueberry pancakes, strawberry shortcake, apple walnut raisin crepes with ice cream, homemade breads, fresh fruits. Served in garden patio or in sun porch breakfast room.
Plus: Hors d'oeuvres by the fire during BYOB cocktail hours. Individual thermostats in some rooms. Ceiling or window fans. Down comforters. Mints on pillow. Guest refrigerator. Bikes. Beach towels.

Guests arrive as strangers, leave as friends.

Bed & Breakfast Cape Cod Host #10

Falmouth, MA

Location: Peaceful. On an ocean inlet that is ideal for swimming, fishing, clam digging, windsurfing. Fifteen-minute walk to Martha's Vineyard ferry landing in Falmouth.

Reservations: Year round through Bed & Breakfast Cape Cod, page 118.
Rates: $85 per room.
🛥 🗡

A private beach. Ocean views from rooms. And your own private entrance.

"Little Jewel," named by the current owners, began in 1960 as a traditional ranch. Now it has guest wings on each end. Throughout, everywhere you look, there are antiques: a Victorian doll carriage, a cradle used as a magazine rack, Sandwich glass shards, a birdcage with dolls, French hats, china birds among bath crystals, decoys, gravy boats with freshly picked yellow roses. And potpourri, lots of lace, monogrammed and ironed sheets, geranium boxes, and many mirrors that reflect the nearby ocean.

"Guests come with great plans and, often, don't go anywhere! They sit, ponder, talk, look, and visit. Occasionally they might join us for clams on the half shell after we've been clamming. For us, this is a storybook come to life," says the the hostess, who wrote real estate ads. Her husband, who has also been in real estate, was in the Connecticut State Police.

Bed and bath: Those two oceanview rooms—one with double bed, sitting area, skylights; one with double bed, working fireplace. Each has a private entrance, private full bath, air conditioning, small refrigerator.
Breakfast: 8–10. Juice, fruit, baked goods, beverages. Served in dining room "always set with silver, crystal, and candles and often photographed" or on deck.
Plus: Warm-water outside shower. Fireworks over the water on weekends from June through early July.

Capt. Tom Lawrence House

508/540-1445
800/266-8139

75 Locust Street, Falmouth, MA 02540-2658

Host: Barbara Sabo-Feller
Location: Set back 100 feet from road that leads to Woods Hole. Within walking distance of restaurants, shops, bus station, and ferry shuttle. One block to bike path and bird sanctuary. Half mile to town beach with warm-water swimming.

Open: Year round except January. Two-night minimum June–October weekends. Reservations preferred.
Rates: Mid-June–mid-October $85–$104. Singles $10 less. $20 additional person. Off-season, $70–$85. MC, Visa.
♥ ♣ 🗡 ⅟

From England: *"We were so impressed . . . that we adjusted our itinerary to visit again the following week."* From New York: *"European charm with New England warmth. . . . Helped with plans for our wedding there in front of crackling fire."* From Germany: *"Tips about interesting places made our holidays unforgettable."* From Ohio: *"A golden anniversary gift, our first B&B, from our children. . . . Beyond expectations . . . restaurant menus . . . took us to ferry . . . like visiting a good friend."* From New Jersey: *"A beautifully kept house with service*

(Please turn page.)

and food to die for." From Cayman Islands: *"Welcomed us with a pot of tea. . . . Son was thrilled to play the Steinway."*

Barbara moved to New England from Europe in 1977. Eight years later she left Boston to open here—with much encouragement and background information shared by Dudley Hallett, the town historian. I heard him get pretty excited about the restoration of this 1861 sea captain's house, which is furnished with some hand-carved antique pieces from Germany and a Steinway baby grand piano. Breakfast specialties include homemade granola and, often, fantastic bread made with organic flour that Barbara purchases in 50-pound sacks and grinds right here.

Foreign language spoken: German.
Bed and bath: Six spacious first- and second-floor corner rooms with private shower baths. Laura Ashley or Ralph Lauren linens. King or queen beds (two with extra-long twin beds); some four-posters; three are canopied.
Breakfast: Full at 9, earlier if requested. Varies daily. Fresh fruit. Low-fat yogurt and homemade granola, an egg dish, quiche, crepes, pancakes or Belgian waffles with strawberry sauce, freshly whipped cream.
Plus: Ceiling fans in all bedrooms and fireplaced living room. Large deck overlooking backyard. Will meet guests at bus station. Ferry tickets, sightseeing, dining assistance.

The Inn at One Main Street   508/540-7469

One Main Street, Falmouth, MA 02540-2652

Hosts: Karen Hart and Mari Zylinski
Location: Can't miss it! With tall white fence, in historic district, "on the bend" where the road to Woods Hole begins. Very close to village green. Walk to ferry shuttle, beaches, dining, shopping, bike path.

Open: Year round.
Rates: Memorial Day–Columbus Day—twin beds, detached bath $75; en-suite bath $85; large turret room $95. Off-season $10 less. Singles $10 less. $20 additional person. MC, Visa.
♥ ❖ ✖ ✕

The Cape's youngest innkeepers, still in their twenties, may win an award for enthusiasm and zest. Everyone asks who did the decorating—in three weeks!—in this 1892 house. An inn for many years, it was vacant when Karen, who knew about innkeeping from her parents (who own The Village Green Inn, down the road), decided to return to her hometown from Colorado. She and partner/longtime friend Mari, an elementary school (substitute) art teacher, painted and freshened everything from ceilings to floors. They furnished—"it helped to have a pretty house to begin with"— with auction finds, some grandmothers' treasures, lots of lace, and, in the soft mauve-colored living room, sofas, wing chairs, and swags. Within their first season (1993), all of their very first guests either returned or referred others who came.

Bed and bath: Six rooms, all private shower baths, on first and second floors. King, queen, double, twins, or queen and twin beds.
Breakfast: 8–9. (Breakfast bag for early departures.) Freshly baked muffins, scones, coffee cakes, fresh fruit. Gingerbread pancakes with freshly whipped cream or orange pecan Belgian waffles.

Plus: Fireplaced dining room. Fans. TV in common room. Afternoon beverage and sweets. Large yard and shaded porch. Fresh flowers and mints in rooms. Suggestions and directions for everything including a very pretty not-so-well-known cycling route.

Mostly Hall Bed & Breakfast Inn 508/548-3786
27 Main Street, Falmouth, MA 02540-2652   800/682-0565

Hosts: Caroline and Jim Lloyd
Location: In historic district, across from the village green. Set back from the road on over an acre of lawn, trees, and shrubs. One mile to town beaches. Around corner from four-mile bike path to Woods Hole and Martha's Vineyard ferry. Two blocks from bus station.

Open: Year round except for January and first two weeks of February. Two-night minimum preferred May–October and weekends.
Rates: May–October $95–$115. Off-season $80–$85. Honeymoon and other packages. MC, Visa.
♥ ✻ ⚞

Unmistakably grand and gracious, even romantic, with 13-foot ceilings, Oriental rugs, antiques, dramatic floral wallpaper, and a cupola "travel room" (with videotapes). A B&B since 1980, the four-storied residence was originally built in 1849 by a sea captain for his New Orleans bride. It was named decades ago by an owner's youngster when he first saw the inside of the new family home.

The Lloyds, avid travelers who have bicycled in many states, including Hawaii, and several countries, including Mexico, Bora Bora, Kenya, and Costa Rica, changed careers in 1984. In Boston Caroline was a department store buyer and planning director; Jim, an avid gardener, was a computer corporate executive.

Foreign language spoken: Some German.
Bed and bath: Six spacious corner rooms, each with private en-suite shower bath and queen four-poster canopied bed.
Breakfast: Full at 9, or "breakfast to go" bags for early travelers. Juice, fresh fruit, homemade sweet breads or muffins. Entree might be Mexicali eggs, stuffed French toast, or cheese blintzes with warm blueberry sauce. Special diets accommodated—with advance notice, please. Served on the covered porch that wraps around all four sides or in living room.
Plus: Central air conditioning plus ceiling fans in most rooms. Sherry and afternoon refreshments. Library/game area. Piano. Gazebo with swing. Croquet. Badminton. Complimentary six-speed bicycles. Cookbook available.

From British Columbia: *"Our ideal prototype of a charming New England B&B experience. We cannot rave about it enough!"*

---

*B*reakfast is where the magic happens.

The Palmer House Inn

81 Palmer Avenue, Falmouth, MA 02540-2857

508/548-1230
800/472-2632
fax 508/540-1878

Hosts: Ken and Joanne Baker
Location: In residential historic district, adjacent to village green. Two blocks to shops and restaurants, three to bike path to Woods Hole. Close to bus station and ferry shuttles. One mile to town beaches.
Open: Year round. Two-night minimum holidays and special events. Some three-night minimums for certain special events.

Rates: June 16–October 15 $75 small double, $85 larger double, $105 queen, $115 corner room with queen bed, refrigerator. Excluding holidays and special events, May–June 15 and late October $10 less; November through April $20–$25 less. Third person $20–$30. Ten percent less for five or more nights. Honeymoon and holiday packages. Amex, CB, Diners, Discover, MC, Visa.
♥ ❖ ♦ ✈ ✗

There's a fountain in front. Inside the turn-of-the-century Queen Anne Victorian, there's original woodwork, old photographs, stained glass windows, lace curtains, silk flowers, potpourri, and lots of Victoriana. A B&B since 1982, the Palmer House is known for elaborate breakfasts that are never repeated as long as you are a guest.

Since coming here from Pennsylvania in 1990, the Bakers, grandparents and newlyweds who wanted to work together, have met guests from all over the world. Ken, the waiter and former truck driver, is pianist/gardener/cyclist/carpenter. Joanne, the chef, was in private practice as a certified public accountant for 13 years.

In residence: Victoria, a Yorkshire terrier, "enjoys playing Frisbee and will pose for photographs."
Bed and bath: Eight rooms with ceiling fans. Four on second floor (two have refrigerator). Up steep stairs to four (one with refrigerator, complimentary sodas and spring water, and candy) on third floor. All private baths (seven are shower without tub). Queen, double, or double and a twin bed.
Breakfast: At 9:15. Sometimes at 8 too. Freshly blended juices (recipe printed in *Gourmet*). Maybe poached pears in raspberry sauce, Finnish pancake with strawberry soup, orange cinnamon rolls, freshly baked breads, a special coffee blend, imported teas. Served on fine china and crystal in candlelit dining room. With classical music.
Plus: Fireplaced living room with upright piano and TV. Guest refrigerator. Mints on the pillow. Wraparound porch. Beach towels. Ferry tickets. Complimentary bikes. Directions to a spectacular (especially in spring) private garden. In winter, hot beverages until 10 p.m. November–May, 3 p.m. tea (extra charge and open to public).

Many B&Bs that allow smoking restrict it to certain rooms and/or public areas. Although some of those B&Bs that have the ✗ symbol allow smoking on the porch and/or patio, others do not allow smoking anywhere on the property.

Village Green Inn
508/548-5621

40 West Main Street, Falmouth, MA 02540-2678

Hosts: Linda and Don Long
Location: On the village green, surrounded by homes and churches dating to early 1700s. Minutes' walk to shops and restaurants, bus station, ferry shuttle; bicycle path to beaches and Woods Hole.
Open: April–December. Two-night minimum on holidays. Reservations recommended.
Rates: Memorial Day weekend–Columbus Day weekend $95 room, $115 suite. Off-season $80 room, $95 suite. Single $10 less. $20 third person.

♥ ♣ ✖ ⊬

> From England: *"Whilst on holiday, touring New England, we stayed at a number of B&Bs. . . . Village Green Inn was the top . . . tastefully decorated . . . 'good-bye hugs' a delightful surprise . . . mints in the room . . . lemonade on the veranda . . . breakfasts were the best anywhere. . . . Truly a relaxing place."*

Many letters about the Village Green Inn give long dissertations about the Longs. Don is one of the few Cape Cod innkeepers who is a native. He is also a skilled craftsman and builder. Linda is decorator, with attention to detail—swags and drapes in the living room, an unusual Victorian rocking chair, Grandfather's high chair in the dining room—and many plants. The hosts are both (early) retired educators who "feel challenged to find new ways to pamper guests, wonderful people—and we learn a lot about history, geography, and various careers." They moved in 1985 from East Falmouth to the 1804 Federal family house that was made into a Victorian in the late 1800s.

Bed and bath: Four large queen-bedded rooms (two on first floor) plus a two-room suite with a queen and a twin daybed. All with private baths (three with shower, two with tub/shower) and ceiling fans. Two rooms with working fireplace.
Breakfast: 8–9. Fresh fruit dishes include hot spiced fruit and tangy ambrosia. Cinnamon/apple-filled oven pancake, banana nut chocolate chip pancakes or cheesy egg puffs. Homemade rolls, breads, and muffins. Teas. Freshly ground coffee. In dining room; coffee on large wicker-furnished porch overlooking green.
Plus: Complimentary seasonal beverages. Magazines. Books. Games. Puzzles. Extra pillows. Chocolate treats. Will meet guests at bus station or ferry. "Breakfast bags" for early departures.

Woods Hole Passage
508/548-9575
800/790-8976
fax 508/540-9123

186 Woods Hole Road, Falmouth, MA 02540

Host: Cristina Mozo
Location: Peaceful. On Woods Hole Road, midway between (two miles to) Woods Hole and Falmouth.
Open: Year round. Two night minimum stay on weekends.
Rates: July–Labor Day $85–$95. Early September–mid-October and
Memorial Day weekend through June $75–$85. Mid-October–late May $65–$75. Singles and senior citizens 10 percent less. $20 third person. Winter packages. Amex, CB, Diners, MC, Visa.

◗ ♣ ♦ ✖ ⊬

(Please turn page.)

Contentment. For guests and the innkeeper too. On grounds with mature trees, a little fish pond, and berry bushes. The main structure is an 1875 carriage house that was converted to a private residence in 1952. And in 1991 Cristina, a graphics designer, realized her dream of working at home; she bought this one-year-old B&B and converted the attached barn by raising the roof (matching the angle and molding—it looks like it was built that way originally) and furnishing with lace curtains, collectibles, and restored pieces. A piano is in the large, comfortably furnished living room with raspberry sherbet–painted walls and a wonderful huge multipaned window overlooking the grounds. Throughout, all art is original.

As Cristina says, "This is the perfect place to do pencil drawing (my old passion!), to take long walks on the beach, to garden, and to paint." Many of her guests are associated with the Woods Hole Oceanographic Institute. And, of course, the island ferry dock is minutes away.

In residence: Camilla, 15-year-old daughter. Lady, "a very sweet dog." Fluff and Nina, "quiet and polite cats."
Foreign language spoken: Spanish.
Bed and bath: Five large rooms. All private shower baths with seats. In main house, room with antique double bed. In barn, two rooms on first floor, two on second (with cathedral ceilings), queen beds. One room has a twin bed also.
Breakfast: 8:30–10. Quiches. Home-baked breads, souffle, French toast, fresh fruit. Juices, tea, coffee. Buffet style. Eat in living room, on patio, or at picnic table on grounds.
Plus: Two rooms with ceiling fans; portable air conditioner available. Plenty of reading material. Fresh flowers. Glycerine soaps.

From Connecticut: *"Welcoming, charming, and helpful hostess . . . impeccably neat and clean . . . comfortable and quiet. . . . Worth staying for the breakfast alone!"*

The Elms   508/540-7232
495 West Falmouth Highway, West Falmouth, MA 02574-0895

Hosts: Betty and Joe Mazzucchelli
Location: On shore route (28A), within walking distance of Chapoquoit Beach. Half hour from departure point (Barnstable harbor) of whale watch trips. Ten minutes to Woods Hole and four public golf courses.

Open: Year round. Reservations required. Two-night minimum weekends, June–October. Three nights on long holiday weekends.
Rates: June 15–Columbus Day $65 shared bath, $85 private. Off-season $55 shared bath, $65 private.
♥ ✻ ✗

Betty was literally born into the business. Her mother had a B&B in Ireland. Still, it was a trip to Europe that spurred the Mazzucchellis to start their own in this country. Perhaps it is no coincidence that many Europeans find their way to The Elms. Those who have written to me from England and France rave about how much at home they felt—and about the food, the food, and the food. They appreciated local suggestions, including a secluded nature walk that leads to a breathtaking view of the ocean.

Betty, formerly a nurse in Boston, and Joe live in a Victorian house that was built in 1739 and added on to in 1850. "It has nooks, unexpected closets, and an alcove that only an old-house sleuth could explain." A large fireplace with crane is in the huge living room. A gazebo and flower and herb gardens are part of the award-winning landscaped grounds.

In residence: Annie, a Lhasa apso.
Bed and bath: Nine rooms, seven with private baths. Two first-floor rooms, one with twin beds and one with a double. Five second-floor rooms have private baths; two share a full bath. Some double four-posters, twin brass beds, and queens; all are antiques.
Breakfast: 8–9:15. Fresh fruits. Juice. Eggs Benedict, bananas Foster served on French toast, or crepes; homemade codfish cakes, Irish bread, blueberry and cranberry muffins. In plant-filled solarium that overlooks deck.
Plus: Sherry. Living room with TV. Deck and lawn furniture. Ironed eyclet-trimmed percale sheets. Will meet guests at Falmouth bus. Bicycles on a first-come basis. Winter "Stressless Weekends" with gourmet dinners.

Sjöholm Inn Bed & Breakfast   508/540-5706
17 Chase Road, West Falmouth, MA 02574-0430

Host: Barbara Eck
Location: In a quiet country area, on 2½ acres, one mile to Chapoquoit Beach. Minutes to Falmouth and Woods Hole.
Open: Year round except for several weeks in winter.
Rates: June 14–September 22, single $40–$50; sail loft $55; carriage house $85 private bath; main house double $65 shared bath, $80–$85 private. November 1–April 15, single $40; double $50 shared bath, $60 private. Rest of year, $40 single; double $60 shared bath, $70 private. $15 extra person in room. Senior citizens and stays over five days, 10 percent discount.
♥ ❖ ✈ ✕

"This is a very relaxed place with very few rules. Guests sit on the porch in their swimsuits. Cycling groups come here. Road racers know they get an early, light, special breakfast. Board sailors know how close we are to their favorite beach. Families feel comfortable. And we have a couple of rooms that are favorites for romantics. Some guests come all scheduled. Others let each day unfold, sleep until noon, or read."

In 1985 Barbara, a nurse and counselor, came here from Boston with her three teenagers. "The name of this inn, built 140 years ago as a farmhouse, was appealing, because I am Swedish on my father's side. It's quiet here. We go to sleep hearing the crickets and wake up hearing the birds."

In residence: The official welcomer is Amber, a female golden retriever. Oliver is a German short-hair pointer.
Bed and bath: Ten in winter, 15 mid-May through mid-October. Beds vary from a single twin to queen size. Some rooms sleep three or four. Private baths for four ground-floor rooms of carriage house and two upstairs in the inn. Four upstairs rooms in the inn share two shower baths. Four unheated (portable heaters available) sail loft rooms plus one four-person room (off the porch) share two baths.
Breakfast: All-you-can-eat buffet. Homemade quick breads, muffins, eggs, quiches, homemade jams, fruit. Homemade granola. Swedish dishes include

(Please turn page.)

rosettes, a deep-fried sugared pastry. Sunday special: Swedish pancakes. **Plus:** Intentionally, no clocks, TVs, or radios in rooms. Outdoor hot/cold water shower, also available for beachgoers late on checkout day. Line-dried linens. Big screened porch with library and games. Ceiling fans in rooms with private baths and common rooms. Cable TV, stereo, books, magazines. Picnic tables. Lawn chairs. Large grass lot for spontaneous ball games. Use of refrigerators, outdoor clotheslines. Beach permits ($3/day).

Dunscroft-By-The-Sea Inn and Cottage

24 Pilgrim Road, Harwichport, MA 02646-2304   508/432-0810
800/432-4345

Hosts: Alyce and Wally Cunningham **Location:** A few steps to private mile-long beach. (Water view from some inn rooms during winter.) In a lovely, quiet residential area. Within walking distance of village. Close to National Seashore and whale watch boat tours. **Open:** Year round. Three-night minimum stay June 20 through Labor Day.

Rates: Mid-June through mid-October, $85–$135 (depending on location in house, bath and bed arrangement, fireplace) queen or king. $25 extra person. $160 cottage. Off-season, $75–$115 queen or king, $125 cottage. Romance packages available. Amex, MC, Visa. ♥ ⁂ ♦ ✠

From Massachusetts: *"Relaxing, clean, homey, nicely decorated."* From Wisconsin: *"Delightful retreat, far enough from the madding crowd, yet within walking distance of enough amenities in the event you tire of silence . . . unassuming yet comfortable . . . lovely ample breakfast . . . friendly hostess with grace."*

Honeymooners, business guests, and vacationers (singles too) come to this weathered-shingled colonial, which has been an inn for 44 years. True to plan, when Alyce and Wally bought the inn in 1987, they were married here. Since, they have made some major renovations and decorated with floral fabrics, heart-shaped accessories, and family treasures. In Connecticut Wally had considerable experience in management for public utilities, and Alyce was a high school teacher of English. As owners of a Cape motel, they were inspired to become innkeepers. Now, in winter and spring, Wally serves in the Merchant Marine. Alyce is currently president of the Harwich Accommodations Association.

Foreign language spoken: Some French.
Bed and bath: Eight rooms plus one cottage; all private baths. First floor—king/twin option (off dining room) with shower bath; queen, full bath, fireplace, private exterior entrance; king canopied, full bath, private exterior entrance. Second floor—king or queen beds (all but one are corner rooms, two with canopied beds), en-suite full or shower baths. Cottage—king bed, living room with wood-burning fireplace, kitchen, color cable TV, full bath.
Breakfast: 8:30–10. Juice, fresh fruit, three or four homemade breads, custards, cottage pudding, fried apples, muffins, cheese molds, cereal, coffee, tea. Egg dishes with breakfast meats. Buffet style in dining room.
Plus: Air conditioning in some rooms. Complimentary sherry. Candy kisses. Wicker-furnished sun porch. Brick terrace, shaded lawn, umbrella tables. Guest refrigerator.

Harbor Walk

508/432-1675

6 Freeman Street, Harwichport, MA 02646-1902

Hosts: Marilyn and Preston Barry
Location: One house in from Route 28, right behind the house known for miles around for its roses. Five-minute walk to sandy beach, restaurants, and shops.

Open: April–November. Two-night minimum June–September.
Rates: July–September 15 $40–$45 shared bath, $50–$60 private bath. Off-season $10 less. $15 extra bed.
♥ ⬥ ⬥ ⬥ ♦ ⚸

"Our guests make every year a new experience. We love it! B&B is just as I imagined it would be when I was a physical therapist in Philadelphia. Every day I used to notice a wallpaper scene of Wychmere Harbor. Why not live near the real thing? We're golfers. And we wanted to be closer to our kids. So when Preston retired as a school administrator in 1978, we opened here, just across the road from the harbor. Although this is a Queen Anne house, it's a summer place, with floors painted navy blue. Walls are stenciled. Log cabin quilts give the color to the lace-canopied pencil-post beds. Breakfast is the time when everyone talks about their first-ever trip to an island, antiquing, shopping, the homes of the rich and famous, restaurants—plain and fancy—and whale watching, which, we found out, is like seeing magic."

Bed and bath: Six rooms, each with at least three windows, on first and second floors. Four with private en-suite shower baths; three have queen canopy beds (one on first floor has private sitting area), one has twin/king bed option. Room with queen canopied bed and one with two twin beds share a full bath. Rollaway available.
Breakfast: 8–10. Two fruit juices, fresh fruit platter or compote, home-baked goods (many requests for kuchen recipe), homemade granola, strawberry yogurt, cheese platter, coffee, tea. On the porch in summer, family style in dining room (with ceiling fan) in spring and fall.
Plus: Turndown service. Flannel sheets. Beach towels. Fresh flowers. Guest refrigerator. Will meet bus from Boston in Barnstable (15-minute drive.)

> From California: *"Cape Cod panache, in a great location.... Rooms are comfortable and airy ... wonderful breakfast." From North Carolina: "It feels like home, only better."*

The Inn on Sea Street

508/775-8030

358 Sea Street, Hyannis, MA 02601-4586

Hosts: Lois M. Nelson and J.B. Whitehead
Location: In a quiet residential neighborhood, 10 minutes from Route 6. Walking distance to beach, Kennedy Compound and Memorial, island ferries, bike rentals, restaurants.

Open: April–November.
Rates: $70 shared bath, $85–$95 private bath. $98 cottage. Singles $5 less. $15 additional guest. Amex, Discover, MC, Visa.
♥ ⬥ ⚐ ⚸

The beach, just steps away, may be a big draw, but the decor, the food, and the innkeepers themselves make this a favorite B&B; guests frequently leave with reservations for next year. The main inn, a Greek Revival house that Lois and J.B. had admired for 18 years, came on the market in 1983, the year

(Please turn page.)

that Lois's job as a director of airline in-flight services was phased out. Thus was born the first B&B in Hyannis. It's decorated with flair, with antique Persian carpets, a crystal chandelier in the foyer, a huge photograph of Grandfather over the mantel—all intentionally "not stuffily elegant." In 1992 more delightful rooms became available when the innkeepers renovated the French mansard-roofed house across the street. It features canopied beds, TVs hidden in armoires, its own living room, and Adirondack chairs on the wraparound porch. Behind that house, the very popular dollhouse of a cottage was opened in 1993.

J.B. is an antique car buff who drives a Model A truck with the inn's logo. When he is home from his job as a pilot with Continental Airlines, guests enjoy a ride in a 1953 yellow Packard convertible.

Bed and bath: Five main house rooms. First-floor room has double bed, private bath. Two second-floor rooms (both have canopied beds) share a bath across the hall. Third second-floor (air-conditioned) room is separated from its private bath by a back stairway. Down a flagstone path and around the barn is garden room with queen canopied bed, TV, private full bath. Across the street—four rooms, canopied queen beds, private baths. In white wicker–furnished cottage—living room with TV, queen bed, shower bath, kitchen.
Breakfast: 8–9:30. Fresh fruit. Homemade baked goods. Served to all guests in main inn's dining room and sun porch at tables set with sterling silver, china, linen, and fresh flowers.
Plus: Floor fans. TV in main inn. Beach towels. Use of refrigerator. Complimentary package of inn recipes. Book with guests' reviews of restaurants. Will meet guests at Hyannis airport or bus or train station.

Academy Place Bed & Breakfast 508/255-3181

8 Academy Place, P.O. Box 1407, Orleans, MA 02653-1407

Hosts: Sandy and Charles Terrell
Location: On the village green, at the edge of Orleans's shopping district. At Route 28 and Main Street. Ten minutes from the National Seashore; ⅜ mile to bike trail; 2½ miles to Skaket (charter fishing boats) and Nauset beaches.
Open: Memorial Day weekend through Columbus Day weekend.

Two-night minimum on weekends and holidays.
Rates: $55 double or twin beds, shared bath. $65 queen or $75 king beds, private bath. $15 extra bed in room. Five-night discount. Off-season (after Labor Day) 10 percent less. MC, Visa.
♦ ❖ ✗ ⅍

"Charles grew up in this authentic 1752 Cape Cod house when his parents ran it as a guest house (1955–75). We exposed beams, painted and papered with colonial colors, and opened as a B&B in 1989. Period furnishings include spool beds, spinning wheels, and a fainting couch. During much of the summer season, Charles commutes from Washington, D.C., where he is the national water quality specialist for the Soil Conservation Service."

When the Terrells were year-round Massachusetts residents, Charles was a college biology professor; Sandy, a registered nurse. Their fascinating house history (a copy is in each room) is complete with sketches and notes about the size of Cape houses—"small, to minimize heat loss." For vacationers they have compiled an extensive suggestion list including a winery, whale watching—"see Sandy for discount tickets"—and even a 1950s drive-in theater (which shows the latest movies).

Bed and bath: Five rooms. Two first-floor queen-bedded rooms overlook the village green; each has nonworking fireplace, private shower bath. Up steep, narrow steps to second floor with skylit guests' lounge, one king-bedded room with private shower bath. One room with two twin beds shares a full bath with double-bedded room. Rollaway available.

Breakfast: Usually 7:30–9:30. Buttermilk bran muffins, chocolate and other homemade breads, or blueberry coffee cake. Freshly brewed coffee or tea. Fruits and juices. By candlelight in beamed dining room.

Plus: Air conditioning in some rooms. Porch rockers. Rear sunken garden with picnic table and barbecue. TV in upstairs lounge. Hot or iced tea. Guest refrigerator. Table fans. Outside hot/cold shower.

> From Illinois: *"Blueberry muffins alone well worth the stay."* From Massachusetts: *"Just as you described it, and we loved it."* From Georgia: *"Comfortable . . . immaculate. . . . Sandy introduced us to beach plum jelly, which we loved . . . plenty of books and magazines to enjoy . . . warm and cheerful."*

Morgan's Way Bed & Breakfast   508/255-0831
Nine Morgan's Way, Orleans, MA 02653-3522   fax 508/255-0831

Hosts: Page McMahan and Will Joy
Location: Rural and peaceful. On four acres of landscaped grounds, one mile from Orleans center. Ten minutes to National Seashore, five to ocean and bay beaches.

Open: Year round. Two-night minimum stay.
Rates: $90 May–October. $75 November–April. $15 additional person in room. Singles $5 less.
♥ ⬛ ⁂ ◆ ✗ ⅄

This architect-designed Cape contemporary has cathedral ceilings; plenty of windows (many arched and half-circled); and a spacious downstairs living room with comfortable seating, porcelains, and original Cape art. An oak spiral staircase leads to an upstairs living room with piano, TV/VCR, wood-burning stove, library, small refrigerator, and a large window seat that overlooks a multilevel flower-filled deck and a 20-by-40-foot heated swimming pool. Beyond the extensive gardens—perennials, annuals, a kitchen garden, and a cut flower garden—are acres of woods and wetlands, a bird-watcher's paradise.

Page, the gardener, sings with several groups and has strong interests in nutrition, fitness, health and human services, and the arts. Will, an outdoorsman, is president of an engineering and surveying firm and is active in the community. They love sharing their property and Cape Cod.

In residence: Kitty-man is "an entertaining Himalayan."
Bed and bath: Two rooms. On first floor, one with queen bed, private shower bath, connects to pool and deck area. On second floor, very large queen-bedded room with private full bath overlooks pool and gardens.
Breakfast: 7:30–9:30. Varies. Fruit dish could be simmered plums with cream or honey walnut baked apples. Pancakes with maple syrup and sausages or Grand Marnier French toast with maple syrup and bacon. Carrot/pineapple bread or apple oat-bran muffins. Hot beverages. Yogurt,

(Please turn page.)

fruit, cereals, Egg Beaters always available. Garnished with fresh fruit, herbs, edible flowers.

Plus: Bedroom floor fans. Guest refrigerator. Mints on pillow. Map of back roads to Provincetown. Complimentary champagne for special occasions. Fresh flowers.

From New Jersey, Washington, Wisconsin, Virginia, Massachusetts, Bermuda: *"In a word, superb . . . gorgeous home, grounds, room . . . remarkable hosts . . . suggestions for every possible activity . . . relaxing . . . glorious breakfasts . . . a gem."*

Bed & Breakfast of Sagamore Beach

One Hawes Road, Box 205   508/888-1559
Sagamore Beach, MA 02562   fax 508/888-1859

Host: John F. Carafoli
Location: Peaceful. On a hill with view of Cape Cod Bay, all the way to Provincetown. On grounds with lawn and vegetable, herb, and flower gardens. Minutes' walk to sandy beach where you can walk for miles. Two miles from Sagamore Bridge ro-

tary; four to Sandwich center via Sagamore Bridge.
Open: Year round. Reservations required. All answering machine messages returned promptly.
Rates: $85 per room.
♥ ⛵ ⁂ ✗ ⌇

"With that smile, you oughta be on television." How often I have said that to John. And it just might be—now that his *Food Photography and Styling,* the first book on the subject, is published. John is a former art director for several publishing companies; his clients include many major food companies, newspapers, magazines, and advertising agencies. "For a quasi-Mexican menu I might make corn muffins, omelets with fresh herbs on a bed of tortilla with fresh salsa, served with cinnamon coffee—all on Fiesta-ware with a bright colored table cloth. When I tested recipes for a microwave cookbook, guests sampled an upside-down peach cake and a cranberry orange coffee roll—and then got to take them all with them."

What was a heatless century-old beach house on stilts when John purchased it in 1973 has been rebuilt and featured in *Better Homes and Gardens* and *Bon Appétit.* Everywhere there's the Carafoli treatment, with much use of fabric and color. Eclectic furnishings include the bedspread Grandmother brought from Italy. In the fireplaced living room there's a huge painting of Carmen Miranda "from my days as a fine artist." French doors lead to a wicker-furnished, flower-bedecked porch, where former guests had their wedding complete with a string quartet.

Bed and bath: Three second-floor rooms, each with an antique double bed (one mission oak, one brass, one four-poster), share one full bath plus, in summer, the big hot-water shower room under the deck.
Breakfast: Usually 8–9. "Healthy." Maybe pancakes, baked French toast made with two eggs plus three egg whites, fresh fruit, raspberry muffins. Sometimes, dairy-free menus. Presented on oak pedestal table or on porch with view of water.
Plus: Hammock. Fresh flowers. Welcoming beverage. Down comforters.

From Ireland: *"A haven."* From New Mexico: *"Perfect."* From Massachusetts: *"Wonderful food, friends, conversation, laughter."*

Captain Ezra Nye House

152 Main Street, Sandwich, MA 02563-2283

508/888-6142
800/388-2278
fax 508/888-2940

Hosts: Harry and Elaine Dickson
Location: In village center. Walk to Sandwich Glass Museum, Heritage Plantation, Thornton Burgess and Yesteryear's Doll museums. Less than a mile to beach.
Open: Year round. Two-night mini-
mum on weekends and holidays.
Rates: June–October, $80 private bath, $65 shared. November–May $10 less. Year round, $90 queen with fireplace, $85 suite, $15 third person.
♥ ❖ ◆ ✗ ⅄

> From New Jersey: *"Elegant but homey . . . attention to detail . . . knowledgeable about the town and antiquing opportunities."* From Canada: *"A treasure."* From New York: *"Just right."* From Massachusetts: *"Six breakfasts and menu never repeated . . . genuine caring."*

Harry and Elaine, world travelers, came to Sandwich on their honeymoon when Harry retired from 10 years as an engineer with GTE (preceded by 25 in the Air Force). "This 1829 sea captain's house on a main street in a small town, near the ocean and surrounded by greenery, gives the feeling of a private home. It is just what we were looking for as a B&B in 1986. There's so much to do right here that you can leave your car for a few days and just walk. Among memorable guests—New Zealanders who were married in our parlor."

They furnished with fine antiques, including some of Harry's family pieces and a collection of Chinese export china. Elaine's paintings (her studio is in the barn) have found a home here too. If you take a tour of the house, you'll see the first owner's name chalked under a roof beam, and the name and date of a subsequent owner etched by diamond on a window pane. Praise has appeared in *Glamour, Innsider,* and *Cape Cod Life*—as "best upper Cape B&B"—magazines.

Bed and bath: Six rooms. Plus first-floor suite with queen bed, sitting room with single sofa bed, private shower bath, outside entrance. Second floor—queen four-poster, working fireplace, private shower bath; three canopied queen-bedded rooms with private shower baths (one has claw-footed tub also). A double-bedded room and one with two three-quarter beds share a shower bath.
Breakfast: Sittings at 8 and 9, earlier by arrangement. Sample menu: orange juice, melon, individual cheese souffles, sausage, zucchini bread, lemon-ginger muffins, coffee and tea.
Plus: Fireplaced living room with piano. Den with games, books, TV, VCR. Large deck. Beach towels. Bicycles. Will meet guests at Sandwich train depot or bus stop.

Ocean Front

508/888-4798

273 Phillips Road, Sandwich, MA
Mailing address: Box 346, Sagamore Beach, MA 02562-0346

Host: Mary A. Blanchard
Location: On Cape Cod Bay with private beach, two miles from Sagamore Bridge rotary. Within walking distance of path along the Cape Cod Canal.
Open: April 15–October 31. Reservations required.
Rates: $55 double bed, $75 king bed, $95 suite.
♥ ◢ ❖ ◆ ✗ ⅄

(Please turn page.)

"'Well, Mary, what are you going to do with your big beautiful home?' my friends asked." And that's how I got the idea of B&B. I can't believe it Bernice, yesterday someone called from Hong Kong with your book in hand. Guests come from Sicily, Rome, and Australia. Some who come to see the Cape just want to stay right here!"

Mary, who grew up on a dairy farm, used to have a restaurant in a small town near Boston. She bought this Cape Cod weathered-shingled house in 1975 and over a 10-year period did extensive remodeling to take advantage of the views. Wicker furnishings add to the summery feeling. Year round, a Christmas tree is in the living room. "And for another year I am renting a six-foot Pinocchio from my grandson."

Foreign language spoken: Italian.
Bed and bath: Three rooms, all private baths. Suite that encompasses an entire floor has a queen and a twin bed, full bath, and sliding glass doors that lead onto a large oceanfront balcony. On lower level, room with king bed, shower bath; room with double bed, shower bath. Rollaway available.
Breakfast: 8–10. Juice, fresh fruit, muffins, toast, and Mary's almost-famous hot cinnamon bread; coffee. Served in dining room overlooking ocean.
Plus: Living room with wood stove, TV, organ. Latticed and flower-bedecked patio. Platform swing facing ocean. Huge decks. Beverages. Babysitting. Use of refrigerator.

> From Massachusetts: *"The panoramic view is spectacular (an understatement)— with the open Atlantic ocean, ocean liners and many ships and sailboats entering and leaving the Cape Cod Canal . . . to the right, sand dunes of Sandy Neck Beach, to the left the White Cliffs of Plymouth. . . . Low tide is a special treat with its huge sandbars for walking. . . . In the morning, beautifully set table, delicious home-baked goods. . . . Immaculately maintained. . . . Mary Blanchard is a very rare person—warm, kind, and compassionate. . . . Little slice of Heaven on Earth."*

Seth Pope House 1699   508/888-5916
110 Tupper Road, Sandwich, MA 02563

Hosts: John and Beverly Dobel
Location: Residential area of road that connects Route 6A and Route 130. On a treed acre overlooking salt marsh. Five-minute walk to museums and gristmill. Short drive to picturesque boardwalk across marshes to beach or to marina.
Open: Year round. Two-day minimum, July–Labor Day weekends.
Rates: Tax included. $75 Memorial Day–Labor Day. $55–$65 off-season.
♥ ⌂ ❀ ✗ ✂

"How long have you lived here?" ask many guests when they enter this rare 295-year-old five-quarter Cape colonial. The house has seven fireplaces (one with beehive oven), gunstock beams, wide board floors that tilt a bit, and some original hand blown glass window panes. After the Dobels, parents of five grown children, moved from Michigan, they, too, were delighted to find that their antiques looked like they belonged "in this historic, perfect-for-B&B house in the perfect location that has everything!" Beverly's ancestors were early Cape Cod settlers, and John was personnel manager with Ford Motor Company. They added many "inn touches" and opened as a warm, inviting B&B in 1990.

Foreign language spoken: A little Portuguese. "We lived in Brazil for two years."
Bed and bath: Three second-floor rooms. All with private shower baths. Twin pineapple four-posters, Victorian queen, or queen pencil-post bed (in room with exposed beams). Rollaway available.
Breakfast: 8:30. Fresh fruit, juice, cereal, homemade banana nut muffins, French toast or savory eggs, coffee or tea. Served in candlelit beamed dining area.
Plus: Cable TV. Wood stove in keeping room. Fresh flowers. Slate patio surrounded by old stone walls and an herb garden.

The Summer House   508/888-4991

158 Main Street, Sandwich, MA 02563-2232

Hosts: David and Kay Merrell
Location: In historic district. Walk to restaurants, museums, shops, pond, and gristmill. One mile to Heritage Plantation and beach.
Open: Year round. Two-night minimum on summer weekends and holidays.

Rates: Double occupancy. $65 shared bath. $75 private bath. November–Memorial Day weekend $10 less. Singles $10 less. $10 rollaway. Amex, Discover, MC, Visa.
♥ ♣ ♦ ✈ ✂

From California: *"We planned to stay for one night and extended to three . . . charming and creative decor. . . . Exquisite quilts . . . a jewel . . . a labor of love. . . . As for Dave and Kay, I wish we were neighbors."* From Florida: *"Traveled around New England . . . breakfasts were superior to places where I paid $175 per night."* From New Jersey: *"I love everything about Summer House . . . checkerboard dining room floor . . . four-poster beds . . . the front porch with its glorious climbing rose just invites you to 'sit a spell.'"*

Conclusion: Summer House guests are ecstatic. The Greek Revival house, built in 1835, features original wavy handmade window glass, detailed moldings, latch hardware, and seven fireplaces. For 10 years while David, a senior scientist, and Kay, an executive secretary, were working for a Los Angeles aerospace firm, they planned on becoming innkeepers. "All that time we collected antiques, Kay made quilts, and in 1988 we took early retirement." Creative changes are constant. And so is the list of delighted guests.

Bed and bath: Five rooms, four with working fireplace. First floor—queen four-poster, private attached shower bath. Second floor—full bath shared by one room with queen bed and one with antique pineapple king/twin four-poster. Queen-bedded room shares shower bath with king/twin four-posters (without fireplace). Rollaway available.
Breakfast: 8–9:30 or by special arrangement. (Prebreakfast coffee on sun porch.) Entree may be quiche, stuffed French toast, strata, eggs Benedict, crepes, or pancakes; garnished with garden vegetables and herbs. Freshly ground coffee. Teas. Fruit juices. Fresh fruit. Two freshly baked items. Served in plant-filled dining room at tables for two set with floor-length cloths, Victorian butter servers, pressed glass plates.
Plus: Afternoon tea (brewed in antique silver pots) with baked goods; served in garden, on enclosed wicker-furnished sun porch, or in guests' room. Beach

(Please turn page.)

towels. Hammocks in secluded garden, "a haven." Umbrella table. Window fans. Transportation to/from local train depot or Sagamore Circle bus. Hints from Dave about scenic jogging routes. Champagne for special occasions.

Bed & Breakfast in Truro   508/349-6610
Castle Road, Box 431, Truro, MA 02666-0431

Host: Tonie Strauss
Location: On a winding picturesque Cape road. Between ocean and bay, next door to the Truro Castle Hill Center for the Arts, in a quiet, rather sparsely settled residential area.

Open: May–October. Two-night minimum stay. Reservations required.
Rates: $75 per room.
♥ ⬛ ✹

Tonie's flair means that the house is comfortable and she welcomes you graciously, but there's nothing formal about the 200-year-old captain's house set among lilac bushes, apple trees, and rolling lawns. Tonie is an abstract colorist who paints in oil. She is happy to show you her studio as well as tell you the history of the house.

"Most guests are seeking a quiet time. They come here because Truro leaves the hectic pace and fast-food concessions behind. They usually leave by 10, enjoy the Cape, come back to get ready for dinner, and retire early."

In residence: Tonie breeds wirehaired dachshunds and has two champion females, Lucy and Sophie, and a toy Pekinese named Lolly.
Foreign languages spoken: French and German.
Bed and bath: Two rooms share one guest bath. Private guest entrance and up a captain's staircase to one room with twin beds and another with a double bed. Furnished eclectically with antiques and "Cape decor." (No food in rooms, please.)
Breakfast: 8–9:30. A specialty such as fruit soup. Fresh fruit and juices, muffins, yogurts, cheese, coffee. Served in a stylish European manner—"no plastic ever"—on the covered porch or indoors at a wonderful big table.
Plus: Bedroom fans. Comforters. Duvets. Flowers. "Mints, of course." Hammock under the apple trees. Landscaped grounds.

> From Massachusetts: *"Tasteful furnishings . . . European-style hospitality . . . quiet and private setting—restorative."* From Georgia: *"Peaceful porch . . . delicious breakfast . . . a lovely introduction to Cape Cod."*

Parker House   508/349-3358
P.O. Box 1111, Truro, MA 02666-1111

Host: Stephen Williams
Location: In the center of this tiny beautiful town. Two miles from Cape Cod National Seashore ocean or bay beaches. Ten minutes' drive to Provincetown (north) or Wellfleet (south). Between the Cobb Memorial Library and the Blacksmith Shop restaurant. Near sailing, tennis, golf,

Audubon sanctuary, whale watches, art galleries, restaurants.
Open: Year round. Two-night minimum on summer weekends.
Rates: $50 single, $55 double, $65 triple. $5 surcharge for single nights and second bed.
⬛ ⁙ ✹ ⊬

The classic full Cape house is filled with history, ancestors' portraits, books, period furniture, and wide painted floors.

"My great-grandmother bought this place for $4,500 in 1920. I have been restoring it over many years, and it's getting there! For the last four years I have been carrying on the B&B tradition established in the 1980s by my mother, Jane Parker, a world traveler and writer."

Stephen, official B&B host/baker, is the town's building commissioner and agent to the board of health. "Guests enjoy a secluded walk, the clean beaches, and the history of the area. Some find that the house offers the perfect opportunity just to think or to curl up and read."

In residence: "One gray cat, a shy female hunter, permanently grounded after getting hit by a car."

Bed and bath: Two second-floor rooms, each with (new) sink, share a full bath with claw-foot tub under a skylight and a shower. A (reinforced) four-poster double and a day couch/single bed in each room.

Breakfast: 7:30–10:30 "to the soft chimes of a ship's clock." Homemade muffins and coffee cakes. Breads for toast. Jams. Cereals. Juice. Fresh fruit. Coffee or tea. By dining room bay window or on screened porch. Can last for hours.

Plus: Line-dried sheets. Private off-street parking. Recipe for orange coffee cake.

Guests wrote: *"Superb accommodations, particularly in the registers of music, atmosphere, directional and transportation resources, and engaging conversation."*

The Towle House Bed & Breakfast

P.O. Box 71, North Truro, MA 02652   508/487-9678

Hosts: Dawn and Harry Towle
Location: On five acres within the National Seashore boundaries. Set on a hill with view of ocean ¾ mile away. Within minutes' walk of the Cape Cod Light and the Highland Golf Course.

Open: Year round. Two-night minimum.
Rates: First-floor room $110; $95 if bath shared with upstairs ($85) room. $50 extra person in adjoining room.
🐾 ✈ 🍴

The National Park Service considers this 1760 vintage full Cape house to be the least altered of the antique homes in the park. The Towles—Harry is a retired biologist who serves on the conservation commission; Dawn has restored several houses and is in the construction business—came for their first Cape vacation 12 years ago. "We were living in a 19th-century house in New Jersey but had not seen such a collection of wonderful old structures as the Cape has. Within four days we bought this structurally sound 12-room L-shaped gem from descendants of the original owners. We put in central heat and redecorated; we furnished with family pieces, many antiques, and some reproductions—and we kept all the handmade doors and latches and wide pine floors. The layout is perfect for B&B, allowing for visiting and plenty of privacy."

A recently completed addition has a 30-foot long kitchen and, for Dawn's oil painting and antiques refinishing, a glorious 800-square-foot studio complete with great ocean view (request a tour). Harry is an ardent surf fisherman and gardener. Word of their warm hospitality (and memorable conversations) brings many relatives and friends of former guests.

(Please turn page.)

Bed and bath: Two rooms. On first floor, one room with double bed and private fireplaced living room, plus single bed in adjoining room for person traveling in same party. First-floor bath with tub and shower shared with second-floor room that has two twin beds.

Breakfast: Usually 8–9. Juice, cold or hot cereal, muffins made with wild blueberries from property, or hosts' own organically grown raspberries or strawberries. Pancakes or French toast, eggs any style, bacon or ham. Special diets accommodated.

Plus: Screened porch. Two guest parlors; one with TV, VCR, wood-burning Vermont cast iron stove.

The Marlborough

320 Woods Hole Road, Woods Hole, MA 02543

508/548-6218
800/320-2322
fax 508/457-7519

Host: Diana M. Smith

Location: Set back from the road on a wooded half acre in a residential area. One mile from town center; 2½ miles to Falmouth. Five minutes to Martha's Vineyard and Nantucket ferries or to bus terminal for New York or Boston.

Open: Year round.

Rates: Memorial Day–Columbus Day $85–$105. October–November and April–May $75–$95. December–March $65–$85. Singles $5 less. Additional person $20. MC, Visa.
♣ ♦ ✗ ⊁

From New York: *"A tranquil, creative atmosphere.... Keeps pulling at my heart strings for return visits.... Early-morning laps with freshly ground coffee waiting at poolside ... a sense of being in heaven ... breakfast is a culinary feast ... big oversized towels."* From Ontario: *"Candlelight breakfasts were romantic."* From Texas: *"We are two 65-year-old ladies ... our first B&B ... a haven, sparkling clean ... charming ... well versed in the area."* From Kansas: *"Took picture of breakfast table before we took a bite."* From Maryland: *"Provided at-home attention for us and our two young daughters."* From Texas: *"Fresh-baked cookies in the evening ... grounds were immaculate ... classical music ... much laughter."* From Massachusetts: *"Picture-perfect room, felt very special and pampered."* From Scotland: *"Obviously the right person in the right job."*

The accolades are endless for the "just right" innkeeper, a longtime area resident, who lives in a 1930s Cape Cod shingled cottage that is decorated with wallcoverings of paper or fabric, collectibles, handmade quilts, cross-stitch samplers, and hooked rugs. Before buying The Marlborough in 1992, Diana had experience as a mother, as a community service worker, and as a "serious bicycle tourist" (who stayed at inns), and as manager of an accounting firm's computer operations.

In residence: Ms. Muffins, a short-haired cat.

Bed and bath: Five air-conditioned rooms on two floors (steep stairway to second-floor dormered rooms); all private modern baths, four with shower only. Rooms have a double and a twin bed; a double bed (one with private entrance); a queen and two twin beds; or a queen with a double daybed, heated towel bar in bath. New: Poolside accommodation with gazebo sitting room.

Breakfast: 8–9:30. Maybe baked Cortland apple stuffed with homemade granola, dates, nuts, and honey, topped with granola, homemade cider syrup,

whipped cream. Or French bread marinated in egg, sauteed in butter, topped with fresh fruit, whipped cream, dash of nutmeg. Served by the pool or parlor fireplace. "Sack surprise" for early ferry departures.
Plus: Kidney-shaped swimming pool. TV in parlor. Coffee and tea always available. Paddle tennis. Gazebo. Hammock. Fresh flowers. Special occasions acknowledged. Spontaneous sightseeing tours or walks along ocean. Directions to "a magic sunset place." Off-season—late-afternoon cream tea; high tea on Sundays. Always bike and walking route suggestions.

Bed & Breakfast Cape Cod Host #71

Yarmouth Port, MA

Location: On a residential side street, a marked "scenic way" in this picturesque village. Four blocks to freshwater lake; half a mile to bay beaches. Within walking distance of fine restaurants and shops. Ten-minute drive to Hyannis and the Martha's Vineyard and Nantucket ferries.
Reservations: Available year round

with some seasonal restrictions through Bed & Breakfast Cape Cod, page 118.
Rates: Queen bed $85 year round. Other rooms $70 in season; $65 October 12–May 25. Single in twin-bedded room $50 year round. Third person $15. ♥ ♯ ♨ ✈

Maybe you, too, will join those who comment on this traditionally furnished Cape house, built in 1800, which "looks like a painting." Among its fans are many B&B guests who leave with the feeling that they have a Cape Cod home to come back to. And it has been a highlight on house tours conducted to raise restoration funds for the historic West Barnstable courthouse.

The impeccable restoration was done by the friendly and knowledgeable hosts, a former senior citizens' services director and her husband, who worked in the industrial sales field. "After all those family vacations on the Cape, these retirement years—combined with our guests from all over the world—are a dream come true," say the former Connecticut residents, who now work in retailing and at a conference center.

In residence: One small dog.
Bed and bath: Three air-conditioned rooms, each with private full bath. One first-floor room with queen bed, fireplace. On second floor—room with two twin beds; one with a double bed and a single bed.
Breakfast: 8:30–9:30. Juice, fresh fruit, baked apple or homemade muffins or breads. Serve in fireplaced dining room.
Plus: Screened porch. Parlor TV. Three working fireplaces. Use of grill.

> From Canada: *"Breakfast was beyond all expectations."* From New York: *"Totally charming . . . clean and comfortable. . . . Hosts were gracious, easygoing, informative, efficient, cheerful."* From Nebraska: *"Exceptional."*

Unless otherwise stated, rates in this book are for two and include breakfast in addition to all the amenities in "Plus."

Liberty Hill Inn

77 Main Street, Yarmouth Port, MA 02675-1709

508/362-3976
800/821-3977

Hosts: Beth and Jack Flanagan
Location: On Old King's Highway (Route 6A), set back on a little hill (site of Revolutionary War rallying point) with views of Barnstable Harbor. Across from a conservation area. Walk to fine restaurants and antiques and crafts shops. Ten-minute drive to Hyannis.
Open: Year round. Two-night minimum on holiday weekends.

Rates: Memorial Day–Columbus Day $115 twin beds or queen, $95 double. $135 bridal suite. $20 extra person. Singles $70. Five-night honeymoon package $575. Off-season $60 and $55, $75 bridal suite; one-night getaway package $99 including dinner for two. Amex, MC, Visa.
♥ ♨ ♦ ✗

From New Jersey: *"I had the pleasure of experiencing a B&B, a kind of establishment I had heard and read about. The service at Liberty Hill was extra special, the rooms well kept and beautifully furnished with lovely antiques and quilts, the food very satisfying, and the atmosphere very homey and friendly. We felt truly welcome."*

Although Beth and Jack had had experience restoring three houses, when it came time for a "retirement occupation" in 1987, they bought an 1825 shipowner's Greek Revival house that had already become a B&B. On the National Register—and featured in *Colonial Homes*—it features a columned veranda, floor-to-ceiling windows, and Queen Anne antiques.

Jack had been an auditor and in real estate in the New York/New Jersey area. (He is a Cape broker.) Beth was an actress and worked in international college admissions. Now the Flanagans conduct seminars for prospective innkeepers. And they give guests great suggestions that include an old-time soda fountain, historic houses, and nature trails.

Bed and bath: Five large rooms with private baths. One first-floor air-conditioned room, three steps up from driveway, with two twin beds and oversized stall shower bath with seat. On second floor, three rooms with sitting areas: two rooms have queen beds and stall shower baths; one is air conditioned with a four-poster double bed and full bath. Third-floor air-conditioned bridal suite has a king bed, nonworking fireplace, and full bath. Rollaway available.
Breakfast: 8–10. Includes recipes tested for Beth's B&B book. Fruit, apple strudel, quiche, meat and cheese casseroles, baked eggs, omelets, French toast, home-baked breads. Cheese, fresh fruit, juice, coffee, tea, and decaf. At dining room tables set with lace.
Plus: Cocktail hour. Tea and cookies on holiday weekends. Veranda chairs. Croquet lawn. Terraced garden. Cable TV in common room. Library includes area restaurant menus and maps. Dinners by arrangement.

*H*eard all over New England: *"Most guests are surprised at all our area has to offer."*

One Centre Street Inn   508/362-8910

One Centre Street, Yarmouth Port, MA 02675

Hosts: Stefanie and Bill Wright
Location: Residential. In historic district, on corner of Route 6A; across from antiques shop. Fifteen-minute walk to "wonderful restaurants," or to little-known beach with great boardwalk and sunsets. Half mile to well-known Parnassus Bookstore for old and new titles.

Open: Year round. Two-night minimum with summer Saturday nights.
Rates: May 15–October 15, shared bath $65 or $75; private bath $85, $95, $110 (suite). Extra person $15. Off-season (all private baths) $65, $75, $85, $110 with fireplace. Amex, Discover, MC, Visa.
♯ ♣ ♦ ⅍

Every day recipes are requested and granted at this restored 1824 colonial inn. Guests often say it is "even nicer than we expected." It has 10-foot first-floor ceilings; refinished pine floors; interesting oak, pine, and mahogany period pieces; some stenciled rooms; overstuffed living room chairs; and, in the dining room, a frequently admired Hoosier cabinet and an 80-inch-long country table.

Stefanie's enthusiasm is contagious—for the Cape, food, the community, vegetable gardening, physical fitness (she taught in New Jersey), and innkeeping. Bill, the friendly evening and weekend cohost, worked for Mobil Corporation and is now plant engineer for Cape Cod Potato Chips. Their B&B, appreciated by families, couples, and many international travelers, evolved in 1987 from their dream to open a restaurant.

In residence: In hosts' quarters—William, age 10; Sarah, 9; Jessica, 8; Dillon ("maybe the only child guests meet"), 3.
Bed and bath: Seven rooms. "Next-door" house—on first floor: queen bed, private shower bath; suite with high double four-poster, living room with double bed, private full bath. Main house—first-floor suite has queen bed, den with double futon and working fireplace, private shower bath. On second floor: queen-bedded room with private shower bath; facing main road, room with a double and a single shares shower bath with double-bedded room; steep back staircase to quiet double-bedded room tucked under eaves, small private full bath.
Breakfast: 8:30–9:30; earlier for ferry-catchers. Fresh fruit. Juices. Homemade breads, muffins, or cakes. Homemade granola. Quiche, pancakes, cheese/vegetable frittata, or Belgian waffles. Buffet style. In dining room with wood stove.
Plus: Parlor piano. Games, puzzles, children's books. Beverages. Suggestions for shoreline walks. Fresh flowers. Horseshoes—"Bill is always looking for partners." Complimentary bikes. Large barn for bikes.

Can't find a listing for the community you are going to? Check with a reservation service described at the beginning of this chapter. Through the service you may be placed (matched) with a welcoming B&B that is near your destination.

The Wedgewood Inn

83 Main Street, Yarmouth Port, MA 02675

508/362-5157
508/362-9178

Hosts: Milt and Gerrie Graham
Location: On route 6A, in the historic district. On two landscaped acres with patios and gardens. An eight-minute drive to island ferries or whale watch boats. Bikes, nature trails, beaches.
Open: Year round. Advance reservations recommended.

Rates: Per room. $130 double with working fireplace, $105 or $115 without. $140 suite, $150 with sitting room. $15 rollaway. November 1–June 1 except holidays, off-season rates available. Amex, Diners, MC, Visa.
♥ ❖ ♦ ✖

"Send me *there!*" said the Boston television interviewer as I was commenting on slides of B&Bs being shown for Valentine's Day suggestions. The touch of elegance in the area's first architect-designed house—built in 1812—was also seen on a *Colonial Homes* cover. And the inn has received a "Best of Cape Cod" award.

Milt, a former professional football player (who now does some mountain climbing), was with the FBI for 20 years. Gerrie taught school in Darien, Connecticut. In 1986, when they saw this inn with working fireplaces, spacious rooms, and wide board floors, the "what next" decision was made. Every guest room has upholstered wing chairs, an antique or handmade bed (many are pencil post), and a handmade quilt—all enhanced by fresh flowers, a late-afternoon tea tray, and fresh fruit. Lovely gardens and a gazebo are on the grounds.

In residence: Tasha, a Shih Tzu dog, "enjoys guests from a distance."
Bed and bath: Six air-conditioned rooms; no two have adjoining walls. All private baths; most have hand-held showers. First-floor suites have fishnet-canopied queen beds, private screened porch, sitting area, working fireplace, full bath. On second floor—two queen-bedded rooms with working fireplace; one room with a double and a twin daybed. Entire third floor (suite) with private exterior entrance accessed by narrow staircase; queen bed and, in the sitting room, a single bed. Rollaway available.
Breakfast: 8–9:30; other times by arrangement. French toast, scrambled eggs on puff pastry, or maybe Belgian waffles. Homemade and English muffins. Cereal. Yogurt. Served on tables for two set with china and flowers in dining room with handcrafted Windsor chairs.
Plus: Individual thermostats. Patio. Gazebo. Lawn seating.

KEY TO SYMBOLS
♥ Lots of honeymooners come here.
⚶ Families with children are very welcome. (Please see page xii.)
⚐ "Please emphasize that we are a private home, not an inn."
❖ Groups or private parties sometimes book the entire B&B.
♦ Travel agents' commission paid. (Please see page xii.)
✖ Sorry, no guests' pets are allowed.
⚕ No smoking inside *or* no smoking at all, even on porches.

Martha's Vineyard
_____ Reservation Services _____

The following reservation services represent B&Bs on Martha's Vineyard:
Bed & Breakfast Cape Cod, page 118
Destinnations, page 118
House Guests Cape Cod and the Islands, page 119

Martha's Vineyard B&Bs

Breakfast at Tiasquam   508/645-3685
RR 1, Box 296, off Middle Road, Chilmark, MA 02535-9705

Host: Ron Crowe
Location: At the top of a hill, surrounded by farms, ponds, woodlands, rolling pastures, scenic roads. Four miles to Menemsha and Lucy Vincent Beach. (Note: Transportation is necessary. See "Plus" below.)
Open: Year round. Two-night minimum for summer and fall Saturdays.
Rates: Early June–mid-September $105–$185. Mid-April–early June and mid-September–October $90–$160. November–mid-April $70–$120. Ages 2–12 $25; two or more, $20 each; under 2 free.
♥ ⅰ⅟ ☼ ✗ ⅟

From Massachusetts: *"A little bit of heaven tucked away . . . presided over by inimitable Ron Crowe . . . 'breakfast' takes on a heightened meaning."*

Two years after Ron, a Massachusetts native, "discovered" the Vineyard during a bicycling vacation with his son, he found this site and left his 19-year position as director of Bowdoin College's dining service. He built the house in seven months, during the 1987 winter of record island snow.

One guest dubbed this built-to-be-a-B&B "the perfect place." It has an enormous bow roof, 20 skylights, many sliding doors, and a two-storied greenhouse atrium. Even with all the public space, there's the feeling of home and privacy. Outstanding craftspeople handcrafted much of the furniture, a graceful spiral staircase, the pottery sinks, 32 paneled cherry doors, and cabinets and woodwork. And there's Ron, the convivial host and cook.

Bed and bath: Eight quiet carpeted rooms; many with skylights, two with private baths. Two handicapped-accessible first-floor rooms, one queen-bedded and one with one twin bed, share a full bath. On second floor, two rooms duplicate first-floor bed and bath arrangement. The master room has queen bed, cathedral ceiling, ceiling fan, wood stove, two skylights, private full bath with two-person Jacuzzi. Another has a queen bed, private full bath, four skylights. Two-room suite has a room with two double beds, one with queen bed plus a single futon, connecting doors, private deck, private full bath (shared bath if two rooms used individually). Rollaway for children.
Breakfast: 7–9:30. "Practically anything you want." Fresh corn (in season), blueberry pancakes with Vermont maple syrup, cinnamon-raisin French toast, fresh fish if available. At kitchen counter, at dining table, or on deck.
Plus: Two outdoor hot/cold showers. Plenty of deck space. Lucy Vincent Beach passes. Beach towels. Ron has one rental car, which includes pickup service at airport or ferry.

*A*ccording to many hosts: *"Guests come with plans and discover the joys of hammock sitting."*

The Arbor   508/627-8137

222 Upper Main Street, P.O. Box 1228, Edgartown, MA 02539

Host: Peggy Hall
Location: Six-minute walk into town, 10 minutes to harbor. On the bicycle path. Shuttle bus to downtown Edgartown, South Beach, Oak Bluffs, Vineyard Haven (in season) stops at front door.
Open: May–October. Three-day minimum July–August; two-day minimum May–June and September–October.
Rates: June 15–September 15, single bed $80. Double, semiprivate bath $85 or $90. Queen $95 or $115 shower bath, $135 full bath. Off-season, $55–$95. MC, Visa.

♥ ❖ ♦ ✈ ⅙

The weathered-shingled house, built in 1880, was moved from the adjoining island of Chappaquiddick in 1910 and added on to through the years. Since Peggy took it over in 1979, she has been in a position to share her love affair with the island and its hideaways. Rooms are decorated with painted walls, stenciling, shutters, ball fringe curtains, vintage furniture, and, in the living room, chintz-covered sofas. "When English guests say it looks like an English country cottage, I feel I succeeded."

It's all because she played an experimental game that asked what you wanted to be doing in 10 years. "The children were grown, so the time was right. After training real estate brokers for 20 years, I can say that work has never been so much fun. . . . I like to tell about the two guests who, upon arrival, walked and talked as though they were in a contest to finish first. By the time they left, they were strolling casually. I told them they would probably be picked up for loitering when they returned to Manhattan. . . . We get a great mix of people—young, retirees, singles, couples, and international travelers too."

Bed and bath: Ten rooms, eight with private baths (four shower only, four are full). Six are queen-bedded rooms. One has a pair of twin beds. One cozy single room. Two double-bedded rooms share a full bath. Designer linens.
Breakfast: 8–10. Juice, homemade corn and other breads or muffins, tea or coffee. Buffet style with linens, cloth napkins, silver service. Eat in fireplaced beamed dining room, outside at umbrella tables, or in the courtyard.
Plus: Adjoining dining room is living room with vaulted ceiling and balcony library. Enclosed outdoor hot/cold shower. Hammock for two suspended from trees. Guest refrigerator. Setups (ice, glasses, mix) 5–7 p.m. Bicycle rack. Antiques shop in former garage.

> Guests wrote: *"Caring hostess who knows her island! Joyful and restful visit . . . Super place either for being alone or for finding people to be with . . . cozy . . . like home."*

In this book a full bath includes a shower and a tub. "Shower bath" indicates a bath that has all the essentials except a tub.

The Shiverick Inn

508/627-3797
800/723-4292
fax 508/627-8441

P.O. Box 640, Pease's Point Way
Edgartown, MA 02539-0640

Hosts: Martin P. and Denise M. Turmelle
Location: With residences and one inn as immediate neighbors. One block from Main Street's dining, shopping, historic area. Three blocks from waterfront.
Open: Year round. Two-night minimum on weekends and June 16–Oc-

tober 12; three nights on major holidays.
Rates: June 16–October 12 $170–$180, $200 private terrace, $225 suite. October 13–June 15 $120–$135, $160 suite. Amex, Discover, MC, Visa.
♥ ♣ ♦ ✗ ✍

Intentionally grand—with crystal chandeliers, brocades, gilt mirrors, Oriental rugs, and ancestral portraits—this 19th-century Victorian was built in 1840, during the height of the whaling era, by Dr. Clement Shiverick, the town's physician. An inn since 1981 and restored (elegantly) in 1987, it is now popular as a romantic getaway complete with a lighted cupola chandelier as an evening landmark.

As Marty, a former utility executive in New Hamphire, says, "In 1992 we looked all over New England for a special place for special people. And we found it!" Denny, the other pamperer, was in real estate sales and development. Their guests, too, are happy the Turmelles made a career change.

Foreign language spoken: A bit of French.
Bed and bath: Ten rooms, all private baths. First-floor air-conditioned rooms—canopied queen, queen four-poster with fireplace, or two twin beds. Second-floor rooms with fireplace—air-conditioned rooms with canopied or four-poster queen (together can be a suite with adjoining sitting room). Queen four-poster. Canopied king. Third floor—air-conditioned rooms with queen or canopied queen (and private rooftop terrace).
Breakfast: 8:30–10. Juices, fruit, two cereals (homemade granola), homemade English toasting bread, homemade pastry, coffee, tea. Served in fireplaced garden room overlooking formal courtyard.
Plus: Fireplaced living room. No TV. Tea and sweets at 4:30. Guest refrigerator. Beach towels. Study on second floor with books and TV. Wraparound outdoor terrace. Robes in rooms.

The Beach Rose

508/693-6135

P.O. Box 2352, Columbian Avenue, Oak Bluffs, MA 02557

Hosts: Gloria and Russell Everett
Location: In a quiet wooded area; 1½ miles to nearest beach, Vineyard Haven ferry, and Oak Bluffs center. (Transportation provided to and from ferry, airport; bicycle, moped, or car rentals; cabs available.) Two miles to Nathan Mayhew Seminars.
Open: May–October. Three-night

minimum on holidays weekends, Memorial Day–Labor Day. Two nights on August weekends.
Rates: Mid-June–mid-September $60 single, $85–$90 double, $20 extra person. Less on July weekdays. Off-season (except Memorial Day weekend) $55 single, $65–$70 double.
♠ ♣ ✗ ✍

What one guest dubbed "a postcard home on a postcard island" is a traditional shingled Cape Cod house with country antiques. A huge quilt hangs above the fireplace of the cathedral-ceilinged living room. Sliding glass doors lead to a wicker-furnished deck overlooking the landscaped yard. Maps, directions, suggestions—even sandpaper requested for a guest's fishing hook—are all part of the personal attention here. The Everetts bought the place after 15 years of vacationing on the island. They made many changes, then opened as a B&B in 1992. In New Jersey Russ was a science teacher. Gloria taught high school English and home economics in addition to sewing and quilting.

Bed and bath: Three rooms. First floor—room with queen four-poster shares a full bath with hosts. One room with twin beds shares full second-floor bath with large second-floor room that has two double beds (white iron and antique rope), skylight, sitting area. Rollaway available.
Breakfast: 7:30–9:30. Announced by school bell. Continental plus. Fresh fruits and juices, a daily entree (baked French toast, baked omelet with salsa), granola, cheeses, cereal. Homemade muffins and jams. Served in fireplaced dining area or on deck.
Plus: Ceiling fans and individual thermostats. Phone jacks in skylight suite. TV in loft sitting room. Afternoon/evening hot/iced tea, lemonade. Use of refrigerator. Laundry facilities. Hot/cold outside shower.

Captain Dexter House   508/693-6564
100 Main Street, P.O. Box 2457, Vineyard Haven, MA 02568

Hosts: Tom Miller and Kimberly Boettcher
Location: One block from ferry dock. In historic residential district that abuts shops, restaurants, beach.
Open: Year round. Three-day mini-

mum on high season weekends.
Rates: Depend on room size and furnishings. May 15–September 30, $95–$165. October–May 14, $55–$125. Amex, MC, Visa.
♥ ♦ ✄

More than a piece of history has changed hands here. When Washingtonians bought the 1843 captain's house in 1988, they acquired all the furnishings of the previous owner, a consultant on 18th-century house restoration and decorating. So the first inn to be part of the Island Historical Society's annual house tour still has the fine antique Sheraton and Chippendale pieces and Oriental rugs.

Romance plays a big part in the current history of the inn. Tom and Kim, who are planning to be married in 1994, note that "at least five couples became engaged here in July 1993. And we've lost count of the number of honeymooners!" Tom worked for 15 years with major hotel corporations in Canada and the United States. Kim, who has a nursing degree, trained with Sheraton ITT and has extensive hospitality industry experience.

Bed and bath: Eight rooms. All private baths; some full, some shower only, some tub only. Two rooms have canopied queen four-poster and fireplace. Suite has a queen canopied bed and living room with queen-sized sleep sofa. Other rooms have king, double, or twin beds. Cot available. (November–April, ocean views from several rooms.)
Breakfast: 8:30–10. Homemade fresh fruit breads and muffins. Freshly squeezed orange juice, coffee, teas. Served in elegant dining room.

(Please turn page.)

Plus: Air conditioners on the third floor; all other rooms have ceiling fans. Fireplace in living room. Afternoon lemonade or sherry. Bedroom ceiling fans. Garden with tables and chairs. Locked garage for bicycles. Off-street parking.

From Connecticut: *"Great place . . . good service . . . lots of nice touches."*

Lothrop Merry House   508/693-1646
Owen Park, Box 1939, Vineyard Haven, MA 02568

Hosts: John and Mary Clarke (April–December). "In winter, inn-sitters who are delighted to be here." **Location:** A quiet spot with harbor view and private beach. A block from ferry dock. Short bus or bicycle ride to public beaches. Across from town park (with summer band concerts some Sunday nights). **Open:** Year round. **Rates:** Double occupancy. $98 for room with double and single bed, shared bath; $108 for double or dou-ble and single with harbor view, shared bath; $155 double, working fireplace, private bath; $165 queen, working fireplace, private bath. Mid-October through early April, about $10–$30 less per room. $20 extra person. $6 child under seven or crib. Summer sails: per person, $50 for three daylight hours or $50 for evening sail. Overnights to Cuttyhunk or Nantucket. MC, Visa.
♥ ♨ ⁂ ✂

From Connecticut: *"A little piece of heaven. . . . The view from my cozy room was of the front lawn stretching down to the harbor full of sailboats. Flowers everywhere. . . . Peace and contentment sustained me all winter . . . charm and beauty surpassed only by John and Mary."*

As Mary says, "We enjoy our somewhat unusual lifestyle, combining innkeeping with sailing. We live aboard our 54-foot ketch, which John captains on day sails here in the summer and on weekly winter charters in the Caribbean."

The Clarkes, a social worker and a teacher, have worked in Afghanistan, Greece, and Japan. Before becoming islanders in 1980, the parents of four grown children ran a New Hampshire ski lodge. Here they have an antiques-filled 1790s shingled house that was moved to its perfect site in 1815 by 20 oxen. It is "settled," with uneven floors, a reception room that doubles as a common room in the winter, and fresh cheerful decor. Adirondack chairs are on the terrace overlooking the lawn and harbor beyond. Guests may use the canoe, Sunfish, and small private beach.

Bed and bath: Seven rooms, five with harbor views, four with private baths. On first floor, off sitting area, canopied queen bed, working fireplace, private shower bath. One room with double bed, working fireplace, private full bath. Plus one room ("perfect for families with children") with a double and a single bed, access to patio. Upstairs, with outside stairway, three rooms; two with a double and a single bed, one with a double. All three share a bath with tub, hand-held shower. (In summer there is also an enclosed outside hot/cold shower plus changing room.) Rollaway and crib available.
Breakfast: Varies daily. Orange juice, homemade baked goods, coffee, teas, cocoa. Outside on patio or (in winter or in inclement weather) in reception room with trays guests may take to their rooms.

Plus: Beach chairs. Garden flowers or dried bouquets. Babysitting. Conference room for about 12.

Pier Side
508/693-5562

P.O. Box 1951, Drews Cove, Lake Tashmoo, Vineyard Haven, MA 02568

Hosts: Phil and Ilse Fleischman
Location: Two miles from Vineyard Haven center on Lake Tashmoo, a beautiful 1½-mile-long saltwater lake open to Vineyard Sound.

Open: Year round. Advance reservations required.
Rates: Per room. June 15–September 14, $100. Off- season, $75.
♥ ✙

> From California: *"Magical. Through quiet woods to a clearing . . . flower-filled patios . . . a warm welcome usually reserved for old friends. . . . The house blends Ilse's European flair with Philip's down-to-earth practicality . . . charming room (more like a studio apartment) with all the comforts of home and a private balcony overlooking sparkling blue water."*

After 17 years of living in the German country-style house they designed and built in Edgartown, the Fleischmans moved to this "forever" spot—where "the total traffic consists of ducks, geese, seagulls, hawks, swans, otters, and a new family of ospreys."

Phil, an architect who has been a yacht captain and boat builder, designed this traditional New England house with cedar shingles and trim, French doors, red brick paths and European details. He built it with Ilse, a kindergarten teacher in her native Germany and also in Greece, and now a travel agent here. Their informal style of hosting provides for opportunities to visit on the porch or in the garden—or even by the boathouse, where Phil is currently restoring some boats, including one that is over 100 years old.

In residence: "One friendly 16-pound gray cat."
Foreign language spoken: German.
Bed and bath: Overlooking the lake, two large rooms, each with private entrance and shower bath. King bed in Balcony Room; queen in cathedral-ceilinged Patio Room.
Breakfast: Full breakfast provided in refrigerator of guests' rooms. Help-yourself arrangement.
Plus: Deep-water pier (guests' boats are welcome) used for swimming. Horseshoes and bocci. Use of grill. Ample parking.

Thorncroft Inn
508/693-3333
800/332-1236
fax 508/693-5419

P.O. Box 1022, 278 Main Street
Vineyard Haven, MA 02568

Hosts: Karl and Lynn Buder
Location: On 3½ acres in a residential area, a half mile beyond the edge of the village. One mile from ferry landing.
Open: Year round. Three-night

minimum on major holiday weekends.
Rates: Mid-June–Labor Day, $149–$349. Off-season, $109–$289. Amex, MC, Visa.
♥ ♦ ✙ ⅙

(Please turn page.)

"It's the type of place where we find ourselves falling in love all over again." Since that comment from a guest appeared in my first B&B book, the Buders have continued to embellish the house, which was built in 1918 for the son of an industrialist. At first Karl, with his father, restored everything and helped to install new baths. Now there are Jacuzzis and hot tubs. To add rooms "and keep the same noncommercial feeling," they bought nearby property. Lynn selected turn-of-the-century lamps, colonial pieces, and beds that include four-posters and high-back Victorians. Now there is air conditioning throughout and each guest room has a telephone. "By popular demand," dinner is served here. And some guests return with colleagues for meetings— and for the hospitality of friendly hosts who share their knowledge "of the wonders of Martha's Vineyard—and career transitions." Thirteen years ago Karl, who has a master's degree in public administration, was a probation officer and marathon runner. Lynn commuted on weekends from her executive position with a Connecticut insurance company.

In residence: In innkeepers' quarters, sons Alex, age nine, and Hans, age seven.
Foreign language spoken: French.
Bed and bath: Thirteen rooms with queen (many canopied) or double bed. Most with working fireplace and/or a balcony. All with private bath; some full, others shower only. Two have two-person Jacuzzi, two have a private 300-gallon hot tub.
Breakfast: (Continental for early ferry departures.) Announced by a breakfast bell when the French doors are opened at 8:15 and 9:30. Buttermilk pancakes and bacon, blueberry or strawberry honey sauces, almond French toast, quiche, croissant sandwiches, baked goods or granola. Classical music.
Plus: Afternoon tea. Turndown service. *Boston Globe* at your door. Color cable TV in some rooms. Screened porch. Wicker-furnished sun room. Victorian reading parlor. Lawn furniture. Extra bath for post-checkout refresher. Option of dinner 6–8 p.m. in inn's 18-seat restaurant.

The Tuckerman House

508/693-0417
800/252-8882
fax 508/693-7654

45 William Street, P.O. Box 194
Vineyard Haven, MA 02568-0194

Hosts: Joe and Carolyn Mahoney
Location: Seven-minute walk from ferry. In historic district, among sea captains' houses. Three miles to gingerbread cottages.
Open: Year round. Two-night minimum weekends April–October; three nights on Memorial Day, July 4th, Labor

Day, and Columbus Day weekends.
Rates: June 15–September 15 $160–$180 king, $150–$170 queen, $130–$150 double, $140–$170 with sitting room, $110 back of house. Off-season $85–$180. Amex, CB, Discover, MC, Visa.
♥ ♦ ✠ ✒

The Greek Revival house was built in 1836 as a wedding gift from mariner Thomas Tuckerman for his bride. The Mahoneys bought it as a one-year-old B&B in 1988. "We had vacationed here since 1976 and find that many travelers are surprised to learn how big the island is, how laid back and idyllic it is, and, at the same time, how many activities it offers. We give them a map, explain the differences of the six towns, and highlight places including our own favorite spots."

The Mahoneys, former Bostonians, furnished with Sheraton, Chippendale, and Victorian antiques. In the winter Carolyn teaches. Joe, a certified financial planner, does consulting.

Bed and bath: Five antiques-furnished rooms, all private modern full baths. King-bedded first-floor room has private entrance. Second floor—queen four-poster canopy bed, two wing chairs, working fireplace. Room with double four-poster, seven windows. Another double-bedded room with Victorian rocker. In rear, private entrance to room with quarter-canopy double bed, shower (no tub) bath.

Breakfast: 8:30–10. Choice of juices and cereals. Fruit. Homemade granola and muffins. Coffee. Herbal tea. Preserves. In the summer, served on veranda; in the winter, in dining room.

Plus: All air-conditioned bedrooms. Tea in winter by fireplace; lemonade in summer on veranda. Cable TV in living room. Guest refrigerator. Guest phone room. Off-street parking.

From a CNN producer: *"Delightful. Couldn't have asked for a nicer time. Highly recommended."* From Massachusetts: *"They go the extra mile . . . felt pampered . . . extremely clean . . . quaint."*

The Bayberry   508/693-1984

Old Courthouse Road, P.O. Box 654, West Tisbury, MA 02568-0654

Host: Rosalie Powell
Location: Down a country lane where there are birds, woods, meadows, horses. Ten minutes to beaches. Five miles from ferry landing.
Open: Year round (except maybe January or February). Two-day minimum on many weekends.

Rates: June–September, semiprivate bath $98 twin beds or queen canopy; private bath $130 double canopy, $138 king. Off-season $75–$95; special rug-hooking workshop rates. Amex, MC, Visa.
♥ ⬛ ⁂ ♦ ✈ ⸆

From Massachusetts: *"Rosalie Powell, a native who is a descendant of Governor Thomas Mayhew, founder of the Vineyard and Nantucket, extends herself in every way possible—from the quaint rooms, to fresh flowers bursting everywhere, to passes to wonderful beaches and tennis courts, to providing sherry and mints, to a gourmet breakfast . . . but most importantly, you feel welcomed and appreciated!"*

Others call The Bayberry "the perfect honeymoon spot." They comment on the "warm and tranquil environment" in this rambling, weathered-shingled Cape Cod–style house built (surprise) in 1972 on land settled by Rosalie's family in 1642. Opened as a B&B in 1984 when the hostess took early retirement from the University of Massachusetts Extension Service, it is filled with family heirlooms and restored antiques. There's an open country kitchen (watch Danish aebleskivers being made); a beamed ceiling with hanging baskets; pottery; quilts; hooked rugs (Rosalie offers workshops here); and lacy pillows (made by Rosalie). The bobwhite calls. The meadow is filled with daisies. Horses graze. The hearth beckons. Joie de vivre.

Bed and bath: Five rooms. On first floor, two rooms share a hall full bath; one has an arched canopied queen bed, the other has two pineapple-post

(Please turn page.)

twin beds. On second floor, two rooms with king beds (one wicker, one high Victorian), private shower baths; one canopied double bed, private full bath. **Breakfast:** Usually 8:30. (Coffeepot on for early risers.) Great variety, including "Dreamboats," named by a guest and almost always photographed before being eaten. Or Belgian waffles with fresh blueberry sauce; bacon, sausage, or ham. Fruit or juice. Homemade muffins and jams. Special diets accommodated. Served with linens and china at fireside tables overlooking gardens or on flower-filled patio by rose garden.

Plus: Outside hot/cold shower big enough for two. Depending on guests' plans, afternoon tea, wine, hors d'oeuvres. Bedroom fans. Grand piano. Library of books on antiques. Croquet. Occasional seafood chowder or barbecues. Champagne for honeymooners. Hints for beaches with shells and fossils. Aromas: "Heavenly today. I am making beach plum jelly from the plums I picked yesterday on the sand dunes at Lobsterville."

___ Nantucket Reservation Services ___

The following reservation services represent B&Bs on Nantucket:
Bed & Breakfast Cape Cod, page 118
Destinnations, page 118
House Guests Cape Cod and the Islands, page 119

_____ Nantucket B&Bs _____

Nantucket's unique characteristics have always been appreciated by its residents. Today the island is loved by off-islanders as well.
  B&B guests are likely to find little need for a car. Advance reservations for autos (carried by the Steamship Authority only) are essential and are often made months before the summer season. The two-hour ferry ride from Hyannis is provided by The Steamship Authority (phone 508/540-2022) and Hy-Line (508/778-2600). Bicycles (extra charge) are allowed on ferries.

Centerboard Guest House

508/228-9696
fax 508/228-1957

P.O. Box 456, 8 Chester Street
Nantucket, MA 02554-0456

Hosts: Marcia Wasserman and Reggie Reid
Location: On edge of historic district, a few blocks from cobblestoned Main Street.
Open: Year round. Two-night minimum on weekends Memorial Day–Columbus Day. "Reserve early for

August and Christmas Stroll."
Rates: Peak season (Memorial Day–Columbus Day) $265 suite, $165 studio, $165 other rooms. Rest of the year $175 suite, $110 studio, $110 other rooms. $25 additional person in room. Amex, MC, Visa.

♥ ❖ ♦ ✈

"People call and ask for our unnamed suite by the name of a famous performer who honeymooned there! And we find that 'old-timers' share all their island 'bests' with first-time guests. We're small. We're both home and a romantic place. We offer privacy and opportunities to mingle. Our linens are spectacular. Most of the quilts are antiques. There are Tiffany oil lamps, Oriental rugs, and painted murals. The floors, except for the century-old inlaid floor in the suite, are pickled. Bouquets of fresh flowers are everywhere. We repaint almost every year. And I am amazed at the details guests notice—even when we change the color of mugs. They bike, walk, have wine on the porch, and at the harbor watch the fish being weighed after a tournament. They relax—and return to this wonderful place." Reggie, who started coming to the island 22 years ago, has been in residence since the day Marcia, a former New York artist and interior designer (who now lives a couple of blocks from the inn) transformed and opened this Victorian house.

Bed and bath: Six rooms, all private baths. One two-room suite with fireplace, queen canopied bed, queen sofa bed, Jacuzzi in full bath. Other rooms have queen bed, queen with twin sofa bed, or two double beds. Studio has two double beds, one platform twin bed, kitchen, private exterior entrance. Crib available.
Breakfast: 8:30–9:30. Fresh fruit. Homemade muffins and breads. Granola. Cereals. Coffees. Teas. At dining room tables with cloths and fresh flowers.
Plus: Air conditioners and ceiling fans in every guest and public room. Each room has individual thermostat, private telephone, and a refrigerator with

fresh fruit, cheese, and sodas. Champagne for honeymooners. Living room with window seat. Down comforters. Plush beach towels.

The Century House
508/228-0530

P.O. Box 603, 10 Cliff Road, Nantucket, MA 02554-0603

Hosts: Jean Heron and (husband) Gerry Connick
Location: In quiet section of historic district. Five-minute walk from steamship landing. At top of the hill, surrounded by sea captains' mansions. Three blocks from town center. Ten minutes to beach.
Open: Spring through December Christmas Stroll weekend. Three-night weekend minimum, late June–late September; shorter stays accommodated when posssible.

Rates: Depend on room size. Late June–late September and holidays, $80–$100 single, private bath; $95–$110 double, shared bath; $95–$160 double, private bath. Off-season $55 single, private bath; $65–$75 double, shared bath; $75–$125 double, private bath. Group rates available. Amex, MC, Visa.
♥ ♨ ♦ ✕ ✄

> From New York: *"Warm and inviting . . . wonderful wraparound porch . . . outrageous breakfasts . . . could make conversation or sit alone and think."* From Pennsylvania: *"Terrific combination of friendliness and service."* From Massachusetts: *"Originally booked for location . . . return for the innkeepers."*

Exuberance—for Nantucket, for the inn, for life! Two former high-tech executives, Gerry (who was trained as an architect) and Jean, answered a "needs work" real estate ad in 1984 and proceded to "plan an inn with special appeal for people with stressful careers. It works! Guests enjoy the tranquillity of the island, the fireplace, the *New York Times* in peace on a Sunday." Nantucket's oldest continuous (since 1833) guest house, decorated "in simple Nantucket country with Laura Ashley highlights" is home to many artists who come to the island for opening nights or private shows; to guests from Japan who read *Spur,* a leading interior design and fashion magazine; and to many returnees, who write limericks about the inn—and its innkeepers.

Foreign languages spoken: Several, according to staffing.
Bed and bath: Fourteen rooms on three floors. Most have private shower baths (three also have tubs). The two third-floor double-bedded rooms that share a bath have sinks in the rooms "and the best harbor views." Other rooms have double, king/twin, or queen beds. Some are four-posters or canopied; many are draped. Some have separate entrances. Cot available.
Breakfast: 8:30–10. Bach music indicates it's time for fresh fruit, juice, English muffins, coffee cakes, granola and cereals, bagels with cream cheese, hot beverages. Eat in pine kitchen or on the veranda or patio.
Plus: Often, BYOB cocktail hour (setups and munchies provided). Coffee and tea always available. Ceiling fans in most rooms; portable fans available. Beach towels. Guests' refrigerator.

B&Bs offer the ultimate concierge service.

Cliff Lodge

9 Cliff Road, Nantucket, MA 02554-4025

508/228-9480
fax 508/228-6308

Host: Gerrie Miller
Location: About a seven-minute walk from ferry; five-minute to town. Residential area with many large homes dating back to whaling era. On a hill overlooking town and harbor.
Open: March–December. Three-night minimum on holiday weekends and in summer.

Rates: Mid-June–late September, Christmas Stroll, Memorial Day, and Columbus Day weekends $100–$150, $65 single. Spring and fall plus Thanksgiving and Christmas, $75–$125, $55 single. Winter $60–$80, $40 single.
♥ ✗ ✍

> From New Jersey: *"After seeing Cliff Lodge in a USA Today article, I called . . . Gerrie Miller enthusiastically explained . . . described. . . . It was all Ms. Miller boasted about and more. Beautifully decorated . . . very clean . . . wonderful aromas from the kitchen made us wish it was morning already. . . . The first evening at dinner my (now) husband proposed to me . . . this is the perfect place, with very personal attention from an innkeeper who makes everyone feel so welcome."* From France: *"There is no other place to which we come with such pleasure and leave with so much regret."*

The 1770s captain's house has been a guest house for over 50 years. The current owner (since 1986) has decorated it with a light and airy feeling, spatter-painted floors, white eyelet bedding, Laura Ashley wallpaper, and rag rugs and dhurries.

In 1988 Gerrie, an interior designer, visited her daughter on the island and, within a matter of weeks, "by accident" (as she says) became the inn's contented—and "perfect" (as guests say)—innkeeper. She suggests the best places to see the sun rise or set, a cemetery "that *is* Nantucket history, a library that is very special, and tips about the famous Nantucket restaurants."

Bed and bath: Twelve rooms (on three floors), each with adjoining private bath, cable TV, phone. Twin, double, queen, and king beds available. Some rooms have views of harbor. Third-floor rooms have air conditioning. Full apartment (often booked a year in advance) has working fireplace, private deck.
Breakfast: 8–10. Homemade bread, biscuits, scones, apple crisp, 14 varieties of muffins, bagels, cream cheese, homemade granola, fresh fruit. Buffet in fireplaced breakfast room with door leading to garden patio. Or on trays to take to your room.
Plus: Widow's walk with panoramic view of harbor is accessible to guests. In summer, afternoon iced tea. Color cable TV. Outside shower. Beach towels. Four common rooms. Pantry with refrigerator and ice maker. Games. Croquet. Parking lot.

Wedding guests love to stay at a B&B.

Corner House   508/228-1530

P.O. Box 1828, 49 Center Street, Nantucket, MA 02554-1828

Hosts: Sandy and John Knox-Johnston

Location: Residential. In Old Historic District. Around corner from village center, on a quiet side street. Few minutes' walk from Steamboat Wharf.

Open: Year round except two January/February weeks. Mid-June through mid-September, four-night minimum including Saturday, three nights during the week. (Inquire about shorter periods, often available.) Other times, two-night minimum required.

(Maximum group size is two couples traveling together.)

Rates: Vary according to room size. Late June–late September and Christmas Stroll, $90, $110, $125, $150; suite $175. Late April–late June, late September through late October, Thanksgiving week, and 12 days of Christmas, $75, $80, $90, $105, $120; suite $135. Winter excluding Thanksgiving and Christmas, $50–$90. Singles $5 less. Third person $15–$20. MC, Visa.
♥ ✗

Gourmet magazine and Swedish and German publications are among many that have raved about everything from the muffins to the decor and hospitality at this B&B, which now has all private baths, skylights, a welcoming hearth, afternoon tea, and English garden terrace. Filled with family antiques, original art, botanical prints, Oriental rugs, antique brass and pewter, and big bouquets of dried flowers, the house built in 1723 is as the hostess hoped it would be: "quintessential Nantucket, without the decorated look." It features knowledgeable concierge service—"better than the Ritz," according to one well-traveled Irish businessman—for everything from sailing lessons to historical walking tours.

It all started in 1980 when Sandy, a designer and restorer of 18th- and 19th-century buildings, was asked to "do up" a former five-room boarding house for selling. "I loved it so I kept it!" she says. British-born John, whom she met in Nantucket, brought country house and rose-growing (and Lloyd's of London) experience—plus acting talent (discovered here) that he didn't know he had. The Corner House is "our home, lifestyle, and joy."

In residence: Summer staff is from England, Scotland, and/or New Zealand.
Foreign languages spoken: Some French and a little German.
Bed and bath: Fifteen rooms. All private adjoining baths; some full, some shower without tub. In main house—eight rooms on three floors. Some with canopied or four-poster bed. King, queen, and twin beds available. In reproduction house nearby—four rooms, each with queen canopied bed, refrigerator, small TV. In Rose Cottage—harborview suite and two queen-bedded rooms (with TV).
Breakfast: 8:15–9:45. Homemade muffins, coffee cakes, granola. Bagels and cream cheese. Juices, coffee, cocoa, teas. Cold cereal. Buffet style in keeping room.
Plus: Two fireplaced sitting rooms. Screened porch with wicker and flowers, overlooking the garden terrace. Cable TV. Library with games, puzzles, books, current magazines. Down pillows and comforters. Beach towels. Window fans. Bike racks.

Four Chimneys Inn

38 Orange Street, Nantucket, MA 02554

508/228-1912
fax 508/325-4864

Hosts: Bernadette L. Mannix and Jimmy Dowdle
Location: Residential. On a street where 126 sea captains built their mansions. Four short blocks to cobblestoned Main Street.
Open: May 15–December 15. Three-night weekend minimum; two nights on weekdays.
Rates: May 15–September 20 $150 canopied double; canopied queen

$165 with dressing room, $200 with fireplace or suite with harbor view, $250 with fireplace, private porch, harbor view. Off-season $130 canopied double; $150 canopied queen with dressing room, $175 fireplace or suite with harbor view, $200 with fireplace, private porch, harbor view. Amex, Diners, MC, Visa.
♥ ❖ ✈

What some travelers call "the ultimate honeymoon place"—many engagements happen here too—has always been known for its gracious style. It was a captain's mansion for about 20 years before being purchased as an inn in 1856 by Freeman Adams, who advertised, "no pains will be spared to insure the comforts of its patrons." The lovely 1980s B&B was embellished in 1990 when Bernie, formerly restaurant/banquet manager at the Metropolitan Museum of Art, became innkeeper at age 27. "I always dreamed of running an inn on Nantucket." Major structural repairs meant raising the entire house from its foundation! From the apartment Bernie grew up in in New York City came gorgeous Oriental rugs and fine antiques. The Ansell Adams photographs and Audubon prints came from the art collection of Jimmy, a landscape designer—"we met on the island in 1987"—who created a Japanese-style garden here. He is also responsible for all the flower arrangements in guests' rooms.

In residence: Liam, a Newfoundland, who spends much of the summer on Bernie's family's farm on the island. "I breed and show Newfies."
Bed and bath: Ten air-conditioned rooms with double or queen canopied bed. Some with working wood-burning fireplace and/or private porch and harbor view; one with sitting room. All private baths (most are shower without tub). On three floors; first and second floors have 12-foot ceilings.
Breakfast: 8–9:30. Homemade muffins, pastries, scones, and granola. Fresh fruit. Juices. In dining room, on wicker-furnished porch, or in your room.
Plus: Harbor and sunset view from cupola. Twin fireplaces in double parlor. Grand piano. TV, VCR. Hors d'oeuvres at 5 p.m. Turndown service. Guest refrigerator. Oversized beach towels. Down comforters. Bike rack. Mints on the pillow. Concierge service for outings.

---

*T*he place to stay has become the reason to go.

Seven Sea Street   508/228-3577

7 Sea Street, Nantucket, MA 02554-3545

Hosts: Matthew and Mary Parker
Location: On a quiet, shady side street in historic district. Two-minute walk to Harbor Beach and Steamship Wharf, five to Main Street and Nantucket Whaling Museum.
Open: Year round. Two-night minimum on April–October weekends, three nights on holiday weekends.
Rates: January–late May $95 room, $125 suite. Late May–late July and early fall $145/$185. Late July–Labor Day and Christmas Stroll weekend $165/$210. Mid-October through December $95/$125. Columbus Day–late June, discounts for week-long stays or Sunday–Thursday three-day stays. $15 rollaway or crib. Amex, MC, Visa.

♥ ♦ ✗ ⅄

From Massachusetts: *"The charm and beauty of the island are matched and exceeded by this inn."*

As Matt says, "In cool weather, guests walk on the beach, use our Jacuzzi, play cribbage, and read by the fire. This year-round inn with a widow's walk, canopied beds, braided rugs, and local art is the realization of my childhood dream." Built in 1987, the year the Parkers were married, it's an early American–style post-and-beam colonial with Scandinavian features (lots of natural wood).

Matt grew up in Rhode Island, vacationed on Nantucket, earned a B.S. in management engineering, and then joined his father in developing Nantucket real estate and designing Seven Sea Street. He met Mary when she was selling advertising for a publication that has become a quarterly magazine, *Nantucket Journal*, published by the Parkers. Seven Sea Street was Matt's project from groundbreaking to working with the crew to assembling all the reproduction furnishings. Now, as co-innkeeper, he finds that guests enjoy cultural activities, art galleries, restaurants—and the suggestion of a secluded beach with moorland views.

In residence: "Puddy, our discreet, lovable tabby."
Foreign language spoken: French.
Bed and bath: Eight rooms plus two two-room suites (all air conditioned); each with queen fishnet-canopied bed, cable TV, sink, private phone, and desk. All private baths with tiled bath floors and two-seat shower stalls. Rollaway and cribs available.
Breakfast: 8–10. Home-baked muffins. Granola. Fresh fruit salad. Juice, coffee, tea, milk. Buffet style in fireplaced breakfast room. Or served in bed, if you'd like.
Plus: Panoramic harbor views from widow's walk. Two common rooms with wood stoves, without TV. Individual thermostats. Guest refrigerators. Beach towels. Wall-mounted hair dryers. Mints on pillows. Babysitting arranged.

*B*ed and breakfast gives a sense of place.

Stumble Inne

109 Orange Street, Nantucket, MA 02554

508/228-4482
fax 508/228-4752

Hosts: The Condon Family—Mary Kay and Mal and daughter Carol
Location: Residential. Ten-minute walk to Main Street, historic downtown, and Tresses Day Spa.
Open: April–December. Two-night weekend minimum late June to mid-September. Three nights July 4, Memorial Day, Labor Day, Columbus Day weekends.
Rates: Vary according to amenities and bath arrangements. Before mid-May and after third week in October, $45–$75. Daffodil weekend, mid-May to late June, and mid-September to late October, $65 (shared bath) to $160 (two-room suite, sleeps four). High season rates, including Memorial Day and Columbus Day, $75–$140 ($225 for suite). Two-room suites in Spring Cottage $110–$185. Off-season special midweek rates. Inquire about Thanksgiving and Christmas Stroll rates. $20 extra adult. $10 child with adult. MC, Visa.
♥ ❖ ♦ ✈

From Massachusetts: *"Wonderful people who make you feel like part of the family. . . . Rooms are relaxing and homelike with fresh flowers, fragrant soaps, charming antiques. On cool afternoons there's hot coffee with cinnamon."*

It's a real family venture, one that was always in the parents' minds during many years of Nantucket vacations. In 1985 the Condons bought the Stumble Inne, a 1704 house later rebuilt in the Greek Revival style, and the Starbuck House, an early 19th-century Quaker-style house. Mal, a technical specialist in the paper industry, became the "technical expert." Carol, a year-round island resident, now hosts Spring Cottage—"we should have named it 'Honeymoon Haven'!"—located just across the street. Added help comes from son Malcolm and his wife, Carolyn. When Mary Kay isn't rearranging new finds—lace, pictures, antique quilts—in the Laura Ashley–styled rooms, some with "undulating random width floors," she's probably suggesting bike routes and dining spots or making her famous muffins (a *Gourmet* magazine–requested recipe).

Bed and bath: Fifteen rooms, on first and second floors. Stumble Inne—seven rooms—queen (with air conditioning) or double beds; all with TV, small refrigerator; most with private bath. Starbuck House—six double-bedded rooms with private bath, ceiling fan; one has sun deck, one is a family suite. Spring Cottage—two-room suites, all private baths, air conditioning.
Breakfast: 8:30 and 9:30 (at 9 in off-season). Fresh fruit and juices. Homemade breads and muffins. Freshly made granola, coffee with cinnamon, and teas. By hearth. (Served in your room in Spring Cottage.)
Plus: Parlor with TV and VCR. Spacious backyards with lawn furniture. Bike racks. Babysitting referrals. Champagne for special occasions.

From Bernice's mailbag: *"The last straw was the classmate from 1935, whom I hadn't seen in 50 years, who read about us in your book. He's been here twice."*

Southeastern Massachusetts
_____ Reservation Services _____

The following reservation services represent some B&Bs in Southeastern Massachusetts:
Bed & Breakfast/Inns of New England, page 259
Bed & Breakfast of Rhode Island, page 307
Bed and Breakfast Associates Bay Colony, Ltd., page 190
Host Homes of Boston, page 192

— Southeastern Massachusetts B&Bs —

Actor's Row   617/383-9200
90 Howard Gleason Road, Cohasset, MA 02025   fax 617/383-2678

Hosts: Maggie and Dick Tibbets
Location: Overlooking harbor and lobstermen at work. In quiet residential neighborhood. Five-minute walk to village and beach. Ten-minute drive to 25-minute ferry ride to Boston. Near fine restaurants, summer concerts and plays, and spectacular cycling route along the coastline.
Open: Year round. Two-night minimum on weekends.
Rates: Queen beds $100, $115, $120. King suite $135; $25 rollaway.
♥ ◆ ✗ ⚬

> From Georgia: *"Everything was perfect, the Tibbetses wonderful . . . I will never forget all those wonderful clocks."* From Texas: *"The house is gorgeous . . . food is delicious . . . I ended up staying 10 days. If I could have sold my house in Texas, I would have moved in permanently."* From New Jersey: *"The grounds are heaven . . . everything spotless, tasteful, comfortable . . . made us feel like we were friends."*

The collection of over 100 antique clocks were photographed for a six-page *Colonial Homes* spread on this rambling harborside 1840s Cape, home to Tibbetses since 1978. It has 10 working fireplaces, exquisite moldings, paintings, antiques, and a wicker-furnished veranda facing the harbor. A 1992 countrywide search (in their own plane) for an ideal B&B led Dick, a steel foundry president, and Maggie, who "always wanted to run an inn," right back home. Their on-the-way-to-Boston, Plymouth, or Cape Cod property is now a destination in itself—with in-ground pool, hot tub, tennis court, gardens, and 10-speed bikes. Some guests who come here for a day or two return the next year for a week.

Bed and bath: Four second-floor queen-bedded rooms; all with private shower bath. Two-room suite with king bed, private full bath. Rooms overlook harbor or pool and gardens. Rollaway available.
Breakfast: 8:30–9:30. Fresh fruit, homemade breads and muffins. Served in fireplaced dining room overlooking harbor or on flower-bedecked patio by poolside.
Plus: Fireplaced living room with piano. Wine and cheese at 4 p.m. Fruit always available. Down comforters. Turndown service. Guest refrigerator. Fresh flowers. Big-screen TV in large entertainment room. Cozy den with TV.

Edgewater   508/997-5512
2 Oxford Street, Fairhaven, MA 02719-3310

Host: Kathy Reed
Location: On the water, facing New Bedford harbor. In a quiet residential neighborhood. Five minutes from I-195, 15 to Martha's Vineyard and Cuttyhunk ferries or to outlets; 75 to Boston. Within 45 minutes of Plymouth, Massachusetts, and Newport, Rhode Island.
Open: Year round.
Rates: $55–$75 single, $60–$80 double. Each extra person $10. Amex, MC, Visa.
♥ ⚬ ◆ ✗

The dining and living room river views give the feeling of being aboard ship. The idea of living in a historic home—and having a B&B—had always appealed to Kathy, a college professor. This one was built in the 1760s by Elnathan Eldridge as his store and home when he was involved in shipbuilding and the East Indies trade. Kathy's home—since 1983—combines a more formal Victorian part with a colonial section that reflects that era with stenciling and simple furnishings.

Fairhaven's architectural gems include a high school with Tiffany windows, Italian marble floors, and intricately carved plaster ceilings. Just across the bridge, within walking distance if you are energetic, is New Bedford, the largest fishing port on the east coast, with its Whaling Museum, cobblestone streets, and manageable historic trail.

In residence: "Sadie, an adorable black and white fluffy dog."
Bed and bath: Three double-bedded rooms (one has canopied bed); private baths. Plus two suites, both with working fireplaces. Queen-bedded suite has full bath; suite with twin beds has private entrance, shower bath, kitchenette.
Breakfast: 7–9:30. Homemade muffins, toasted Portuguese sweet bread, juice, jams, butter shaped as daisies, swans, roses.
Plus: Spacious lawns bordering water. Upper deck with sunsets.

From Massachusetts: *"Out of a fairy tale . . . decorated to soothe rather than astonish . . . perfect setting. . . . Our daughters made us promise that we would visit in winter and enjoy the fireplace and the view of water edged by snow."* From Texas: *"A tub with a view! . . . Restful."*

1810 House Bed & Breakfast   617/659-1810
147 Old Oaken Bucket Road, Norwell, MA 02061

Hosts: Susanne and Harold Tuttle
Location: Residential. Five-minute drive to ocean or to three excellent restaurants. Near antiques shops, Routes 3 and 3A; 20 miles south of Boston.
Open: Year round.
Rates: $50 single, $55 double.
🛥 ⚘ ✖ ⽱

From Rhode Island, Florida, New Jersey, Maine: *"Delightful accommodations . . . hospitable hosts who love what they do . . . worth spreading the word in your book . . . filled with antiques and personal touches. . . . At (delicious) breakfast, watched cardinals feeding in the snow."*

Wedding guests are among the travelers who discover that this B&B is a great place from which to explore the south shore. The house, featured on a holiday tour and in *Country* magazine, has colonial decor, antiques (35 years of collections), stenciling, hand-crocheted bedspreads, and Oriental rugs. Originally a full Cape, it was cut in half at the turn of the century. Additions were made in the 1970s.

Harold, who works in industrial sales, is a woodworker and antique car buff. He and Susanne, a dental hygienist, have been hosting since 1986. "If time and weather permit, we take our guests in Harold's 1915 restored Model T depot hack along the nearby Cohasset and Hingham coast. A gorgeous route!" (It is.)

(Please turn page.)

Bed and bath: Three rooms. On air-conditioned second floor, double-bed-ded room has private modern full bath; can be shared arrangement for same party that books other second-floor double-bedded room. First-floor room (canopied double or two twins) with ceiling fan shares first-floor full modern bath with hosts.
Breakfast: 7:30–9. Omelets with local farm eggs, waffles, pancakes, quiche, homemade bread and muffins, fresh fruit, juice, coffee. Served in fireplaced kitchen or on screened porch.
Plus: Fireplaced and beamed family room with spinet piano, TV, VCR. Individual thermostats on second floor. Evening beverage. Down comforters. Fresh flowers. Candy.

The Onset Pointe Inn

508/295-8442

9 Eagle Way, Onset, MA 02558-1450   (U.S./Canada) **800/35-ONSET**

fax (call first) **508/295-8442**

Hosts: Toni and Carl Larrabee
Location: Nontouristy. On a sandy point with a mile of beach (and gorgeous sunsets) in quiet neighborhood of summer homes. "On near side of the canal." Five-minute walk to town and restaurants; 20 minutes to fine dining. Within 30 minutes of Tabor Academy or Massachusetts Maritime Academy, antiques shops, Cape Cod.

Open: Year round. Two-night minimum on major summer holidays.
Rates: Mid-May–mid-September $75 (small room) to $140 (large rooms with sitting area). Off-season $75, $85, $95. Inquire about winter specials. Ten percent discount for five or more nights. Senior and corporate midweek rates. Amex, MC, Visa.
♥ ⁂ ♦ ✈

This 1992 first-prize winner in the National Trust for Historic Preservation Great American Home Awards competition has quickly become a haven for returnees who send or bring their friends. A Victorian (1880s) complete with Adirondack chairs on the veranda and in the waterside gazebo, it has terra-cotta roof tiles and stucco finish. Inside it is bright and light with florals and chintzes and intentionally elegant comfortable furnishings.

When the Larrabees, experienced weekend hosts, left Manhattan after 25 years of running their own film and video production firm, they "ran a Connecticut restaurant; participated in public service projects in Idaho, where we skied; worked in Stockbridge, Massachusetts, and in Martha's Vineyard real estate; and then heard of this restoration opportunity." Now they sail their own boat "right here in the bay."

In residence: Muggs, 11-year-old Lhasa apso, "sits at your feet."
Bed and bath: Seven mansion waterview rooms (one with turreted sitting area) on second and third floors; two with private balcony. All private tub/shower or shower baths. Queen four-posters or antique double beds. Two queen-bedded cottage accommodations (one has kitchen) with full bath, patio. Five guest-house accommodations (some with kitchen).
Breakfast: 8:30–10. Mid-May–mid-September for mansion guests only. Buffet with juices, fresh fruits, croissants, muffins, rich blend of Colombian coffee, teas. Off-season for all guests—pancakes, croissant French toast (secret shared), or scrambled eggs. In dining room or wicker-furnished sun parlor.

Plus: "No TV or phones in rooms." Fireplaced living room. Beach towels and sand chairs. Hammock.

Pilgrim's Place   508/747-0340
264 Court Street, Plymouth, MA 02360-4038

Hosts: Kathleen Herlihy and Gilbert Fox
Location: On main road (Route 3A), one block from ocean. One mile north of town center, 35 miles south of Boston.

Open: April–November. Reservations preferred.
Rates: $58 shared bath. $65 private bath. $8 third person.
♥ ⊶ ⊸ ⁂ ✗

Step through the double entry to be greeted in the hall with grandfather clock, winding staircase, and window seat. On a clear day you can see the tip of Cape Cod from the upper floors. This shingled Federal-design house was built in 1904 for the president of the world's largest rope company, for 124 years the largest employer in town.

Kathleen says, "B&B is really my fourth career. I started as a chemist, brought up a family in New Jersey, and became a counselor. Now, back in my native state and with a view of the lighthouse I knew from childhood summers, I am a psychotherapist, B&B host, and grandmother to six. Sharing this (traditionally furnished) home and seeing the interaction—as I have since 1987—makes me think that we could avoid wars with such communication." As cohost, Gilbert, a retired salesman, also enjoys sharing local lore with "wonderful people, B&B travelers"—including many returnees.

Bed and bath: Three rooms. Double-bedded with modern shower bath on second floor. On third floor, old-fashioned tub bath shared by two rooms, each with two twin beds. Rollaway and crib available.
Breakfast: 8–9. Juice, fruit, homemade muffins, cereals, coffee, tea, milk. Served in formal dining room.
Plus: Gazebo. Backyard. Rocking chairs on front porch. Bedroom window fans. Guest refrigerator.

Remembrance Bed & Breakfast Home
265 Sandwich Street, Plymouth, MA 02360-2182   508/746-5160

Host: Beverly Bainbridge
Location: Residential. One mile from historic Plymouth, Plimoth Plantation, and Route 3; a little more to beach. Five-minute walk to ocean (walking area) or local bus stop (to Boston). Near Jordan Hospital. Twenty-minute drive to Cape Cod, one hour to Boston.

Open: Year round. Two nights appreciated on major holidays.
Rates: $55 single, $60–$65 double. Twin-bedded room $12 in conjunction with another room, $45 as a single. $5 floor mattress or sleeping bag for child.
♥ ⊶ ⊸ ⁂ ✗ ⚥

From Connecticut: *"Definitely a spread-the-good-word place!"* From Arizona: *"Charmed by her beautiful house as well as her tasteful decorating style."* From Nova Scotia: *"Felt as if we were visiting an old friend."* From Mississippi: *"[while] I served as Surgeon General to the Society of Mayflower Descendants . . .*

(Please turn page.)

stayed in other enjoyable places, but we enjoyed this one far more than others."
From Georgia: *"Immaculate . . . well-stocked library. . . . breakfasts enticing to
the palate and eye. . . . My sons decided to call her 'Aunt Bev' . . . she took them on
walks, taught them how to make shortbread . . . a treasure."* From Florida: *"Had
birthday cupcakes waiting for our daughter who had just turned nine!"* From
England: *"Met me at bus station, showed me around Plymouth . . . felt very much
at home . . . fine colonial-style home."* (All echoed by many more.)

Beverly has experience as mother to two, art teacher, department store
display designer, herb lady and open hearth cook at Plimoth Plantation,
picture framer, and, now, as a calligrapher working at home. Her handmade
gifts have sold in museum gift shops. Her sense of display, color, and
style—with wicker, antiques, original art, and plants and flowers—is everywhere in the 1920s center chimney cedar-shingled Cape-style house.

In residence: Tyler, "a gentlemanly old sheltie." Two cats, Pandora and
Morgan.

Bed and bath: Three second-floor rooms with sloping ceilings share one
full bath and a downstairs half bath. Two with antique brass double bed, air
conditioning. One with a twin bed. Child-size floor mattress and lined
sleeping bag available.

Breakfast: At guests' convenience. Repertoire includes fruit salad, apple
crisp, homemade muffins (lemon-ginger a specialty) and scones, French toast
with a variety of toppings, feather-bed eggs, cereal, freshly ground gourmet
coffee, teas. Served at Victorian ice-cream table in greenhouse overlooking
gardens (and birdfeeders) by old dry-stone wall; in winter, in the kitchen.
Special diets accommodated.

Plus: Fireplaced living room. VCR, films, music, books, magazines, toys.
Beach towels. Tea with shortbread or cookies.

Gilbert's Bed & Breakfast   508/252-6416

30 Spring Street, Rehoboth, MA 02769-2408

Hosts: Jeanne and Pete Gilbert
Location: On 100-acre tree farm in
a rural town, 35 minutes from Great
Woods Center for the Performing
Arts, 20 from shopping outlets, Bat-
tleship Cove (Fall River), and Providence. Near clambakes, hay rides,
and hot-air balloon rides.
Open: Year round. Two-night minimum Memorial Day and Columbus

Day weekends. Advance reservations, even last-minute ones, required. (Please do not arrive at door
unannounced.)
Rates: $32 single, $50 double ($45 if
two or more nights). Additional person over age five, $10; $5 if younger.
Two horse stalls ($15 each includes
shavings and water).
♯ ⬛ ♦ ✈ ✂

Guests who are just here overnight often wish they could stay to enjoy all (see
"Plus" below) that the Gilberts have to offer—far beyond the basics of B&B.

Remembering a trip to Vermont, Jeanne knew that she would like to host
in her in-laws' 13-room farmhouse. Ever since the "someday" idea began in
1984, guests have written to me.

From New York: *"Simple, friendly, reasonably priced, well located."* From
Massachusetts: *"Rooms were private, quiet, and cozy. Jeanne took a lot of time*

showing our daughters around the horses, took them for rides in the pony cart, and found books and games for them to play with. We returned home rested, relaxed, and well cared for." From New York: *"Greeted us with lemonade, and within a half hour we were helping Jeanne walk her Shetland ponies to another field."* From Michigan: *"Reminded me of B&Bs in Ireland."*

Jeanne, a local newspaper reporter and photographer, is an avid equestrian who teaches riding. Pete, named Massachusetts Tree Farmer of the Year, is a pipe organ repairman and plays bluegrass music on banjo and bass— sometimes with guests.

In residence: Daughter Amy is a college student. Son David plays drums in a band. John, age 15. Four registered Shetland ponies, three horses.
Bed and bath: Three second-floor rooms tucked under the eaves share a full bath. Two rooms have a double bed, one has two twin beds. Cot and crib available.
Breakfast: Menu varies. Eggs, bacon, blueberry pancakes, sausage, home-made muffins, fresh fruit, juice, coffee or tea.
Plus: Horses welcome! In-ground pool. Air-conditioned guest sitting room that also displays saddles and bridles. Popcorn. Mints. Fresh wildflowers. Bedroom fans. Babysitting. Piano, 95-year-old reed organ. Hiking and bridle paths. Cross-country ski trails. Cabin (12 feet square) in the woods for listening to the great horned owl.

Perryville Inn

157 Perryville Road, Rehoboth, MA 02769

508/252-9239
(from Boston) 800/439-9239

Hosts: Betsy and Tom Charnecki
Location: Quiet. In rural community seven miles east of Providence. Within an hour of Boston, Plymouth, Newport. Twenty minutes from Great Woods Center for the Performing Arts. Across from an 18-hole golf course open to the public. Near antiques shops.

Open: Year round. Minimum two-night stay on summer and fall weekends. Reservations not required but please call first.
Rates: $50 semiprivate bath, $65–$85 private bath. $10 third person. Amex, MC, Visa.
♥ ♯ ♣ ♦ ✈ ✂

Brass, oak, and canopied beds. (Locally) refinished and reupholstered antiques. Locally handmade quilts. A huge wonderful kitchen. Immaculate housekeeping combined with comfortable country charm and family hospitality. All discovered by wedding guests, lots of first-time B&B travelers, many business people, and my neighbors. For their impressions (and fascinating reading), check out the Secret Drawer Society diaries in the night tables.

You can hardly imagine the abandoned farmhouse that the Charneckis bought in 1984. That was the year Tom, a Colorado bank president, returned here to his childhood hometown, ending a countrywide search for a B&B location that would provide a desired small-community lifestyle. The Charneckis' Massachusetts home, now on the National Register of Historic Places, consists of two top floors built in the 1820s, and a bottom floor built in 1897! The third floor, reached by a private staircase, was originally used for hired hands. "Still is," says Betsy, a registered nurse and four-time

(Please turn page.)

marathon runner, referring to the family's quarters. Now Tom is a financial planner. Both hosts are active with the local historical society.

In residence: Sara during college vacations. Tim is 18. Tina is 12. Two cats, Horsefeathers and Junior.
Bed and bath: Five rooms on two floors. Three rooms with private, two with semiprivate baths. Queen, double, or twin beds. One room has both a queen and a double bed. Cot and crib available.
Breakfast: Usually 8–10. Freshly squeezed orange juice, seasonal fruit, croissants, homemade bread, muffins and sticky buns. Served in dining room or, weather permitting, on screened porch.
Plus: First-floor sitting room with piano. Second-floor sitting/game room. Four acres of wooded grounds with trout stream (fishing allowed). Access to additional 30 acres with ponds and old mill site. Tandem bicycle. Within minutes, clambakes, hay and sleigh rides, and even champagne (after landing) hot-air balloon rides, all by arrangement. Bedroom fans.

The Allen House Bed & Breakfast
18 Allen Place, Scituate, MA 02066-1302   617/545-8221

Hosts: Christine and Iain (Ee-ann) Gilmour
Location: On a hill overlooking harbor of this "wonderful quiet very New England town." Two-minute walk to shops, restaurants, commuter bus to Boston (30 miles). Ten miles to Hingham for commuter boat to Boston; 35 to Cape Cod Canal.
Open: Year round.

Rates: $79–$89 shared bath, $89–$99 private bath. May–October $20 extra for one night only on Friday or Saturday; $10 less for two or more weekday nights. November–April $10 less if Friday or Saturday night included; $20 less for two or more weekdays. Amex, Discover, MC, Visa.

♥ ❖ ◆ ✈ ✂

From Maryland, New York, British Columbia, Kentucky, Minnesota, Ohio: *"So wonderful that our planned one-day stayover lasted for three days! . . . awoke to chirping of songbirds and fresh ocean breezes . . . tray outside door with coffee and flowers . . . beautiful, comfortable, relaxing, accommodating . . . felt as if we knew them for years . . . expertly prepared, beautifully presented breakfast with freshly cut flowers—even edible ones! . . . tea with wicked chocolate torte. . . . All the little touches make one feel very pampered."*

In Hertford, England, Christine, a caterer, and Iain, a journalist who worked in worldwide communications for Polaroid Corporation's medical department, were delighted with their role as summer hosts for European students (up to 10 at a time!) who wished to improve their English. When Iain transferred to Polaroid's U.S. headquarters in 1976, the Gilmours settled here on the south shore, where Christine gained fame as "the Cake Lady." In 1989 they opened this B&B, a 1905 gabled Victorian furnished with early 19th-century English antiques. And Iain became a piano tuner.

In residence: Two cats, Jellicoe and Delius.
Foreign languages spoken: A little French, German, and Spanish.

Bed and bath: Four second-floor rooms (two with ocean view) with queen or double bed. Two share a full bath (robes provided); other two have shower baths en suite.

Breakfast: 7:30–9:30. (Coffee and juice 5:30–7:30.) Pineapple spears with rum sauce or strawberries with sorbet. Homemade granola with yogurt. Waffles, cheese and mushroom strata, or German potato pancakes with sour cream and salsa. In fireplaced dining room or on plant-filled porch.

Plus: A highlight—5 p.m. tea with sandwiches, cakes, sorbets. Evening wine. Fireplaced living room with Estey Cottage organ. Turndown service. Guest refrigerator. Extensive classical music CD collection.

Salt Marsh Farm Bed & Breakfast

322 Smith Neck Road, South Dartmouth, MA 02748-1402   **508/992-0980**

Hosts: Sally and Larry Brownell
Location: Serene. Just over a mile to beach. Three miles from scenic Padanaram harbor; 15 minutes from I-195, New Bedford's historic district and waterfront, Martha's Vineyard and Cuttyhunk ferries. Walk to locally famous ice cream sold from art deco bottle–shaped stand featured in *New York Times*.

Open: Year round. Two-night minimum on holiday weekends and May–September weekends.

Rates: Tax included. $65–$80 per room. Varies according to season. MC, Visa.

Whatever your definition of "real New England" may be, it fits this B&B. A freshly decorated 200-year-old weathered-shingled Federal house on 90 acres with chickens, an old-fashioned flower garden, fruits, vegetables, and trails through a nature preserve with woods, wetlands, salt meadows, and tidal marshes. Cozy bedrooms. "Hardly a straight line in the house." Working fireplaces in the living and dining rooms. Enough family antiques to arouse your curiosity for hours. A visiting octogenarian mother (Sally's) who arranges spectacular bouquets in every room (bathrooms too). And much more—including an apron-wearing hostess who greeted us with clothes basket in hand. "I love to listen to the foghorn and gulls while hanging out the sheets." And an enthusiastic, knowledgeable, sharing host, the organic gardener, who is active in local land conservation efforts.

Before the Brownells, descendants of Plymouth colonist John Smith and parents of four grown children, returned to the family homestead in 1987, they lived in the Philadelphia area. There Larry was a banker and fund-raiser; Sally, a librarian. "We hosted so many out-of-town visitors that B&B here just seems natural." The neighbors, corporations, wedding parties, and vacationers from all over the world are grateful.

In residence: Two cats. Lady Jane is long-haired, George's hair is short.
Bed and bath: Two rooms, each with private bath, hall, and stairway. One room has two twin four-poster beds, bath with large old-fashioned tub. Second room—choice of one double bed or two twin four-poster beds; full bath.
Breakfast: Full 8–9, continental after 9. Earlier by request. Prizewinning blueberry muffins. Farm-fresh eggs or maybe Portuguese or herb omelets or
(Please turn page.)

French toast with special sauce. Heart-shaped waffles for honeymooners. Fruit; in season, homegrown cantaloupe. Special diets accommodated.
Plus: Afternoon sherry, tea, or lemonade. Beach pass and towel. Use of three-speed and tandem bikes (for marvelous country roads). Flannel sheets. Books everywhere.

> From New York: *"[Hosts] are veritable history books about the area. . . . For first time, could imagine myself, a city mouse, converting to country for good."* From New Jersey: *"The most hospitable, relaxing, and just plain wonderful B&B."*

In this book a full bath includes a shower and a tub. "Shower bath" indicates a bath that has all the essentials except a tub.

__ Boston Area Reservation Services __

AAA Accommodations

2218 Massachusetts Avenue, Cambridge, MA 02140-1836

Phone: 617/491-6107 or 800/232-9989, 8 a.m.–10 p.m. daily.

Fax: 617/868-2848.

Listings: About 100. Mostly private residences. Some inns and some un-hosted residences. Most are in Boston (including the waterfront) and Cambridge; others are in Arlington, Brookline, Lexington, Medford, Newton, and Somerville.

Reservations: Last-minute callers often accommodated. Usually, two-night minimum; $10 one-night surcharge.

Rates: $50–$70 single, $60–$95 double. For cancellations received at least 10 days before arrival date, refunds made less a $10 processing fee; for less than 10 days, refund made less the sum equal to one night's stay for each room booked. Amex, MC, Visa. ◆

Since Ellen Riley and Tony Femmino restored a historic house that has become an acclaimed B&B in Cambridge, they have had requests for many more accommodations than they could provide. The result is this reservation service, based in their B&B, A Cambridge House Bed & Breakfast (page 201).

Plus: Car rentals, tours, "and whatever else the traveler wants. We'll get it done!"

A Bed & Breakfast Agency of Boston (and Boston Harbor B&B)

47 Commercial Wharf, Boston, MA 02110-3801

Phone: 617/720-3540 or 800/CITYBNB (or 248-9262), 9 a.m.–9 p.m. daily. Free from United Kingdom: 0800 89 5128.

Fax: 617/523-5761.

Listings: 145. Most are located in downtown Boston—on the historic water-front (a few on boats, many with harbor views from 1840 lofts as well as new buildings); in Faneuil Hall/North End areas of the Freedom Trail; Back Bay; Beacon Hill; Copley Square; and the South End. All are private air-conditioned residences near public rapid transportation. Most are hosted B&Bs, but in addition there are a wide variety of unhosted studios and one- and two-bedroom condominiums (nightly, weekly, monthly).

Reservations: Last-minute callers accommodated. Two-night minimum preferred.

Rates: $60–$85 single, $70–$110 double. Weekly rates available. November 15 through February, three nights for price of two (based on availability).

Nonrefundable deposit of 30 percent of entire cost of booking required. For cancellations made less than 10 days before expected arrival, entire deposit forfeited. MC, Visa. ◆

Ferne Mintz, an experienced host (whose lively beagle, Fanny, is still on many guests' Christmas card lists), features placements with "hosts who put you in close touch with the city." Before starting the reservation service, Ferne did public relations, advertising, and special events. Her latest offerings: some 40-foot cabin cruisers with sun deck, TV, air conditioning, and galley kitchens. "And one architecturally designed houseboat is very popular."

Plus: Tours arranged. Short-term (one week to six months) hosted and unhosted downtown housing available.

Bed and Breakfast Associates Bay Colony, Ltd.
P.O. Box 57166, Babson Park, Boston, MA 02157-0166

Phone: 617/449-5302 or 800/347-5088. Monday-Friday, 9:30–5:30. In winter, 10–12:30 and 1:30–5. Answering machine at other times. Closed Christmas week.

Fax: 617/449-5958.

Listings: 150. Mostly historic properties—hosted private residences and some small inns. Many are in downtown Boston—in Back Bay, Beacon Hill, South End, and Copley Square areas. A large number of private residences are in adjacent Cambridge and Brookline. Others are in a total of 35 eastern Massachusetts communities, extending to coastal towns on the north and south shore and including many on Cape Cod, Martha's Vineyard, and Nantucket. Free descriptive listings available.

Reservations: Most hosts require a two-night minimum stay, May–October. "We try to accommodate last-minute callers (for one or more nights) but prefer a week's notice." Available through travel agents, but service prefers direct contact with guests.

Rates: $50–$90 single, $60–$125 double. Family and weekly rates available. Some homes offer the seventh night free and reduced winter rates. $15 per booking agency service fee. Thirty percent of total is required as a deposit. Full advance payment required on one-night stays and on special event weekends. Deposit minus $25 processing fee refunded on cancellations received at least 14 days prior to arrival. Amex, MC, Visa. ◆

Arline Kardasis and Marilyn Mitchell focus on minute details that even the experienced traveler may not think of. Hosts, many of whom have been with Bay Colony since it started in 1981, often speak of the professional, personal, and efficient service that the agency performs. While maintaining high standards, they offer wide variety—"unforgettable luxury as well as basic comfort and convenience at a modest rate. For our guests, bed and breakfast is a preference, not simply an alternative."

This reservation service is one of the founding members of Bed & Breakfast—The National Network (B&Bs throughout the United States, Canada, and United Kingdom).

Plus: For short-term stays (one week to several months), there are house-sharing opportunities as well as unhosted apartments.

Bed & Breakfast Cambridge & Greater Boston/ Minuteman Country

P.O. Box 1344, Cambridge, MA 02238

Phone: 617/576-1492 or (outside 617) 800/888-0178. Monday–Friday 10–6. Saturday 10–3.

Fax: 617/576-1430.

Listings: 65. Mostly hosted private residences. A few unhosted furnished apartments. Although most are in Boston, Cambridge, Lexington, and Bedford, there are some in Arlington, Brookline, Concord, Somerville, and Waltham. "For many that are located near good public transportation, you may not need a car." Generous continental breakfasts include fruit and cereal as well as juice, rolls and/or baked goods, hot beverages.

Reservations: Advance notice always preferred, but they will do their best to accommodate last-minute requests. Two-night minimum with occasional one-night bookings (usually for last-minute) possible.

Rates: $50–$95 single, $60–$105 double. Senior citizens (over 65), 10 percent less. $10 one-night surcharge. Weekly rates depend on length of stay, location, and season. Confirmed reservations require 30 percent nonrefundable deposit. Amex, MC, Visa for deposit only.

"A personalized service with each home unique and wonderful, with attention given to individual needs." Pamela and Tally Carruthers have been making careful, appropriate matches of host and traveler since 1987. They accommodate tourists in the historic Boston/Cambridge/Lexington area, visitors to area universities, and business travelers who work along Route 95/128. In addition, the agency works with high-technology companies that need short- and long-term housing for business consultants and visiting executives.

Plus: Air conditioning available in most homes. Unhosted apartments and houses available for up to two months.

Boston Reservations/Boston Bed and Breakfast, Inc.

1643 Beacon Street, Suite 23, Waban, MA 02168-1545

Phone: 617/332-4199, Monday–Friday, 9–5.

Fax: 617/332-5751.

Listings: Most are in Boston (Beacon Hill, Back Bay, and the South End); included are hosted private residences (also available in Cambridge and Brookline) as well as some inns, private clubs, and fully furnished unhosted apartments. All are within walking distance of public transportation; most are within walking distance of major hotels.

Reservations: At least a few days' notice required.

Rates: At hosted private homes, $60/$70 single, $70/$80 double. At un-hosted residences, club facilities, and small inns, $60–$135. One-night sur-charge $5. Full amount is due as deposit. If stay is longer than 20 nights, billing is done weekly. Deposit less $15 processing fee is refunded if cancellation notice is received at least three business days before arrival date; otherwise one night's deposit is retained. Amex, Diners, MC, Visa.

Liz Moncreiff and Cynthia Spinner have offered accommodations since 1980, when they started their business at the request of the Continuing Education Department of the Harvard Medical School. Now, in addition to booking reservations for professionals attending courses, conferences, and seminars, they accommodate the general public as well.

Plus: Short-term (up to three months) hosted and unhosted housing available.

Greater Boston Hospitality

P.O. Box 1142, Brookline, MA 02146

Phone: 617/277-5430. Monday–Friday, 8–5:30; Saturday 8:30–1. Answer-ing machine at other times.

Listings: 100. Mostly hosted private residences. Some inns and unhosted private residences. Located mostly in and around Boston—in the city; in Brookline, Newton, Needham, Cambridge, Somerville, Lexington, and Ar-lington; and north in Danvers, Lowell, Marblehead, Gloucester, and Swampscott. Free directory describes homes and includes rates.

Reservations: Advance notice preferred. Sometimes, last-minute reserva-tions accommodated. Two- or three-night minimum stay, May–October.

Rates: $40–$145 single or double. $10 one-night surcharge. Family and weekly (seventh night free) rates. $50 nonrefundable deposit required. For cancellations made at least 15 days before arrival date, refunds minus deposit made. For inn reservations—MC, Visa ◆

Lauren Simonelli offers a broad range of homes but tries to select hosts who are close to major hospitals, schools, and tourist attractions. Most hosts have been on her roster for two years. "Amenities differ. Most hosts are native Bostonians; all are congenial hosts who make that extra effort for the comfort and convenience of guests."

Plus: Walking tours of historic Boston. Dining in exclusive private city clubs may also be arranged with advance notice. Short-term (two weeks) hosted and unhosted housing available.

Host Homes of Boston

P.O. Box 117, Waban Branch, Boston, MA 02168-0001

Phone: 617/244-1308. Monday–Friday 9–noon and 1:30–4:30; reduced live hours November–March. Answering machine at other times. (Prompt re-sponse.) Closed December 23–January 2.

Fax: 617/244-5156.

Listings: 50. Located in Boston area plus some on Cape Cod and the north shore. They are in Boston (Beacon Hill, Back Bay, and South End); in Brookline, Newton, and Cambridge; and in Cohasset, Hamilton, Milton, Needham, Quincy, Sudbury, Swampscott, Wellesley, Westwood, and Weymouth; and on Cape Cod in Sandwich and Waquoit. Mostly hosted private residences. A few inns and one city club. Free booklet directory.

Reservations: At least two weeks' advance notice advised. Two-night minimum stay required with the exception of reservations made within two days of arrival; $10 one-night surcharge for those last-minute bookings.

Rates: $48–$95 single, $57–$125 double. $15 extra adult or child (infants excepted). Winter weekly rates available. Deposit of one night's lodging required; half of total required for short-term housing. Balance of payment (or cancellation) is due to the office at least 72 hours before arrival, or seven days before arrival if stay is five or more days. For cancellations received within that time, all monies, less $20 service fee per room, refunded. Amex, MC, Visa.

Marcia Whittington has carefully selected hosts who live in city brownstones or in close-to-Boston (older Victorian and colonial) homes where guests can leave their car and use public transportation. Some "country feeling" homes are within a half hour's drive of downtown Boston. Marcia has lived in Boston more than 30 years and knows the territory. Since 1982 she has managed all B&B inspections and reservations, giving personalized attention to both hosts and guests. It's a spirit and style that is appreciated by visitors from all over the world.

Plus: Highlighted road and subway maps with reservation confirmations. Relocation assistance for short-term hosted housing (over 10 days) arranged.

University Bed & Breakfast, Ltd.

P.O. Box 1524, Brookline, MA 02146

Phone: 617/738-1424.

Listings: 50. Most are private residences; some are inns. They are located in the metropolitan Boston area—in downtown Boston, Brookline, Cambridge, Jamaica Plain, Lexington, Newton, and Somerville. They offer the ambiance of the countryside and convenience to the city, and are accessible to public transportation or within walking distance of universities and other meeting places.

Reservations: A minimum of two days' notice is preferred.

Rates: $45–$75 single, $70–$100 double. $10 one-night surcharge. Prepayment required. If cancellation is received at least 14 days before expected arrival date, refund less $20 processing fee is made. MC, Visa. ◆

Ruth Shapiro and Sarah Yules accommodate visiting professionals and accompanying spouses and/or traveling companions who come to the Boston area for academic or other reasons. They also accommodate relatives and friends of area students.

Boston Area B&Bs

B&Bs are in all downtown Boston neighborhoods—including Back Bay, Beacon Hill, and the waterfront—in brownstones and penthouses, high-rise buildings and converted warehouses. Many are in restored Victorians in the South End, the fashionable place to live before the tidal flats of the Back Bay were filled in the 1800s. Scene of many changes, the South End in its latest renaissance is the city's most culturally diverse neighborhood, complete with a full array of shops and restaurants, and abuts the expanded Hynes Convention Center and Copley Place shops.

For many, the convenience of being in the city is primary. The Greater Boston area, however, is compact; several hosts in "outlying" (mostly suburban) areas are actually closer to downtown Boston than many who live in the city. If you have time to commute, many of these B&Bs are less expensive than in-town locations. Traffic and parking in the city can be time-consuming and frustrating. The public transportation system, relatively simple and color coded, has convenient routes. Its schedules are not as dependable as those Europeans are used to; even so, the "T" is recommended.

Beacon Hill Bed & Breakfast   617/523-7376
27 Brimmer Street, Boston, MA 02108

Host: Susan Butterworth
Location: Overlooking Charles River. On quiet street in historic downtown residential neighborhood. Walk to everything, including Boston Public Garden, shopping, restaurants, Hynes Convention Center, Freedom Trail, subway system.
Open: Year round. Two-night mini-

mum stay (one-night bookings at last minute only). Three-night minimum on holiday weekends.
Rates: Single or double occupancy. $120–$145 second-floor rooms, $115–$135 third floor. $20 rollaway or sofa bed. Ten percent less on stays over seven nights.
♥ ◀ ✻ ◆ ✈ ✂

From Ohio: *"An elegant, well-appointed six-story home . . . superb creative breakfasts."* From Alabama: *"Delightful. Personable, knowledgeable, talented, and interesting hostess."* From Massachusetts (via Louisiana): *" . . . even acted as liason to realty companies."*

Built in 1869 with elegant details, this very large and beautiful brick row house has marble fireplaces, high ceilings, and deep moldings. The French touches reflect this San Francisco–born hostess's many years of living in France. A professional caterer, Susan trained at La Varenne in Paris and has taught French in several New England schools.

Foreign language spoken: French.
Bed and bath: Three large air-conditioned rooms, all private baths. Third floor—two spacious rooms with nonworking fireplaces, full baths. One with river view has a queen bed and a double sofa bed; one that overlooks Beacon Hill has a double bed and queen sofa bed. Second floor—queen-bedded room, shower bath, nonworking fireplace.

Breakfast: 8:30–9 weekdays, 9–9:30 weekends. Extremely popular home-made granola. Muffins or coffee cake. Eggs or French toast or waffles, fruit, and "good strong" coffee. Under crystal chandelier from Loire chateau. In large dining room overlooking the Charles River.
Plus: Elevator for luggage. Near guarded parking lot, $15 per 24-hour day.

Bed and Breakfast Associates Bay Colony Host #M128

Boston, MA

Location: On Beacon Hill. "You can walk to anywhere in town (including Faneuil Hall Marketplace, theater, restaurants, Freedom Trail sites), and we are minutes from three different subway lines."

Reservations: Year round through Bed and Breakfast Associates Bay Colony, page 190.
Rates: $95 for suite. Cot, $10 for children (only).
♥ ⬤ ♦ ✄ ⅄

"A couple of years ago we moved from nearby Back Bay to this well-built c. 1835 townhouse, which is authentic with lovely features—six fireplaces, original floors and moldings. For B&B we designated the original parlor floor, the one with the prettiest fireplaces, and furnished with English antiques. The bedstead is 150 years old, about the same age as the house."

The hostess, a writer who participates as a guide for special tours of Beacon Hill homes, has lived in the Boston area all her life. Her husband is an interior designer. His special, helpful map for guests highlights points of interest in the city.

In residence: Three school-aged children. Three cats and a dog.
Foreign languages spoken: French and Spanish.
Bed and bath: Entire air-conditioned second floor with double-bedded room, sitting room, dressing area, full bath, small refrigerator.
Breakfast: Usually 7–9. Homemade muffins, fresh fruit, juice, coffee. Served on tray in room.
Plus: A warm welcome with beverage at dining room table, an orientation map, and, if you'd like, an explanation of (uncomplicated) subway system.

From California: *"Generous hospitality . . . consider ourselves lucky to have stayed here."* From Texas: *"Made our vacation memorable."* From Georgia: *"Felt like home."* From Louisiana: *"Wonderful accommodations."* From Wisconsin: *"Delicious breakfasts."*

Coach House

Boston, MA

Location: Quiet gaslit street in historic district. Two blocks to Boston Common on Freedom Trail. Walk to Quincy Market, fine shops and dining, theaters, convention hotels, Red (20 minutes to Harvard Square) and Green subway lines.

Reservations: Available year round through Host Homes of Boston, page 192. Two-night minimum.
Rates: $95 single, $115 double.
⬤ ✄ ⅄

(Please turn page.)

"When we moved from Montreal for business reasons 17 years ago, we looked for a family home that was downtown in an American city. By the time those business reasons were no longer relevant, we had come to appreciate Boston, a top-drawer city that has a unique quality of life, flavor, and history, all here within a few blocks. A few years ago we started to share all of this with guests, interesting people from all over the world."

The hosts, world travelers who have lived in several countries, reside in a converted 1870s coach house that once held 12 coaches, with staff living on the upper floors. In the early 1900s the ground floor was a concert hall for a well-known pianist as well as a puppet theater. A townhouse since the 1930s, the house is decorated with antiques and an eye for color and detail. The host is in the air pollution control field. His wife is a builder and marketing consultant.

In residence: One 14-year-old son. Two Siamese lynx cats who do not go above the first floor.
Foreign languages spoken: Fluent French, some Spanish.
Bed and bath: Two air-conditioned rooms; TV in each. Second-floor room has one twin bed, private en-suite shower bath. Third-floor room has queen bed, private en-suite full bath.
Breakfast: 7:15–8:30. Fresh fruit, cereals, juice, baked goods with jams and jellies. Freshly ground coffee. Tea. Served in dining room.
Plus: Use of formal living room. Clock radios.

> Guests wrote: *"Comfortable. . . . Clean. . . . A delightful family. Made to feel right at home."*

Greater Boston Hospitality Host #29
Boston, MA

Location: In historic district, within walking distance of theaters, fine dining, historic sites.
Reservations: Year round through

Greater Boston Hospitality, page 192.
Rates: $80 single, $85 double.
♥ ⅶ ◆ ✄ ⅍

For an experience in elegance and a sense of old Boston, this B&B is the home of a host who provides a flexible breakfast arrangement (in your own apartment area)—appreciated by honeymooners who are looking for privacy as well as by tourists who seek suggestions and information. The 1790 townhouse is furnished with an outstanding collection of European antiques. Off the living room there's a roof deck with flowers, blue spruce, and an interesting view of the city.

Bed and bath: The entire floor is for you, with double bedded room, living room with daybed, dining room, modern kitchen, full bath.
Breakfast: Served 8–9:30; or, if you prefer, help yourself from stocked kitchen. Fresh fruit, muffins, croissants, jams, jellies, butter, coffee, tea.

> From Maryland: *"This is one of the finest homes we have every stayed in."* From California: *"An outstanding cosmopolitan European hostess."*

Bed and Breakfast Associates Bay Colony Host #M416

Charlestown, MA

Location: In historic district, one block from the Freedom Trail. A 15-minute walk or 5-minute bus ride to Faneuil Hall Marketplace.
Open: Year round through Bed and

Breakfast Associates Bay Colony, page 190.
Rates: Single $50. Double $70 suite, $65 third floor.
♥ ⬛ ⁂ ♦ ✙ ⚋

From Florida: *"Ironically, we were most concerned about staying in the city, but this turned out to be the most charming of all the New England B&Bs we stayed at. . . . One of the high points of our vacation was the evening we sat on the deck atop our hosts' townhouse. There we overlooked Boston harbor and the masts of the USS Constitution while we enjoyed refreshments and chatted with our hosts."* From Switzerland: *"Loved this place. . . . It was hard to leave."*

"Before moving here in 1979, we lived in the suburbs. Here, I still have a garden, but it's more private. I walk to work in Boston. And we are in a perfect place [with the perfect arrangement] for B&B."

The hostess first came to America as an exchange student in 1956. Shortly after returning to the United States in 1965, she met her husband, an engineer who was born of Polish parents in India and brought up in Afghanistan. They have made some exciting changes in their lovely home, an 1846 brick townhouse. It has been appreciated by many international travelers, a well-known film actress, honeymooners, marathon runners, medical interns-to-be, and professional innkeepers too.

Foreign languages spoken: French, Polish, and Turkish.
Bed and bath: A second-floor suite has a room with a double bed, adjoining sitting room with TV, and private full bath. On third floor, room with an antique brass double bed and private shower bath, plus, off the hall, a library with TV.
Breakfast: Weekdays, self-service at guests' convenience. Continental with freshly squeezed orange juice and homemade cake, croissants, or Irish bread. Weekends, more elaborate menu. With classical music.
Plus: Use of deck. Storage for bicycles. A shared love of the city.

Bed and Breakfast Associates Bay Colony Host #M314

Boston, MA

Location: On a quiet residential street in historic South End. Five minutes from Back Bay Amtrak/subway station, Copley Square, Hynes Convention Center. Within 15 minutes' walk (no car needed here) of Faneuil Hall Marketplace, Beacon Hill, and the waterfront.

Reservations: Year round through Bed and Breakfast Associates Bay Colony, page 190.
Rates: Vary according to season. $97–$125. Weekly and monthly rates available.
♥ ⁂ ♦ ✙ ⚋

(Please turn page.)

From California: *"Marvelous . . . delicious breakfasts at a beautifully set table."* From Michigan: *"We would recommend this B&B to anyone, especially first-time visitors to Boston . . . wonderful restoration."* From Maryland: *"Made us feel like members of their family . . . decorated with a comfortable elegance."*

A very popular B&B. Remembered by many, especially the couple who came to get away from decision-making days of planning a wedding. They did— with a spontaneous decision to be married here that very weekend with the hosts as attendants.

The 1863 red brick row-style townhouse, restored in 1980, was fully renovated and refurbished in the late 1980s so that each guest room has a new bath. The interior design fulfills the expectations of many who anticipate a decorated, inviting B&B with floral drapes, period furnishings, marble mantels, color-coordinated linens, and Oriental rugs.

For an orientation to the city, the hosts, a retired city administrator and an artist, utilize a large framed map of Boston. Many guests follow their custom-designed day trip suggestions to nearby historic communities that can be reached by public transportation.

In residence: Sylvester, the cat, "official greeter who loves attention."
Foreign language spoken: A little French.
Bed and bath: Five rooms, all with brass queen beds, private shower baths with granite floors. On second floor, two rooms with hidden kitchenettes. On third floor, two more rooms with kitchenettes. On the fourth (penthouse) floor, "room with a view" with exposed brick wall, antique armoire, adjacent hall skylit bath.
Breakfast: Usually 8:30. Menu could include almost-famous blueberry buttermilk pancakes, French toast with fruit compote, or apple crepes. Served family style.
Plus: Phone, air conditioning and ceiling fan in each room. Fresh flowers. Nearby parking garage ($15–$20 for 24 hours).

The Terrace Townehouse   617/350-6520
60 Chandler Street, Boston, MA 02116

Host: Gloria Belknap
Location: In a row of South End Victorian houses, minutes from convention center. Two blocks from Copley Place, home of Neiman Marcus. Half block from Amtrak/subway station. The ethnically diverse neighborhood is always changing and currently includes longtime residents, families, and young professionals.
Open: Year round. Reservations required. Two-night minimum in summer and on fall weekends.
Rates: Per room. May–November, $115 and $140. December–April, $105 and $130.
♥ ♣ ✈ ✁

Romantic. Elegant. Luxurious. Private. And just when Gloria has every last accessory in place, she finds another fine antique and there's a change! New Yorkers love to come here and walk to restaurants, museums, the theater. When a horse-drawn carriage arrived to take a bride to a Back Bay church, the neighbors gathered to wish her well. Executives appreciate the private phones. And honeymooners, too, stay in the "fantasy rooms" that Gloria has created with marble mantels, an antique Waterford chandelier, a mirrored armoire, shuttered windows, and fresh flowers.

The 1870 townhouse, found in 1986 when a daughter came to Boston to go to college, ended the Belknaps' five-year search for a neighborhood location in a cosmopolitan city. In California Gloria, a graduate (two diplomas) of La Varenne in Paris, was a successful caterer. Here she became a house restorer who selects Pierre Deux fabrics and goes to auctions. And she serves afternoon tea in the library with its collection of more than 1,000 volumes. Guests leave with the ultimate compliment: "Thank you for having us."

In residence: One cat "who tells us he doesn't go into guests' rooms."
Foreign languages spoken: Some Spanish, French, and Portuguese.
Bed and bath: Four rooms on first two floors. All private shower baths. Beds are king, canopied queen, or double. (Inquire about garden apartment.)
Breakfast: 8:30 (8:30–9 weekends). Freshly squeezed orange juice, fresh fruit, granola, yogurt, "just out of the oven" scones, "special surprises," coffee or tea. Served in your room on antique china with crystal and silver.
Plus: Air-conditioned bedrooms in summer. Bathrobes. Down pillows and comforters. Common room, the library, is available until 7 p.m. Three parking lots within a two-block radius.

The Bertram Inn　　　　617/566-2234
92 Sewall Avenue, Brookline, MA 02146　　(U.S./Canada) **800/295-3822**

Hosts: Bryan and Sierra Austin
Location: On a corner in a lovely residential neighborhood (private homes and some condominiums) with tree-lined streets, just one block from fine shops, restaurants, and trolley (10-minute, 85-cent trolley ride to downtown Boston). Within walking distance of Boston's Longwood medical area.
Open: Year round.
Rates: March–October, shared bath $59 single, $69 double, $79 queen; private bath $89 double, $94 queen, $104 king. November–April $10 less. $10 cot. MC, Visa.
♥ ♣ ♦ ✂

This attractive 1908 Victorian/Tudor style house is, as Bryan surmised it would be in 1986, "perfect for B&B." Now it has all new systems, many new baths, fresh decor, and antiques—without clutter—everywhere. Old velvet drapes are in one room, fresh white curtains in another. The first-floor oak floors are refinished; upstairs there is carpeting. You almost have the feeling that Bryan, now in his thirties, updated Grandmother's solidly built residence with its leaded windows, stone fireplaces, and grand staircase complete with landing.

He was the youngest of four boys and in high school when his mother, an antiques collector, bought an old house and enlisted her sons' assistance for restoration. After Bryan received his English degree, he restored and sold houses. Now that he has earned his MBA, he and/or his wife, Sierra, a landscape designer, are the daytime innkeepers—natives who happily share their knowledge of the city with travelers from all over the world.

In residence: A full-time manager. (The Austins live nearby.)
Bed and bath: Twelve rooms with color TV and phones (for outgoing calls); mostly private baths. First floor—king and two twins, working fireplace, private full bath; queen and double sofa bed, private hall full bath. Second

(Please turn page.)

floor—king or queen (some four-posters) and double beds; private baths (some shower without tub). Third floor (steeply sloped ceilings)—one double-bedded room and two with twin beds (all with ceiling fans) share one full bath plus a half bath.

Breakfast: 8–9. Fresh fruit, juice, breads and jams, coffee cakes, muffins, bagels and cream cheese, hot beverages. Buffet style in large fireplaced living room.

Plus: Most rooms are air conditioned. Great front porch (glassed in winter). Flowers arranged by Sierra. Daily papers.

Sarah's Loft
Brookline, MA

Location: Quiet residential street. One mile to Boston University, Longwood Medical Area, Fenway Park, Boston College. Two blocks to village shops, restaurants, Beacon Street (Green line) trolley.
Reservations: Through Host Homes of Boston, page 192. Two-night minimum.
Rates: $75 single or double with one bedroom. $25–$20 per extra guest for second bedroom. $15 crib.
♯ ♦ ✗ ⚭

> Guests wrote: *"Much more comfortable and hospitable than [major hotel]. . . . We had a wonderful experience . . . helped make our time in Boston very special. . . . We've stayed in many B&Bs and this is one of the nicest by far."*

The 800-square-foot guest floor offers plenty of privacy. A separate stairway leads to a comfortably furnished skylit cathedral-ceilinged sitting room, two bedrooms, and bath. The suite was created in 1988 in this stucco and frame house, built 25 years ago on the site of a Victorian that had been leveled. The hostess, who grew up in Maine, is a law professor. The host, a software consultant from New York who was born into a bilingual family, lived in Taiwan for two years so that he could learn a different Chinese dialect. While there, he also became a master of Chinese cuisine. They both enjoy sharing their knowledge of Boston area restaurants, attractions, and (readily accessible) public transportation arrangements.

In residence: In hosts' quarters—a seven-year-old daughter and a two-year-old son.
Foreign language spoken: Chinese.
Bed and bath: On private third floor—one bedroom has traditional queen bed, wall-to-wall carpeting; the other has queen-sized futon on a platform, area rugs on hardwood floor. One full bath.
Breakfast: 8–8:30. Brought to your sitting room on a tray. Freshly squeezed orange juice, fruit, homemade granola, breads—often homemade. Hot beverages, milk.
Plus: Stereo and TV. In the winter, a view of Boston skyline from sitting room. One off-street parking space.

---

*T*hink *of bed and breakfast as a people-to-people concept.*

A Cambridge House Bed & Breakfast

2218 Massachusetts Avenue, Cambridge, MA 02140   617/491-6300
    800/232-9989
    fax 617/868-2848

Hosts: Ellen Riley and Tony Femmino
Location: On a main street with a smorgasbord of residences and businesses and restaurants. From front door, short bus ride to Harvard Square. Five-minute walk to subway stop that is one stop from Harvard Square; from there, a 10-minute subway ride to downtown Boston.
Open: Year round.
Rates: May–November—$79–$145 single, $89–$185 double. Rest of the year—$69–$139 single, $89–$169 double. Vary according to size and amenities in room. Amex, MC, Visa.
♥ ❖ ◆ ✂ ⚕

"It happens all the time. People realize that we're here. They are curious. They ring the bell, request a tour, and then book family or business associates."

The Hartwell and Richardson–designed house, built in 1892 and on the National Register of Historic Places, has been a featured B&B on BBC in Europe and on Boston's WBZ-TV. Completely redone in 1986 (with more recent embellishments), it has hundreds of yards of fabric—on windows, on walls, in entryways. Chinese vases are on pedestals. There are Oriental rugs and, throughout, antiques. Of the six fireplaces in the house, the tall intricately carved one in the den is the most outstanding. And then there's the showplace carriage house created from a shell.

Ellen, former membership director of the Boston Chamber of Commerce, and Tony, former investment property broker, are Realtors.

Foreign language spoken: Italian.
Bed and bath: Fourteen air-conditioned, carpeted rooms; described in detail on phone. Several with canopied four-poster beds. Bed sizes include queen, double, and twins. Nine (all with private baths, some with working fireplaces) on three floors of main house. On first and second floors of carriage house—five rooms share four baths.
Breakfast: 7:30–9 weekdays, 8–10 weekends. Elaborate. Fresh fruit. Freshly squeezed juice. Belgian waffles, crepes, omelets, or frittata. Served in living room under crystal chandelier with classical music.
Plus: Evening white wine or sherry. Afternoon coffee, tea, or mulled cider with freshly baked pastries. Background jazz. Cable color TV with remote control in each guest room.

Guests come from as close as 10 minutes away or from around the world.

Just a Little West
_____ Reservation Services _____

The following reservation services represent B&Bs in the areas just a little west of Boston:

AAA Accommodations, page 189

Bed & Breakfast Cambridge & Greater Boston/Minuteman Country,
   page 191

Bed & Breakfast Cape Cod, page 118

Bed & Breakfast Folks, page 208

Bed & Breakfast Marblehead, page 208

Destinnations, page 118

Greater Boston Hospitality, page 192

Host Homes of Boston, page 192

House Guests Cape Cod and the Islands, page 119

——— Just a Little West B&Bs ———

Hawthorne Inn   508/369-5610
462 Lexington Road, Concord, MA 01742

Hosts: Gregory Burch and Marilyn Mudry
Location: In historic district of must-see picture-perfect New England town. Across from Nathaniel Hawthorne's "Wayside." On grounds with marvelous old trees. "Four museums—all the staffers are walking libraries—in the eight-tenths of a mile between here and town center." Twenty-minute walk to Old North Bridge; 10-minute ride to bicycle rentals; two miles to Walden Pond; 20 minutes to Harvard Square (Cambridge); 35 to Boston (45-minute train ride).
Open: Year round. Two-day minimum during fall foliage.
Rates: January–March $75–$85 single, $85–$95 double. April, May, December $85–$110/$110–$125. June–August and November $110–$125/$125–$140. September, October $125–$150/$150–$160. Amex, Discover, MC, Visa.
♥ ♨ ❀ ♦ ✈ ⚜

A sense of history (Gregory's ancestors settled in Concord in 1637), peace and relaxation, family, privacy, and community too. It's all here in the 18-room altered colonial (1920s stucco exterior over 1870 clapboard) that Marilyn, a hospice volunteer, quilter, and Realtor, and Gregory, a sculptor and painter, restored in 1976 after searching for an old house that would provide studio space. Their haven, on land once owned by Emerson, the Alcotts, and Hawthorne, is furnished with a blend of antiques, 18th- and 19th-century Japanese prints, and Gregory's works. Business travelers return as tourists. Scholars and historians love it here. (Gregory and Marilyn wrote and produced a one-hour video history of Concord.) And families are warmly welcomed too.

In residence: In hosts' quarters—Ariel Zoe, age 11; Ezra Avery, 9; Jasper Gardener, 7. (All began their music studies with the Suzuki method.) Three cats. One friendly German shepherd.
Bed and bath: Seven rooms, all with private baths (some tub and shower, others shower only). First floor—three double-bedded rooms (three are canopied). Four on second floor (three with skylights)—king, double, double and a single bed, and twin beds. Rollaway and crib available.
Breakfast: 8:30–10. Expanded continental with homemade honey molasses or Portuguese sweet bread, pound cake with yogurt topping, fresh fruit, cereal, homemade jams, French roasted/ground coffee.
Plus: No TV. Books and poetry collections in each room. Fireplaced living room. Window fans. Air conditioning in some rooms. Beverages. Fine toiletries. Games. Yard. Treehouse. Sandbox. "Recommendations for best bookstores and antiques shops; places to canoe, fish, walk in the woods; a great deli, a fine reasonably priced restaurant, ice cream stands."

Brock's Bed & Breakfast   617/444-6573
60 Stevens Road, Needham, MA 02192-3314

Hosts: Anne and Frank Brock
Location: In a quiet residential neighborhood, half a mile from Route 128, two miles from the Massachusetts Turnpike (I-90). To Boston, nine driving miles, one-half mile to commuter train, or three miles to subway station with parking. Four miles to Wellesley College; 15 minutes to Boston College, 35 to Cambridge.
Open: Year round.
Rates: $55 shared bath, $60 private. $20 rollaway. $5 surcharge for one-night booking.
♥ 🏠 ❋ ✗ ⌿

> From Wisconsin: *"They don't charge enough!"* From Texas: *"A soothing backdrop to the fast pace of Boston . . . breakfasts made to order with healthy doses of friendliness."* From New York: *"My husband stayed there rather than the upscale hotel his expense account would have covered."* From New Jersey: *"Your books have guided our way to many wonderful B&Bs, but our favorite is the Brocks'."* From Connecticut: *"The feeling of coming home."*

Those are just a few excerpts from a huge stack of letters written to me. What started with area colleges in 1984 has become "a wonderful people business" for the Brocks. Their house, the first by Royal Barry Wills, was built in 1922 when Wills was an architecture student at MIT. It was built Cape style, with nooks and crannies, lots of built-ins, and high ceilings. The flagstone walk, landscaping, and Williamsburg decor have all been done by the Brocks, second owners of the house as of 1966. Guests have much privacy; since becoming a B&B, the hosts have established their own quarters on the lower level. Before retirement, Anne worked in the medical field and Frank in human resources.

Bed and bath: Three rooms, each with cross-ventilation, share a full bath and a half bath. One on first floor with double four-poster. On second floor, one with two twin beds; one with queen bed; both with ceiling fan.
Breakfast: 6–9. Juices, fresh fruit cup, cereals, homemade muffins. Eggs with bacon or sausage; 24-hour French toast (marinated in eggs, cream, orange juice, vanilla, and sugar), blueberry or pecan pancakes; or Brocks' crepes. Hot beverages.
Plus: First floor is air conditioned; separate air conditioners in second-floor rooms. Electric blankets. Portable TV by request. Rear sun deck. Good neighborhood for walking and jogging. Guest den with books and TV.

Rockledge
Newton, MA

Location: One block from 20-minute trolley ride to downtown Boston, Hynes Convention Center, Copley Square. On a quiet residential street. Walk to lake (swimming), village shops, restaurants.
Reservations: Year round through Host Homes of Boston, page 192.
Rates: $59 single. $64 double.
🏠 ✗ ⌿

Here in the same friendly neighborhood where our own children were brought up are two popular hosts who came to Boston for college and stayed—with the exception of periods when they lived in several countries. The host, a professor, and his wife, a community activist/house restorer and "longtime piano student," share their knowledge of the area. "The Isabella Stewart Gardner Museum, unknown to many of our guests, is a big hit." (And should you decide to take up bread making, the hostess will share her starter with you.)

Their large Victorian house is filled with books, Oriental rugs, and antiques. The unusual front hall mural was painted by a friend who, in all likelihood, inspired one of the hosts' daughters to study art.

In residence: Two affectionate cats, Chloe and Clementine.
Foreign languages spoken: French, German.
Bed and bath: Two second-floor rooms (at most) booked at a time. Shared hall shower bath. Choice of queen, double, or two twin beds.
Breakfast: Usually 7:30–9. Homemade breads (sourdough a specialty) and jams. Cereal. Cheese. Yogurt. Juice. Fresh fruit. Freshly ground or decaf coffee. Tea. In breakfast area of worth-a-magazine-feature kitchen overlooking garden, or in dining room. Hosts often join guests.
Plus: Bedroom ceiling fans. Clock radios. Second-floor guest sitting room with TV. Wicker-furnished covered front porch. Off-street parking.

> Guests wrote: *"Marvelous ... with a real angel! ... warm, welcoming, convenient to public transportation ... filled with original artworks ... Chloe adopted us and made us feel one of the family."*

Sage and Thyme Bed & Breakfast

P.O. Box 91, Newtonville, MA 02160-2244   617/332-0695

Hosts: Edgar and Hertha Klugman
Location: On a hill in a lovely residential neighborhood. Six miles from downtown Boston; 1½ miles from I-90 (Massachusetts Turnpike). Within walking distance of restaurants, a cafe, and Boston College's Newton campus.
Open: Year round. Two-night mini-

mum preferred. Reservations requested; will accommodate last-minute guests when possible.
Rates: $49 single, $59 double. $20 third person in double room. Under age five, no charge. One-night surcharge, $10 per room.
🛋 🍴 ⚬⚬ ✗ ✂

From New York, Florida, Montana, Vermont, Tennessee, California, Rhode Island, Canada, Germany, England: *" Their home is your home. . . . Suggested great places to go. . . . More than you could ever want to eat. . . . Peaceful and quiet . . . comfortable. . . . Respect your privacy. . . . Articulate and interesting, not overbearing, but very natural. . . . Made our stay in Boston memorable . . . reasonable rates . . . meditated in living room . . . ran along [nearby] Boston Marathon course . . . I wish this was my home."*

Guests from all over the world continue to write to me about Ed, a college professor at Wheelock College in Boston, and Hertha, who has taught on the college level as well. The eclectic decor of their center entrance colonial reflects some of their own travel and living in other countries. Their activities reflect their concern for our total environment.

(Please turn page.)

In residence: "Takara, our six-year-old granddaughter, is a part-time resident. Our gentle cat, Betsy, is shy but friendly."
Foreign languages spoken: German. Plus some French, Italian, and Persian.
Bed and bath: First-floor room with two twin beds, adjacent half bath, overlooking yard and garden. Second-floor room with double bed, sofa, full guest bath (shared if both guest rooms occupied). Crib and cot available.
Breakfast: Usually 7–9. Juice and fresh fruit cup. Thereafter, menu varies. Freshly made bread or muffins, croissants, toast, pancakes or waffles, hot or cold cereals, hot beverage. "Requests cheerfully accommodated."
Plus: Fireplaced living room. Bedroom air conditioners. Fans. Evening beverages. Portable black/white TVs. Screened porch. Yard. Off-street parking.

Amerscot House   508/897-0666
P.O. Box 351, 61 West Acton Road, Stow, MA 01775   fax 508/897-2585

Hosts: Doreen and Jerry Gibson
Location: Quiet rural setting bordered by stone wall, wagon wheel by sign, lovely grounds. Next door to a farm; across from apple orchard. "Minutes to private airfield with helicopter service to Logan Airport, winery, excellent restaurants, three top golf courses, canoeing." Fifteen minutes to Concord or Sudbury, 45 to Boston or Sturbridge. Five miles from Routes 495 and 2.
Open: Year round.
Rates: $80 double, $95 suite. Single $5 less. Amex, MC, Visa.
♥ ⁂ ◆ ✳ ⅄

"You're missing a great place!" said our well-traveled neighbors, who have joined the Gibsons for Scottish country dancing in their barn room used for weddings and meetings. This "great place" is in Bostonians' apple country, in a 1734 center chimney farmhouse that has been the Gibsons' home "and our restoration project" for 25 years. The keeping room Rumford fireplace glows on winter nights. There's a blend of antiquity and modern comfort, with wide board floors, Dutch ovens, beds with handmade quilts and electric mattress pads, private phone lines, and, in armoires, cable TV. Maybe you'll meet Carlo, a business traveler from Italy who loves to cook ravioli. Or grandparents visiting local families, tourists, or getaway guests.

Scottish-born Doreen, a registered nurse who also worked with Jerry in his accounting and consulting business, has experience as a midwife and airline stewardess. The Gibsons, parents of four grown children, opened as a B&B in 1990 on Robert Burns's birthday.

Bed and bath: Three large air-conditioned rooms with individual thermostats and nonworking fireplaces; all private baths. First-floor room has two twin beds, private exterior entrance. Second floor—queen four-poster and adjacent loft with two twin beds. Suite has queen canopied bed, sitting room, and "our Taj Mahal bath" with Jacuzzi, shower stall, marble walls, nonworking fireplace.
Breakfast: 7–9. Orange juice, fruit, granola. Pancakes, eggs Benedict, orange French toast, Dutch babies, scrambled eggs with cream cheese and vermouth. In fireplaced dining room or in greenhouse.
Plus: Croquet court. Individual thermostats. Beverages. Turndown service. Guest refrigerator. Fresh flowers.

From Germany: *"Despite some luxury hotels . . . Amerscot House was the best overnight stay—and most friendly hostess and host—in all our five-week visit in the U.S.A."*

Webb-Bigelow House   617/899-2444

863 Boston Post Road, Weston, MA 02193

Hosts: Jane and Bob Webb
Location: Hidden from road (Route 20) by high fence and hemlocks. On 3 acres adjacent to 800-acre forest. Twelve miles west of Boston; 20 minutes to Harvard, Boston University, Boston College; less than 10 to Brandeis, Wellesley, Regis, and several private secondary schools. Close to restaurants.

Open: Year round. January–March, weekends only. Two-day minimum in October and at Thanksgiving, Christmas, and New Year's.
Rates: $85 double, $90 twin beds. Singles $5 less.
📪 🏹 ⚱

Ever since the historic Longfellow's Wayside Inn asked the Webbs to take overflow guests in 1982, travelers from all over the world have appreciated the hospitality in this large 1827 Federal house, home to the Webbs since 1961. It has 14-foot ceilings, triple-hung (floor-to-ceiling) windows, grand porches, and a swimming pool. Furnishings include fine antiques and family portraits.

Bob is a retired business executive. Jane, a social history writer and peace activist who has worked with the American Friends Service Committee, has taught at Boston University and Wheaton College.

In residence: Two "elderly, personable-with-guests" Australian sheepdogs.
Bed and bath: Three air-conditioned second-floor rooms. Double-bedded room and one with two twin beds connected by a full bath. Other double-bedded room has private hall bath with tub, no shower.
Breakfast: 8–9:30. Eggs, sausages, rolls, muffins, fresh fruit, juice, coffee, tea, and decaf. Served in formal dining room or on pool deck.
Plus: Fireplaced living room and library. TV in family room. Late-afternoon beverage. Down comforters. Robes. Turndown service. Guest refrigerator. Fresh fruit and flowers. Complimentary laundry service for guests staying more than four days. Off-street parking.

From New York: *"A wonderful discovery . . . away from the madding crowd . . . close enough for easy access to Boston . . . gracious and caring . . . Breakfast is imaginative . . . final garnish to a most pleasant stay."*

---

*U*nless otherwise stated, rates in this book are for two and include breakfast in addition to all the amenities in "Plus."

North of Boston
_____ Reservation Services _____

Bed & Breakfast Folks

48 Springs Road, Bedford, MA 01730

Phone: 617/275-9025. Answering machine messages responded to on same day—until 11 p.m.

Listings: 25 and growing. Mostly hosted private residences north and northwest of Boston and Cambridge. Within 30–60 minutes' drive of Boston and Cambridge and convenient to southern New Hampshire. Communities represented include Acton, Bedford, Billerica, Burlington, Chelmsford, Concord, Groton, Lexington, Lowell, Newton, Pepperell, Reading, Stow, Tyngsboro, and Westford.

Reservations: Advance notice is requested. Last-minute calls accommodated when possible.

Rates: $40–$50 single. $50–$75 double. $10 crib or extra bed in room. Deposit equal to one night's lodging required. Full refund, less $10 handling charge, if cancellation is received at least 48 hours prior to arrival.

Phyllis Phillips lists hosts who enjoy sharing their New England homes with tourists and business travelers, and with newcomers who are relocating. Her agency fills a very special need in a historic area that is also known for its rural character (tap maple syrup or feed animals), high technology firms, and the Lowell National Historic Park. Listings include locations where you can swim in a private pond, relax in a hot tub, or enjoy water views.

Plus: Monthly hosted housing available.

Bed & Breakfast Marblehead & North Shore/ Greater Boston & Cape Cod

P.O. Box 35, Newtonville, MA 02160

Phone: 617/964-1606 or (in Canada and in U.S. outside Massachusetts, for reservations only) 800/832-2632. Monday–Friday 9–5; also 7–9 p.m. Monday–Thursday. Saturday 9–12 noon. Sunday 9–12 noon and 7–9 p.m. Off-season hours may vary.

Fax: 617/332-8572.

Listings: 70. Many are within 15 minutes of Boston and Logan Airport—in oceanside towns and historic homes, convenient to colleges, universities and business areas. Many are north of Boston, including the shore communities of Gloucester, Marblehead, Newburyport, Rockport, and Salem. Others are in Cambridge; west of Boston in Concord, Newton, and Sturbridge; in Brewster, Chatham, Eastham, Harwichport, Orleans, and Provincetown on

Cape Cod; and on Martha's Vineyard. Plus a few in coastal Maine communities; in Portsmouth and some ski areas in New Hampshire; and in Vermont.

Reservations: Advance notice preferred; last-minute bookings are possible. Two-night minimum on holiday weekends year round, and throughout the summer, during fall foliage, and for special events such as Haunted Happenings in Salem. (A few hosts accept one-night reservations during those periods.)

Rates: $45–$75 single. $50–$165 double. Family, weekly, and long-term rates available. Deposit of 25 percent required. $15 booking fee (but $10 for one-night reservations) waived for members who pay an annual fee of $25 (unlimited bookings). For special events and wedding parties, a $50 fee entitles all attendees to use the service without a booking fee. For any cancellation received at least two weeks before expected arrival, refund less $15 per room per night is made; $15 booking fee is nonrefundable. If cancellation received with less than two weeks' notice, refund given only if room(s) rebooked. Amex, MC and Visa accepted (5 percent service charge) for late bookings and to secure reservation. ♦

Accommodations "ranging from the reasonable to the regal" are in private residences and inns that are inspected annually by Suzanne Ross and Sheryl Felleman, two professionals who have always had people-oriented careers. They make arrangements for tourists (including families), business travelers, groups (up to 16 people), government agencies, and educational institutions. "We know our hosts and their wonderful and unique homes and inns. After we place guests according to their needs, the result seems to be a mutually unforgettable experience: The stay is a memorable visit for guests, a highlight for hosts too."

Plus: Many are accessible by commuter rail and bus from Boston. Many hosts provide complimentary transportation to and from train or bus stations; to/from Logan Airport for a fee. Some offer private tours. And they acknowledge special occasions.

KEY TO SYMBOLS
♥ Lots of honeymooners come here.
♯ Families with children are very welcome. (Please see page xii.)
♠ "Please emphasize that we are a private home, not an inn."
✤ Groups or private parties sometimes book the entire B&B.
♦ Travel agents' commission paid. (Please see page xii.)
✗ Sorry, no guests' pets are allowed.
✗ No smoking inside *or* no smoking at all, even on porches.

—————— **North of Boston B&Bs** ——————

George Fuller House   508/768-7766
148 Main Street, Route 133, Essex, MA 01929-1304

Hosts: Cindy and Bob Cameron
Location: On main causeway, with views of marsh. Within walking distance of antiques shops (there are 50 in town) and lobster-in-the-rough and other seafood restaurants. Ten-minute drive to Crane's Beach, whale watch excursions, deep-sea fishing. Thirty miles north of Boston, three from Route 128.

Open: Year round. Two-night minimum on holiday and summer weekends.
Rates: $75 double bed; $86 king, queen, or twins. $110 suite. $10 additional person. Off-season, 10 percent less. Midweek sailing packages; sails are $45/hour, three-hour minimum. Amex, Discover, MC, Visa.
♥ ❖ ♦ ⚓

> From Illinois, Washington state, California: *"Beautiful home. . . . Returned with my husband and he was thrilled. . . . Excellent breakfast was beautifully presented. . . . Super. . . . We'll be back for sailing lessons, history, hospitality, and Cindy's breakfast crepes."*

This "happy place" is a house tour hit. It's appreciated by wedding guests. Romantics. Tourists (some on their way to Maine). Antiques lovers. Business travelers. And food and fun lovers too. It's an 1830 shipbuilder's Federal house restored in 1988 by Essex-born Cindy, a registered nurse turned chef, and Bob ("I do what Cindy says to do"), who operates a sailing school. Bob also offers day trips on his 30-foot sailboat. Aunt Blanch, age 92, contributed braided rugs, antiques, and those glorious handmade quilts that set the tone and color scheme for each picture-perfect room. All the caning was done by Cindy's mother, age 86, who also serves as a part-time innkeeper. Returnees abound.

In residence: Mittens, a double-pawed calico cat, "meanders around evaluating guests."
Bed and bath: Five large rooms and one suite. All with air conditioning, TV, private baths, phones and jacks. On first floor—cathedral-ceilinged room with partial-canopy queen bed, shower bath, Palladian window overlooking marsh. Queen canopied bed, Indian shutters, fireplace, shower bath. Double bed, marsh view, full bath. Second floor—two rooms with king/twins option; one with working fireplace shares deck overlooking marshes with suite that has queen canopied bed, working fireplace, shower bath, sitting room with day bed. Rollaway available.
Breakfast: 7:30–9:30. Pina colada pancakes, Belgian waffles with yogurt and orange sauce, or French toast with brandied lemon butter. Juice, fruit, home-baked breads. In dining room or guests' room.
Plus: Individual thermostats. Fireplaced living room. Late-afternoon beverages and homemade cookies. Porches and decks. Bicycle and camping equipment storage space.

Miles River Country Inn

508/468-7206

823 Bay Road, P.O. Box 149, Hamilton, MA 01936   **fax 508/468-3999**

Hosts: Gretel and Peter Clark
Location: In estate and horse country. Down a long driveway, past fields, apple orchard, caretaker's house. On 30 acres of lawn, gardens, mature trees, outbuildings, two ponds, meadow marshes. Ten minutes to renowned six-mile-long Crane's Beach, 25 to Gloucester, 5 to dozens of antiques shops, 4 to Hamilton train station. Forty minutes from Logan Airport.
Open: Year round.
Rates: Single $50 or $60 ($5 less if bath shared), double $75–$85. Extra bed or crib $15.
🏡 🛥 ♣ ♦ ✈ ⅍

The rambling 200-year-old colonial, home to the Clarks for 20 years, has 24 rooms (each quite different—one has walls covered with 19th-century bedsteads from Brittany) and 12 fireplaces. Family heirlooms are among the eclectic furnishings. B&B guests are welcome to bird right here on the Atlantic flyway, hike, cross-country ski, and enjoy the landscaped grounds, even a secret garden that has formal flower beds and a statued fountain. Sometimes, colorful carriage-driving competitions from nearby Myopia Hunt Club can be viewed.

Gretel, the beekeeper, recently retired as bilingual specialist for the State Department of Education. Peter is a major energy developer in Latin America. Through their earlier careers, they lived in France, Germany, Norway, Chile, and Nigeria.

In residence: Lady, "spitting image of dog from *Lady and the Tramp*." Tess, a German shepherd. Tinuchen, a Burmese cat. A flock of chickens.
Foreign languages spoken: Spanish, French, and some German.
Bed and bath: Eight rooms (four with working fireplaces) with queen, double (one extra-long), or twin beds on second or third floors. Rollaways and crib available. Room size and decor vary. Three rooms have private baths; rest share two baths.
Breakfast: 7–10. Croissants, homemade muffins, scones and coffee cakes. Fresh egg/vegetable/cheese casserole, pancakes, or waffles. Homemade fruit preserves and honey. On terrace, in glassed-in alcove with expansive view of lawns, or in fireplaced dining room with original colonial paneled walls.
Plus: Fireplaced living room. Baby grand piano. Window fans. Late-afternoon tea or wine with cookies and fruit. Fresh fruit and flowers. Garden terraces. Trail maps. Bike routes. In season, a jar of honey. Weddings and family reunions booked.

From England: *"Fabulous house and gardens. Extremely hospitable, friendly, and helpful hosts. Home-baked breakfasts. Wonderful view from the rooms. Fantastic birds and wildlife . . . saw an otter in the pond one evening."*

Wedding guests love to stay at a B&B.

"The Very Victorian" Sherman-Berry House
508/459-4760

163 Dartmouth Street, Lowell, MA 01851-2425   fax 508/459-4760

Hosts: Susan Scott and husband David Strohmeyer
Location: In a quiet residential neighborhood of a city known for its 19th-century cotton mills and as birthplace of Jack Kerouac and Bette Davis. (The country's first planned industrial city has retained miles of canals, part of an extraordinary park system that is still being discovered by many Bostonians.) Minutes' drive to New England Quilt Museum and Lowell National and State Historic Parks' (very reasonably priced) museums and guided tours (some include canal and open-air trolley rides. Seven miles to New Hampshire; 26 miles northwest of Boston.
Open: Year round except Christmas.
Rates: $45 single. $50 double. $5 one-night surcharge. Family rates available.
♦ ♦ ♦ ♦ ♦

Guests wrote: *"Breakfasts were extravaganzas . . . thoughtful personal touches in each room. . . . Our granddaughter loved it. . . . For any antiques lover, this is a must-see . . . 19th-century books, hats, dolls, silverware, player piano. . . . Charm and hospitality beyond compare . . . spirit is relaxed, happy, and adventurous . . . clean and lovely . . . superb museum suggestions. . . . Wonderful!"*

After many years in Alaska, David, "a computer guru," and Susan, a therapist, were transferred to his company's headquarters in Lowell. They bought "a mostly restored grand old house— but not a mansion," toured New England in search of appropriate furnishings, and then commissioned a spectacular stained glass window that has a story of its own. Susan became the prime mover behind a neighborhood drive to create the Tyler Park Historic District. There's more—worth a special trip.

Bed and bath: Two second-floor rooms. One with a double bed; the other has two twins. Victorian Murphy bed and crib available. Shared full bath (hand-held shower).
Breakfast: 7–9, at mutually agreed upon time. Could be popular Irish oatmeal; Alaskan reindeer sausage and eggs with garden grown herbs; eggs Benedict; or Lowell Mill Girls' Breakfast—ham, baked beans, apple pie. Susan cooks weekdays, David on weekends.
Plus: Susan's award-winning walking tour. Moxie, a Lowell-developed drink. Use of tandem bicycle. Stereopticon viewer. Access to computer, copier, fax. Extensive library on restoration and Victoriana. Hard-wired smoke detectors. Babysitting by prior arrangement.

Harborside House
617/631-1032

23 Gregory Street, Marblehead, MA 01945-3241

Host: Susan Livingston
Location: In historic district of this yachting center, which is four square miles in all. Thirty minutes north of Logan Airport, downtown Boston, I-95.
Open: Year round.
Rates: April–December and holidays $70. Off-season $50 single, $65 double. $5 one-night surcharge.
♦ ♦ ♦ ♦

From this comfortable mid-19th-century house, built by a ship's carpenter, there are views of hundreds of sailboats in the famous harbor. In 1985 Susan, mother of three grown children, made her home into a B&B, a welcoming place that blends her interests—sewing (she's a professional dressmaker), baking (recipes shared), arranging homegrown flowers, and history (she's a former historic house guide). Rooms are furnished with antiques and period wallcoverings. Many guests follow her suggested walking route (sometimes by moonlight) along winding streets, past old-fashioned doorways and interesting gardens, to historic sites, shops, restaurants, and the beach.

Susan's major avocational interest is competitive Masters swimming; she's among the country's top 10 in her age group.

Foreign language spoken: "Un petit peu de francais."
Bed and bath: Up steep stairs to two second-floor rooms—each with desk, clock radio, TV—that share a full bath. Large (14 by 20 feet) harborview room with two antique twin beds tucked under the eaves; floor mattress for child. One room with double bed, garden view.
Breakfast: Usually 7–9. Juice. Fresh fruit in season. Homemade applesauce; warm home-baked raisin bran, blueberry, or cranberry muffins; banana, muesli, or cranberry bread. Cereals. Yogurt. Coffee and teas. On covered porch or in dining room with harbor view.
Plus: Third-story deck. Fireplaced beamed living room. Flagstone patio. Secluded yard with gardens. Afternoon tea and cookies. Mineral water. Specialty chocolates. Menus of local restaurants.

From Michigan: *"A calm and lovely place."* From Oklahoma: *"Just as we imagined New England would be."* From Washington state: *"A warm, friendly home."*

Spray Cliff on the Ocean

508/744-8924
800/626-1530
fax 508/744-8924

25 Spray Avenue, Marblehead, MA
Mailing address: c/o Salem Inn, 7 Summer Street
Salem, MA 01970-3315

Hosts: Diane and Dick Pabich
Location: In a residential neighborhood, 2½ miles outside of town, 15 miles north of Boston. Steps away from Preston Beach, atop a 20-foot seawall "with views that extend forever."
Open: Year round. Two-night minimum June–October weekends. Reservations strongly suggested along with estimated arrival time, please, so someone will be on hand to greet you.
Rates: April 15–November 15 $130–$150 oceanfront; $125–$150 street side; $175–$200 suite. Off-season $100–$125, suite $175. Third person in room $25. Amex, CB, Diners, Discover, MC, Visa.
♥ ❖ ♦ ✄

"When a public television crew filmed a Doris Day special, they interviewed John Updike, a Doris Day fan, from our seaside patio with the surf crashing in the background. Some academic institutons come here for a retreat. Honeymooners love this place. And landlocked people from other parts of the country never want to leave!"

(Please turn page.)

Once the scene of many fashionable weddings and graduation parties, the 18-room Tudor mansion, built in 1919 as a summer home, became an inn in 1940. It was a rooming house "in shambles" when the Pabiches bought in 1976. After they repaired it for their own home, Dick, a software manager for Raytheon, and Diane, a real estate developer, opened a 23-room inn in nearby Salem. "So as our children went off to college, opening our waterside home as a B&B was a natural."

In residence: Daffodill is the family's chocolate Labrador retriever.
Bed and bath: Seven spacious rooms; five with ocean views. All with private baths, antiques, wicker, chintz curtains. First floor—queen-bedded suite with fireplace, full bath, private oceanfront deck. Street-side room has one king, one double bed, shower bath, working fireplace. Second floor—king bed, working fireplace, shower bath; two queen-bedded rooms, full baths. Third floor—two king-bedded rooms, shower baths.
Breakfast: 8–10:30. Buffet style in the fireplaced oceanfront breakfast/sitting room. Baked goods, cold cereal, fresh fruit, juice, coffee and tea.
Plus: Patio with that mesmerizing view. Refrigerator and toaster available. Gardens. Fruit bowl. Aperitifs. No cigars or pipes, please.

From Michigan: *"Better than the Ritz!"* From California: *"Idyllic escapism."*

Ten Mugford Street Bed & Breakfast
10 Mugford Street, Marblehead, MA 01945-3449   617/639-0343
                                                    617/631-5642

Hosts: Liz and Mike Mentuck
Location: In historic Old Town section, one block from town landing on harbor. On a bus line from Boston (30 minutes). Eighteen miles north of Boston. Near antiques shops, historic sites, restaurants—everything.
Open: Year round. Two-night mini-

mum on some weekends.
Rates: In hosts' residence—$75 per room, $95 suite (two bedrooms and a bath). $525 weekly rate in season. Special rates for groups (e.g., wedding guests or family reunions) that book entire B&B.
♥ ⬛ ✲

"In 1986 we bought the perfect house for B&B." That may sum things up for the first B&B in a four-square-mile charming town that needed lodging facilities. This "19th-century beauty" was a home for elderly women, originally donated to the Marblehead Female Humane Society by a local family. It was restored by the Mentucks, who decorated in Grandmother's-house style—comfortable and fresh-looking with books and antiques. In 1988 the Mentucks, lifelong Marblehead residents (a marina owner and an enthusiastic hostess), gutted and rebuilt a three-story Federal-style house (that began as a 1700s carriage house) located across the street. "Typically New England" furnishings are in this all-suite property, which is popular with families and with business and weekly guests. In both locations there's a casual, friendly atmosphere—with lots of assistance for day-trip planning.

Bed and bath: In the main house—four second-floor rooms with double or twin beds share three baths. Across the street—four two-room suites with king or queen bed. Each has refrigerator and, overlooking the garden, a

balcony. Two suites (booked by week) have kitchenette, cathedral ceiling, skylight, full bath; two have shower bath.
Breakfast: 7:30–10:30. Fruit, muffins, cereal, coffee, tea, juice. Buffet in Ten Mugford family room (no smoking allowed) with TV and refrigerator. Suite guests eat at several smaller tables set in annex dining room.
Plus: Night parking provided. Make-yourself tea or coffee. Yard and garden. Private guest entrance. Use of dining room for take-out food; deli is half block away.

The Windsor House

508/462-3778

38 Federal Street, Newburyport, MA 01950   fax 508/465-3443

Hosts: Judith and John Harris
Location: Within walking distance of the harbor, shops, performance center. Across from historic Old South Church. Five-minute drive to ocean, Parker River Wildlife Refuge, and Maudslay State Park (magnificent grounds on the Merrimack River).
Open: Year round. Two-day minimum on weekends and holidays, May–December.

Rates: Tax and service charge included. $75–$90 shared bath, $115 private. Singles $62–$70 shared bath, $85 private. Family suite $170 (four persons). Less November–April. $25 additional guest. No charge under age three. Corporate rates and winter packages. Amex, Discover, MC, Visa.
♥ ♨ ♣ ♦ ⚮

Guests feel as if they have come home to an English country house—with a courtyard and garden, traditional Cornish breakfast, afternoon tea, a portrait of HM Queen Elizabeth II, British publications—and John, a retired Royal Navy senior communications officer. He lived in a lovely cottage not far from King Arthur's castle when Judith met him (at a B&B in Tintagel, Cornwall, England) while she was studying Megalithic Britain. "We courted on the high cliffs of North Cornwall, married in 1990, and returned to this inn that I established in 1979."

Recently refurbished, the former 1786 mansion/chandlery is a three-storied brick building that combines colonial, Georgian, and Federal styles of architecture.

In residence: Trelawny, the cat. Lilabet, a toy poodle, age 17.
Foreign languages spoken: A little French, less German.
Bed and bath: Six large rooms; some with sleigh or four-poster beds. First floor—double and a twin bed, private shower bath, private street entrance. Second floor—queen, private full bath. Suite (can be separate rooms)—room with double bed and another with a double, a twin, a crib, lots of toys; hall full bath shared with third-floor king-bedded room. Other third-floor room—king bed, private shower bath.
Breakfast: 8–9. Traditional English menu—eggs, turkey ham, tomatoes, mushrooms, beans. Sometimes pancakes or waffles. Bread and muffins. Their own brew of coffee. Watch preparations and chat with innkeepers (occasionally in Cornish dress) in huge brick-walled kitchen that has 14-foot ceiling.
Plus: Gracious common room with TV and VCR. Formal dining room. Window fans.

Inn on Cove Hill

508/546-2701

37 Mount Pleasant Street, Rockport, MA 01966-1727

Hosts: Marjorie and John Pratt
Location: One block from village, harbor, and shops. Bus servicing Cape Ann goes by the inn. One mile to train to Boston.
Open: April–October. Two-night minimum in July and August and on

September and October weekends.
Rates: April–early June (excluding Memorial Day), $45 shared bath, $56–$77 private bath. Late June–October, $48 shared bath, $63, $75, $93, or $98 private bath.
♥ ✈ ⅄

They took a trip around the world and stayed in many B&Bs. John, a civil (geotechnical) engineer specializing in soils and foundations, and Marjorie, a registered nurse in public health and home care, found that the idea of "being together, sharing a business in a lovely location" had strong appeal.

Since their 1978 career change, the Pratts have become parents (Michelle is 11 now), moved to a nearby residence, and completely restored this classic square, three-story 205-year-old Federal home, the very inn where Marjorie and John spent their own honeymoon. What they offer all guests is a friendly atmosphere and the option of privacy. Their attention to architectural detail can be seen in the wood-shingled roof, pumpkin pine floorboards, H and L hinges, dentil molding, and a spiral staircase with 13 steps symbolizing the original 13 colonies. Furnishings include fine family antiques, reproductions, and paintings—some done by artist guests. English travelers wrote, "Beautifully decorated room . . . a lovely restful atmosphere. Heaven on earth, what more can I say?"

Bed and bath: Eleven rooms on three floors. Nine with private bath. One first-floor room has private entrance. Third floor reached via a steep narrow stairway or outside metal spiral staircase. Rooms (some are very small) have queen bed (some canopied), queen and trundle, a double bed, or a double and a twin; some are four-posters or cannonball.
Breakfast: 8–9:30. (Coffee at 7.) Continental with one of seven varieties of muffins. Served around the pump garden (weather permitting), in living room, or on individual trays in guest rooms.
Plus: Bedroom fans. Legendary saga of how the mansion was built with pirates' gold. Third-floor porch with harbor view. Hot spiced cider in fall. Will meet guests at train station. Parking.

Old Farm Inn

508/546-3237

291 Granite Street, Route 127
Rockport, MA 01966-1028

(U.S./Canada) 800/233-6828

Hosts: The Balzarinis—grandma Mabel; son Bill and wife Susan
Location: Quiet country setting on the northernmost tip of Cape Ann. Next to Halibut Point State Park and Reservation, one of my family's favorite ocean viewpoints (with tidal pools). Two and a half miles to town center.

Open: April–November. Two-night weekend minimum, three nights on most holiday weekends.
Rates: $78–$108 July–October. $68–$98 off-season. Amex, MC, Visa.
♥ ✈

It's a picture-perfect landmark. A red New England farmhouse built in 1799, bordered by an old stone wall, with extensive lawns and gardens. Inside there's an eclectic blend of primitive and country antiques, a beamed and fireplaced living room, print wallpapers, and some dramatic and romantic touches. ("Bernice, please keep some as surprises.") Many guests take nature walks (one leads to a quarry) in the adjacent state park before breakfast. Or visit Folly Cove for lobster in the rough and sunsets. They relax. They bicycle in this gorgeous and interesting area. They become mesmerized by the ocean view (five-minute walk) free of shops or crowds. And they return "home" to a peaceful, friendly environment.

Bill, a native Rockporter, and his parents established the inn in 1964. Susan, a Pennsylvanian until she married Bill in the 1960s, is responsible for the decor. "It's amazing how many people dream about this lifestyle."

Foreign languages spoken: Susan is trying to learn Spanish.
Bed and bath: Nine rooms (eight are air-conditioned); all with private bath, TV, fans (some are ceiling). Four barn rooms on two levels; one king-bedded room with kitchenette, three with a queen and twin bed each. In main inn, on first floor, one two-room suite with queen bed, two twin daybeds in sitting room, full bath. Upstairs, two cozy double-bedded rooms with shower baths; one has private sitting room. "Especially romantic" room with queen canopied bed, antique love seat, shower bath. Plus cottage that sleeps up to six; rented weekly in summer, two-night minimum rest of year. Rollaway and crib available.
Breakfast: 8:30–9:30. Fresh fruit, juice, cereal, homemade muffins and granola, bread, coffee cake, yogurt, herbal teas, hot chocolate, Sanka. Buffet style on black iron stove in sun room with floor-to-ceiling windows overlooking gardens.
Plus: Off-the-beaten-path suggestions. Hotpots, mugs, coffee and tea, and small refrigerators in most rooms. Library nook. Beverages and cookies. "Collection of old magazines—some from 1919!" Iron and hair dryer by request. Bike rentals delivered to inn.

Pleasant Street Inn

17 Pleasant Street, Rockport, MA 01966-2152

508/546-3915
800/541-3915

Hosts: Lynne and Roger Norris
Location: Residential. Two blocks from the center of town with its shops, beaches, galleries, restaurants. Set back and up from the street, overlooking church-steepled profile of the village with Sandy Bay beyond.
Open: Year round. Three-night minimum on Memorial Day, July 4, Labor Day, and Columbus Day weekends.
Rates: July and August $78 smallest room; $88 turret room or room with whirlpool tub; $98 largest room, full bath. All others $80–$85. $10 third person. January–June $69–$75. September–December $65–$85. Singles $3 less. MC, Visa.
♥ ♣ ❖ ♦ ✈

From England: *"A delightful house, stylish, tasteful, and extremely comfortable . . . the best homemade muffins we tasted in the USA!"* From Massachusetts: *"He's in the business (a remodeling contractor) and did the beautiful work on the huge Victorian . . . wonderful moldings and woodwork . . . polished floors . . . traditional and simple furnishings. . . . Just right!"*

(Please turn page.)

The Norrises, longtime Rockport residents, were looking for a larger house. "Ten years ago we found one that we decided to share." It's a Shingle Style 1893 Victorian with huge front lawn. One guest room has a tin ceiling. Another has a spiral staircase leading to its own turret with futon. Some have a window seat and/or a bay window. There's a popular front veranda with overview of town. And as one experienced guest observed, "They know how to host too."

In residence: Son Curt, 18, and daughter Brett, 14. Toddy, Lynne's mother. Duke, "our Labrador, who craves attention."
Bed and bath: Eight rooms, all with private baths, on three floors. (Steep stairs to third floor.) One room with whirlpool tub, color TV, refrigerator, private entrance. Queen or double bed; some rooms with two single beds also. Rollaway available. Carriage house apartment (weekly) with one or two bedrooms (sleeps seven) includes laundry.
Breakfast: 8:30–10. Juice. Fruit. Homemade baked goods—recipes, including one for pecan cornbread, shared. Yogurt. English muffins. Cereals. Coffee and tea. In dining room or on veranda.
Plus: Ceiling fans in all third-floor rooms. Window fans. Some rooms with individual thermostats. Beverages. Guest refrigerator. A green cloth sack to carry wine or beer to restaurant in this dry town. TV in guest living room. Off-street parking.

Seacrest Manor   508/546-2211
131 Marmion Way, Rockport, MA 01966-1988

Hosts: Leighton T. Saville and Dwight B. MacCormack Jr.
Location: About 300 yards from the ocean, overlooking spectacular rocky coastline. On two acres of gardens and woodland. On scenic (seasonal) trolley route. One mile from center of Rockport, off Route 127A.

Open: April through November. Three-day minimum on holidays, two-day on weekends. Reservations required.
Rates: $88–$120 depending on bath arrangement. Singles $10 less.
♥ ✈

Leighton and Dwight host in an English style intended as "concierge-type guest assistance." Hence the attention to turned-down beds, tea at four, shined gentlemen's shoes (when left outside door at night), and peace and quiet in a beautiful setting. In an English guest's words, "Seacrest Manor must be heaven—came for one, stayed for seven!"

The part-Georgian, part-Federal-style house, built in 1911 and an inn since the 1940s, was for many years the summer home of Arthur Park of Boston's Durgin-Park restaurant family. In 1973 the two current hosts took it over when Dwight, an ordained Congregational minister, was looking for an alternative career. (He had lived in England for a few months and was on the faculty of three area colleges.) Leighton's family home is three doors away. (He retired from his NBC executive position in 1985.)

Recent changes include fresh classic wallcoverings, additions from family art collections, and still more prizewinning gardens. Furnishings, a mixture of traditional and antique, include a dramatic gold-leaf-framed floor-to-ceiling living room mirror that came from the old Philadelphia Opera House. And then there's that endless ocean view from the big second-story deck.

In residence: Tansy, a 13-year-old black Lab mixture, really does greet guests with a paw-shake.

Foreign languages spoken: Some French.

Bed and bath: Eight carpeted rooms; two on first floor, rest on second (two are seaside with picture windows and deck). Six with private bath; one two-room suite with shared bath. Queen bed or king/twins option.

Breakfast: 7:30–9:30. A different specialty each day. Fresh fruit cup, juices, spiced Irish oatmeal with chopped dates, dry cereals, bacon and eggs, toast and sometimes muffins. Coffee, English tea, chocolate. At tables set with fine china and linens.

Plus: Mints on pillow with quote from Shakespeare. Huge living room with books, magazines, English publications. Bedroom oscillating fans. Hammock between trees. Library. Complimentary newspapers Monday–Saturday. Beach towels. Bicycles ($5 for half day). No cigar or pipe smoking indoors.

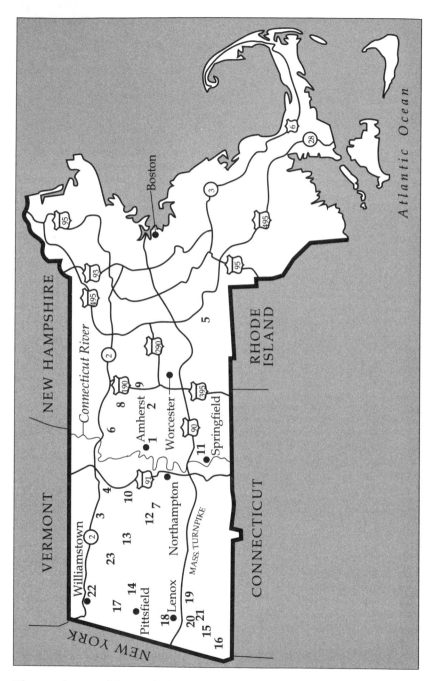

The numbers on this map indicate the locations of Central Massachusetts, Connecticut River Valley, and Berkshires B&Bs described in detail in this chapter.

Central Massachusetts, Connecticut River Valley, and Berkshires

Please see page 115 for Cape Cod, Martha's Vineyard, and Nantucket; Southeastern Massachusetts; Boston Area; Just a Little West; North of Boston.

Central Massachusetts and Connecticut River Valley
———— Reservation Services ————

Folkstone Bed & Breakfast Reservation Service

Darling Road, Dudley, MA 01571-9703

Phone: 508/943-7118 or 800/762-2751. (Machine messages returned promptly.)

Fax: 508/949-3652.

Listings: 15. Most are hosted private residences. A few inns. Several are in the Worcester/Sturbridge area of Central Massachusetts and in the "quiet corner" of northeastern Connecticut. They range from in-town to mountainside locations, from colonial to Victorian, from remodeled farmhouse to "elegant modern."

Reservations: Most hosts appreciate at least 24 hours' notice. Some long-term housing available; host on premises.

Rates: $45–$60 single, $55–$80 double. $3 surcharge for one-night stay. Monthly and weekly rates available. Cost of first night's lodging is required as a deposit. Deposits (less $15 service fee) are refundable if cancellation is made at least seven days in advance. Amex, MC, Visa.

Priscilla Van de Workeen (featured in *'GBH* magazine) traveled all over the world as deputy director of the Harkness Fellowships. A couple of years ago, she and her husband moved from Manhattan to his grandmother's Central Massachusetts farmhouse, which they transformed (rebuilt). Then, utilizing her considerable experience as both B&B traveler and host, Priscilla took on this personalized reservation service. (She gives much credit to her mother, who at age 72 opened and ran a successful B&B in the 1980s.) She has continued to add new listings, all interesting homes and hosts.

Other reservation services with some B&Bs in Central Massachusetts and the Connecticut River Valley:
Bed & Breakfast/Inns of New England, page 259
Berkshire Bed & Breakfast Homes, page 234

Central Massachusetts and ___ Connecticut River Valley B&Bs ___

Allen House Victorian Inn   413/253-5000
599 Main Street, Amherst, MA 01002-2409

Host: Alan and Ann Zieminski
Location: In town, on three acres. Across the street from the Emily Dickinson House. Within walking distance of Amherst College; Hampshire College; University of Massachusetts; galleries, museums, shops, restaurants. Ten miles to Deerfield Village. On five-college (free) bus route.

Open: Year round. Two-night minimum on college and foliage weekends.
Rates: Tax included. Vary according to season and length of stay. $45–$85 single. $55–$95 double.
♥ ✖ ✔

The hand-carved cherry mantels of this Queen Anne Stick Style house are pictured in the Metropolitan Museum of Art catalog. Some of the wallpapers were designed by William Morris and Walter Crane. Built in 1886, the house still has original woodwork. The antiques have been collected through the years by Alan; he "has a perfect eye for spotting Aesthetic Period (1880s) pieces," according to his brother, Jonas, assistant innkeeper, who has helped to research the "Oscar Wilde period." Ann (a dental hygienist), other family members, museum staffers, and guests have also exchanged information with Alan, a biochemist who lived in the house as a student before he bought it "with the desire to make an 18-room Victorian into other than student housing." For his efforts he received the Amherst Historic Commission's Preservation Award.

Bed and bath: On first and second floors—five rooms, all private baths, with a queen, a double, or a double and one twin bed. Rollaway available.
Breakfast: At guests' convenience. Perhaps eggs Benedict, Swedish pancakes, stuffed French toast, or Southwestern-style eggs.
Plus: Central air conditioning. Bedroom ceiling fans. Beverages. Goose down comforters and pillows. Tea and refreshments.

> From Connecticut: *"Beautiful . . . hearty and healthy breakfasts. . . . Warm hospitality."*

*I*f you have met one B&B host, you haven't met them all.

Jenkins House Bed & Breakfast Inn

Barre Common, P.O. Box 779, Barre, MA 01005   508/355-6444
800/378-7373

Location: In the center of this small town, at one end of common at main road. Walk to gourmet restaurant (established 1992 with tavern downstairs, fine dining upstairs) in restored business block; summer Sunday night common gazebo band concerts; Saturday (Mother's Day–Halloween) farmer's market. Minutes to Audubon sanctuary, Barre Falls, herb farm, horseback riding, antiquing, apple orchards, the country's oldest agricultural fair (in Hardwick). Twenty miles northwest of Worcester, 30 north of Brimfield, 20 south (a pretty ride) to Sturbridge; 90 minutes from Boston.

Reservations: Year round. Two-night Columbus Day weekend minimum.

Rates: $60 single, $95 double.
⁂

"That would make a perfect B&B," said the innkeeper-to-be when he first saw this Victorian (in 1987), not knowing that this was the very house the Realtor was about to show him. Although David Ward grew up in Worcester, he had never been to this "lost-in-time uncommercialized town." He and cohost Joe Perrin (from New York and Connecticut), both experienced in the hospitality industry, revitalized the property and furnished eclectically. They established an English garden. And on both the front and back porches they put tables and chairs and a swing. "Always, first-time guests are amazed that there is no traffic light for miles around!"

In residence: One dog in hosts' quarters.
Bed and bath: Five second-floor rooms; three with air conditioning. Private tub/shower bath for room with queen bed, small fireplace (Duraflame log burns for almost two hours), ceiling fan, balcony. Room with canopied queen bed, 11 windows, private tub/shower bath. Canopied queen and king/twin option; private shower baths. Two double-bedded rooms, each with ceiling fan, share a full bath.
Breakfast: 8–10. "Menu differs every day of your stay." Chef's choice. Maybe apple cinnamon or light chocolate waffles or French toast made with homemade bread. Homemade muffins or scones. At individual tables in fireplaced breakfast room that has 10 windows.
Plus: Two fireplaced common rooms. TV (three are color) in all guest rooms. Mints on the pillow. Directions to country store in Petersham.

1797 House

413/625-2975

Charlemont Road, Box 23, Buckland, MA 01338

Host: Janet Turley
Location: Rural. West of Greenfield, 5 miles from nearest village; 17 miles from historic Deerfield. About 30 minutes to University of Massachusetts, Smith College, Williams College, Deerfield Academy, Stoneleigh-Burnham, Eaglebrook, Amherst. Minutes to Shelburne Falls' Bridge of Flowers or to Berkshire East or Swift River Inn (cross-country).
Open: Year round.
Rates: Single $60–$65. Double $75 one night, $70 per night for two nights, $65 three or more nights.
♥ ◀ ⁂ ✈

"Even New Englanders are surprised at how 'terribly New England' it is here. The church bells chime three times a day. Two couples have bought or built within a few blocks. Many guests come for academic-related reasons. And we've become known as a romantic getaway and honeymoon spot!"

Janet, recently retired from teaching, lives in a large two-story 1797 colonial. Mary Lyon, the founder of Mount Holyoke College, used the house for the Winter School for Young Ladies in 1829–31. Today the neighborhood is one of 18th- and early 19th-century homes together with a traditional spired white New England church, a historical society, and some properties with horses and sheep.

Before restoring and adding here, Janet had experience redoing an abandoned seven-bedroom house. She now consults for remodeling, decorating, and B&B.

From California: *"Spacious yet cozy and comfortable. We stayed one night but wished it were a week."*

In residence: Janet's mother, who has her own apartment in the house, is a big hit with guests. (So are her hand-stitched items and English garden.)
Bed and bath: Three second-floor rooms. Private full bath for double-bedded (one brass, one four-poster) rooms; private shower (no tub) bath for room with a double and a twin bed.
Breakfast: 8–9:30. Served in 18th-century fireplaced dining room or on large screened porch. Juice, fresh fruit, beverage. Stuffed croissants, sausage/apple ring or sauteed ham strips; French toast with local syrup and bacon; mushroom egg casserole with baked tomatoes; or fresh blueberry pancakes.
Plus: Beverages. Sometimes a guided tour of area. Lots of suggestions—including auctions. Big screened porch with wicker furniture, plants, overlooking old cemetery and abandoned orchard. Bedroom fans.

Hitchcock House
                   413/774-7452
15 Congress Street, Greenfield, MA 01301

Hosts: Betty and Peter Gott
Location: Ten-minute walk to town. "Ten-minute drive to five miles of woodland trails with breathtaking views and pond." Near whitewater rafting, skiing, colleges, schools. Three miles to Historic Deerfield and Deerfield Academy.

Open: Year round.
Rates: King $70 shared bath, $90 private bath. Queen $55 shared bath, $75 private. Double $60 shared, $75 private. Single $45 shared bath. MC, Visa.
♥ ♦ ♠ ♣ ♦

From Massachusetts: *"Three comfortable floors in a beautiful Victorian, just past the center of town, decorated with a lot of love."* From England: *"We now feel we know what the famous American hospitality is all about. . . . Not surprising that other guests all seemed to be on return visits."*

Caught in the rain while walking? The Gotts provide taxi service. And if you need a golf, tennis, or horseshoe partner, you'll find one here. Newlyweds are greeted with champagne. Betty shares recipes. Since 1989 the Gotts have been hosting in the style that they experienced on an Irish B&B trip. Their turreted 1881 Victorian is across the street from the high-rise where they met.

(Please turn page.)

Peter, a town councilman who was a teacher, headmaster, and NASA electronics engineeer, has nearby Stonehenge-type obelisks on his places-to-see list. Betty, "a lover of interior design," recently retired as a University of Massachusetts lab technician.

Foreign language spoken: French, "haltingly."
Bed and bath: Five rooms (two on first floor) share three baths; private bath possible. King, queen, double, or twin beds. Cot and portacrib available.
Breakfast: 8:30 "or as requested." Continental earlier. Fruit, juices, hot or cold cereals, yogurt with toppings, bacon, eggs, cheeses, meat and vegetable casseroles, apple or blueberry pancakes. In dining room or on adjacent enclosed porch.
Plus: Third-floor rooms are air conditioned. Three living rooms (two with fireplaces). Two enclosed porches. Hammond electric organ. Handmade quilts. Guest refrigerator. Croquet. Horseshoes, lawn swing, patio, toys. Fresh flowers in season.

The Brandt House
29 Highland Avenue, Greenfield, MA 01301

413/774-3329
800/235-3329
fax 413/772-2908

Host: Phoebe Compton
Location: Quiet. High on a hill, surrounded by 3½ acres of lawns and century-old evergreens. Hiking trails from here lead to panoramic views and town park. Five-minute walk to town and lighted skating pond. Five-minute drive to Historic Deerfield; within 15 minutes of cross country ski center in Northfield and many private schools; 20 to Amherst and Northampton. Within two miles of I-91 and Route 2.

Open: Year round. Two-night minimum on May and October weekends.
Rates: Weekends: May–September $85 shared bath, $105 private; October $100 shared, $125 private; November–April $75 shared, $90 private. Weekdays: $10–$20 less. Corporate and long-term rates available. Amex, MC, Visa.
♥ ♠ ✿ ♦ ✍

This estatelike turn-of-the-century 16-room Colonial Revival is made for entertaining, for B&B, for business meetings, and for weddings too. It fits Phoebe's style—as did her Boston area brownstone, where she hosted before she moved here in 1986. An interior designer (with computer industry experience in sales and marketing), she has decorated the spacious, light-filled tall-ceilinged rooms with a blend of contemporary and antique pieces, Oriental rugs, and works by local artists. The beamed living room has a fireplace, bay windows, and wonderful valley views. A regulation pool table and fireplace are in the library. Wicker furniture and a swing are on the huge, inviting covered porch.

In residence: Sheba, a "can-be-outdoors-if-guests-prefer" cat.
Foreign language spoken: A little German.
Bed and bath: Seven large, centrally air-conditioned rooms (two with working fireplace) on second and third floors. Five with private full baths. Two share large full bath. King, queen, double, twin, and extra beds available; all with feather beds and down comforters. Some suite options.

Breakfast: Usually 7:15–9. Juice, fresh fruit, homemade granola, home-made baked goods, freshly ground coffee. Plus, on weekends, cheese blintzes, Moravian frittata with cheese sauce, or French toast, all with bacon. At large oak dining room table overlooking terrace, in living room at table for two overlooking valley, or on covered porch.

Plus: Clay tennis court. Private phones in some rooms. Upright piano. Down comforters. Guest refrigerator. Fresh fruit and flowers. Dinners for special occasions.

From New Mexico: *"Beautiful home, wonderful breakfasts, and a most gracious staff make this B&B hard to leave."*

Arnold Taft House   508/832-7282
166 Millville Street, Mendon, MA 01756

Hosts: Diedre and Michael Meddaugh
Location: In the soon-to-be-discovered (go now!) Blackstone Valley. On a country road in good bicycling country (Diedre has maps that include routes taking you from one B&B to another). Short drive to walking paths along river, canoeing, summer canal tour boats, museums, National Park Service talks. Two miles to New England's largest zoo. Fifteen minutes to commuter train to Boston (37 miles to northeast); 24 miles north of Providence.
Open: Year round, by reservation only.
Rates: $60 queen, private bath. Shared bath $55 queen, fireplace; $50 twins. Singles $10 less. $10 trundle or crib.
♦ ♣ ✴ ⊁

Many guests ask Diedre if she went to cooking school. One from British Columbia borrowed Michael's bicycle to trace his roots and the town's history. The Meddaughs' brick 1820 Federal house has two beehive ovens, seven staircases, 12-over-12 windows, and original wide board floors. It is decorated with colonial colors, antiques and reproductions, hooked and Persian rugs.

"This was a dream since our first B&B visit in 1984. After two years of restoration, we opened in 1990." Diedre, a former computer designer, now has a decorating business. Michael is a software manager for a computer company.

In residence: Son Urik, age 15. Mouchie, a mutt. Floppy, a rabbit.
Foreign language spoken: A little French.
Bed and bath: Three second-floor rooms. Two large queen-bedded rooms (one with private full bath); each with wood-burning fireplace and window air conditioner. Room with four-poster shares full bath with room that has two twins.
Breakfast: 8–9:30. Cheese omelet with salsa, apple pancakes, almond French toast, or cinnamon blintzes. Fresh fruit. Home-baked surprises. Sausage, bacon, or ham.
Plus: Fireplaced common room. Books. Games. No TV. Beverages. Flannel sheets. Croquet and badminton.

(Please turn page.)

From New York: *"Charming hosts, excellent breakfast . . . immaculate . . . lovely antiques . . . [in-ground] pool beautifully maintained."* From Illinois: *"Elegant and homey . . . shared knowledge of rich historical background of house and area . . . superb!"* From Washington, D.C.: *"Exceptional. . . . Please put this B&B in an inconspicuous place in your book. I don't want my chair at the breakfast table to be taken."*

Bullard Farm Bed and Breakfast 508/544-6959
89 Elm Street, North New Salem, MA 01364   fax 508/544-6959

Host: Janet Kraft
Location: On 300 acres, in a town of 50 people. Three miles to Route 2. One mile to Route 202, Lake Mattawa, and Quabbin Reservoir; 13 miles to Northfield Mountain (cross-country skiing); 25 to Historic Deer-field and Northampton; 18 miles northeast of Amherst.
Open: Year round.
Rates: $65. $15 three-quarter bed. $20 rollaway. Corporate rates. MC, Visa.

♯ ⛴ ⁂ ◆

"The Bullard family were lumbermen and have been in this 200-year-old Federal house for 127 years. My mother and her three sisters were born and married here. For my third career, I restored the house, which has been filled with vibrant people for as long as I can remember. It has family treasures including ancestral portraits (everyone asks). After opening as a B&B in 1991, I converted the barn into a modern conference center that can accommodate 150 people. Sometimes we have ski touring clinics, art shows, sleigh and hay rides (with Charlie, a 25-year-old workhorse), stargazing parties, or open hearth cooking weekends. One field here leads to the river, another to a wooded ridge with scenic waterfall and gorge. Guests pick blueberries (100 cultivated bushes), find the old swimming hole, explore Quabbin Reservoir. It's just 90 minutes from Boston—and into another world!"

Janet, a church organist, is a former piano teacher and retired human services counselor.

Bed and bath: Four large second-floor rooms. One with twin beds (and a phone) shares bath with room that has double bed, working fireplace. Room with a double and a three-quarter bed, working fireplace, and phone shares a full bath with air-conditioned queen-bedded room. Rollaway and crib available.
Breakfast: 8–10. Cheese strata or blueberry pancakes. Apple coffee cake, muffins, cran/applesauce, homemade breads and pastries. In dining room (with organ) overlooking field, or in fireplaced breakfast room with exposed beams.
Plus: Fireplaced living room. Tea, wine, or hot mulled cider. Robes provided. Badminton. Croquet. TV. "I can usually borrow playmates for children over three." Liquor license.

From Utah: *"A very special place."* From Virginia: *"Charming house . . . delicious food."* From Washington, D.C.: *"It's terrific—and so is Janet."*

The Knoll   413/584-8164

230 North Main Street, Northampton, MA 01060-1221

Hosts: Lee and Ed Lesko
Location: In Florence, a section of Northampton. Set far back from the road, on a knoll (an acre of lawn) overlooking 17 acres of farmland and forest. Three miles from Smith College, 9 from Amherst, 15 from Mount Hol-

yoke, 12 from Deerfield. Five-minute walk to beautiful public park.
Open: Year round. Reservations preferred.
Rates: $40 single, $45 double, $50 twins.
🛡 ⅍

The Leskos talk of their four-year guests—those who bring their freshman children to school and stay for every visit through graduation. We stayed during a spring cycling trip when the magnificent two-story high Michigan redbud blossoms were peeking into our room. The strawberry beds, later to be pick-your-own, had just been set out. For the evening activity, we had our choice of contra dancing or a concert.

Time has brought a few changes. The strawberry beds have been discontinued. Ed, a former Air Force pilot, is retired from his window and door sales. Many more B&B guests have discovered the Leskos, Ed a Northampton native and Lee originally from Biloxi, Mississippi. Their spacious 12-room English Tudor is furnished with many Oriental rugs. In the corner of their large living room is a striking (in every sense of the word) seven-foot-high grandfather clock made in Germany around 1900. Traditional furnishings are in the guests' (formerly the children's) rooms. Housekeeping is impeccable.

Bed and bath: Three second-floor bedrooms share two tub baths. One room with twin beds, the others with double beds. Cot available.
Breakfast: 8–8:30. Lee will usually join you for coffee after you have had your cereal, fresh fruit, their homegrown raspberries, strawberries, fresh farm eggs any style, bacon, homemade bread, muffins or coffee cake, and jam.
Plus: Large screened porch. Oscillating room fans. Tour of the house and grounds, if you'd like. Paths for jogging or walking. Walk to Look Park for its beautifully landscaped grounds, plenty of running and roaming space, playground, picnic grounds, and tennis courts.

Harrington Farm Country Inn   508/464-5600

178 Westminster Road, Princeton, MA 01541   (outside 508) **800/736-3276**

Hosts: John Bomba and Victoria Morgan
Location: Serene. On winding country road. Surrounded by thousands of acres of reservation land. On the western slope of Wachusett Mountain; 45 miles west of Boston, 10 north of Worcester. Short walk to

Wachusett Audubon Sanctuary. Cross-country skiing from front door.
Open: Year round.
Rates: Per room. $67.50 shared bath. $75 private bath. $100 suite. MC, Visa.
♥ ⁂ ⅍

(Please turn page.)

"A lot of guests oversleep because it's so quiet here! After breakfast, some just sit on the porch or lawn and read. Others go antiquing or go to Boston or to Old Sturbridge Village; or they hike, bird-watch, cycle, jog, or ski. They leave rejuvenated."

Vicki, a horticulturist, and John, a Culinary Institute of America graduate who has been chef in gourmet restaurants from coast to coast, liked the idea of working in their hometown, a resort at the turn of the century. In 1987 they bought the Harrington property (the oldest part is a 1762 saltbox), which had been a working farm and, for a century, a summer lodging place. A lot of work was done. Rooms were stenciled. *Worcester Magazine* gave "best" awards in the "romantic" and "restaurant" categories. Extensive herb, vegetable, and flower gardens were planted. Now, thanks to a solar greenhouse, there are enough greens and herbs to market to Boston restaurants. Once again, Princeton has become a destination.

In residence: Three cats. "Mika, a Siamese; Bill loves guests; Willey, black with white bibs and socks."

Foreign languages spoken: "Vicki speaks enough German to get by. French, Dutch, and/or Spanish depending on staff."

Bed and bath: Five second-floor rooms, some over dining area, all with views of gardens, lawn, or pond. Suite with queen bed, sitting room, and private full bath. One room with extra-long double bed, private full bath. Three (two available to restaurant guests) second-floor baths are shared by room with a queen, one with an extra-long double, and one with extra-long double and a single bed.

Breakfast: 8–9:30. "Visiting time with innkeepers." Fresh fruit. Juice. Homemade granola and muffins. "Fabulous coffee."

Plus: Huge front porch. Two acres of lawn. TV in third-floor common room. Gazebo. Down comforters. Flannel sheets. Discount coupons for Wachusett Mountain ski area. Herbs, plants, and perennials for sale. Dinners (35-seat restaurant) Wednesday–Sunday 5–8:30 p.m.; entrees $16–$21.

The Rose Cottage   508/835-4034
24 Worcester Street, Routes 12 and 140, West Boylston, MA 01583-1413

Hosts: Michael and Loretta Kittredge
Location: Country setting on landscaped grounds overlooking Wachusett Reservoir. Forty-five minutes west of Boston. Ten minutes to Worcester, Wachusett Mountain ski area (snowmaking), or winery (tours and picnic area); 40 to Sturbridge Village.

Open: Year round. Two-night minimum on holiday, college graduation, and college parents' weekends. Reservations required.
Rates: $65 double. $10 extra person in room.
♥ ♨ ☆ ✕ ⅙

Home to the Kittredges since 1984, this antiques-filled classic Gothic Revival cottage has lots of gingerbread, tall windows, wide board floors, white marble fireplaces, electrified gas fixtures, and lavender glass doorknobs. Many of the "comfortable kind of Victorian furnishings" are the kind Loretta had in her barn antiques shop right here. Loretta, a West Boylston native, changes the seasonal decor. She makes the wreaths and silk flower baskets (and provides lunch and/or dinner for weddings or business groups). Mike is a semiretired engineer; he is very involved in the community, "and he is a very active cohost!"

Bed and bath: Five rooms. Private full bath for first-floor room with iron-and-brass double bed. Upstairs, three double-bedded rooms and one room with twin beds share two baths. Apartment for longer stays.

Breakfast: Usually 7:30–10. Everything is garnished. Perhaps cheddar-bacon quiche with homegrown herbs, hot muffins. Or French toast and homemade pastry. Cereals—with cholesterol- and diet-conscious guests in mind. Served by candlelight in air-conditioned (and fireplaced) dining room.

Plus: Welcoming beverage. Fruit bowl. Candy. Fresh herbs year round. Fans in some bedrooms. Larger dining room for meetings. Three porches. Large yard with umbrella tables and swings.

From California: *"Helped rejuvenate me . . . in middle of a business trip."*

Sunnyside Farm   413/665-3113
11 River Road, Whately, MA 01093
Mailing address: P.O. Box 486, South Deerfield, MA 01373

Hosts: Mary Lou and Dick Green
Location: In a farming community, next door to Nourse Strawberry Farms. Five miles south of Deerfield, 15 minutes from Northampton and Amherst, near many colleges and private schools. Along a wonderful cycling route that is flat, very rural, very much old New England.
Open: Year round. Reservations required. All answering machine messages returned promptly.
Rates: $65 double bed, $70 twin beds. $40 single.
♥ ⬛ ✻

If you've never had grandparents who lived in a big yellow farmhouse with a red barn complete with big letters that spell out its name, here's the place, and it's well maintained and loved by family and B&B guests. The 14-room home was previously owned by Mary Lou's grandparents. "This is one of the reasons I want to stay here and hand it down to our children and (10) grandchildren. I spent summers here as a child and have wonderful memories . . . We have been living here since 1972 when we moved up from North-ampton, with our four children. (Two have been married on the grounds.) Except for extensive redecorating and recent redoing of the kitchen, the house is basically the same as when my grandparents remodeled it in 1920.

"My husband, a former comptroller at Amherst College, visits with guests in the evening when I am working as head nurse in the emergency depart-ment of Northampton's Cooley Dickinson Hospital. Breakfasts are a fun time for me. In season, not only do guests wake up to the aroma from one of the largest strawberry (and raspberry) farms in the Northeast, but some join me in picking before breakfast."

(Please turn page.)

In residence: Dick hopes to quit smoking someday.
Bed and bath: Three rooms, all with cross-ventiliation (and window fans), share two baths (one full, one shower only). Two large rooms with twin beds. One room with a double bed. Cot available.
Breakfast: 8:15–9:30. Seasonal fruits, homemade muffins and jams, eggs, bacon or sausage, or a cheese strata. Please indicate special diets in advance. Served in country kitchen or dining room.

> From Manhattan: *"Peaceful, pretty, comfortable. . . . The children loved the sense of freedom that they lack living in the city . . . breakfasts are wonderful too, but our favorite thing about Sunnyside is the hospitality of Mary and Dick Green."*

Berkshire Bed & Breakfast Host #GS8
Wilbraham, MA

Location: Spectacular. On three mountainside acres, 900 feet up, with gardens, walking paths—and, in the distance, Mount Tom. Fifteen minutes to Brimfield, 25 to Eastern States Exposition. Ten miles from downtown Springfield.

Reservations: Year round through Berkshire Bed & Breakfast Homes, page 234.
Rates: $70 double or twin room. $125 king. $10 per child.
♥ 🛥 ⚓ 🐾 ✖

What a place to unwind. And oversleep. (Everyone does.) "Guests love the quiet, the view of the valley below, the west-facing hot tub with magnificent sunsets, the pool with fountain. And the cottagelike pool house has a daybed—great for a nap. When we bought the land in 1989, this was a funny little Cape built onto a tiny 1920s brick building with a loft (now a TV room with wood stove). From this, my husband, a real estate director who was a developer, created our 6,000-square-foot house. Double French doors in the living room [20 by 40 feet] lead to our summer outdoor living room: a 60-foot-long covered porch that has a swing chair, a hammock, and lots of wicker and flowering plants. When we lived in Marblehead, we had an antiques store. Our eclectic collections are everywhere in this house!"

Throughout there is stenciling done by the hostess. As many guests say, "This house has everything—including a welcoming, sharing host family." It's a perfect place for wedding parties. The king-bedded room is a favorite for getaways. And young guests are often taken in hand by the host children.

In residence: Two children, ages 11 and 13. Four cats.
Bed and bath: Three carpeted rooms. First-floor double-bedded room and one with two twins share a full bath. Huge second-floor treetop room has two skylights, eight double windows, private bath with Jacuzzi, steam shower, dressing room.
Breakfast: At guests' convenience (from dawn to brunch!). Fresh fruits. Juice. Homemade sticky buns. French bread French toast or bacon and eggs. Cereals. Coffee. Tea.
Plus: Fruit and sparkling water in room. Each room has ceiling fan, cross-ventilation; "Even in 95-degree weather, guests sleep under a light blanket." Fireplaced living and dining rooms. Grand piano. Game room. Area restaurant menus.

Twin Maples 413/268-7925

106 South Street, Williamsburg, MA 01096

Hosts: Eleanor and Martin Hebert
Location: Two miles from village, surrounded by fields, gardens, stone walls—and mountain view. Seven miles from Northampton, 9 miles to I-91 interchange, and 25 miles to Springfield.
Open: Year round. Two-night mini-mum on holidays and for college commencements.
Rates: $50 single, $55 double. Large room $55 single, $60 double. $5 surcharge for one-night stay. $15 cot (child only) or crib.
🛏 ✈ ⚓

What started out to be a sometime-maybe activity has almost become the headquarters—or at least a model—of B&B in the area. Eleanor, a former Williamsburg librarian, is very involved with the expanded B&B scene in the Hampshire Hills as well as in the Berkshires. Martin, a design engineer, recently launched his own company. The parents of five grown children have renewed their interest in farming with a new (1993) sugarhouse, and with haying, extensive gardens—and Romney sheep being bred for their wonderful wool.

The restored—inside and out—200-year-old farmhouse has exposed beams in the dining room, a kitchen with large fireplace and Dutch oven, and antique as well as colonial reproduction furnishings. We are among the guests who have found everything, including hospitality, "just perfect." Or, as guests from New York wrote, "Like the candy on the pillow . . . 'mint'!"

In residence: Toby, a miniature sheltie. "Six sheep as starters."
Bed and bath: Three rooms in a guest wing share a full updated bath. One room has restored iron-and-brass double bed, nonworking fireplace. Another has twin iron-and-brass beds, nonworking fireplace. Third room has restored double brass bed. Cot and crib available.
Breakfast: 7:30–9 on weekdays, until 10 on weekends. "We cater to vegetarians." Juice, fresh fruit; buttermilk pancakes (with or without blueberries), sausage, homemade sweet breads; coffee, tea, and milk; homemade maple syrup. Served on table set with flowers, linens, and handcrafted pottery, in dining room or on screened porch.
Plus: Flannel sheets and electric blankets in winter. Guests' sitting room with TV and games. Wood stove in huge country kitchen. Screened porch. Picnic table. Bedroom fans.

Guests arrive as strangers, leave as friends.

___ Berkshires Reservation Services ___

Berkshire Bed & Breakfast Homes

P.O. Box 211, Williamsburg, MA 01096

Phone: 413/268-7244. Monday–Friday, 9–6; Saturday 10–12 noon. Year round.

Fax: 413/268-7243.

Listings: 90. Located in Massachusetts—North and South County Berkshires (many near Tanglewood and Williams College), Pioneer Valley and Hampshire Hills (close to the five-college area), greater Springfield (some near Civic Center and Big E), and Sturbridge. Also eastern New York state. Mostly hosted private residences, some unhosted private residences plus inns. Free (partial) list includes rates.

Reservations: Two weeks' advance notice is recommended. In the Berkshires, two-night minimum stays are often required on weekends or holidays and during the Tanglewood season.

Rates: $45–$185 single, $50–$185 double. $8 booking fee. For some locations, $5, $10, or $15 surcharge for one-night stays. One night's rate required as deposit. Deposit minus $25 processing fee refunded if cancellation is received at least two weeks prior to arrival date. "For less than two weeks' notice, no refund unless our office or your host can rebook your reserved room; full refund if room is rebooked." Amex, MC, Visa. ◆

Attention to detail is a hallmark of this highly regarded service. For eight years it has been owned and run by Eleanor Hebert, an experienced B&B host who was, for many years, a professional librarian. She is aware of the importance of meeting the needs and expectations of hosts and guests. She knows what needs to be done and does it—well.

Plus: Short-term (several weeks) hosted and unhosted housing also available.

Other reservation services with some B&Bs in the Berkshires:
The American Country Collection, page 343
Bed & Breakfast/Inns of New England, page 259
Covered Bridge, page 2

─────────── Berkshires B&Bs ───────────

Cumworth Farm   413/634-5529
Route 112, RR 1, Box 110, Cummington, MA 01026

Hosts: Ed and Mary McColgan
Location: On a scenic rural road with mountain views, 3.4 miles from town center. Hiking trails nearby; 45 minutes to Tanglewood, Williamstown, Amherst; 30 to Northampton. Near Hickory Hill and Swift River Inn for cross-country skiing.
Open: Year round. Reservations preferred.
Rates: $60 double. $40 single. $10 one-time charge for a cot. ♨ ⛴ ✿ ⚵ ✄

> From New Jersey: *"Cross-country skied right across the street—with their Border collie. Much joy."* From New Hampshire: *"From good conversation we were lured to the fields . . . lost ourselves in rows upon rows of raspberries . . . walked two miles on the property."* From Connecticut: *"Went at maple syrup time with our children for a pancake breakfast and tour of sugarhouse [many do] . . . a very special place . . . the best of outdoor living with a warm home environment."*

We too have experienced this traditional European-like B&B. You'll get tips about restaurants, a great cycling route, and a fun Tuesday night auction. You can enjoy the hot tub with views of fields, rolling hills, and gardens. Read by the parlor stove. Have tea by the kitchen stove. And get to know multifaceted hosts who, for good reason, have a lengthy roster of fans.

As a youngster Ed worked on potato, dairy, and tobacco farms. As an adult he has experience as college history professor, Massachusetts Bicentennial director, state legislator, and Department of Public Health executive. Parents of seven grown children, Ed and Mary have both been Northampton city councilors. Since buying this 200-year-old farmhouse in 1979, they have had many animals and held a barn roofing (complete in one weekend). Mary still works as a congregate housing coordinator.

Now they concentrate on maple sugaring—using wood to boil sap that is collected from 4,000 taps. From the 1,000 blueberry and 2,500 raspberry bushes, there's plenty of jam and jelly for the newest enterprise, gift packs of Massachusetts-grown products.

In residence: Neil, a Border collie. Barn cats. Sheep in season.
Bed and bath: Six second-floor rooms—with either a double bed or two twins. Four rooms share a full bath. Two share a tub bath. Four have ceiling fans.
Breakfast: 7–9. Pancakes with homegrown berries and McColgans' syrup. Also cereal, fruit, and muffins. Served around the claw-footed oak table in kitchen with restaurant stove and dozens of hanging baskets.
Plus: Beverages. Patio with lounge chairs. Dinner by advance arrangement.

The Dalton House   413/684-3854
955 Main Street, Dalton, MA 01226-2100

Hosts: Gary and Bernice Turetsky
Location: On the main street of a small town that is the home of the company that makes all the paper for U.S. currency. Close to Tanglewood and to cross-country and downhill skiing at Jiminy Peak and Brodie Mountain.
Open: Year round. Two-night minimum in July and August and on holidays.
Rates: Double occupancy. Varies according to room size. $78–$100 summer, $68–$85 fall, $58–$75 winter/spring. Suites $75–$100. $10 extra person. Ten percent discount for five-night stays, Monday–Thursday.
✳ ✌

"We were doing B&B before we knew what a B&B was. We have made so many changes that we have torn down walls that we put up!" The 20-by-40-foot swimming pool, a deck with colorful striped awning, extensive gardens, and a large breakfast room with skylights are among the additions to this B&B, a main house with wing and a converted carriage house.

The Turetskys moved from Freehold, New Jersey, in 1971 to be in the flower business in "this quaint town." Innkeeper friends in Vermont provided the inspiration for converting this 1810 colonial home to a B&B. Now the three daughters are grown and gone. The flower shop was sold and moved in 1990. Guests, including campers' parents and skiers, speak of "visiting" with Bernice and Gary at "my place in the Berkshires."

In residence: "Pumpkin is our retired 15-year-old cat."
Bed and bath: Nine carpeted rooms with two twin beds or a double bed. Plus two suites with very large rooms and sitting areas. All with private shower baths. One suite has double beds, the other, a twin and a double. Cots available.
Breakfast: Continental buffet. Hot and cold cereals. Blueberry, cranberry nut, and banana muffins. Toast-your-own English muffins and bagels. Fresh fruit in season. Juice, coffee, hot chocolate, teas.
Plus: Air conditioning and individual heat control in bedrooms. Large sitting room with fireplace, old beams, piano. Patio. Picnic area in the woods. Appalachian Mountain Club seminars. (Gary is a rock climber.)

> From England: "*Recommend it for amenities, comfort, homey atmosphere, friendly hosts.*" From California: "*Shared lots of interesting facts about the area and Crane Company.*" From New York: "*Very, very pleasant rooms.*"

Elling's Guest House B&B   413/528-4103
RD 3, Box 6, Great Barrington, MA 01230

Hosts: Josephine and Raymond Elling
Location: On six acres of lawns, gardens, and wooded areas, one mile west of town on Route 23, 300 feet from the main road. Twenty minutes to Rockwell Museum, 25 to Tanglewood. Close to Butternut Basin and Catamount ski areas, and to small river beach.
Open: Year round. Two-night minimum on summer weekends.
Rates: $85 June–October and holidays. $65 November–May. Singles $15 less Monday–Thursday.
✳ ✈ ✌

> From Rhode Island: "*Peaceful surroundings . . . warm, comfy feeling. . . . There's nothing like waking up to Jo's freshly baked muffins or scones.*"

This B&B is almost a legend. "When our summer-only address turned out to be a nonpaying guest house, we decided that running a B&B would be the thing to do. Now, 20 years later, we still have wonderful guests!"

And now, thanks to the town historian who found the original deed, the Ellings have learned that the frame house that they updated was built in 1742 (for a woolen-mill owner), making it Great Barrington's oldest lived-in house. "Among family pieces is our pride—an 1820 tall clock that strikes each hour." Ray is a do-it-yourself buff. Jo gardens, hooks rugs, and makes wreaths. They will suggest "anywhere in the Berkshires" as a favorite place, "but we are partial to the small back roads. If you get lost, you'll enjoy it anyway."

Foreign language spoken: Some Italian.
Bed and bath: Four cozy rooms with air conditioning; private guests' entrance and parlor. King/twins option, queen, or double beds available. Private full baths; two with tub and shower, two with shower only.
Breakfast: 8–9:30. "Abundant continental." Fresh fruit, hot muffins or biscuits with homemade jam, juice, and a bottomless pot of coffee or tea. In lovely dining room. In summer, eat on the wicker-furnished porch or on lawns.
Plus: Garden swing suspended from an old maple. Adirondack lawn chairs. Fireplaced common room with TV, games, cards. Badminton, horseshoes. Guest refrigerator. Apres-ski hot beverage. An invitation to see the original cooking fireplace in the Ellings' part of the house.

Littlejohn Manor   413/528-2882
31 Newsboy Monument Lane, Great Barrington, MA 01230

Hosts: Herbert Littlejohn, Jr., and Paul DuFour
Location: On spacious grounds with views of hills and cornfields. One mile west of downtown. Across lane from the Newsboy Monument. Within a mile of tennis, golf, and swimming; five miles to Butternut Basin or Catamount; 20 minutes to Tanglewood.

Open: Year round. Two-night minimum on summer weekends, and in foliage and ski seasons; three nights on holiday weekends.
Rates: $65–$85 Memorial Day weekend–October. $60–$75 November–May. Midweek $5 less except in July, August, and October and holiday weekends. Singles $5 less.
♥ ⬥ ✿ ✈

From Massachusetts: *"Rooms are absolutely charming. . . . A wicker-furnished front porch that begs you just to sit a spell . . . immaculate. . . . Hosts who make hospitality look easy."*

The innkeepers, who prepare breakfasts that are almost famous, have experience that includes 15 years as owners of a Maine summer resort, 20 years as Harvard University food service administrators, and considerable international travel. They invite guests to take garden tours and to taste, touch, and smell many of the more than one hundred herbs and edible flowers. Drying herbs are in the colonial-style dining room, which features a chandelier, "a whimsical concoction of Viennese and Baccarat crystal, cleverly brought together by the head designer for Tiffany." The house, a combination of American Shingle and Greek Revival architecture, is furnished with early American and Victorian pieces, European and Oriental accents, and dried arrangements.

(Please turn page.)

Herb is an officer of the local historical society and garden club. Paul, a master gardener, is past president of the Berkshire Concert Choir and Berkshire Bach Society, a notary public, and a justice of the peace (some weddings held in gardens here).

In residence: Maine Coon cats, Maid Marion and Robin Hood.
Foreign languages spoken: Minimal German and French.
Bed and bath: Four second-floor carpeted rooms share two full baths. Two double-bedded rooms. One with king/twins option. One with working fireplace has twins/king bed option.
Breakfast: 8:30–9:15. Memorable. Eggs with ham, bangers (sausages), sauteed mushrooms, grilled tomato, potato. Garnished with flowers. English muffins. Homemade marmalades and jams. Coffees and teas.
Plus: Air conditioner in every room of house. Chocolate on the pillow. Tea at 4 p.m. if arranged by noon—perhaps with marigold or lemon thyme and lemon balm scones. Fireplaced living room with color cable TV. Bus or airport (1.5 miles) pickup to rental car.

Seekonk Pines   413/528-4192

142 Seekonk Cross Road   (for reservations only) **800/292-4192**
Great Barrington, MA 01230

Hosts: Linda and Christian Best
Location: Just off Route 23, bordered with pine trees. Two miles west of town and Route 7. Fifteen minutes to three state forests. Eight miles to Stockbridge, 5 to Butternut Basin and Catamount ski areas, 16 to Tanglewood.
Open: Year round. Depending on room, two- or three-day minimum July, August weekends, and most holidays; two nights on June, September, and October weekends.
Rates: November–May $70–$85. June and September–October $75–$95. July–August $85–$99. Singles $25 less. $20 extra adult, $15 extra child, $10 crib, $5 cot (if not extra person). Ten percent less for stays of one week or more, 5 percent if five or six nights.
♥ ✿ ✖ ⅄

They met while playing the lead roles in *Damn Yankees*. Now Linda and Chris perform year round in the area—and they give unscheduled performances at the inn. In addition to their perennial gardens, an attraction for passersby, they grow raspberries, strawberries, rhubarb, and squash—for jams and jellies—sold to guests only, by popular demand. Guests often ask about the stenciling, the handmade quilts, the dollhouse that Linda and her daughter decorated, or Linda's watercolors. Auction acquisitions emerge in a reconditioned state from Chris's barn workshop. All these projects are part of "the continuing creative process" started in 1979 when the Bests converted the expanded 1830s house to an inn. It was featured in *Country Inns* magazine for its "country-comfortable atmosphere" and "unaffected pristine charm."

In residence: Grown daughter, Jill. Ivory, "a lively white shepherd/yellow Lab mix." Ebony, a Belgian shepherd.
Foreign language spoken: German.
Bed and bath: Six rooms, all private baths. First floor—queen bed, shower bath, private exterior entrance. Second floor—a queen and a double bed, full

bath; queen and twin, ceiling fan, shower bath; queen, full bath; queen, shower bath; king/twins, full hall bath. Rollaway and crib available. **Breakfast:** 8–8:45. Heart-healthy menus with whole grains. Homegrown fruit; yogurt, granola; maybe corn pudding, oatmeal souffle, oatmeal–brown rice flour–crushed almond pancakes, hot cereal, stuffed French toast. Special diets accommodated. **Plus:** In-ground swimming pool. Hammock. Fireplaced common room with piano. Decks overlooking gardens. Extensive lawn area. Picnic tables. Cross-country ski trails from the door. Portable fans. Bicycles. Guest pantry with refrigerator and hot water dispenser. Iced tea or hot mulled cider.

From Connecticut: *"Great food, wonderful conversations, cozy atmosphere."*

The Turning Point Inn   413/528-4777

RD 2, Box 140, Great Barrington, MA 01230-9808

Hosts: Irving and (daughter) Jamie Yost
Location: On 11 acres with nature trails. Close to the Appalachian Trail. Fifteen minutes from Tanglewood. On a well-traveled road, just down the road from lake swimming and Butternut Basin.
Open: Year round. Two- or three-day minimum on summer, fall, and holiday weekends; sometimes, one-nights are available.
Rates: $80 semiprivate bath, $100 private. Singles $10 less. $200 cottage for four; optional breakfast, $5 per person. $5 crib. $10 cot under age 12, $15 if over 12. Seventh night free. MC, Visa.
♠ ♣ ✟ ⊁

Returnees abound. They send friends and relatives. "Everyone" seems to know this inviting inn, which was one of the first in the country to feature marvelous whole-grain and sugarless creations at breakfast. In 1977 Irv was an architect in New Jersey; his wife, Shirley—who died from injuries in a 1993 automobile accident—was an arts-oriented teacher of gifted and learning-disabled children. They bought "the mess," an old tavern/inn, with plans to establish a vegetarian restaurant. During conversion they discovered a beehive oven and two fireplaces. The warm innkeepers with contagious enthusiasm became year-round Berkshire residents in 1982. Baker Jamie, a nursing student scheduled to graduate in 1994, has been innkeeper-in-residence since 1988.

In residence: Alana, 14-year-old granddaughter.
Bed and bath: Six cozy second-floor rooms, attractively furnished with "19th- and 20th-century furniture." Four with private bath; two share one full bath. King/twin option or double beds. Cribs and cots available. Two-bedroom cottage (with or without breakfast provided) has living room, kitchen, and sun porch.
Breakfast: Usually at 8:30 and 9:30. Bountiful. Served in dining/common room. Maybe Irv's own blend of whole-grain hot cereal; bran and whole wheat pancakes; eggs with veggies; or Jamie's hot baked fruit, bran muffins, or zucchini and date bread. Tofu and tofu salad too. Special diets accommodated.

(Please turn page.)

Plus: Fresh fruit always available. Fireplaces in three common rooms. Piano. Library. TV. Refrigerator. Laundry facilities. Picnic table. Hammock.

Baldwin Hill Farm Bed & Breakfast

Baldwin Hill Road, Egremont   **413/528-4092**
Mailing address: Box 125, RD 3, Great Barrington, MA 01230-0125

Hosts: Richard and Priscilla Burdsall
Location: Spectacular. On a hilltop with 360-degree view of hills, fields and valleys. Surrounded by 500 acres with gardens, orchards. Hiking and un-groomed cross-country ski trails right here. Five miles west of Great Barrington; 25 minutes to Tanglewood.

Open: Year round. Two-night stays preferred on weekends.
Rates: June through October and holiday weekends, $95 private bath; $85 shared bath with sink in room; $75 shared bath. Rest of year, $10 less. MC, Visa.

♥ ⁂ ♦ ✈ ⅍

Surprise! Many who come with a list of planned activities spend much of their time right here. *Country* magazine, *Travel Holiday* and *Newsday* have also discovered this white clapboard Victorian farmhouse with its views of rolling hills—views from the bay windows and screened porch, from the heated swimming pool surrounded by orchards, and on the trails too. It was this countryside that drew the Burdsalls back to the farm where they had lived in their early years of marriage and where Richard was born and raised. He has experience as a farmer (who sometimes takes guests on a tour of the huge red barn complex and its carriages, sleighs, tools, and old farm machinery) and as a banker. Currently he is teaching college English part time. "And many guests ask about wildlife, conservation, and the local history."

Richard and Priscilla did most of the restoration work before opening as a B&B in 1990. All the furnishings—antiques, paintings, and Orientals—are family pieces.

Foreign language spoken: "A bit of French."
Bed and bath: Four second-floor rooms. One double-bedded room has private bath with full-sized shower. Three rooms—one with two twin beds and sink/vanity, one with king/twins option and sink/vanity, and one with a double bed—all share a full bath and a half bath.
Breakfast: Usually 7:30–9:30. Choose from menu. In season, "fruit from our orchards." Blueberry or apple pancakes; whole wheat or regular pancakes; white or whole wheat French toast; fresh farm eggs. Juices. Hot or cold cereal. Homemade muffins. Bacon, sausage, or creamed dried beef. In dining room under Tiffany chandelier.
Plus: In-ground concrete pool. Welcoming beverage. Two living rooms, one with fieldstone fireplace. Down comforters. Color TV, VCR, piano, books, games. Wicker-furnished screened porch. Spacious lawns. Picnic table. Hiking and biking maps.

---

*A*ccording to many hosts: "Guests come with plans and discover the joys of hammock sitting."

Bread & Roses   413/528-1099
Route 71, Corner Baldwin Hill Road, Egremont
Mailing address: Star Route 65, Box 50, Great Barrington, MA 01230-0050

Hosts: Elliot and Julie Lowell
Location: On three acres with gardens and brook.
Open: Year round. Three-night min-

imum on July and August weekends.
Rates: $95 July–October. $75 November–June. $15 extra bed in room.
♥ ♦ ✈ ⊬

One couple presented the Lowells with a "best B&B of our trip" certificate complete with seal. A honeymoon couple wrote to me about "a lovely old farmhouse . . . charming hosts . . . unexpected gift . . . delicious breakfast." Put simply, Julie says, "We love people, and I got tired of computers (as a data processing manager) as a way of life. I did the renovation, not a slavish restoration, as a wonderful home to enjoy. Many people come here just to relax. And lots of cyclists stay with us."

Just looking at the bridge that arches over the brook is enough to make guests unwind. Inside, the focal point is the large brick fireplace, a divider between the living and dining rooms. To the 1813 farmhouse, once used as a school, the Lowells added lots of new plumbing and a wraparound porch.

Julie is active with the League of Women Voters. Elliot was an attorney in Long Island; he now practices law here.

In residence: "Artemis is a friendly tiger cat."
Foreign languages spoken: French. Some Spanish and German.
Bed and bath: Five air-conditioned second-floor rooms accessible by stairs or inclinator. All with private baths. Shower baths for rooms with a queen bed, a queen and a twin, or king/twin beds. Full baths for two queen-bedded rooms. Rollaway available.
Breakfast: 8:30–10 with Mozart accompaniment. Freshly squeezed orange juice, fresh fruit, homemade breads (including chocolate) and rolls. Entree could be French toast Grand Marnier, apple souffle, or lemon ricotta pancakes. Special diets accommodated. Served in dining room or on porch.
Plus: Steinway piano. Screened porch. Plenty of books. Tea. Robes. Telephones and radios in rooms.

The tradition of paying to stay in a private home—with breakfast included in the overnight lodging rate—was revived in time to save wonderful old houses, schools, churches, and barns all over the country from the wrecking ball or commercial development.

Townry Farm   413/443-9285

Greylock Road, Lanesborough, MA 01237-0155

Hosts: Barbara and Clifford Feakes **Location:** Rural. Just off Route 7 between Pittsfield and Williamstown, on a well-maintained road. At base of Mount Greylock State Reservation, "with the highest peak in Massachusetts and the most wonderful (and free) nature lectures and walks, blueberry picking, hunting in legal season, and cross-country skiing." Three miles to Brodie Mountain, four to Jiminy Peak; 20 minutes to Tanglewood. **Open:** Mid-December–March and mid-May–October. Two-day minimum on July and August weekends. **Rates:** $45 single, $50 double. $15 third person in room.
♥ ⊄ ⁂ ⅏

From Sweden: "Unique experience representing the best of New England. Warmth, comfort, hospitality, and beauty."

What fun to follow these hosts, who are especially popular with travelers looking for the original B&B style. Only one family had owned the 1750 farmhouse when, in 1971 Barb and Cliff switched from the women's apparel business to this working farm. They found time to listen to classical music and do some dance skating. They established a breeding sheep flock and raised Labrador retrievers and registered Morgan horses. As the children grew older and left, B&B was added. It seems to Barbara that everyone must wish they could "move to the Berkshires and live our lifestyle." As of 1993 the last of the animals is gone. "And I no longer put the bakery sign out, but the smell draws people in. And to think when we started I couldn't even boil water! We hike four miles a day here, and on our semiannual hiking trips to Switzerland and Austria, we meet some former guests as well as others whom we subsequently welcome here. It's such fun!"

In residence: Two Labradors, one yellow and one black.
Foreign language spoken: Some French and German.
Bed and bath: Three first-floor rooms (with 18-inch-wide floorboards) share one full bath. One room has a double bed; two have a double and a single.
Breakfast: 8–10. Fresh fruit. Homemade granola. Barb's famous oatmeal toast or blueberry crunch and cranberry muffins. At dining room table set with lace tablecloth and fine china.
Plus: Guest den with color TV. Bread-making demonstrations. Recipes shared. Directions to "bargain of the century, the Clark Art Institute," and to daughter's Truffles and Such, a restaurant (kitchen tours given to B&B guests) that won the Seafood Challenge Trophy over the Chatham Bars Inn and Boston's Four Seasons Hotel.

*H*ospitality *is the keynote of B&B.*

Birchwood Inn

7 Hubbard Street, P.O. Box 2020
Lenox, MA 01240-2330

413/637-2600
(U.S./Canada) **800/524-1646**

Hosts: Joan, Dick, and Dan Toner
Location: On a hill on a corner of Main Street. Steps to hiking and cross-country ski trails. A few blocks to shops and restaurants; 1.5 miles to Tanglewood.
Open: Year round. Three-night minimum in July and August.
Rates: July and August $85–$95 shared bath, $125–$195 private

bath, $165–$195 carriage house. October $70–$80 shared bath, $100–$150 private, $125–$150 carriage house. Other months $50–$60 shared bath, $60–$120 private, $80–$120 carriage house. Weekday specials. MC, Visa.
♥ ♣ ✗ ✄

From Tennessee: *"Comfortable and beautiful inside and out . . . modern baths . . . fireplaces made each night special . . . breakfast tides you over to way past lunch."* From Maryland: *"Called to check on ski reports, museums, restaurants; gave us maps."* From Virginia: *"Jogged in woods across the street . . . memorable view of distant lake shrouded in mist, with leaves just starting to turn."* From New York: *"Especially warm hospitality."*

"After Dick retired from the military, we got hooked at an innkeeping seminar. Our son, Dan, manager of a large hotel, urged us to find the perfect place. We did in 1991."

The Toners bought this 225-year-old former tavern, which had been a private home until being converted to a B&B in 1981. Now it is filled with many antiques and with collectibles acquired in Europe and the Far East when Dick was a general in the U.S. Air Force. Joan was a teacher and real estate agent "wherever we lived."

In residence: Seamus, a chocolate Labrador. Chablis and Cognac, Himalayan cats.
Foreign language spoken: Some French.
Bed and bath: Ten rooms plus two carriage house suites. Main house second floor—king (one has fireplace and TV), queen (two with canopy and fireplace), double, or twin beds. All private baths; four are shower only. Third floor—private bath for room with queen or king/twins option. One double-bedded room shares (robes provided) bath with queen-bedded room. Queen or double bed in carriage house efficiency suites. Rollaway available.
Breakfast: 8:30–10. Dick's international repertoire includes huevos rancheros, tarte d'Alsace, cranberry pancakes, eggs Benedict. Homemade muffins, breads, croissants. Fruit, juice, cereal, hot beverages. In fireplaced dining room.
Plus: 5–6 p.m. tea or wine and snacks. Fireplaced living and TV rooms. Front porch with rockers. Massage therapy here, $70/hour. Access to health club and tennis courts, $6/day; indoor tennis, $10/hour. Picnic baskets, $13.50/person.

Brook Farm Inn

413/637-3013
15 Hawthorne Street, Lenox, MA 01240   800/285-POET

Hosts: Joe and Anne Miller
Location: In a quiet wooded glen. Ten-minute walk to village center. One mile to Tanglewood.
Open: Year round. Three-night weekend minimum July–Labor Day. Two nights on other weekends.
Rates: Vary according to room size, fireplace, floor location. Tanglewood season: $95–$115 Monday–Wednesday, $105–$170 Thursday–Sunday. Foliage: $75–$110 Monday–Thursday, $95–$135 Friday–Sunday. September: $65–$90 midweek, $95–$110 weekends. November–June: $65–$100 midweek, $75–$110 weekends. Discover, MC, Visa. ♥ ♣ ✗ ✔

This attractive century-old home, in a peaceful location complete with in-ground pool, is filled with antiques, traditional pieces, framed old posters, turn-of-the-century programs, and a collection of carved shorebirds. During Tanglewood season chamber recitals are given here to accompany Sunday morning breakfast. Poetry readings are offered on Saturday afternoons. Every day a personal favorite poem of the day (from a collection of hundreds of books) is placed on a podium. The "total relaxation" felt by guests—including Tanglewood performers, honeymooners, and wedding parties—is precisely what the Millers dreamed about. "We just always wanted to be innkeepers." They moved here in 1992 from New Jersey, where Joe was in commercial construction; Anne was a real estate paralegal.

In residence: Buster and Agnes, Labradors. Bob, the "mascot" cat.
Bed and bath: Twelve rooms (most have ceiling fans; six have working fireplace) on three floors. All private baths (some shower only). King/twin option, queen (some canopied), or double bed. Third-floor rooms are air conditioned; one has skylights and fireplace; two are tucked under the eaves. Rollaway available.
Breakfast: 8:30–10. Freshly squeezed orange juice. Homemade granola. Bread pudding (recipe shared), quiche, egg casserole, or French toast. Served in breakfast room overlooking woods.
Plus: Sherry. Fireplaced library with upright piano. No TV. (Very sociable) afternoon tea with homemade scones and jam. Guest refrigerator. Champagne for birthdays or anniversaries. Valentine's Day roses.

From Massachusetts: *"It is lovely. And the innkeepers have just the right touch."*

---

*T*he place to stay has become the reason to go.

The Gables Inn

413/637-3416

103 Walker Street (Route 183), Lenox, MA 01240

Hosts: Mary and Frank Newton
Location: In the village center, one mile from Tanglewood.
Open: Year round. Three-night minimum in July and August; two nights in October and on holiday weekends.

Rates: Vary according to room size, amenities, time of year, weekday or weekend. $60–$140. Suite (summer only) $195. $20 additional person.

"Young man, I see you have kept the Whartons' red damask wallpaper," said the 82-year-old Lenox resident while visiting with Frank Newton in this former home of famed novelist Edith Wharton (author of *The Age of Innocence*).

For their eighth house restoration (six were Manhattan brownstones done while they lived in them), the Newtons, both former bankers, took on this elegant Queen Anne Berkshire Cottage built in the Gilded Age of 1885. In addition to hanging fresh red damask wallpaper, they restored the eight-sided library (which had become a restaurant with bar) and added a tennis court, a greenhouse with solar-heated 40-foot pool (I loved the prebreakfast swim), a Jacuzzi, and, most recently, two 500-square-foot suites. "The Teddy Wharton Suite is very masculine, with leather furniture; Edith Wharton Suite is feminine and flowery." The Presidents' Room is complete with a collection that delights history buffs. The Show Business guest room has signed photos (plenty of nostalgia) and an extensive library. Throughout, there are period furnishings and examples of Mary Newton's painting, pierced lampshades, and quilting.

Depending on the season or year, Frank—the official baker, who gave/produced a B&B cooking demonstration in Manhattan's Abraham & Strauss—finds time to write and produce shows and recordings; play piano; lecture on restoration and period style; and create even more area cultural events.

In residence: "'Cat' is shy."
Foreign language spoken: Spanish.
Bed and bath: Seventeen air-conditioned rooms—including three suites—on three floors; nine have working fireplaces. All queen beds; some are canopied. All private baths.
Breakfast: 8–10. Fruit, juice, homemade bread and pastry, coffee, tea. Cereal in the summer. At tables for 2, 4, or 20. Note to summer guests: "We love the *Times* too! Please read it in the library rather than in the dining room."
Plus: Afternoon or evening wine. Lounge chairs in quiet garden.

According to guests (many are preservationists and/or house restorers), there ought to be a medal for the meticulous work—everything from research to labor—done by B&B owners. Indeed, many have won preservation awards.

Garden Gables Inn

413/637-0193

141 Main Street, P.O. Box 52, Lenox, MA 01240   fax 413/637-4554

Hosts: Mario and Lynn Mekinda
Location: In historic district of village. Set back from the main road on five wooded acres with gardens, fruit trees, and huge old pines and maples. One mile from Tanglewood.
Open: Year round. Three-night minimum weekends July–August and on holiday weekends; two-night minimum weekends June and September–October.

Rates: Late June–Labor Day and late September–October: weekends $110 (double bed, smaller room) to $185 (king four-poster, whirlpool bath, porch), most rooms $130–$140; weekdays $90–$165. Mid-September and winter months: weekends $70–$135, weekdays $65–$100. Third person $25. Amex, Discover, MC, Visa.

♥ ♣ ♨

It's home. It has white clapboards and green shutters. The gabled part with low ceilings was built in 1780. Subsequent additions were made to the private estate, which was an inn for 35 years before the Mekindas bought it in 1988.

"A tinkerer," Mario says he is. Every old-house owner would appreciate a Mario-in-residence. The results of his efforts include fresh, inviting rooms, tile baths, a homelike atmosphere. There are books, fireplaces, comfortable sofas, a very unusual 1924 handcrafted Steinway baby grand piano, English antiques, Dutch and English 18th-century watercolors, and, in the guest rooms, early American furniture. On the spacious grounds there are gardens, that 72-foot-long in-ground pool with umbrella tables on the deck, and many trees.

In Canada Mario was a professional engineer. Lynn worked in public relations. Here Lynn writes and is active with the historical society. Mario is active with several arts organizations.

In residence: Two teenagers, Emma and Jonathan. Also, two nameless 16-year-old turtles.
Foreign language spoken: French and German.
Bed and bath: Fourteen cozy rooms on first and second floors with king (four are canopied and have Jacuzzi baths), queen, double, or twin beds. All private baths. Rollaway available.
Breakfast: 8–10. Buffet. Homemade bran and blueberry muffins, cantaloupe and native berries, farm-fresh eggs, healthy cereals, cheese-filled crumb cakes, yogurts, croissants. In dining room overlooking gardens and pool.
Plus: Phone in all rooms. Individual thermostat in some rooms. Bedroom window fans. Guest refrigerator. Late-afternoon wine or tea. Down comforters. Beach towels. Flannel sheets. Games. TV and VCR. Mints on pillow.

If you've been to one B&B, you haven't been to them all.

Rookwood Inn   ·   **413/637-9750**
19 Old Stockbridge Road, P.O. Box 1717   **800/223-9750**
Lenox, MA 01240

Hosts: Tom and Betsy Sherman
Location: On a quiet road, half a block from town center, dining, shopping. A mile to Tanglewood. Twenty minutes to five major ski areas, golf, hiking.
Open: Year round. Three-night minimum on summer weekends.
Rates: June 30–Labor Day: Thursday–Monday $120–$225; Tuesday,

Wednesday $75–$110. September and June: Friday and Saturday $70–$120; Sunday–Thursday $55–$110. Late September–October: weekends $90–$160; Sunday–Thursday $65–$110. November–May: weekends $60–$110; Sunday–Thursday $65–$85. Holidays $80–$150. Singles $10 less. Amex.

♥ ♫ ✿ ♦ ✈ ✂

This is the kind of place where guests relax enough to ask "What time is it?" Named after an eclectic kind of Victorian pottery, it was referred to as "the place run by the wonderful couple who made fantastic changes" when the Shermans completed the restoration, which included a historically accurate "painted lady" exterior. The 1886 summer "cottage," built onto an 1820 colonial structure (the town's oldest building), is decorated with Oriental rugs, antiques the Shermans bought in England, "comfortable-not-high-Victorian" American pieces, and period wallcoverings. An integrated addition complete with second turret was built in 1992.

In Boston Betsy was a nurse who always wanted to become an innkeeper. Now the Shermans help prospective innkeepers make their decisions. After eight years of hosting, Tom, an investment advisor with a stock brokerage, says, "We both enjoy this great place, which is home for our family and our guests."

In residence: Brooks, seven, and Hannah, five.
Foreign language spoken: "A small amount of Spanish."
Bed and bath: Nineteen air-conditioned rooms on second and third floors with ceiling fans and individual thermostats. Some with working fireplace and/or private balcony. All private baths. Queen, double, and twin beds; some four-posters, some canopied. Daybeds and crib available.
Breakfast: 8–9:30 or 10. Buffet of homemade muffins, eggs, cereal, fresh fruit, cheese, juice, yogurt, coffee, and milk. In fireplaced dining room at individual tables.
Plus: Verandas with striped awnings. Wicker-furnished screened porch. Lawn for lounging or picnicking. Fireplaced living room. Late-afternoon tea or lemonade with cookies or cakes. Down comforters. Formal gardens. Transportation to and from bus stop.

Innkeeping may be America's most envied profession. As one host mused, "Where else can you get a job where, every day, someone tells you how wonderful you are?"

Walker House

64 Walker Street, Lenox, MA 01240-2735

413/637-1271
(U.S./Canada) **800/235-3098**
fax 413/637-2387

Hosts: Peggy and Richard Houdek
Location: On a main street, set on three gorgeous acres. Within walking distance of shops, restaurants, and cross-country skiing. Within 25 minutes of Brodie, Jiminy Peak, and Butternut mountains. Buses from New York and Boston stop a block away.
Open: Year round. Three-night minimum in July and August and on all holiday weekends.

Rates: Late June–Labor Day: $95 and $170 Thursday–Sunday, $70–$90 Monday–Wednesday. Early September: $70–$90 Friday and Saturday, $50–$70 Sunday–Thursday. Late September–October: $95 small room, $135 larger, $145 with fireplace. November–late June: $70–$90 weekends, $50–$70 Sunday–Thursday; winter theme packages available.
♥ ❊ ⅙

They were a successful arts-oriented couple living in a Spanish-style house on a southern California hill and looking for adventure. Once the Houdeks decided on the Berkshires, they set out to establish a B&B that would give them the feeling of having some friends visit for a few days. And it has been that way—"an ongoing open house"—since 1980. It is the sought-after change from when Peggy was managing editor of *Performing Arts* magazine. Dick was director of public affairs at the California Institute of the Arts, a *Los Angeles Times* contributing critic, and a Long Beach Opera consultant. Now he's an arts consultant as well as a columnist whose observations—everything from town hall restoration/conversion to arts center to walking tours (map available)—appear in a weekly Berkshires newspaper. (January–April, he makes frequent trips south.)

The art- and antiques-furnished 1804 house, once the house of the headmaster of the private Lenox School (disbanded in the early 1970s), is one of the last remaining examples of Federal architecture in Lenox. Each spacious guest room (returnees have their favorites) is named and decorated for a composer. "Whenever we have a request, we feature good films, operas, plays, concerts, and TV shows on a 100-inch (7 by 5.5 feet) screen in the Library Video Theatre."

In residence: "Six friendly but unobtrusive cats."
Foreign languages spoken: French and Spanish.
Bed and bath: Eight rooms, five with working fireplace; one also has private veranda. All with private baths (two are shower only) and radios. One or two doubles, two twins, or queen.
Breakfast: 8–10. Juice, fresh fruit, several kinds of muffins and biscuits, cold cereals, freshly ground coffee, many teas. Served around large oak tables (displacing huge seated stuffed animals) in dining room, or on wide plant-filled veranda overlooking acreage.
Plus: Bedroom air conditioning. Tea at 4. Parlor grand piano for professional performances or impromptu ones by guests or, occasionally, for accompanying Peggy, a trained singer. Old-time radio cassette library. Guest refrigerator. Large lawn for picnics. Ten bicycles.

Joyous Garde
Olde Quarry Road, Otis, MA 01253-0132

413/269-6852
fax 413/269-7207

Host: Joy Bogen
Location: On 130 beautiful acres with horses and sheep in the fields. Ten-minute walk through woods to an old quarry. Just off Route 23. Five minutes to Otis Ridge ski area, canoeing, swimming. Ten minutes to Jacob's Pillow.
Open: Year round. Three-night minimum on July, August, and holiday weekends.
Rates: Include breakfast, sandwich lunch, late-night snacks. Memorial Day–October: Thursday–Sunday (Monday–Wednesday) $165–$175 ($125–$145) king, $155–$325 ($125–$165) queen, $135–$175 ($115–$145) twins. $35 ($30) extra person. November until Memorial Day weekend: Friday and Saturday (Sunday–Thursday) $125–$170 ($100–$140) king, $145–$300 ($125–$145) queen, $100–$155 ($85–$125) twins, $25 ($20) extra person. Amex, CB, Diners, MC, Visa.
♥ ✿ ⚲ ⚼

Joy, an opera singer who was the only student of Lotte Lenya and sang unpublished music of Kurt Weill, bought this property as a retreat in 1975. When a friend suggested she turn it into a B&B in 1991, she did—that very weekend. Since, she has embellished it with private baths (some with chandeliers), a tennis court at the end of a wooded path, a heated pool with waterfall, antiques and art (all for sale), designer linens, and a staff. "It's sort of a miniresort where people get to know one another, go to Tanglewood together, take massages and tennis instruction, and simply relax."

Foreign languages spoken: Portuguese, Italian, French.
Bed and bath: Nine air-conditioned, carpeted rooms with king, queen, or twin beds; TV; private baths. Converted 1770 barn with original beams has queen bed, tiled bath, sauna. Three second-floor rooms in converted 1770 house that has TV/sitting room and terrace with outdoor hot tub. 1885 house has five bedrooms, some with canopied bed and/or fireplace).
Breakfast: 7:30 continental. Full 9–10:30: caviar or Spanish omelets; blintzes; smoked salmon; blueberry, strawberry, banana nut pancakes with orange sauce. Rhubarb pudding, baked bananas, apple crisp, or bread pudding. Homemade breads. Yogurt, goat cheese, fruits, oatmeal. Served in crystal-chandeliered dining rooms by uniformed staffers.
Plus: Fieldstone fireplace and upright piano in main house. Option of dinner on Friday in summer, on Saturday in ski season. Special occasions acknowledged. One free tennis court hour per day. By request, Joy's tapes played.

From New York: *"A hidden oasis."*

Heard from one host's son: "I'm sure you're good at B&B, but a honeymoon in our house? I cannot imagine it."

Merrell Tavern Inn

Route 102, Main Street
South Lee, MA 01260-0318

413/243-1794
(U.S./Canada) **800/243-1794**
fax 413/243-2669

Hosts: Charles and Faith Reynolds
Location: On a main street in small village. An informal restaurant next door; a more elegant one across the street. One mile to Norman Rockwell's Stockbridge, five miles to Tanglewood; three from I-90, Lee exit. Ten minutes to ski areas (with snowmaking).

Open: Year round. Two-night minimum (three in July and August) on weekends.
Rates: July–October $95–$105 weekdays, $115–$145 weekends. November–June $95 double bed, $120 queen with fireplace. $15 third person. MC, Visa.
♥ ♨ ✥ ♦ ✈

From Connecticut: *"Captures the feeling of the 19th century while more than satisfying the expectations of 20th-century travelers by anticipating all of their needs."*

Happy 200th (1994) birthday to this inn, once a stagecoach stop. Authenticity, charm (even a screened gazebo by the river), and old-fashioned hospitality are evident from the moment you sign in at the only surviving circular colonial bar in America. The grandfather clock in the central hallway dates from the late 1700s, when the building was constructed. Authentic colors, researched by Faith and Charles, are a background for their period Hepplewhite and Sheraton furniture. The inn is on the National Register of Historic Places and is under historic covenant with the Society for the Preservation of New England Antiquities.

One guest room was a ballroom. One parlor was the keeping room, with cooking fireplace and beehive oven. The work of the innkeepers, two former Rochester, New York, teachers, was recognized when they received the 1981 Massachusetts Historical Society Preservation Award. After complete redecoration and much landscaping in 1992, the innkeepers received the Berkshire Visitors Bureau Beautification Award.

In residence: Two cats and one golden retriever—not in guests' areas.
Bed and bath: Nine air-conditioned rooms (each with phone, three with fireplace) on three floors. All canopied beds (queen, double, twins, or double and twins) with private tiled shower baths (one has tub) and wing chairs or Chippendale sofas. Cribs and cots available.
Breakfast: 8:30–10. From an open menu cooked to order. Cereal, ham or cheese omelets with local pure maple syrup, or sausage with French toast and almond garnish. Juice. Hot beverage. Served in original fireplaced Tavern Room with 1817 birdcage bar.
Plus: Afternoon tea served from 200-year-old breakfront and heirloom tea set. Lemonade in summer. Guest refrigerator. TV room. Grounds with old stone walls, English garden, two acres of lawns to banks of Housatonic River. Two gazebos.

From Argentina: *"Slept in eight cozy inns and this is the best. . . . Not a dream. It's true and it's great."* From Massachusetts: *"Like the Berkshire Hills . . . soothing, peaceful, inviting, and refreshing . . . a great place to escape to."*

The Golden Goose   413/243-3008

Box 336, Main Road, Tyringham, MA 01264-0336

Hosts: Lilja and Joseph Rizzo
Location: Quiet. In town center, "protected from—though so near to—all the Berkshires have to offer." Across from steep beautiful Tyringham Cobble (for hiking) and Hop Brook (trout fishing). On great cycling route. Six miles to Stockbridge; eight to Tanglewood.
Open: Year round. Two-night min-imum Tanglewood weekends; three nights on holidays.
Rates: Semi-private bath $75. Private bath $85–$95 double, $90 king, $100 two twins. Studio apartment $120, $10 extra person. $10 less May 15–November 30, excluding holidays. $5 single night surcharge. Amex, Discover, MC, Visa.
♥ ♨ ⁂ ♦ ✱

A baby grand piano is the latest addition to the music room, where guests sometimes play—even before breakfast. The Rizzos' warm welcome begins with the front-porch flags on the 200-year-old white colonial farmhouse: "Swedish (for me); the state flag; the 13-star American flag; and the Italian for New York-born Joe, who left his engineering management position for innkeeping/groundskeeping and, when time permits, some cello study. I am a Californian whose checkered career includes public relations, multimedia production, and Victorian antique furniture in Manhattan. (My struggles with violin continue with frustration and joy.)"

Wide plank floors are refinished. Beveled French glass doors now lead to the deck. Antiques are everywhere. As guests wrote, "A bit of the old country . . . casual . . . know how to make people feel special . . . authenticity, charm, warmth. . . . A little spot of Eden along the Appalachian Trail."

In residence: One cat, Bubula, "not around guests very often."
Bed and bath: Six second-floor rooms, up a steep, narrow staircase; four have private full or shower bath, two share a full bath. An extra shower bath available at foot of stairs. Private bath with double sinks, tub, and shower in minisuite with double bed. Other rooms have double bed or king/twins. First-floor studio apartment—queen bed, double sofa bed, kitchen, shower bath, private entrance.
Breakfast: 8–9:30. "Sometimes 'til noon!" Mufskits (an eggless muffin/biscuit) homemade jams, and applesauce. Fruit breads. Fresh fruit. Cold or hot cereal or rice dish. Varies according to whim of chef. Juices, teas, coffee, hot chocolate.
Plus: Hot or cold apple cider, tea, or wine with hors d'oeuvres. Two fireplaced common rooms. Bedroom table fans. Guest refrigerator in barn. Barbecue. Near swimming pond and nine ski slopes, plus parks and golf courses for cross-country.

*B*ed and breakfast gives a sense of place.

Goldberry's   413/458-3935
39 Cold Spring Road, Williamstown, MA 01267-2750

Hosts: Bev and Ray Scheer
Location: On Routes 7 and 2. Three-block walk to the campus, village, Williamstown Theatre Festival, Clark Art Institute. Twenty-minute drive to Brodie Mountain and Jiminy Peak ski areas; 40 minutes north of Tanglewood.

Open: Year round. Two-night minimum on summer and October weekends.
Rates: $65 shared bath, $75 private bath. Futon $10 third party. February and March ski weekend packages.
🛏 ⛵ ☆ ✗ ✗

From North Carolina: "Breakfast, beautifully presented, was best we've ever had, and we've stayed in many B&Bs . . . coddled us, fed us tea and wonderful cakes [at 4 p.m. every day], tucked us into dear rooms with antiques and quilts . . . lovely backyard." From New York: "Suggested superb restaurants . . . area highlights as well as hideaways known only to locals. . . . So taken with a lithograph [in B&B] that we requested directions for museum." From New Jersey: "Spacious . . . clean . . . a real knack for making guests feel completely at home."

"This is something I have wanted to do since I read Tolkien's *Fellowship of the Ring*. In it, a character named Goldberry takes in some weary hobbits and they instantly forget their troubles. I thought, 'That's for me!'"

In New Jersey, Bev, who writes poetry, taught English. Ray was a history teacher. They retired, came to Williamstown in 1988, redecorated this 1830 Georgian house, and opened as a B&B in 1991. Now they are very involved with the Berkshire Food Project initiated by Williams College students. As hosts, they meet students' parents, some guests who come for cultural events, some who "head for the hills," others who "collapse in the living room and read," and many who write enthusiastic letters to me.

Bed and bath: Three large second-floor rooms with antique beds. One with two twin beds shares connecting full bath with double-bedded room. Queen-bedded room has private full bath.
Breakfast: Until 9:30. Frittata or pancakes (lemon ricotta or pumpkin) and Canadian bacon. Freshly baked muffins. Juice. Fresh fruit (organically grown berries in summer). In stenciled dining room or on back porch overlooking garden.
Plus: Fireplaced 32-foot-long living room. Coffee and tea always available.

All the B&Bs with this ⛵ symbol want you to know that they are a private home set up for paying guests, not an inn. Although definitions vary, these private home B&Bs tend to have one to three guest rooms. For the owners—people who enjoy meeting people, B&B is usually a part-time occupation.

Steep Acres Farm B&B   413/458-3774
520 White Oaks Road, Williamstown, MA 01267-2227

Hosts: Mary and Marvin Gangemi
Location: High on a hill with panoramic views of New York, Vermont,
and Massachusetts. Two miles from
Clark Art Museum and Williamstown Theatre Festival. Adjacent to
Appalachian and Long trails. Forty

minutes to Tanglewood. Many
downhill ski areas within 20-mile-
radius.
Open: Year round.
Rates: $50 single, $70 double.
♥ ⬛ ⁂ ✻ ⊬

"Our guests love the pond. They explore the 50 wonderful acres. The apple,
cherry, peach, pear, and nut trees are flourishing. We no longer have cows
or sheep and I don't churn butter any more, but there are turkeys, chickens,
ducks, and pigs. And the bountiful gardens get a boost from the greenhouse.
And yes, B&B is a grand fit, because we have the room and have found that
every guest has been wonderful."

The Gangemis bought this great site with house and three barns after they
sold the summer camp where their six kids were first campers and then staff.
Son Daniel, a professional landscaper, the only grown child who lives on the
property, helps to keep things going. Marvin, the beekeeper, is a teacher.
Mary, the creative chef, is a nurse.

In residence: Two dogs plus. (They breed Labrador retrievers.)
Bed and bath: Four rooms with antique beds share two full baths and a
half bath. Two double-bedded rooms, one room with single bed, one with
two twins.
Breakfast: Full. Varies. "Today's menu started with a half pineapple (per
person), sliced bananas, and strawberry garnish. Oatmeal blackberry pancakes are this year's hit. Sometimes I make a Mexican egg dish or breakfast
puffs." Plus homemade muffins and breads. Eat by dining room fireplace in
winter or on the glassed porch with its tri-state view in summer.
Plus: Ceiling fans on porch and in upstairs hall. Canoe, rowboat, and raft
with diving board. Five kilometers of hiking and cross-country ski trails.

The Williamstown Bed and Breakfast
30 Cold Spring Road, Williamstown, MA 01267-2751   413/458-9202

Hosts: Kim Rozell and Lucinda
Edmonds
Location: In a neighborhood of
1800s homes on the main road. Just
off village green. With gardens,
shade trees, red barn. Minutes' walk
to college campus, theater, museums, village center.

Open: Year round. Two-night minimum on summer and holiday weekends and during foliage season.
Rates: April–October, $70 single,
$80 double. November–March, $60
single, $70 double.
⬛ ⁂ ✻ ⊬

From Michigan: *"Really first class . . . Kim and Lucinda, delightful young ladies,
have done great things with the house."* From Pennsylvania: *"Sparkling clean
. . . special antique pieces, old photographs, and lovely wallpaper. . . . Beds are*
(Please turn page.)

among the most comfortable in which we've slept . . . breakfasts, excellent . . . provide individualized and extra services . . . uniformly top-notch."

Stays at Irish B&Bs inspired these innkeepers "to change careers and pace. We looked at Massachusetts' college towns and fell in love with Williamstown, a terrific community with a rich history and wonderful cultural and recreational opportunities." In 1989 they restored this Victorian—"not the ornate kind." Area antiques dealers (hints shared) helped to add to their furnishings. For four years Kim, a former meeting planner, was solo weekday innkeeper while Lucinda continued to commute on weekends from her environmental services executive position. Now they're both here full time. Guests can tell that they enjoy doing what they do.

In residence: Two cats in hosts' quarters.
Foreign languages spoken: "None fluently, but we have had numerous foreign guests . . . wonderful time exploring sign language and language dictionaries."
Bed and bath: Four second-floor rooms; all private baths. Twin four-posters with tub/shower. Double four-poster with shower bath. Queen and a twin, hall shower bath. Queen-bedded room (with connecting double can be a suite) with shower bath.
Breakfast: Usually begins at 8. Hot dishes 8:30–9:30. Oven-puffed pancakes with fresh fruit, cheese blintzes, baked eggs with hot salsa sauce, French toast, or blueberry pancakes. Freshly baked muffins, bread (oatmeal is a favorite), scones. Cereals. Juices, freshly ground coffee, teas. Family style in dining room.
Plus: Hot or cold afternoon beverages. Spring water in rooms. Large front porch.

Windfields Farm   413/684-3786

154 Windsor Bush Road, Windsor, MA
Mailing address: 154 Windsor Bush Road, Cummington, MA 01026

Hosts: Carolyn and Arnold Westwood
Location: On dirt road. From West Cummington off Route 9, two miles uphill (winter guests should have snow tires!). Twenty miles west to Pittsfield, 25 east to Northampton, 8 miles to Swift River Inn's cross-country ski area; 40 minutes to Tanglewood.

Open: May–February. Two-night minimum on most weekends. Reservations required.
Rates: $45 single, $60 double. $15 cot. Special winter weekends, $250 for two couples includes two nights, two breakfasts, and your own kitchen.
♥ ⬤ ⁎⁎ ✈ ⅄

Just thinking about this B&B makes me feel good all over. The interesting house is a haven, way up and away, with scenic surroundings—but, in true B&B style, the hosts make the difference.

Arnold, retired as a Unitarian Universalist minister, now edits the town (pop. 600) newsletter and founded the town land trust. With the help of his youngest (then college-age) son, he built most of the solar addition, the Westwoods' part of the residence. The maple syrup—500 taps, sugarhouse, and mail order—is Carolyn's responsibility. Vegetables from her organic garden win prizes at regional fairs—as do her flowers, bread, pies, syrup ("first prize in 1991 after trying since 1975!"), and jam. Their 200-acre homestead borders an Audubon sanctuary, part of which was donated by the Westwoods, hosts who are concerned with conservation, building community spirit, and ending the arms race.

Carolyn refers to "living in a sculpture," a summer retreat—"a mess" purchased in 1962—that became, after 10 years of family work, a year-round "joyous house." The active/passive solar addition retains the pressed tin ceiling, paneled doors and hand-hewn beams of the original c. 1815 cottage. The connecting (c. 1830) farmhouse is now for guests, who have their own private entrance and living and dining rooms. Furnishings include many family antiques, carved pieces done by both Arnold's and Carolyn's mothers, and paintings done by artists the Westwoods know.

In residence: On the Westwood settlement—"Elsie, an English pointer/black Labrador, and Pushamet, a four-way mix, are often within call of the megaphone to act as B&B guide dogs."

Bed and bath: Two spacious corner bedrooms, "your castle as long as you're here." One with 1818 canopied double bed that belonged to Carolyn's great-great-great-grandmother. Queen walnut bed in other. Shared full bath with old-time barber's sink and claw-foot tub with shower.

Breakfast: 7:30–9. "Announced to strains of Mozart and Bach." Homegrown organic produce, berries, eggs. Pancakes, yogurt, maybe Irish oatmeal topped with granola, natural grain homemade muffins or popovers, Windfields' low-sugar jams. Served in guests' dining room.

Plus: Bedroom fans. Cross-country skiing and hiking trails (with blueberries for picking). Spring-fed swimming pond with sandy beach. A short walk to waterfall in the state forest. Beverages. Piano, hi-fi, fireplace, extensive library. Sun-dried towels.

From New York: *"The world's most effective therapy for urban stress."*

Can't find a listing for the community you are going to? More Berkshires B&Bs are available through reservation services. Please see page 234.

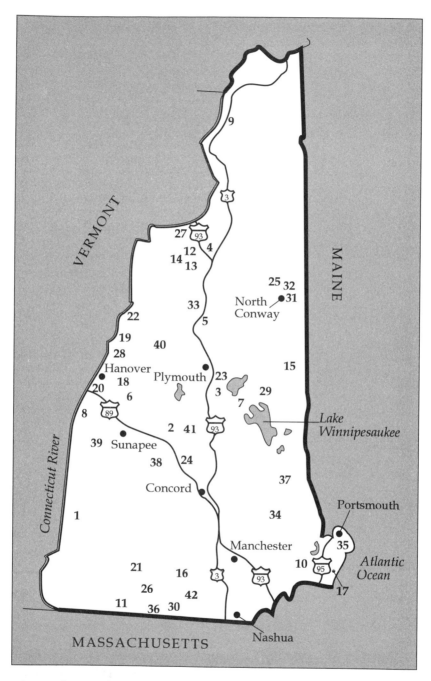

The numbers on this map indicate the locations of B&Bs described in detail in this chapter.

NEW HAMPSHIRE

KEY TO SYMBOLS
♥ Lots of honeymooners come here.
♯ Families with children are very welcome. (Please see page xii.)
♯ "Please emphasize that we are a private home, not an inn."
⁂ Groups or private parties sometimes book the entire B&B.
♦ Travel agents' commission paid. (Please see page xii.)
✗ Sorry, no guests' pets are allowed.
✌ No smoking inside *or* no smoking at all, even on porches.

New Hampshire
———— Reservation Services ————

Bed & Breakfast/Inns of New England
329 Lake Drive, Guilford, CT 06437

Phone: 603/279-8348 or 800/582-0853 (U.S./Canada). Daily 9 a.m.–9 p.m.

Listings: 100+ B&Bs and inns. Located throughout the state (and New England) in and around cities and towns. Included are hosted private residences and small inns—restored colonials, farms, and mountainview, lakeside, oceanfront, and island homes. Directory ($1).

Reservations: Two-day minimum stay required on holiday weekends. Short-term (one month plus) hosted housing available.

Rates: $35–$65 single. $45–$85 double. Suites from $85. Weekly rates available. Some hosts accept credit cards. Deposit required is first night's rate plus tax or 50 percent of multinight reservation. If cancellation is received at least 14 days before expected arrival, refund made, less $15 service fee. ♦

Ernie Taddei, an experienced innkeeper, has a growing list of hosts who believe in hearty breakfasts and "the friendly way to travel." Since becoming owner/director of this personalized New Hampshire–oriented reservation service in 1990, he has added listings in the five other New England states. Some hosts offer cross-country skiing, tennis courts, and swimming pools on the premises. Reservation confirmations arrive with helpful brochures about area attractions.

Plus: Some hosts offer picnic lunches, musical breakfasts, sleigh rides, theater ticket pickups, babysitting, and transportation to/from bus, train, and/or plane.

Other reservation services with some B&Bs in New Hampshire:
The American Country Collection, page 343
Bed and Breakfast of Rhode Island, page 307

Six weeks *after* one B&B opened, a neighbor inquired: "I need lodging for visiting relatives. When are you going to open?" This was the same neighbor who, during a zoning hearing, had expressed great concern about traffic and noise that a B&B would create!

——— New Hampshire B&Bs ———

Darby Brook Farm   603/835-6624
Hill Road, Alstead, NH 03602

Host: Howard C. Weeks
Location: Rural. On a town road, 2 miles from the village. Six miles west of Connecticut River Valley, 15 north of Keene.

Open: May–October.
Rates: $25 per person.
👭 🛥

Authentic. A classic 18th-century Georgian house. Discovered by relatives and friends of area residents, who sometimes say that it is a bit like being in a museum. Every room except the kitchen has raised paneling. Moldings are beveled. There's stenciling. And beams. Other than plumbing and electricity and one kitchen window, everything is original. Where the wide floorboards (mostly painted) have been scuffed by boots, knots are exposed. The 19th-century furnishings were put in place when Howard's parents bought this house in 1929. A few newer pieces were made by Howard, who was a furniture designer in New York. Since 1980 he has become a farmer, with sheep and chickens, a vegetable garden, apple orchard, berry bushes, and some maple trees (for syrup). He takes his produce to the Keene farmer's market. He directs guests to antiques shops, scenic roads, and the local lake. In the winter he is a cabinetmaker and lives in the house next door.

In residence: Queenie, the dog. Barney, the cat.
Bed and bath: Three rooms share one large full bath. One with two twin four-poster beds, working fireplace. One with double half-canopied bed, working fireplace. One room with a twin four-poster. Rollaway and crib available.
Breakfast: "Anything you wish." Cereal, fruit juice, bacon and eggs, muffins, toast, coffee. Howard joins guests.
Plus: Fireplaced living and dining rooms, a treat in the fall. Tea or soft drinks. Beverages. Down comforters. Fresh flowers.

The English House   603/735-5987
P.O. Box 162, Main Street, Andover, NH 03216-0162

Hosts: Ken and Gillian Smith
Location: In village center with Ragged Mountains behind, Mount Kearsarge view in front. Next to Proctor Academy. Within 15 minutes of King Ridge, Ragged Mountain, Norsk Cross-Country Ski Center; 20 minutes to Mount Sunapee. Near fishing, golf, water sports.

Open: Year round, except late March. Reservations advised. Two-night minimum on foliage, holiday, and special school weekends.
Rates: $55 single. $75 double. $20 extra person. MC, Visa.
✳ 🏸 ⅄

From Connecticut: *"A successful combination of old-world innkeeping with attention to detail and warm American hospitality . . . privacy in (well-insulated) rooms . . . beautifully renovated dwelling. . . . Breakfast is sumptuous."*

What was a big old unoccupied and neglected house has gone through a metamorphosis, thanks to Ken, a retired British army officer/former cross-country ski coach/gardener, and Gillian, a needlecrafter (featured in *Quilt* magazine and juried shows) who creates wearable art in her adjacent carriage house studio. The maple, birch, and oak woodwork is no longer black. Now there are Oriental and other area rugs, rocking chairs, plants everywhere, and traditional prints, all giving the feeling—embellished by afternoon tea—of an English country house.

Foreign languages spoken: Simple French and German.
Bed and bath: Seven rooms, each with private shower bath. One on first floor with two twin beds. Three with queen and one with two twins on second floor. Two large third-floor rooms, each with a queen and a twin bed. Rollaways available.
Breakfast: Usually 8:30. All homemade. Breads, rolls, muffins, jams, jellies, marmalades, yogurt, granola. Entree repertoire includes whole-meal pancakes with homemade sausage patties, honey-pecan sauce; elaborate omelets; or kedgeree with smoked fish and rice. Fresh fruit.
Plus: Rear deck accessible from guest sitting room. Landscaped grounds with fruit trees. Heated ski storage and waxing area.

Glynn House "Victorian" Inn

603/968-3775
43 Highland Street, P.O. Box 719   800/637-9599
Ashland, NH 03217-0719   fax 603/968-9338

Hosts: Betsy and Karol Paterman
Location: Residential, two-minute walk from the village. In the Golden Pond/White Mountains area; 2-minute drive to Squam Lake swimming; within 30 minutes of Waterville, Loon, and Tenney mountains. One mile from I-93. Ten minutes to Plym-outh State College and Holderness School.
Open: Year round.
Rates: $85 private bath. $95 bridal suite. $10 third person. Third floor, $150 for up to six people. MC, Visa.
♥ ⬤ ♣ ♦ ✈

From the turret to the oak foyer, from the square piano (bought at auction from area historical society) to ornately patterned wallpaper, Victoriana is the theme at this B&B restored and opened in 1989. The hosts, former restaurateurs, are auction buffs and know which auctioneer specializes in furniture, Depression glass, or porcelain. They have this week's auction schedule (and a story about last week's find)—as well as books and magazines about antiques. They'll direct you to fine restaurants and the rolling waters of the Basin, their favorite scenic spot. Karol, the chef/plumber/electrician/gardener, enjoys his role as full-time host. Betsy is regional sales manager for a food company.

In residence: In hosts' quarters, Gracie, age 14; Christopher, age 5. One cat, Muffin.
Foreign languages spoken: Polish and Russian.
Bed and bath: Four rooms and a suite, all with air conditioners and new private baths. Bridal suite with queen canopied bed, Jacuzzi/shower bath. Room with double bed, fireplace, shower bath. One room with queen bed,

(Please turn page.)

tub and shower bath. One room with queen and a single bed, sofa, shower bath. Entire third floor—suite with two bedrooms (One with a king and a single bed, one with double bed), air conditioners and ceiling fans, sitting room with cable TV, shower and tub bath.
Breakfast: Usually at 9 (coffee and tea an hour earlier.) Whim-of-chef menu. Belgian waffles, thick French toast, or eggs Benedict. Maybe muffins or apple strudel.
Plus: Beverage. Fruit basket. Fresh flowers. Mints on pillow.

Haus Trillium B&B   603/968-2180

RR 1, Box 106, Sanborn Road, Ashland, NH 03217-9740

Hosts: Susy and Roy Johnk
Location: On a hillside with old apple trees, wildflowers, gorgeous view of valley. One mile to village center; 3 to Squam Lake and public beach. Fourteen miles west of Lake Winnipesaukee and east of Newfound Lake. Two miles to I-93; 30 miles south of Waterville Valley and Loon Mountain. Ten minutes to Plymouth State College and Holderness School.
Open: Year round.
Rates: Private bath $50. Shared bath $45, $50 with fireplace. $10 child's cot.
♯ � 💤 ⚥

From New Mexico, Kentucky, Maryland, Nebraska: "*Old world charm. We would definitely return if we ever get within a hundred miles of Ashland, N.H. . . . A wonderful deck surrounded by trees and a meadow . . . birds at the feeders . . . wind chimes . . . refreshments before we went out to dinner. . . . We could tell a lot of thought had gone into making the room cozy and comfortable. . . . Super breakfast served with a gracious European flair. . . . Interesting couple. . . . A serene setting enhanced by attention to detail and a gracious hostess.*"

It's a century-old farmhouse with 1970s addition. It's the fulfillment of German-born Susy's long-held dream. The Johnks, who are interested in "all things connected with nature," opened in 1992 after Roy retired first from the U.S. Army (15 years on military intelligence assignments in Germany) and later from a supermarket headquarters position in Maryland. Furnishings include comfortable seating and Oriental rugs in the living room, Susy's grandparents' Flemish-style dining room set, and beds with upholstered headboards. And Susy has a pottery workshop on the premises.

In residence: Dolly, a 15-year-old bichon frise.
Foreign language spoken: German.
Bed and bath: Three rooms. On first floor, private exterior entrance to double-bedded room with private shower bath. On second floor, "in tree-tops," large queen-bedded room with working fireplace shares connecting shower bath with another queen-bedded room. Cot available.
Breakfast: Until 9:30. Juice, gourmet coffee, tea, fruit, meat and cheese platter, Apfelkuchen and other German pastries, pancakes, muffins, omelet, quiche, French toast, homemade jams and jellies. Buffet style in dining room or on deck.
Plus: Fireplaced living room with cable TV. Afternoon tea. Down comforters. Behind B&B, a well-kept trail.

Adair

P.O. Box 359, Old Littleton Road
Bethlehem, NH 03574-0359

603/444-2600
fax 603/444-4823

Hosts: Patricia and Hardy Banfield; daughter Nancy, house manager
Location: On 200 acres. Adjacent to another estate (open to public) on 1,200 acres with Christmas tree farm, more views, and two miles of hiking/ cross-country ski trails. Near Franconia, Littleton, and four-star dining. Ten minutes to Cannon Mountain, 20 to Bretton Woods, 30 to Loon Mountain.

Open: Year round. Three-night minimum on holiday weekends.
Rates: January–mid-March, mid-June–October, December 16–31 $125; with fireplace $145; suite with fireplace $175. Late March–mid-June, November–mid-December $105; with fireplace $120; suite with fireplace $145. Amex, MC, Visa.
♥ ✧ ◆ ✗

An estate. A getaway. Dubbed "a destination" by guests. With spectacular views from every room. With grounds that were originally designed by the Olmsted brothers of Boston's Emerald Necklace and Manhattan's Central Park fame.

Built for Dorothy Adair as a wedding gift in 1927—she celebrated her 80th birthday here in 1982—the Georgian Colonial Revival is furnished with antiques and reproductions and has three very large gathering rooms in addition to the dining room; also a patio, gardens, and a tennis court.

The Banfields spent seven months redecorating before opening in 1992, after Hardy, who had 20 years' experience in his Maine commercial construction company, earned a degree in hospitality management. Patricia owned the well-known Portland knitting shop, The Wool Room. Nancy managed a Mailboxes, Etc. Here, in the first place seen during their property search, the Banfields greet returnees "who feel like family."

In residence: Roosevelt, a black poodle. Sydney Adair, a black Labrador.
Bed and bath: Eight large rooms; all with individual thermostats, private full baths. Second floor—four queen-bedded rooms, three with working fireplaces. Third floor—one queen and three with king/twin option. Rollaway available.
Breakfast: 8:30–9:30. Coffee and tea available at 8. Granola, oatmeal made with maple syrup, popovers with hand-whipped butter and preserves, fresh fruit, eggs Benedict with spiced potatoes, or cinnamon apple pancakes, cob-smoked Vermont bacon. Very social time.
Plus: Tea at 4 p.m. Hors d'oeuvres at 5:30 in fireplaced granite Tap Room, which has setups, TV/VCR and movies, upright piano. Guest refrigerator. Dinner for groups of six or more. Access to PGA golf course. Photos of original construction. A guest's compilation of hiking trails.

To tip or not? (Please turn to page xi.)

The Gables Bed & Breakfast   603/869-5780

Main Street, Bethlehem, NH 03574-0190

Hosts: Dawn M. Ferringo and William K. Demers
Location: On main street of small village with a restored 1914 movie theater (open in summer), a general store, a video shop, restaurants, and some antiques shops. Walk to PGA golf course, tennis, antiques shops, restaurants. Fifteen miles to Bretton Woods, 36 to Mount Washington Auto Road, 48 to North Conway.
Open: Year round.
Rates: Tax included. Double $60–$70, singles $5 less. Dinner packages available. MC, Visa.
♥ ♣ ⋈ ⊱

"It's a marvelous big old Victorian with lots of carved wood [oak and yellow birch], plenty of Victoriana, a pool and hot tub, wicker chairs on a wrap-around porch, and great food too. It belongs in your next book."

The recommendation, first of many, came from an L.L. Bean shopper while I was in the Freeport, Maine, store, introducing B&B to travelers from all over the world.

In Bethlehem's heyday as a pollen-free resort, this was a hotel annex; hence the two-digit room numbers. Vacant for 32 years, it opened as a B&B in 1991 after Dawn's parents spent 7 years on the restoration, which included a new four-paneled stained glass window on the stairway landing. They furnished with period pieces, plants, and dried arrangements. Dawn, an experienced restaurant manager, took it over in 1993. Bill, an EMT, is a certified nurse's aide.

In residence: Two cats—Yincenzo and Prudence.
Bed and bath: Four second-floor rooms; all with mountain views. All share full bath with shower and deep old-fashioned claw-footed tub. One queen with private half bath. Two other queen-bedded rooms, each with sink in room. One double-bedded room with balcony overlooking pool, hot tub, tennis courts. Rollaway available.
Breakfast: 8–11. Freshly baked muffins, croissants stuffed with berries, or scones. Apple walnut pancakes, spiced rum French toast, quiche. In ornate fireplaced dining room.
Plus: Fireplaced living room. Game/TV room. Poolside refreshments or evening cider. Setups provided. Flannel sheets in winter. Fresh flowers in summer. Dinner by arrangement. Babysitting. Transportation to/from Littleton.

Mountain Fare Inn   603/726-4283

Mad River Road, P.O. Box 553, Campton, NH 03223

Hosts: Susan and Nick Preston
Location: At the edge of the small village. Surrounded by six acres. Ten miles east of Waterville Valley, 15 north of Squam Lake, 20 miles south of Loon and Cannon mountains and Franconia Notch.
Open: Year round. Two-night minimum during ski season, holiday weekends, and vacation weeks.
Rates: $35–$40 single. $80 family-sized rooms; $70 other rooms with private bath; $56 shared bath. April–June and November–December 15—about $8 less.
♥ ⅋ ♣ ♦ ⋈ ⊱

The Prestons coach competitive skiers including U.S. Ski Team members. They grow their own vegetables and herbs. Susan dries flowers and crafts arrangements. And they meet many outdoors-oriented guests who envy their "simple, down-home lifestyle." The lifestyle has evolved since 1982, when they were boarders here and found an old brochure; it made them realize the potential of the country cottage that has lodged paying visitors since the 1880s. Wes, age 12, and Tim, 9, have grown up in the inn, which now has a welcoming red enamel wood stove in the entry room. Furnishings are family treasures, country pieces, printed fabrics, and a collection of wildlife art prints. Guests remember moose sightings; being snowed in (1993); recommendations for back roads, hiking trails, waterfalls, and antiques dealers. And relaxation.

In residence: Three cats—mostly outdoors.
Foreign language spoken: Some French.
Bed and bath: Eight rooms, varying in size and decor; one with air conditioning. Five with private en-suite baths; one bath down the hall has tub, no shower. Four are family-sized rooms with two or three beds; first-floor suite has room with double and a twin bed, room with sitting area and double daybed; private full bath. Another has queen, twin, bunk alcove, sitting area, private shower bath. Cribs available.
Breakfast: 7:30–9 (ski season 6:30–9), coffee until 10:00. "Hearty, wholesome natural foods for outdoors people." Eggs any style, herb and cheese omelet, blueberry muffins, French toast, pancakes. In dining room, air conditioned in summer, that has an upright piano.
Plus: Fireplaced living room with TV. Guest refrigerator. Room for ski tuning and Ping-Pong. Apres-ski refreshments. Window fans. Babysitting. Soccer and volleyball fields. Swing set. Laundry service; $3 per load. Dinner for family reunions and ski, hiking, or biking groups. "A porch for 'settin.'"

The "Inn" on Canaan Street   603/523-7310
RD 1, Box 92, Canaan Street, Canaan, NH 03741-9761

Hosts: Lee and Louise Kremzner
Location: By lake. At the foot of Mount Cardigan on 14 acres. Two and one-half miles up hill. Around corner from Cardigan Mountain School. Five minutes off Route 4; 25 minutes from Dartmouth College.

Open: Year round. Reservations required.
Rates: $65–$75 single. $75 double, shared bath, $75–$85 private. $150 two bedrooms as a suite—$95 if fireplaced room only—with private bath. $15 cot.
♥ ♯ ☆ ♦ ✗ ⊬

Guests are always asking, "How did you ever find this lovely place?" Located on a 1788 street that is in the Federal Register, it's the home of a Columbia professor emeritus and his wife, a former nutritionist/consumer publicist (two terrific people who gave a wonderful cooking demonstration in my first Bloomingdale's Meet-the-Hosts program). Since the Kremzners restored the "Federal but country-style house" 10 years ago, they have become very involved in this wonderful community. As hosts they meet many "Cardigan School parents, folks from Dartmouth, many notables—how did they ever find us?—and lots of people who come to catch their breath, to enjoy the views and the lake. We love pampering them, sharing this area, laughing at

(Please turn page.)

ourselves, solving the world's problems, and relaxing over a fun breakfast." (It's all true. My husband and I loved our stay.)

In residence: Labradors Snickers and Ginger are "lovable wigglebottoms."
Foreign language spoken: A little French.
Bed and bath: Five second-floor rooms, all with desk and comfortable chairs. Private baths; one shower only, rest are full. One single bed. One canopied queen, working fireplace. Three king/twin options. Two rooms can be a suite. Cot available.
Breakfast: 8–9:30. Juice, fruit, toast. Homemade sweet breads, muffins, or popovers. Egg dishes and herbs. Scones—"best west of London's Brown Hotel," said one guest. Blueberry pancakes, yogurt, granola. Prepared by Louise, who has a collection of 800 cookbooks. Served in Garden Room that opens onto porch.
Plus: Books everywhere. Swimming. Cross-country skiing right here. Tea. Fruit. Library, games, movies. Ping-Pong, badminton. Dinner during inclement weather and with theme weekends (antiques, auction, gardening, cooking, reading series). Barn antiques shop.

Watch Hill Bed and Breakfast 603/253-4334
Old Meredith Road, P.O. Box 1605, Center Harbor, NH 03226

Host: Barbara Lauterbach
Location: On the same road as post office and a farm. (Ask about the night the cows came.) Five-minute walk to village, Keepsake Quilting (country's largest quilt supply shop), and beach. Just off Route 25, on the northernmost end of Lake Winnipesaukee, near MS *Mount Washington* excursions.

Open: Year round. Two-day minimum on July 4th and Columbus Day weekends.
Rates: $65 includes state meals and room tax. Single $5 less. Rollaway $15. Three nights or more, $5 less per night.

From Georgia: *"Of course the syrup was from New Hampshire, but how many B&Bs make their own sausage?"* From Vermont: *"Bright, cheerful, cozy, comfortable, friendly, excellent."* From Massachusetts: *"A real home . . . terrific view of the lake and mountains beyond."*

Some guests place orders for a case of Barbara's tomato jelly before the tomatoes are even planted. Barbara, too, is enthusiastic—about the view of the MS *Mount Washington* "precisely at 9:40 a.m.," about "the ancient locust trees of mammoth proportions," and about how her interests dovetailed into her 1989 B&B opening. A 1772 Cape with Victorian additions, the house is furnished with many English and American antiques, dog prints, and Staffordshires. (Barbara was a breeder of champion bullmastiffs.) She is a world-trained chef and food consultant, a former Ohio cooking school director, a spokesperson for King Arthur flour, a local historic district commission officer, and a New Hampshire League of Craftsmen board member. She enjoys meeting guests who talk about "getting centered in Center Harbor."

In residence: Martin, an Amazon parrot, "imitates female guests' laughter." Two cats: "super friendly" Frank, and Moxie, an orange Morris.

Foreign languages spoken: Fluent French. Some German.
Bed and bath: Four second-floor rooms; two have slanted ceilings. Two shared hall baths—one full, one shower only. King, queen, or two twin beds. Rollway available.
Breakfast: Usually 7:30–9:30. Belgian waffles, maple French toast, sausage, "muffin du jour," eggs, home fries, mulled cider applesauce, homemade breads, jams, and jellies. In paneled room with fresh flowers, sterling silver, and linens or on screened porch with that lake view.
Plus: Beverages. Fruit bowl. Beach towels. Horseshoes. Bocci balls. Quilting parties in dining and living rooms. Off-season cooking weekends.

The Barberry House   603/675-2802
70 Saint Gaudens Road, Cornish, NH 03745

Hosts: Becky Rice-Mesec and Don Mesec
Location: Peaceful. Without a neighbor in sight. On a dirt road, almost a mile from well-traveled Route 12A. Five-minute walk to the Saint-Gaudens National Historic Site (house tour, gardens, walking trails).

Four miles across Connecticut River to Windsor, Vermont, shops, museums, restaurants; 30 minutes south of Dartmouth College.
Open: Year round.
Rates: $85 shared bath. $95 private bath. Singles $40 less. MC, Visa.

Spectacular grounds with perennial gardens, terraced lawn, a fountain, and reflecting pool surround this 200-year-old colonial farmhouse. It's been discovered by wedding and reunion guests, Dartmouth college visitors, and many others who wish they had time to stay right here. Opened as a B&B in 1991, the house was once part of Cornish Art Colony and was also the home of Homer Saint-Gaudens, son of the famous sculptor Augustus.

Don, a carpenter for the current owners, worked on this 18-month restoration project. An interior designer furnished the lovely rooms with period antiques. Cohost Becky is office manager of Dartmouth College's athletic department.

In residence: Two cats, Marty and Bug.
Bed and bath: Five rooms. Second-floor beamed rooms have canopied beds. One has king bed, private full bath. Room with queen bed shares a full bath with a room that has two twin beds. On dormered third floor, double-bedded room shares tub and shower bath with large queen-bedded room. Rollaway available.
Breakfast: 8–10. Juice, fruit dish, egg dish with cheese, pancakes or waffles or muffins, tea, coffee, milk, decaf. Served in fireplaced dining room.
Plus: Fireplaced living room, library, and reception room. Standing fans available. Evening coffee or hot chocolate. Down comforters. Fresh flowers.

According to guests (many are preservationists and/or house restorers), there ought to be a medal for the meticulous work—everything from research to labor—done by B&B owners. Indeed, many have won preservation awards.

Rooms with a View

603/237-5106

RR 1, Box 215, Forbes Road
Colebrook, NH 03576-9718

(N.H. only) **800/499-5106, ext. 1**

Hosts: Sonja and Charles Sheldon
Location: Very much off the beaten path. On a hillside of a former dairy farm. On a snowmobile trail system. Six miles east of Colebrook center, shops, restaurants. Ten miles to skiing at The Balsams in Dixville Notch.

Near fishing, canoeing, hiking, golf, hunting. Two and one-half hours from Montreal; 4½ from Boston.
Open: Year round.
Rates: $60 shared bath, $65 private. Singles $15 less. MC, Visa.
♥ ♨ ⚓ ⁂ ✗ ⅙

From New Hampshire: *"Hospitality, food, and view are unsurpassed!"* From Michigan: *"Walked in wildflower garden before scrumptious breakfast."* From Arkansas: *"Felt like visiting family."* From Maine: *"Worth finding."*

"People wonder at the quiet and solitude and beautiful views that abound. Some stay on the porch with a book. Artists paint the countryside. One Viennese opera singer came on her honeymoon. Snowmobilers leave from our door. After we fell in love with this area while vacationing one winter at The Balsams, we built this farmhouse B&B in 1991 with wraparound porch. A Russian fireplace (which heats about half of the house) is in the living room. Everyone gathers in the kitchen, especially when I'm cooking at the three-ton soapstone stove that also heats the house."

In Massachusetts Sonja worked with medical records at a nursing home; Charlie was a carpenter. Here, Charlie is a groundskeeper at The Balsams; Sonja is fulfilling a 10-year dream.

Bed and bath: Seven rooms, all with Sonja's handmade quilts. Second floor—three rooms with king/twins option and two double-bedded rooms share two full baths. Third floor—two rooms, each with a double and two twin beds, one with private full, other with private shower bath.
Breakfast: 6–11. Homemade muffins, bread, waffles, pancakes. Eggs any style, hot or cold cereal, coffee, tea, milk, juice. Homemade jellies and honey. In dining room with more views.
Plus: Den with entertainment center that includes nature and children's videos; satellite system. Down comforters. Flannel sheets. Drying room for wet clothes. Croquet. Volleyball. Horseshoes. Bocci. Dart area. Gift for returnees.

The Curtis Field House

603/929-0082

735 Exeter Road, Hampton, NH 03842

Host: Mary Houston
Location: Route 27 east. On five wooded acres, on Exeter line. Three miles to Exeter Academy, 7 to ocean, 10 to Portsmouth.
Open: May–October. Two-night

minimum on holidays and Academy weekends. No check-ins after 8 p.m. please.
Rates: Per room. $65 including tax. MC, Visa.
✗

Mary's ancestors were Exeter's first settlers in 1638. Her father, "a master craftsman by hobby" built this Royal Barry Wills Cape with wide floorboards in 1954. Often, during the 1980s restoration, carpenters commented on the attention to detail. Now the house has antiques, reproductions, and hooked, braided, and Oriental rugs. The gardens too, receive loving care.

Mary, a retired decorator, opened the house as a B&B in 1988. Her own extensive travels include trips to China and Japan and, still, an annual ski trip to Europe. And she describes cooking as "pure enjoyment."

Bed and bath: Three rooms, all with air conditioners and window fans. On first floor, room with double four-poster shares shower bath with hosts. On second, room with two canopied twin beds, private full bath; room with queen bed, shower bath.
Breakfast: 7:30–9. Omelet, bacon or ham and eggs, strata, or French toast. Fresh fruits, yogurt, Swiss familia cereal, juice, coffee, tea, coffee cake. In dining room or on sun deck.
Plus: Piano. Down comforters. Ping-Pong. Croquet. Badminton. Flower and vegetable gardens. Smoking on enclosed porch only.

Hannah Davis House   603/585-3344

186 Depot Road, Route 119, Fitzwilliam, NH 03447-9625

Hosts: Kaye and Mike Terpstra
Location: A few steps from common of this small New England town. In the historic district, on a scenic route (119). Twelve miles south of Keene; 28 miles east of Brattleboro, Vermont. "Within 45 minutes of enough antiques shops to keep dealers busy for three days."

Open: Year round. Two-night minimum for college weekends (two in October, one in May).
Rates: Per room. $55 double bed, $65 queen bed, $80 carriage loft and suite. $20 third person, $10 fourth person. Singles $5 less.
♥ 🛏 ♣ ♦ ✈ ⊁

Everything. It's all here. Enjoyed by the "Good Morning America" staff when they were broadcasting from Fitzwilliam: this c. 1820 Federal house with its original kitchen/hearth room, added baths with brass and porcelain fixtures, demolished and restored you-name-it, all embellished with antique furnishings and linens, country quilts, and braided rugs. It is the home—a B&B since 1990—of an engineer and a social worker who owned and operated a small Brookline, New Hampshire, grocery store until they began work on this house six years ago. Kaye and Mike welcome you with cider or coffee and a treat. They turn down your bed and leave homemade cookies. They love the smell and feel popcorn gives the house. These two sharers—cooking tips, carpentry lessons, local history, a secluded waterfall, a covered bridge—give B&B mentoring credit to a neighbor at The Amos Parker House, where you are invited to see extraordinary gardens.

In residence: "Sadie, a shy red setter/black Lab. Toby, a gregarious collie/shepherd mix. Tabatha, a happy, fluffy sheltie."
Bed and bath: Five rooms. All private full baths. First-floor suite, private entrance, extra-long twins/king option, sitting room with double-size sleep sofa, fireplace. On second floor, one queen canopied four-poster; one queen plus a twin bed, working fireplace; one "snug" double-bedded room. In carriage shed, queen bed in cathedral-ceilinged loft with queen-size sleep sofa in sitting room below.

(Please turn page.)

Breakfast: "The main event." Usually 8–10; tea and coffee earlier. Fresh fruit. Juices. Homemade granola, chunky applesauce, sour cream/poppyseed or blueberry bread. Elaborate entrees (demonstrated in Jordan Marsh's Meet-the-Host program) such as stir-fry chicken wrapped in crepes or stuffed French toast with cheesy Dijon sauce.

Plus: Sitting room with stereo and piano, "but everyone ends up in the kitchen or on its long screened porch." Lots of pillows. Down comforters. Forgotten items.

Blanche's B&B   603/823-7061

351 Easton Valley Road, Franconia, NH 03580

Hosts: John Vail and Brenda Shannon
Location: Set in a meadow along a country road. Backyard is Kinsman Ridge, part of Appalachian Trail. Near working farms. Five miles from I-93 and Franconia village; 6 to Franconia Notch; 20 to Bretton Woods.

Open: Year round. Two-night minimum in foliage season, during holiday weeks, and on major holiday weekends.
Rates: $60–$65 double room. $35–$40 single. $20 third person.
❊ ✹ ⊁

> From Vermont: *"Brenda and John, with their warmth and friendship, are probably the primary attraction . . . I have reviewed inns for* Ski *magazine and other publications . . . there is something special, very special, about Blanche's."*
> From Massachusetts: *"Decorated in an artistic, homey, inviting style, all fitting together beautifully . . . breakfast alone is worth going for."*

"One particular British B&B inspired us to leave our Boston area jobs. Using parts salvaged from other old houses, we have restored the unadorned farmhouse to a glory it probably never had. John does carpentry here. I am a decorative painter who makes colorful floorcloths and hand-painted furniture. We furnished with family treasures and auction finds. Guests gather round the living room wood stove. Even though we have separate quarters, it's B&B in a traditional style."

In residence: Daughter Ruby is two. Blanche, a black dog, is "a respected member of the family who greets guests, gives a house tour, and poses for photos."

Bed and bath: Five rooms with Brenda's hand-painted and stenciled walls. Two shared baths—one with claw-foot tub and separate tiled shower with built-in bench; one with shower only. Large first-floor room with hand-carved double four-poster. On second floor—canopied double bed and single in alcove; antique double sleigh bed; single four-poster; queen bed.

Breakfast: Usually 8–9. Maybe fresh fruit salad with maple yogurt dressing, spinach omelets, stuffed French toast with kiwi; pumpkin ginger muffins or honey nut rolls. Served at big round antique dining room table.

Plus: No TV. Yard. Games. Books. Sheets of 100 percent cotton. Pickup arranged at Franconia bus station. Dinner to groups by reservation only.

The Inn at Forest Hills

603/823-9550

P.O. Box 783, Route 142, Franconia, NH 03580-0783   **fax 603/823-8701**

Hosts: Gordon and Joanne Haym
Location: On five wooded acres with three ponds, hiking, and ungroomed cross-country trails. Along a little-traveled road—with gorgeous mountain views—between Franconia and Bethlehem. Half mile from I-93. Five minutes to Cannon Mountain; 10 to fine dining in Franconia, Sugar Hill, or Littleton.

Open: Year round. Two-night minimum on peak season weekends.
Rates: Private bath $95 king, $75–$85 queen, $75 double bed. Shared bath $55 queen. $40 single room. $20 extra bed. Senior citizens and AARP, 10 percent less. MC, Visa.
♥ ♦ ✂

From England: *"As we were passing the inn, a voice spoke, saying 'come and visit'—the type of silent voice heard by those who are fortunate enough to hear the words of Burns, Blake, and Wordsworth. This invitation and the overall ambiance and hospitality induced us not only to stay but to embark upon matrimony while resident in this beautiful place."*

Birders, sports enthusiasts, and antiquers too have discovered this spacious English Tudor, which the Hayms moved into in 1993, just five weeks after they saw it—empty. Built in 1894 as a lodge for a grand summer hotel, it was the residence for Franconia College's president in the 1960s and '70s. Now everything is redone. Furnishings are a blend of country casual, modern, turn-of-the-century pieces, and local craftsmen's works.

In New Jersey Joanne, originally a home economics major, was a corporate officer in finance. Gordon, a small business specialist who has consulted worldwide, was a chemical corporation executive. "With our children grown, we chose this wonderful lifestyle, a lifestyle that seems to be the dream of many guests, our extended family."

In residence: "Tiffany, our fat cat, seldom in guests' area."
Bed and bath: Eight rooms. First floor—queen, private full bath. Four large second-floor rooms, all private baths—double-bedded room has shower bath; full baths (two en suite, one across the hall) for queen-bedded room and king suite. Third floor—two large queen-bedded rooms share (robes provided) full bath with single-bedded room.
Breakfast: 8:30; coffee at 7:30. Orange juice. Granola with milk or yogurt. Fresh, baked, or poached fruit. Homemade bread or muffins with honey, strawberry butter, or vanilla cream cheese. Possibilities include Belgian waffles; buttermilk and honey pancakes with apples or walnuts and blueberries; curried cream eggs in puff pastry; French toast. By fire in winter. Next to open French doors and bird feeders (finches and hummingbirds) in warmer months.
Plus: Fireplaced living room. Oversized fireplace in Alpine Room. Solarium and Alpine Room have VCR, TV, games. Covered porch overlooking mountains. Individual thermostats on all radiators. Badminton. Croquet. Inquire about option of dinner for skiers and cyclists. Printouts of recipes.

The Bungay Jar

603/823-7775
fax 603/444-0100

Easton Valley Road, Easton, NH
Mailing address: P.O. Box 15, Franconia, NH 03580

Hosts: Lee Strimbeck and Kate Kerivan
Location: Gorgeous. Franconia range of the White Mountains. Tucked back from the road on 12 wooded acres with hiking path to a stream. Six miles south of Franconia. Ten minutes to I-93, Sugar Hill, Cannon Mountain, Lost River; 30 to Loon, Bretton Woods.

Open: Year round. Two- or three-night minimum during foliage season and on holiday weekends.
Rates: Foliage season $75 and $85 shared bath, $95–$120 private bath. Winter $60–$100. Summer and holidays $65–$105. Third person $20. Amex, MC, Visa.
♥ ♣ ✈ ✄

Guests wrote: *"Could look around for days and not see everything. . . . Surpassed your glowing recommendation . . . picturesque . . . most charming proprietors we have met in our extensive travels."*

A treat. A *Country Accents* cover story. Built from an 18th-century post-and-beam barn, it is filled with antiques and collectibles, stained glass windows, quilts, English pub panels, Benny Goodman's six-foot-long soaking tub, glass-topped lightning rods that hold up one railing . . . all arranged by Kate, the landscape architect, who has become innkeeper/gardener (the herb and perennial gardens are spectacular) and chef (who uses a commercial stove) and craftswoman (wreaths, dried flowers). Lee, a patent attorney, recently built stone walls and a pergola. Getaway guests, honeymooners, and many returnees enjoy the two-storied fireplaced living room, a sauna, a small library, and multiple decks that offer mesmerizing mountain views.

In residence: Kyle, age seven. "Lila, our standard poodle; Checkers, the cat."
Bed and bath: Six rooms, four private baths. First floor—room with two twin beds shares a bath with double-bedded room. Second floor—Victorian queen bed with private balcony, bath with six-foot tub; one king canopied bed and daybed, full bath, interior reading balcony. Third floor—Stargazer suite with four skylights, king bed, tub bath; another skylit room with double bed, shower bath, French doors to private balcony. Plus a private cottage in the woods that sleeps two or more.
Breakfast: 8:30–9:30. Full. Blueberry pancakes with local maple syrup. Popovers. Local smoked meats and salmon. Fresh fruit. In dining room or on porch overlooking gardens and mountains.
Plus: No TV. Tea or cider with homemade snacks 3–5 p.m. Coffee or tea anytime. Flowers in season. CD player. Games. Croquet. Hammock.

*T*he place to stay has become the reason to go.

The Hilltop Inn

603/823-5695

Sugar Hill, NH 03585

Hosts: Mike and Meri Hern
Location: In this tiny village with cheese store, post office (open three hours a day), and a historical museum. Ten minutes from Franconia Notch.
Open: Year round. Two-night minimum during fall foliage and holiday weekends.
Rates: Late May–late September, late October, and December 24–

January 1, $65 double, $80 queen, $90 suite. Late September–mid-October, $85 double, $100 queen, $110 suite. January 2–late May and late October–December 23, $60 double, $75 queen, $85 suite. Additional guest $15 ($20 during foliage). Singles $10 less. Pets $10 per evening. Discover, MC, Visa.
♥ ♣

"Nearby there's a lover's lane—really!—with benches placed for sunset views."

Outside and *Yankee* magazines have featured this inn, which is owned by hikers and cross-country skiers. "Last winter we added 20 acres of cross-country ski trails right from our door. Guests (and their pets—one even came with a llama) comment on the homey Victoriana, our Garland kitchen stove, the handmade quilts, the lace—and, outside, the perennial gardens and hummingbirds. Many guests come for one night and stay several. We love them, the inn, the town."

Meri discovered Sugar Hill when she visited a college friend more than twenty years ago. ("I never left.") She and Mike, a former electrical engineer, are caterers who, in the last nine years, have made many changes in the 1895 inn.

In residence: Boop, a 13-year-old black Labrador mix. Lucy and Elphie, sister cats.
Bed and bath: Six second-floor rooms, private full baths. Double beds in smaller rooms; queens in others. Rollaway and crib available.
Breakfast: 8:30–9:30. Hearty buffet. Cinnamon French toast, farm eggs, raspberry and wild blueberry pancakes, local berries and maple syrup. Locally smoked ham and bacon. Homemade jams and muffins. By dining room wood stove or on deck or porches.
Plus: Large deck with sunset views. Porch rockers. Ceiling fans. TV with VCR (250 movies) in fireplaced sitting room. Flannel sheets. Teas or local cider with snacks. Transportation to/from Franconia bus stop. Option of dinner by candlelight.

Sugar Hill Inn

603/823-5621
800-548-4748

Sugar Hill, NH
Mailing address: Route 117, Franconia, NH 03580

Hosts: Barbara and Jim Quinn
Location: On 16 acres—half rolling lawns with flowers, half wooded—with spectacular mountain views. "Our only neighbor is a goldsmith's studio/shop." Four miles from Franconia Notch and the White Mountains.
Open: Year round except April and

mid-November–December 27. Two-night minimum stay in foliage season.
Rates: Per room, $90 (without mountain view) to $115 (queen bed, mountain view). Working women's weekend getaway packages.
♥ ♣ ✗ ✗

(Please turn page.)

"So many of our guests began to say that this was the quintessential country inn that I looked quintessential up in the dictionary! 'The purest essence of a country inn' is just what we have tried to create ever since we ended our eight-year search in 1986. [Returnees find some major change every year.] Jim spent 28 years in the grocery business in Rhode Island. Here, he and guests, too, are delighted with his role as chef. *Bon Appétit* and *Yankee* magazines have published some of his recipes."

Barbara has stenciled most of the rooms (others have small-print wallcoverings) and furnished them with antique or period reproductions. The dining room has Rockwell prints, an old spinning wheel—and lots of light, thanks to windows on three sides, complete with those mountain views. For a better look, use the telescope. You might focus on the tram going up Cannon Mountain.

Bed and bath: Eleven rooms (15 in summer and fall); all private baths. In main inn, first-floor room with two twin beds, shower and small tub bath. Second floor, 10 rooms with queen, double, or twin beds; most have full bath with reglazed 1930s deep soaking tub, 2 have shower without tub. May until mid-November, 4 large king-bedded cottage rooms, each with separate exterior entrance, modern full bath.
Breakfast: 8–9:30. Full country menu. Could be juice, pumpkin raisin or blueberry muffins, egg/cheese/cream souffle, breakfast meats, hot beverages.
Plus: Afternoon tea. Antique player piano with rolls in fireplaced living room. Four working fireplaces. Wicker-furnished wraparound porch. Cribs and rollaways available in cottages. Candlelit dinners (menu announced on chalkboard in morning) by reservation only.

Freedom House   603/539-4815
P.O. Box 478, 1 Maple Street, Freedom, NH 03836-0478

Hosts: Bob and Marjorie Daly
Location: In a quiet country village, by the millpond. Half hour south of Conways' outlets and ski slopes. Half hour east of Wolfeboro.
Open: Year round. Two-night minimum September 15–October 15.
Rates: $40 single, $60 double. MC, Visa.

Small town, U.S.A. With a genuine Old Home Week and Fireman's Parade in August. With summer crafts shows, yard sales, and, in a converted barn, an antiquarian bookshop.

Within walking distance of church, town hall, library, post office, and a lake, is this B&B. It's a white Victorian house with bay windows, gray shutters, and an American flag. The comfortable Victorian/country decor includes Marjorie's own handmade quilts.

Since 1985, when the Dalys left their resort management positions, the world has come to their doorstep. And now Bob, retired from the U.S. Coast Guard, serves as a selectman.

In residence: Muffin is a friendly and declawed black house cat "who helps show guests to their rooms."
Bed and bath: Six rooms share two second-floor baths (one with tub, one with shower), one first-floor half bath, and one third-floor half bath. On second floor—two rooms, each with two twin beds; two double-bedded

rooms. On third floor, one room has a double bed and antique crib for infant; one room is a single. Cot available (no charge).
Breakfast: 7–9. Homemade muffins, pancakes with Freedom's own maple syrup, French toast, farm-fresh eggs, bacon, ham, sausage. Served in breakfast room (with ceiling fan).
Plus: Welcoming beverage. Portable fans in guest rooms. Swimming passes to lake located along a dirt road.

Greenfield Bed & Breakfast Inn

603/547-6327
800/678-4144
fax 603/547-2418

Town Center, Forest Road
Routes 136 and 31 North, Greenfield, NH
Mailing address: P.O. Box 400, Greenfield, NH 03047-0400

Hosts: Barbara and Vic Mangini
Location: On three acres of lawn in center of small town. On main road, next to the library. Three minutes from 400-acre Greenfield State Park; 15 from Peterborough and from Crotched and Temple mountains, 90 from Boston.

Open: Year round. (No phone calls or arrivals after 9:30 p.m.)
Rates: Per room, double occupancy. $69 private bath, $49–$59 shared (with one other room) bath. $20 each additional person. MC, Visa.
♥ ♯ ⁂ ♦ ✈

Twenty minutes after the Manginis' B&B sign went up in 1986, the first guests—honeymooners—arrived. That couple and many others celebrating anniversaries return annually. And, as you'll see (mementos), Bob and Dolores Hope have come twice.

The "for sale" sign on the big beautiful white Victorian, built in 1817, was too much to resist just about the time the parents of six grown children were about to retire to their nearby farm. Barbara decorated with plenty of white wicker, Laura Ashley linens, antiques, dolls, wallpapers, crystal, and laces. Vic ("I leap out to the driveway to greet guests"), who has spent 30 years in advertising and marketing, has found that corporate executives, too, enjoy the ambiance here—"especially the rocking-chair strategy meetings in the glass-walled deck house with mountain views."

Bed and bath: Nine rooms; eight are air conditioned, all have phones. Large first-floor room has two twin beds, TV, private full bath. On second floor—king, double, or twin beds; most have private shower baths, one is a tub bath. Two rooms share a full bath. One twin-bedded and one double-bedded room form a suite with private hallway. Sleep-six hayloft suite, private entrance, TV. Rollaways available. (Infants must have own portable crib and high chair.)
Breakfast: 7:30–9:30. "A party." Egg casseroles, strata (meatless or with sausage, ham, chicken). Barbara's home-baked muffins, one kind known as "miracle muffin." Bagels. Cereals. Fresh fruit. Buffet style in the garden room.
Plus: Bedroom ceiling fans. Games. Books. Mountainview sun deck. Fireplaced living room with TV. Access to fax, copier, video player, movie screen.

B&Bs offer the opportunity to get away without going away.

The Inn at Elmwood Corners

603/929-0443
800/253-5691

252 Winnacunnet Road, Hampton, NH 03842

Hosts: John and Mary Hornberger
Location: In residential area, on main street, 1½ miles from Hampton Beach. Walk to village theaters, antiques shops, restaurants.
Open: Year round. Two-night minimum on May–October holiday weekends.

Rates: June–October, $55 single, $65 double, $85 studio. November–May, $40 single, $50 double, $75 studio. $10 extra person. Discounts for three or more days. MC, Visa.
♥ ♨ ❖ ✈

Wyoming, where are you? At press time, that was the only state missing from the guest list—a list that includes many "who tell us that we are living their dream of a lifestyle."

John, an avid freshwater fisherman, had experience as a restaurateur. Mary, a computer analyst who has learned how to upholster, enjoys creating a casual country ambiance. They spent a year on restoring and opened the century-old former sea captain's house in 1988—with braided rugs, stenciled walls, and quilts. Some rooms have exposed beams. The parlor has a floor-to-ceiling sea-stone fireplace and a wall filled with books. (Take the paperback home with you.) And now traditional New England dinners are an option here.

In residence: "Assistants" Keith, 11, and Kevin, 8. Alex, yellow Lab, loves to be petted; not allowed in guest rooms.
Bed and bath: Seven rooms. Five second-floor rooms—with queen or a double bed—share (robes provided) two shower baths and one half bath. Two studio suites on the third floor include queen beds, private shower baths, air conditioning, and kitchenettes. Rollaways available.
Breakfast: 8–10. May include eggs Benedict, cheddar-and-chive omelet, French toast, pancakes, or huevos rancheros. Home fries, juice, fresh fruit. Plum/oatmeal or banana nut bread. In dining room or on enclosed sun porch.
Plus: Nighttime homemade cookies. Large yard. Games. Weddings catered on or off site. Dinner, $25–$30 per person.

From Vermont: *"Large, comfortable rooms . . . delicious, copious, and varied breakfasts."* From Massachusetts: *"Welcoming family . . . plenty of privacy . . . breakfast (freshly caught trout this particular morning) first-class."*

Looking for a B&B with a crib? Find a description with the ♨ symbol and then check under the "Bed and bath" description.

Moose Mountain Lodge   603/643-3529
P.O. Box 272, Etna, NH 03750-0272

Hosts: Kay and Peter Shumway
Location: One mile up a winding dirt road (winter shuttle provided) to 350 acres with a view of Connecticut River valley below, Green Mountains beyond. Eight miles from the Dartmouth College campus and Connecticut River in Hanover. The Appalachian Trail crosses lodge property and continues over Moose Mountain.
Open: June 1–October 20 and December 26–March 15. Two-day (Fri-

day and Saturday) weekend reservations required.
Rates: Per person. $60 B&B, $38 age 14 or under. $80 ($48 age 14 and under) includes breakfast and dinner. (B&B usually not offered in winter, when $75–$95 per person includes three meals here "on the top of the world.") Ten percent discount for three or more nights. MC, Visa.
♥ ⚏ ⚏ ♦ ✈ ⚏

One of a kind. A hit for the first New England REI (sporting goods store) ski trip. Hailed by *Condé Nast Traveler*. Established by the Shumways 20 years ago.

Devotees—including cyclists—come for these easygoing folks who have time to listen. "We love to share this tranquil place, to introduce people to the beauty of our trails and the Beaver Pond with its wonderful animal and bird life."

Their rustic building, built as a ski lodge in 1938, has a massive stone fireplace, pine walls, and couches and four-poster beds made of logs. Peter, the vegetable gardener/song leader/former wholesale lumber businessman, took tap dancing lessons to celebrate his 60th birthday and recently skied in the Swiss Alps and northern Quebec. Kay, a skier too, is the good cook who wrote the *Moose Mountain Lodge Cookbook*. Before breakfast she spins her goats' mohair. The Shumways' guests come looking for peace and quiet and relaxation—and find it.

In residence: Tulla, a gray weimaraner, the perfect guide for walks. Four angora goats, Tom, Billy, Lenny, and Eddie. One pig named Sylvia Pigioli.
Foreign languages spoken: French; some Spanish and Swedish.
Bed and bath: Twelve rooms, all with views, share five full baths. Queen, double, double and twin, or two twins; one room has a double and two bunks.
Breakfast: 8–9. Huge. Could include homemade granola, fresh farm eggs, turkey sausage, black bean hash, hot cereals, or pancakes with Shumways' own maple syrup.
Plus: No TV. Player piano. Filled cookie jar. Huge porch with 100-mile panoramic view. Hiking, cross-country skiing, and snowshoesing trails start at the front door. Three fireplaces used almost year round, even in summer on cool evenings.

From Bernice's mailbag: "Guests tell us that your book answers all the questions they usually ask on the phone. Still, it's kind of amazing to have them arrive as old friends because they know so much about us."

The American Country Collection Host #178
Orford, NH

Location: Spectacular. On 125 pastoral acres (with hiking trails) overlooking Orford. Three miles across Connecticut River to Fairlee, Vermont; 15 north of Dartmouth College. Near antiquing; restaurants; golf course; pond swimming; canoeing, boating on Connecticut River.

Reservations: Year round through The American Country Collection, page 343.
Rates: Shared bath $51 single, $60 double. Private bath $56–$72 single, $65–$85 double. $10–$15 more September and October.
♠ ❖ ◆ ✄ ⅄

A B&B special. Pass through the village of Orford, known for a row of beautiful Federal style houses built in the 1800s. Turn onto a dirt road and savor the mile-long uphill drive under ancient maples. At the secluded end there's a dramatic view of open fields with cows and red deer, a backdrop of woods and mountains—and, on the hillside, a gambrel-roofed house, built in the 1930s, with terrace, rock-walled gardens, and huge sloping lawn. It is furnished with Oriental rugs, brass lamps, comfortable seating, and original art. A massive stone fireplace is in the large living room. Hand-hewn beams and wood stove are in one sitting room. TV and VCR are in a second-floor sitting room.

The hosts have lived in several foreign countries, including Chile, Venezuela, Nepal, Brazil, and England. Before moving here two years ago, they lived in Vermont and Washington, D.C.

Foreign language spoken: Spanish.
Bed and bath: Five rooms. First floor—suite with queen bed, working fireplace, private shower bath. One double-bedded room, private full bath. Second floor—huge very private room with queen bed, sitting area with sunrise view, private full bath. Two rooms, each with two twin beds, share full bath.
Breakfast: 6:30–9:30. Coffee in your room followed by juice, fruit, cereal, yogurt with maple syrup, muffins, toast, beverage, in dining room with large picture window or on terrace.
Plus: Down pillows and comforters. Individual room thermostats. Window fans. Large screened veranda with those views.

White Goose Inn
Route 10, P.O. Box 17, Orford, NH 03777

603/353-4812
fax 603/353/4812

Hosts: Manfred and Karin Wolf
Location: Fifteen miles north of Hanover, across the bridge from Fairlee, Vermont, on the outskirts of an unusual town that is essentially a street of elegant Bulfinch mansions.
Open: Year round. Two-day mini-

mum on some weekends.
Rates: Per room, double occupancy. $75 twin beds, shared bath. $85 double bed, private bath. $95 queen, private bath. Plus $15 for air conditioning. $20 third person. MC, Visa.
♥ ❖ ✄ ⅄

What a setting for antique cars! Some are here when the Wolfs host the cocktail party the night before the show on the Orford Common.

In 1987 *Country Living* featured the rooms of the 1833 brick house, which the Wolfs furnished with family heirlooms from Germany, auction and antiques shop finds, and Karin's pierced lampshades and other country crafts. The neighboring gambrel-roofed air-conditioned Cape house, Gosling House, was built in 1988—complete with a common room, a dining room, and a deck with a marvelous view of extensive grounds and flower gardens.

Guests usually ask for "the story," one that begins in 1983. Karin, who was working in retailing, and Manfred, a Firestone production supervisor, stayed in inns while looking for an old New England property as a second residence. When they walked into what had become an apartment house and saw the potential of the beamed rooms, the wide-planked floors, and the many fireplaces, they knew that they had found new careers as well as a new location.

In residence: Three sheep. Schnapps, a schnauzer. Fleury, a West Highland terrier.
Foreign language spoken: German.
Bed and bath: Fifteen rooms. Ten in old brick house. Five second-floor rooms in new Gosling House. Most with private shower bath, two with old-fashioned tub (only). Two rooms share one bath. Bed sizes include queen, double, and twins; some four-poster beds.
Breakfast: 8–9:30. Waffles, eggs, or French toast. Fresh fruit in season. Homemade muffins.

Stonecrest Farm Bed & Breakfast

119 Christian Street, Wilder, VT	802/296-2425
Mailing address: P.O. Box B1163	800/369-2626
Hanover, NH 03755-1163	fax 802/295-1135

Host: Gail Sanderson
Location: On two country acres with classic red barns. Near I-91 and I-89; 3.7 miles south of Dartmouth College, 13.5 east of Woodstock, Vermont.
Open: Year round. Two-night minimum on Dartmouth's parents' weekends and September 15 through October.
Rates: Private bath $110 double, $100 single. Shared bath $100 double, $90 single. MC, Visa.
♥ ♨ ☀ ♣ ♦ ✗

From New York: *"Antiques . . . fresh flowers . . . floor-to-ceiling bookcases . . . care for details . . . impeccably clean . . . warm and friendly . . . delicious breakfast . . . peaceful country setting . . . highly recommended!"*

Following years of world travel and academic administration, the Sandersons moved to this stately 1810 house. It has much stonework, a curved oak staircase, and a 34-foot-long beamed living room with French doors that lead to a terrace. Paintings, Oriental rugs, and window treatments add to the ambiance.

Since Gail redecorated and opened as a B&B, she has also become a practicing attorney. She hosts inn-to-inn canoeing groups, sings with choral groups, enjoys hiking, and often suggests visiting the Saint-Gaudens National Historic Site with its lovely gardens; the tour of the sculptor's studio includes the showing of a film produced by Gail's son, Paul.

In residence: Tessa, an affectionate collie. McDougel is a friendly Border terrier.
Foreign language spoken: "Very limited German and French."

(Please turn page.)

Bed and bath: Five rooms. First floor (honeymooners' favorite)—queen bed, private full bath. Second floor—one queen- and one king-bedded room, each with private cedar shower bath. Room with grandparents' mahogany canopied double bed and one with twin beds share a full bath.
Breakfast: 7:30–9 weekdays; 8–9:30 weekends. Could be freshly squeezed orange juice, fresh strawberries with rhubarb sauce, homemade lemon yogurt muffins, local honey spread. In fireplaced dining room with individual bouquet at each place, or served on flower-filled terrace.
Plus: Living room fireplace/wood stove. Baby grand piano. Bedroom ceiling or floor fans.

The Harrisville Squires' Inn Bed & Breakfast

Keene Road, Box 19   (voice or TDD) **603/827-3925**
Harrisville, NH 03450-0019

Hosts: Doug and Pat McCarthy
Location: Tranquil. On 50 acres. One-half mile from idyllic 19th-century textile village, a National Historic Landmark, with nine lakes and, in center, a mill over canal, a weaving center, and a supply shop. Five miles to Mount Monadnock, 12 to Crotched and Temple mountains.
Open: Year round.
Rates: Shared bath $45 single, $50 double. Private bath $55 single, $60 double. Third person $25. Tour planning, $30–50, includes maps and reservations. MC, Visa.
♥ ❖ ◆ ✈

The century-old caretaker's quarters, once part of a working farm, are now the home of Monadnock Bicycle Touring. Doug plans custom-designed day or overnight routes, both on- and off-road, through covered bridges and small villages. Guests also come to this B&B for getaways, reunions, and small weddings (Pat is a justice of the peace). "Some cross-country ski or hike on our trails. Others relax—for days!—by the fire or in our gardens."

With the help of their three adult sons, the McCarthys completed their third house restoration in 1985. Located in one of the most photographed towns in New England, it is decorated in country style with hats, wreaths and potpourri.

Before hosting, Pat was an interpreter for the deaf and a Hilton Hotel restaurant manager. Doug was a special needs teacher for the deaf in the Boston area. Both know American Sign Language.

In residence: Sable, Cocoa, and Inky—"three lovable cats."
Bed and bath: Five large rooms. First-floor wheelchair-accessible room has double four-poster bed, private full bath. Second floor—three queen-bedded rooms share full skylit bath; one room has two twins/king bed, sitting area, private full bath. Two rollaways.
Breakfast: 8–9. Juices. Fruit. Homemade breads, muffins. Entree changes daily; hosts' own maple syrup. Cereals. Hot fruit dessert. In dining room or country kitchen by fire.
Plus: Tea with cakes, breads, and cookies. Swimming in nearby pond. Gift shop in the largest barn left in town.

> Guests wrote: *"Comfortable, charmingly decorated, reasonably priced. Delicious breakfast. . . . A warm, friendly couple who go 'the second mile' to make your stay a more memorable one."*

Haverhill Inn   603/989-5961
Dartmouth College Highway, Haverhill, NH 03765-0095

Hosts: Stephen Campbell and Anne Baird
Location: On main route N.H. 10, with a wonderful view of Connecticut River valley and Vermont hills. Half a mile south of the double common. Half hour north of Dartmouth College.

Within an hour's drive of five major ski areas. Antiquing in town.
Open: June through February. Two-day minimum in foliage season.
Rates: $85 double occupancy, tax included.
♥ ❀ ✗ ⚭

There's a sense of place in this gracious 1810 Federal house, one of 40 buildings in a National Historic District. In the living room you'll see antique maps on the walls, area history books, and two volumes on the history of the house. There are wide board floors, painted-grain interior doors, solid panel interior (Indian) window shutters, and the warmth of antique furnishings. The recently rebuilt open kitchen—still with enormous old hearth and bake-oven—is a popular gathering place.

Steve and Anne are among the friendly and helpful innkeepers who participate in an acclaimed inn-to-inn canoeing program. Both professionals at Dartmouth College, they are members of community groups that sing mostly classical music "one evening a week, when we alternate as innkeepers."

In residence: Two dogs and one cat.
Foreign language spoken: Steve knows some Spanish; Anne, some German.
Bed and bath: Four large rooms with working fireplace, private bath. First-floor room has twin canopied beds. Upstairs, one double, one queen, and one with a pair of double beds. Two full baths, two with showers only.
Breakfast: 8–9. Always a full meal. Fresh bakery, locally smoked bacon, freshly brewed coffee.
Plus: Afternoon tea. Other meals prepared for inn-to-inn canoeing participants. Cross-country ski trails at the door.

The Inn on Golden Pond   603/968-7269
P.O. Box 680, Holderness, NH 03245-0680

Hosts: Bill and Bonnie Webb
Location: On 50 wooded acres with trails. Across the street from Squam Lake, setting for the film *On Golden Pond.* Twenty minutes to White Mountain National Forest, 15 to Tenney Mountain. Four miles from I-93. Near many maple sugaring shacks and great 45-minute (gradual) hike to mountaintop for "unsurpassed view of 50–60 islands."

Open: Year round. Two-night minimum on holiday weekends and on weekends between May 15 and October 30.
Rates: Double $95. Suite $120 main house; $135 with separate entrance, full kitchen. Third person $25. Some ski, honeymoon, anniversary, or birthday package rates. MC, Visa.
♥ ♦ ✗ ⚭

If you have seen the film, your expectations of a fairly undeveloped area will be fulfilled. And if you're looking for a family-run inn where you get to know the

(Please turn page.)

innkeepers and other guests (and still there's a respect for privacy), this is the place—immaculate and comfortable (not lavish) in a location that appeals to outdoor-oriented and international travelers, including many honeymooners.

Bill and Bonnie changed careers in 1984, when they left their California jobs in guidebook publishing and data processing. Since Becky and her brother Ricky arrived from Korea seven years ago, they have taken to the worlds of innkeeping, skiing, and cycling. The country home, built in 1879, is surrounded by stone walls, antique split rail fences, flowers, bushes, and shade trees.

In residence: Ricky, age 12; and Becky, 11.
Bed and bath: Nine rooms (two are suites). On second and third floors. All private baths (some full, some tub or shower only). King, queen, or double beds; two rooms with a queen and a twin bed.
Breakfast: 8:30–9:30. Cooked by Bonnie. Entree such as apple pancakes or eggs and bacon. Homemade bread and muffins. Fresh fruit. At individual tables. Usually a very social time. Innkeeper/waiter Bill joins guests for coffee.
Plus: Turndown service; homemade mint on the pillow. Fireplaced living room. Hair dryers. Picnic tables. Lawn games. A 60-foot screened porch. Ice and glasses. Swimming (small fee) at town beach just around the corner.

Windyledge Bed & Breakfast   603/746-4054
1264 Hatfield Road, Hopkinton, NH 03329   fax 603/746-4052

Hosts: Dick and Susan Vogt
Location: Fifteen minutes west of Concord. On an old country road. Less than two miles from Routes 202 and 9. Four miles from I-89, 10 from I-93. Five minutes to New England College, 10 to Saint Paul's School. Within 7 miles of three award-winning restaurants.

Open: Year round.
Rates: Double $55 shared bath, $75 private. Single $10 less. Rollaway $15. No charge for crib. Monday–Thursday, 10 percent less for senior citizens, business travelers, and families. Discover, MC, Visa.
♥ ♦ ♣ ✿ ♦ ✈ ⌘

From Canada, New York, Michigan, California, Vermont, Maryland: *"We use it as our country retreat . . . rode my first horse, hired from a local stable . . . Messrs. Hyatt and Hilton take note: Dick and Susan have a better mousetrap! . . . Even the drive to find it is fun. . . . Spotless. . . . Minor weight gain from eating too well. . . . As a frequent business traveler, I consider Windyledge a rare find. . . . Sent out their rescue unit when we stalled at steep incline on bicycle trip. . . . Our eight-year-old was thrilled to gather fresh eggs for breakfast. . . . Perfect example of what a B&B should be."*

Perfect by design. With handmade quilts, Oriental rugs, a beamed sitting room adjoining the open kitchen, a swimming pool, and lots of amenities. All planned by the Vogts, a retired Digital Equipment Corporation manager and a dental receptionist, about the time their youngest was getting ready to leave for college. That's when they rearranged/rebuilt their 1970s all-electric colonial house (which is heated primarily with two wood stoves)—even though a local official had asked, "Who in the world would want to go out to Hatfield Road, anyway?" Since 1990 lots of delighted guests have come to Hopkinton!

In residence: On the property: Margot, 25-year-old horse; two barn cats; a dozen chickens.

Bed and bath: Three second-floor rooms, all with desks and phone jacks. One with queen pencil-post bed, adjoining private shower bath. Two rooms—one with handmade Victorian double bed, one with twins/king bed with handmade pine headboard—share a double-sinked hall tub-and-shower bath. Extra twin, rollaway, and crib available.
Breakfast: Flexible schedule. Dick's repertoire includes apricot glazed French toast; asparagus and eggs goldenrod; German apple pancake; ginger pancakes with lemon sauce. Muffins and sweet breads. On deck, in sun room, or in dining room at table set with linen, silverware, china, antique pressed glass, and fresh flowers.
Plus: In-ground pool. Ceiling fans. Individual thermostats. Satellite dish. Refreshments. Guest refrigerator. Flannel sheets. Turndown service. Fresh flowers. Candy. Pool towels. Beamed sitting room. Video film and book library. Piano. Extensive gardens. Suggested cycling routes. When you leave, a gift of muffins and jar of homemade jam.

Ellis River House

603/383-9339
P.O. Box 656, Route 16   (U.S./Canada) **800/233-8309**
Jackson, NH 03846-0656   fax **603/383-4142**

Hosts: Barry and Barbara Lubao
Location: Set back from the road, overlooking the river. Ten minutes to Attitash, Wildcat, Black Mountain, Tuckerman's Ravine. On Ellis River Trail to Jackson Cross-Country Ski Foundation.
Open: Year round. Two-day minimum on December–March and holiday weekends.
Rates: Vary according to season and

whether it's midweek or weekend. Highest in September and October. Per person, double occupancy—shared bath $25–$60, private bath $38–112. Age 12 and under free in parents' room. Suite (sleeps six) $95–$175 for two; cottage (sleeps four) $75–$150 for two. $20 each additional person. Amex, Discover, MC, Visa.
♥ ♯ ⁂ ◆ ⠵

The farm and the farmhouse continue to grow. Barry was chief engineer for the Sheraton Hotels when the family came here nine years ago. Now he tends award-winning organic gardens and a small vineyard. There are chickens (gather your own breakfast eggs), geese, ducks, rabbits, a pig, and a pony. There's an atrium with Jacuzzi spa (where hot mulled cider is enjoyed in winter) and a sun deck that also has river and mountain views. The cottage down by the river is ideal for honeymooners and families—and even pets too. The biggie was built in 1993: a 14-room addition with "everything"—sound-proofing, central air conditioning, a sprinkler system, rooms with amenities galore, a heated outdoor swimming pool. Staff, too, has been added.

Still, decor is farmhouse style, with many crafts made by Barbara. Enthusiasm is Olympic style—for the area, for river swimming and fishing (trout), for skiing, and for a wide variety of guests.

In residence: Barry (Jay), age 19, and Jennifer, 13.
Foreign language spoken: Polish.
Bed and bath: Eighteen rooms. Farmhouse—rooms on second and third floors. One private bath; three rooms share two baths, each with claw-foot tub and shower. Queen, queen and twin, double, or double and twin beds.

(Please turn page.)

Suite has queen bed, four twins, private balcony, shower bath. Cottage has spiral staircase, queen bed plus queen sofa bed, full bath. New rooms on three floors have cable TV, private full baths; some with two-person Jacuzzi, gas or wood-burning fireplace, riverside balcony or patio. One room handicapped accessible. One honeymoon suite; others for families.

Breakfast: 7:30–9:30. Juices, fruit, homemade muffins; Barry's cinnamon, oatmeal raisin, and beer breads. Hot and cold cereals. Farm-fresh eggs, sausage, bacon; French toast or pancakes.

Plus: Popcorn and hot toddies by the fire. VCR. Wraparound screened porch. Piano. Playground. Horseshoes. Croquet. Volleyball. Terry robes. Five-course dinner ($24.50) by reservation only.

Paisley and Parsley   603/383-0859
Box 572, Jackson, NH 03846-0572

Hosts: Beatrice and Charles Stone
Location: High on a country road, Route 16B, with an "exclusive view" of Mount Washington. Surrounded by birch trees and herb and perennial gardens. Within walking distance of village. Near five major ski areas.
Open: Year round except May–late June. Two-day minimum on July 4, Labor Day, and Thanksgiving week-ends, and September 16–October 15.
Rates: Late September–mid-October, $85 doubles, $95 queen, $115 king. Mid-October–December 22, $55–$75. June 15–September 15 and January 2–February 28, $20 less. March 1–May 5, $30 less. Singles $15 less. $15 additional guest. $10 children up to age 14. MC, Visa.
♥ ⚏ ⚐ ⚒ ♦ ✕ ⚛

This new contemporary Cape house, filled with early colonial antiques, textiles, folk art, and books, is the home of Bea, who was a school librarian in New Jersey; Chuck, an environmental planner in New York; and Bridget, their full-sized doll. They vacationed here, loved the area, "retired," built the house (after searching for a "right" old house), and began hosting corporate transferees. As a next step, B&B was a natural. One guest took photographs and measurements and had a similar house built—complete with skylights. Many, even those who come for outdoor activities, "just relax." They remember the food, the pampering, the privacy, the views, the grape arbor with mountain backdrop, the hammock—and the hosts.

Foreign language spoken: A little French.
Bed and bath: Three rooms, all private baths. Handicapped-accessible first-floor room has twins/king bed, two-person whirlpool, ceiling fan. On second floor—one room with queen canopied bed; one with two double beds, sitting area with TV and VCR. Rollaway available.
Breakfast: 7:30–9. Special. Crepes, omelet with feta cheese and herbs, shellfish quiche, poached pears. Served on English bone china in dining room by full-length windows or on deck. Special diets accommodated.
Plus: Afternoon tea or mulled cider. Beach towels. Terry robes. Croquet. Fruit basket. Flowers. Terrace. Shortbread recipe.

> From New Hampshire: *"An exceptional job of blending old New England charm with the luxury of contemporary style and comfort. . . . A breakfast that held us through a good long hike."*

Benjamin Prescott Inn

603/532-6637

Route 124 East, Jaffrey, NH 03452-1810   fax 603/532-6637

Hosts: Jan and Barry Miller
Location: Overlooking a working dairy farm on Route 124, 2.3 miles east of town center. Near Cathedral of the Pines, Mount Monadnock, Sharon Art Center.
Open: Year round. Two-night mini-

mum on summer and fall weekends.
Rates: $60–$80 single. $60–$130 double. $15 cot or extra person. Ten percent senior citizen discount. Weekly/monthly available. Amex, MC, Visa.
♥ ❖ ◆ ✄

TLC in the form of nightly homemade chocolate truffles in a basket. Fresh berries in the fruit breads. And, if you'd like, advice (often sought) about innkeeping; but most guests come for a getaway, mountain views, antiquing, hiking or local colleges.

After Barry, an avocational wood-carver, had spent 26 years in the corporate hotel world, the Millers moved in 1988 from Michigan to this 1853 Greek Revival house, once owned by Vannevar Bush, inventor of the computer. They created a warm, inviting ambiance with country antiques and decorated some rooms with Jan's stenciling and needlepoint. Each spring they tap the 300-year-old maple trees. Each day, guests are grateful that the Millers are doing what they do.

Bed and bath: Nine rooms; all private baths. First floor—queen, double, or twin beds. Second floor—king, queen, double. Rollaway available. Third-floor suite has room with canopied king four-poster bed, two double beds in alcoves, queen bed in other room, cathedral ceiling, skylight, private balcony with fantastic countryside views, wet bar.
Breakfast: 8–9:30. Juices. Fruit breads. Jan's creations include cinnamon sourdough French toast, Dutch apple pancakes, and egg croquettes.
Plus: Ceiling fans. Portable telephone available. Down comforters. Local restaurant menus. Transportation to and from Jaffrey airport. Executive conference room available.

The Galway House

603/532-8083

247 Old Peterborough Road, Jaffrey, NH 03452

Hosts: Joe and Marie Manning
Location: On a quiet woodland road 10 minutes from the villages of Jaffrey and Peterborough. In foliage and ski country. Near Cathedral of the Pines, Mount Monadnock, beaches.

Open: September–June. Two-night minimum, September and October.
Rates: $40 single, $50 double. $10 per extra person.
⚑ ◀ ❖ ✄

The Mannings have hosted guests from as close as the next town (while their house was being readied) and as far away as mainland China. Their oversized Cape house was built in 1974 on a now-paved 1760s road. Joe is semiretired. He and Marie think that the people-to-people concept of B&B makes it a great way to travel.

Bed and bath: Two large second-floor rooms share full bath. One has a double bed and two twin beds, the other a double and a single bed. Cot. Two cribs.

(Please turn page.)

Breakfast: 7–9. A full country breakfast including juice, hot and cold cereal, pancakes or eggs, homemade muffins, and hot beverages.
Plus: Afternoon tea. Will meet guests at Logan Airport (Boston) or the Fitzwilliam bus for an extra fee. Babysitting available. TV. Sun deck.

Guests wrote: *"The Mannings have a rare sixth sense that makes one feel that she 'belongs'. . . . House is lovely—an unspoiled rural delight with nearby wooded paths for an early morning wander. . . . At night, only noise comes from a wind in the trees. . . . Room was huge and pleasant. . . . Breakfast was a treat in the bay-windowed dining room where we watched the birds. . . . After juggling juice, coffee, eggs, and toast, Mr. Manning, a state senator, is happy to sit down and tell you anything you want to know about local weather, news, events. . . . On maps they showed us back roads for bicycling and trails for hiking that were less crowded during peak fall season. We plan on returning this winter to cross-country ski on the trails leaving from their backyard."*

Lilac Hill Acres Bed & Breakfast   603/532-7278

5 Ingalls Road, Jaffrey, NH 03452

Hosts: Frank and Ellen McNeill
Location: Two miles from historic Jaffrey center. Overlooking Gilmore Pond. Surrounded by Monadnock, Pack Monadnock, and Temple mountains.
Open: Year round except Easter,

Thanksgiving, Christmas, New Year's. Reservations required. Two-night minimum, October weekends.
Rates: Shared bath—$50 single, $60 double. Private—$60 single, $70 double. $25 extra person in room.
♥ 🏠 ♣ ✈ ⚕

"When we looked up the hill and saw this marvelous old 1740 white farmhouse, we knew we had found a new family homestead and lifestyle. There's always family around."

At Christmastime all the grandchildren and their parents fill the house. (But the thousands of decorations—inside and out—are up at least through the month of January.) Frank, now retired, has an enormous (and ever-expanding) garden with vegetables and many berries that keep Ellen busy in the wonderful open country kitchen. All the McNeills visit with guests in the comfortably furnished common rooms, which are filled with antiques, Oriental rugs, and a glowing fire. There's an apple orchard, a stocked spring-fed pond that you can swim in, and open hay fields. As the McNeills notice, "Guests feel very relaxed here." (We did, after a day of cross-country skiing.) "They sit on the porch. They read." And when in Boston, some travelers from other parts of the country drive up just to visit and catch up.

In residence: Bengie, a dog, and four or five cats. Some years, many farm animals.
Bed and bath: Five rooms. Second floor—private shower bath "and a superior view" for room with king bed. Two baths (one with tub and shower, one shower only) shared by three rooms that have either a king or two twin beds. Third floor—"superior view" double-bedded room, private shower bath.
Breakfast: 8:30–9:30. Full country. The record length is four hours!
Plus: Fireplaced living room. Tea or mulled cider. Bedroom ceiling fans.

The Beal House Inn   603/444-2661
247 West Main Street, Littleton, NH 03561

Hosts: Catherine and Jean-Marie Fisher-Motheu
Location: Ten-minute walk to village shops, restaurants, movie theater; 15 minutes north of Franconia Notch; 15 south of Cannon Mountain; 25 minutes east of Bretton Woods and Mount Washington; 35 to Loon Mountain; 10 from Bethle-

hem. One mile from Route 93.
Open: Year round except November.
Rates: December–June $55 or $60 weekdays, $55 or $65 weekends. July, August $55 or $70. September, October $55 or $80. Additional person $15. MC, Visa.
♥ ♨ ♣ ♦ ✗ ✁

Interesting combination: Catherine has a degree in philosophy, experience in the printing business, and an interest in storytelling and art. Jean-Marie, a former professional soccer player in Belgium, is a wine connoisseur (more than 200 wines are offered at dinner) who has been associated with restaurants and hotels in 30 countries. When they decided in 1991 to work together "in a place of our own," they bought this 1833 Federal farmhouse; built in 1833, the place had seen constant changes since 1938 as an inn, B&B, and/or antiques shop. Recent guests have included the White House press corps, a poet who presented a reading, and guitarists who have given impromptu concerts. Decor is a blend of Victoriana and colonial, sometimes formal, sometimes casual, with old hats here, 1950s battery-operated toys there, and, everywhere, works—all for sale—done by local artists. The restaurant that seats 20 in the converted garage became so popular that a second dining room was built for functions in 1993.

Foreign language spoken: French.
Bed and bath: Thirteen rooms on first and second floors; 11 with private baths. King/twin, queen, or double beds (some canopied and some four-posters) and rollaway available. Some rooms have additional twin bed and some have connecting bath arrangement for families.
Breakfast: 7:30–9:30. Belgian waffles with various toppings. Muffins, breads, toast, cereal, fresh fruit, juices. Candelit. With music. Served by Catherine and Jean-Marie in fireplaced breakfast room.
Plus: Decks. Enclosed porch. Game room. No TV. Bedroom table fans. Beverages. Down comforters. Mints on pillows. Dinner entrees $12–$17, Wednesday–Sunday 6–9 p.m.

Loch Lyme Lodge   603/795-2141
RFD 278, Route 10, Lyme, NH 03768   800/423-2141

Hosts: Paul and Judy Barker
Location: On a spring-fed lake surrounded by hills. On Route 10, one mile north of the village. Eleven miles from Dartmouth College, four miles from Dartmouth Skiway.
Open: Year round. Closed Thanks-

giving and Christmas days. Three-night minimum on Columbus Day weekend.
Rates: $36 single, $48 double. $7 age 7 and under, $14 ages 8–15. One-time charge of $5 for crib.
♨ ♣ ✗

"Immediately after Labor Day we close the cabins (some are booked into the year 2010!) and move from the barn (the location of our summer apartment)

(Please turn page.)

into the main Lodge. We move all the tables and chairs out of the dining rooms (which become our living room and piano room) and reopen as a bed and breakfast."

By 1923 the 1784 farmhouse had become part of a boys' camp and a lodging place for campers' parents and tourists too. Eventually Judy's parents ran it as a resort. When Judy and Paul left their teaching careers in 1977, they took over and added B&B in their home.

In residence: Jon Paul, age 12. Joshua, age 6. Two cats, Beefer and Princess.
Foreign languages spoken: Paul speaks Spanish, Judy a little French.
Bed and bath: Three second-floor rooms—with king, double, or two twin beds—share two full baths, one upstairs, one downstairs. Cot and crib available.
Breakfast: Usually 8–9; flexible. Full country breakfast served family style on the sun porch. Busy bird feeder in view.
Plus: Fireplaced living room. Beverages. Woodlands, fields, and lake shore on 125 acres. Informal cross-country lessons and tours. No TV. Babysitting possible.

From Massachusetts: *"On a warm early spring weekend, we loved all that space in the great outdoors; a canoe; the welcoming family environment; a beautifully served, substantial breakfast; and a great suggestion—the Dartmouth Pow Wow. Marvelous."* From New Jersey: *"Accommodations with a relaxed, old-fashioned flair.... Enjoyed sledding—and, on the frozen lake, cross-country skiing."* From Connecticut: *"Entered the ambiance of a Grandma Moses farmhouse after a brisk fall walk."*

Olde Orchard Inn

RR Box 256, Moultonborough, NH 13254

603/476-5004
800/598-5845

Host: Mary Senner
Location: Along a country road, on 12 acres with meadows, orchards (100 fruit trees and more being planted), pond, and brook (for fishing). One mile from Route 25 and from 200-year-old country store and the town's one blinking light. Five-minute walk through orchard across the street to "a very good restaurant"; 15 to Audubon Society's just-opened 200-acre Loon Center with nature trails, picnicking, lake frontage, gift shop; 20-minute walk to quiet Lake Winnipesaukee beach. Ten-minute drive to country's largest quilt supply shop.

Open: Year round.
Rates: $70 or $80 per room. $130 suite. Off-season, $10 less. $15 third person. $5 crib.
♥ ❖ ✂

After looking "all over," the Senners bought this restored early 19th-century Cape in 1992. They painted inside and out, planted an English garden, and furnished in colonial and "foreign service eclectic we gathered over a 25-year period while living in Afghanistan, India, Nepal, Sudan, and Finland." Mary, a quilter and former first-grade teacher, did all the stenciling. The wooden part of this house was built in 1790. In 1812 an addition was built with bricks fired from clay on the property.

Foreign language spoken: Jim speaks Farsi and some Arabic and Finnish.
In residence: Husband Jim (on weekends now; full time when he retires from the foreign service). Rosie, Jim's mother, an inspiration for Mary's genealogical work. Laura, age 16. Katy and Alison during college vacations.

Bed and bath: Five rooms in private wing with private entrance. (Plus a double-bedded room with hall bath in older section.) Three first-floor double-bedded rooms, one with fireplace; all with en-suite full tile baths. Second-floor suite has two rooms (double bed and two twin beds), each with half bath, connected by hall with shower room. Cot and crib available.
Breakfast: 7:30–9:30. Juice, fruit, sticky buns or other baked goods. Pancakes, omelets, or eggs.
Plus: Guest sitting room with fireplace. TV. The fragrance and sight of spring orchard blossoms.

> From Texas: *"A charming, charming inn. Wonderful hospitality. Delicious breakfast. We hated to leave."*

The Inn at New Ipswich   603/878-3711

P.O. Box 208, Porter Hill Road, New Ipswich, NH 03071-0208

Hosts: Ginny and Steve Bankuti
Location: Up the hill from the village center, on a peaceful road. Abutting an old cemetery. Near antiquing; 15 minutes to Mount Monadnock trails.
Open: Year round. Advance reservations preferred. Two-night mini-mum during foliage season and on holiday weekends.
Rates: $45 single, $65 double. $10 cot for child. $95 suite. $5 use of guest room fireplaces. MC, Visa.
♥ ❖ ✗ ⅍

"B&B was our justification for buying this splendid 1790 farmhouse with its fireplaces and wide plank floors. Although we added baths and redecorated, we have kept the 'Grandma's house' feeling. [The Bankutis have seven grandchildren.] Steve, who grew up on a farm in Hungary, continues to enlarge the garden—and to send guests home with zucchini. Innkeeping is so different from our days of rushing off to the office and the garage and towing business. The world comes to us—even bridal parties, and for one Christmas, a South African family who joined us for a sleigh ride."

In residence: "Star is our gentle, affectionate yellow Labrador."
Foreign language spoken: Steve speaks Hungarian.
Bed and bath: Five rooms, all private baths. First-floor room with two twin canopied beds, working fireplace, shower bath. Three second-floor queen-bedded rooms (one with working fireplace), shower baths (one has tub and shower). Family suite has a queen-bedded room (space for cot, too) with adjoining double-bedded room, shower bath.
Breakfast: 8:30–9. (Continental thereafter.) Fresh fruit, juices, oven-puffed pancakes, bacon or sausages, fresh eggs, home-baked muffins and breads. In season, homegrown berries and rhubarb. Special diets accommodated.
Plus: Welcoming refreshments. TV in living room. Quiet second-floor sitting room. Books. Games. Screened porch. Front porch rockers. Lawn chairs. Horseshoes.

> From Rhode Island: *"Artistic and delicious breakfasts. . . . Great location for running, cross-country skiing, hiking."* From New Jersey: *"Warm, hospitable, delightful people. . . . Felt spoiled."* From Maryland: *"Hosts were walking resources . . . Ginny's cookies should be marketed."* From California: *"Spotlessly clean."* From Texas: *"Homey, elegant, charming."*

The Buttonwood Inn

P.O. Box 1817, Mount Surprise Road
North Conway, NH 03860-1817

(in N.H.) **603/356-2625**
(U.S./Canada) **800/258-2625**
fax **603/356-3140**

Hosts: Hugh and Ann Begley
Location: Secluded. At top of hill, on five acres of woods and spacious lawns. Two miles from Route 16 and village; one mile to downhill skiing.
Open: Year round. Two-night minimum preferred on winter and holiday weekends.
Rates: Per person, double occupancy. April 1–June 23 and October 25–December 23, $25 shared bath,

$35 private bath. $10 more June 24–September 15; $20 more, September 16–October 21. $25–$35 midweek January–March. $30–$40 Christmas week and March weekends. $85–$100 January and February weekends includes two nights and breakfasts, Saturday dinner. Singles $15 extra. Third person $18. Ski and family packages. Amex, MC, Visa.
♥ ⚕ ❖ ♦ ✄

From Massachusetts: "Cozy . . . relaxing . . . spotless . . . informal. The entire atmosphere is simply one of warmth and hospitality."

That atmosphere was captured for a New England feature on British television. It's all part of the fun for the Begleys, sports-oriented hosts who hike, ski, and fish.

After working with innkeepers while booking tours for a New Jersey bus company, Ann, together with Hugh, a school equipment salesman, opened this B&B in 1984. To this day they tell of their introduction to country plumbing—a waterfall in the newly done living room—and calm plumbers—"If that don't beat all." The 20-room added-on-to 1820s Cape farmhouse has wide board floors, country antiques, print wallpapers. There's a 40-foot swimming pool. "The real hit is Penny, who will walk, hike, or cross-country ski with any guest who will take her—and just about everyone does."

In residence: Penny is a retriever and Lab mix dog. Icis, a cat. Six grown children and six grandchildren "are always coming and going."
Bed and bath: Nine second-floor rooms, some dormered, three with private (mostly shower) baths. Three shared baths (two shower, one full). Two queen-bedded rooms have sinks. Others have a double, two twins, or a double and a twin bed. Cot available.
Breakfast: Usually 8–9:30. Full country breakfast—a popular low-cholesterol menu or thick French toast stuffed with preserves and fruit. At tables set with linen, fresh flowers. Sometimes granddaughters Marisa, age 11, and Jessica, 5, assist.
Plus: Game room with open fireplace. Horseshoes, badminton, croquet. Dryer. Guest refrigerator. Two TV rooms. Barbecues for summer groups. Hiking and 60 km of groomed cross-country trails from the door.

The place to stay has become the reason to go.

Nereledge Inn Bed & Breakfast   603/356-2831

River Road, P.O. Box 547, North Conway, NH 03860-0547

Hosts: Valerie and Dave Halpin
Location: Just off Route 16, on the road to Echo Lake State Park and Cathedral Ledge; 100 yards from Saco River. Within walking distance of village.
Open: Year round. Two-night minimum on weekends.

Rates: Per couple. Shared bath $59 twins or double bed; $64 queen. Private bath $69; $75 larger room. $10 more on holidays. Singles $45 when available (seldom on weekends). Extra adult $15. Children $1 each year of age up to 12. Amex, MC, Visa.
♥ ♨ ♯ ✗ ✗

From Canada, California, Pennsylvania, Connecticut, Massachusetts, Indiana, New Hampshire, Texas: "Not the fanciest but by far the most hospitable B&B we ever stayed in. A casual open atmosphere that still allows privacy. . . . Outstanding, imaginative, diverse breakfasts. . . . Family friendly. . . . Firm beds. . . . Impeccably clean. . . . Peaceful. . . . Dry sense of humor. . . . Advice about hiking trails."

Continually, from all over the country, letters extol every aspect of this old-fashioned inn built in 1787. In 1981 Valerie, a beginning skier and classical music lover, established the B&B style she knows from her native England. (In England she was a teacher; in Florida, a commodities broker.) Here she met Dave, expert skier, mountain bike rider (sometimes with guests), runner (with Loki), professional landscaper, and former Hawaii resort manager (and now deputy fire chief). And the letters go on: "My daughter wanted to stay forever. . . . Walls lined with photos of climbers . . . extras like second pillows and alarm clocks. . . . Accommodated our low-fat diet. . . . However, their cribbage board and cards favor female players over male ones."

In residence: Loki and Pinga, "large photogenic dogs."
Bed and bath: Nine rooms (some with individual thermostats) on second and third floors. Private shower baths for queen-bedded room and one with two double beds. Private full bath in second-floor wing with queen bed, sitting room. On each floor, three rooms—with queen, double, or twins/king option—share a full hall bath and one half bath. Plus full bath on ground floor. Crib and rollaway available.
Breakfast: 7:30–9:30. Juices. Eggs, French toast, pancakes, omelet (a meal in itself). Home fries. Homemade muffin or toast. Apple crumble and vanilla ice cream. In room with wood stove, sunny exposure.
Plus: Welcoming beverage. Two sitting rooms. Window fans. Sprinkler system. Bicycle shed. Ski-waxing area. Guest refrigerator. Gardens. Game room includes darts, backgammon, piano. Babysitting arranged. Option of packed lunch. By reservation, dinners for groups of 12 or more.

As Valerie says, "B&B is like having a large family and getting them off to school in the morning."

The Victorian Harvest Inn   603/356-3548
Bed & Breakfast   800/642-0749

28 Locust Lane, Box 1763, North Conway, NH 03860-1763

Hosts: Linda and Robert Dahlberg
Location: Quiet side street, off Route 16/302. Short walk to shops, eateries, park, and scenic railway. Three miles to Mount Cranmore, 10 to Attitash, 20 to Jackson.
Open: Year round. Two-day mini-
mum on foliage and winter weekends.
Rates: $55 single. $65–$90 double; $55–$70 double midweek or off-season. $20 extra person. Amex, Discover, MC, Visa.

♥ ♨ ✿ ♦ ✈ ✀

Welcome home. Enter through the kitchen, renovated by the Dahlbergs' son after Linda changed careers (a nurse manager) and Bob fulfilled the dream from all those inn stays that the family had experienced. (Midweek he is still sales manager for a building supply company.) In addition to completely redoing this 1850s house, they added an in-ground swimming pool with Victorian fence. Inside there are (still changing) collections of eclectic "family treasures" gathered from 26 years of marriage. If you'd like, Bob will play some cylinders on the 1905 graphophone.

In residence: Tuckerman, a collie/husky mix, is one of the reasons guests return.
Bed and bath: Six rooms, each named by guests. First-floor room has a queen and a twin bed, private full bath, 1930s weathered cast aluminum carousel horse in bay window. Second floor rooms have slanted ceilings: king bed with private shower bath; two queen-bedded rooms (one with a sink) share connecting tub bath (robes provided). Through fireplaced living room and up narrow back stairs to two more rooms (ceiling fan in each): large room has king bed, twin bed, single futon, shower bath, mountain views; smallest (and most popular) "Nook and Cranny Room" has double bed, balcony, tub bath, mountain views. Rollaway available.
Breakfast: 7:30–9. Fruit plate. Apple cake or cranberry shortbread. Belgian waffles, cinnamon French toast, or omelets.
Plus: Room air conditioning. Fireplaced living room. Spinet piano in library. TV. Hot chocolate or cider at 5 p.m. Mints. Two guest refrigerators. Nordic Track. Use of canoe. Impromptu barbecues.

> From Massachusetts, Rhode Island, Connecticut, New Hampshire: *"Spotless, cozy, comfortable. . . . Gigantic blueberry waffles. . . . Warm welcome. . . . Old-time charm with air conditioning and a pool. . . . Tuckerman is a favorite playmate for our nine-year-old daughter."*

Can't find a listing for the community you are going to? Check with a reservation service described at the beginning of this chapter. Through the service you may be placed (matched) with a welcoming B&B that is near your destination.

Wyatt House Country Inn

603/356-7977
P.O. Box 777, Route 16   (U.S./Canada) 800/527-7978
North Conway, NH 03860

Hosts: Bill and Arlene Strickland
Location: On an acre along Route 16, with backdrop of woods (path to river for fishing or swimming) and mountains. Short walk to village, restaurants, Saco River, outlet shopping. Minutes to four major ski areas.
Open: Year round.
Rates: $55 single. $65 double bed.

$75–$95 queen bed. $85–$95 suite with private deck. $15 additional person. $15 less per room April and May. Ten percent AAA discount except April and May. Valentine's packages with flowers and chocolates. Discover, MC, Visa.
♥ ♣ ♦ ✈ ✂

Lace. Fringe. Ruffles. Antique photographs. Victoriana everywhere. A breakfast that is intentionally memorable. Almost-famous chocolate chip cookies at Victorian teatime. Bedtime sherry. Always, plenty of pampering.

All offered in this 1870s home, which became a B&B in 1985. Since the Stricklands, parents of grown children, purchased it in 1992, they have found "pure joy" in helping guests to unwind. It's just the lifestyle they hoped for when they decided to stop the 23-year two-hour (each way) commute to their Manhattan jobs as American Express Company director and paralegal. In New York Arlene also served as president of the Babylon Historical and Preservation Society.

In residence: Spats, a popular, declawed cat, greets guests.
Bed and bath: Six large rooms; four with private baths and air conditioning. First floor—queen-bedded room, private shower bath, private exterior entrance and porch. Second floor—breakfast in bed in large suite, queen canopied four-poster bed, private shower bath, private deck. Another two-room suite has queen bed, queen sofa bed in adjoining room, private shower bath. Two double-bedded rooms share hall full bath. Third-floor suite has double bed, sitting area, cable TV, private full bath.
Breakfast: Seatings for eight at 8 and 9:30. (Coffee and muffins available at 6.) Spinach and cheese quiche, shirred eggs with sausage, or souffle. Homemade granola, muffins, bread, and jams. Juice. Fresh fruit. Freshly brewed coffee. Served on English Wedgwood by candlelight with chamber music. In dining room or on porch.
Plus: Fireplaced living room. Down comforters. Flannel sheets. Turndown service. Beach towels. Guest refrigerator. Games, books, magazines. Fresh fruit. Candy. Box lunches. Restaurant menus. Porch rockers. Hammock. Picnic tables. Adirondack chairs. Champagne for honeymooners.

From Canada: *"A little bit of heaven."* From New York: *"Five-star breakfast."*

---

*B*reakfast is where the magic happens.

The Forest, A Country Inn

603/356-9772
800/448-3534

P.O. Box 1736, Route 16A at the Intervale
North Conway, NH 03860

Hosts: Ken and Rae Wyman
Location: On 25 wooded acres on a quiet country road. With 65 km of groomed cross-country trails at the door. Between (minutes from) Jackson and North Conway village, near Mount Washington.
Open: Year round.
Rates: May and June $50–$80 in inn, $80–$90 cottage. July–October $60–$85 inn, $85–$95 cottage; peak foliage $82–$98 inn, $98–$125 cottage. November–mid-December $60–$80 inn, $80–$110 cottage. Mid-December–April $70–$90 inn, $90–$120 cottage. Singles $10 less. Midweek and ski weekend packages. Thanksgiving weekend includes three nights and holiday dinner: $200–$276 inn, $276–$336 cottage. Amex, MC, Visa.

♥ ⅰ ♣ ✻ ✔ ✄

Twice, *Bon Appétit* has featured the Wymans' afternoon tea. Their well-kept century-old inn is also known as a place for relaxation, for its inn-to-inn cycling and cross-country ski programs, and for its innkeepers, who are active mountain climbers (48 peaks over 4,000 feet), skiers, and cyclists.

In 1986 Ken was a vice president of a Boston area life insurance company, and Rae managed a dentists' office. They created a casual atmosphere in the mansard-roofed inn with Victorian and colonial antiques and a quilt collection. They installed a solar-heated outdoor swimming pool, established a picnic area with lawn chairs and gas grills, and blazed a nature/cross-country ski trail through the forest.

Bed and bath: Eleven rooms (two are suites that accommodate three or four) plus stone cottage; all private baths. On second and third floors—queen, double, or twin beds. Cottage—queen-bedded rooms with private entrance and bath; one has fireplace, screened porch. Rollaway available.
Breakfast: 8–9. Eggs, rum raisin or amaretto French toast, spiced Belgian waffles, apple or blueberry pancakes, homemade yeast and sweet breads, muffins and doughnuts, fruits.
Plus: Ceiling fans. Afternoon tea during foliage season. Candy. Fruit. Guest refrigerator. Fireplaced common room. Glassed/screened porch with wood stove. Hot beverages with sweet bread or homemade doughnuts. Option of candlelit Saturday dinner in ski season. Access to three clay tennis courts.

From New Jersey: *"Warm welcome. . . . Scrumptious breakfast . . . quaint and comfortable."* From Massachusetts: *"Romantic cottage for first wedding anniversary."*

---

*H*eard all over New England: "Most guests are surprised at all our area has to offer."

Wildflowers Guest House   603/356-2224
Route 16, P.O. Box 802, Intervale, NH 03845-0802

Hosts: Eileen Davies and Dean Franke
Location: On the main road, fronted by award-winning gardens with a mountain range backdrop. Minutes to shops, outlets, and restaurants. One and a half miles north of North Conway village and Saco River.

Open: May–October.
Rates: May 1–July 15, $60 private bath, $50–$55 shared. July 16–September 25 and October 16–31, $80 private, $60–$68 shared. September 26–October 15, $92 private, $72–$80 shared. Single rate (when available) $40. Extra person $15. MC, Visa.
♥ ⛵ ✿ ✗

This traffic stopper fulfilled the name Eileen and Dean gave to it when, in 1978, they left the corporate world and bought their "jewel in the rough." As Eileen says, "'Wildflowers' seemed to have the right aura for this house, built in 1878 with wonderful woodwork, six fireplaces, and six-foot windows." It was several years before Dean (an avid fisherman too) discovered his horticultural talent. Today the front gardens are a photographer's delight, with about 75 varieties of perennials. From the first floor with its 11-foot ceilings, a U-shaped staircase leads to a square hallway and corner guest rooms, many with dramatic, colorful wallpaper. Furnishings include Oriental rugs, a working Victrola, marble-topped bureaus, and Dean's paintings of familiar local scenes. "We have stayed small so that we can spend time with our guests—often sharing information about waterfalls and ponds, restaurants and cycling routes."

In residence: Three cats who spend the entire summer outside.
Foreign language spoken: "Enough French to relay area information and directions."
Bed and bath: Six carpeted bedrooms. Private shower baths for two second-floor double-bedded rooms. Semiprivate shower baths for other rooms on second and third floors, which have a queen, a double, or a double and a twin bed. Rollaway available.
Breakfast: 7:30–9:15. Juice, homemade sour cream coffee cake, seasonal fruit, hot beverages. In plant- and flower-filled fireplaced dining room.
Plus: Individual thermostats. Window fans. Magnificent view of Mt. Washington. The Intervale Cathedral Ledge and the Moat Mountains back the house. Transportation to and from center of North Conway.

From New York: *"A storybook house . . . absolutely immaculate . . . a superb B&B."* From Massachusetts: *"Memorable hospitality . . . not very large . . . intimate . . . Eileen has a definite knack for baking."* From Germany: *"Beautiful house, excellent recommendations . . . interesting conversations."*

In this book a full bath includes a shower and a tub. "Shower bath" indicates a bath that has all the essentials except a tub.

The Wilderness Inn
603/745-3890

Routes 3 and 112   (U.S./Canada) **800/200-WILD (9453)**
RFD 1, Box 69, North Woodstock, NH 03262-9709

Hosts: Michael and Rosanna Yarnell
Location: Residential, with river in back yard. At intersection facing a spired church and Loon Mountain's south peak. Three miles to Loon Mountain, eight to Cannon, 20 to Bretton Woods and Waterville Valley.

Open: Year round. Two-night minimum during foliage and on holidays.
Rates: Per room. $40–$60 shared bath, $50–$75 private bath. $60–$85 suites and cottage. $10–$15 additional person. Winter and spring midweek discount.
♥ ♨ ⁂ ♦ ✖

The shingled cottage-style house, built by a lumber baron in 1912, has mahogany-trimmed living and dining rooms and, in guest rooms, examples of the Yarnells' stained glass work. Michael, a Cornell-trained hotelier who teaches downhill skiing at Cannon Mountain and plays the violin, was with the Los Angeles Biltmore. Rosanna, a French teacher of Italian and Indian parentage, was born and raised in Ethiopia. Summers, students from France help, learn English, "and teach our guests French!"

In residence: Charles Orion, age four; Pia Camille, age two. "Our cat, Madiera, the concierge."
Foreign languages spoken: French, Italian, Bengali, Amharic.
Bed and bath: Seven rooms on two floors. Two double-bedded rooms share a full bath. One queen-bedded room, private shower bath. One room with two double beds, private shower bath. Two suites, each with a queen bed, two twin beds, and private full bath. Plus the queen-bedded cottage with beamed ceiling, built by Michael, which overlooks river. Crib available.
Breakfast: 8–10. Fresh fruit compote, juice, homemade breads, teas, hot milk with freshly ground coffee. Entrees include several varieties of pancakes, crepes with homemade applesauce, French toast. In warm weather, served on long enclosed porch. Option of continental breakfast in bed.
Plus: Tea or mulled cider with snacks. Stenciling and comforters. Fruit basket. Backyard (river) swimming hole. Winter dinners ($10–$20) and babysitting by arrangement.

> From Massachusetts: *"An aura of warmth radiates from both the sitting room hearth and the Yarnells' quiet loving care. . . . Gourmet meals . . . a little piece of paradise."*

Meadow Farm
603/942-8619

Jenness Pond Road, Northwood, NH 03261-9406   **fax 603/942-5736**

Hosts: Doug and Janet Briggs
Location: Quiet. Lake frontage, 50 acres of field and woods. Five-minute drive from Route 4; 25 minutes east of Concord, west of University of New Hampshire; 45 minutes to Gunstock ski area. Near Shaker Village in Canterbury, and antiquing.

Open: Year round. Reservations preferred.
Rates: $45 single, $60–$65 double. $10 third person. Children under three free. Family and weekly rates available. Amex.
♨ ⚓

Pretty as a picture. Authentic. And it keeps getting even better. The 1770 center chimney colonial with old beams, four fireplaces, and original paneling has been restored, stenciled, and painted over a period of 16 years by the Briggses. The added screened porch, overlooking the meadows, perennial gardens, and more than 100 old garden rose bushes, is furnished with handmade twig furniture. There are fruit trees and raspberry bushes for preserve making. A lake for swimming (private beach and dock), fishing, and canoeing (canoe provided). And even a pony for children to ride. When they aren't hosting or skiing or gardening, Janet is director of the University Program of Horsemanship, and Doug manufactures and markets equipment for agricultural research.

In residence: Nifty, a Jack Russell terrier with lots of personality.
Bed and bath: Three antiques-filled rooms. First-floor single room shares shower bath with hosts. On second floor, two double-bedded rooms share a full bath. Cot available.
Breakfast: 7:30–9. Homemade breads, muffins and preserves. Specialties such as bismarcks, German pancakes, Belgian waffles with New Hampshire maple syrup. Served in keeping room with fireplace and bake-oven or on screened porch.
Plus: Window fans. Marked cross-country trails.

From New York: *"An exciting trip back in time in a very old home, yet with modern comforts and a great breakfast."* From Massachusetts: *"Interesting hosts. Marvelous home. We loved it."*

Governor's House Bed & Breakfast
32 Miller Avenue, Portsmouth, NH 03801-5130   603/431-6546
fax 603/427-0803

Hosts: John and Nancy Grossman
Location: Residential. In historic district. With huge pines and a 75-year-old rhododendron "forest." Ten-minute walk to the harbor, shops, restaurants, and Strawbery Banke, a 10-acre (42 buildings) museum community.

Open: Year round.
Rates: $90. $110 with double-headed shower, $140 with Jacuzzi. Singles $10 less. November–May $20 less. MC, Visa.
♥ ♣ ◆ ✗ ⅄

A magic touch combined with joie de vivre. A stately 1917 Georgian colonial, all redone in 1992 but with the feeling that the Grossmans, parents of five grown children, have always lived here. The first New Year's Eve a caterer turned the preservation award–winner into a one-night four-star restaurant. The local chamber proudly hosted a reception here for legislators and corporate executives. A visiting musician practiced on the grand piano that has been here since the house was owned by Charles Dale, governor in the late 1940s. Applesauce—what an aroma—was being "put up" the day I arrived.

All the antiques were collected at auctions during the "four months flat" that it took to create new baths, redesign existing ones, and install wainscoting, wonderful wallcoverings, and a sprinkler/alarm system. Before "retiring," John, an Ohioan, was an educational publishing executive in California.

(Please turn page.)

Nancy, a Connecticut native who was inspired by an adult education course, is a professional tile painter and artist whose extraordinary creations can be seen in the bathroom murals, on the living room fireplace, and in private commissions on both coasts.

In residence: Chinook, an American Eskimo dog, age two.

Bed and bath: Four air-conditioned queen-bedded rooms (two are canopied), one with an extra single; all with ceiling fan. All private shower baths (worth a magazine feature) with individual thermostats—one with double head and one with Jacuzzi.

Breakfast: Usually 8:30 weekdays, 9:15 Sundays and holidays. (Coffee earlier in second-floor library.) In the fireplaced dining room with mural, a true conversation piece, complete with signatures of every local craftsman who worked on the restoration.

Plus: Coffee or tea and home-baked cookies. Tennis court. A "Did you forget" closet. Vintage magazines. Fresh flowers. Laundry facilities. Transportation to C&J bus stop and Pease Airport. An antiques "shop" in a breakfront with "must-bargain-for" prices.

> From New Hampshire: *"They make everyone feel right at home and, at the same time, special. Delicious breakfast and gorgeous rooms—or should that be gorgeous breakfasts and delicious rooms."*

Grassy Pond House   603/899-5166
Rindge, NH 03461-9520   603/899-5167

Hosts: Carmen Linares and Bob Multer
Location: Quiet. On 150 acres of woods and fields on an unspoiled lake. Minutes' walk to groomed cross-country trails and Cathedral of the Pines. Three miles from junction of U.S. Route 202 and N.H. 119.

Open: Year round. Reservations required. Two-night minimum October 5–20.
Rates: Tax included. $45 single. Double $55 shared bath, $65 private bath.
♥ ⬤ ✗. ⌇

"A secluded place where folks come just to hide away. Others come for weddings, for area schools, or for the outdoors. We are a traditional (small) B&B, with a layout that allows guests to have their own wing with pocket doors to our older part of the house."

There's a story for each antique, quilt, or mantel in the 1831 farmhouse, which has been carefully restored by Carmen, "the aesthetic one," a former management consultant, and Bob, "the scientific partner," a chemical engineer. Both hosts have had work assignments in various parts of the United States and abroad. Here, on the site of Rindge's first sawmill, where the dam is now maintained by beavers, Carmen and Bob have taken on the roles of builders, landscape designers, and historians. They added porches that look out over the pond to Cathedral of the Pines. And, "for a joyful summer," between the house and the pond there's a screened octagonal gazebo with a cupola, surrounded by perennials.

In residence: One or two cats.

Bed and bath: Three first-floor rooms, private entrance. Room with two twin beds shares connecting full bath with double-bedded room. One room with double bed, private shower bath. Second-floor double-bedded room, private shower bath.

Breakfast: Usually 8–9. In dining room overlooking pond, Carmen and Bob join you for juice, baked apple or poached pear, buckwheat pancakes, French toast or pecan waffles, breakfast meats, local maple syrup; Colombian coffee, decaf, or tea.

Plus: Beverages. Fruit. Thermostats in each room. Fans. Wool blankets. Terry robes. Audiocassette player, games, piano, books, magazines in fireplaced common room. Extensive gardens.

> From New York: *"Beautiful country B&B gave us a tremendous feeling of serenity . . . an enjoyable way to slow down . . . delicious home-cooked breakfasts . . . interesting conversations . . . wonderful experience."*

Province Inn   603/664-2457

Box 309, Province Road, Bow Lake, Strafford, NH 03884

Hosts: Steve and Corky Garboski
Location: Pastoral setting on a cove of a quiet lake with beavers and herons; 120 wooded acres with trails and waterfall. Near summer theater, weekend dancing and sing-alongs, restaurants, country stores, antiquing, cross-country skiing. Half hour to Portsmouth, Concord, University of New Hampshire.
Open: Year round. Two-night minimum on Columbus Day weekend.
Rates: $65 per room. $12 cot. $7 crib. $5 one-night surcharge.
♥ ♨ ⛵ ♣ ♦ ✈ ⚹

In a "not totally isolated" rural setting, the Garboskis offer a family atmosphere. Nine-year-old daughter Bethany sometimes visits at the table, two dogs lead guests to the waterfall, and a Siamese cat is "known to sleep at the foot of a guest's bed or knock on the window to be let in." Among the available "toys" for guests' use: A one-of-a-kind electric-powered sailless catamaran and paddleboards with seats, all designed by Steve.

Corky is an airline stewardess, a justice of the peace, and a former ice skating instructor. Steve, an airline pilot, is a former Olympic class bicyclist. They combined all their interests and expanded their skills in 1984 when they bought and restored their 18th-century center chimney colonial. The living room has Victorian furnishings and swags. The den is more casual.

In residence: Daughter Bethany. Two dogs. One cat.
Bed and bath: Four second-floor rooms share two full baths plus one half bath. Three rooms with double beds, one with twin beds. Two rooms have nonworking fireplaces. One child in a crib or cot (provided) in room with parents. Maximum of three persons per room.
Breakfast: Usually 8:30–9. Full country meal with eggs or pancakes, bacon, fruit, muffins. In fireplaced keeping room.
Plus: Enclosed heated swimming pool. Lighted tennis courts. Use of mountain bicycles (it's three miles to beach) and canoe. The catamaran and paddleboards. Snacks. Fruit. Guest refrigerator. Use of barbecue. Babysitting possibility.

Mountain Lake Inn

603/938-2136

P.O. Box 443, Route 114, Bradford, NH 03221   800/662-6005

Hosts: Carol and Phil Fullerton
Location: On 165 acres of lawns, woods, trails, streams, waterfalls. Within 15 minutes of Pat's Peak, Sunapee, King Ridge. Near Indian Museum and antiquarian bookstores.
Open: Year round, except April and part of November. Two-night mini-

mum on holiday weekends and in fall.
Rates: Double occupancy $85–$95. Third person $25. Single $70. Family room $110 for quad occupancy. Discover, MC, Visa.
♥ ✚ ❖ ◆ ✈

From Massachusetts: *"It's like going home for a visit with family."*

Uncommon and loved: A good old-fashioned inn with pine-paneled living room and a screened front porch facing the lake. A four-room "hotel" when built in 1764. And changed a couple of times over since Carol, a caterer, and Phil, a stockbroker, came from Boston in 1987. The parents of five grown sons now boil maple syrup in the spring. They have the waterfront location (a private swimming beach) they wanted. Their tree work has resulted in snowshoe trails (snowshoes provided). They offer cooking-on-wood-stove, innkeeping-seminar, and family-reunion weekends as well as hike and bike tours (with maps that include back roads along 18- to 55-mile-long routes) and, as one guest wrote, "a wonderful sense of peace."

In residence: Parker, a friendly English springer spaniel, "a real inn dog." One cat, Pepper, also great with kids.
Bed and bath: Nine rooms (one on first floor), all private baths (most en suite, some shower without tub). King, queen, or double beds with quilts. Family room—two twin beds plus a queen sofa bed. Rollaway and crib available.
Breakfast: 8–9:30. Juice, fresh fruit, homemade muffins and coffee cake. A different hot entree every morning.
Plus: Tea, wine, hot cider. Babysitting. Canoe, horseshoes, badminton, croquet. Fishing. An 82-year-old pool table. Option of dinner ($15 per person); dinner arranged for company and seminar groups too. Plenty of New Hampshire information. (Phil, organizer of B&B–Country Inns Association of New Hampshire, has also been state travel council president.)

The Inn at Coit Mountain

800/367-2364

523 North Main Street, Newport, NH 03773   (in N.H.) 603/863-3583
fax 603/863-7816

Hosts: Dick and Judi Tatem
Location: Two miles north of Newport on Route 10, with mountain and river views. Seven miles west of Sunapee. Cross-country skiing at the door.
Open: Year round.
Rates: Singles $70 double or queen, $110 queen with fireplace, $100 king

with fireplace. For two—$85 double or queen, $100 queen with fireplace ($125 with private bath), $115 king with fireplace ($140 with private bath). Two-room suite $135 single, $175 for two, three, or four people. $20 rollaway. $10 crib. MC, Visa.
✈

From the outside, it's the quintessential New Hampshire inn. Inside, the 1790 Georgian features spacious and inviting rooms. But the real magnet is the turn-of-the-century addition, a 35-foot, two-storied library with a Palladian window, lots of books, and a huge stone fireplace. "Often, guests who come with a long list of things to do settle in there and really relax." In 1878 the developer of Coney Island and the Long Island Railroad bought the house as a wedding present for his daughter. It has been home to the Tatems since a B&B trip to England influenced their 1985 move from rural northeastern Connecticut. A former artist's studio is now Dick's art gallery and custom frame shop. Chef Judi is a professional retouch artist.

In residence: Dan, 19, and Melissa, 18. Becky, a red setter. Rascal, an old orange tabby. Spooky, a black Lab born on Halloween. Two horses. A family of English game hens.
Bed and bath: Six rooms, two with working fireplaces. A first-floor room has a double and a twin bed, shared shower bath. On second floor—queen bed, fireplace, bath with footed deep tub. Queen-bedded room and a room with two double beds (can be a suite) share a full bath. King-bedded room with fireplace and a queen-bedded room (can be a suite) share a tub bath. Rollaways and crib available.
Breakfast: Usually 7:30–9. Freshly squeezed orange juice, fruits, bacon and eggs, breads and muffins, plus a specialty such as sherried creamed eggs and mushrooms on toast or pecan waffles with honey butter.
Plus: Turned-down beds. Refrigerator in each room. Grand piano. Two-storied porch. Large yard and garden. Dinner ($18) by prior arrangement.

> Guests wrote: *"Gourmet breakfast . . . warm hospitality . . . beautiful home. . . . And don't forget to mention the light with wide glass shade directly over one bath tub. The lady of the house used to read there."*

Hilltop Acres   603/764-5896
Box 32, Eastside and Buffalo Road, Wentworth, NH 03282

Hosts: Cecilia and Marie A. Kauk
Location: Minutes off Route 25. On 20 acres with lawn, pine forest, and brook. Close to antiquing and three river swimming holes. Within 30–60 minutes' drive of White Mountains and lake attractions; 25 to Plymouth State College, I-93, or I-91; 10 minutes to Appalachian trail.

Open: Year round.
Rates: $65 per room. $10 extra adult, $5 extra child (ages 6–12). Cottages (breakfast option, $5 per person)—$80 for two, $20 extra adult, $10 extra child (ages 6–12); weekend and weekly rates available. Amex, MC, Visa.
♥ ♯ ♣ ♦ ✂

An American flag, a little windmill, and a wooden gnome are in front of this 1806 farmhouse, the childhood home of Marie and Cecilia. They remember when their parents ran it as an inn and served three meals a day to guests. Eventually it became the family's summer retreat. And in 1990 the sisters opened it as a B&B furnished simply with antiques, older pieces, and plants. The lodgelike beamed, pine-paneled recreation room, a popular gathering place, has a big stone fireplace, an upright piano, and sliding glass doors.

(Please turn page.)

Now Cecilia and her teenage daughters live here full time. Marie dovetails hosting with her Manhattan legal support services position.

Foreign languages spoken: German and some French.
Bed and bath: Four first-floor rooms—three double-bedded, one with two twin beds—all private full baths. Plus two pine-paneled housekeeping cottages with fireplace, kitchen unit, separate bedroom, screened porch. Rollaway available.
Breakfast: 8–9. Gourmet coffee, fruits, cereal, bagels, muffins, cheese, pastries. By request, eggs with ham or sausage. In dining room with picture windows facing field and gardens.
Plus: TV and VCR. Indoor and outdoor games. Lawn chairs. Ceiling fans in guest rooms; window fans in cottages. Refreshments.

> From New York: *"Decor in typical New England fashion . . . cleanliness beyond reproach . . . charm and hospitality outstanding . . . super place to get away from it all."*

The Atwood Inn

Route 3A, RFD 2
West Franklin, NH 03235-9361

603/934-3666
fax 603/934-6949

Hosts: Phil and Irene Fournier
Location: Wooded acreage with river. Twenty miles north of Concord. Within 30 minutes of Gunstock, Sunapee, and King Ridge mountains and Canterbury Shaker Village; 17 miles northeast of International Speedway in Loudon; 20 to five lakes, including Winnipesaukee. Ten minutes to Tilton School or Proctor Academy.

Open: Year round. Two-night minimum in October and on holiday weekends.
Rates: $55 single, $70 double. $75 The Room. $20 per extra person in room. $10 more for fireplaced rooms. Amex, Diners, MC, Visa.
♥ ❖ ♦ ✗ ✂

> From Massachusetts: *"Thoughtfully decorated . . . surpassed expectations that Bed & Breakfast in New England set for us."* From Rhode Island: *"Made us feel welcome. . . . Phil knew all about the best ski conditions. . . . Breakfast was a treat."*

First-time B&B guests are "won over" at this B&B that has welcoming candles in each window. The 1830 Federal brick building was restored in 1984 with great attention to authenticity, colonial colors, and wallpapers. Six fireplaces, wide board floors, and Indian shutters form the backdrop for comfortable chairs, many antique four-poster beds, and an eclectic collection of artwork and antique bric-a-brac.

Ever since Phil, an insurance adjuster, and Irene, a former educational administrator and college instructor who now has an antiques booth in a cooperative shop, took early retirement in 1986, they have been receiving rave reviews for their breakfasts, for their hints about restaurants and scenic routes, and for, as one guest said, "pampering guests to life."

In residence: Mini, a miniature schnauzer, a favorite with guests.
Foreign languages spoken: French and Greek.
Bed and bath: Seven rooms on three floors. All private shower baths. Full

bath with very large room with a double and a twin bed. Four double-bedded rooms with working fireplace. One room with a double and twin beds; one with a queen and twin beds.
Breakfast: 7:30–9. Pancakes, French toast, quiche, or omelets. Fresh fruit, juice, breakfast meats, muffins, breads. Served by fireplace or on patio.
Plus: Snacks and beverages always available. Cable TV. Popcorn. Games. Bedroom window fans. Bicycle and ski storage. Patio (with bug zapper). Umbrella table amidst gardens.

Stepping Stones   603/654-9048

RFD 1, Box 208, Bennington Battle Trail, Wilton Center, NH 03086-9751

Host: D. Ann Carlsmith
Location: Quiet country setting in Monadnock hills. Facing a reservoir. Near historic Frye Mill, Monadnock Music concert series, Wapack (hiking) Trail. Two minutes from a picture-book village; 15 to Peterborough. Six miles to Temple Mountain,

20 west of Nashua, 60 north of Boston.
Open: Year round. Reservations recommended.
Rates: $50 private bath, $45 shared bath. $35 single, shared bath. Seventh night free.
♥ ♦ ♣ ✄

From Manhattan, Massachusetts, Michigan, and Connecticut: *"A home that is a masterpiece of Ann's work. . . . Warm and welcoming in every detail. . . . Enchanting. . . . Peaceful. . . . Art, flowers, and handweaving everywhere . . . Winding paths and terraces among spectacular perennial gardens . . . Warm and snug in winter . . . A guest is reminded that some people and some places are still extra special."*

Glowing letters continue to arrive, all praising the landscape designer and garden consultant who spends winters weaving (rugs, throws, pillows) on the many looms in her 19th-century house. Perhaps you have come for concerts, weaving lessons, antiquing, puppet opera, or theater—or for rejuvenation. When you tear yourself away, Ann can direct you to a 30-foot waterfall or to a back road lined with farms. People from all over the world—"people whom I never would have met otherwise"—have found this haven.

In residence: Caprice and Vivace, the cats, and Stanza, a dog, "all kept out of bedrooms." Bantams and ducklings in the yard.
Bed and bath: Three second-floor bedrooms. One with two twin beds shares full hall bath with room that has a double-sized spindle bed. Queen-bedded room has a private shower bath.
Breakfast: By 10. Belgian waffles or French toast with maple syrup or homemade preserves, sausages, omelets, croissants, quiches, fruit and nut granola with yogurt, homemade muffins and sweet breads, seasonal fruit and orange juice. In solar breakfast room that has plants, pottery, a wood stove, and a view of garden.
Plus: Beverages and ginger cookies. An opportunity to visit gardens and to observe weaving. Extensive garden library. Down comforters. Window fans. Guest refrigerator. Color TV, stereo, books and magazines in fireplaced living room. Cone and herbal wreaths for sale.

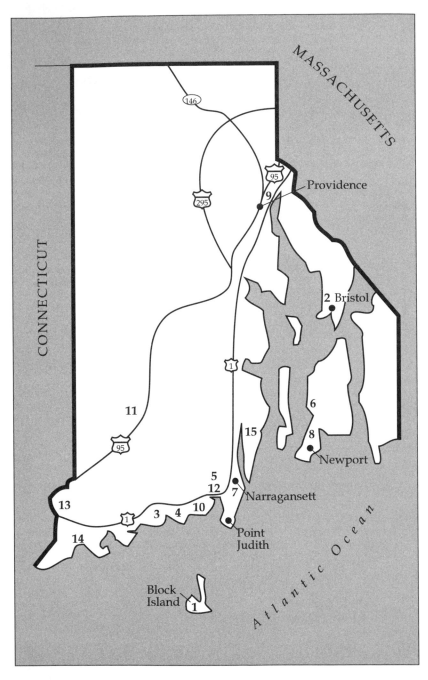

The numbers on this map indicate the locations of B&Bs described in detail in this chapter.

RHODE ISLAND

KEY TO SYMBOLS
♥ Lots of honeymooners come here.
⚰ Families with children are very welcome. (Please see page xii.)
⚱ "Please emphasize that we are a private home, not an inn."
⁂ Groups or private parties sometimes book the entire B&B.
♦ Travel agents' commission paid. (Please see page xii.)
✂ Sorry, no guests' pets are allowed.
✄ No smoking inside *or* no smoking at all, even on porches.

Rhode Island
_____ Reservation Services _____

Anna's Victorian Connection

5 Fowler Avenue, Newport, RI 02840

Phone: 401/849-2489, 24-hour live answering service. Reservations made daily in May, June, September, and October, 9 a.m–9 p.m.; July and August 8 a.m.–10 p.m.; November–April 12 noon–8 p.m.

Fax: 401/847-7309.

Listings: 200. Some inns; mostly private residences within 15 minutes of downtown Newport. Some are in unhosted, self-catered houses and apartments. A few are in other parts of Rhode Island and in southeastern Massachusetts border communitiies.

Reservations: Advance notice preferred. Some available through travel agents.

Rates: $25–$150 single. $50–$200 double. One night's lodging rate required as a deposit. Balance due upon arrival. Refunds of 90 percent for cancellations made at least two weeks before scheduled arrival date. Amex, CB, Diners, Discover, En Route, MC, Visa.

A wide variety of annually inspected properties—a place on the harbor, a Cape Cod–style home, an antebellum Ocean Drive mansion, neighborhood Victorian houses, and historic inns—are represented by Susan White, creator of this 10-year-old service. A school guidance counselor, she still hosts in her own Victorian home and teaches a how-to-run-a-B&B course. Her four children are grown, and they—together with one grandson—assist in making "careful matches" for lodgings as well as restaurant reservations and activity arrangements.

Bed & Breakfast, Newport Ltd.

33 Russell Avenue, Newport, RI 02840-1723

Phone: 401/846-5408 or 800/800-8765, 9 a.m.–8 p.m. daily.

Fax: 401/846-1828.

Listings: 60+ private residences. Most are in Newport, but several are in Wickford, Saunderstown, Providence, and Block Island.

Reservations: Two weeks' advance notice suggested.

Rates: $75–$85 shared bath, $95–$120 private bath. Some with family and weekly rates. One night's lodging rate is a required deposit. (Balance due in cash or travelers' checks upon arrival.) For cancellations made more than a week before scheduled arrival, deposit refunded less $15 service charge. If cancellations made within seven days of scheduled arrival date, refund less

$15 service charge made if filled by another reservation. Amex, Discover, MC, Visa.

As owner/hostess of Bluestone, page 323, Cindy Roberts found that she was booking so many Newport area residents with her overflow that she established this attentive service. "We inspect and interview. We are concerned about cleanliness and friendliness. Every one of my listings is special—whether right in town within walking distance of everything or in quiet residential sections with extensive gardens." The homes range from modest to luxurious, from urban to rural, from waterfront to hilltop. Many are historic; some are contemporary. Free directory of sample listings available.

Plus: Dinner reservations, floral arrangments, champagne . . . "whatever you wish."

Bed & Breakfast of Rhode Island

P.O. Box 3291, Newport, RI 02840-0993

Phone: 401/849-1298 or 800/828-0000. Monday–Friday 9–5; Saturday 9–12.

Fax: 401/849-1306.

Listings: 120. Most are hosted private residences; some inns.

Reservations: Two-night minimum stay required on summer weekends in resort areas.

Rates: $38–$225 single. $50–$225 double. Weekly and monthly rates available. Required deposit is one night's lodging rate plus one-half of each additional night. If cancellation is received at least two weeks prior to reservation date, refund is given minus $20 processing fee. No refunds within two weeks of scheduled arrival date unless room is rebooked. Amex, MC, Visa usually accepted for last-minute reservations only.

Rodney and Barbara Wakefield acquired this reservation service in 1991, and since then they have expanded into many areas of the hospitality industry. Together with their daughter Amanda, they now book weddings and special events. Packages include discounts to attractions and concerts. Tours are booked for British travelers coming to New England as well as for travelers to England. The service's American B&B listings go beyond Rhode Island to all parts of New England.

Other reservation services with some B&Bs in Rhode Island:
Bed & Breakfast/Inns of New England, page 259
Covered Bridge, page 2

Rhode Island B&Bs

The Barrington Inn   401/466-5510

P.O. Box 397, Beach and Ocean Avenue, Block Island, RI 02807

Hosts: Joan and Howard Ballard
Location: On a knoll overlooking Great Salt Pond. Three-quarters of a mile from ferry (departs from Point Judith, 30-minute drive from Newport); one-half mile from island airport. Five-minute walk to beach.
Open: April–October. Advance reservations necessary for summer weekends. Two-night minimum July, August, and weekends; three nights on holiday weekends spring through fall.
Rates: Weekends in season $90, $120, $135, $145; May 1–mid-June, September, October $70–$95; April $45–$70. Monday–Thursday $5–10 less. $20 third person in room. MC, Visa.
♥ ♣ ✕ ⚬

From New Hampshire: "We found a home . . . comfortable, spotless, and the views superb . . . delicious breakfast . . . highly recommended for those who like a personal greeting, privacy, and a firm bed."

I concur. All in a great location for a before-breakfast beach walk. With a host whose family has vacationed on the island since the turn of the century. Still, Howard never had any idea—not even a dream—that he would be doing what he is. When the Ballards lived in Michigan, Joan was mother to four and a secretary. It's a long story, but it ends (or begins really) with the purchase of what was a family summer home. "We were sort of thrown into this. Howard, a former shipyard manager, has always repaired everything we own. Now he has his own home maintenance business, he handles all the repairs at the inn, and our family is grown. The vacation atmosphere is very different from working in an office. I love it!"

Furnishings include wicker and antiques—all in keeping with a big old farmhouse, "but we're constantly making changes and redecorating." Old photographs include one of the original 1886 house. Other photographs—of tall ships, sunsets, and island scenes—are Howard's work. On the grounds there's an old apple orchard favored by many colorful birds.

Bed and bath: Six carpeted rooms of various sizes on three levels. All with private shower baths and ceiling fans. On second floor, double or queen bed, sliding glass doors to private deck, water views. Third floor—two rooms with sitting areas; one has queen bed, the other a queen and a twin; both with wonderful water views. Plus two apartments.
Breakfast: 8–9:30. Fresh fruit, juices, cereal; homemade muffins, breads, and jams. Sometimes blackberry cobbler or apple Betty. Hot and cold beverages. Served by Joan and Howard in dining room and/or on deck.
Plus: Good map of island. Beverages. Well water. Two living rooms, one with color TV, VCR, games. Guest refrigerator. Ice. Deck with water view and sunsets. Outside shower. Bike rack. Off-street parking. Off-season, will meet guests at ferry or airport.

The Sasafrash   401/466-5486

P.O. Box 1227, Center Road, Block Island, RI 02807

Hosts: Shirley and Sanford Kessler
Location: Quiet country setting along main road. About a mile from town and beaches in what was, in the 1800s, the center of town. Between the old and new harbors.
Open: Year round. Two-night minimum on weekends, three nights on holidays.

Rates: Memorial Day–Labor Day semiprivate bath $85–$95, private bath $100–$110. April, May, September, October semiprivate bath $65–$75, private $85–$95. Winter rates.
♥ ⬦ ⁂ ♦ ✄

"When guests enter this former church, for a moment a quiet comes over them. They look up at the choir loft, the original stained glass windows, the raised pulpit platform, and the communion rail. Built in 1907 by and for its 125 parishioners, it was active until 1975. The entire building was our antiques shop until 1987, when we began the four-year conversion to a residence/antiques shop."

Architects, historians, island aficionados, and romantics are among guests who appreciate the Victorian ambiance in this fascinating structure, which is furnished with many cottage antiques acquired over several decades from Block Island homes and hotels. Rhode Island artists are represented in the extensive collection of 18th- and 19th-century paintings. Shirley, a former school administrator and college professor, is a third-generation Block Island resident, active as president of the Friends of Island Free Library and as a member of the school committee, ecumenical church groups, and the historical society. Sanford, a Realtor, volunteers with FISH, walkathons, and the Nature Conservancy. The enthusiastic hosts share recipes, sunset viewing spots, and their love for the island.

Foreign language spoken: Spanish.
Bed and bath: Four large corner rooms. All baths are large, with oversized stall shower. Private baths for one room with double bed and one with two twins. One bath shared by one double-bedded room and one with two twins. All custom-made mattresses and antique quilts.
Breakfast: 8–9:30. Juice. Hot or cold cereal. Fresh fruit. "A surprise dish." Homemade breads and muffins. Served by Sanford on antique china in living/dining room, former sanctuary. Option of hot beverage on large deck.
Plus: Setups, cold drinks, snacks, 5–6 p.m. Outside dressing room and hot shower. Portable fans. Books (many first editions), games, and cards in second-floor common room. No TV. Landscaped yard. Lawn games. Directions to private walkways accessible to guests. Transportation to/from ferry or airport.

From Massachusetts: *"Charming building, spacious rooms, comfortable beds . . . interesting and helpful host. . . . My wife says it's the cleanest place she's ever seen. . . . Everything was perfect."*

The Sea Breeze

401/466-2275

Spring Street, P.O. Box 141, Block Island, RI 02807-0141   **800/786-2276**

Hosts: The Newhouse family with Allan McKay
Location: On the crest of a hill overlooking a two-acre meadow and pond, with broad view of the ocean and coastline. Five-minute walk to restaurants, shops, and ferry landing.

Open: Year round. Two-night minimum; three nights on holiday weekends Memorial Day–Columbus Day. **Rates:** $80–$110 shared bath. $140–$170 private bath. Less off-season. MC, Visa.
♥ ♣ ♦ ✗ ⚬

"The gardens are just as we planned—with several hundred varieties of perennials, roses, and flowering shurbs. They make the perfect spot for small weddings. And the five original cottages are now four, completely renovated with the feel of seaside cottages."

Mary Newhouse, a Manhattan artist, and her physician husband—gardeners who really love this island—listened when one of their daughters suggested B&B for the compound of five very tired houses purchased in 1979. Together the family, known for their decorating service and the Sea Breeze Gallery (located in an old harbor area building), planned and redid. Rooms were enlarged and filled without clutter but with flair—with English chintzes, country antiques, and contemporary art. The latest addition: June and September painting and environmental workshops led by visiting instructors in this spectacular natural setting.

Foreign languages spoken: German, French, some Spanish and Italian, depending on family members in residence.
Bed and bath: Ten rooms—some with cathedral ceilings—with double or twin beds, on first and second floors. All shower baths; five are private. Six rooms have ocean views; four have private porches.
Breakfast: 8:30–9:30. Viennese coffee, English tea. Freshly baked croissants or muffins, homemade preserves, fruit, juice. Served on trays in the sitting room or in baskets brought directly to rooms with private baths. May be taken to rooms or onto porch or lawns.
Plus: Sitting room. Sitting and writing area on the second floor. Library. Guest refrigerator, sink, and glasses provided.

The Sheffield House

401/466-2494

P.O. Box C-2, High Street, Block Island, RI 02807   **fax 401/466-5067**

Hosts: Steve and Claire McQueeny ("daughters host during the one or two off-season months when we're in Ireland.")
Location: In historic district, one block from ferry landing. Two blocks from beach.
Open: Year round. Two-night minimum on June, July, August, and September weekends; three nights on holiday weekends.
Rates: Summer $80–$100 shared bath, $95–$140 private. Spring and fall $60–$90 shared bath, $80–$125 private. Winter $40–$50 shared, $50–$70 private. Amex, MC, Visa.
♥ ♣ ♦ ✗ ⚬

"Aunt Claire," as one guest dubbed the enthusiastic hostess, has a very big family these days. When the McQueenys started B&B, this was a casual second home, with Claire spending winters as a florist in Connecticut. In 1987 they became permanent residents. ("How lucky we feel.") Their family pieces and antiques add to the home-away-from-home atmosphere of the summer cottage built in 1888 for a Providence doctor.

"The wraparound front porch has been rebuilt complete with gingerbread. Steve, now chairman of the planning board, continues with his worldwide brokerage firm. As gardener, he added zillions of daffodils. The perennial gardens are flourishing. Through my flower business, I design wedding arrangements. Our oldest daughter, also a permanent resident, is in her eighth season with a gift shop. Lots of guests are returning, but we still see new faces every year. And please remind your readers that the Nature Conservancy declared Block Island 'one of the Ten Great Places in the Western Hemisphere.'"

In residence: "Heather, our aging calico cat, sunbathes on her back. Maggie, our black golden retriever, gets lots of attention." (Neither allowed inside.)
Bed and bath: Seven rooms on first and second floors. Queen or double beds. Five private baths (one has tub); four en suite, one across hall.
Breakfast: At 8:30. Juices, coffee, herbal tea, fruit, homemade muffins. Buffet style in country kitchen that has a bottle collection from all over the world.
Plus: Bedroom ceiling fans and heat. Books. Games. Refrigerator, ice, and glasses. Grill. Picnic table. Porch rocking chairs. Bike rack. Sometimes, a (fascinating) island tour. One room becomes a library in winter. Will meet guests at airport or ferry.

> From Rhode Island: *"Pampered for the entire weekend . . . house and hosts a little piece of heaven."*

Rockwell House Inn   401/253-0040
610 Hope Street, Bristol, RI 02809-1945

Hosts: Debra and Steve Krohn
Location: On a half acre with the state's largest tulip tree. On a main street block of large historic homes. Around corner from 99-cent movie theater. One block to harbor; to 14-mile bike path (to Providence); and to restaurants, antiques shops, and five museums, including America's Cup International Hall of Fame.

Twenty minutes to Providence, Newport, winery tour.
Open: Year round. Two-night minimum on holidays and local special events.
Rates: Tax included. $100 king/twins, $90 queen. Less off-season. $15 extra person. Corporate discounts. Amex, MC, Visa.
♥ ❖ ◆ ✄ ⅍

This "wedding cake house" began as a traditional Federal-style house. For its now eclectic architecture—with some Georgian, Greek Revival, Italianate, and Victorian features—it has been featured in *Smithsonian*. And now wedding planners, too, are happy that it was saved by the family who restored it in 1973. Everyone asks about the spectacular stencils throughout. As Debra says, "The designs were researched, cut by hand, and done by the 1984 buyer, who spent seven years on a ladder!

(Please turn page.)

"In California Steve worked for Gallo wines and I was a speech pathologist. When we moved to Rhode Island from upstate New York three years ago, Steve became sales manager (still is) for the Sakonnet Winery, and I worked as an assistant innkeeper in Newport. In 1991 we bought this wonderful pink house. It has eight-foot pocket doors, high ceilings, intricate parquet and inlaid floors, and a fireplaced courting corner. We furnished it eclectically— and love sharing it with travelers."

In residence: "Many guests want to take Misha, our oft-photographed bichon frise, home!"
Foreign languages spoken: Spanish.
Bed and bath: Four large rooms with private baths. On first floor— king/twins option, full bath, gas fireplace. On second floor—room with king/twins option, shower bath. King/twins option, gas fireplace, sink in room, shower bath. Queen bed, sink in room, shower bath.
Breakfast: 7–10. Homemade granola, bread, muffins, preserves, lemon poppyseed cake. Yogurt. Fresh fruit cup. Freshly ground and brewed gourmet coffees. Served on 30-foot-long terrazzo-tiled porch or in candlelit dining room.
Plus: Parlor TV and parlor/library. Bedroom ceiling fans. Afternoon tea, sherry, or wine. His and hers robes. Turndown service. Specialty mints. Terrace. Wine tasting and tour weekends. Tented weddings booked here.

From Texas: *"Both the inn and the town are picture perfect. . . . Excellent hospitality . . . relaxing and comfortable."*

William's Grant Inn

154 High Street, Bristol, RI 02809

401/253-4222
800/596-4222

Hosts: Mike and Mary Rose
Location: On the July 4th parade (seen by 250,000 people) route. In quiet old neighborhood with many restored homes. Five-minute walk to Bristol harbor, Lobster Pot Restaurant, antiques shops, town common with gazebo. Five blocks to 99-cent movie theater. Short drive to 33-acre Blithewold Gardens, museums, "and a park with incredible water views, beaches, and bike path."
Open: Year round. Two-night minimum on July 4th, Roger Williams graduation, Newport Jazz Festival.
Rates: Per room. May–October $85 shared bath, $95 private bath. November–April $65 shared bath, $75 private bath. Amex, Diners, Discover, MC, Visa; 5 percent surcharge.
♥ ♣ ♦ ✗ ✄

Complete with picket fence, this 1808 Federal/colonial house is the Roses' dream come true. They opened in 1992 after Debra Krohn, page 311, Mary's assistant at a Newport B&B, "discovered untouristy Bristol" and encouraged the Roses to move. Mary's mother painted the entry hall with a mural of Bristol harbor. Mike, a swimming pool manufacturing company accountant, renovated and refinished. (He makes his own kayak paddles too.) Mary, a former special events coordinator, made all the window treatments—"I've been sewing since the fourth grade,"—and painted. Furnishings are from grandparents and from auctions. Here Mary plans theme weekends, exhibits local artists' work, volunteers with the animal shelter, and does fun activities with two adopted grandparents.

In residence: Chloe, a Jack Russell mix, "a thinker." Tadger is a short mixed terrier who "loves to sleep."
Foreign languages spoken: "None. We have English/French and English/Spanish dictionaries and our pantomime is pretty good!"
Breakfast: 8–10. Fresh fruit. Homemade muffins, coffee cakes, breads. Gourmet coffee; blended teas. Repertoire includes huevos rancheros, pesto spinach quiche, or Belgian waffles. Mary is weekday chef; on weekends it's Mike. Served in great room kitchen or on patio.
Bed and bath: Five queen-bedded rooms with nonworking fireplaces. Three first-floor rooms; two with shower baths (one is handicapped accessible). The room with private hallway has tub and shower. Two second floor rooms (can be a suite) share a tub bath; robes provided.
Plus: Fireplaced living room. Bedroom ceiling fans. No TV. Tea, wine, or sherry. Patio. Wine buckets and glasses.

> From Massachusetts: "*Nicely decorated . . . immaculate . . . comfortable . . . friendly . . . four-star breakfast. . . . Lots to do in Bristol.*" From Texas: "*Hesitate to write . . concerned one of my favorite B&Bs will be booked when I visit next.*"

One Willow by the Sea   401/364-0802
1 Willow Road, Charlestown, RI 02813-4162

Hosts: Denise Dillon Fuge
Location: On a quiet road. Bordered by a large meadow and wilderness area. Seven-minute drive to "impeccable white-sand beaches," 5 miles to wildlife refuges, 4 to Theatre-By-The-Sea, 10 to University of Rhode Island, 25 to Mystic and Newport, 11 to Block Island ferry.

Open: Year round. Two-day minimum on summer weekends, national holidays, and University of Rhode Island and Brown University graduations.
Rates: April 15–October 31, $55 double, $50 single. Off-season, $10 less.
♯ ♨ ◆

A flexible hostess. A comfortable kick-off-your-shoes-and-relax split-level house furnished with "good" antiques and comfortable sofas and lots of books and flowers. A deck and gardens where you can "hear the sea and smell the sea breezes."

Denise spent 31 years in New York City. As a teenager in London during World War II she was inspired by the suffragists. In the 1980s she was president of the New York City NOW chapter and a national NOW board member. She also helped create the National Women's Health Network. Denise has experience in publishing, speaking, and lobbying—and, since coming here, as a library trustee and literacy volunteer. For winter beach walks, she "borrows a dog." Next? Inquire about owl prowl or bird migration theme weekends along with other off-beach activities.

In residence: Lizzie, "a 12-year-old Russian blue ex-Manhattanite cat." Minou, a Siamese, "takes role of discreet morning greeter seriously." Joe, another Siamese, "keeps the two females on their toes."
Foreign languages spoken: "Slightly fractured French, some understanding of Danish-Norwegian/Swedish."

(Please turn page.)

Bed and bath: Three rooms plus family room. Main floor, two queen-bedded rooms share a full bath. Lower level, room with two twin beds, adjacent shower bath. Family area with double bed, space for two cots and a crib.
Breakfast: 6:30–10. Cantaloupe with ginger, vanilla yogurt, fresh fruit, bagels, blueberry muffins, and "my son's killer croissants from the best deli in town." Juices. Gourmet coffee and tea. Upon request, French crepes; Irish oatmeal; English scrambled eggs with sausages, ham, or bacon. On sun deck or in dining room on glass-topped table with fine china.
Plus: Thick bath sheets. Sun-dried sheets. Terry robes. Window fans. Bedside radio. Boat trailer parking. Champagne for special occasions. Will meet train or plane. Wood stove in winter. Dinner and theater reservations. Discount beach passes and bridge tokens.

Fairfield-By-The-Sea   401/789-4717
527 Green Hill Beach Road, Green Hill, RI 02879-5703

Host: Jeanne Ayers Lewis
Location: Secluded country setting. Between Westerly and Wakefield, ¾ mile from ocean beach, 2 miles from Theatre-By-The-Sea, 10 from University of Rhode Island. Twenty miles east of Mystic; 25 west of Newport. Near Block Island ferry and family-oriented Yawgoo ski area.
Open: Year round. Two-night minimum on weekends, three nights on most holiday weekends.
Rates: Per room. $60 May through October. Less off-season. Cot $10 child under six, $12 anyone over age six.
♥ 🛏 ⊁

Zest, here art thou! A creative home economist who has been a nationwide consumer consultant and has edited national publications. A retired teacher, considered Rhode Island's B&B dean, who has given hundreds of workshops on food, crafts, stitchery, use of phyllo leaves. A poet, avid gardener, watercolor artist, and grandmother who has explored "every inch of this culturally rich state, where everything is nearby."

The contemporary country home, one of our havens on a B&B-to-B&B cycling trip, was designed and built by Jeanne's husband. It is a lovely place, filled with a varied library (many current titles), art, maps, family pictures, quilts, and silhouettes. "Stress reduction" is a theme, especially in winter. Guests bird-watch, bicycle, walk on the beach, sit by the fire, enjoy breakfast conversations—and return.

In residence: Murphy, a friendly terrier, "looks like old-fashioned teddy bear." Harrington is a life-sized soft sculpture butler.
Bed and bath: Two "treetop" rooms reached by a living room spiral staircase. One with twin/king option, one with double share a full bath and a half-bath.
Breakfast: 8–10 but flexible. Fresh fruit. Freshly baked goods, maybe fruit tarts. Egg dishes (farm-fresh eggs) or waffles. Eat in dining room or on an open deck.
Plus: Wonderful hot/cold outdoor shower. Picnic deck. Use of gas grill (for lobsters, if you wish).

From New Jersey: *"We have rarely been in a place where the outside and the inside blend so beautifully and creatively."* From California: *"Well worth the 2,500-mile trek from Los Angeles."* From Maine: *"Pampers by paying attention to people and by leaving them room to go their own way."*

Hedgerow B&B
1747 Mooresfield Road, P.O. Box 1586
Kingston, RI 02881

401/783-2671
800/486-4587

Hosts: Ann and Jim Ross
Location: On two beautiful acres with trees and gardens. One-half mile from University of Rhode Island entrance. Fifteen minutes to beaches, Block Island ferry; 25 to Newport, 30 to Providence.

Open: Year round. Two-night minimum on holiday weekends.
Rates: $55 single, $60 double. Cot $10 or $15 depending on age. Crib, under age five, free. Discover.
♯ ✿ ✕ ⚞

The colonial house built in 1933 by an Olympic medal winner/URI coach was exactly what Ann had in mind for a B&B when Jim, an insurance executive, pursued his dream of earning a doctorate so that he could teach (he is associate professor now) on the university level. That was in 1987, and the 2 youngest of 11 Ross children were in college. All the comfortable and refinished family treasures (with new bedding) from the big Victorians the family had lived in fit beautifully. Three daughters were married here. (One lives in Tunisia.) And now the Rosses enjoy seeing other weddings that are booked on the lovely terraced grounds. University of Rhode Island visitors come. And so do day-trippers. And then there are those who pace themselves—read on the porch, play tennis, go to the beach and out to dinner. Warm hospitality reigns.

In residence: One grown daughter and one grandchild (of 23).
Bed and bath: Four second-floor rooms. "Lots of hot water" baths. Queen-bedded room shares connecting full bath with room that has two twins. One double-bedded room shares full hall bath with room that has two twins.
Breakfast: Usually 7:30–9. Banana, blueberry, or apple pancakes; French toast with fruit and whipped cream; egg-and-cheese souffle; or eggs Benedict. Bacon, sausage, or ham. In dining room or on porch.
Plus: Fireplaced living room with grand piano. Late-afternoon happy hour; setups provided. Den with TV. Game room. Long wicker-furnished back porch overlooking formal gardens. Grill. Picnic table. Transportation to/from train station or airport.

Lindsey's Guest House
6 James Street, Middletown, RI 02842

401/846-9386

Host: Anne Lindsey
Location: In residential area. Ten-minute walk to Second Beach, restaurants, Norman Bird Sanctuary, Sachuest Point Wildlife Refuge. Two miles to Newport's harbor, shops, entertainment; 1½ to its Bellevue Avenue mansions, Tennis Hall of Fame, Cliff Walk.
Open: Year round. Two-night mininum on holiday weekends.

Rates: July and August $65 weekends; $10 one-night stay surcharge; $55 weekdays. May, June, September, October $5 less; add $5 for private bath. November–April $10 less. $20 extra person. $10 under age 12 (with two adults). MC, Visa.
♥ ♯ ☎ ✿ ◆ ✕ ⚞

(Please turn page.)

Over 30 years as a B&B, this split-level house has seen conversation run the gamut—from family to Newport attractions, from hints about bargain hours at good restaurants to Elderhostel, from gardening to shell collecting.

"Three grandchildren now assist—remembering how grandfather shared sightseeing tips and history of this wonderful area. Folks from all over the world balance the headline news and show how much we as humans are all alike." Anne has 7 grown children and 13 grandchildren.

Bed and bath: Three rooms. One on street level with double bed, private entrance, private bath (handicapped accessible, 28-inch access). Queen-bedded room and one room with two twin beds; two full baths (one can be private). Rollaway and crib available.

Breakfast: Usually 8–10. Juice, cereal, fruit in season, English muffins, bagels and cream cheese, homemade jams and coffee cake, coffee, tea, and milk. In dining room with linens, candles, and color-scheme-of-the-month flowers.

Plus: Ceiling fans in guest rooms, dining room, kitchen. Off-street parking. Wraparound deck. Large yard. Swing.

From New York: *"Warm, friendly hospitality."* From Virginia: *"Helped me get acquainted with the area."* From Missouri: *"Felt at home. A relaxing atmosphere with clean, comfortable rooms."*

Ilverthorpe Cottage   401/789-2392
41 Robinson Street, Narragansett, RI 02882

Hosts: Chris and John Webb; Jill Raggio
Location: On a residential street in historic district. Three blocks to shops, restaurants, The Victorian Towers. Five-minute walk to beach.

Open: May–November. Two-night minimum on summer weekends.
Rates: Per room. $65–$70 shared bath, $70–$75 private.
♥ ⊶ ⊷ ⁂ ◆ ✈

From Massachusetts: *"A most gracious breakfast. Every bit of of the house artistically beautiful . . . all wonderful."*

Those artistic touches change as Chris, a first-grade teacher, finishes a new (gorgeous) basket or is inspired to redecorate a wall or even an entire room—with stenciling or small-print wallpaper, dried or fresh flower arrangements, messages written in calligraphy, lace, or many pillows. The Victorian house is furnished with an eclectic collection of family pieces and antiques. From the flower, vegetable, and herb gardens come garnishes and flavorings for the breakfast, one of the features shown on an NBC television news segment. Cohost John, a retired army officer, is a commercial banker. Teenaged daughter Jill, who has grown up as "assistant innkeeper," often greets guests and helps with the morning meal.

Bed and bath: Four second-floor rooms. Of the two with private baths, one room has king bed; the other has canopied double four-poster bed. Room with two twin beds and five windows shares a full bath with adjoining double-bedded room. Cot available.

Breakfast: "Meant to spoil each and every guest." At 8:30. Maybe breakfast pizza, cheese souffles, pocket omelets, baked eggs, blintzes. Fresh fruit, juices, coffee, and regular, herbal, or English tea. Homemade breads; could be fruit flan, French egg puff, poppyseed bread. In the dining room or on the veranda. **Plus:** Wraparound porch; screened half is accessible from living room French doors. Wine. Foyer ceiling fan. Will meet guests at the Greene airport, Kingston train station, or bus stop. Bus to Newport passes by the street. Babysitting. Off-street parking. Use of refrigerator, dishes, and glassware. Outdoor children's gym set. Games for adults and children.

Murphy's B&B   401/789-1824
43 South Pier Road, Narragansett, RI 02882

Hosts: Martha and Kevin Murphy
Location: One block from mile-long seawall, which leads to "our beautiful Narragansett Beach (10-minute walk)." Set back from the street in the shade of two stately maples. Walk to restaurants, shopping, and cinema. Small boat launch with fishing pier at end of street.

Open: May–October; weekends rest of year. Two-night minimum on peak season weekends, three nights on holiday weekends.
Rates: $50–$60 single, $65–$80 double. $10 more holiday weekends. Discount for one week or longer.
♥ ⅎ ✗ ⅒

> From Connecticut, California, New Jersey, Colorado, Pennsylvania: *"A haven. . . . Everything I dreamed my vacation would be. . . . Simple elegance warmed by Martha's generosity and superb culinary talent. . . . Lovely . . . immaculate . . . Martha was friendly yet gave us the privacy we needed. . . . Daughter likes the Orange Julius. My husband has 'borrowed' Martha's scone recipe. I enjoy everything!"*

Martha's impeccable touches are everywhere—from the fuchsia-colored porch geraniums and front door to the room with Laura Ashley fabrics on the walls and bed. Built in 1894 as a summer residence, it's a comfortable Victorian restored with care by Martha, a teacher and writer, and Kevin, a commercial fisherman and artist. It has oak parquet floors, a massive stone fireplace, Waterford crystal sconces, and antique furnishings; but this B&B's latest claim to fame is the *The Bed & Breakfast Cookbook,* which features hundreds of recipes—submitted from B&Bs all over the country—that Martha tested and guests critiqued. Kevin's scrimshaw pieces, some of which have been exhibited at Mystic Seaport, are etched on cured swordfish swords that have the look of ivory.

In residence: "Some guests never see our two sweet dogs, who live in fenced-in backyard."
Foreign languages spoken: Very little French and German.
Bed and bath: Two third-floor rooms with no common wall. Large private full baths. Queen-bedded room (and its bath) have an ocean view. One room with two twin beds convertible to king.

(Please turn page.)

Breakfast: Full 8:30–9:30; continental 9:30–10:30. Repertoire from "The Book." Fresh fruit in season, juice, pastries, pancakes, French toast or waffles, freshly ground coffee. Murphys' own herbs, vegetables, and raspberries. Presented at table with linen, silver, fresh flowers.
Plus: Third-floor sitting area with lots of sightseeing information. Color TV in each bedroom. Much reading material in guest rooms. Cafe tables on porch. Cookbooks, antique silver, and Kevin's scrimshaw for sale.

The 1900 House
401/789-7971

59 Kingstown Road, Narragansett, RI 02882-3309

Hosts: Bill and Sandra Panzeri
Location: On a side street (Victorian homes) that leads to ocean wall. Five-minute walk to shops, fine dining, historic Towers, ocean beach.
Open: Year round. Two-night minimum May 15–October 15 weekends.

Rates: $60 shared bath. $65 private bath. Singles $10 less. Additional futon $10 per person. Seventh night free May 15–October 15. Off-season, $10 less per room; stay two nights, receive third night free.
♥ ⁂ ✈ ⌇

"Through our own travels we became addicted to the B&B concept, and started our own in 1989. Since we restored this Victorian house and furnished it with treasures of the past, Bill, who coaches middle school girls' softball, has established marvelous flower and vegetable gardens. Guests ask about restaurants, about relocating here—and about our favorite little-known place (South County nature trails). Strangers who met at our breakfast table had, by the time they had consumed the last waffle, made plans to meet in Barcelona, Spain!"

Sandy is a counselor/watercolorist/museum board member.

In residence: Chrys and Fred, two cats restricted from guest rooms.
Bed and bath: Three second-floor rooms. One room with canopied double bed, TV, private bath with claw-foot tub and hand-held shower. Two rooms, each with antique double bed, share shower bath.
Breakfast: 8:30–9:30. Unlimited refills. Juices. Strawberries (from Bill's garden) and cream, or baked stuffed apple. Homemade muffins. Belgian waffles, guavaberry French toast and ham, or tarragon eggs and bacon. Hot beverages (mulled cider, too, in winter). In dining room with wood stove.
Plus: Screened wraparound porch. Guest refrigerator. Outside hot/cold shower. Bike and surfboard storage. Special occasions acknowledged.

From California: *"So wonderful I returned to stay another three nights. . . . Friendly, gracious, helpful . . . layout provided privacy and space . . . wonderful morning kitchen smells."* From New York: *"Filled with family treasures . . . tea and cookies when we came in late at night."*

Newport is just 20 minutes away from Narragansett, a community that has long been known for its beaches.

The Old Clerk House   401/783-8008

49 Narragansett Avenue, Narragansett, RI 02882-3386

Host: Patricia Watkins
Location: One block from Narragansett Beach and mile-long seawall walk. In residential pier section. Six miles to Block Island ferry. Fine restaurants, shops, cinema within four-block radius.

Open: Year round. Two-day minimum on weekends May 1–October 15.
Rates: May 1–October 15 $65 single, $75 double. Off-season $10 less.
♥ ✿ ◆ ✗ ✂

Professional photographers and artists, too, have discovered this house with its gold leaf sign, white picket fence, and lots of flowers, particularly roses. The "warm glow" c. 1890 house, the former home of a succession of town clerks, was completely redone over a period of three years by Pat, a former technical reference specialist with an international development organization. Here she is a computer consultant and Friends of Oceanography board member, and she shares her lovely home with beachgoers and Block Island visitors—and with business guests, who feel comfortable enough to spread out their work on the oak dining room table. The guests' living room has leather sofa and chairs. Guests ask about the clocks, admire the "very English" yard, and request recipes. For someplace different, Pat will suggest "a delightful nearby village huddled around a cove" and "a historic house nestled in a woody hollow with millstream."

In residence: Four cats live in own outdoor quarters in summer. "Max is the car inspector. Persian Miss Moppet is chief inspector of guests and their luggage, if given the opportunity. Pansy, her daughter, was born April Fool's Day, 1990. Tigger is a flame-point Himalayan. Billy is a friendly, quiet collie dog."
Foreign languages spoken: French and "rusty" German.
Bed and bath: Two air-conditioned second-floor rooms, private full baths. Front room with cannonball double bed and twin bed. "Romantic" room with dormer windows, twins/king bed. Both rooms have a color TV.
Breakfast: 7:30–9:30. All "from scratch, no mixes." Menu includes cranberry or orange juice. Fruit. Cereal. Banana bran, lemon poppyseed, apricot almond, or walnut cream cheese muffins. English toast with butter, homemade jams. Crepes with strawberry sauce, mushroom and cheese omelet, French toast, Belgian waffle, or blueberry pancakes.
Plus: Refreshment tray. Acknowledgment of celebrations. Patio with chaises, picnic table with umbrella. Video library. Record and CD player; classical to pop music. Games. Transportation from bus (three blocks away) or from Kingston train station. Half-price beach passes.

The tradition of paying to stay in a private home—with breakfast included in the overnight lodging rate—was revived in time to save wonderful old houses, schools, churches, and barns all over the country from the wrecking ball or commercial development.

The Richards
401/789-7746

144 Gibson Avenue, Narragansett, RI 02882

Hosts: Steven and Nancy Richards
Location: On a quiet, private, dead-end road. One mile from center of town. One-quarter mile from ocean; one mile to beach.
Open: Year round. Two-night mini-

mum stay on weekends; three nights on holiday weekends.
Rates: $80 private bath, $65 shared bath.
♥ ◀ ⅄ ⅃

The gabled 1884 stone house, dubbed "Nancy's dream" from the day she first saw it, has become a destination for many guests. A circular gravel driveway leads to an entrance topped by a copper cupola. The only other house in sight is the former caretaker's house of what was a 20-acre estate. Inside there's a grand 40-foot-long entrance hall (with elevator, no longer used, such as you have never seen); 11 fireplaces; deep windowsills; spectacular kitchen (now); and, every year, more drapes sewn by Nancy, more self-custom-mixed paints, and more gardens too.

Since purchasing the house (that process is part of the interesting history), the Richardses have decorated with Oriental rugs and antiques. And they have established and reestablished gorgeous gardens. "Still, after 16 years of hosting (including 10 in a Narragansett Cape-style house), we are constantly amazed and delighted with guests. One musician, thinking no one was home, sang while she went up and down the steps. Another time we heard great sound from saxophone player. The grounds have been used for wedding photographs."

Steven, weekend co-chef and former director of a state legislature program, is in real estate sales and development.

In residence: Assistant innkeeper daughters are living in Italy this year. Two cats; not allowed in guest areas.
Bed and bath: Four large second-floor rooms, all with working fireplaces. (Inquire if a suite is done and waiting.) One room with king and one with queen canopy bed, each with private bath (tub, hand-held shower). One double-bedded room shares a bath with a room that has two twin-sized antique sleigh beds. Cots available.
Breakfast: 8:30. Fresh fruit. Repertoire may include eggs Florentine, baked apple pancakes, seafood strudel, Steven's johnnycakes, cheese blintzes. Homemade (raspberry) muffins or bread. Freshly ground coffees. In formal dining room under crystal chandelier.
Plus: Working fireplaces everywhere. Guest refrigerator. Library. Down comforters. Patio. Badminton. Sherry. Bench in shade garden. Newport Bridge tokens.

> From Tennessee: *"Stately . . . fantastic breakfasts . . . they obviously enjoy sharing their lovely home and gardens."* From New York: *"A visit to the Richardses is truly a special occasion. Quiet . . . private. . . . A perfect honeymoon retreat."*

---

*I*s B&B *like a hotel?*
How many times have you hugged the doorman?

Stone Lea

401/783-9546

40 Newton Avenue, Narragansett, RI 02882-1368

Hosts: Carol and Ernest Cormier
Location: Surrounded by lawn, on two oceanfront acres. Residential neighborhood. Five-minute drive to beach, 10 minutes to Block Island ferry.
Open: Year round. Two-night minimum on weekends in season.
Rates: Tax included. Memorial Day,

June and September weekends, July and August, $85–$95 queen bed, ocean view. $105 two twins, oceanfront. $125 queen and two twins, oceanfront. $95 double, attached bath. $105 suite with queen and two twins, attached bath. Off-season, $60–$100. $25 third person.
♥ ⬤ ◆ ✈ ⚊

Drive up to the porte cochere of this stone and shingled mansion built in 1884 by McKim, Mead and White, the same architectural firm that designed the Rhode Island state house, the Towers in Narragansett and the Boston Public Library. Enter the grand central hall with its magnificent staircase and English sideboard. Sit on the patio and watch the surf against the rocky shore.

"Stone Lea was a B&B when we fell in love with it seven years ago," says chef Carol. "We sold our company and became full-time hosts. We meet many guests who arrive with plans to do everything. They take nature walks, watch the sunset over the water—and leave, slowed down and unstressed."

Cohost Ernie, "an antique and classic car lover," is volunteer administrator for a nonprofit educational corporation that offers apprenticeships in the metal working industry.

In residence: Brandy, a nine-year-old black dachshund "who thinks guests have come to see him."
Foreign language spoken: French.
Bed and bath: On second and third floors—eight rooms, more simply furnished than common areas. Some rooms oceanfront; others, ocean view. All private full baths (one has shower, no tub); some attached, some in hall. Queen, double, or twin beds.
Breakfast: 8–9:45. Fresh fruit. Juice. Homemade coffee cakes, breads, muffins, or sticky buns. Puffed apple pancakes, French toast, or quiche. At tables for four in fireplaced dining room.
Plus: Upright piano, TV, and vintage pool table (very popular) in enormous antiques-filled living room. Sun room with floor-to-ceiling windows. Croquet. Fruit. Special occasions acknowledged.

> From New York: *"Location reminds me of estates in Ireland. . . . Clocks chiming at different intervals were delightful . . . indescribable breakfast. . . . Used binoculars for the 'spectaculous' view of bay from the picture window. . . . We are still not over having to leave after one heavenly week in Nirvana!"*

---

*U*nless otherwise stated, rates in this book are for two and include breakfast in addition to all the amenities in "Plus."

Swan Cottage

401/783-4391

16 Betty Hill Road, Narragansett, RI 02882

Hosts: Nancy and Bill Bivona
Location: Mesmerizing. Off the beaten path. On Point Judith Pond (known locally as Salt Pond). In residential area with homes built in the 1950s and 60s. Five-minute drive to beach.

Open: Year round. Two-night minimum preferred.
Rates: $65 per room. $15 child on couch or cot. $15 crib.

♥ ♨ ⬛ ❖ ✦ ⅄

When Nancy says, "Look! The world is a hundred diamonds!" she is repeating the comment made by her young daughter (now grown) about the glistening water view.

You feel as if you're on a ship in the huge cathedral-ceilinged, glass-walled living room of this unusual house built in 1951. It has been home to the Bivonas since 1962, when they moved to the area to work at the University of Rhode Island. Through ongoing creative changes, they have retained the original six levels. ("I can't find my room," said one guest upon returning from the beach.) Today there are many antiques "that have survived three kids and 100 of their most intimate friends"; three fireplaces; hardwood floors throughout; extensive landscaping and beautiful gardens—"our passion"; and that view, often complete with blue herons, egrets, swans, gulls, cormorants, loons, ducks, and osprey too.

Foreign language spoken: A little German.
Bed and bath: Four rooms. On uppermost level—waterview room with queen bed (and wicker sofa that sleeps one child) and a double-bedded waterview room share a shower bath. On lowest level—one waterview room with twin beds shares a full bath with room that has high-headboard Victorian double bed and walls of windows overlooking pond.
Breakfast: Until 10. Menu by popular demand. Juice, fresh fruit, dry cereal, coffee cakes and Danish, herbal teas, gourmet-flavored coffees, skim and whole milk and cream. On patio, on lawn by water, in greenhouse, or in fireplaced dining room.
Plus: TV. Restaurant recommendations. Guest refrigerator. Guests' den.

Anna's Victorian Connection Lighthouse

Newport, RI

Location: On a small Narragansett Bay island "with the best views of the bay." A mile from Newport and Jamestown; just south of Newport Bridge.
Reservations: Year round through Anna's Victorian Connection, page 306. (If the weather is too rough, Anna's Victorian Connection will arrange for mainland accommodations.)
Rates: May–September weekends

$140 double, $115 single; weekdays (excluding holidays) $115 double, $90 single. Rest of year $25 less. Foundation members ($15 individual, $30 families) $20 less. Apartment booked by the week ($600) in summer; monthly, rest of year. Transportation (extra charge) via scheduled launch. Mainland parking fee charged in season.

♥ ❖ ✦ ⅄

Fall asleep to the sound of waves, foghorn, and bell buoy. Wake up in your high brass bed to a fantastic view of the boat-filled bay. Since 1992 these cozy overnight accommodations complete with turn-of-the-century ambiance have been discovered by romantics, historians, and adventurers.

Here, away from it all, is this two-storied 1869 mansard-roofed house topped by a light tower that was deactivated in 1971. Thanks to the nonprofit Rose Island Lighthouse Foundation, the property has been restored as a public site and self-sufficient environmental center. (Some summer day-trippers come for a picnic, bird-watching, and a tour of the working lighthouse and the grounds.) Now the first floor has an in-floor radiant heating system. The small museum area has natural history exhibits in addition to photographs and memorabilia that have been provided by grandsons of two long-term lighthouse keepers.

Bed and bath: Two first-floor waterview rooms, each with an extra-long double bed, share a WC that has an "ecologically sound pump-your-own toilet." (Full bath available at mainland Seamen's Institute.) Second-floor keeper's apartment has a room with queen bed and sofa bed; one huge kitchen/living/dining room with microwave, wood stove for heat, gas cooking stove, refrigerator; hot and cold running water, tiled full bath.
Breakfast: Juice, muffins, fruit, cereal, coffee, tea, cocoa. Serve yourself. (Use of gas hot plate or outdoor grill, old-fashioned ice box; ice provided in warm weather.)
Plus: Summer outdoor solar shower. Down comforters.

Bluestone

401/846-5408

33 Russell Street, Newport, RI 02840-1723

Hosts: Cindy and Roger Roberts
Location: A quiet residential area. A mile from downtown Newport.
Open: Year round. Two-night minimum stay on weekends, three-night on holiday weekends.

Rates: March 15–November 15, $75 and $95. November 15–March 15, $65–$75.
◆ ✖

Country Almanac magazine photographed the country store decor in this 1905 Victorian, which was owned by one family until the Robertses bought it in 1983. "It is like stepping back to a quieter time, and just the right place for our collections of country antiques and refinished furniture." Natural woodwork is throughout. The focal point is an old Newport store tobacco case filled with Bennington pottery.

When the Robertses lived in Massachusetts, Cindy was in restaurant and hotel management work. Roger, the gardener, is a retired electrical lineman. "We are Newport natives who moved back here with the idea of having a rooming house. When friends sent us our first (unplanned) B&B guests, we were hooked!" Soon Cindy found herself was placing so many overflow guests with selected private home B&Bs that she established a reservation service (described on page 306).

In residence: One dog, Ms. Daisy, a Shar Pei. Grandchildren, ages 12–24, are occasional visitors.

(Please turn page.)

Bed and bath: Two air-conditioned rooms. One large room with double bed, private shower bath. One with queen bed, private full bath.
Breakfast: 8–9:30. Entree might be strawberry waffles with fresh whipped cream, strata, or Monte Cristo French toast. Served in dining room surrounded by stoneware, samplers, baskets, and quilts.
Plus: Beverages. Porch. Yard. Will meet guests at the Newport bus. Guest refrigerator for beverages only.

Guests wrote: *"Proved that it takes more than interesting antiques to run a B&B . . . friendly, kind . . . marvelous cook . . . knowledge of sights, shops, restaurants, and activities helped us make efficient use of limited time."*

Cliffside Inn

2 Seaview Avenue, Newport, RI 02840

401/847-1811
800/845-1811
fax 401/848-5850

Hosts: Annette and Norbert Mede
Location: In a quiet residential area, a half block from Cliff Walk. Six blocks to Bellevue Avenue mansions; 15 minutes' walk to waterfront, 5 to First Beach.
Open: Year round. Two-night minimum May–October weekends; re-quested for other weekends.
Rates: Queen bed $125 with shower bath, $155 tub/shower, $185 whirlpool or steam bath. $205 queen or king with whirlpool or in suites. $20 less November–April weekdays. Amex, Diners, MC, Visa.

♥ ❖ ◆ ✗ ✄

What became known as "one of Newport's best-kept secrets," thanks to a reader of this book, is a haven—sort of a small hotel—for romantics and art lovers too. It is filled with period furnishings and decorated with wonderful wallcoverings and fabrics. "Good Morning America" and *Country Inns* magazine have featured the works of Beatrice Turner, who lived and painted in the house for the first half of this century. Reproductions of her self-portraits are throughout the high-ceilinged, bay-windowed summer "cottage," which was built in 1880 by the governor of Maryland.

Norbert and Annette had experience in the hospitality industry in California. In 1992 they became innkeepers for Win Baker, Cliffside's owner, who has researched the few remaining Turner works. Since then, the Medes have become immersed in the history of the artist, the house, and Newport.

Bed and bath: Twelve rooms; some are suites. Four with working fireplaces; all with air conditioning plus ceiling or window fan. All rooms pictured on rate card (call 800 number). King, queen (one canopied), one or two double beds, or two twins. On three floors. All private baths; some with whirlpool; some shower only. One room with king bed, cathedral ceiling, four skylights, French doors to whirlpool bath and shower.
Breakfast: 8–10. Homemade granola, muffins, and coffee cakes. Fruit. Yogurt. Quiche, French toast, eggs Benedict, walnut pancakes or waffles. Freshly squeezed orange juice. Freshly ground coffee.
Plus: Individual thermostats. Afternoon hors d'oeuvres. Front porch. Beach towels. Bicycle storage. Off-street parking.

From Georgia: *"Grand and wonderful."*

1855 Marshall Slocum House

29 Kay Street, Newport, RI 02840-2735

401/841-5120
401/846-3787
800/372-5120

Host: Joan Wilson
Location: Canopied by a copper beech, on a street of Victorian homes. Five-minute walk to waterfront, shops, beaches, and harbor.
Open: Year round. Reservations preferred. Two-night minimum on

summer weekends, three nights on holidays.
Rates: (Include lobster dinner with three-day midweek stay.) Per room. $80 shared bath. $90 private half bath. Amex, Visa.
✿ ✹

"Yes, this really is my home, but it has turned out to be home away from home for sailors, students, writers, artists, croquet players, musicians, and lots of international visitors . . . every one with an interesting tale to tell, and many return every year . . . I've tried to take breakfast to state of the art. Guests have shared their expertise, and I share my recipes, some of which are painted on the kitchen wall tiles."

Before buying this restored Victorian in 1985, Joan managed an orange grove in Florida. And then there was a short interlude as a travel agent. Now she is a craftswoman who makes jam, reads, fishes in the Florida keys, and visits children and grandchildren in California and Europe. Her friendly house is furnished with family heirlooms, antiques, and collectibles.

In residence: One cat, Buttons, "a true professional in the feline world of hospitality who graciously accepts pats from kitty lovers."
Bed and bath: Five large rooms, one skylit, on two floors; two with private half bath. Three shared full guest baths, one with claw-foot tub, shower, sink set in antique server. Queen, double, or twin beds.
Breakfast: 8–10. (Coffee earlier.) Perhaps Belgian waffles with fresh strawberries or peach French toast. Plus homemade bread, fruit, juice, cereal. Served in dining room or on back deck overlooking large shaded backyard.
Plus: Afternoon refreshments. Off-street parking. Bedrooms have ceiling or window fans. Down comforters and pillows. Library. Front porch rockers. Parlor with TV, VCR, movies (including *The Great Gatsby*) made in Newport. Dinner and picnics (extra charge) by request.

From South Africa: *"An ideal base during my visit, which was in connection with a book I was writing . . . [located] in an attractive and quiet part of town . . . tastefully furbished and well run . . . Joan Wilson is a most friendly and knowledgeable person . . . breakfast a full and tasty meal."*

☀

"A genial greeting? The only person around was a workman on a ladder, so I left," read one complaint. "Bernice, I was the workman," replied the innkeeper/handyman/chef.

Elm Tree Cottage

336 Gibbs Avenue, Newport, RI 02840

401/849-1610
800/882-3ELM

Hosts: Thomas and Priscilla Malone **Location:** On a lovely acre of land in estate neighborhood, 1½ blocks from the ocean and Cliff Walk. Within 15-minute walk of restaurants. One mile from mansions. **Open:** Year round. Two-night weekend minimum; three on July and August, holiday, and special event weekends. **Rates:** Memorial Day through October, weekdays $150–$300; weekends $150, $185, $300 (Windsor Room). Off-season, weekdays $100–$225; weekends $135, $165, $250. ♣ ⋈ ⅄

A true story that sounds a bit like fantasy. Two personable Long Island stained glass artists/designers (for religious, commercial, and residential buildings) fell in love with Newport and innkeeping. In 1989, when they were substitute innkeepers for one week, they took time for a bicycle ride and found this 1882 Shingle Style summer "cottage" surrounded by weeds and in need of everything. A year later, having used their talents, skills, and advanced degrees in interior design, fine arts, and woodworking, they furnished with fine antiques from auctions and estate sales. And soon after its opening, the elegant B&B, with a marvelous open-style floor plan, was discovered by the staff of *Mirabella* magazine. The spacious (enormous) and gracious (welcoming) living room—with grand piano and Oriental rugs—overlooks Easton Pond and First Beach. The hosts' eye for color, design, and texture is everywhere—in linens and fabrics in English and French country styling, in the window treatments and Louis XV French beds. To this day the rooms keep getting more lavish. Here the cuisine, too, is a fine art.

In residence: In hosts' quarters, three daughters—Keely, 12; Briana, 9; Erin, 7.
Bed and bath: Five second-floor rooms—with more stained glass windows each year. All private baths. Windsor Room, 39 by 20 feet, with king crown-canopied bed, fine linen, crystal-chandeliered full bath, working fireplace, two living room arrangements, winter water views. Queen beds in three rooms, two with working fireplace. Room with king, working fireplace, private bath across the hall. Rollaway available.
Breakfast: 8:30–9:30, Sundays until 10. Intentionally special. Fruit. Homemade breads, muffins, and granola. Perhaps fruit-stuffed crepes, French bread/toast with amaretto syrup, sausage in puff pastry, or fresh fruit in wine custard. Served at candlelit dining room tables set with flowers, lace, and china.
Plus: Air-conditioned bedrooms. Floor fans. Coffee always available. Mints. Amenities basket. BYOB bar. By request, tour of hosts' workshop. Off-street parking.

From New York: *"Rooms are romantic and exquisitely done. Tom and Priscilla made our vacation perfect."* Another from New York: *"Best business trip in ten years. . . . Can't wait to return to the beautiful home for a vacation."*

B&Bs offer the opportunity to get away without going away.

Flag Quarters   401/849-4543
54 Malbone Road, Newport, RI 02840-1746

Hosts: Joan and Rich Hulse
Location: On a corner in a residential neighborhood. About a 15-minute walk to shops, restaurants, and harbor.
Open: Year round. Two-day minimum, June–September weekends.

Rates: January–March, $75. April–May, $85. June–October 15, $95–$110. October 16–January 1, $85–$95. Amex, Diners, MC, Visa.
♥ ⫱ ♦ ✕ ⚮

One guest called the breakfast "culinary artistry." Another wrote, "The Vanderbilts can have their mansions. We can't wait to return here." Many comment on the "romantic rooms," which are decorator-finished with drapes, wall-to-wall carpeting, some antiques, some reproductions.

Rich, a retired navy captain and carrier pilot, is an international marketing representative in the defense industry. Joan, a native Newporter who has taught English in four states, has a flair for silk and dried flower arranging that is growing into a secondary business. "Our first-time weekend guests find they can't 'do all of Newport.' We assist with the high spots and save some of the out-of-the-way places for veterans. Ever since our stays in European B&Bs, we wanted to run our own with all the warm fuzzies together with the privacy and amenities of a hotel. Five years ago we found this 1880 former gardener's house, perfect for suites and a landscaped yard."

Foreign language spoken: "Minimal German."
Bed and bath: Via private exterior entrance and onto an interior narrow former servants' staircase to two third-floor suites. Each has tall slanted ceilings, double bed, scented lace or embroidered linens, satin quilt, private shower bath, living room area.
Breakfast: 8:30–9. In a Victorian basket with lace and Wedgwood china; left at your door with bell announcement. Juice, fruits in silver compote, baked goods. Entree might be eggs in pastry shell with bacon or baked apple-rum French toast. Coffee or tea.
Plus: Air conditioning. Individual thermostat. Ceiling fans. Color TV with movie channel. Private phone. Small refrigerator. Microwave. Perrier on silver tray with crystal glasses. Mints. Forgotten-items basket. At Christmas, award-winning decor with candle lights in every window. Off-street parking.

From New York: *"Enchanting. . . . Felt spoiled. . . . Magical."*

Hydrangea House Inn
16 Bellevue Avenue, Newport, RI 02840-3206

401/846-4435
800/945-4667
fax 401/846-4435

Hosts: Grant Edmondson and Dennis Blair

Location: On top of Newport's historic hill (in center of walking district), with brick sidewalks, gas lighting, old trees, and shops. Across from Viking Hotel. Five-minute walk to harbor, 10 to first mansion on Bellevue Avenue and to the beach.

Open: Year round. Two-night minimum on weekends.

Rates: May through October, $89 and $125 double bed, $139 two doubles or one queen. $15 extra person. Off-season, $55–85 double, $95 queen. Deposit required. MC, Visa.

♥ ♠ ✿ ♦ ✕ ⚡

A transformation by Newport antiques dealers. Here in an 1876 building that was, in 1988, shops, apartments, and offices, is a gracious B&B—"not a mansion"—created by Dennis, a former customer service administrator, and Grant, a former construction company owner.

Now the first floor is a contemporary fine arts gallery, the breakfast room for overnight guests. Antiques, sculpture, paintings, fine fabrics, and attention to detail are throughout. In the rear, a 500-square-foot veranda overlooks hydrangea gardens. It's the "special place with a welcome mat out for new friends" that Grant and Dennis imagined during their long property search.

In residence: Two cats. "Miss Kitty is suave and sophisticated. Chester is fat and lazy."

Bed and bath: Six carpeted second- and third-floor rooms. All private baths; some full, some shower only. Queen or double beds. One room has two double beds.

Breakfast: 8:30–9:30. Homemade everything. Freshly squeezed juice. Fruit salad. Granola. Raspberry pancakes or seasoned egg entree. English muffins and breads. "Our own blend of coffee." In gallery or on veranda.

Plus: Air-conditioned bedrooms. Down comforters. Afternoon refreshments. Crystal water glasses. Fresh flowers. Bedtime chocolate chip cookies and milk. Guest refrigerator. Picnic baskets ($12). Spontaneous "turn-of-the-century gossip." Off-street parking. Tour bus, city bus, and airport shuttle leave from the door.

From France: *"Un charmant petit nid."*

Inn at Old Beach
19 Old Beach Road, Newport, RI 02840

401/849-3479
fax 401/847-1236

Hosts: Luke and Cyndi Murray

Location: In a lovely residential neighborhood just around the corner from Newport Art Museum. Seven-minute walk to harbor, shops, restaurants; 10 minutes to mansions or beach.

Open: Year round. Two-night weekend minimum April–June, September, October; three nights on weekends in July and August and on holidays.

Rates: Per room. $125–$135 May–October. $100–$110 April and November. $75–$95 December–March. $20 third person. Amex, MC, Visa.

♥ ✿ ✕

Flair everywhere. And an obvious love of design, flowers (and floral prints), whimsy—and people. The 1879 Gothic Victorian was just what the Murrays were looking for shortly after they were married in 1989. Since, they have enlarged their collection of antiques and hand-painted furniture; and they've done wonderful things to the yard, which now has a pond and gazebo backed by a fabulous remodeled carriage house complete with carriage lights.

In addition to innkeeping, Cyndi gardens and is full-time manager at the University of Rhode Island oceanography information center. Her mother has created the curtains and duvets, the dolls and cloth rabbits. Multifaceted Luke is bar manager at the Black Pearl Restaurant.

In residence: In carriage house, Callan, two-year-old son.
Bed and bath: Seven rooms, all private baths, all with deep wall-to-wall carpeting. Main house—first-floor room with queen bed, private full bath. On second floor: queen or double bed; one full bath, three shower baths. Three rooms with working fireplace or stove. In carriage house—private exterior entrance for each of two queen-bedded rooms, each with shower bath, individual thermostat, TV. Rollaway available.
Breakfast: 8:30–10. Freshly squeezed juice, fresh fruit and yogurt, granola, locally made baked goods, toast-your-own bread and bagels, coffee, tea. At individual tables in elegant dining room; French doors lead onto flower-filled back porch overlooking grounds.
Plus: Fireplaced living, sitting, and dining rooms. Air conditioning in six guest rooms. Chocolates. Patio with wrought iron chairs. Transportation to/from bus. Off-street parking.

The Melville House

39 Clarke Street, Newport RI 02840-3023

401/847-0640
fax 401/847-0956

Hosts: Vincent DeRico and David Horan
Location: Terrific. On a quiet one-block-long street with many restored colonial houses. One block from harbor. Around corner from shops and restaurants. Short walk to Touro Synagogue and Trinity Church.
Open: Year round. Two-night minimum on weekends, three nights on holidays and events.
Rates: Memorial Day weekend–mid-September: Friday, Saturday, holidays $95 shared bath, $110 private; mid-week $85 shared, $95 private. January–March, November, December: weekends/holidays $55 shared, $60 private; midweek $45 shared, $50 private. April: weekends/holidays $60 shared, $70 private; midweek $50 shared, $55 private. May and mid-September–October: weekends/holidays $80 shared, $90–$95 private; midweek $70 shared, $80 private. Singles $5 less. Amex, MC, Visa.
♥ ❖ ◆ ✗ ✂

Attractive and welcoming. It's an unpretentious restored 1750 house with oak pieces, braided rugs, lace curtains, and collectibles. This "historic and urban" established B&B—dubbed a mini-museum by one guest—is just what Dave (an endangered species biologist who has attended chef training school) and Vince, both former national park rangers and restaurant managers, were looking for in 1993.

(Please turn page.)

In residence: Dewey and Spike, "friendly brother and sister cats from a Vermont farm."
Bed and bath: Seven rooms. A first-floor double-bedded room has private shower bath. On second floor, four rooms, each with a double bed, have private shower baths. A large shower bath is shared by one double-bedded room and one with two twin beds, nonworking fireplace.
Breakfast: 8–10. Homemade granola and yogurt. Muffins, corn bread, homemade bread, scones, cinnamon buns, bagels. On weekends, Rhode Island johnnycakes, crepes, stuffed French toast or quiche.
Plus: Fireplaced living room. Complimentary 4–6 p.m. tea, sherry, and homemade biscotti. Use of gas grill. Sometimes, hosted barbecues here. Off-street parking. Recommendations for a secluded beach and "the best undiscovered restaurant."

> From Florida: *"It felt good to have two friends in Newport."* From Michigan: *"Absolutely delightful. Full of country charm."* From Sweden: *"Excellent. Well kept."* From California: *"Superb food."*

Polly's Place   401/847-2160
349 Valley Road, Route 214, Newport, RI 02840

Host: Polly Canning
Location: On the Newport-Middletown line, a mile from Newport harbor. On Route 214, set back from the road. Fronted by split rail fence and rose bushes. In back, large backyard and brook.

Open: Year round. Two-night minimum July and August weekends.
Rates: Memorial Day–September 30, $75 and $80. Off-season, $50–$65.
♥ 🏶 ❖ ◆ ✈

As a Newport Realtor and B&B hostess, Polly has met many America's Cup and other sailing crew members as well as croquet players who participated in championship games. Her own extensive travels have taken her as far as Australia, where she visited some guests who have stayed in her comfortably furnished extended Cape house.

"Sometimes guests linger in the kitchen or on the deck. They enjoy sitting on the Adirondack chairs in the yard, under the weeping willow by the brook. I love to bake and to garden and to suggest cycling routes, picnic spots, or concerts. It's a good feeling to see people who arrive as strangers leave as friends."

Bed and bath: Four rooms. Two first-floor rooms, one with a double, one with two twin beds, share a shower bath. On second floor, two large rooms, each with king-sized bed, private full bath. Plus suite with kitchen.
Breakfast: 8–9:30. Strawberry waffles, stuffed French toast, garden quiche, or frittatas. Juices, fruit salad, yogurt, cereal, breads, homemade muffins and jams, coffee, tea. In dining room or on deck overlooking yard and brook, birds, and sometimes fox.
Plus: Egg-crate foam on all beds. Bedroom ceiling fans. Down comforters. Fresh flowers. Thick towels. Sometimes, in season, take-home veggies from the garden. Living room with brick fireplace and grandfather clock. A delicious parting gift.

> From Philadelphia: *"Gracious hostess. Clean, comfortable, beautiful surroundings. Very quiet and relaxing."*

Rhode Island House　　　　401/848-7787
77 Rhode Island Avenue, Newport, RI 02840-2761

Hosts: Michael Dupré and John Rich
Location: Quiet Victorian estate neighborhood. Ten-minute walk to beaches, Cliff Walk, mansions; 15 to shops and waterfront.
Open: Year round. Two-night minimum on weekends, three nights on holidays.

Rates: Memorial Day–Labor Day weekdays $115 (for room with tub, no shower) to $185, weekends $135–$200. Off-season weekdays $85–$145, weekends $105–$165. Vary according to amenities.
🛥 ⁂ 🎿 ⚵

Timing. A big, beautiful, light-filled private Victorian house with multipaned wide bay windows, many fireplaces, paneled French doors to large common rooms, and arched hallways. All done over with new wiring et al. 10 years ago. All for sale in 1993 when Michael, a classical French and contemporary chef with experience at Hammersmith Farm and other Newport estates, and John, a university career counselor with some inn-sitting experience, were interested in opening a B&B.

Furnishings are a combination of family antiques and treasures and auction finds—rattan, Chippendale, and Americana, with paintings and some bronze sculptures. There's a Garden Room, an Auchincloss Room, a Hunter Room with lots of leather, and a color-filled dining room. Windows have sheers and lace; some have "treatments." John is the official perennial and herb gardener. Off-season, Michael offers cooking classes here.

Foreign languages spoken: French and Spanish.
Bed and bath: Five carpeted second-floor rooms with queen beds (two are four-posters), all private baths. All firm custom bedding with designer linens. Some rooms with nonworking fireplace, separate dressing area, separate marble and mirrored Jacuzzi room. One bath has shower only, one has tub only.
Breakfast: 8:30–10. (Coffee at 7:30.) Buffet sideboard with fresh fruit, granola, juice, homemade breads, muffins. Individually prepared hot entrees such as eggs Florentine, blueberry/lemon French toast, cheese souffle, sometimes served by John's three teenage daughters. In fireplaced color-filled dining room.
Plus: Fireplaced living room, library, morning room. Late-afternoon tea available. Fresh fruit. Mints. Cookie jar. Turndown service. Beach towels. Picnic baskets arranged. Off-street parking. Video tour of Hammersmith Farm showing Michael preparing a formal dinner there.

Stella Maris Inn　　　　401/849-2862
91 Washington Street, Newport, RI 02840-1531

Hosts: Dorothy and Ed Madden
Location: In the historic, quiet Point section, across from a small park overlooking the bay. On about an acre of land with beach and sycamore trees. Within 10 minutes' walk of harbor.
Open: Year round. Two-night mini-

mum, May–October weekends.
Rates: Per room. November–April, $75 room with garden view, $85 room with bay view. May–October, $125 ($75 weekdays) garden view, $150 ($85 weekdays) bay view.
♥ ⁂

(Please turn page.)

It's a big beautiful French Victorian mansion built as a summer residence in 1861 with Connecticut fieldstone and, throughout, 13-foot ceilings. A convent for about 60 years—and unoccupied most of the late 1980s—the structure was purchased and renovated completely by the Maddens, including one son who is an architect and another who restores old houses. Before opening here in 1990, Dorothy and Ed had a smaller B&B in Newport, and one on Cape Cod before that.

Dorothy, an antiques dealer when the six grown children were younger, has decorated with Victorian antiques, many upholstered pieces, fine art, and French lace. Here she combines her loves of "people and cooking." Ed, an orthopedic surgeon, cohosts in evenings and on weekends.

Bed and bath: Eight large rooms on second and third floors; all with private baths, some shower only. All with queen beds except two with two twin beds. Four rooms with working fireplaces. Rollaway available.

Breakfast: 8–9:30. Juices, fresh fruit, cereals, homemade breads and muffins, coffee, tea, milk. In formal dining room with fireplace or on porch overlooking the bay.

Plus: Wraparound porch with garden and sunset views. Fireplaced living room. TV. Late-afternoon wine or tea. Ceiling fans in guest rooms. Off-street parking.

From Massachusetts: *"The Maddens are the nicest people! . . . breakfast table set with a banquet of foods . . . stimulating conversation . . . beautifully decorated in an understated style."* From California: *"Wonderful respite from usual business trip stays."*

Anna's Victorian Connection Host #193

Providence, RI

Location: In a diverse neighborhood that is home to many college faculty members. Less than a mile to Brown University or Rhode Island School of Design.
Reservations: Year round through

Anna's Victorian Connection, page 306. Two-night minimum on graduation and parents' weekends.
Rates: $55 single, $65 double, $10 third person.

♥ ⬛ ✗ ✂

Books, art, and photographs are everywhere in this 1904 14-room shingled house, home to a host who has just experienced her first "graduate" guests—parents who began to stay here when their child began college.

This is a home away from home. It has a light and airy first floor that has leaded and stained glass windows; archways instead of doorways; refinished furniture; a wonderful sense of color and space; and art that reminds the host of previous residences in Japan and France and "all over the United States." When in Florida she was an art critic. Here she teaches academic writing at Rhode Island College and at Boston University. And she is active in the Green Party.

Bed and bath: Three second-floor rooms with Laura Ashley linens. "Honeymoon suite" is a queen-bedded room with working fireplace and private full bath. Double-bedded room (with sink) and room with two twin beds share a full bath. Cot available.

Breakfast: Usually around 8:30. Juice or fruit. Homemade muffins and scones. Coffee. Teas.

Plus: Fireplaced living room. Wicker-furnished enclosed porch. TV and VCR. Laundry facilities. Restaurant menus. Off-street parking.

Admiral Dewey Inn

401/783-2090
800/457-2090

668 Matunuck Beach Road
South Kingstown, RI 02879-7021

Host: Joan LeBel
Location: In a small village, one straight mile from Route 1, 75 yards to the surf and great beach with boardwalk. Fifteen-minute walk to wildlife refuge. Ten miles to University of Rhode Island; half mile to Theatre-By-The-Sea; 20 miles to Mystic, Connecticut, and Newport; 4 to Block Island ferry.

Open: Year round. Two-night minimum on weekends May–November.
Rates: May–November, $80–$120. December–April, $40–$60. Single 15 percent less. $20 rollaway. Amex, Discover, MC, Visa.
♥ ♣ ♦ ✻ ✮

If you arrive on the wraparound porch and tell Joan that you drove beyond the inn to the dead end point, turned around, and found the (lovely oval) sign facing the wrong way, she'll respond that the local landscaper put it that way "because it's right architecturally, and besides," he said, "they'll see it on the way back."

That sign is in front of a Victorian showcase, a former beach boarding-house, a plumbingless wreck in 1987. Saved from demolition by the LeBels who had the 137-ton house moved onto a new foundation (see pictorial history album), it now has indoor baths, claw-footed tables, brass and tall-headboard beds, overstuffed living room chairs, Victorian wallpaper, and lace curtains. Joan, a former antiques dealer and Realtor who has taught in Hawaii, Japan, and Europe, furnished the inn with fine old pieces.

In residence: "Brat and Cat, twin black fluffy litter mates." Joan smokes.
Foreign languages spoken: Polish and French.
Bed and bath: Ten rooms, each furnished in a different period; most with ocean view. Eight with private shower bath. Two share a full bath. Queen, double, or twin beds. Rollaway available.
Breakfast: 8:30–11. Buffet on 1840s table. Fresh fruit, juices, homemade breads and muffins, English muffins or bagels, coffee and tea.
Plus: Fruit, beverages, munchies always available. Outside shower. Beach towels. Down comforters. Special occasions acknowledged. Pickup at Amtrak station or Westerly airport. Porch rockers. Off-street parking.

> Guests wrote: *"Ten plus . . . great haven near a spectacular beach . . . spacious, clean, comfortable . . . absolutely delightful innkeeper . . . like your favorite aunt . . . wonderful food. . . . Highly recommended."*

According to guests (many are preservationists and/or house restorers), there ought to be a medal for the meticulous work—everything from research to labor—done by B&B owners. Indeed, many have won preservation awards.

The Cookie Jar Bed & Breakfast   401/539-2680

64 Kingstown Road, Route 138   (U.S./Canada) **800/767-4262**
Wyoming, RI 02895-9710

Hosts: Dick and Madelein Sohl
Location: Set back from two-lane Route 138, main road to nearby University of Rhode Island (10 minutes) and Newport (35 minutes). Fifteen minutes northeast of Westerly and northwest of South Kingstown; 25 to Block Island ferry; less than a mile from I-95.

Reservations: Year round. Two-night minimum on summer weekends; three nights on holidays.
Rates: $60 queen or twin room. $65 (two people) second-floor room; $15 extra person. Singles 10 percent less; November 15–April 15, 20 percent less.
♯ ⌂ ❖ ♦ ✗ ⊱

One five-year-old guest adopted Dick as "Grandpa." Since, the Sohls have visited him in California!

Dick is the chief cook and bottle washer (and an old-house renovator/perfectionist) and has had considerable experience as a hotel manager, accountant, and furniture manufacturer. Madelein, a former nun, teaches psychiatric nursing at the Community College of Rhode Island.

Their immaculate, homey farmhouse began in 1732 as a blacksmith shop on a plantation. The original wood ceiling, hand-hewn beams, and granite walls remain in the living room. The forge has been replaced by a large stone fireplace built by an American Indian stonemason. Today the property has two homes, a barn, and a swimming pool. One of the three acres is grass. Among "Grandpa's" latest projects: 50 fruit trees, grapevines, berry bushes and a flower garden.

Bed and bath: Three rooms. On first floor, one queen-bedded room and one with two twin four-poster beds; both are handicapped accessible and have a sink. They share a huge bath that has shower with bench seat. On second floor, room with a double and a king bed, sink in room, private shower bath.
Breakfast: 8–10. Select from menu night before. Juice. Cereal. Waffles, pancakes, or eggs, bacon or sausage, toast or blueberry muffin. In season, homegrown fruits. Coffee and tea.
Plus: Fireplaced living room. Porch, sun room. A 29-foot (diameter) in-ground circular pool.

The Gardner House   401/789-1250

629 Main Street, Wakefield, RI 02879-4012

Hosts: Nan and Will Gardner
Location: On two acres along what was known as Old Post Road. Bordered by stone walls, rhododendron, and woodlands. Two miles to beach, Block Island ferry, summer theater, fishing villages. Five minutes to University of Rhode Island, 20 to Newport, 40 to Mystic Seaport. Near wildlife sanctuary and fine restaurants.

Open: Year round. Two-night minimum on summer weekends and during holidays and URI commencement.
Rates: Tax included. $65 twins, $75 double, $85 suite. $10 child as third occupant. Deposit required for one-night stay.
♥ ♯ ⌂ ✗ ⊱

What a pleasure to visit with the Gardners in what one guest rightfully dubbed "a happy house." Nan speaks of "this gem of a history-filled 1818 Federal period house," which have been their home since 1986. It is the perfect place for sharing art, music, garden horticulture—and "collections of yesteryear, everything from birdcages to rocking horses—gathered over 42 years." (*Country Interiors* and *Decorating* photographed many for a Christmas feature.)

Next to people, Nan, a former antiques shop owner who has a flair for displaying and utilizing hundreds of fascinating items, specializes in designing rugs and teaching rug braiding. Will, retired from the telephone company, is "full-time pool cleaner, creative handyman, and internationally known chef." (It's true.) Nearly every guest—from 30 countries and 45 states—is in their photo album.

Bed and bath: Three rooms (with stool for climbing into the highest antique bed). All private baths. On second floor, one room with antique cannonball bed, adjoining room-sized full bath. One room with antique double bed, full bath, adjoining room with twin bed. Third-floor room has two twin beds, tub bath.
Breakfast: 8–9. Menu varies daily. Fruits, tipsy toast, "dreamboats," Belgian waffles. Homemade muffins. Rhode Island johnnycakes with Rhode Island maple syrup, eggs, bacon, ham, sausage. "Best coffee around." Served by candlelight with music and fresh flowers.
Plus: In-ground pool (with a necessary set of rules). Porch. Many books. Down comforters. Spectacular gardens near house, around pool, in woodlands—everywhere.

Grandview Bed & Breakfast

212 Shore Road, Westerly, RI 02891

401/596-6384
fax: call to activate
800/447-6384

Host: Patricia Grande
Location: High on a hill, set back from Route 1A, overlooking Block Island Sound and Winnapaug Pond. Within walking distance of golf courses and tennis courts; short drive to beaches, restaurants, Newport, Mystic Seaport, Foxwoods Casino.
Open: Year round. Advance reservations required. Two-night mini-

mum on weekends Memorial Day–Labor Day.
Rates: $75–$95 Memorial Day–Labor Day, $60–$80 off-season. Families in more than one room and senior citizens and returning guests, 10 percent less. $15 extra person. Amex, MC, Visa.
♥ ♨ ⬛ ⁂ ◆ ✗ ⅄

Guests wrote to me about "the quintessential hostess . . . perfect spot . . . good food . . . unpretentious . . . comfortable and spotlessly clean rooms . . . a brilliant choice for our family reunion . . . for our wedding . . . a 4:30 a.m. coffeepot for my fisherman husband . . . the 'at home' place to book our actors and theater guests . . . a base for our birding group." Retreat groups have been known to break into song before each discussion or art session.

The inn consists of a main house that, legend says, was moved from Connecticut by barge and a wing built in 1910. Pat, a library trustees' board member and former chamber of commerce president, was a teacher before working in broadcasting. In 1986 she fell in love with this "big house with wraparound stone porch and ocean view," and innkeeping became her third career.

(Please turn page.)

In residence: Nike, a black Labrador retriever, an outdoor dog, "sulks on summer Sunday afternoons when guests leave."
Bed and bath: Ten rooms (one suite possibility) with a double or two twin beds. Some with porch and/or water view. Private baths for four annex rooms. Private shower baths for the two third-floor main house rooms with sitting room. On second floor, room with double bed and one with two twins and cable TV share a full bath. Two double-bedded oceanview rooms share a bath. Rollaway available.
Breakfast: 8–9:30. Fresh fruit pies, strawberry shortcake, blueberry cobbler, or hot cranberry apple crisp with whipped cream. Freshly baked muffins, bagels, English muffins, jams, fruit, yogurt, cereals, juices, coffee, tea. Buffet on sun porch or on open wraparound porch.
Plus: Welcoming beverage. Fruit. Living room fieldstone fireplace. Family room in wing with player piano, cable TV, games. Lounge chairs on spacious grounds. Outside shower. Babysitting with notice. Fax available.

From New York: *"To me, it is a place to relax and be surrounded by (new) friends. To my son, it is a place to explore inside and out. To him, it is a wonder."*

The Villa

190 Shore Road, Westerly, RI 02891

401/596-1054
800/722-9240

Host: Jerry Maiorano
Location: On 1.5 landscaped acres with gardens, fruit trees, spacious lawns. Along scenic Route 1A. Five minutes to Watch Hill; 1½ miles to beaches; 20 minutes to Mystic, Connecticut; 50 to Newport.
Open: Year round. Two-night minimum on summer weekends and holidays.

Rates: Memorial Day–Labor Day weekends, shared bath $95 and $105; private bath $105; Jacuzzi suite $150; fireplace suite $165; midweek 20 percent less. Off-season weekends $75, suites $135; less midweek. Singles $5 less; additional person $15. Amex, MC, Visa.
♥ ⁂ ◆

A villa indeed—with archways, porticoes, and verandas. It's a Dutch Colonial with Mediterranean flair complete with pool surrounded by deck, umbrella tables, and glorious gardens established by Jerry's father.

When Jerry bought the house 20 years ago, he was an engineer. A call from a Watch Hill inn with overflow guests changed his career. In season, there's a complimentary Thursday evening poolside buffet; on off-season Saturdays, coffee and dessert; year round, "loving Italian hospitality."

In residence: Blackie, a Boston bull terrier, visits frequently.
Foreign language spoken: Italian.
Breakfast: 8–10:30. After 6 a.m. coffee brought to room by request. Orange juice, cereals, homemade muffins or sweet breads, toast-your-own bagels, freshly ground coffees, teas, hot chocolate. In your room, in informal poolside cafe, or by pool.
Bed and bath: Seven rooms—each with refrigerator and remote-control cable. First floor—private exterior entrance to two fireplace suites, each with queen bed, queen sofa bed, private shower bath, working fireplace. On second floor—three double-bedded rooms; one has private shower bath, two

share large tiled full bath. Suite has double bed, oversized Jacuzzi tub, microwave, private phone. Third-floor suite with ocean view, low angled ceilings has double bed, queen sofa bed in sitting area, private shower bath, microwave.

Plus: Pool shower and changing room. Garden flowers. Upright piano in casual poolhouse. Outdoor Jacuzzi. Chocolates. Free shuttle service to/from Amtrak. Special occasions acknowledged.

From Massachusetts: *"Hospitality very warm without being overdone."* From New Jersey: *"Appreciated restaurant tips, breakfast buffet, fresh flowers arranged with care . . . too much to list!"*

Woody Hill B&B   401/322-0452

149 South Woody Hill Road, Westerly, RI 02891-5901

Host: Ellen L. Madison
Location: Just off busy Route 1, but really in the country. Two miles from ocean beaches. Minutes from Mystic Seaport, Newport, casino.
Open: Year round. Two nights pre-

ferred for summer and holiday weekends.
Rates: $70–$80 for two. $10 additional person in room. One night free for a week's stay. Off-season, less.
♥ ♨ ⬛ ⁂ ◆ ✗ ⅄

From New Hampshire: *"A cozy, warm feeling. We booked a return visit with friends . . . hard to find such a memorable place in these days of rush, rush, rush."* From Massachusetts: *"Our eight-year-old daughter fell in love with the darling antique dolls. Suggestions for restaurants and sightseeing were 'right on.'"* From New York: *"Breakfast pleases the eye and palate as Ellen, a gastronomical intellectual, serves her unique creations."*

We loved our stay during a marvelous cycling/swimming vacation. Another time I met Virginians on a genealogical mission, who were here because they had read that Ellen's family has lived within a two-mile radius of her house since 1636.

The house is an Ellen-designed gambrel-roofed you-can-hardly-tell colonial reproduction. It features early American decor, fireplaces made with old bricks, wide floorboards, and nooks and crannies. Four walls of books, shuttered windows, and window seats are in the library. (The hostess, a high school English teacher with a Ph.D., is very involved with Connecticut's program for mentoring with new teachers.) Summer guests enjoy the 40-foot in-ground pool. Winter guests—including those on a romantic getaway— might be treated to fireplace cooking weekends where you do as little or as much as you wish.

In residence: Three cats. Treasure "cozies up to anyone and molds himself to that person. Lady's aloof and skittish, although less than usual because of her total deafness. Tomasina is frustrated in dealing with the other two."
Bed and bath: Four second-floor guest rooms. All private baths. In "original" house, one double-bedded room and, at opposite end of hall, another corner room with a double and a 3/4 bed. In new addition (in process as we go to press), two double-bedded rooms, private shower baths.
Breakfast: 8–9. Huge repertoire from hundreds of cookbooks. Maybe strawberry nut or blueberry ginger muffins, seasonal fruit with interesting sauces,

(Please turn page.)

pear sauce and waffles or apple crisp, "anything but eggs!" Served in "new" breakfast room with walk-in fireplace.
Plus: The pool. Yard with flower and herb gardens, privacy, "and sometimes mosquitoes." Porch swing. Fireplaced living room. Pump organ.

Rockbound

Haversham, RI

Location: Rural. At the end of a narrow country road, minutes from Westerly, with view of saltwater pond and ocean beyond. Ten minutes by car, bike, or rowboat to beaches (private one available in off-season). Within 15 minutes of restaurants, Theatre-By-The-Sea; 25 to Mystic, Connecticut; 45 to Newport.

Reservations: Available year round through Covered Bridge, page 2. Two-night minimum on weekends and holidays.
Rates: Main house $95–$110 per room. Cottage $100 for two; breakfast extra.
♥ ⚐ ⚑

A find. All done by an artist/gardener/gourmet cook described in my first B&B book as a host in a passive-solar contemporary home. An architectural designer now, she has remodeled her grandfather's summer residence, an Arts and Crafts–style farmhouse, by making the first floor one long flowing spectacular space. A huge fieldstone fireplace defines areas. The floor is Mexican tile. Everywhere there are windows with water views, "quadrillions of books," the hostess's paintings, and antiques—Queen Anne, Chippendale, and Sheraton. And examples of trompe l'oeil and faux finishes. Outside, a wisteria-covered pergola is built over the wicker-furnished brick terrace, "which everyone uses."
The hostess invites guests to feel at home, to enjoy the surroundings and the privacy.

Bed and bath: Two second-floor rooms; private baths. (Plus a summer cottage.) One room, treehouselike, with four-poster double bed, claw-foot tub bath (no shower), antique spinet desk, love seat, high ceiling, porch overlooking pond and ocean. One larger room with two double beds, shower bath, lots of windows, armoire, wing chairs. Private cottage has three bedrooms, fieldstone fireplace, full kitchen, laundry.
Breakfast: 7:30–9:30. Fresh fruit, cheese and/or yogurt, homemade muffins, coffee, tea, juice. Served on china and silver in dining room or on terrace overlooking water.
Plus: Down comforters. Use of entire house. TV. Hammock. Perennial gardens. Setups. Option of private dinner by prior arrangement.

*B*ed and breakfast gives a sense of place.

Anna's Victorian Connection Host #105

Saunderstown, RI

Location: Spectacular. High on a cliff on six waterfront acres with marvelous view of Narragansett Bay. At the end of a rural road. Ten minutes to Newport, Wickford, beaches; 20 to Theatre-By-The-Sea.

Reservations: Available year round through Anna's Victorian Connection, page 306. Two-night minimum on weekends and holidays.

Rates: $65–$85 single, $75–$95 double. Off-season, $5 less. ♥ ◗ ✗

This place to stay has become the reason to go. "Many who come to rush off to Newport return here, sit by the water, use the cabana, and have a picnic," says the hostess, a well-traveled (former airline stewardess) Realtor "who loves to walk the mile-long Narragansett Beach."

Arrive by boat, if you wish. Look over Narragansett Bay from the wraparound stone porch—built with cedar limbs from the yard atop this 50-foot cliff. Or take in the view from the benches along the long terraced walkway that leads through the woods and down to the water.

The one-of-a-kind country house with its huge quarry stone living room fireplace was built over a quarry in 1910 by a Philadelphia lawyer. Since, beams have been put in first-floor ceilings and the living room has been paneled in walnut. It's wonderful—with traditional country pieces, many oil paintings, and Oriental rugs. And on the hillside heather, planted by Scottish builders of the Jamestown Bridge, blooms.

In residence: Fetch, the dog.

Bed and bath: Two large lovely second-floor rooms with water views. Each with two twins or one king, antique furnishings. One with private full bath; one with shared shower bath.

Breakfast: 8–10. Juice, fruit, muffins and breads, gourmet coffees and teas. Served on veranda or in dining/living room area overlooking the water.

Plus: Complimentary sherry hour. Private beach. Use of mooring; use of cabana with refrigerator and bathroom.

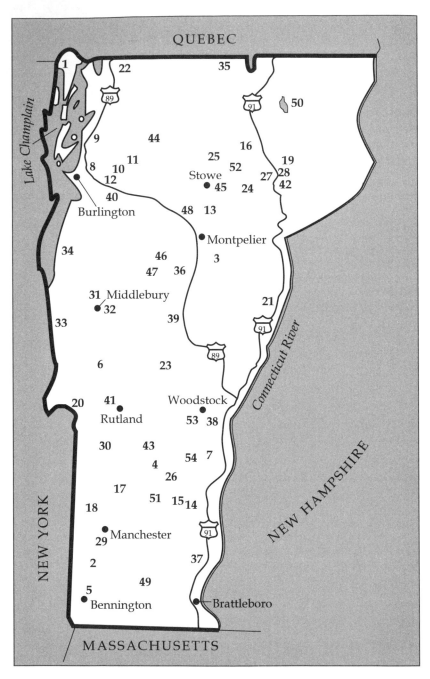

The numbers on this map indicate the locations of B&Bs described in detail in this chapter.

VERMONT

KEY TO SYMBOLS
♥ Lots of honeymooners come here.
♯ Families with children are very welcome. (Please see page xii.)
▰ "Please emphasize that we are a private home, not an inn."
♣ Groups or private parties sometimes book the entire B&B.
♦ Travel agents' commission paid. (Please see page xii.)
✗ Sorry, no guests' pets are allowed.
⌇ No smoking inside *or* no smoking at all, even on porches.

——Vermont Reservation Services——

The American Country Collection

The Willows, 4 Greenwood Lane, Delmar, NY 12054-1606

Phone: 518/439-7001 Monday–Friday 10–1, 2–5. Closed holidays and last week of March.

Fax: 518/439-4301.

Listings: 110. Mostly hosted private residences; a few unhosted. Many are inns. A great number are on the National Register of Historic Places. Most New England listings are in Vermont and New Hampshire, and in the Berkshires of western Massachusetts. A few are in the Connecticut River Valley sections of Massachusetts. In New York State, most are in the Albany/Saratoga, Hudson Valley, Catskill, Central Leatherstocking/Utica/Syracuse, Lake George, and southern and eastern Adirondack regions. Directory ($7.25).

Reservations: Two weeks in advance preferred. Last-minute accepted when possible. Two- to three-day minimum stay at some locations in season.

Rates: $30–$70 single, $40–$185 double. Some weekly rates. Senior citizen discounts midweek (excluding foliage season, holidays, and Saratoga in August). Deposit required is equal to one night's lodging or half of total stay, whichever is higher. If cancellation made no less than 14 days prior to scheduled arrival, deposit refunded less $20 service fee; same refund policy for less than 14 days if room is rebooked. For August–October bookings, refunds less $20 cancellation charge made only if notice received at least 30 days prior to arrival; if less than 30 days, deposit refunded (less cancellation charge) if room is rebooked. Four percent fee for credit cards, Amex, MC, Visa. ◆

Arthur Copeland's hosts are attentive to guests' needs but aware of their desire for privacy. They present homemade foods, know their area, and often help guests to plan an itinerary.

Plus: "Ski 'n' B&B," romance, and dinner packages available. Pickup at transportation points provided by some hosts. Short- and long-term (up to several months) hosted and unhosted housing booked for relocation and business purposes.

Other reservation services with some B&Bs in Vermont:
Bed & Breakfast/Inns of New England, page 259
Bed & Breakfast of Rhode Island, page 307

_____Vermont B&Bs_____

Thomas Mott Homestead

Blue Rock Road, Route 2, Box 149B
Alburg, VT 05440-9620

802/796-3736
(U.S./Canada) **800/348-0843**
fax **802/796-3736**

Host: Patrick J. Schallert
Location: All by itself on Lake Champlain, with wonderful mountain views, sunrises, sunsets. An hour to Montreal Island, Burlington, Adirondack Mountains; 1.8

miles east of Highway 2.
Open: Year round.
Rates: $55–$70. $10 for extra person. Discover, MC, Visa.
♥ ♣ ♦ ✗ ✍

From dozens of guests' notes written to me: *"One of the most delightful times in our lives. . . . A full moon glistening on the lake. Gentle wind and water equaled by tender care of Pat. . . . Sensitive about allowing private time yet available. . . . Funny and warm. . . . The place has a special spirit and great French toast . . . Grandma, mother and daughter loved it. . . . A magical charm. . . . Asparagus cut five minutes before being cooked . . . gourmet breakfasts, helpful knowledge of area, and directions . . . fantastic for the soul . . . spotless, beautiful, lots of windows . . . lovely decor. . . . Perfect."*

Exuberant Pat loves making guests happy. Ben & Jerry's delivery truck comes every Thursday to refill the help-yourself ice-cream freezer. The 1838 farmhouse was totally renovated (beams still show) in 1987 after Pat retired from his travels to French chateaux and German estates, where he purchased premium wines to distribute through his Los Angeles–based company. (He is also a ham radio buff—K6KAG/1—and has a master's degree in criminology.) Here he cooks, raises quail (lets them go at summer's end), takes pictures of every guest (for you and the album), provides canoes and bicycles, and greets many who come to "do everything" and then just stay here. That's what I would like to do.

Bed and bath: Five lakeview rooms, all with handmade quilts and private baths. First-floor corner room with a queen and a twin bed, full bath. Second floor—twin beds, queen (one is extra long, one has fireplace and private balcony), or king "that Kareem could get lost in"; private entrance.
Breakfast: Usually 8–9:30. "Like a Chinese meal, with everyone trying something different." Entrees include berry pancakes; decadent French toast with five kinds of nuts, cream cheese, pure vanilla from Mexico, home-ground nutmeg; omelets with fresh crab or shrimp.
Plus: Fireplaced living room. Upright piano. Ceiling fans. Individual thermostats. Lawn games. Three porches. Greens to feed quail. Fresh fruit. Flowers for honeymooners. Gazebo. Cross-country skiing and snowmobiling.

The tradition of paying to stay in a private home—with breakfast included in the overnight lodging rate—was revived in time to save wonderful old houses, schools, churches, and barns all over the country from the wrecking ball or commercial development.

Hill Farm Inn
RR 2, Box 2015, Arlington, VT 05250-9311

802/375-2269
800/882-2545

Hosts: Regan and John Chichester
Location: At the foot of Mount Equinox. Bordered by Battenkill River (fishing). Surrounded by 50 acres of lawns, gardens, and farmlands. Large red barn with silo in back. Old gas pump in front. Between Bennington and Manchester, one-half mile off Route 7A.
Open: Year round. Two-night

weekend minimum in summer and in fall foliage and ski seasons.
Rates: $70 shared bath, $85 private bath, $100 suite. Singles $20 less. Discount for children under 12; age 2 and under free unless crib ($5) is required. Cabins $70, $75, or $85 for two; $20 additional person. Amex, Discover, MC, Visa.
♯ ⁂ ♦ ⅄

They hardly make them like this anymore. In the Hill family from 1775 until 1983, the property has been a farm inn since 1905. Since the Chichesters took over in 1993, they have welcomed skiers, sightseers, and shoppers in addition to many who choose to take walks, read, and relax right here. In Manhattan Regan was color stylist and dye-lab coordinator for a large textile manufacturer. She has also been a weaver, professional cook, baker, and crepe chef. Originally from London, John was with Christie's auction house for 14 years in New York City. Before that he was a tour manager in the rock and roll business, a professional musician, a graphic designer, and a photographer. They are continuing the inn's traditions of good food, unpretentious country decor, and warm hospitality.

In residence: In hosts' quarters, Nigel, born April 16, 1993; and Congo, the cat.
Foreign languages spoken: Some French and some Spanish.
Bed and bath: Eleven rooms plus two suites (with skylight, ceiling fan, porch) and four cabins (each sleeps two to six). On first and second floors of main inn and guest house. Eight private baths; rest are semiprivate baths. King, queen, double, or twin beds available.
Breakfast: 7:30–9:30. Cooked to order from menu for each guest. Buttermilk blueberry pancakes, French toast, farm-fresh eggs. Homemade toast, muffins, and granola. Country sausage and bacon. Oatmeal. Juices. Hot beverages. In fireplaced dining room with classical music.
Plus: Upright piano, fireplace, and TV in parlor. Fans provided. Fresh fruit in rooms. Complimentary afternoon snacks. Wine or beer available. Games cupboard. Lawn games and swing set. Dinner option, $20 per adult.

> From New York: *"Beautiful setting, very friendly hosts, excellent meals . . . very clean . . . peaceful . . . homey . . . perfect."*

Woodruff House
13 East Street, Barre, VT 05641-3806

802/476-7745

Hosts: Robert and Terry Somaini
Location: Near center of the city, on a quiet old-fashioned park. Halfway between Boston and Montreal. Near the state capital, Montpelier; the largest granite quarries in the

world; and Sugarbush, Mount Mansfield, and Stowe ski areas.
Open: Year round.
Rates: $50 single, $70 double.
♠ ⅋ ⅄

(Please turn page.)

From Oregon and Connecticut: *"A very beautiful place . . . full of antiques and ornate decoration . . . more importantly, the beds were very comfortable . . . breakfast in the dining room surrounded by gleaming silver, tea before bed in the upstairs drawing room, feather pillows, the finest all cotton percale sheets, perfectly white towels, wonderful breakfast by candlelight. . . . It's obvious that they truly enjoy people and the art of conversation. . . . Go! You will be wrapped in fun and happiness and warmth."*

From the Somainis' point of view: "After 15 years of hosting, we have many rich and precious memories." Their home, an 1883 Victorian in a National Register historic district, is filled with an eclectic, ever-changing collection of antiques. Robert, a native Vermonter and local history buff, is an interior design consultant who owns an antiques mall. Terry is a CPA with an insurance firm.

In residence: Daughter Katie, during college vacations.
Bed and bath: Two rooms with private shower baths. Cozy first-floor queen-bedded room. Large second-floor room—two twin-size beds on king headboard, sitting porch.
Breakfast: At 8 weekdays, 9 on weekends. In one of two candlelit dining rooms. Menu varies from simple to fancy. French toast, fruit, ham or bacon, juice, coffee or tea.
Plus: Fireplaced living room. TV upstairs. A large wood furnace. Dessert often served in the evening.

The Leslie Place

Box 62, Belmont, VT 05730

802/259-2903
800/352-7439

Host: Mary K. Gorman
Location: On undeveloped (west) side of Okemo Mountain. On a quiet dirt road, minutes from a paved one, with meadows, mountain views, and, in summer, cows. Fifteen minutes to Weston Priory and Okemo ski area; 30 to Killington ski area; 25 miles from Route 91.
Open: Year round. Advance reservations recommended. Two-night minimum for foliage and ski season weekends. Three nights for national holiday weekends.
Rates: Mid-September through October and mid-December through February $72 queen bed; $77 room with queen and twin beds; $67 suite. Rest of year $10 less. Each additional guest $12. Singles $8 less. MC, Visa ✻ ✖ ✂

Oh, for the opportunity when fleeting weekends can stretch to more abundant weekdays for Re-creation.
The Leslie Place is my farmhouse for all seasons.

So concludes a warm, enthusiastic poem enclosed in one guest's letter I received. Others reminisced about tranquillity; beauty, peace, and friendship; old-fashioned flower gardens; homemade ornaments on the hand-cut Christmas tree; charming, spacious, uncluttered yet Old World style; real Vermont. "It's tempting never to leave the house."

It was different when Mary moved in 19 years ago. "The house had been empty for 16 years. No bathrooms, water, heat, or electricity! I was young and determined, I guess. Although my family had doubts, I didn't, as I milked cows next door and restored this house. Everything was done by the Gorman Method, mixed with tears, laughter, frustration, and pleasure. I furnished with a rescued schoolhouse piano, hooked rugs, some of my own oil paintings, and a Kalamazoo cookstove. Now I sell firewood in the fall, make maple sugar in the spring, and, year round, share my home with guests, each one a wonderful surprise."

Bed and bath: Four rooms. First floor—queen-bedded room with phone, private shower bath. Second floor—a queen and a twin bed, private shower bath. Suite—a double bed in one room, a double and two twins in the other, shower bath. Crib available.

Breakfast: Until 9:30. Menu varies daily. French toast, pancakes, or apple crisp. Homemade muffins or breads, maple syrup, and granola. Cereals. Juice. Coffee.

Plus: Phone in first-floor guests' sitting room. Guest kitchenette. Barbecue and picnic table. Books. Games. TV and fans available.

Molly Stark Inn

802/442-9631

1067 East Main Street, Bennington, VT 05201

800/356-3076

Host: Reed Fendler
Location: On landscaped acre along Route 9 (look for gold leaf sign, sometimes with cow flag); 1.2 miles from town center and shops, 5 to Bennington College. Thirty minutes south of Manchester and Arlington. Four miles to Appalachian Trail.
Open: Year round.

Rates: (All plus 5 percent gratuity.) $65–$85 Memorial Day–September 15. $80–$95 September 16–October 25. $60–$68 rest of year. Singles $10 less. Extra person $10. Champagne/restaurant dinner package. Amex, Discover, MC, Visa.
♥ ♣ ✖ ⊱

The brick front walk and wraparound front porch lead to comfortable surroundings with classical and jazz music playing in the background. Collectibles and antiques—most acquired at area auctions and sales—are everywhere in this 1890 country home "possibly built from a Sears kit." It's just the way Reed imagined it when he saw the *New York Times* ad in 1988. That was the year he, a political science major (in his twenties then), decided it was time to change careers—from retail manager to "manager of everything": the wood stove; the three common rooms; the braided and hooked rugs on gleaming hardwood floors, patchwork quilts, and claw-footed tubs; and the cuisine. Landscape photography is his main hobby. And he volunteers with the court system and children's youth services.

Bed and bath: Six rooms on three floors. First floor—antique double oak sleigh bed, private full bath. Second floor—rooms with a queen, a double, and two doubles share one full and a half bath. Third-floor suite with a queen and a double bed, private full bath, air conditioning. Rollaway available.

Breakfast: 8–9:30. Puffed apple pancakes, oatmeal/wheat germ pancakes, herbed cheese omelets, "exotic muffins," or the hallmark blueberry Belgian buttermilk waffles with pure Vermont maple syrup. Williams Smokehouse bacon and sausage. Juice, fresh fruit cup, homemade granola.

Plus: Welcoming beverage. Ceiling fans in several rooms. Herbal teas and coffees. Games, puzzles, TV, books. Rockers and wicker on wraparound porch.

Hivue Bed and Breakfast Tree Farm

RR 1, Box 1023, High Pond Road
Brandon, VT 05733-9704

802/247-3042
800/880-3042

Hosts: Wini and Bill Reuschle
Location: Rural and peaceful. On 76-acre tree farm with panoramic views; 3.5 miles to Brandon center and fine restaurants, 18 to Killington ski area, 10 to Lake Champlain, 16 to Middlebury.

Open: Year round.
Rates: $50 per room. $10 each additional person. Seventh night free. Retreat and executive meeting rates available.
♥ ♦♦ ♦ ✻ ✄

A good reason to leave the beaten path. You're surrounded by nature in this hemlock glen, which has a 1.5-mile marked interpretive trail developed by the hosts since they retired in 1984. Guests from all over the world—many are returnees and Middlebury parents—appreciate the expansive layers of views from the deck and from the large windows of the raised ranch house. There are meadows, a forest, hay fields, and a trout-stocked stream.

In New York Bill was assistant general surface superintendent with the Transit Authority. Wini, a Marine during World War II, was a YMCA program developer in New Jersey.

In residence: Wini's brother, Larry, retired from the computer industry. Dogs—old Tina (terrier) and young Patchie (dalmatian/spaniel). Two ponies. One shetland mare.
Bed and bath: Three rooms, all private baths. Private entrance for ground-floor suite with double bed, sun room, tub bath, TV, VCR, double sleep sofa, ceiling fan, exercise bike. Second level—twin beds, TV, four windows, full hall bath. King bed, en-suite shower bath, studio couch, TV, VCR, four windows, view of sunrise and mountains. Rollaway available.
Breakfast: At guests' convenience. Country meal—"a brunch." Fruit; juices; cereals; muffins; eggs, blueberry pancakes, or French toast; sausage or bacon. "Bill asks a blessing before the meal, entertains with stomper doll collection, and gives his original 'thumb-twister' stress reliever to each guest."
Plus: Fireplaced living room. Wood stove in family room. Window fans. Flannel sheets. Beverages. Shaded patio. Bird feeders. Picnic baskets, $4/person; dinner, $10 with advance arrangement. Hints for antiquing, Brandon's historic districts, museums, canoeing, Long Trail hiking, and skiing.

> Guests wrote: "*An engaging weekend. [It happened here.] . . . Wonderful hospitality and warmth . . . quiet . . . great entertainment, food, and laughter . . . Everything is beautiful.*"

I'll just sleep in the morning," said one college-age son, until the next day when he smelled the muffins.

Old Mill Inn   802/247-8002

Stone Mill Dam Road, Brandon, VT 05733

Hosts: Karl and Annemarie Schrieber
Location: Quiet. Ten acres with brook, woods, meadows, farmland. Near swimming hole and Blueberry Hill cross-country ski center. One mile from village. Twenty minutes to Killington, 45 to Shelburne Museum. Public golf course borders property.
Open: Year round. Two-night mini-mum September 15–October 20. Three-night minimum December 24–January 3.
Rates: Per room. $75 weekdays, $85 weekends. $95 September 10–October 10 and December 20–February 28. Singles $20 less. Extra person in room $20.
♥ ♨ ❖

From Massachusetts: *"Hospitality that makes for intriguing conversation, diet-defying dining, and a desire for lifelong friendship. . . . Decor represents the finest collection of country-style antiques outside of a museum! . . . I caught a very nice rainbow trout on the property while others were making friends with Ben and a couple of curious goats."* From California: *"The unanimous first choice of all my tour participants . . . warm, enchanting atmosphere."*

"Paradise" is the way some others have summed up this 1786 colonial, a former dairy farm, the Schriebers' B&B for 7 years. They came here after 25 years in Los Angeles, where they were in the automobile business. Annemarie also did interior design work. Here she has a painting studio (early American folk art) and antiques shop in the barn. Karl is an accomplished woodworker. In summer they have barbecues; in August, a pig roast. Year round, they have ecstatic, articulate guests who write glowing comments to me.

In residence: Ben, a golden retriever. Some horses, goats, chickens, ducks, pigs, and cats.
Foreign language spoken: German.
Bed and bath: Six rooms, all with private baths, antique beds, handmade quilts, and sitting rooms. One has a working wood stove. First-floor triple (one double and one twin bed) with full bath. Three double-bedded rooms with en-suite shower baths. On second floor—one room with three single beds, one with a double and a twin bed. Rollaway and crib available.
Breakfast: 8–9:30. French toast, eggs Benedict, German apple pancakes, farm-fresh eggs and sausage, or strata. Homemade muffins and jams (farm-grown berries). Juice, fruit, hot beverage. In breakfast room/folk art gallery.
Plus: Fully air conditioned. Individual thermostats. Wine and cheese hour. Beamed living room with ceiling fan and wood stove. Bathrobes. Down comforters. Flannel sheets. Beach towels. Mints on pillow. Champagne for special occasions. Option of dinner, $15 per person.

---

*T*hink *of bed and breakfast as a people-to-people concept.*

Rosebelle's Victorian Inn   802/247-0098

Route 7, 31 Franklin Street, Brandon, VT 05733-1111

Hosts: Ginette and Norm Milot
Location: On main road. In historic town. Minutes' walk to town center and fine restaurants. Close to Killington, Pico, and Sugarbush downhill and cross-country skiing. Fourteen miles north of Rutland, 13 south of Middlebury.

Open: Year round. Two-night minimum on holiday weekends.
Rates: Weekends $65 shared bath, $75 private. Midweek $5 less; singles $15 less. Foliage season and Presidents' week $10 more. Summer and winter packages. MC, Visa.

The 1860 French Second Empire mansard-roofed mansion made a perfect setting for the waiting horse and carriage on the Milots' wedding day. Since 1990, when they bought this National Register property (which was converted to a B&B in 1985) they have redecorated and furnished the inn with many Victorian pieces.

Norm, a state college food service director, has been in the food service industry for over 30 years. He and Ginette have lived in Canada, New York, New Jersey, and Massachusetts.

In residence: One dog—Heidi, a black female pug. Rosie, a tiger cat.
Foreign language spoken: Ici on parle Francais.
Bed and bath: Six spacious rooms with individual thermostats. Second floor—four rooms with queen, double, or twin beds share two baths (one could be private); one bath has shower, the other a claw-foot tub. Third floor—private shower baths for room with extra-long twin beds and one with queen bed; intricate custom-made tin ceilings with fans.
Breakfast: 7:30–9:30. Seasonal fresh fruit, juices, gourmet flavored coffee, homemade pastries. Cooked-to-order omelet or waffles with Vermont maple syrup.
Plus: Flower gardens and sitting areas. Fireplaced living room. Afternoon tea, fresh fruit, candies. Flannel sheets. Croquet. Picnic baskets available. Friday and Saturday candlelight dining; $25 per person includes tax and gratuities.

From Rhode Island: *"The company . . . the meals . . . the decor . . . loved every minute."*

Mill Brook B&B   802/484-7283

Route 44, P.O. Box 410, Brownsville, VT 05037-0410

Host: Kay Carriere
Location: Across from Mount Ascutney, in a rural village "with famous summer baked bean suppers; back roads for walking or mountain cycling; and, next to property, a brook." Ten miles from I-91, 14 south of Woodstock, 30 to Dartmouth College. Walk to covered bridge.
Open: Year round. Two-night minimum preferred on weekends, including Christmas and holidays.
Rates: Vary according to room size.

Most midweek days $48–$55 shared bath, $58–$62 private. All weekends and midweek foliage $52–$62 shared, $65–$72 private. Columbus Day and Presidents' weekends and Christmas holiday week $55–$65 shared, $70–$77 private. Singles $5–$10 less. Extra person $13. $10 one-night surcharge on weekends, holidays, and foliage season. Discounts for senior citizens, families, extended weekends. MC, Visa.
♥ ♯ ❖ ♦ ✁

"We are a farmhouse—not a mansion—with a down-home feeling. We have a wood burning stove, board games, croquet and volleyball, a hammock, picnic tables, a grill—and, on the deck, a hot tub. The bathrooms were recently redecorated. Sheets are line dried year round. Cloth napkins are used, even for tea [served with cake in summer; skiers enjoy soup]. You can go anywhere and have a Sara Lee cake, but not here. You can feed a horse and a goat. (Map and apples provided.) There's a mountain to climb and a brook to fish or swim in. Need a thermos, backpack, fishing pole? It's yours for the borrowing."

Kay, "Mom" or "Aunt Kay" according to guests, is a food writer/cookbook author, a New Orleans native who was a college hospitality instructor and hotel salesperson in New Jersey. She makes all her jellies, pies, and omelets with native apples, berries, and vegetables.

In residence: Son Mike is a chef. "Neither the Philadelphia street cat rescued by my daughter nor our black Lab is allowed inside."
Foreign languages spoken: A very little Spanish, Italian, and French.
Bed and bath: Eight rooms (some adjoin as family suites) on three floors. Six baths. Private baths for room (up narrow steep staircase) with king bed; room with queen; and one with double bed, double sofa bed, and single futon. Shared baths for double/double or twin beds.
Breakfast: 7:15–9 and "to go." Hot cereal, fruit, juice, meat dish, egg dish or pancakes, coffee cake or home-baked bread. Buffet—with entree served in dining room.
Plus: Ceiling fans in two of six gathering rooms. Ceiling or or standing fans in guest rooms. Playpen. Babysitting. TV. Microwave and refrigerator in tea room. Ten percent discount at five area restaurants. By popular demand, an in-house bakery.

Country Comfort Bed & Breakfast

36 Old Stage Road   802/878-2589
Essex Junction, VT 05452-2509

Hosts: Eva and Ed Blake
Location: Quiet, with mountain views. On a high plateau, way back from the road "with a barn, grazing sheep, and clucking chickens." Across the road from a church. Five minutes to fine dining, 15 to Burling- ton, 35 to Shelburne Museum, 9 to University of Vermont.
Open: Year round.
Rates: $50–$55 shared bath, $55–$65 private bath. Singles $10 less. $10 extra bed/crib. MC, Visa.
♥ ♯ ✉ ♣ ♦ ✗ ⅄

Since the Blakes built this Cape house in 1967, all four children have grown. Country antiques—"a lifetime of collecting"—are displayed against a backdrop of traditional wallcoverings, light colors, and stenciled walls. B&B guests enjoy the view, the home-away-from-home ambiance, and the scene-stealing sheep. Before they opened as a B&B in 1989, Eva, a craftswoman, was a dental hygienist and owner of a florist shop. Ed, a civil engineer who manages a large water supply system, hired one young guest from Pennsylvania!

Bed and bath: Three rooms. Private full hall bath for first-floor room with Jenny Lind double bed. Up steps with stenciled risers to second floor—
(Please turn page.)

Country Room with double bed shares full bath with Victorian Room that has two twin beds. Rollaway and crib available.
Breakfast: 8–9. Maybe fruit cup, pumpkin pancakes with homemade apple cider syrup, low-fat sausage. Or eggs Florentine with homemade muffins, juice or fruit. Freshly brewed coffee. Special diets accommodated.
Plus: Ceiling fans in upstairs rooms. Selected reading material according to your interests. Carpeted guest living room with peaked beamed ceiling, TV, VCR with movies, piano. Homemade mints or cookies.

The American Country Collection Host #149
Fairfax, VT

Location: Peaceful. On 400 spectacular acres of open fields and dense woods with not another house in sight, with a sometimes-view of Jay Peak from the rear of the property. Thirty minutes north of Burlington; 70 from Montreal; 15 to Saint Albans, 30 to Mount Mansfield.

Reservations: Available year round through The American Country Collection, page 343.
Rates: $48 single, $58 double, $78 suite.
♥ ♨ ♣ ✗ ✗

Maybe you saw the host on an Oprah Winfrey show that featured people who have made a significant lifestyle change. In Rochester, New York, he was a successful lawyer; his wife, a microbiologist in dental research. After they bought this property in the late 1980s, they blended and completely renovated two buildings to create a B&B. The very private guest rooms are in the former carriage house, which has original beams and a wood-burning stove. An open-hearth stove and refreshment area are in the slate-floored sun room. Furnishings include antiques and country collectibles.

Shortly before this book went to press, the hostess entered medical school; the host, who now practices law here in Vermont, completed his CIT (cook-in-training) course "well enough to talk and cook at the same time." They meet guests who hike; swim in the pool; see their kids enjoy pony rides and the fenced-in play area; shop; go to the Shelburne Museum; and relax back here "at home, where they feel a million miles from nowhere."

In residence: In hosts' quarters, "assistant innkeepers"—seven-year-old son, six-year-old daughter. Two horses. Two ponies. Four sheep "at the moment." Four cats. One dog.
Bed and bath: Four queen-bedded rooms with remote-controlled color TV. Two (one with sofa bed) on first floor share full bath. Two on second floor share full bath.
Breakfast: 8–9. Blueberry pancakes (most frequently requested by returnees), "Grandma's bread pudding," French toast, or cheese strata. An antique cherry table in dining room with sliding glass doors.
Plus: Outside—a 40-foot heated pool with two decks. Two-person Jacuzzi inside. Hammock between two trees overlooking perennial gardens. Hiking/cross-country ski trails. Complimentary pony rides. Sleigh rides arranged. In the spring, watch the maple sugaring here.

Homeplace Bed and Breakfast

802/899-4694

RR 2, Box 367, Jericho, VT 05465

fax 802/899-4883

Hosts: Hans and Mariot Huessy
Location: Very quiet. "Way in the woods, down a half-mile-long driveway." One and one-half miles off Route 15, 15 miles to Burlington, half hour to Shelburne Museum, ¾ hour to Stowe and Mount Mansfield. Near University of Vermont, Ben &

Jerry's ice cream factory.
Open: Year round. Reservations appreciated.
Rates: Shared bath $45 single, $55 double. Private bath $55 single, $65 double.
♥ ♫ ♯ ⁂ ♦ ⅙

More recent guests have a hard time outdoing the Ohio couple who wrote an 82-line poem on everything from "appointments fit for bride and groom" to "A flock of sheep with bells and bleat. They seemed to say, 'We're glad to meet.'"

Spring is the season for sugaring and newborn lambs here. When the Huessys built this wonderful modern country home "with more window than wall" on 100 acres of woodland in 1968, they furnished it with lovely antiques from Mariot's American family and Hans's European family. Hans is "slightly retired" from his teaching position at the University of Vermont Medical School. Mariot, mother to 11 grown children, is caretaker of the farm.

In residence: Two friendly dogs—a golden retriever and an Australian shepherd. Two cats. Horses, donkeys, sheep, chickens, and ducks.
Foreign language spoken: German.
Bed and bath: In a separate wing, four ground-floor rooms share two full baths (can have private or shared bath). One room has two antique twin beds; another has twin beds made by a local craftsperson. A third room has a double bed, a twin bed, and a crib. One room with double bed. Crib and cot available.
Breakfast: Usually 7:30–9:30. Juice, fresh fruit, "homegrown" eggs, Vermont smoked bacon, pancakes, homemade muffins or breads, and freshly ground coffee. By wood stove or in dining room.
Plus: Fireplaced living room with flagstone floor, Oriental rugs, floor-to-ceiling windows, book-filled shelves. Hiking and cross-country skiing trails (maps provided). Pond for swimming (at your own risk). Their own wool, fleeces, and maple syrup for sale.

Sinclair Inn Bed & Breakfast

802/899-2234

RD 2, Box 35 (Route 15)
Underhill, VT 05489-9318

(U.S./Canada) 800/433-4658

Hosts: Jeanne and Andy Buchanan
Location: Four-minute walk to village green. Five miles to Underhill State Park (Mount Mansfield trails); 13 to Smugglers Notch (return via Ben & Jerry's ice cream plant); 14 northeast of Burlington. "One mile to excellent restaurant."

Open: Year round. Two-day stay appreciated on holiday weekends.
Rates: $55 double bed, $65 queen (smaller room), $75 queen (larger room) or king. MC, Visa.
♥ ⁂ ✈ ⅙

(Please turn page.)

"I never want to leave," said one guest upon entering this Queen Anne gem. It's Victorian inside and out, with turrets and towers, leaded and stained glass, a fretwork stairway valance, nine kinds of rich woodwork, and octagonal bedrooms. When the Buchanans bought "this house that hugs you" in 1993, they completely redecorated the first floor with large-floral papers, lace curtains, Oriental rugs, and Andy's mother's silver service. By the time you read this, the outside may be freshly painted in Victorian white with cranberry and teal green trim. In time, the second-floor rooms will also have "Jeannie's treatment."

Here in the Buchanans' fifth house restoration, Andy, a civil engineer who oversaw Vermont bridge and road construction, has added an interior stairway and done some stained glass work too. Jeannie has experience in innkeeping as well as decorating. You can tell that these hosts, parents of eight grown children, are in their element with their "expanded family."

Bed and bath: Six air-conditioned rooms, all private en-suite baths. Handicapped-accessible first-floor room with queen bed and wheelchair-accessible shower. Second-floor rooms have a king, a queen, or a double and a single bed.
Breakfast: 8:30. Blueberry pancakes, Belgian waffles, cinnamon-raisin French toast, or eggs Benedict. Vermont maple syrup and meats. Orange juice, fresh fruit, breads and homemade muffins. In chandeliered dining room. Special diets accommodated.
Plus: Fireplaced living room. Library. Fresh flowers. Afternoon refreshments. Guest refrigerator. Wicker-furnished porch. Lawn chairs by gardens with bird feeders.

Partridge Hill Bed & Breakfast   802/878-4741

P.O. Box 52, 102 Partridge Hill, Williston, VT 05495-0052

Hosts: Roger and Sally Bryant
Location: Up a dirt road to 900 feet above sea level for a panorama of the Green Mountains. Eight miles east of Burlington, 30 minutes from Shelburne Museum, one-half mile from Route 2 in Williston village.

Open: Year round.
Rates: Tax included. $65 double, $35 single. (UVM parents are encouraged to invite their child to breakfast at no charge.)
♥ ✖ ✕

"The view." The Bryants, too, marvel at it. When Roger became head athletic trainer at the University of Vermont in 1965 (he retired in 1992), they built a contemporary chalet. Now the parents of four grown children and 10 grandchildren enjoy sharing the sun that pours in from the east through those big glass windows.

Bed and bath: Off of guests' common room are one queen-bedded room and one room with king bed, vanity, and sink; these share the only guest bath (tub and shower). In addition, for families, there is a suite of two small rooms, one with two twin beds, one with a queen bed.
Breakfast: Usually at 8. Freshly squeezed orange juice. Fresh fruit. French toast, waffles, or pancakes with Vermont maple syrup. "Surprise" muffins. Homemade strawberry jam (a hit). Vermont Cabot cheeses, Vermont ham and bacon made without preservatives. Hot cereals and eggs. Served in

fireplaced dining room or on the deck overlooking the view. "Guests usually have plans and are on their way by 10."
Plus: Large fireplaced common room with TV. Fresh flowers. Electric blankets.

Guests wrote: *"Welcomed to a scrumptious morning repast. . . . Read late into the night in front of a blazing fire with freshly baked brownies and coffee. . . . Found our car (windshield too) cleaned when we left. . . . A real find!"*

Northview Bed & Breakfast   802/454-7191

Lightening Ridge Road, Calais, VT
Mailing address: RD 2, Box 1000, Plainfield, VT 05667-9802

Hosts: Joani and Glenn Yankee
Location: Off a rural country road, eight miles north of Montpelier in a historic, picturesque town. On a hill, surrounded by stone walls and white fences, with meadows and mountain views. Five minutes to swimming, boating, horseback riding, summer theater; 15 to Montpelier or Barre granite quarries.
Open: Year round. Reservations required.
Rates: $40–$45 single. $40–$50 double. Less for stays that are longer than three nights. Cot $15 adult, $10 child; under age five, free.
♥ ♨ ♨ ♨ ✄

From Texas: *"Just what I always pictured New England to be—stenciled walls, tab curtains, antiques, dried herbs, theorem paintings, French toast with Vermont maple syrup, freshly picked blueberries in muffins . . . I loved the countryside and quiet."* From Massachusetts: *"The Yankees were warm. The blizzard was cold. We'll be back."*

Other guests, who cross-country skied from the door, wrote about getting engaged on "Huggers' Hill." A family from Pennsylvania recalled "hosts who outdo themselves, sledding, cross-country skiing, spacious and beautiful rooms, and a roaring living room fire." Another from New Mexico borrowed the Yankees' big deep boots so that they could tromp around on the quaking bog a five-minute walk from the house. Glenn, a school superintendent and licensed pilot, and Joani, a teacher who lists windsurfing among her interests, sometimes join visitors in the unusual bog nature preserve, which has carnivorous plants, orchids, and other rare flowers.

In residence: "Beaver is a friendly, comical cat. Tucker is a placid one."
Bed and bath: Three antiques-filled rooms share a second-floor full bath and a first-floor half bath. Two corner rooms, each with double bed (one is canopied). One room with two twin beds. Cot available.
Breakfast: 6–9. (At 7:15 on school days.) Beautifully served in country kitchen with potbellied stove, in stenciled dining room, or on the garden patio. Juice. Fruit. Homemade coffee bread and muffins, eggs, breakfast meats, homemade jams; Dutch babies (souffle), a recipe sent by a guest.
Plus: Beverages. Beamed living room. Fresh flowers. Mints. Picnic area with table and fireplace. Yard games.

---

*T*o tip or not? (Please turn to page xi.)

Chester House

802/875-2205

Main Street, P.O. Box 708, Chester, VT 05143

Hosts: Irene and Norm Wright
Location: Across from the village green in this lovely village.
Open: Year round. Two-night minimum on major holiday and foliage season weekends.

Rates: $75 queen, $65 king, $60 double, $55 twin beds. Singles $10 less. $10–$15 third person.
♥ ✿ ✗

"B&B fulfills the idea that came to us in 1984 while I was working as a Mobil employee relations manager in Saudi Arabia. [Before that, Norm was at corporate headquarters in Manhattan.] When I retired early, we moved to Vermont, 12 miles from where I was born, where we still have family. Irene is from Algona, Iowa, an area that has provided some small-world stories around our breakfast table." They looked at several places before buying this c. 1780 colonial, now restored and furnished with Oriental rugs and early American antiques.

In residence: One "extremely friendly" husky/collie mixed-breed named Kiela, "not allowed in guest areas."
Bed and bath: Four rooms, all private baths. First-floor room with canopied double bed. Second floor—king-bedded room with sitting area; room with canopied queen bed and large Jacuzzi; another with twin beds.
Breakfast: 7:30–9. Varies. Could be waffles with fried apples or scrambled eggs with home fries. Always fresh coffee, tea, juice, fruit dish, homemade breads and muffins. In dining room with two-tiered brass chandelier, wainscoting, and French print wallpaper.
Plus: Individual thermostats. Fans. TV in guest living room. Gathering room with fireplace. Down comforters. Flannel sheets. Turndown service. Front porch rockers. Fresh flowers.

Greenleaf Inn

802/875-3171

P.O. Box 188, Chester, VT 05143-0188

Hosts: Elizabeth and Dan Duffield
Location: Just off Main Street. Surrounded by spacious lawn, old apple trees, and, in back, a babbling brook. Within 30 minutes of Okemo and Bromley ski areas; 45 to Stratton. Walking distance to restaurants. Close to three cross-country centers.

Open: Year round except April. Two-night minimum on winter holiday weekends.
Rates: $65 dormer room. $70 others. $20 rollaway. $5 less for singles. "Rent-an-inn" (10 people) $325. MC, Visa.
♥ ✿ ✗

The Duffields, parents of a grown family, looked at 50 inns before returning, in 1986, to Dan's "unchanged childhood summer territory." He had retired as colonel from the Marine Corps and worked for a defense contractor when he and Liz decided to work together. To their "dream" Liz brings diverse experiences. She was "a navy officer way back." After marrying Dan, she cooked and entertained all over the world, did newspaper reporting, and became a full-time antiques dealer. Family heirlooms and some of Liz's paintings are in the 1850 Victorian home that the Duffields restored.

In residence: "Our two cats are restricted to first floor. Becket is a super-friendly golden retriever."
Bed and bath: Five second-floor rooms, each with private full bath. Two four-poster twin beds in large corner room. Four rooms have queen beds: one large room with old harpsichord; one dormer room with large bath across hall; one room with high four-poster and footstool. Rollaway available.
Breakfast: 7–9. Vermont bacon and sausage, scrambled eggs, pancakes. Cinnamon oatmeal in winter. Homemade muffins and breads. On Sundays sausage, egg-and-cheese casserole. Juice and hot beverages.
Plus: Iced mint or hot spiced tea and cookies. Morning papers. Bedroom window fans. Storage space for skis and bicycles. Fireplaced living room and den. Games. Books. Magazines. Classical music. Small art gallery.

Guests wrote: *"What a B&B is supposed to be. . . . Wonderful innkeepers. . . . Appreciated the closet and drawer space. . . . Beautifully furnished and homey. . . . Spotless. . . . Tall showers. . . . Peace and quiet. . . . A breakfast that will get anyone out of bed."*

Inn Victoria

802/875-4288
On the Green, P.O. Box 788, Chester, VT 05143   800/732-4288
fax 802/875-4323

Hosts: K.C. and Tom Lanagan
Location: "With the purple shutters at end of village green. In the Vermont you've been hoping to find."
Open: Year round. Depending on season or holiday, some two or three-day minimums.

Rates: (High tea or apres ski included.) Queen $85, $125 with Jacuzzi or soaking tub, $150 queen and double room as suite. Double-bedded room—$65 shared bath, $75 private. Theme weekend packages. MC, Visa.
♥ ❖ ✻

Talk about a magic wand! This elegant Second Empire house with damasks and moires and soft shades of mauve, purple, and lavender was gutted and without a kitchen when, in 1988, the Lanagans bought it "because we fell in love with the town." Silver is polished. Embroidered linens are ironed. High tea is served with style in the 35-foot-square living room. And now, by popular demand, there are Saturday night dinner parties complete with champagne.

In New Jersey Tom was president of a computer company. Now he dovetails innkeeping with consulting in telecommunications. K.C. is an antiques dealer, paints in her studio, runs a teapot shop next door, and has started (with two others) an art gallery. She also makes costumes for the Chester Players.

In residence: Son Tom, during college vacations. Baby Face, a Himalayan cat, "maybe the most remembered part of a visit and definitely the inn's Queen Victoria."
Bed and bath: Seven rooms on second and third floors. All private lavish baths, some with Jacuzzi, one with large soaking tub and separate shower; some hall baths. Queen or double bed; some are canopied. Two rooms can become a suite. Rollaway available.

(Please turn page.)

Breakfast: 8–10. Cinnamon raisin French toast with maple butter, eggs Benedict, scones, crumb cake. Served in the formal dining room (with armchairs that invite lingering) under a huge antique chandelier. Recipes shared. (Everyone asks.)
Plus: Fireplaced living room with melodeon. Wicker-furnished screened porch. Window fans. TV. Fruit, tea, coffee, mulled cider, brandy. Maple hearts on pillows. In renovated barn—cathedral-ceilinged great room for beer-making and cooking classes and bicycle group suppers.

The Madrigal Inn and Fine Arts Center

61 Williams River Road, Chester, VT 05143-9304   802/463-1339
800/854-2208

Hosts: Ray and Nancy Dressler
Location: On 60 acres, a former farm, with mountain meadows, woods, wildlife, and, in every direction, marvelous views. Five miles east of I-91, exit 6; 20 minutes to Okemo Mountain.
Open: Year round. Three-day minimum on holiday weekends.

Rates: $65 single, $85 double. $20 additional adult, $10 ages 5–12, free under 5. Special rates for three to seven consecutive nights, excluding holiday weekends and foliage season. Ten percent less for clergy, military, and seniors.
♥ ♣ ♦ ✖ ✗

The ultimate—by design. A post-and-beam building with huge Palladian windows, French doors, and a three-storied living room brick fireplace. With deep green carpeting. Wing and Windsor chairs. And a seven-foot antique Steinway grand piano. And to think it was an idea sketched on a drugstore napkin on the Dresslers' second date when they were in college in the 1950s. The Vermont dream became a reality after the family (four children) lived in 22 homes during the years when Ray was a pastor in the Midwest and then a navy chaplain. Since the inn's opening on Christmas eve, 1992, retreats and group seminars have been held here. All the Dresslers paint. The family includes a composer and a porcelain doll maker. Inquire about planned chamber concerts and crafts workshops. Or even your own wedding on site.

In residence: Prince, a tricolored collie, "a wonderful greeter."
Foreign languages spoken: A little German, French, and Japanese.
Bed and bath: Eleven rooms on three levels; all private full baths. King/twins option with private exterior entrance. Queen-bedded handicapped-accessible room. Queen and double sofa bed plus room for two rollaways. Four-poster and canopied queens. Twin beds. Extra-long king/twins option.
Breakfast: 7–10. Pancakes or French toast with Vermont maple syrup. Or eggs and bacon or sausage. Homemade muffins. Juice, fruit, coffee, tea, cocoa. In fireplaced dining room by candlelight.
Plus: Fireplaced library. Wood stove in conference room. Individual thermostats. Down comforters. Window fans. No TV. Refreshments. Fresh fruit. Mints. Picnic baskets, $15 for two people. Light fare dinner ($10 adult, $8 under age 12) by request. Use of sleds, toboggans, and fishing poles. Five kilometers of hiking and cross-country ski trails being developed.

From Virginia: *"Magnificent!"* From New Jersey: *"Fresh, charming, immaculate, comfortable, inviting . . . warm friendly atmosphere."*

The Inn at High View

RR 1, Box 201A, Andover, VT 05143

802/875-2724
fax 802/875-4021

Hosts: Greg Bohan and Sal Massaro
Location: On a quiet country road with panoramic mountain views. Just outside small village; six miles northwest of Chester. On 52 acres with hiking and cross-country ski trails that connect to 15-km network. Fifteen minutes to Okemo Mountain, 25 to Bromley, 35 to Stratton, 45 to Killington. Near golf, antiquing, Weston Playhouse (10 minutes).

Open: Year round except for two weeks in April. Two-night minimum most winter weekends; three nights on Columbus Day, Martin Luther King, and Presidents' Day weekends.
Rates: $90–$105 double or queen bed, $125 suite. $20 extra person. April July $80 per room or suite. Packages available. MC, Visa.
♥ ♨ ❉ ♦ ⚰

The post-and-beam farmhouse—the original part was built in 1789—is comfortable, with Oriental rugs, a curved white modern living room sofa "where some guests curl up with a good book by the fire," some antiques, and Queen Anne dining room furnishings.

Greg, a former partner in a New York accounting firm that specialized in the hospitality industry, "had B&B in the back of my mind even when I attended the Cornell School of Hotel Administration." Now he conducts innkeeping-as-a-career sessions here and is president of the Chester Innkeepers Association. Since Greg and Sal, a native of Luzzano, Italy, bought this B&B in 1991, it has become known for its hospitality and food. As one guest from Virginia wrote, "On any scale, top billing. . . . Our stay was just too short."

In residence: Max, "a beautiful blond cocker spaniel."
Foreign languages spoken: Italian and Spanish.
Bed and bath: Eight rooms on first and second floors. (Some with slanted ceilings.) All private baths (some shower without tub), most en suite (robes provided for two hall baths). Double (some canopied), queen (private entrance and pool view), or king/twin beds (with treehouse feel). Two two-room suites, each with private entrance and an antique rocking horse. One has two doubles and a double daybed; other suite has double bed and a single daybed.
Breakfast: 7:30–9. French toast, pancakes, or waffles with fruit; stuffed French toast with cream cheese and apricots and raspberries; bacon and eggs with homemade biscuits.
Plus: Hot cider or mulled wine by the fire. Down comforters and quilts. Upright piano. Coffee and tea always available. Gazebo. Rock garden pool. Sauna. Option of weekend (usually Italian) dinner, $25 per person. Transportation to/from Bellows Falls Amtrak. Meeting room with conference table.

Innkeepers are great sharers. One recalls the guest who arrived for a wedding only to find he'd left his dress pants at home. The innkeeper wore the same size. The guest appeared at the wedding properly dressed in borrowed pants.

Craftsbury Bed & Breakfast on Wylie Hill

Craftsbury Common, VT 05827 802/586-2206

Host: Margaret Ramsdell
Location: High. Rural. Peaceful. About a mile from Craftsbury Common, two from Craftsbury Sports Center (whose groomed and tracked cross-country ski trails pass through fields of this B&B). Near miles of back roads (good for mountain bikes) and lakes. Thirty miles from Stowe. One mile from Sterling College.
Open: Year round. Reservations preferred.
Rates: $45 single room, $60–$70 double. $5–$15 crib or rollaway.
♥ ♦ ♦ ♣ ✗ ⊁

From New Hampshire: *"Drink coffee in the kitchen while she prepares the best breakfast I've ever had."* From Massachusetts: *"An excellent and sensitive conversationalist who knows when to give 'space' to guests."* From Vermont: *"Excellent knowledge of area. . . . Her house is a home."*

The hostess, too, enjoys her 1860s farmhouse. "I feel so peacefully in tune with my surroundings, the views, sunrises, sunsets, rainbows, and startlingly beautiful moonrise seen through slats of our barn. It is a joy to share this with guests. . . . When the family was young, we had a summer residential riding camp here. Since converting [10 years ago] to a B&B, I've met an octogenarian who came for one week and stayed for six, honeymooners, and many returnees who come for relaxation."

In residence: Willoughby, a golden retriever.
Foreign language spoken: French.
Bed and bath: In separate wing—four ground-floor rooms with individual thermostats and queen, double, or twin beds share two shower baths. Main house—second-floor queen-bedded room and room with extra-long double bed share full bath with hostess. Rollaway and crib available.
Breakfast: Usually not before 8. Juice, fruit. Cinnamon apple pancakes or French toast with hot applesauce. Or cinnamon apple coffee cake and omelets with Vermont cheddar. Homemade corn bread. In dining room (off country kitchen with wood stove) on table set with hand-thrown pottery, silver, fresh flowers; view of bird feeder outside window.
Plus: Wood stove in guests' living room. No TV. Flannel sheets. Dinner for cyclists or groups arranged; babysitting too.

Quail's Nest B&B Inn

802/293-5099

P.O. Box 221, Main Street, Danby, VT 05739-0221

Hosts: Anharad and Chip Edson
Location: In a quiet village, surrounded by mountains. Between Manchester and Rutland, just off Route 7. Walk to crafts and antiques shops. Three miles to Appalachian Trail; within 20–45 minutes of five ski areas, water- falls, country auctions, alpine slide.
Open: Year round except two weeks in April and December 24–26.
Rates: $60 shared bath, $75 private. $10 less April, May, June, November. $10 third person. MC, Visa.
♣ ✗ ⊁

From New Jersey: *"A peaceful, gentle place to reflect and unwind . . . full of country atmosphere . . . gave my brother and his wife a gift certificate to spend their 25th anniversary there."* From New York: *"A delight to the senses."* From Illinois: *"Breakfasts are phenomenal, in quantity as well as quality. . . . Art and old quilts everywhere."* From California: *"Cozy and homey. . . . Memories of antiques, exploring, a quaint old village, and people who leave us feeling sentimental and nostalgic."*

One television producer was so impressed with "everything, including the artistry and the coming-home-to-mom feeling," that she wanted to do a B&B segment.

When Anharad (a Welsh name meaning "country flower") and Chip, a former art teacher, moved from New Jersey to Vermont 10 years ago, they blended their talents in this 1835 house. Now Chip dovetails hosting with a folk art shop in the barn where he carves and paints wooden signs and furniture.

In residence: In hosts' quarters—Aubrey is seven; Chelsea, five; Ethan, two. Pumpkin, a yellow Lab retriever, "is as sweet and plump as my apple pie!"
Bed and bath: Five second-floor double-bedded rooms; two have a twin bed also. Three have private shower bath, two share a full bath.
Breakfast: Usually 8–9 (7:30 in winter). Cheese baked eggs, apple muffins, waffles with fresh strawberries and whipped cream, fresh fruit or apple puff pancakes, banana bread, and homegrown raspberries. Cereals, juice, coffee, tea, milk. Served family style in dining room.
Plus: Living room fireplace. Hammock. Front porch chairs. Lemonade, mulled cider, or tea with home-baked goodies. Guest refrigerator. Restaurant recommendation where "Mom and Pop do the cooking."

Cornucopia of Dorset   802/867-5751

P.O. Box 307, Dorset, VT 05251-0307

Hosts: Bill and Linda Ley
Location: In National Historic District. Walk to pubs, restaurants, Dorset Theatre. Ten minutes to Manchester.
Open: Year round. Two-night minimum on weekends and during fall foliage; three-night minimum on holiday weekends.

Rates: $95–$105 king, $105–$120 four-poster king/twins option or four-poster queen, $105–$135 canopied queen with fireplace, $165–$185 cottage suite. Some seasonal specials. Amex, MC, Visa.
♥ ♨ ❄ ✈ ✂

"It really is *marvelous*, with very caring innkeepers," said the fussy Boston innkeeper who sometimes hosts the Leys on their own getaways.

And to think that the Leys, now known for their personalized attention to detail, were looking for a much larger property in January 1987. That's when they happened upon "this country village, a great community with wonderful dining and a professional theater," and this 19th-century clapboard colonial with just four large guest rooms and one cathedral-ceilinged cottage.

In New York Bill and Linda had experience working together in the travel industry. Here they furnished with comfortable antiques, a huge (14 by 26), gorgeous "very old" Oriental dining room rug, and some reproductions.

(Please turn page.)

Turndown service includes freshened everything, a "sweet dreams" sweet, and tomorrow's breakfast menu. There's welcoming champagne (with fresh berries); a Ley-written "guidebook" to the area; your own advance copy of a specific menu if you have dinner reservations; good conversation; plenty of pampering—and privacy too.

In residence: Kitt, "our 100 percent purebred Vermont mutt, loved by all."
Bed and bath: Four air-conditioned second-floor rooms with sitting areas, private full baths (one has shower only). King bed; canopied queen with wood-burning fireplace; four-poster queen; four-poster king/twins option. Sensational cottage has queen-bedded skylit loft with air conditioning, fireplaced living room with ceiling fan, large full bath, fully equipped kitchen, private patio.
Breakfast: 8–9:30. (Wake-up tray with coffee or tea and fresh flowers for main house guests.) Repertoire includes warmed spiced fruit compote with sour cream and almonds, baked croissant a l'orange with creme fraiche, baked raspberry puff pancakes with pecans, warm maple syrup, sausage links. "Cookbook in the works."
Plus: Fireplaced library and living room. VCR. Sun room. Self-serve beverages and cookies. Fresh fruit. Flowers. Robes. Wool mattress covers. Down comforters. Fine wines and champagne available.

Dovetail Inn

P.O. Box 976, Main Street, Route 30
Dorset, VT 05251-0976

802/867-5747
fax 802/867-0246

Hosts: Jean and Jim Kingston
Location: Across from village green (on the main road) in historic district "free of architectural intrusions." Walk to summer theater and fine restaurants. Within 30 minutes of Bromley and Stratton mountains; 7 minutes to Merck Forest (hiking and cross-country skiing). Six miles north of

Manchester's designer outlets.
Open: Year round except for late fall and early spring. Two-night minimum most weekends.
Rates: $60–$80 smallest rooms, $65–$90 average room, $80–$125 with fireplace and wet bar. $15 extra person. Crib free. MC, Visa.
♥ ⁂ ✗

What's it like to live in such a pretty village year round? It offers the strong sense of community that the Kingstons hoped for when they moved here from Connecticut with their teenagers in 1984. Guests are welcome to attend a town meeting with the hosts—and/or you might meet local residents when they drop into the inn for coffee. The Kingstons are active members of the local historical society (museum is next door to the inn). Jim, an engineer and woodworker who has served as a town lister, is a freelance building inspector and property manager. Jean wears aprons (really!) and is the inn's official gardener/seamstress/ baker.

The inn, two buildings that served as the annex and tearoom of the Dorset Inn (located across the street), is warm and comfortable, with country decor.

In residence: Alice, "our regal Irish setter/golden retriever mix."
Bed and bath: Eleven rooms (10 are air conditioned) on first and second floors; all private baths. One bath has shower only, others are full. King, queen (one with fireplace and wet bar), double, or twin beds. Cot and crib available.

Breakfast: 8–9:30. Fruit. Juices. Yeast breads, muffins, or coffee cakes. Locally made jams and jellies. Plenty of coffee and tea. Served by the fireplace in the keeping room during cool months, by the pool in summer.
Plus: Ceiling fans. Free use of pool (unguarded). Guests' pantry with microwave, refrigerator, sink; coffee, tea, juices, and soda always available. Cable TV. Games. Library nook.

The Little Lodge at Dorset   802/867-4040

Route 30, Box 673, Dorset, VT 05251

Hosts: Allan and Nancy Norris
Location: Set back from road on a rise, one block from village green. A pretty pond in front, mountain view beyond. Across from oldest nine-hole golf course in the country and adjacent to hiking and cross-country trails. Close to craft and antiques shops and summer theater; 15 minutes to Bromley, 30 to Stratton, 6 to Manchester. "Excellent biking terrain."
Open: Year round (usually). Two-day minimum in foliage season and on some holiday weekends.
Rates: $80–$90 for two. $30 extra person. Discount for extended stays. Amex, Discover (preferably for deposits only).
♥ ♦ ♣ ♦ ✂ ✁

Just five guest rooms, but so much space for relaxation: an antiques-filled living room with stenciled wallpaper and wood stove; a five-sided sun porch screened in summer, glassed in winter; a unique barnboard den; and all that lawn. The inn's original part, c. 1810–20, was moved here in the 1930s from Hebron, New York. Subsequent additions resulted in an unusual and interesting arrangement of windows, staircases, and halls. Country decor includes Nancy's stenciling and quilts, some fine antiques, and bedspreads crocheted by Allan's sister.

Since the Norrises moved here from Baltimore, Maryland, in 1981, their between-season travels have included Kenya, Egypt, China, Yugoslavia, India, South Africa, and Turkey.

In residence: A very friendly dog "whom the guests love."
Foreign languages spoken: Some Spanish and French.
Bed and bath: Five rooms, each with twins/king option (three are air conditioned), on first (one room with private exterior entrance) and second floors. All with private baths; some full, some shower only. Cot and crib available.
Breakfast: 8–9:30. Juice, ccreals, unusual toasted homemade breads, muffins (many made from recipes exchanged with guests), beverage. In antiques-filled dining room.
Plus: Tea, coffee, and hot chocolate always available. Late-afternoon cheese and crackers. Refrigerator and (BYOB) wet bar. Turned-down beds. Mints on your pillow. Dartboard, games, books, puzzles, mini–pool game. Terrace. Skating on the pond. Barn for bikes and skis.

From New York: *"Charming . . . friendly . . . hosts who anticipate every need."*

Mountain View Creamery   802/626-9924
Box 355, Darling Hill Road, East Burke, VT 05832   fax 802/626-9924

Hosts: Marilyn and John Pastore
Location: Spectacular. On 440 acres with gorgeous huge red stable, carriage houses, barns—including the state's largest cow barn. Five minutes to Burke Mountain; 15 to Lake Willoughby.
Open: Year round.

Rates: Vary according to size of room. $90–$120. Fifteen percent less for three or more nights, for singles, and for everyone March 15–June 15 and November–December 15. Midweek Burke Mountain ski packages. MC, Visa.

♥ ✲ ◆ ✖ ✄

From Vermont Bicycle Touring: *"Lovingly, authentically, and elegantly restored . . . warm and gracious welcome . . . one of the favorites on our list!"* From North Carolina: *"Felt very relaxed . . . setting captured our hearts."* From Massachusetts: *"Both quaint and elegant. Food exceptional."* From Minnesota: *"View was awesome . . . acres delightful for walks."*

Count the ways! Guests extol (at length) this 1890 red brick Georgian colonial building opened as a B&B in 1990. Once part of Elmer Darling's gentleman's farm, which produced butter and cheese for his New York City Fifth Avenue hotel, the entire enormous property had fallen into a sad state of disrepair. Then the Pastores took over, and restoration became a labor of love for Marilyn, who remembers writing contracts for her immigrant grandmother/builder. Now the creamery is filled in country manor style with antiques, chintzes, quilts, and stenciled floors.

A former teacher of Russian, Marilyn accompanied John, a Boston cardiologist, on many trips to Russia when he was secretary of the Nobel Prize–winning International Physicians for the Prevention of Nuclear War. The Pastores, parents of three grown children, and Joy, an almost-native Vermonter who grew up on a farm, are thanked by guests for "peace, quiet, and beauty."

In residence: Joy Chesley, manager. Roxie, a Scottish terrier. "John's herd"—four cows. Joy's horse, Penny.
Foreign language spoken: Russian.
Bed and bath: Seven second-floor rooms, all private shower baths. Queen, double, or twin beds. Rollaway and crib available.
Breakfast: 8–9. Home-baked breads, fresh fruit, yogurt, frittata with red pepper, hot/cold cereals, apple pancakes with maple syrup. In brick-walled breakfast room with views; classical music plays.
Plus: No TV. Extensive hiking and cross-country trails right here. Fireplaced living room. Down comforters. Upright piano. Individual thermostats. Soup on wood stove. Fresh fruit. Beverages. Guest refrigerator. Two Ping-Pong tables. Quilting classes. Huge vegetable gardens.

*M*any B&Bs are perfect for family reunions.

Maplewood Inn & Antiques   802/265-8039

Route 22A South, RR 1   (U.S. except Vt., and Canada) 800/253-7729
Box 4460, Fair Haven, VT 05743-9721

Hosts: Cindy and Doug Baird
Location: Pastoral, with mountain views. From Route 4, exit 2, it's one mile south of historic village center. Minutes to Lakes Bomoseen and Saint Catherine. Forty minutes west of Killington and Pico ski areas.
Open: Year round. Two-night mini-

mum during foliage season and some holidays.
Rates: $70–$75 double bed. $85 queen. $105 suite. $175 expanded suite for four. $20–$30 third person. Singles $5 less. Five nights or more, 10 percent less. Discover, MC, Visa.
♥ ❖ ♦ ✈

The sunsets from the front porch, the traditional decor, and the many amenities all get high marks from guests who enjoy the hospitality at this B&B. It was the Maplewood Dairy homestead from 1880 until 1979. Since Cindy bought the three-part Greek Revival house and red barn, she has restored, redecorated, and added fireplaces and cable TV to guest rooms—and now the barn is her antiques shop, with collectibles, folk art, and crafts.

On Long Island Cindy had her own restaurant/cafe. Doug, a native Vermonter, "is a treasure trove of information—for cycling routes, hidden waterfalls, and fishing coves."

Bed and bath: Five rooms (four with fireplaces) including two suites. One suite via private steep stairway has double sofa bed in living room. All private baths (all en suite except one) with shower/tub or shower without tub. Double or queen beds. Rollaways available.
Breakfast: 8:30. Juices. Fruit course. Homemade bread and muffins, homemade granola, cereals, yogurt, meat and cheese. Hot beverages.
Plus: Air conditioning in four rooms; fans in all. In-room phones ($2/day) with private number. Complimentary cordials, sherry, teas, mulled cider, coffee, cocoa always available. Fireplaced sitting room with cable TV and stereo. Board games. Stereopticon viewer and slides. Gathering room with library. Croquet.

Guests wrote: *"Tasteful . . . not overdone! . . . very clean . . . enthusiastic, friendly innkeepers."*

Silver Maple Lodge & Cottages   802/333-4326

RR 1, Box 8, South Main Street, Fairlee, VT 05045   800/666-1946

Hosts: Sharon and Scott Wright
Location: One mile south of town center; close to I-91. Close to Leda's Pizza Restaurant (popular with local residents and tourists). Opposite open farmland with barn. Views of White Mountains to the east, Green Mountains to the west; 17 miles from Dartmouth College.
Open: Year round.

Rates: In inn (no smoking)—shared bath $42 single, $48 double; private bath $52–$58 single, $54–$62 double. Cottages (smoking and pets allowed)—$56–$62 single, $60–$66 double. Ten-speed bicycles $10/day (includes shuttle, if needed). Canoes $30/day. Special packages offered. Amex, Discover, MC, Visa.
♥ ⅃ ❖ ♦

(Please turn page.)

Restored and refurbished. With crisp, simple country decor. All done by Scott, the award-winning pumpkin grower who grew up on a nearby farm, and Sharon, the official baker, a young couple who publish an enticing seasonal newsletter. They have great suggestions for do-it-yourself tours, for cycling, for canoeing, and for walking from inn to inn or from Silver Maple as a base. They'll direct you to antiques auctions; suggest a wild game, lobster, clam, or steak supper; or arrange for a champagne hot-air balloon ride or for delivery (at the inn) of a Vermont-grown turkey.

The 1790s farmhouse became an inn in the early 1900s. Pine-paneled cottages were added in the 1950s. Since the Wrights bought the property in the mid-1980s, they have added baths, a common room fireplace, and, in the cottages, air conditioning.

In residence: "Our cat, Albert Riley, has the life of Riley."
Bed and bath: Eight second-floor rooms (all with mountain views) in the inn; four rooms with sinks. All private baths (with tub or shower) except for two rooms that share a full bath. King, double, or twin beds. Cottages (nostalgic for some people) with private baths have three twins, a double bed and a twin, two doubles, or one king. Two cottages have kitchenettes, one has working fireplace. Cot available.
Breakfast: 7–9. Juice, fruit, homemade breads and rolls, coffee or tea. Self-served in the dining room.
Plus: Ceiling fans in two guest rooms. Screened wraparound porch. Piano. Games. Croquet, badminton, shuffleboard, volleyball. Picnic tables among the apple trees. Babysitting arranged.

Fair Meadows Farm B&B   802/285-2132

Box 430, Route 235, Franklin, VT 05457

Hosts: Terry and Phil Pierce
Location: In the land of "big sky" (spectacular views) and big hills (for cycling). Minutes to Canadian border. Three miles west of Franklin; 12 miles from I-89; 65 to Montreal, 50 to Burlington International Airport.
Open: Year round.
Rates: $35 single, $45 double.
🛥 ✳✳

Rare. The kind of reasonably priced B&B that is getting harder to find. The comfortable and immaculate farmhouse has been in the family since 1853. The five Pierce children, educated at five different colleges, are now in five different states.

During two B&B-to-B&B cycling trips—10 years apart—we appreciated Phil's sense of humor and his perspective on the changes in dairying through the years. Although he is retired now, a nephew is continuing the family tradition. Terry continues her gardening and cooking and community involvement. Recipes are shared. And so are practical hints—everything from changing currency at a bank before entering Canada to alternative routes going south.

Foreign language spoken: French.
Bed and bath: Four rooms, each with double bed except for one upstairs room with two twin beds. Rooms share two full baths, one upstairs and one downstairs. First-floor room has private half bath. Two cribs available.

Breakfast: At guests' convenience. A real farm breakfast including home-made muffins and butter. Served in the pine-paneled room off the kitchen and overlooking the meadow.
Plus: Large living room. TV. Garage for bicycles.

From Vermont: *"A visit—my first B&B—that is a very happy memory for my grandson and me."* From England: *"We felt sad when we left because they made us feel so welcome."*

Cobble House Inn
802/234-5458
P.O. Box 49, Childrens Camp Ground Road, Gaysville, VT 05746

Hosts: Beau and Phil Benson
Location: Atop a mountain road. Six miles west of Bethel; 15 from Killington and Pico ski areas; 5 from lake; 9 miles from I-89. Within 12–20 miles of four golf courses.

Open: Year round. Two-day minimum on most weekends and during foliage season.
Rates: Include tax and service—$80 porch room, $100 queen bed.
♥ ♨ ✿ ✗ ⚡

From Massachusetts: *"A treasure . . . perfect hosts."* From New York: *"One of our favorite places (we also liked Florence, Italy!). . . . Words cannot describe the food . . . served with impeccable style and grace . . . handsome rooms . . . total relaxation."*

It all happens "off the beaten track, on a river and in the mountains," the very location the Bensons searched for in 1985. They bought this house with cupola and huge barn, did the house (even the foundation) all over, and furnished with antique bedsteads and lots of country touches. Recent "discovered joys" include expanded gardens and trompe l'oeil painting as well as graining and marbleizing techniques. (Yes, hints shared.) Sam has become star tour leader for wooded and river trails, rock-finding expeditions, and great swimming holes.

Now the Bensons have an ardent following of die-hard skiers, cyclists (mountain bikes, helmets, and maps delivered here); "foodies" (Beau is a trained chef); and people who only want to relax. Now the "city boy" who was president of a small Washington-based research company is called "Farmer Phil." He raises livestock naturally, trains Morgan horses, and uses felled trees for fencing. As guests can tell, you couldn't find a family that is happier doing what they do.

In residence: Son Sam is nine years old. In barnyard—pigs, calves, turkeys, horses, muscovy ducks, cats.
Bed and bath: Six rooms; all new private (two tub/shower, four shower) baths. Private veranda entrance to small double-bedded rooms. Queen bed and sitting area in each second-floor room; rollaways available.
Breakfast: Usually 8–10. Belgian waffles, sourdough French toast, omelets, whole-grain pancakes. Bensons' own pork products. Outdoors in warm months. In bed, if you'd like.
Plus: Afternoon hors d'oeuvres. Fireplaced dining room. Porch rockers. If requested, morning coffee outside your door. Two fishing rods. "We'll cook and store your catch for you." Use of refrigerator. Two miles of hiking and cross-country trails right here. Picnic service. Option of acclaimed dinner ($18–$25) Thursday–Sunday with advance arrangements. Beer and wine for sale. Sometimes, four-wheel drive tours of the area.

Carolyn's Bed & Breakfast

802/472-6338

15 Church Street, P.O. Box 1087, Hardwick, VT 05843-1087

Host: Carolyn Hunter Richter and daughters Emily and Anna
Location: In a small Vermont town, 20 miles northeast of Stowe, 5 miles to Caspian Lake. Within five miles of three cross-country ski centers. Walk to free tennis courts. Bike touring country.

Open: Year round. Two-night minimum in foliage season and on major holidays.
Rates: $45–$50 single, $70–$80 double. $25 each child six and older in parents' room, $10 under age six. MC, Visa.
♥ ♨ ☀ ✈ ⚥

From Vermont: *"Pampered with every conceivable amenity . . . chocolates in our room, huge selection of lush towels . . . everything you might want and had forgotten . . . decor reflects Carolyn's gracious and fun-loving nature. . . . Gorgeous rooms . . . memorable breakfasts . . . a real treasure."*

The cottage Victorian has original cherry woodwork, hardwood floors, cypress staircase, and oak wall-to-wall bookcase. Many of the antiques acquired at area auctions came complete with a "story." Carolyn, a former elementary school counselor, is a mountain biker, skier, and children's therapist who enjoys cooking and baking. Guests from several continents, including an Egyptian princess and her family, have enjoyed the hospitality since this B&B opened in 1986.

In residence: Anna is 16. Emily is home during Washington State University breaks.
Foreign languages spoken: A little French, Italian, and Russian.
Bed and bath: Four second-floor rooms (accessible by two interior stairways)—all with feather beds—share one second-floor full bath and one first-floor half bath. Two rooms have king beds, one with a crown canopy. One room with twin pineapple beds. One with double four-poster, ceiling fan, and a sink. Rollaway and crib available.
Breakfast: 8–10; other times arranged. Maybe homemade lemon poppyseed French toast with local strawberry jam or banana walnut pancakes with Vermont maple syrup; or soufflelike casserole with French bread, cheddar cheese, eggs, and smoked ham. Juices, granola, cereals, seasonal fruits, rhubarb coffee cake, lemon/blueberry muffins, homemade breads and scones.
Plus: Tea and sweets upon arrival. Evening sherry by fire or in library. Bedroom fans. Porch rockers. Children's crib, toys, high chair. Guest refrigerator. Dinner ($12.50). Victorian cream teas, $15.

All the B&Bs with this ♨ symbol want you to know that they are a private home set up for paying guests (rather than an inn). Although definitions vary, these private home B&Bs tend to have one to three guest rooms. For the owners—people who enjoy meeting people—B&B is usually a part-time occupation.

Fitch Hill Inn

RFD Box 1879, Fitch Hill Road
Hyde Park, VT 05655-9733

802/888-3834
802/888-5941
800-639-2903

Hosts: Richard A. Pugliese and Stanley E. Corklin
Location: Rural. On four hilltop acres with hiking and cross-country ski trails. Spectacular mountain views. Five-minute walk to historic Hyde Park (pop. 475) and (summer) opera house. Four miles from Long Trail and from a reservation with "no development and plenty of loons." One-third mile off Routes 100 and

15. Fifteen minutes north of Stowe.
Open: Year round. Two-day minimum December 25–January 3 and on Presidents' and Columbus Day weekends.
Rates: $50 twin, $55–$60 double, $60 king. Less in November and April 15–June 15. Singles $5 less. Extra person $15. Skiing, canoeing, bike, and golf packages. MC, Visa.

♥ ⁂ ♦ ✈ ⊬

From California, Ohio, Illinois, New York, Oklahoma, New Hampshire, Washington state, Canada: *"Best vacation of our lives . . . Richard was like a personal tour guide . . . provided excellent hints, hidden secrets, cycling routes and maps . . . very clean, nicely decorated . . . tea and cookies at end of day . . . superb and creative food . . . different breakfast every day for seven days . . . tranquil . . . well-maintained grounds . . . spectacular front porch view. . . . Among the best of more than 50 B&Bs we have stayed in."*

Richard has "always had a summer camp in Vermont" and is now doing what he "always wanted to" (run an inn). Stanley teaches at Stowe Middle School. In Illinois they were both Episcopal clergymen. In 1991 they restored this c. 1794 Federal house and furnished with period antiques.

In residence: Richard's sons Jeremy, age 20, and Joshua, 18. Brandon, a golden retriever.
Foreign languages spoken: Spanish and some French.
Bed and bath: Six second-floor rooms share three upstairs baths plus one first-floor half bath. King, double (plus space for rollaway in one room), or twin beds.
Breakfast: 8–10. Caramel French toast, blueberry pancakes with Vermont maple syrup, berry strata, sausage and crescent roll bake, fresh orange juice, cereals, Green Mountain coffee.
Plus: Late-afternoon tea or sherry. Color cable TV; 250 videos. Quilts and down comforters. Window fans. Picnic baskets ($5 for two). Dinners by reservation, $40 for two. Complimentary maple syrup.

*H*eard all over New England: "Most guests are surprised at all our area has to offer."

The Andrie Rose Inn

13 Pleasant Street, Ludlow, VT 05149

802/228-4846
(U.S./Canada) **800/223-4846**
fax **802/228-7910**

Hosts: Ellen and Jack Fisher
Location: One-half block off Main Street, one-half mile to Okemo ski mountain. Ten minutes north of Weston.
Open: Year round. Two-night minimum on fall and winter weekends.
Rates: Main inn—spring/summer $75–$85, $95 with Jacuzzi. Fall/win-

ter $95–$110, $120 with Jacuzzi. Family suites up to four guests spring/summer $200, fall/winter $250. $25 additional guest. Luxury suites—spring/summer $148, fall/winter $185. Discounts for senior citizens and for extended stays.

♥ ♯ ⚜ ♦ ✗ ⅀

"Better than four- and five-star hotels that we've stayed in during our extensive travels." That's what the Fishers saw in this 1829 colonial-style house in 1993, after looking at 60 inns. The Fishers had been living in Palm Beach, Florida, having owned a Budget Rent-a-Car franchise and one of Philadelphia's largest health care agencies. Here they redecorated the B&B, making the carriage house suites "lush and plush."

Guests tend to gather in the kitchen. Jack studies at the Culinary Institute of America. Ellen, too, enjoys pampering romantics and families.

In residence: Schultz, a dachshund.
Bed and bath: In inn—10 double-bedded rooms (two with sloped ceilings and skylights). All private full baths; five with whirlpool tubs, one with claw-foot tub. Guest house luxury suites have granite fireplaces, whirlpool tubs, TV, VCR, stereo, private phones. Family suites have granite kitchen, dishwasher, microwave, whirlpool tubs, washer/dryer, gas grill on deck.
Breakfast: Blueberry pancakes, buttermilk waffles with Ben & Jerry's ice cream, or cinnamon walnut French toast. Juices, teas, Colombian and espresso coffees, yogurt, cereals, fresh fruit, homemade bread.
Plus: Cookie-filled jars. Fresh fruit. Cocktail hour. Hot chocolate, coffee, apple cider. Special occasions acknowledged. Porch rockers. Saturday and holiday candlelight dinner, $50 per couple. Free ski shuttle to Okemo Mountain. Individual thermostats. Down comforters. Turndown service with Vermont mints on pillow.

Fletcher Manor

1 Elm Street, Ludlow, VT 05149-1301

802/228-3548

Hosts: Bob and Jill Tofferi
Location: In center of town, with free ski season shuttle from door to Okemo Mountain. Bordered by Black River. Minutes' walk to shops, restaurants, antiquing. Four miles to Ludlow lake region, one to Fox Run Golf Club. Thirty minutes to hiking (Long Trail, Coolidge State Park).

Open: Year round. Two-night minimum on weekends September 15–April 15, three nights on holiday weekends.
Rates: Mid-April–mid-September $75. Winter and foliage months $95. Singles $10 less. MC, Visa.
⚜ ✗ ⅀

From New York: *"My husband and I picked Fletcher Manor for New Year's Eve because it was small (only four guest rooms) . . . went back to visit in April . . . like being in a friend's home . . . beautifully decorated . . . nicely presented, satisfying breakfast . . . relaxing, down-to-earth yet elegant place."*

The Tofferis had always admired this 1837 brick Federal/Greek Revival house. And some local B&B owners knew that they would love hosting. "We do." After the redoing was done in 1992—the oak staircase railing, too, is handsome—they decorated every room with Oriental rugs, formal antique furnishings, and swags. Upstairs, the beds have quilts—some are on walls too—all made by Jill, who owned a quilt shop in Ludlow for eight years. Bob, who is a postmaster for the Postal Service, is a Ludlow native.

In residence: Jenna Lyn, age six. Kodiak, a golden retriever. Cats, Zag and Whiskers.

Bed and bath: Four second-floor rooms (two with mountain views) with double or queen bed share two baths—one with shower, the other with claw-foot tub. Rollaway available.

Breakfast: 7–9:30 depending on season. Homemade breads and muffins. Locally made baked goods. Vermont jellies and cheeses, fresh fruit, juice, yogurt, cereal, beverages. Continental buffet in formal Victorian dining room with crystal chandelier.

Plus: Fireplaced parlor. Baby grand piano in adjoining music room. Ceiling fans in two guest rooms. Guest refrigerator. Wicker-furnished porch. Information about state parks, auctions, cycling routes.

Branch Brook Bed & Breakfast   802/626-8316

South Wheelock Road, P.O. Box 143   800/572-7712
Lyndon, VT 05849-0143

Hosts: Ted and Ann Tolman
Location: In the village. Walking distance of two covered bridges. Half a mile from I-91, exit 23. Two miles to Lyndon State College, 8 to Burke Mountain ski area, 35 to Canadian border. Near restaurants and (other) antiques shops.
Open: Year round.
Rates: $55 shared bath, $60–$70 private. $10 crib or rollaway. Singles $5 less. MC, Visa.
♥ ♨ ♣ ✕ ⊁

"Our favorite place is our log cabin on 23 acres, located eight miles west. If guests want to cross-country ski, watch the maple sugaring operation, hike, or just relax there, we take them to it. To reach the cabin, we often passed by 'this old (1830s) house,' which had been vacant for eight years. In 1986 we spotted a FOR SALE sign in the tall grass. 'You don't want it,' said the Realtor. We did. After three years of renovating (rebuilding), we furnished with many of the antiques we had in our restored 1760 Connecticut house. Guests are welcome to try using our AGA cooker, our only cooking source. Shortly after we purchased it, an AGA importer used our kitchen to film a video for an owner's manual."

In Connecticut Ted was assistant food service manager for an insurance company. Ann was director of the state's child nutrition programs.

(Please turn page.)

Bed and bath: Five second-floor rooms. One room has queen canopied bed, private shower bath. Two rooms, each with two twin beds, share a shower bath (robes provided). Two queen-bedded rooms have beamed ceilings, private baths (one with tub and shower, one with claw-footed tub). Rollaway and crib available.
Breakfast: 8–9:30. Pancakes or French toast with "our own" maple syrup. Muffins or scones. Fresh fruit. Cereals. Yogurt. Eggs any style on toast. Bacon or sausage. Juices. In fireplaced dining room with full-length windows.
Plus: Window fans. TV with cable, VCR. Games. Books. Late afternoon coffee, tea, or hot cider. Cookies. Phone jacks and individual thermostats in some rooms. Transportation to/from Vermont transit bus stop or Lyndonville airport. Antiques shop in restored barn.

> From Florida: *"They love to cook and I love to eat. . . . I think they introduced me to half the town of Lyndon; I'll have to go back to meet the other half."* From Canada: *"Spotless, charming decor . . . breakfast was a unique experience . . . but most important were the hosts, who made me feel special and right at home."*

Wildflower Inn
Darling Hill Road, Lyndonville, VT 05851

802/626-8310
800/627-8310

Hosts: Jim and Mary O'Reilly
Location: On 500 gorgeous Northeast Kingdom acres with mountain views overlooking valleys. Four miles from I-91.
Open: Year round except three weeks in April and November. Two-night minimum on Saturdays and in foliage season.
Rates: Include breakfast, snacks, dinner, taxes, gratuities. Year round,

age 5 and under free. In season, first two occupants in rooms $140 or $150; in suites $170, $190, $200, $260; $30 more in foliage season. Third or fourth occupants $40 adult, $30 ages 13–17, $20 ages 6–12. Less off-season. Special packages offered. Discounts for stays longer than three nights.
♥ ♫ ♣ ✗ ✶

A find. Found first by romantics and now by families. Acclaimed on Boston's "Chronicle" (WCVB-TV). Created as a B&B by a couple who wanted to be "at home" with their kids (Jim was a traveling civil engineer), it is now a destination, a personalized miniresort where ideas grow and flourish along with the O'Reilly family. In the beginning (1984) they planted wildflowers, built stone walls, and stenciled the 1850 farmhouse. They furnished with antiques, four-posters, and quilts. Now there's a variety of rooms and suites in four converted buildings. There are pony rides, fishing trips, nature walks—all "togetherness low-key activities." An outdoor (summer) heated swimming pool and a baby pool. And sledding, cross-country skiing, skating (on the duck pond), horse-drawn wagon and sleigh rides, bonfires, face painting, children's menus—and even an order-ahead no-wait family dinner hour with vegetarian option. Everyone meets Jim. The O'Reilly kids are great guides and playmates. Mary, the newsletter-writing mom, has begun a home schooling program.

In residence: In O'Reillys' house—Sean, Anna, Kevin, Danny, Brian, Tom, ages 4–14. In petting barn—donkey, pony, calf, lamb, goat, Peter Cottontail. Also Belgian horses—Molly, and Sally and daughter Rosie.
Bed and bath: Twenty-three rooms or suites, some with shower and tub, with shower only, or with Jacuzzi. Honeymoon cottage has queen bed, French doors onto deck, kitchenette, two-person Jacuzzi. Four shared-bath farmhouse rooms soon to be converted to two-room suites. Family suites with kitchenettes accommodate four to eight. Three have washer and dryer; another, two bathrooms, TV and VCR, deck. Handicapped-accessible room has double bed, bunk beds, room for cot or portacrib.
Breakfast: 8–9. (Coffee at 7.) Buttermilk pancakes with strawberries and whipped cream, farm-fresh eggs or "teddy bear" pancakes. Fresh fruit, cereals, granola, yogurt, homemade muffins or coffee cake.
Plus: Call 800 number for current activity schedule. Snacks by living room wood stove, 3–5 p.m. Sauna and hot tub. Children's recreation room with dress-up clothes and reading loft. Playground. Babysitting. Family evening movies. Children's musical theater workshops. Christmas Nativity Play. Tennis courts under construction. Summer snack bar, open 11–3; sandwiches, beverages, cocktails. Public dining room (not open Sundays) seats 40.

The American Country Collection Host #080

Manchester, VT

Location: Tranquil. On five acres with babbling brook at the foot of the Green Mountains. One mile to Manchester center; 5 to Long Trail, 6 to Bromley, 10 to Dorset Theatre; 15 to Weston Playhouse or Stratton.
Reservations: Year round through The American Country Collection, page 343.
Rates: $55 single, $60 double.

> Guests wrote: *"Our first B&B and we loved it. . . . Scones were superb . . . hospitality beyond our expectations. . . . Talented people who added much to our stay."*

They were among many guests who are fascinated by the carvings done by the hosts, ex-advertising executives. The host creates interesting pipes and does swordfish-bone scrimshaw. The hostess carves birds. Their house, built for a tenant farmer in 1890 and added on to through the years, has wide board floors and beamed ceilings. It is furnished eclectically—with comfortable old pieces, antiques, sculpture, and art. The property includes a barn with many original features intact.

In residence: One dog.
Bed and bath: Two second-floor rooms. One with one double bed and attached private shower bath. One with king/twins option, private full bath on first floor at bottom of stairs.
Breakfast: Flexible hours. Juice, fresh fruit, homemade scones and muffins, and coffee. Served in the dining room or on the deck.
Plus: Afternoon tea on the deck beside the brook, or by dining room wood stove or living room fireplace. Perhaps a tour of their workshop.

The American Country Collection Host #147
Middletown Springs, VT

Location: On 12 acres with a stream for wading, open fields for cross-country skiing, and neighboring woods for walks. Among other large older homes in a town with 640 residents, a green, a museum open on Sundays, and a little park where the mineral spring house is being restored. Half hour north of Manchester outlets, 15 minutes east of Lake St. Catherine, 8 east of Green Mountain College. Twenty minutes to Long Trail and Merck Forest. Good cycling country.
Reservations: Year round through The American Country Collection, page 343.
Rates: $55 single, $65 double. $20 third person.
🛥 ⁂ 🏕 ⚰

"'Did you buy it furnished? It's just like my grandmother's!' And even 'It's nicer than we expected!' That's what we hear in this big Victorian house, which was built with wonderful architectural details by the son of the inventor of Gray's horsepower machinery. It's furnished mostly with Victorian antiques, and now it is mostly redecorated. Some of the baths have high-tank toilets and claw-foot tubs. No chocolates on the pillow. It's a very get-togetherish place with basic hometown fun." Breakfast discussions run the gamut. People seem to be comfortable here. One woman, used to being on a schedule, made her husband take his watch off. "Another, who loved outlet shopping, gave us a fashion show every morning." Aromas seem to draw guests into the kitchen, the entryway for returnees who declare "We're home!"

This cheerful hostess, a Britisher who tends a lovely garden, converted this National Register house to a B&B in 1986 when she moved from North Carolina.

Bed and bath: Six rooms, five with queen bed, one king/twins option. All private baths (three en suite, three hall).
Breakfast: 8:30ish. Flexible. Fruit, juice, granola, waffles, sausages. Home-baked scones, muffins, or bread. At one table in sun room or in fireplaced dining room.
Plus: Fireplaced living room. Basement game room with pinball machines, foosball, player piano, jukebox, table tennis. Front porch rockers. Back porch (eclectic seating) overlooking garden. VCR with tape library. Dinner, $15 per person.

From Vermont: *"A real treat. Don't miss it!"*

Brookside Meadows   802/388-6429
RD 3, Box 2460   (U.S./Canada, for reservations) **800/442-9887**
Painter Road, Middlebury, VT 05753-8751

Hosts: Linda and Roger Cole
Location: Set back from lightly traveled road on meadowland with view of pond, brook, and Green Mountains beyond. Less than three miles from village and college. Within 45 minutes of Shelburne Museum, UVM Morgan Horse Farm, ski areas.
Open: Year round. Two-night reservations preferred. Two-night minimum on weekends and in summer and fall.
Rates: $75–$90. $15 cot. $135–$150 suite (up to four people).
♥ 🛥 ⁂ ◆ ⚰

From Maine: *"Excellent, modern, clean, efficient, comfortable."* From Australia: *"Our family was made to feel so welcome . . . breakfasts were delicious . . . relaxed surroundings with beautiful people."* From New York: *"Thought of everything."* From Massachusetts: *"An oasis in a meadow."*

Travelers from all over the world have declared that Linda, a former teacher, and Roger, a retired Middlebury College administrator, are gracious and helpful. Their house is designed on the lines of a late-1800s colonial story-and-a-half farm home. Linda worked closely with the architect when it was built in 1979—and she helped coordinate the recent addition and renovation. The decor is fresh; the gardens, beautiful. The barn behind the house is an oldie built in 1876 and moved in the 1980s from 12 miles away. Whether you want to watch maple sugaring or find a local swimming hole (with view of covered bridge), a lighted cross-country ski area, or a wide variety of restaurants, the hosts are prepared with more than directions.

In residence: Giant schnauzer, Tux(edo). Cat in hosts' quarters. Outside, two white China geese.
Bed and bath: Three rooms plus a suite, all private baths. First-floor room with queen bed, old wide pine floors. Upstairs—room with two twin beds, large full bath, double sink. One large king-bedded room. In suite, one room with queen bed, one with two twin beds, private entrance, bath, living room, dining area, and kitchen.
Breakfast: Usually at 8:30. Juice, cereal, fresh eggs or French toast with local maple syrup, coffee or tea.
Plus: Tea, wine, or soft drinks. Wood stove and cable TV in family room. Mints. Transportation from local bus stop or for bicyclists. Walking or cross-country skiing along brook with beaver dams.

October Pumpkin Inn

P.O. Box 226, Route 125E
East Middlebury, VT 05740

802/388-9525
(U.S./Canada) 800/237-2007

Hosts: Eileen and Charles Roeder
Location: "A quiet apple-pie-and-wooden-screen-door American village setting on a historic stagecoach road in Robert Frost country." Four miles south of Middlebury Village, then one mile east on Route 125.
Open: Year round.
Rates: $50 shared bath, $90 private. Less in off-season. $15 third person. Extended stay rates available.
♥ ❖

Staffers of major book companies looking for the "real Vermont" stay here. So do business travelers who have become B&B fans. It's a completely redone (by the Roeders), immaculate 1850 Greek Revival house furnished with colonial and English antiques, wing chairs, and Eileen's quilts.

Eileen and Charles have recreated the Renaissance era: In the early 1980s they had a B&B/farm in Vermont where they raised all their own produce and meats. They have been inn managers. And in the 1970s they were New Jersey–based antiques dealers. Here they did the stenciling seen throughout the inn.

(Please turn page.)

In residence: "Two neurotic ducks." Guests' polite pets accepted.
Bed and bath: Five air-conditioned rooms. Two first-floor rooms, each with queen bed, sitting area, private full bath. On second floor, canopied double bed, private full bath. Room with antique cannonball double bed, private bath. Room with two single wicker beds, shared bath. Cot available.
Breakfast: At guests' convenience. Continental, featuring Charles's cast iron–baked corn sticks and homemade jellies and jams. Served by dining room wood stove.
Plus: Air-conditioned common rooms. Cozy parlor with piano and abundant reading material. Carriage house hosts guests' bicycles, skis, canoes, and vintage autos. Gazebo.

From Massachusetts: *"As inviting as the name and exterior color."*

Shoreham Inn & Country Store   802/897-5081
On the Village Green   (U.S. except Vt., and Canada) **800/255-5081**
Shoreham, VT 05770

Hosts: Fred and Cleo Alter
Location: In small village in apple country. On Route 74 west. Five miles east of Lake Champlain ferry to Fort Ticonderoga; 12 "soul-enrich-
ing" miles south of Middlebury.
Open: Year round except November.
Rates: $40 single, $75 double.
♦ ♦ ♦ ♦ ♦

Good old-fashioned hospitality with homey eclectic decor have been the Alters' hallmarks since 1973 when they, silver anniversary celebrants, left Long Island and bought the rambling 1791 Shoreham Hotel, an added-on-to post-and-beam structure that had become apartments. They had both worked in Cleo's parents' Brewster, New York, hotel, and they had experience in advertising, publishing, public relations, and graphic design. Here they became do-it-yourselfers, retained the balustrade that was originally in a local church, and furnished with an assortment of country auction finds. (You're welcome to try on some vintage clothing.) Fred and Cleo juggle roles as Mr. and Mrs. Fix-it/Innkeepers/Realtors and as next-door Country Store shopkeepers who make sandwiches, salads, and pizza for locals and travelers. Also caterers and Elderhostelers, the Alters share hints for cyclists (tour companies book here), hikers, sightseers, and parents of college students—and for the many dreamers who want to become innkeepers.

Bed and bath: Eleven simply furnished rooms (double and/or twin beds) with shared baths. Nine rooms on second floor, two (can be a suite with private full bath) on third. First-floor bath has separate shower. Second floor has two full baths and one with separate shower.
Breakfast: Baked French toast, eggs, or quiche. Croissants, muffins, or orange date bread. Fresh fruit. Yogurt. Raisins. "Our own blend of coffee." In large, fireplaced beamed dining room.
Plus: Classical music. Fireplaced living room. No TV. Guest refrigerator. Rear deck. Sometimes, Sunday art exhibitions and/or tea. Picnic tables on the green.

Emersons' Guest House   802/877-3293

82 Main Street, Vergennes, VT 05491-1155

Hosts: John and Pat Emerson
Location: On the wide main street of this Champlain Valley city of 2,300. Six miles to Lake Champlain. Near Shelburne Museum, Shelburne Farms, and Morgan Horse Farm.

Open: April–December.
Rates: $35–$45 single, $45–$60 double with shared bath. $75 room with private bath. $10 rollaway.
♥ ⅆ ⅆ ⁂ ⅙ ⅙

Quick! Get thee to a rarity: a family home that became (in 1980) a B&B as the children grew up and moved out. Now the youngest of nine Emersons is in college. The spacious 1850 home has refinished floors and fresh paper and paint—and it is impeccably clean. Sometimes Pat tells the story of having to convince John, a high school math teacher who retired in 1988, to host; soon thereafter she was kicking him under the table as a signal "to stop the interesting conversation and get on with the day!" We had one of those fascinating discussions. And so have hundreds of others —before and after a profile of the Emersons appeared in *Family Circle*.

Bed and bath: Five rooms. Large first-floor room—double bed, private full bath. Second-floor rooms (three are very large) with double, queen, or two single four-posters share two guest baths. Rollaways available.
Breakfast: Usually 7:30–8:30. Eggs, pancakes, waffles or French toast with Vermont maple syrup. Eggs, juice, homemade muffins and toast, jams and jellies from the hosts' berries. Bottomless cup of coffee or tea. Served in the country kitchen.
Plus: Bedroom window fans. Lawns. Porches. Babysitting can be arranged. Community pool, tennis courts, public playground nearby.

Strong House Inn   802/877-3337

82 West Main Street, Vergennes, VT 05491-9531

Hosts: Mary and Hugh Bargiel
Location: Rural. On Route 22A between two working farms. One mile west of Vergennes center. Twenty-two miles south of Burlington; 15 to Shelburne Museum or Middlebury; 7 to Lake Champlain, 30 to Sugarbush resort. Ten-minute drive to New York state ferry.

Open: Year round.
Rates: ($20 more, mid-September–October.) Shared bath $65. Private bath $80 double bed, $90 king; $120 canopied queen, fireplace. Suites: $110 double and sofa bed; queen suite $140 for two, $170 for four. $15 additional person. Amex, MC, Visa.
♥ ⅆ ⁂ ♦ ⅙ ⅙

From New Hampshire: *"Charming hosts who made sure that our every need was met. Their home is elegant and comfortable. My husband and I came with our baby and parents; the suite in one wing of the house was perfect. The rest of the house was beautiful too."*

Maybe you've seen this 160-year-old National Register Greek Revival house pictured in cycle touring company catalogs. When the Bargiels found it "complete with so many wood-burning fireplaces" in 1992, their search for "the perfect B&B for pampering" ended. They furnished with antiques and

(Please turn page.)

traditional pieces. In Florida, Mary had experience in real estate and catering. Here she has already received the Small Business Administration person-of-the-year award. Hugh works in corporate purchasing.

In residence: Teenage daughter, Melissa. Pandy, a black house cat. Missy, an outside dog.

Bed and bath: Seven rooms on first and second floors. Private baths—king bed; canopied queen, fireplace; two double-bedded rooms; and two suites. One suite has queen bed, library, queen sofa bed, fireplace, sun room. The other has double four-poster, living room with double sofa bed, cable TV. Full bath shared by double-bedded room and one that has two twin beds. Rollaway available.

Breakfast: 8–9. Quiche, omelets, crepes, eggs Benedict, French toast, fresh-baked muffins, fresh fruit, bacon or sausage. On fine china and pewter in formal dining room.

Plus: Suites are air conditioned. Fireplaced living room and library. Upright piano. Individual thermostats. Window fans. Evening tea, appetizers, or desserts. Turndown service for suites. Guest refrigerator. Picnic baskets, $15 per person. Dinner option (winter months) $25 per person.

Whitford House   802/758-2704
RR 1, Box 1490, Vergennes, VT 05491-9521   fax 802/758-2704

Hosts: Barbara and Bruce Carson
Location: Quiet. On a country lane off the beaten path. With 180-degree view of Adirondack Mountains. (Sometimes, in foreground pasture, a "horse" built from sticks.) Fifteen miles to Middlebury and Vergennes center, 20 to Ticonderoga, 25 to Shelburne Museum, 2 to Lake Champlain.
Open: Year round.
Rates: Shared bath $70–$90 twins or double bed; $50–$60 single. Private bath $100–$125 king bed; $25 extra bed.
♥ ⅙ ♣ ⅙

> From Illinois, Colorado, New Jersey, California, Ohio, England: *"Very excited to have discovered them . . . epitomizes 'Vermont's best.' Our favorite B&B on a bike tour . . . immaculate . . . eclectically decorated without clutter . . . terrific views from veranda. . . . Felt nurtured by more than the lovely breakfast on beautiful china. It was hard to leave. . . . Lots of good conversation, rest, food my husband is still talking about . . . a gem."*

It's a fantasy retirement place complete with hosts who, happily for travelers, thought it a natural for B&B. In California Barbara taught English; Bruce was an electromechanical engineer. When they bought this restored 200-year-old added-on-to farmhouse in 1988, they placed antique Oriental rugs on the wide pine board floors, comfortable Morris chairs by the fire, and, throughout, a blend of antiques and modern pieces.

In residence: Lane, a beagle.
Foreign languages spoken: A little Spanish and French.
Bed and bath: Four second-floor rooms. King-bedded room (space for rollaway), private attached full bath. Rooms with double, twin beds, and single share (robes provided) full bath and first-floor half bath.

Breakfast: Usually 8–9. Scalloped apples or fresh fruit. Frittatas, Belgian waffles, or French pancakes with fresh blueberries. Homemade breads, muffins, jams.
Plus: Refreshments with garden herb hors d'oeuvres or homemade cookies. Fireplaced living room with baby grand piano. Extensive library. Use of canoe and bicycles. Window fans. Down comforters. Fresh fruit. No TV. Picnic baskets and dinner arranged.

Rose Apple Acres Farm   802/988-4300

East Hill Road, RR 2, Box 300, North Troy, VT 05859-9719

Hosts: Jay, Cam, and (son) Courtney Mead
Location: Rural and quiet, with spectacular views of Canadian Sutton Range. "To Canada, one mile as the crow flies; two hours' drive to Montreal." Five miles to end of Long Trail. Ten miles to Jay Peak ski area. Less than a mile from Route 105. Near antiquing, covered bridges, Big Falls on Missisquoi River. "Great chefs at many restaurants within 10 miles."
Open: Year round. Reservations recommended.
Rates: Per room. $42 shared bath. $52 private bath. With adjoining room $77 for three, $100 for four. Amex.

♥ ⬛ ⁂ ♦ ✗ ⚥

From Canada: "Unspoiled charm, magnificent setting, reasonable rates, comfortable living arrangements, great food, myriad of activities—even sleigh rides . . . very relaxing, beyond our expectations . . . feel like you're staying with friends."

"No, you don't have to dress for dinner," laughs Cam when she gets a call from someone who hasn't been to "a real B&B" before. "Here you can take a hayride, pick apples or berrries, swim in a farm pond, learn to milk a cow or goat, help bale hay (done with antique equipment), cross-country ski, or try spinning yarn. Or enjoy the farmers' porch in a rocker." Courtney's Lincoln flock, a rare breed of sheep, has grown to 16. Clara and Gypsy just kidded, "so hurray—goat milk again!"

Recently the farm was highlighted in *Country* magazine. On Cape Cod Cam was a music and choir director; Jay, a building materials buyer.

In residence: Mollie, a collie. Augér, a Himalayan cat. S.S., a barn cat. "Jimmy (should be called James) is an aristocratic Afghan." Two Belgian horses pull antique sleighs, plow, and harrows.
Bed and bath: Three second-floor rooms. One with double bed and private full bath has adjoining room with two twin beds. Two rooms, each with one double and two twins, share a full bath.
Breakfast: 8–9. "Homemade granola and maple muffins are favorites." Maybe mapled apples or blueberry buckle. Served in tin-ceilinged kitchen or candlelit dining room.
Plus: Directions to hidden (and marvelous) swimming hole with waterfall. Living room with Franklin fireplace, TV, piano. Huge (take a tour) barn for bicycles and skis. Butter making in antique swing churn. Cider making in antique press. Transportation provided to/from end of Long Trail; small fee charged to trails that are 50 miles south.

Northfield Inn   802/485-8558

27 Highland Avenue, Northfield, VT 05663-1448

Hosts: Aglaia and Alan Stalb
Location: In historic district. Overlooks village and Norwich University. Five miles west of I-89; 9 south of Montpelier; 23 south of Stowe; 16 miles to Sugarbush.
Open: Year round. Minimum stays for events such as quilt festival and art workshops.

Rates: Queen bed $85 private bath, $75 shared; singles $10 less. Single bed $55. Two-room suite $140. Three-room suite $225. Getaway packages. MC, Visa.

♥ ⁂ ✖ ⌇

From the porches, there are panoramic views of gardens, mountains and sunsets. A welcoming fireplace blazes in the winter. Opened in 1990, this pride of the community is a totally restored 25-room Victorian with Palladian windows in four gables, lots of natural woodwork, and now even baseboard heating. Decor features floral wallcoverings, Oriental rugs, antiques, and period lighting fixtures.

Aglaia, formerly a section head with Grumman Aerospace Corporation, has worked as an interior designer. She owned and managed a construction company and has experience in real estate sales and investments. Alan, the chef, was a navy nuclear submarine specialist. Currently he is an engineer and operations manager with Grumman. Here the Stalbs enjoy "an intellectually stimulating and culturally fascinating" career hosting travelers, business retreats, family reunions, and some beautiful weddings.

Foreign language spoken: Greek.
Bed and bath: Six large rooms plus a two-room suite (sleeps three; can be two separate rooms) and a three-room suite (can be three private rooms that share bath). All queen beds with feather bedding; private baths with glass-enclosed showers, one with claw-footed tub.
Breakfast: 7–10. Crepes, stuffed French toast, German apple pancakes, eggs Benedict, souffle, or stuffed omelets. Fresh fruit and homemade jams. Special ethnic menus prepared. Table is set with bone china, crystal, linen, fine lace.
Plus: Afternoon tea. In winter, soup at noon. Butler's pantry with refrigerator, fresh fruit, home-baked goods, snacks—"make yourself at home." Ceiling fans. Down comforters and pillows. Two parlors. Game/exercise room. Library. Croquet. Horseshoes. Dinners for groups.

Guests wrote: *"Beautiful . . . congenial . . . peaceful."*

The American Country Collection Host #176

Putney, VT

Location: Rural. On 10 acres of fields, meadows, and hills. With paths down to the river road for 20 miles on cycling route. Near antiquing, theater, music, boating, fishing, canoeing (in Putney or 15 minutes south in Brattleboro). Twenty-five miles to Okemo Mountain, 1.5 miles to Santa Land.

Reservations: Year round through The American Country Collection, page 343. Two-night minimum on holiday and foliage weekends.
Rates: $55 single, $65 double. October—$75 per room. Third guest $15 adult, $10 child.

♥ ⊷ ⁂ ✖ ⌇

One young guest returned to write her dissertation here—in peace and quiet. Honeymooners love it. Canoeists and cross-country skiers are among the returnees here. The oversized center chimney cape was designed to be a B&B by the hosts, who camped on this land when their children were younger. In southeastern Massachusetts the hostess was in accounting; her husband worked in the space and aircraft industry. Here he is a manager in the jewelry industry. She works part time at a nursery. "Now, seven years later, our own gardens are beginning to mature." The living room is furnished traditionally with Oriental rugs and wing chairs. The dining room is "country" with a fieldstone fireplace. Outside there's a three-tiered deck. Down by the herb gardens there's a gazebo. And everywhere—those views.

In residence: Five cats, not allowed in bedrooms. Two dogs.
Bed and bath: Three first-floor rooms, all private full baths. King/twins option, queen, or double bed. Rollaways available.
Breakfast: 8–9:30. Juice. Eggs, pancakes, or French toast with bacon or sausage. Homemade muffins and jam. Coffee and tea.

Hickory Ridge House   802/387-5709
RFD 3, Box 1410, Putney, VT 05346-9326

Hosts: Jacquie Walker and Steve Anderson
Location: Quiet. On 12 acres with perennial gardens, woods for hiking, views of rolling meadows and hills. Two miles to Putney Village, I-91, and Connecticut River; 10 to Brattleboro.
Open: Year round. Two-night mini-

mum on holiday weekends.
Rates: With fireplace, $85 private bath, $70 shared. Without fireplace, $70 private bath, $45–$60 shared. $18 each additional person. $10 crib. Four or more days, 10 percent discount. MC, Visa.
♥ ♚ ♣ ✗ ⅍

Jacquie and Steve were chimney sweeps with previous careers in college teaching (political science), administration (Planned Parenthood), and parenting when they acquired this well-maintained and little-altered 1808 Federal brick country manor. Once a college president's residence, this architectural gem features spacious rooms and halls, a grand stairway and Palladian window, country and Federal furnishings. The books, decor, and cuisine reflect the innkeepers' interest in other cultures and world affairs. There is a piano in the living room and impromptu music is encouraged. Steve plays viola and violin.

Since they became innkeepers in 1986, Jacquie and Steve's own extensive travels have taken them to China, France, the American Southwest, and Czechslovakia. Nature lovers too, they, together with guests, sometimes ski on moonlit fields or swim at the nearby swimming hole.

In residence: "Aging Trevor and matronly Gretchen, our fun-loving golden retrievers, provide company on walks along woodland trails."
Foreign languages spoken: "Steve can greet you in German, Russian, or French; hopes to learn some Czech and Slovak."
Bed and bath: Seven rooms, three with private baths. Of the four with working fireplaces, the first-floor one is handicapped accessible and has a private shower bath. Rooms have queen, double, a double and a single, or

(Please turn page.)

two twin beds. Rollaways, futons, and crib available. (Families with children booked only in rooms without fireplace.)
Breakfast: 8–9:30. Fruit compotes, hot applesauce, poached pears, or baked grapefruit. Homemade stollen, muffins, or coffee cakes. Eggs (gather your own here), pancakes, cheese souffle, or Belgian waffles. In fireplaced dining room or on large deck.
Plus: Wood stove. Fireplaced parlor. Hot cider or mulled cranberry-lemon drink. Tea, coffee, ice cubes always available. Guests' refrigerator. Croquet. Horseshoes. Line-dried sheets.

Quechee Bed & Breakfast   802/295-1776

753 Woodstock Road, Route 4, P.O. Box 80, Quechee, VT 05059-0080

Hosts: Susan and Ken Kaduboski
Location: On 2½ acres with spectacular cliff-edge views of Ottauquechee River. Half mile west of Quechee Gorge. Walk to Simon Pearce glass blowing in village; 6.5 miles to Woodstock, 30–45 minutes to Killington, Pico, Okemo ski areas;

15 to Dartmouth College.
Open: Year round. Two-night minimum during foliage and Christmas seasons, and most weekends June through October.
Rates: $85–$135 depending on view and room size. MC, Visa.
♥ ❖ ♦ ✄

As one Rhode Island innkeeper said, "There's only one word for it—'fabulous.'" And that was before the latest major changes were made by the Kaduboskis—"we think we got it right this time"—in the 1795 colonial that was once a coach stop. There's a combination of antiques and contemporary art, dried flowers and baskets, stenciled curtains and braided rugs. And there's Susan, who grew up in Latin America. "It's exciting to learn to downhill ski at my age!" Ken remembers, "Prior to this, we led a very corporate life. Our intial exposure to B&Bs was in England, where we lived for three years." Here they answer *Gourmet*'s request for a recipe; *Glamour* and *Elle* like them too. They garden and feel lucky to live in this beautiful area. "And to meet such wonderful people."

Foreign language spoken: "Slightly rusty fluent Spanish."
Bed and bath: Eight air-conditioned rooms on first and second floors. All private full baths. Queen four-poster or two twin beds in main house. In renovated attached barn, king bed, refrigerator, spectacular view; up steep stairway, queen four-poster in cozy room.
Breakfast: Presented 8–9:30. Apple cinnamon pancakes, buttermilk waffles, or whole wheat French toast filled with cream cheese; Vermont cob-smoked bacon. Fresh fruit; homemade frozen yogurt or steel-cut oatmeal.
Plus: Living room with oversized brick-and-granite fireplace. Setups in each room. Refrigerator space. Lawn chairs. Midweek golf and tennis privileges at (private) Quechee Club.

Guests arrive as strangers, leave as friends.

Placidia Farm Bed and Breakfast

RFD 1, Box 275, Randolph, VT 05060-9413   802/728-9883

Hosts: Viola Frost-Laitinen and Don Laitinen
Location: Six miles north of Randolph, 1½ miles up a dirt road. On 81 quiet acres with mountain views, pond, and brook. Near alpine and cross-country skiing areas.
Open: Year round. Two-night minimum on holiday weekends.
Rates: $80–$90. $25 each additional guest. $10 per child ages 2–12.
♥ ◢ ✗ ⅍

From Massachusetts: *"Much more than we expected. Vi's house was so beautiful—to go along with her smile and hospitality."* From Connecticut: *"Exquisite flower beds, a manicured lawn, breathtaking views . . . welcoming goodies . . . breakfast in room with windows on three sides . . . hummingbirds sipping nectar just 10 feet away."* From New Jersey: *"Makes you want to move to Vermont."* From California: *"First class."*

Once a weekend retreat, the hand-hewn log house is home to Vi, a former federal government tax adjuster, and Don, a retired occupational health engineer. "Depending on the season, you might see a farmer harvesting hay. His cows graze in the meadow. Recent additions include a Christmas tree farm and a workshop for woodworking and stained glass. Guests tell me they rest body and soul here."

In residence: Three cats—Fawn, Cato, and BD.
Foreign language spoken: A little German.
Bed and bath: In private apartment—large bedroom with double bed and rollaway, queen sofa bed in living room. Fully equipped kitchen with microwave. Full bath. Private entrance and deck.
Breakfast: Usually 8–9. Omelets, German apple pancakes, fresh eggs, or waffles. Popovers or homemade muffins. Fresh fruit and juices. On plant-filled sun porch with linen and fine china.
Plus: Living room with TV, radio, books, cards, games. Fans. Aquatic garden. Hiking. Make-your-own cross-country trails on property.

The Richmond Victorian Inn

802/434-4440
fax 802/434-4410

Main Street, P.O. Box 652
Richmond, VT 05477-0510

Hosts: Ron and Vicki Williamson
Location: In the village on Route 2, one mile east from I-89, exit 11. Fifteen miles to Shelburne Museum, 12 to Burlington, 7 to Bolton Valley, 30 to Stowe. Two miles to Long Trail at Jonesville.
Open: Year round. Two-night minimum in foliage season and on major holidays.
Rates: $65 private bath, $50 shared. $85 large room with a double and a queen bed. $135 suite. MC, Visa.
♥ ⁂ ⅍

"I had one just like it," said the elderly guest who was admiring the 1931 Model A Ford. The Williamsons offered him a ride. "As we drove through town and back again he grinned from ear to ear."

The Williamsons' 1880 turreted Victorian house was another major restoration project. "Done with TLC, it was decorated with warmth and comfort in mind."

(Please turn page.)

Vicki, a native Vermonter, is a property manager who does old-house restoration. Previously she owned and managed a natural food store. Ron, a longtime Vermont resident, is an electrical contractor who also restores old lighting fixtures.

In residence: Two cats. Callie "is an old hand at charming guests. Tigger is very curious and loves to play."

Bed and bath: Six second-floor rooms with queen or double bed. Two with private bath. Two share a hall bath. Two double-bedded rooms share a connecting bath. Rollaway available.

Breakfast: Usually 8:30. Fresh fruit. Juice. Quiche, cheese strata, sourdough cream cheese French toast, waffles, or pancakes and Vermont maple syrup. Giant fruit muffins and sour cream coffee cake. Harrington smoked sausage, ham, and bacon. Family style in dining room.

Plus: Welcoming beverage. Living room with TV, VCR. Champagne for newlyweds. Fans. Mints on pillows.

From England: *"The kind of house you'd like to own. Well recommended."* From New York: *"Warm hosts. . . . Highest standards."*

Hillcrest Guest House   802/775-1670

RR 1, Box 4459, Rutland, VT 05701

Hosts: Bob and Peg Dombro
Location: Two miles from the junction of Routes 4 and 7, .3 mile (and into another world) from Route 7. About 20 minutes to Pico, half hour to Killington ski areas.

Open: Year round. Advance reservations preferred. Two-night minimum in foliage season and on ski weekends.
Rates: $40 single. $45 double.
🛥 🛩 ⚡

From New York: *"Never enjoyed a B&B more. Large, attractive, clean rooms . . . restaurant suggestions and directions to points hitherto unknown. A sumptuous healthy breakfast."* From Massachusetts: *"Generous hospitality."* From Germany: *"Almost a museum . . . warm-hearted, open-minded people."*

"Several years ago I stayed with Peace Corps volunteers in Central America. As B&B hosts, we operate in the same fashion as our foreign friends: sharing our home, learning about other hometowns, and exchanging ideas."

The Dombros have been "blending two cultures" for over a decade in their welcoming mid-19th-century post-and-beam farmhouse furnished with a wonderful collection of country antiques. Herb and vegetable gardens grow on the site of the old dairy barn. Plants thrive inside and out.

Bob has directed a school and rehabilitation agency for exceptional children. Now he is coordinator of an art gallery and guardian ad litem for Rutland Family Court. Peg is active in community theater, and then there's horticulture, her year-round love. *Country Living* should come here! We did—and loved it.

In residence: "One beautiful fat and lazy cat."
Bed and bath: Three second-floor rooms share one full guest bath with tub and hand-held shower. Two double-bedded rooms. One room with one twin bed.

Breakfast: 7–9. "We emphasize fresh fruit, homemade low-fat muesli granola, and high-carbohydrate breakfasts. Meat and eggs are not served." Served on screened porch or in country dining room.
Plus: Line-dried sheets when weather permits. Two porches. Wood stove and fireplace in living room. Books. Fresh flowers. Down comforters.

The Looking Glass Inn   (voice and TTY) 802/748-3052

RFD 3, Box 199, St. Johnsbury, VT 05819

Hosts: Barbara and (son) Christopher Haas
Location: On 34 acres with views of mountains, pastures (used by some cross-country skiing guests), and cows. Three miles from town center, museum, library, art gallery, and Main Street old mansions. Near Maple Grove Farms (maple syrup products) tour. Just a few feet from I-93. Four miles from I-91. Within 20 minutes of Burke and Cannon mountains and two gourmet restaurants in restored old homes.
Open: Year round.
Rates: $60 shared bath, $80 private bath. Single $40 shared bath, $50 private. MC, Visa.
♥ ❖ ♦ ✖ ⊬

"People think we have been here forever, because there are family collections and books everywhere. We had always wanted to live in a big old house in the country. Our Second Empire brick Victorian with classic mansard roof was built in 1806 as a tavern with 15-foot high first-floor ceilings. Many returnees are hikers, cyclists, and those on a getaway."

The Haas family moved from Morristown, New Jersey in 1986. Barbara, a craftsperson, is a nursing supervisor at the community hospital. Chris has experience as a case-worker for New Hampshire and is studying to be an interpreter for the deaf.

In residence: "Five huskies and two cats, never ever allowed in the inn, can be visited in the yard."
Bed and bath: Six rooms, each with an antique double bed. Private bath (1900 fixtures include long tub and shower) for one on first floor, one on second. Four rooms share two full baths.
Breakfast: 7:30–9. "All you can eat." French toast—"Chris's secret recipe"—with Vermont maple syrup. At least three kinds of fruit. Hot breads and muffins. Freshly brewed hazelnut coffee.
Plus: Wood-burning stove in guests' parlor. TV in sitting room. Coffee always available. Sherry in room. Mints on pillows. Down comforters. TV. Volleyball. Badminton. Lawn chairs and swing. Dinner (at least three hours' notice required) $20 per person.

Buckmaster Inn   802/492-3485

Box 118, Lincoln Hill Road, RD 1, Shrewsbury, VT 05738-9711

Hosts: Grace and Sam Husselman
Location: On a paved country road in the Green Mountains; 20 minutes to Killington and Okemo mountains. Two miles north of Cuttingsville.
Open: Year round. Reservations preferred. Two-night minimum on holiday weekends.
Rates: $50 shared bath, $60 private bath. $15 cot.
♥ ◗ ❖ ✖ ⊬

(Please turn page.)

Just as they dreamed, "It's country living at its best—with homemade breads and muffins and rural mountain scenery." In New Jersey Grace was a teacher and a director of a public library. Sam was an engineer. Their "gorgeous and functional" 10-room house, originally a coach stop and known as Buckmaster Tavern in the early 1800s, has a grand staircase and wide floorboards. Family heirlooms grace every room, yet Grace and Sam still "hunt for antiques."

Sam enjoys golf, chess, and fishing, "anything outdoors." In winter he (and guests) appreciate the extensive grounds for cross-country skiing. Grace enjoys knitting Icelandic sweaters as well as other handwork; many of her framed crewel pieces are throughout the house.

In residence: Patty Patience, an old English sheepdog.
Foreign language spoken: Dutch.
Bed and bath: Four rooms. On second floor, two rooms share a bath; one has a queen bed, the other has two twin beds. One room with four-poster double bed and private bath. On third floor, a huge beamed-ceiling hideaway with king bed, private bath with shower. Cot available.
Breakfast: 8–9. If later, self-service continental. Homemade Vermont jams and jellies, sweet breads and muffins and/or Vermont cheddar-and-egg casserole, hot beverages. Served in the country kitchen with wood-burning stove, in dining room, or on porch.
Plus: Tea and cookies upon arrival. "Special goodies and wedding bells, if we know honeymooners are arriving." Use of entire house, TV, library, and fireplace. Outdoor grills, picnic tables and umbrellas, and screened porches. Badminton. Croquet.

Guests wrote: *"We wished our minivacation could have been longer!... immaculate yes, but cozy too.... My in-laws from Wales and England thoroughly enjoyed themselves."*

Maple Crest Farm   802/492-3367
Shrewsbury, VT
Mailing address: Box 120, Cuttingsville, VT 05738

Hosts: Donna, William, and (son) Russell Smith
Location: High, with great views and Long Trail hiking (and cross-country ski) trails right here. Ten miles south of Rutland, 10 north of Ludlow. Near Killington and Okemo ski areas.

Open: Year round. Two-night minimum during holidays and foliage season.
Rates: $30 single, $54 double. One night's deposit required.
♥ 🛏 ✱ ♦ ✗

This B&B has been discovered by *Country Living.* And by artists and photographers, who comment about "true Vermont hospitality" where farming and sugar making are carried on by a fifth and a sixth generation. The antiques and personal treasures reflect Smith activities through the years.

Except for the first 20 years, when it was run as a tavern, this 27-room landmark built in 1808 has been a private home, each generation welcoming guests on a small scale. Robert Frost and past governors slept here.

Donna, a former town treasurer who is a bank director, met Bill when she was working at a nearby inn. In 1969 she started B&B at Maple Crest as "a real home away from home, the way B&B started. To this day, we enjoy this noncommercial style of hosting." Guests of all ages, quilting groups, and retreat planners do too.

In residence: K.C., a Labrador retriever. Tyler, an Airedale. About 80 cattle in the meadows.

Bed and bath: Six large rooms (two are suites with private half baths), each with a double and a single bed; some with wood stoves. One first-floor room with half bath shares full bath with second-floor rooms. Two apartments; each sleeps five. Cot and crib available.

Breakfast: 8–9:30. Full country meal with bacon and eggs, pancakes with Smiths' award-winning maple syrup, homemade muffins and jams.

Plus: Seasonal flowers. Beverage. Tour of farm and maple sugaring operation.

From Washington, Rhode Island, California: *"The most memorable part of the trip. . . . I had to arrive late at night and leave early in the morning, yet was met with great warmth. In that short time I knew it was a place that I wanted to return to with my family. . . . Snowed in during a blizzard and loved it."*

Kelldarra, A Vermont Bed and Breakfast

P.O. Box 197, Jeffersonville, VT 05464-0197   **802/644-6575**

Host: Darra Kell
Location: Rural. On Route 109. On four hillside acres beside Lamoille River. Six miles to Smugglers Notch, 20 to Stowe, 1½ to village. Near sugarhouses and a covered bridge.
Open: Year round. Two-night min-

imum; three nights for legal holidays and October weekends.
Rates: Per room. $50 double bed. $60 queen. $70 queen with Jacuzzi or room with two double beds. Single $10 less.
♥ ⬛ ⁂ ✈

From New York: *"We felt so at home in this big, beautiful house sharing wonderful moments with Darra and her family."* From Arizona: *"Top quality of everything, from the freshly prepared gourmet food to the lovely furnishings and Waterford crystal."* From England: *"Truly exceptional and unique establishment."* From Canada: *"Told us about many interesting places to shop and visit . . . a wonderful place to call home."*

"A passion for cooking and people." Love of the outdoors and water sports. Joie de vivre. Darra brought all of that to her c. 1826 colonial brick post-and-beam farmhouse. There are wide floorboards, stenciled walls, and a welcoming kitchen with a wall of bricks from the original cooking hearth. Most of the antiques come from England. In the 1970s Darra lived in London and Paris, where she "entertained extensively." Here, since 1990, she has welcomed many guests who call this "the best B&B ever." Now she is working on a master's degree in counseling psychology. And just as this book went to press, she acquired a cruising sailboat.

In residence: Daughters Hilary, 17, and Kendra, 11.
Bed and bath: Four large rooms. On first floor, one double-bedded room and one with two double (antique iron) beds share a full bath. On second floor, one with queen four-poster, private bath with Jacuzzi. One with queen bed, shared full bath.

(Please turn page.)

Breakfast: Until 11. Perhaps pancakes with spiced apple-cinnamon sauce. Scones with jam and clotted cream. Fruited breads with savory butter. Vermont cheeses. Fresh fruit. Vermont smoked breakfast meats. Darra-blended and ground hazelnut coffee. Served by candlelight under early 18th-century English brass chandelier.

Plus: Fireplaced, brick-walled, and book-lined living room. Down comforters. Flannel sheets. Turndown service. Mints on pillows. Evening refreshments. Champagne for honeymooners. Sports equipment storage. Bicycle rentals right here. June–October, Lake Champlain three-hour sunset supper cruise, $40 per person; two-hour moonlight cruise, $30 per person.

Guest House Christel Horman
4583 Mountain Road, Stowe, VT 05672

802/253-4846
800/821-7891

Hosts: Christel and James Horman
Location: On Mountain Road (Route 108), 1½ miles to Mount Mansfield, 5¼ from Stowe village. Walking distance to Stowe's recreation path and some restaurants. Near theaters, Mozart festival, shops, golf, tennis, antique car show.

Open: Year round. Two-night minimum on weekends.
Rates: Per person, double occupancy. $30–$33 spring and summer. $40 fall and winter. $35 ski week. Holidays higher. $20 cot in same room. MC, Visa.
❖ ♦ ✗

When the Hormans had the Swiss chalet–style house built in 1980, they finished the interior as a home away from home. They decorated with handmade items and collections from Australia (where Jim was an auto mechanic and ski instructor) and Germany (where Christel was an accountant and secretary). They traveled all over the United States before settling in Stowe. Jim still works for the Mount Mansfield Company, but Christel is full-time innkeeper, "meeting people from all over the world. Even when we do not speak the same language we understand and enjoy one another."

Foreign language spoken: German.
Bed and bath: Eight large carpeted rooms (on first and second floors), each with two double beds, private full bath, individual thermostat.
Breakfast: 8–10. Apple pancakes; French toast; eggs and bacon. Toast and marmalade. Juice and hot beverages. Served outside in summer.
Plus: Guest living room with hearthstone fireplace. Color TV and VCR. Cross-country skiing from the door. Small pool. Trout fishing in brook behind the house. Babysitting possibilities. Use of outdoor grill.

Unless otherwise stated, rates in this book are for two and include breakfast in addition to all the amenities in "Plus."

Inn at the Brass Lantern

717 Maple Street, Stowe, VT 05672-4250

802/253-2229
800/729-2980
fax 802/253-7425

Hosts: Andy and (teenaged son) Dustin Aldrich
Location: Half a mile from village center. Within 10 minutes of "everything," including restaurants, skiing, tennis, golf, hot-air ballooning, concerts, theater, sleigh and surrey rides, antiquing.
Open: Year round. Two-night minimum during foliage and on holiday and ski season weekends. Four-day minimum Christmas–New Year's week.
Rates: (For stays of two or more nights, include health club, half mile away.) $65–$85 double bed. $75–$95 queen bed. $100–$120 queen bed with fireplace. $25 third person. Singles, $10 less. Packages include skiing, golf, honeymoon/anniversary, fly/drive. Amex, MC, Visa.
♥ ♣ ♦ ✗ ✄

Andy hosts many honeymooners and other guests who appreciate his recommendations for everything "from spa to sleigh rides to candlelit restaurants." An active farm from 1800 until 1950, this was a lodge and then a restaurant before the Aldriches made it into an inn, an award-winning restoration with wainscoting, wide planked floors, and a beamed living room that has a view of Mount Mansfield. There's stenciling, small-print wallpapers, and handmade quilts. Andy dovetails innkeeping with his Burlington-based construction business. Dustin, in charge of the gift shop, is an avid hockey player.

Bed and bath: Nine air-conditioned antiques-furnished rooms; some with canopied beds, most with view of Mount Mansfield. Cozy farmhouse double-bedded gable rooms have private shower baths. Larger rooms, some with fireplace, in farmhouse and attached renoved barn, have queen bed, private full bath.
Breakfast: 8–9:30. All homemade. Entree made with Vermont produce and products might be French toast, apple crepes, blueberry pancakes, or omelets. Fruit, juice, hot beverages. Special diets accommodated.
Plus: Patio. Tea and dessert. Individual thermostats. Guest refrigerator. Maps for self-guided walking, driving, hiking, and biking tours. Bath with shower for after checkout. Transportation arranged to/from airport, train, or bus. Fresh fruit. Chocolates. Picnic baskets.

Ski Inn

802/253-4050

Route 108, Stowe, VT 05672

Host: Harriet Heyer
Location: Set back from the highway on 27 wooded acres, 5.2 miles to Stowe village. Five-minute drive to Mount Mansfield.
Open: Year round. May–November as a B&B; dinners served in winter.
Rates: Per person, double occupancy. $20–$22.50 shared bath, $25–$30 private bath. In winter (includes breakfast and dinner) $45–$50 shared bath, $55–$60 private bath.
♠ ♣ ♦ ✗ ✄

(Please turn page.)

A legend. An old-fashioned inn with a big fieldstone fireplace, knotty pine walls, and a Ping-Pong table. It was built by Larry Heyer in 1941 when Stowe was primarily a summer resort, when some folks weren't quite sure that skiing would be more than a fad. Fifty years later, Larry and Harriet, parents of Lyndall, a former U.S. ski team member, were still saying, "We started the trend of intimate country inns and have refused to expand."

In the 1940s, Harriet had public relations experience in Manhattan. In the 1990s, between seasons, she bicycles in the United States and Europe. In the winter she downhill skis every day—and sometimes hosts returnees who represent three generations. Now she's planning to take up cross-country skiing.

Bed and bath: Ten large rooms on two floors, each with a double and a single bed. Some rooms have private full baths.

Breakfast: In B&B season, continental with homemade jellies and preserves from wild elderberry, chokecherry, blueberry, or rhubarb. In winter, full meals with homemade everything.

Plus: Air-dried cotton sheets. Flat hiking road on property. More than 50 km of cross-country ski trails outside the back door. Outdoor fireplace and patio. Trout stream. Game room with "in tune" upright piano.

> From New York: *"Into the driveway, over a wooden bridge, and you're into another world. . . . Roomy, charming, comfortable, spotless . . . Harriet's unique ability to combine guests of varied and interesting backgrounds . . . excellent, plentiful food, not gourmet but touched up with homemade and homegrown goodies. . . . Location may be best in whole area."*

Inn at Round Barn Farm   802/496-2276(B-A-R-N)
East Warren Road, RR 1, Box 247   fax 802/496-8832
Waitsfield, VT 05673-0247

Hosts: Jack and Doreen Simko and (daughter) AnneMarie DeFreest
Location: Dramatic. Less than two miles from Route 100, through the covered bridge and over a hill to 85 acres of gardens, ponds, meadows, and woods. Fifteen minutes from Sugarbush (North and South) and Mad River ski areas.
Open: Year round. Two-night mini-

mum preferred on weekends.
Rates: Double or twin beds $95. Queen bed $105; $120 canopied with Jacuzzi; $150 with fireplace, steam shower, cathedral ceiling; $165 canopied with oversized Jacuzzi; $120 with daybed ($20 extra person). King canopied $135 with Jacuzzi. Singles $10 less. Amex, MC, Visa.
♥ ♦ ✗ ✄

Everything. It's all here: Cows in the meadows. A 30 km cross-country ski center. A 19th-century farmhouse rebuilt with superb craftsmanship by the Simkos to a style it had never known. It's furnished with a marvelous blend of textures and colors, with country antiques, whimsy, and contemporary crafts. There's a 60-foot-long lap pool in the huge 12-sided tri-level former dairy barn, which is now booked for concerts, lots of weddings, business conferences, and art shows and for cooking, photography, and watercolor workshops. (Climb to the cupola for an incredible view.) Extensive press coverage has included *Colonial Homes, Country Inns,* and the *New York Times.*

In New Jersey Jack established a floral business. Here he grows papyrus, water lilies, and the inn's edible flowers. The family has created what many guests—including romantics—consider the ultimate inn.

In residence: Patches, a calico cat. J.B., a black Lhasa-type terrier. AnneMarie and her husband, a dairy farmer, live nearby; their two-year-old daughter, Elizabeth Anne, often visits at the inn.

Bed and bath: Eleven rooms, some with working fireplace. All private baths, all brass fixtures; some with Jacuzzi or steam shower. Some canopied, antique, or custom-made beds. Luxury rooms have original beamed cathedral ceilings, gas fireplaces, air conditioning, floor-to-ceiling windows, phone jacks, paddle fans.

Breakfast: 8:30–9. Maybe cottage cheese pancakes with raspberry sauce, blueberry Belgian waffles, or French toast with Grand Marnier. Homemade muffins. Baked fruit in winter. Cinnamon coffee. Served in sun porch or on terrace.

Plus: Late-afternoon hors d'oeuvres. Individual thermostats. Wicker-filled solarium. Pool table. Classical music in fireplaced library. Snowshoe and cross-country ski rentals and instruction. Learn-to-ski packages and valley-wide cross-country ski pass available. In winter, dinner option three nights a week.

Lareau Farm Country Inn
802/496-4949

Box 563, Route 100, Waitsfield, VT 05673-0563   800/833-0766

Hosts: Dan and Susan Easley
Location: Rural setting. In a large open meadow (with horses and, in back, a soaring rock face), one mile south of Waitsfield. Along "crystal clear Mad River" for swimming, canoeing, fishing. Near soaring, horseback riding, antiquing. Five miles to Mad River Glen and Sugarbush downhill skiing; 45 minutes to Shelburne Museum and Lake Champlain.

Open: Year round. Two-day minimum on weekends and holidays.
Rates: Jacuzzi suite $90/$110/$125 (weekday/weekend/holiday). Private baths $70/$80/$100. Shared bath $60/$70/$80. Discount on five-night (Sunday–Thursday) stays. Singles $10 less during nonholiday periods. ($1 of every reservation donated to Nature Conservancy.) MC, Visa.
♥ ⚐ ❀ ♦ ✗

The Easleys are as much a draw as their inn. Since the experienced house restorers came here (from Pittsburgh and jobs as bank training director and science teacher) in 1984, they have created a comfortable country look. They added a wonderful large many-windowed dining room with Oriental rugs and a gazebo-styled porch with hanging flower baskets that attract hummingbirds in the summer.

Susan makes the hand-tied quilts and designs the menus with Vermont products. Dan, an elementary school counselor, bales hay and drives carriages and an old-fashioned sleigh. And he has a fabulous collection of jazz classics. The Easleys host memorable spontaneous happenings and lovely weddings. Guests hike and cross-country ski through the "enchanted forest." And many write to me about loving "the relaxed atmosphere" at their "home away from home."

In residence: "Our zoo": There are four dogs, three cats. Horses—Holly and Dolly, "the driving duo," and Molly, "filly in training."

(Please turn page.)

Bed and bath: Thirteen rooms of various sizes with king, queen, double— plus one or two singles—or twin beds. Eleven with private baths (with tub or shower); one suite with double Jacuzzi, high Victorian queen bed, ceiling fan. Two double-bedded rooms share a shower bath.
Breakfast: Generally 8–9. Fresh fruits or hot compote. Homemade muffins— sometimes made from Easleys' pumpkins. Egg souffles or "Dan's famous light-as-a-feather blueberry pancakes." Farm-fresh eggs. Green Mountain coffee.
Plus: In winter, afternoon hors d'oeuvres; cross-country skiing and sleigh rides right here. Room fans. Bocci. Horseshoes. Walking path. By arrangement, dinners for groups.

The Mad River Inn Bed-n-Breakfast

Tremblay-Pine Road, P.O. Box 75   802/496-7900
Waitsfield, VT 05673-0075   800/TEA-TART

Hosts: Luc and Rita Maranda
Location: Overlooking a dairy farm. Along the Mad River. On paved country road, one-fifth of a mile off Route 100. One mile north of village. Seven miles to Sugarbush, six to Mad River Glen ski area.
Open: Year round. Three-night minimum on holiday weekends; four nights during Christmas–New Year's week.

Rates: $115 queen bed, en-suite bath; $125 king or king/twins bed, en-suite bath; $75 second-floor queen, downstairs bath; $95 queen, hall bath. Midweek $35 less (except holidays and foliage). Singles $20 less. For triple or quad occupancy $20 more. $10 under age 12. Amex, MC, Visa.
♥ ♨ ♣ ♦ ✗

Family getaways. Pick-your-own raspberries (mid- to late summer). Garden gazebo weddings (tent provided). Heart-shaped almond cake for honeymooners. Daily afternoon teas featuring baked goods by Rita's sister, Annie Reed, a creative and successful chef. Flower-bedecked porches with views of farmland and mountains. A swimming hole on the river where, in August, you can watch jumpers at the horse show. And groomed snowmobile and cross-country trails.

It's all here, in a renovated 1860s farmhouse decorated in country Victorian style with yards of floral print fabrics throughout. Each guest room reflects the interests of an ancestor—a railroad engineer, a colonel, the founder of organized baseball. Before becoming innkeepers the Marandas lived in south Florida, where Luc was a nightclub manager and Rita marketed luxury real estate.

In residence: Son Jessee Roland, age six.
Foreign languages spoken: French (Luc lived in his native Canada until he was 15) and some Spanish.
Bed and bath: Nine rooms, all private baths. Feather beds (unless you request otherwise). First floor—king/twins or queen bed. Second floor— queen, king, or king/twins option. Single (feather) daybeds available.
Breakfast: 8–9:30. Coffee at 7. Fresh orange juice. Muffins made with homemade maple and berry butter. Fruit dish with colorful edible pansies. Main course may be oven-baked French toast, eggs with Vermont cheddar cheese sauce, blueberry and ginger pancakes, or fresh (homegrown) fruit crepes. In dining room or on back porch.

Plus: Large TV and wood stove in BYOB lounge. Sandbox. Swing set. Billiard table. Knockabout rumpus room. Babysitting. Beach towels. Grill. Hammock. Extensive organic gardens. Kitchen and laundry facilities. Candlelit Saturday dinners ($20/person). Picnic baskets ($10 per person).

Newtons' 1824 House Inn

802/496-7555
Route 100, Box 159   800/426-3986 (42 NEWTON)
Waitsfield, VT 05673-9802   fax 802/496-7558

Hosts: Nick and Joyce Newton
Location: On Route 100, along the Mad River. Two miles from town center. Surrounded by working farms. Minutes to Sugarbush golf club, Sugarbush and Mad River ski resorts.
Open: Year round. Two-night minimum during foliage, summer, and winter weekends. Two- or three-night minimum on holiday weekends.
Rates: $75–$90 smaller double room. $85–$100 standard double. $95–$115 king bed, $105–$115 queen-bedded suite. Singles $10 less. Additional person $20. Midweek packages $60 up. Amex, Discover, MC, Visa.
♥ ✳ ♦ ⊱

Incredible stuffed pears. Enormous muffins. Organic gardening (watermelons, berries, asparagus, and more). Haying with a neighbor. A vintage tractor. A sledding hill. A private swimming hole on the Mad River. It's all a long way from the Manhattan lifestyle Nick knew as an investment banker and Joyce as a stockbroker. But not so far from the California farm life Nick knew as a boy, or from the horseback riding Joyce recalls from camp days.

    The farmhouse has had many additions through the years. Now it is filled with all kinds of collections—antiques, souvenirs, birds, and, in the living room, contemporary art.

In residence: Daughter Ashley, nine. Bonita, "the most lovable golden retriever." Three horses.
Foreign languages spoken: Spanish and limited French.
Bed and bath: Six carpeted rooms (various sizes), one on first floor, five on second. All private baths with tub and shower, except one that is shower only. King (with feather bed), queen, double, or twin beds. Rollaway available.
Breakfast: Usually 8–9. Oatmeal souffle, featherbed eggs, corn meal/buttermilk/blueberry pancakes, crepes, bacon or sausage, homemade muffins, fresh fruits, freshly squeezed orange juice. In fireplaced dining room.
Plus: One room is air conditioned. Fireplaced living room with TV. Upright piano. At 5, hot spiced cider in winter or lemonade on terrace in summer with homemade cookies. Evening sherry. Down comforters. Turndown service. Chocolate hearts on pillow. Guest refrigerator. Babysitting. Outdoor hot tub. Volleyball, badminton, horseshoes.

In this book a full bath includes a shower and a tub. "Shower bath" indicates a bath that has all the essentials except a tub.

Beaver Pond Farm Inn   802/583-2861
RD Box 306, Golf Course Road, Warren, VT 05674-9622

Hosts: Bob and Betty Hansen
Location: On a quiet dirt road, minutes to restaurants and shops. On 40 kilometers of groomed cross-country ski trails. One mile to Sugarbush downhill ski area; 200 yards from the first tee of Club Sugarbush Golf Course (open to the public), designed by Robert Trent Jones.
Open: Year round except mid-April

to mid-May. Reservations required. Two-day minimum during fall and winter.
Rates: Per person, double occupancy. $36–$45 private bath; $32–$40 shared bath. Thanksgiving, ski, golf, fly-fishing, and summer concert packages available. MC, Visa.
♥ ❖ ♦ ✈

From England: *"Full of atmosphere and magic, but also very comfortable . . . picturesque surroundings."* From New York: *"Betty is an incredible cook—energetic and creative . . . interesting, witty, and intelligent hosts."*

Other Manhattanites are still talking about the B&B cooking demonstration Betty, a cooking school instructor, gave in Abraham & Strauss. Europeans, too, appreciate the hospitality in this lovely vacation home turned B&B. When the Hansens created the inn from a vacant farmhouse in 1977, they furnished with "antiques acquired over the years."

In New Jersey Betty was a caterer; Bob a banker for 27 years. They ski; play golf (Betty wins championships); fish (Bob will guide you); travel extensively; and enjoy classical music.

In residence: Jesse, a yellow Labrador retriever, and Jasper, a gray cat.
Foreign language spoken: French. (Betty attended the Sorbonne.)
Bed and bath: Six carpeted rooms, one on first floor with French doors, private deck. Queen or twin beds. Four private baths, one semiprivate; all with hair dryers. Cot available.
Breakfast: 8–9:30. Four choices offered each morning! Maybe smoked salmon "caught and smoked by Bob" and scrambled eggs. Or amaretto French toast, orange-yogurt pancakes, or apple-raisin-walnut pancakes. Homemade Danish pastries. Vermont sausage. Served on antique china with sterling silver in dining room or on large deck.
Plus: Beverages. Setups and hors d'oeuvres. Bedroom fans. Down comforters. Hair dryers. Suggested bicycle routes (15–70 miles). In winter, dinner served on Tuesdays, Thursdays, and Saturdays, and on Thanksgiving and Christmas.

*O*ne out of five guests leaves with the dream
of opening a B&B.

The Sugartree Inn
RR Box 38, Sugarbush Access Road, Warren, VT 05674

802/583-3211
800/666-8907

Hosts: Frank and Kathy Partsch
Location: Wooded. With panoramic mountain views. Three miles west of Waitsfield, one-quarter mile to Sugarbush resort area. Near championship golf course sports center.
Open: Year round. Two-night minimum on foliage and winter holiday weekends.

Rates: Per person, double occupancy. $40–$45 summer, $45–$52 winter, $55–$62 foliage and holiday periods. Singles $60–$66. Triple $35–$52. Midweek, three-to-five day stay, 10 percent less. Amex, Discover, MC, Visa.
♥ ♣ ♦ ✗ ✓

Frank is a banker turned innkeeper/woodcarver; Kathy, who worked in insurance, is co-innkeeper/chef. The two skiers came from Boston in 1992 to this property (once a lodge) with its gingerbread gazebo on landscaped grounds "where chipmunks eat out of your hand in summer." There are quilts and needlepoint pieces, some made by Frank's grandmother. Lots of ruffles. And antiques. A tall clock made by Frank. Flower-filled window boxes with hummingbirds. A guest from Pennsylvania reminisced: "The inn was beautiful, the atmosphere romantic, and the food delicious, but what really made the visit special—Frank and Kathy, friendly, helpful and fun."

Bed and bath: Ten carpeted and wallpapered rooms; one is wheelchair accessible. All private full or shower baths. Antique beds are canopied, four-poster, or brass. First-floor rooms have both a double and a single canopied bed. Second-floor rooms have a double and a single, a queen, or a double. Rollaway available.
Breakfast: 8:30–9:30; 8–9 in ski season. Waffles, three-cheese egg casserole, Dutch apple puff pancake, or pancakes with Vermont maple syrup. Homemade fruit sauces and butters. Homemade breads.
Plus: Fireplaced living room with TV and games. Individual thermostats. Table fans. Hair dryers. Late-afternoon snack for skiers. In summer, lemonade and sweets in gazebo. Down comforters. Special occasions acknowledged. Sauna, hot tub, pool, tennis (fee charged) at nearby sports center. Wicker-furnished porch. Directions to waterfalls and swimming holes.

Grünberg Haus Bed & Breakfast
Route 100 South, RR 2, Box 1595
Waterbury, VT 05676-9621

802/244-7726
800/800-7760

Hosts: Christopher Sellers and Mark Frohman
Location: In Ben & Jerry's hometown, on acres of meadows and woodlands. Within a five-minute drive of Green Mountain Chocolate Company. Twenty miles to Sugarbush, Stowe, Mad River Glen ski resorts.
Open: Year round.
Rates: $55–$70 queen bed. $55–$75

two double beds. $55–$65 one double or two twin beds. $35–$55 single. Extra person in room $7 "permanent" bed, $15 rollaway. Private baths $20–$50 more. Ten percent less for senior citizens, military personnel, and travel industry professionals. Amex, Discover, EnRoute, MC, Visa.
♥ ♠ ♣ ♦ ✗ ✓

(Please turn page.)

What a setting for a convention of harpists; an annual Octoberfest; Shakespeare-in-the-Woods (amphitheater by campfire); and, now, a cross-country ski center. A long lane, a dramatic approach, leads up to this Tyrolean-style chalet built by hand in 1971 and bought by Chris and Mark in 1989. In the living room, a massive fieldstone fireplace faces an eight-foot grand piano, an antique carved pump organ, and a huge picture window with bird feeders beyond. Chris, a professional musician, plays and sings during breakfast and many evenings. As Mark says, "Full house turns into a party." And still the imaginative innkeepers find time to schedule fund-raisers such as Christmas caroling to the animals at four different farms or a "Volksmarch"—a 10-kilometer noncompetitive walk through the woods.

In residence: Two cats, Fritz and Mama. Chickens (both innkeepers had chickens when they lived in the Midwest), doves, fancy pigeons, quails. Ike and Tina are turkeys who peek into the dining room (built on a hillside).
Bed and bath: Ten second-floor rooms, each with access to balcony. One shared bath between every two rooms. Rooms have double bed (one canopied), two twins, (one pair in antique brass), or two double beds. Rollaways available. Just added: Carriage house and cabins in secluded woods.
Breakfast: 7:30–9:30. Fresh eggs for sure. Entree might be ricotta-stuffed French toast or fresh spinach frittata. Fresh fruit creations. Carrot-walnut muffins or peach yogurt bread. In dining room by a 21-foot-wide window.
Plus: Beams everywhere. Hot soup or cider by wood stove in BYOB pub. Hot tub, sauna, and tennis court. Greenhouse library. Guest refrigerator. Snowshoes for rent. Window fans. For groups, family-style dinners, $15 per person. Transportation to/from airport, bus, or train.

Inn at Blush Hill

Blush Hill Road, Box 1266, Waterbury, VT 05676

802/244-7529
800/736-7522
fax 802/244-7314

Hosts: Gary and Pamela Gosselin
Location: At the top of a country road, overlooking golf course and mountains. One mile from I-89, off Route 100. Within 20 minutes of Stowe, Sugarbush, and Bolton Valley ski areas. Adjacent to Ben & Jerry's ice cream plant; two miles to Cold Hollow Cider Mill.

Open: Year round.
Rates: $75–$95 private bath. $55–$70 shared bath. $20 higher in foliage season and Christmas week. $15 rollaway or extra person. Golf and ski packages. Amex, Discover, EnRoute, MC, Visa.
♥ ♣ ♦ ✈ ✄

The grounds and gardens make this a perfect place for a wedding—according to Vermonters and people from many other states too. Honeymooners, skiers, and canoeists have also discovered the 1790s Cape with four fireplaces and wide board floors—all decorated with warm colors, country prints, and auction finds.

From New Hampshire and Washington, D.C., the Gosselins brought 25 years of experience in the hospitality field. Since arriving on a 20-degrees-below-zero day in January 1988, they *almost* feel like natives. They helped to develop a tourism association "to let people know how much there is to do here." Bostonians heard about it when Pam gave a well-received B&B

cooking demonstration in Jordan Marsh. Gary, a commercial real estate broker who specializes in country inns and B&Bs, also consults with prospective innkeepers. "And our whole family skis every chance we can!"

In residence: Christopher is 10; Tyler is 4.
Bed and bath: Six rooms. The first-floor room has double bed, working fireplace, ceiling fan, private shower bath. Upstairs, queen canopied bed, 150-inch-wide window with mountain view, private full bath. Two double-bedded rooms share full bath with claw-foot tub and shower. Room with antique queen bed and room with a double and a twin share a full bath. Rollaway available.
Breakfast: 8–9. French toast or apple pancakes topped with Bed & Jerry's ice cream, Vermont maple syrup, and fresh fruit. Homemade breads and muffins. Juice. Homemade granola. Served at 10-foot-long farm hands' table in country kitchen overlooking mountains.
Plus: Heated mattress pads. Porch rockers. Games. Piano. TV. Afternoon and evening refreshments.

> From Massachusetts: *"An incredible setting, a charming home, and the hosts are terrific."* From New Jersey: *"The breakfast was so good, we decided to stay another night."*

Weathervane Lodge   802/464-5426
Dorr Fitch Road, Box 57, West Dover, VT 05356

Hosts: Liz and Ernie Chabot
Location: One mile off Route 100, up a hill, in peaceful countryside with a panoramic view of mountains and valleys. Within minutes of Mount Snow, Haystack, and Maple Valley ski areas. Near Marlboro Festival, golf, tennis, lake swimming, horseback riding, hiking, museums.
Open: Year round. Two-night minimum Friday/Saturday weekend in ski and foliage seasons, all holidays.

Rates: Vary according to room and season. Winter weekdays are lower than weekends and holiday weeks. Winter rates with shared bath $25–$32 per person. Suite with private bath $40–$44 per person. About 15 percent less in other seasons except foliage. Singles, add $10.
♥ � ✻ ✈

"Returnees ask which room is available, and they know just where to settle in. That's the way my wife and I intended it to be. I built this Tyrolean-style place (with balconies) as my second home in 1962, and if you want, I can tell you how many nails there are, how I laughed, and how I cried. The four fireplaces—for atmosphere—burn 10 cords of wood a year. In summer there's a profusion of flower beds on the landscaped grounds of this comfortable, tranquil place."

Now that Ernie has retired from his work in fine metals, work that took him to places all over the world, "the world comes to me—even from Russia, thanks to a copy of *Bed & Breakfast in New England* at the embassy!"

In residence: Spooky, the cat, and Copper, a golden retriever. Two horses (not for riding).
Bed and bath: Ten rooms and a suite. Most rooms have shared baths. Suite has a room with double bed, living room with double sofa bed, private bath.

(Please turn page.)

Another room has two doubles, a sleep sofa that makes up into a double, and a private bath. Others have two twins, double, set of twin bunks, double and a bunk, double and single, or four singles. Cot and crib available. **Breakfast:** 7–9. The "skip-lunch" variety. Almost-famous blueberry pancakes, French toast, eggs any style—including poached in pure Vermont maple syrup. In beamed and fireplaced dining room with bentwood chairs, white cedar walls, 30-gallon fish tank, antique clocks, atmosphere. **Plus:** Beverages. Lounge with fieldstone fireplace, microwave, and setup bar. Use of refrigerator. Trails, open field, and old town roads are on the property for walking and cross-country skiing.

Fox Hall Inn   802/525-6930

Willoughby Lake, Westmore, VT
Mailing address: RR 1, Box 153E, Barton, VT 05822-9611

Hosts: Ken and Sherry Pyden
Location: Spectacular. On 76 rural acres bordering Lake Willoughby. Twenty miles to Burke Mountain, 40 to Jay Peak. Eight miles off I-91. Two hours from Montreal. "A naturalist's paradise. No shops. Only quaint country stores. (Gasoline available.) Great for water sports, hiking, walking, cycling, reading, cross-country skiing, ice fishing, snowmobiling, or just relaxing. Good restaurants within one mile." Willoughby Lake (summer) Playhouse right here.
Open: Year round. Two-night minimum on fall weekends.
Rates: July–October 15 and December 24–January 2—$70 shared bath, $90 private. Other times—$60 shared bath, $74 private. Singles $10 less. Senior citizens' discount given. $99 three-night double occupancy winter midweek (Christmas week excepted) special. Free use of boats. MC, Visa.

♥ ♫ ✿ ♦ ✗ ✄

This is the ultimate viewing spot, overlooking what is often called one of the world's most beautiful lakes. Guests sit for hours on the wide, partially covered wraparound veranda, which faces the fjordlike scene of Lake Willoughby flanked by Mounts Pisgah and Hor. At the edge of a sweeping lawn, a wooded path (berry picking allowed) leads to the private waterfront (swimming in clear spring-fed lake) with boathouse, dock, canoes, paddleboat, and windsurfers.

The turn-of-the-century mansion with two domed towers (lots of bays inside) was part of a girls' camp that was unoccupied from 1975 until 1986, the year that Ken retired as a millwright with the Ford Motor Company. That's when the Pydens came "way out here, to rehabilitate the property Sherry fell in love with." They opened in 1988 with ruffled tieback curtains on all the windows, plenty of comfortable chairs, and many moose items. "Sometimes guests feel so much at home, they want to help with dishes!"

In residence: Two dogs, Sugar Bayer and Aloysious. Four horses. Arthur, the potbellied pig.
Bed and bath: Nine rooms. First-floor room with a double bed and a three-quarter bed, private full bath. Second-floor rooms with private baths have a stall shower. Five rooms that share a full bath plus a shower bath have marble sink in room. Turret rooms with private bath, magnificent views, are favorites. Beds are queen and a twin, double, double and a twin, or two twin beds.

Breakfast: 7–9. Juice, fresh-baked homemade muffins, fresh fruit salad, pancakes or French toast, hot beverages. In dining room or on veranda. **Plus:** Afternoon snack. Grand piano. Turndown service. Down comforters. Flannel sheets. Guest refrigerator. Mints on pillow. Gas grill, picnic table. Croquet. Volleyball.

The Darling Family Inn

802/824-3223

815 Route 100, Weston, VT 05161-9801

Hosts: Chapin and Joan Darling
Location: Half mile north of village, with panoramic view of mountains and farmland. Near Bromley, Stratton, and Okemo mountains; summer theater, antiques, crafts, art exhibits. Three miles from Weston Priory.

Open: Year round except Christmas eve and Christmas night. Two-night minimum on weekends.
Rates: $75–$95 per room depending on size and location. Special rates for a stay of five or more nights.
♥ ♣

This style of country living was lauded by *Gourmet* magazine. American and English antiques are in a colonial setting created and recreated by Chapin, a skilled woodworker who was a Connecticut life insurance executive until 1980. To the 160-year-old farmhouse he has built an addition, "one that still allows us to stay small so that we can continue to provide surprises for our guests." The hardware is fashioned in the barn forge by son Jeff, a blacksmith. Another son, Eric, created detailed handcrafted wooden items. Dried flower wreaths, hand-painted wood and tin items, even thimbles are examples of Joan's artistry. Also on the property—two housekeeping cottages where pets are welcome.

In residence: Mandy, the dog; Sasha, the cat. Any or all of the four grown Darling children might be visiting.
Bed and bath: Five second-floor rooms, all private full baths. Canopied queen bed, twin beds, and double beds (one canopied) available.
Breakfast: 8–10. Juices (freshly squeezed orange juice), bacon, ham and sausage, any style eggs, omelets, home fries, French toast or berry pancakes. Cloth napkins. Chapin cooks. Joan serves by candlelight.
Plus: Swimming pool. In season, hayrides and sleigh rides nearby (fee charged). Beverages. Fireplaced living room. Library with wood stove. Chapin's guitar accompaniment for impromptu sing-alongs. Four-course candlelit dinners (extra charge) with advance notice.

The Wilder Homestead Inn

802/824-8172

25 Lawrence Hill Road, Box 106D, Weston, VT 05161

Hosts: Roy and Peggy Varner
Location: Next to the historic Church-on-the-Hill. Around the corner from Weston Playhouse. Just off Route 100; turn at post office, go over the bridge. Four miles south of Weston Priory.
Open: Year round. Two-night mini-

mum on July–October weekends and winter weekends.
Rates: $75–$95 private bath. $60–$65 shared bath. $25 third person in room. Special rate (not in peak season) for four or more nights.
♥ ♦ ♦ ♣ ♯ ✂

(Please turn page.)

"It was like having Moses Eaton here, as all the stencils used in 1992 were copies of his 1830 originals." That's the latest project in this Federal brick house bought by the Varners in 1985. The dining room is beamed. There are colonial colors, quilts, tab curtains, and pierced lampshades.

For 33 years the Varners, grandparents of 10, had been in the construction business in northeastern Pennsylvania. Here, Roy has transformed the old woodshed into a crafts shop. And he has helped to build sets for the Weston Playhouse, where Peggy's dream came true when she made her stage debut in *The Music Man.*

In residence: In hosts' quarters, two friendly cats who love visitors who ask to meet them.
Bed and bath: Seven rooms on second and third floors. Five with private bath (all shower except for one full). Two rooms share hall full bath. Beds are twins/king, canopied queen, double, or twins. One room has a queen and a twin bed, ceiling fan. Rollaway available.
Breakfast: 8–9. Fresh fruit, juices, homemade jams and biscuits, pancakes or French toast. Eggs ("try Roy's Vermont cheddar cheese omelet, yummy"), home fries. Brewed coffee. Teas. Served by dining room fireplace.
Plus: Tea or wine and cheese tray. Porch rockers. Player piano.

> From New York, Pennsylvania, Connecticut: *"Treat every guest as if they are special . . . fireplaces, antiques, crisp linen, thick towels, a sense of peace. . . . Warm, beautiful people. . . . Hale and hearty breakfasts."*

Golden Maple Inn   802/888-6614
Route 15, P.O. Box 35, Wolcott Village, VT 05680-0035

Hosts: Dick and Jo Wall
Location: On Route 15, in small village along the Lamoille River, "great for trout fishing; canoeing; and observing beaver, river otter, blue heron, and deer and fox in evening." Near country's last remaining covered railroad bridge, cross-country ski trails; 18 minutes to Stowe,

Craftsbury, Cabot Creamery.
Open: Year round. Two-night minimum on foliage weekends.
Rates: Private bath $52 single, $68 double. Shared bath $47 single, $59 double. $15 cot. Amex, Discover, MC, Visa.
♥ ♣ ♦ ✄ ⊁

> Guests wrote: *"No one could make a stay in magical Vermont more wonderful . . . honeymoon as romantic as we hoped . . . fantastic breakfasts . . . comfortable antiques . . . obviously much love and TLC here."*

Why Vermont? Dick is a retired competitive sailor and mountain climber who worked for many years in the ship- and yacht-building industry. He says, "I picked up an oar, put it on my shoulder, and walked inland until someone asked what it was. That's where I settled down in 1990."

In Yarmouth, Maine, Jo managed computer operations for a national footwear company. She and Dick are parents of three grown children and world travelers who, as guests can tell, love what they are doing.

In residence: In carriage house—Missy, "our bashful calico."
Bed and bath: Three spacious rooms. One ground-floor honeymoon suite with double bed, private full bath with Victorian tub and hand-held shower. One second floor, room with double four-poster bed and another with two twin four-poster beds share a shower bath. Rollaways available.
Breakfast: 7–9. Freshly baked bread. Fresh fruit, homemade granola, oven-baked French toast with blueberries and local maple syrup. Spicy baked farm-fresh eggs. Filled croissants. Bacon-mushroom quiche and scones. Juice. Hot beverages.
Plus: Library. Flagstone terrace with Adirondack chairs. Afternoon tea and homemade sweets. Down comforters. Ceiling fans. Turndown service. Flowers and vegetables from Jo's river gardens. Optional dinner ($19) by reservation.

The Charleston House   802/457-3843
21 Pleasant Street, Woodstock, VT 05091

Hosts: Barbara and Bill Hough
Location: In historic district with shops, restaurants, and galleries within a four-block walk. Twenty minutes to Killington; 10 to Suicide Six. One mile to Woodstock Country Club—tennis, cross-country skiing, Robert Trent Jones golf course open to the public.

Open: Year round. Two-night minimum on weekends and in foliage season.
Rates: Vary according to room size. $110, $130, $145. April–November about $20 less. MC, Visa.
♥ ❖ ♦ ✠ ⊬

"After living in Vail, Colorado; Annapolis, Maryland; and on our sailboat, we became innkeepers in 1987. And all because a friend of a friend told us that the Charleston House might be for sale. With art and antiques befitting the 1835 frame and brick Greek Revival house, Barbara, a Virginian, embellished the southern charm for which the inn was known. Since we acquired the nearby 1880 Canterbury House, her recognized flair for elegance, using Laura Ashley fabrics and period furniture, has been extended to that acclaimed seven-room B&B."

Style, food, and hospitality have become Hough hallmarks. Bill, sometimes called the resident raconteur, is a former executive, stockbroker, salesman, and Realtor.

Bed and bath: Seven air-conditioned rooms on first and second floors. All private full baths. Six queen-bedded rooms (one with private entrance, one with cable TV) plus one with twin four-posters.
Breakfast: 8:30 and 9:30. Varies. Entree repertoire includes baked strata and blueberry French toast. Served in dining room under colonial chandelier.
Plus: Patio. Champagne for anniversary and honeymoon couples. Profits from Barbara's cookbook, *Breakfast at the Charleston House*, are contributed to David's House, a charitable lodging facility for parents of severely ill hospitalized children.

B&Bs offer the ultimate concierge service.

Deer Brook Inn

802/672-3713

HCR 68, Box 443 (Route 4 West), Woodstock, VT 05091

Hosts: Brian and Rosemary McGinty
Location: Rural. On five acres by the Ottauquechee River. Four miles west of the village. Thirty minutes to Dartmouth College, 20 to I-89 and I-91; eight miles to Killington ski area.
Open: Year round.

Rates: Sunday–Thursday $70 ($50 single). Friday and Saturday $85. Foliage season and Christmas $95 ($60 single). $10 extra person over five years old. MC, Visa.
♥ ⌂ ❊ ✖ ✄

From many letters: *"The McGintys have restored the essence of New England and hospitality to their corner of Vermont. . . . Exposed beams, beautiful stenciling, handmade (by Rosemary) quilts, wide pine floors. . . . Homey, comfortable, clean accommodations. . . . Came to Vermont [from Hawaii] planning to get married. Chose the yard of the inn. Perfect. . . . Brian and Rosemary are there if needed but not overbearing . . . a creative home-style breakfast, a feast . . . a roaring fire at the slightest chill. . . . Made our anniversary special. . . . The dogs, too, are great . . . fell asleep to the sound of the brook across the road."*

Restoration was a year-long task before the McGintys opened in 1988. In Breckenridge, Colorado, Rosemary, a nurse, and Brian were on the ski patrol.

In residence: James is six years old; Kelly is three. Golden retrievers, Sage (mother) and Nutmeg (daughter).
Bed and bath: Four (two with skylights) second-floor riverview rooms, all private full baths. Three queen-bedded rooms (one has additional twin bed). One with a double and a twin bed. Rollaway and crib available.
Breakfast: 8–9. Hot entree may be featherbed eggs or baked apple pancake (most-requested recipes). Fresh fruit. Juice. Homemade muffins, breads, or coffee cake.
Plus: Window fans. Air conditioning in living and dining areas. Individual thermostats. Complimentary champagne for honeymooners. Front porch.

Jackson House Inn

802/457-2065

37 Route 4 West, Woodstock, VT 05091-1243

Hosts: Bruce McIlveen and Jack Foster
Location: On three acres with gardens, a brook, a pond (for swimming), walking trails, mountain views. One and one-half miles west of Woodstock village.

Open: Year round. Two-day minimum on weekends and holidays.
Rates: Per room or suite. $125, $130, $135, $150, $175, $225.
♥ ♦ ✖ ✄

"I'd like to keep this as my own secret," said the guest taped at the inn for Boston's award-winning "Chronicle" television show. "Everything is done with such style," exclaimed the Bloomingdale's public relations director who is responsible for many *Bed & Breakfast in New England* programs.

Created by a banker from San Francisco and an airline director of marketing from New York, this elegant inn is an exquisite example of the Colonial Revival architecture built in 1890. In 1984, following 14 months of renovation, Bruce and Jack furnished with museum-quality antiques—Oriental carved rugs, Baccarat and Lalique crystal, French Empire, Victorian, and New England country. Since, they have added and embellished and been dubbed "most romantic" by *Glamour* magazine.

In residence: A cat named Chester.
Bed and bath: Twelve rooms, each in a different period or style, on three floors. All with ceiling fans. Double, queen, or twin beds. Two third-floor queen-bedded suites have French doors leading to decks that overlook landscaped grounds. One fireplaced four-room suite. All private baths, showers with glass doors.
Breakfast: 7:30–9:30. "Memorable." Varies. Santa Fe omelets, crab polenta, breast of chicken with poached egg on buttered fettucini, champagne sauce. Homemade scones, muffins, banana bread. Fruit compote with peach schnapps. Freshly squeezed juice. Family style in Queen Anne dining room.
Plus: A brochure that will make you want to book immediately. Wine and champagne with hors d'oeuvres at 6, with harpist on Saturdays. Godiva chocolates. Video library.

The Woodstocker Bed and Breakfast

61 River Street, Woodstock, VT 05091   802/457-3896
                                                    fax 802/457-4432

Hosts: Liza Deignan and Romano Formichella
Location: At edge of village, on Route 4; five-minute walk to restaurants and shops. Hiking trail up Mount Tom is just around the corner.
Open: Year round. Two-night minimum during foliage season and most weekends.

Rates: Spring, November, early December $75 rooms, $85–$100 suites, $10 less midweek. Summer and winter $85 rooms, $95–$110 suites, $10 less midweek. September, October, holiday weeks, $95 rooms, $100–$120 suites. $10–$20 additional person. MC, Visa.
❖ ♦ ✖ ✄

What to do? Consult the innkeepers, who have experience as chairmen of the Woodstock Chamber's hospitality committee (in charge of the information booth on the green) and who are on several boards, including the Council on the Arts and Chamber of Commerce.

Liza and Romano came to this "wonderful community in which to live" after years of working together in the computer software field. They bought this B&B, a 150-year-old Cape with renovated attached barn, previously owned by someone in the plumbing business. (The cedar room with whirlpool is a big hit.) And they have surprised themselves (and Liza's mother) with their gardening and culinary skills. Enthusiasm is contagious here.

In residence: Zucchina, "our black Lab, who doesn't go into the guest quarters but waits patiently for visitors outside."
Foreign languages spoken: Italian. Some French, German, Spanish.
Bed and bath: Nine rooms, all private full baths. First floor—twins and doubles; suite with kitchen and two double beds. Second floor—doubles or queens. Two suites (one with TV, other with deck) with a double-bedded bedroom, kitchen, living room, dining area. Rollaway and crib available.
Breakfast: 8–9:30. Homemade granola, cereal, muffins, breads, coffee cakes. Quiche. Fresh fruit, juice, bagels, English muffins, breakfast bread pudding (a

(Please turn page.)

hit), gourmet coffee. Buffet style with dining tables set in living room. For special occasions, breakfast in bed.
Plus: That whirlpool. Teatime with homemade goodies. Some bedrooms air conditioned or equipped with window/ceiling fans. Books. Games. TV with VCR.

The Peeping Cow Bed & Breakfast

Route 106, P.O. Box 178, Reading, VT 05062-0047   802/484-5036
fax 802/484-9558

Hosts: Nancy and Frank Lynch
Location: Peaceful dairy country, 11 miles south of Woodstock. Surrounded by meadows, stone walls, brook, and forest. Five minutes to Mount Ascutney, 30 to Dartmouth College. Green Mountain Horse Association, horseback riding, hiking, and skiing "down the road."

Open: Year round. Two-night minimum preferred during fall foliage and Christmas week, and on holiday weekends.
Rates: Per room. $75 queen bed, $65 double. $5 one-night surcharge.
♥ ♣ ✈ ⅙

Along with some of the country's finest lodging places, this "top-class B&B" (as one Irish guest dubbed it) participated in a Manhattan fund-raiser conducted by Christie's (fine art auctioneers). The c. 1830 farmhouse, a B&B since 1976, has been renovated over the last 20 years by Frank, a consulting engineer, who has been an old-car buff since his youth in Scotland. "From our Palladian living room window we see pasture, brook, and forest. Handmade nails are in the old pine random-width floors. Only wood heat is used. Fireside chats are a major indoor activity. Some guests browse in nearby old cemeteries, visit Ogden's Grist Mill, or find '20 Foot,' the village swimming hole."

Nancy, a writer, occasionally attends European trade shows for her children, who are exporting Vermont quilts and products for children. She was a film extra in a Fred Astaire film shot in Woodstock in 1982 and in *Funny Farm* with Chevy Chase, shot three miles north of here at the most photographed farm in the country.

Foreign languages spoken: French and Spanish; some German, Italian.
Bed and bath: Three rooms on first and second floors. One double-bedded room and one queen-bedded room, each with private bath. Another queen-bedded room has a private bath except in summer and foliage season, when it shares bath with a room that has two twin beds.
Breakfast: Usually 8:15; early "plane catchers" accommodated. Fresh fruits. House granola. Homemade rolls, muffins, jams, honey, fruit juice. Yogurt and cheeses. "We think our pure (well and spring) water is what makes the fresh-brewed coffee and steeped tea extra great." In dining room furnished with English antiques and oil paintings.
Plus: Down comforters. Air conditioning in two queen rooms. No TV but plenty of books. Piano, mandolin, ukulele yours to use. Chess. Picnic lunch (advance notice, small fee). Quilt orders taken at discounted prices.

American white-on-white quilted coverlet, ca. 1800. A detail of this quilt appears on the cover. Photo by E. Irving Blomstrann. Courtesy Wadsworth Atheneum, Hartford, Connecticut; gift of Mrs. Frederic J. Agate.

INDEX

NEW HAMPSHIRE

ABOUT THE AUTHOR

Bernice Chesler, "America's bed and breakfast ambassador," has appeared on dozens of television and radio programs including "CBS This Morning," CNN, and NPR's "Morning Edition." She is known for her personalized approach and attention to detail. Guests from all over the world write to her about their B&B experiences. She shares their impressions—and her own, gathered through hundreds of stays and extensive interviews—in her books; in Meet-the-Hosts programs conducted at such major retailers as Bloomingdale's, L.L. Bean, Filene's, and Macy's; in workshops; and in lectures at bed and breakfast conferences from Maine to California.

Recipient of the nation's first B&B Achievement Award and first B&B Reservation Service Award, the author has served on the Advisory Board of the Professional Association of Innkeepers International. She has written for 'GBH, Yankee, Country Almanac, Family Circle, and Innsider magazines and for the Boston Globe and the Washington Post.

BBB—Before Bed and Breakfast—Ms. Chesler conducted thousands of interviews throughout the country for documentary films seen on national public television. As publications coordinator for the Emmy Award–winning television program "ZOOM," produced at WGBH, Boston, she edited twelve books emanating from the series. She is also the author of the classic guide In and Out of Boston with (or without) Children.